Pro Oracle Database 18c Administration

Manage and Safeguard Your Organization's Data

Third Edition

Michelle Malcher
Darl Kuhn

⟨IOUG⟩
Independent oracle users group

Apress®

Pro Oracle Database 18c Administration: Manage and Safeguard Your Organization's Data

Michelle Malcher
Huntley, IL, USA

Darl Kuhn
Morrison, CO, USA

ISBN-13 (pbk): 978-1-4842-4423-4
https://doi.org/10.1007/978-1-4842-4424-1

ISBN-13 (electronic): 978-1-4842-4424-1

Managing Director, Apress Media LLC: Welmoed Spahr
Acquisitions Editor: Jonathan Gennick
Development Editor: Laura Berendson
Coordinating Editor: Jill Balzano

Cover designed by eStudioCalamar

Cover image designed by Freepik (www.freepik.com)

Distributed to the book trade worldwide by Springer Science+Business Media New York, 233 Spring Street, 6th Floor, New York, NY 10013. Phone 1-800-SPRINGER, fax (201) 348-4505, e-mail orders-ny@springer-sbm.com, or visit www.springeronline.com. Apress Media, LLC is a California LLC and the sole member (owner) is Springer Science + Business Media Finance Inc (SSBM Finance Inc). SSBM Finance Inc is a **Delaware** corporation.

For information on translations, please e-mail rights@apress.com, or visit http://www.apress.com/rights-permissions.

Apress titles may be purchased in bulk for academic, corporate, or promotional use. eBook versions and licenses are also available for most titles. For more information, reference our Print and eBook Bulk Sales web page at http://www.apress.com/bulk-sales.

Any source code or other supplementary material referenced by the author in this book is available to readers on GitHub via the book's product page, located at www.apress.com/9781484244234. For more detailed information, please visit http://www.apress.com/source-code.

Printed on acid-free paper

Dedicated to my daughters.
They believe in me just like I believe in them.

Table of Contents

About the Authors..xxix

About the Technical Reviewer xxxi

Acknowledgments...xxxiii

Introduction xxxv

Chapter 1: Installing the Oracle Binaries...1

Understanding the OFA 2

    Oracle Inventory Directory...4

    Oracle Base Directory...4

    Oracle Home Directory 5

    Oracle Network Files Directory...6

    Automatic Diagnostic Repository 6

Installing Oracle 7

    Step 1. Create the OS Groups and User..8

    Step 2. Ensure That the OS Is Adequately Configured 11

    Step 3. Obtain the Oracle Installation Software..12

    Step 4. Unzip the Files..13

    Step 5. Creating oraInst.loc File 14

    Step 6. Configure the Response File, and Run the Installer..15

    Step 7. Troubleshoot Any Issues 20

    Step 8. Apply Any Additional Patches 21

Installing with a Copy of an Existing Installation 22

    Step 1. Copy the Binaries, Using an OS Utility..22

    Step 2. Attach the Oracle Home..24

Installing Read-Only Oracle Home 25

Upgrading Oracle Software..26

Reinstalling After Failed Installation 27

Applying Interim Patches 28

Installing Remotely with the Graphical Installer 30

Step 1. Install X Software and Networking Utilities on the Local PC 31

Step 2. Start an X Session on the Local Computer 31

Step 3. Copy the Oracle Installation Media to the Remote Server 32

Step 4. Run the xhost Command 33

Step 5. Log In to the Remote Computer from X 33

Step 6. Ensure that the DISPLAY Variable Is Set Correctly on the Remote Computer 33

Step 7. Execute the runInstaller Utility 34

Step 8. Troubleshoot 35

Installation in the Cloud 35

Summary... 36

Chapter 2: Creating a Database 39

Setting OS Variables... 40

A Manually Intensive Approach 41

Oracle's Approach to Setting OS Variables 41

My Approach to Setting OS Variables 43

Creating a Database.. 46

Step 1. Set the OS Variables 46

Step 2. Configure the Initialization File.. 47

Step 3. Create the Required Directories 50

Step 4. Create the Database.. 50

Step 5. Create a Data Dictionary 56

Configuring and Implementing the Listener.. 57

Implementing a Listener with the Net Configuration Assistant.. 58

Manually Configuring a Listener... 59

Connecting to a Database through the Network 61

Creating a Password File 62

Starting and Stopping the Database 64

    Understanding OS Authentication 64

    Starting the Database 65

    Stopping the Database 68

Using the dbca to Create a Database 70

Dropping a Database 73

How Many Databases on One Server? 74

Understanding Oracle Architecture 77

Summary 80

Chapter 3: Configuring an Efficient Environment **83**

Customizing Your OS Command Prompt 84

Customizing Your SQL Prompt 87

Creating Shortcuts for Frequently Used Commands 89

    Using Aliases 89

    Using a Function 91

Rerunning Commands Quickly 93

    Scrolling with the Up and Down Arrow Keys 94

    Using Ctrl+P and Ctrl+N 94

    Listing the Command History 94

    Searching in Reverse 95

    Setting the Command Editor 95

Developing Standard Scripts 96

    dba_setup 97

    dba_fcns 98

    tbsp_chk.bsh 99

    conn.bsh 102

    filesp.bsh 103

    login.sql 106

    top.sql 107

    lock.sql 108

    users.sql 110

Organizing Scripts 111

    Step 1. Create Directories 112

    Step 2. Copy Files to Directories 112

    Step 3. Configure the Startup File 113

Automating Scripts 114

Summary 114

Chapter 4: Tablespaces and Data Files 117

Understanding the First Five 119

Understanding the Need for More 120

Creating Tablespaces 122

Renaming a Tablespace 127

Changing a Tablespace's Write Mode 128

Dropping a Tablespace 129

Using Oracle Managed Files 132

Creating a Bigfile Tablespace 133

Enabling Default Table Compression Within a Tablespace Tablespace 134

Displaying Tablespace Size 135

Altering Tablespace Size 137

Toggling Data Files Offline and Online 138

Renaming or Relocating a Data File 141

    Performing Online Data File Operations 142

    Performing Offline Data File Operations 142

Using ASM for Tablespaces 148

Summary 149

Chapter 5: Managing Control Files, Online Redo Logs, and Archivelogs 151

Managing Control Files 151

    Viewing Control File Names and Locations 155

    Adding a Control File 155

    Moving a Control File 159

    Removing a Control File 160

Online Redo Logs 162

    Displaying Online Redo Log Information 166

    Determining the Optimal Size of Online Redo Log Groups 168

    Determining the Optimal Number of Redo Log Groups 169

    Adding Online Redo Log Groups 172

    Resizing and Dropping Online Redo Log Groups 172

    Adding Online Redo Log Files to a Group 175

    Removing Online Redo Log Files from a Group 175

    Moving or Renaming Redo Log Files 176

    Controlling the Generation of Redo... 177

Implementing Archivelog Mode 179

    Making Architectural Decisions 179

    Setting the Archive Redo File Location 181

    Enabling Archivelog Mode 186

    Disabling Archivelog Mode 187

    Reacting to a Lack of Disk Space in Your Archive Log Destination................................. 188

    Backing Up Archive Redo Log Files 190

Summary.. 190

Chapter 6: Users and Basic Security 193

Managing Default Users.. 193

    Locking Accounts and Expiring Passwords 196

    Identifying DBA-Created Accounts 198

    Checking Default Passwords.. 199

Creating Users.. 200

    Choosing a Username and Authentication Method... 201

    Assigning Default Permanent and Temporary Tablespaces.. 206

Modifying Passwords.. 209

Schema Only Account 210

Modifying Users 212

Dropping Users 213

Enforcing Password Security and Resource Limits 214

Basic Password Security 215

Password Strength 219

Limiting Database Resource Usage 221

Managing Privileges 223

Assigning Database System Privileges 224

Assigning Database Object Privileges 225

Grouping and Assigning Privileges 226

Summary 229

Chapter 7: Tables and Constraints 231

Understanding Table Types 232

Understanding Data Types 233

Character 234

Numeric 236

Date/Time 237

RAW 238

ROWID 239

LOB 240

JSON 241

Creating a Table 241

Creating a Heap-Organized Table 242

Implementing Virtual Columns 246

Implementing Invisible Columns 250

Making Read-Only Tables 251

Understanding Deferred-Segment Creation 252

Creating a Table with an Autoincrementing (Identity) Column 253

Allowing for Default Parallel SQL Execution 256

Compressing Table Data 257

Avoiding Redo Creation 260

Creating a Table from a Query 263

Modifying a Table 266

Obtaining the Needed Lock 266

Renaming a Table 267

Adding a Column 267

Altering a Column 268

Renaming a Column 270

Dropping a Column 270

Displaying Table DDL 271

Dropping a Table 273

Undropping a Table 274

Removing Data from a Table 275

Using DELETE 276

Using TRUNCATE 276

Viewing and Adjusting the High-Water Mark 278

Tracing to Detect Space Below the High-Water Mark 279

Using DBMS_SPACE to Detect Space Below the High-Water Mark 280

Selecting from Data Dictionary Extents View 282

Lowering the High-Water Mark 282

Creating a Temporary Table 286

Creating an Index-Organized Table 288

Managing Constraints 289

Creating Primary Key Constraints 289

Enforcing Unique Key Values 291

Creating Foreign Key Constraints 293

Checking for Specific Data Conditions 295

Enforcing Not Null Conditions 296

Disabling Constraints 297

EnablingConstraints 299

Summary 302

Chapter 8: Indexes 303

Deciding When to Create an Index 304

   Proactively Creating Indexes 305

   Reactively Creating Indexes 306

Planning for Robustness 308

   Determining Which Type of Index to Use 308

   Estimating the Size of an Index Before Creation 311

   Creating Separate Tablespaces for Indexes 313

   Creating Portable Scripts 316

   Establishing Naming Standards 317

Creating Indexes 318

   Creating B-tree Indexes 318

   Creating Concatenated Indexes 322

   Implementing Function-Based Indexes 324

   Creating Unique Indexes 325

   Implementing Bitmap Indexes 327

   Creating Bitmap Join Indexes 328

   Implementing Reverse-Key Indexes 329

   Creating Key-Compressed Indexes 330

   Parallelizing Index Creation 331

   Avoiding Redo Generation When Creating an Index 331

   Implementing Invisible Indexes 332

Maintaining Indexes 335

   Renaming an Index 336

   Displaying Code to Re-create an Index 336

   Rebuilding an Index 337

   Making Indexes Unusable 338

   Monitoring Index Usage 339

   Dropping an Index 341

Indexing Foreign Key Columns 341

Implementing an Index on a Foreign Key Column 342

Determining if Foreign Key Columns Are Indexed 344

Summary.. 347

Chapter 9: Views, Synonyms, and Sequences 351

Implementing Views... 351

Creating a View.. 352

Checking Updates... 354

Creating Read-Only Views 355

Updatable Join Views 356

Creating an INSTEAD OF Trigger.. 358

Implementing an Invisible Column 360

Modifying a View Definition 362

Displaying the SQL Used to Create a View... 363

Renaming a View.. 364

Dropping a View 365

Managing Synonyms.. 365

Creating a Synonym 366

Creating Public Synonyms.. 367

Dynamically Generating Synonyms 368

Displaying Synonym Metadata 369

Renaming a Synonym... 370

Dropping a Synonym 370

Managing Sequences.. 371

Creating a Sequence 371

Using Sequence Pseudocolumns 373

Autoincrementing Columns 374

Scalable Sequences 375

Implementing Multiple Sequences That Generate Unique Values 376

Creating One Sequence or Many 377

Viewing Sequence Metadata 378

Renaming a Sequence... 379

Dropping a Sequence 379

Resetting a Sequence... 379

Summary.. 381

Chapter 10: Data Dictionary Fundamentals 383

Data Dictionary Architecture 384

Static Views 384

Dynamic Performance Views... 387

A Different View of Metadata 389

A Few Creative Uses of the Data Dictionary.. 392

Derivable Documentation 392

Displaying User Information 394

Displaying Table Row Counts.. 398

Showing Primary Key and Foreign Key Relationships....................................... 401

Displaying Object Dependencies 402

Summary.. 406

Chapter 11: Large Objects 407

Describing LOB Types.. 408

Illustrating LOB Locators, Indexes, and Chunks 409

Distinguishing Between BasicFiles and SecureFiles 411

BasicFiles 412

SecureFiles.. 412

Creating a Table with a LOB Column 413

Creating a BasicFiles LOB Column 413

Implementing a LOB in a Specific Tablespace... 415

Creating a SecureFiles LOB Column 416

Implementing a Partitioned LOB 417

Maintaining LOB Columns 419

Moving a LOB Column 420

Adding a LOB Column 420

Removing a LOB Column 421

Caching LOBs 421

Storing LOBs In- and Out of Line 422

Implementing SecureFiles Advanced Features 424

Compressing LOBs 424

Deduplicating LOBs 425

Encrypting LOBs 426

Migrating BasicFiles to SecureFiles 428

Loading LOBs 432

Loading a CLOB 432

Loading a BLOB 434

Measuring LOB Space Consumed 435

BasicFiles Space Used 436

SecureFiles Space Used 437

Reading BFILEs 439

Summary 440

Chapter 12: Partitioning: Divide and Conquer 441

What Tables Should Be Partitioned? 443

Creating Partitioned Tables 445

Partitioning by Range 445

Placing Partitions in Tablespaces 450

Partitioning by List 453

Partitioning by Hash 454

Blending Different Partitioning Methods 455

Creating Partitions on Demand 457

Partitioning to Match a Parent Table 462

Partitioning on a Virtual Column 466

Giving an Application Control Over Partitioning 467

Maintaining Partitions 467

Viewing Partition Metadata 468

Moving a Partition 469

Automatically Moving Updated Rows 471

Partitioning an Existing Table 472

Adding a Partition 474

Exchanging a Partition with an Existing Table 476

Renaming a Partition 479

Splitting a Partition 479

Merging Partitions 480

Dropping a Partition 482

Generating Statistics for a Partition 483

Removing Rows from a Partition 484

Manipulating Data Within a Partition 485

Partitioning Indexes 486

Partitioning an Index to Follow Its Table 486

Partitioning an Index Differently from Its Table 490

Partial Indexes 492

Partition Pruning 494

Modifying the Partition Strategy 496

Summary 496

Chapter 13: Data Pump 499

Data Pump Architecture 500

Getting Started 505

Taking an Export 505

Importing a Table 509

Using a Parameter File 509

Exporting and Importing with Granularity 511

Exporting and Importing an Entire Database 511

Schema Level 513

Table Level 514

Tablespace Level 515

Transferring Data 516

Exporting and Importing Directly Across the Network 516

Copying Data Files 519

Features for Manipulating Storage 521

    Exporting Tablespace Metadata.. 522

    Specifying Different Data File Paths and Names... 522

    Importing into a Tablespace Different from the Original.. 523

    Changing the Size of Data Files.. 524

    Changing Segment and Storage Attributes 525

Filtering Data and Objects... 526

    Specifying a Query 526

    Exporting a Percentage of the Data.. 528

    Excluding Objects from the Export File.. 528

    Excluding Statistics 530

    Including Only Specific Objects in an Export File 531

    Exporting Table, Index, Constraint, and Trigger DDL 531

    Excluding Objects from Import.. 532

    Including Objects in Import... 532

Common Data Pump Tasks 533

    Estimating the Size of Export Jobs.. 533

    Listing the Contents of Dump Files... 534

    Cloning a User 535

    Creating a Consistent Export 535

    Importing When Objects Already Exist.. 537

    Renaming a Table 539

    Remapping Data 539

    Suppressing a Log File 541

    Using Parallelism... 541

    Specifying Additional Dump Files 543

    Reusing Output File Names 543

    Creating a Daily DDL File 544

    Compressing Output... 545

    Changing Table Compression Characteristics on Import....................................... 546

    Encrypting Data... 546

    Exporting Views as Tables 548

Disabling Logging of Redo on Import 548

Attaching to a Running Job 549

Stopping and Restarting a Job 550

Terminating a Data Pump Job 550

Monitoring Data Pump Jobs 551

Data Pump Log File 551

Data Dictionary Views 552

Database Alert Log 553

Status Table 553

Interactive Command Mode Status 554

OS Utilities 554

Summary 555

Chapter 14: External Tables 557

SQL*Loader vs. External Tables 558

Loading CSV Files into the Database 560

Creating a Directory Object and Granting Access 561

Creating an External Table 561

Generating SQL to Create an External Table 563

Viewing External Table Metadata 565

Loading a Regular Table from the External Table 566

Performing Advanced Transformations 568

Viewing Text Files from SQL 570

Unloading and Loading Data Using an External Table 572

Enabling Parallelism to Reduce Elapsed Time 575

Compressing a Dump File 576

Encrypting a Dump File 577

Summary 580

Chapter 15: Materialized Views 581

Understanding MVs 581

MV Terminology 584

Referencing Useful Views 585

Creating Basic Materialized Views 586

 Creating a Complete Refreshable MV 587

 Creating a Fast Refreshable MV 591

Going Beyond the Basics 598

 Creating MVs and Specifying Tablespace for MVs and Indexes 598

 Creating Indexes on MVs 598

 Partitioning MVs 599

 Compressing an MV 600

 Encrypting MV Columns 600

 Building an MV on a Prebuilt Table 602

 Creating an Unpopulated MV 603

 Creating an MV Refreshed on Commit 604

 Creating a Never Refreshable MV 605

 Creating MVs for Query Rewrite 606

 Creating a Fast Refreshable MV Based on a Complex Query 607

 Viewing MV DDL 611

 Dropping an MV 611

Modifying MVs 612

 Modifying Base Table DDL and Propagating to MVs 612

 Toggling Redo Logging on an MV 617

 Altering Parallelism 618

 Moving an MV 610

Managing MV Logs 619

 Creating an MV Log 620

 Indexing MV Log Columns 622

 Viewing Space Used by an MV Log 622

 Shrinking the Space in an MV Log 623

 Checking the Row Count of an MV Log 624

 Moving an MV Log 625

 Dropping an MV Log 626

Refreshing MVs 627

Manually Refreshing MVs from SQL*Plus 627

Creating an MV with a Refresh Interval 629

Efficiently Performing a Complete Refresh 630

Handling the ORA-12034 Error 631

Monitoring MV Refreshes 632

Viewing MVs' Last Refresh Times 632

Determining Whether a Refresh Is in Progress 632

Monitoring Real-Time Refresh Progress 633

Checking Whether MVs Are Refreshing Within a Time Period 634

Creating Remote MV Refreshes 635

Understanding Remote-Refresh Architectures 636

Viewing MV Base Table Information 638

Determining How Many MVs Reference a Central MV Log 639

Managing MVs in Groups 641

Creating an MV Group 642

Altering an MV Refresh Group 642

Refreshing an MV Group 643

DBMS_MVIEW vs. DBMS_REFRESH 643

Determining MVs in a Group 644

Adding an MV to a Refresh Group 645

Removing MVs from a Refresh Group 645

Dropping an MV Refresh Group 645

Summary 646

Chapter 16: User-Managed Backup and Recovery 647

Implementing a Cold-Backup Strategy 649

Making a Cold Backup of a Database 649

Restoring a Cold Backup in Noarchivelog Mode with Online Redo Logs 652

Restoring a Cold Backup in Noarchivelog Mode Without Online Redo Logs 653

Scripting a Cold Backup and Restore 655

Implementing a Hot Backup Strategy 660

Making a Hot Backup 660

Scripting Hot Backups 665

Understanding the Split-Block Issue 668

Understanding the Need for Redo Generated During Backup 672

Understanding That Data Files Are Updated 673

Performing a Complete Recovery of an Archivelog Mode Database 675

Restoring and Recovering with the Database Offline 676

Restoring and Recovering with a Database Online 681

Restoring Control Files 682

Performing an Incomplete Recovery of an Archivelog Mode Database 687

Summary 691

Chapter 17: Configuring RMAN 693

Understanding RMAN 694

Starting RMAN 699

RMAN Architectural Decisions 700

1. Running the RMAN Client Remotely or Locally 704

2. Specifying the Backup User 704

3. Using Online or Offline Backups 705

4. Setting the Archivelog Destination and File Format 705

5. Configuring the RMAN Backup Location and File Format 706

6. Setting the Autobackup of the Control File 709

7. Specifying the Location of the Autobackup of the Control File 710

8. Backing Up Archivelogs 711

9. Determining the Location for the Snapshot Control File 711

10. Using a Recovery Catalog 712

11. Using a Media Manager 713

12. Setting the CONTROL_FILE_RECORD_KEEP_TIME Initialization Parameter 714

13. Configuring RMAN's Backup Retention Policy 715

14. Configuring the Archivelogs' Deletion Policy 717

15. Setting the Degree of Parallelism 718

16. Using Backup Sets or Image Copies 719

17. Using Incremental Backups 720

18. Using Incrementally Updated Backups 721

19. Using Block Change Tracking 721

20. Configuring Binary Compression 722

21. Configuring Encryption 723

22. Configuring Miscellaneous Settings 724

23. Configuring Informational Output 725

Segueing from Decision to Action 727

Summary 732

Chapter 18: RMAN Backups and Reporting 733

Preparing to Run RMAN Backup Commands 734

Setting NLS_DATE_FORMAT 734

Setting ECHO 735

Showing Variables 736

Running Backups 736

Backing Up the Entire Database 736

Backing Up Tablespaces 738

Backing Up Data Files 739

Backing Up the Control File 739

Backing Up the spfile 740

Backing Up Archivelogs 740

Backing Up FRA 741

Excluding Tablespaces from Backups 742

Backing Up Data Files Not Backed Up 743

Skipping Read-Only Tablespaces 743

Skipping Offline or Inaccessible Files 744

Backing Up Large Files in Parallel 745

Adding RMAN Backup Information to the Repository 745

Taking Backups of Pluggable Databases 747

While Connected to the Root Container 747

While Connected to a Pluggable Database 748

Creating Incremental Backups 749

    Taking Incremental-Level Backups 750

    Making Incrementally Updating Backups 751

    Using Block Change Tracking 753

Checking for Corruption in Data Files and Backups 754

    Using VALIDATE 754

    Using BACKUP...VALIDATE 756

    Using RESTORE...VALIDATE 756

Using a Recovery Catalog 757

    Creating a Recovery Catalog 757

    Registering a Target Database 759

    Backing Up the Recovery Catalog 760

    Synchronizing the Recovery Catalog 760

    Recovery Catalog Versions 761

    Dropping a Recovery Catalog 761

Logging RMAN Output 762

    Redirecting Output to a File 762

    Capturing Output with Linux/Unix Logging Commands 763

    Logging Output to a File 764

    Querying for Output in the Data Dictionary 764

RMAN Reporting 765

    Using LIST 765

    Using REPORT 766

    Using SQL 767

Summary 772

Chapter 19: RMAN Restore and Recovery 773

Determining if Media Recovery Is Required 775

Determining What to Restore 777

    How the Process Works 777

    Using Data Recovery Advisor 779

Using RMAN to Stop/Start Oracle..783

　　Shutting Down..783

　　Starting Up...783

Complete Recovery...784

　　Testing Restore and Recovery...785

　　Restoring and Recovering the Entire Database...787

　　Restoring and Recovering Tablespaces..789

　　Restoring Read-Only Tablespaces..790

　　Restoring Temporary Tablespaces..791

　　Restoring and Recovering Data Files..791

　　Restoring Data Files to Nondefault Locations...793

　　Performing Block-Level Recovery...794

　　Restoring a Container Database and Its Associated Pluggable Databases..........796

Restoring Archivelog Files...799

　　Restoring to the Default Location...800

　　Restoring to a Nondefault Location..800

Restoring a Control File..801

　　Using a Recovery Catalog...801

　　Using an Autobackup..802

　　Specifying a Backup File Name..803

Restoring the spfile..803

Incomplete Recovery..805

　　Determining the Type of Incomplete Recovery...808

　　Performing Time-Based Recovery..808

　　Performing Log Sequence-Based Recovery..809

　　Performing SCN-Based Recovery...810

　　Restoring to a Restore Point...811

　　Restoring Tables to a Previous Point...811

Flashing Back a Table...813

　　FLASHBACK TABLE TO BEFORE DROP..813

　　Flashing Back a Table to a Previous Point in Time..815

FLASHING BACK A DATABASE 816

Restoring and Recovering to a Different Server 819

Step 1. Create an RMAN Backup on the Originating Database 821

Step 2. Copy the RMAN Backup to the Destination Server 821

Step 3. Ensure That Oracle Is Installed 822

Step 4. Source the Required OS Variables 822

Step 5. Create an init.ora File for the Database to Be Restored 822

Step 6. Create Any Required Directories for Data Files, Control Files,
and Dump/Trace Files 823

Step 7. Start Up the Database in Nomount Mode 824

Step 8. Restore the Control File from the RMAN Backup 824

Step 9. Start Up the Database in Mount Mode 824

Step 10. Make the Control File Aware of the Location of the RMAN Backups 824

Step 11. Rename and Restore the Data Files to Reflect New Directory Locations 825

Step 12. Recover the Database 828

Step 13. Set the New Location for the Online Redo Logs 829

Step 14. Open the Database 830

Step 15. Add the Temp File 831

Step 16. Rename the Database 831

Summary 834

Chapter 20: Automating Jobs 837

Automating Jobs with Oracle Scheduler 839

Creating and Scheduling a Job 839

Viewing Job Details 841

Modifying Job Logging History 842

Modifying a Job 842

Stopping a Job 843

Disabling a Job 843

Enabling a Job 843

Copying a Job 844

Running a Job Manually 844

Deleting a Job 845

Oracle Scheduler vs. cron 845

Automating Jobs via cron 846

How cron Works 847

Enabling Access to cron 849

Understanding cron Table Entries 850

Scheduling a Job to Run Automatically 851

Redirecting cron Output 855

Troubleshooting cron 856

Examples of Automated DBA Jobs 857

Starting and Stopping the Database and Listener 858

Checking for Archivelog Destination Fullness 859

Truncating Large Log Files 862

Checking for Locked Production Accounts 864

Checking for Too Many Processes 865

Verifying the Integrity of RMAN Backups 866

Autonomous Database 868

Summary 869

Chapter 21: Database Troubleshooting 871

Quickly Triaging 871

Checking Database Availability 872

Investigating Disk Fullness 875

Inspecting the Alert Log 878

Identifying Bottlenecks via OS Utilities 882

Identifying System Bottlenecks 883

Mapping an Operating System Process to an SQL Statement 888

Finding Resource-Intensive SQL Statements 891

Monitoring Real-Time SQL Execution Statistics 891

Running Oracle Diagnostic Utilities 894

Detecting and Resolving Locking Issues 899

Resolving Open-Cursor Issues 902

Troubleshooting Undo Tablespace Issues 904

Determining if Undo Is Correctly Sized 904

Viewing SQL That Is Consuming Undo Space 907

Handling Temporary Tablespace Issues 908

Determining if Temporary Tablespace Is Sized Correctly 909

Viewing SQL That Is Consuming Temporary Space 910

Summary 911

Chapter 22: Pluggable Databases 915

Understanding Pluggable Architecture 919

Paradigm Shift 922

Backup and Recovery Implications 924

Tuning Nuances 925

Creating a CDB 926

Using the Database Configuration Assistant (DBCA) 927

Generating CDB Create Scripts via DBCA 928

Creating Manually with SQL 929

Verifying That a CDB Was Created 932

Administrating the Root Container 934

Connecting to the Root Container 934

Displaying Currently Connected Container Information 935

Starting/Stopping the Root Container 936

Creating Common Users 936

Creating Common Roles 937

Creating Local Users and Roles 938

Reporting on Container Space 938

Switching Containers 940

Creating a Pluggable Database Within a CDB 941

Cloning the Seed Database 942

Cloning an Existing PDB 943

Cloning from a Non-CDB Database 945

Unplugging a PDB from a CDB 947

Plugging an Unplugged PDB into a CDB 948

Using the DBCA to Create a PDB from the Seed Database 949

Checking the Status of Pluggable Databases 950

Administrating Pluggable Databases 951

Connecting to a PDB 951

Managing a Listener in PDB Environment 952

Showing the Currently Connected PDB 954

Starting/Stopping a PDB 955

Modifying Initialization Parameters Specific to a PDB 956

Renaming a PDB 957

Limiting the Amount of Space Consumed by PDB 957

Restricting Changes to SYSTEM at PDB 958

Viewing PDB History 958

Dropping a PDB 959

Refreshable Clone PDB 960

Databases in the Cloud 961

Summary 961

Index 963

About the Authors

Michelle Malcher is a security architect for databases at Extreme-Scale Solutions. Her deep technical expertise from database to security, as well as her senior-level contributions as a speaker, author, Oracle ACE director, and customer advisory board participant have aided many corporations in the areas of architecture and risk assessment, purchasing and installation, and ongoing systems oversight. She is on the board of directors for FUEL, the Palo Alto Networks User community, as well as volunteering for the Independent Oracle User Group (IOUG). She has built out teams for database security and data services and enjoys sharing knowledge about data intelligence and providing secure and standardized database environments.

Darl Kuhn is a senior database administrator working for Oracle. He handles all facets of database administration from design and development to production support. He also teaches advanced database courses at Regis University in Colorado. Darl does volunteer DBA work for the Rocky Mountain Oracle Users Group. He has a graduate degree from Colorado State University and lives near Spanish Peaks, Colorado, with his wife, Heidi; and daughters, Brandi and Lisa.

About the Technical Reviewer

Arup Nanda has been working in database management for 25 years and counting. With 6 books, more than 700 published articles and 500 presentations in 22 countries, he is very well known in the database area in general and Oracle technologies in particular. Today he is the Chief Data Officer of Priceline.com in New York area. He blogs at arup.blogspot.com.

Acknowledgments

Every time I sit down to write or prepare a presentation, I spend a few minutes reflecting on how I got to this place in my career. There are many people that I am thankful for: to have their influence, guidance, and encouragement in my life. A few of these people I might have told I was done writing books, four books ago. I enjoy seeing their smiles and getting teased when they hear that another one is done.

The friendships that I have made in the database community have encouraged me to learn more and share. I appreciate each of these fun database people who are passionate about what they do and enjoy bringing along others by teaching, mentoring, and supporting others. What an opportunity to be in this career and working with others passionate about databases and being the best guardians of the data! Thank you!

Introduction

Cloud, automation, artificial intelligence, and machine learning are all keywords for the direction of technology. The interesting thing about these areas is that data is still plays a very important role. Obviously, it is something good for the database administrator or the guardian of the data.

With these new environments and Oracle's Autonomous Database in the cloud, the question is being asked if DBAs are needed. Self-driving, tuning, and provisioning of databases are the future of the environment. However, there are definitely different tasks that the DBAs are going to be performing along with being the people to go to for migrations to the cloud and automating processes.

So, why write a book about Oracle 18c database administration? This is an easy question to answer. Even though the tasks are changing, understanding the database is critical. Even with processes being automated, there are issues that might need troubleshooting and automations put into place. Applications need database objects designed, created and maintained, and tuned for performance. Is the job now just troubleshooting issues and automating the rest? No, there are design and strategy for data, application, and security. But this book is not just about the transitioning role of the DBA, but to provide administration skills that are still relevant in the database environment. It is also important to know that the internal understanding of the database helps with all of these areas including previous versions.

Data are being integrated, migrated, and maintained in several databases. The structures of these environments are what is needed and what it takes to create consistent, reliable, and always-accessible data. Administration is needed for these systems and support applications with database design and development.

This book provides details about the tasks that are needed to create Oracle 18c databases and provide administration for the environments because it is more than just building a database but managing it with the data and active applications. It provides an inside look of the Oracle database, hardware, storage, and servers that are required to run Oracle. Some of the tasks that are presented are now and should be done through automated processes but stated in ways to being able to work through issues and troubleshoot any problems.

There was careful consideration for including chapters and sections in this book to make sure it was providing the right topics to understand the database along with previous versions, support the design and performance tuning of database objects, and give DBAs the tools they need to be successful.

Backups and recovery are discussed heavily because scenarios of recovery are difficult to automate. There are consistent themes throughout the book to look to create repeatable tasks for automation, securing the environments, and utilizing the new features and tools that come with the new releases of the database. DBAs play an important role in creating backup and security strategies as there are several discussions that support this.

Many of these topics are the same if the database is on-premise or in the cloud. Understanding the difference and how the DBAs can support the migrations to the cloud are included in the notes and sections of the chapters. Databases in the cloud serve many purposes in the enterprise, and DBAs are the perfect resource to assist in migrations and make sure the data are secure and integrated from the cloud environment.

There are many examples, tips, and notes to provide any DBA with Oracle database the tools they need to design, implement, and administer Oracle 18c database environments.

CHAPTER 1

Installing the Oracle Binaries

Oracle installations of the past can be large, complex, and cumbersome. The Oracle database administrator (DBA) plans and performs the installation because he or she knows how to troubleshoot and address problems as they arise through the steps. There are several configuration and installation options that need to be reviewed, so installing the Oracle software (binaries) is a task that requires proficiency by every DBA. Now with Oracle 18c and even with 12c, Oracle software installations have become more automated, but understanding the steps and configurations of installing is going to be important for the DBA. The installation of the Oracle binaries should be repeatable for large environments, and the DBA needs to set up the installs to be able to provision databases on-demand and consistently.

Tip DBA tasks are changing and in cloud environments, the DBA tasks might be preparing self-service databases or not even needing to install Oracle binaries. Also, if you're fairly new to Oracle, some of the overwhelming parts of Oracle installation have been simplified. Chances are that another DBA has probably already installed the Oracle binaries, and databases will just need to be created as needed. However, it is valuable to understand the component of the installation and the next section, "Understanding the Optimal Flexible Architecture."

Many DBAs don't use techniques for automating installations. Some are unaware of these methods; others perceive them as unreliable. Therefore, most DBAs typically use the graphical mode of the Oracle Universal Installer (OUI). Although the graphical installer is a good tool, it doesn't lend itself to repeatability and automation. Running the graphical installer is a manual process during which you're presented with options to

1

© Michelle Malcher and Darl Kuhn 2019
M. Malcher and D. Kuhn, *Pro Oracle Database 18c Administration*,
https://doi.org/10.1007/978-1-4842-4424-1_1

choose from on multiple screens. Even if you know which options to select, you may still inadvertently click an undesired choice.

The graphical installer can also be problematic when you're performing remote installations, and the network bandwidth is insufficient. In these situations, you can find yourself waiting for dozens of minutes for a screen to repaint itself on your local screen. You need a different technique for efficient installation on remote servers.

This chapter focuses on techniques for installing Oracle in an efficient and repeatable manner. This includes silent installations, which rely on a response file. A response file is a text file in which you assign values to variables that govern the installation. DBAs often don't realize the powerful repeatability and efficiency that can be achieved by using response files.

Note   This chapter only covers installing the Oracle software. The task of creating a database is covered in Chapter 2. The cloud also changes the tasks and viewpoints of software and database creation, which will be discussed later in this chapter under the section, "Installing in the Cloud and Responsibilities of the DBA."

Understanding the OFA

Before you install Oracle and start creating databases, you must understand Oracle's Optimal Flexible Architecture (OFA) standard. This standard is widely employed for specifying consistent directory structures and also the file-naming conventions used when installing and creating Oracle databases.

Note   One irony of this ubiquitous OFA "standard" is that almost every DBA, in some manner, customizes it to fit the unique requirements of his or her environment.

The OFA standard provides ways to understand where log files are available on a consistent basis. If standards are followed, security, migrations, and automations are going to be easier to implement because of consistency across the environments. The consistent locations of the log files allow for the files to be used by other tools as well as being secured. The ORACLE_BASE directory in 18c provides a way to separate the

ORACLE_HOME directories for read-only directories and have the writable files in the ORACLE_BASE. Read-only ORACLE_HOME directories allow for implementing separation of installation and configuration, which is important for the cloud and securing the environment. This simplifies patching as one image can be used for a mass rollout and distribute a patch to many servers and reduces downtime for patching and updating of the Oracle software.

Because most shops implement a form of the OFA standard, understanding this structure is critical. Figure 1-1 shows the directory structure and file names used with the OFA standard. Not all the directories and files found in an Oracle environment appear in this figure (there isn't enough room). However, the critical and most frequently used directories and files are displayed.

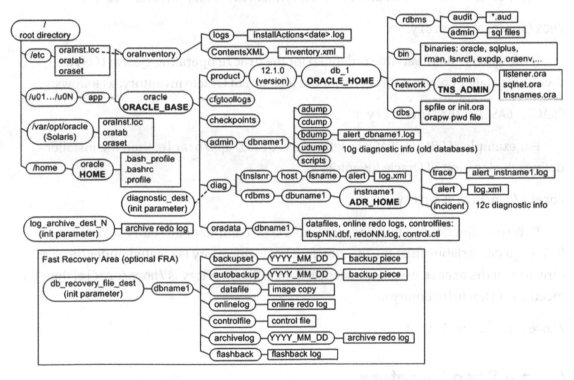

Figure 1-1. *Oracle's OFA standard*

The OFA standard includes several directories that you should be familiar with:

- Oracle inventory directory

- Oracle base directory (ORACLE_BASE)

- Oracle home directory (ORACLE_HOME)

- Oracle network files directory (TNS_ADMIN)

- Automatic Diagnostic Repository (ADR_HOME)

These directories are discussed in the following sections.

Oracle Inventory Directory

The Oracle inventory directory stores the inventory of Oracle software installed on the server. This directory is required and is shared among all installations of Oracle software on a server. When you first install Oracle, the installer checks to see whether there is an existing OFA-compliant directory structure in the format /u[01-09]/app. If such a directory exists, then the installer creates an Oracle inventory directory, such as

/u01/app/oraInventory

If the ORACLE_BASE variable is defined for the oracle operating system (OS) user, then the installer creates a directory for the location of Oracle inventory, as follows:

ORACLE_BASE/../oraInventory

For example, if ORACLE_BASE is defined as /ora01/app/oracle, then the installer defines the location of Oracle inventory as

/ora01/app/oraInventory

If the installer doesn't find a recognizable OFA-compliant directory structure or an ORACLE_BASE variable, then the location for Oracle inventory is created under the HOME directory of the oracle user. For instance, if the HOME directory is /home/oracle, then the location of Oracle inventory is

/home/oracle/oraInventory

Oracle Base Directory

The Oracle base directory is the topmost directory for Oracle software installation. You can install one or more versions of the Oracle software beneath this directory. The OFA standard for the Oracle base directory is as follows:

/<mount_point>/app/<software_owner>

Typical names for the mount point include /u01, /ora01, /oracle, and /oracle01. You can name the mount point according to whatever your standard is for your environment. I prefer to use a mount-point name such as /ora01. It is short, and when I look at the mount points on a database server, I can immediately tell which are used for the Oracle database. Also, a short mount-point name is easier to use when you're querying the data dictionary to report on the physical aspects of your database. Additionally, a shorter mount-point name makes for less typing when you're navigating through directories via OS commands.

The software owner is typically named oracle. This is the OS user you use to install the Oracle software (binaries). Listed next is an example of a fully formed Oracle base directory path:

```
/u01/app/oracle
```

Oracle Home Directory

The Oracle home directory defines the installation location of software for a particular product, such as Oracle Database 18c or Oracle Database 12c. You must install different products or different releases of a product in separate Oracle homes. The recommended OFA-compliant Oracle home directory is as follows:

```
ORACLE_BASE/product/<version>/<install_name>
```

In the previous line of code, possible versions include 18.1.0.1 and 12.2.0.1. Possible install_name values include db_1, devdb1, test2, and prod1. Here is an example of an Oracle home name for a 18c database:

```
/u01/app/oracle/product/18.1.0.1/dbhome_1/db1
```

Note   Some DBAs dislike the db1 string on the end of the ORACLE_HOME directory and see no need for it. The reason for the db1 is that you may have two separate installations of binaries: a development installation and a test installation. If you don't require that configuration in your environment, feel free to drop the extra string (db1).

Oracle Network Files Directory

Some Oracle utilities use the value TNS_ADMIN to locate network configuration files. This directory is defined as ORACLE_HOME/network/admin. It typically contains the tnsnames.ora and listener.ora Oracle Net files. The listener.ora files are now typically with the Oracle Grid installation and not in the database home. The listeners are normally maintained by the system that manages the grid, cluster, and ASM software. The tnsnames provide ways to connect to other databases so these files are part of the centralized directory or part of the database network files.

Tip   Sometimes DBAs will set TNS_ADMIN to point at one central directory location (such as /etc or /var/opt/oracle). This allows them to maintain one set of Oracle network files (instead of one for each ORACLE_HOME). This approach also has the advantage of not requiring the copying or moving of files when a database upgrade occurs, potentially changing the location of ORACLE_HOME.

Automatic Diagnostic Repository

Starting with Oracle Database 11g, the ADR_HOME directory specifies the location of the diagnostic files related to Oracle. These files are crucial for troubleshooting problems with the Oracle database. This directory is defined as ORACLE_BASE/diag/rdbms/ lower(db_unique_name)/instance_name. You can query the V$PARAMETER view to get the values of db_unique_name and instance_name.

For example, in the next line, the lowercase database unique name is db18c, and the instance name is DB18C:

```
/u01/app/oracle/diag/rdbms/db18c/DB18C
```

Or with a clustered environment, the lowercase database unique name is db18c, and the instance name is DB18C01:

```
/u01/app/oracle/diag/rdbms/db18c/DB18C01
```

You can verify the location of the ADR_HOME directory via this query:

```
SQL> select value from v$diag_info where name='ADR Home';
```

Here is some sample output:

```
VALUE
-------------------------------------------------------------
/u01/app/oracle/diag/rdbms/db18c/DB18C
```

Now that you understand the OFA standard, you'll next see how it's used when installing the Oracle binaries. For instance, you'll need to specify directory values for the ORACLE_BASE and ORACLE_HOME directories when running the Oracle installer.

Tip   See the *Oracle Database Installation Guide* for full details on OFA. This document can be freely downloaded from the Technology Network area of the Oracle web site (http://otn.oracle.com).

Installing Oracle

Suppose you're new on the job, and your manager asks you how long it will take to install a new set of Oracle Database 18c software on a server. You reply that it will take less than an hour. Your boss is incredulous and states that previous DBAs always estimated at least a day to install the Oracle binaries on a new server. You reply, "Actually, it's not that complicated, but DBAs do tend to overestimate installations, because it's hard to predict everything that could go wrong."

When you're handed a new server and are given the task of installing the Oracle binaries, this usually refers to the process of downloading and installing the software required before you can create an Oracle database. This process involves several steps:

1. Create the appropriate OS groups. In Oracle Database 18c, there are several OS groups that you can form and use to manage the level of granularity of SYSDBA permissions. Minimally, you'll need to create an OS dba group and the OS oracle user.

2. Ensure that the OS is configured adequately for an Oracle database.

3. Obtain the database installation software from Oracle.

4. Unzip the database installation software.

5. If using the silent installer when first installing Oracle software on the box, create an `oraInst.loc` file. This step only needs to be done once per server. Subsequent installations do not require this step to be performed.

6. Configure the response file and run the Oracle silent installer.

7. Troubleshoot any issues.

8. Apply any additional patches.

These steps are detailed in the following sections.

Note   Any version of the database that Oracle designates as a base release (10.1.0.2, 10.2.0.1, 11.1.0.6, 11.2.0.1, 12.1.0.1, 18.1.0.1, and so on) can be freely downloaded from the Technology Network area of the Oracle web site (`http://otn.oracle.com`). However, be aware that any subsequent patch downloads require a purchased license. In other words, downloading base software requires an Oracle Technology Network (OTN) login (free), whereas downloading a patch set requires a My Oracle Support account (for fee).

Step 1. Create the OS Groups and User

If you work in a shop with a system administrator (SA), then steps 1 and 2 usually are performed by the SA. If you don't have a SA, then you have to perform these steps yourself (this is often the case in small shops, where you may be required to perform many different job functions). You need `root` access to accomplish these steps.

In the old days, a typical Oracle installation would contain one OS group (dba) and one OS user (`oracle`). You can still install the Oracle software, using this minimalistic, one-group, one-user approach; it works fine. If there is just one DBA in your shop, and you don't need a more granular division of privileges among team members, then go ahead, and create only the dba group and the `oracle` OS user. There is nothing wrong with this method.

Nowadays, there are multiple OS groups that Oracle recommends you create—the idea being that you can add different OS users and assign them to groups on an as-needed basis, depending on the job function. When an OS user is assigned to a group, that assignment provides the user with specific database privileges. Table 1-1 documents the OS groups and how each group maps to corresponding database privileges. For example, if you have a user that is only responsible for monitoring a database and that only needs privileges to start up and shut down the database, then that user would be assigned the oper group (which ensures that subsequent connections to the database can be done with sysoper privileges).

Table 1-1. *Mapping of OS Groups to Privileges Related to Backup and Recovery*

OS Group	Database System Privilege	Authorized Operations	Where Referenced
oinstall	none	OS privileges to install and upgrade Oracle binaries	inst_group variable in oraInst.loc file; also defined by UNIX_GROUP_NAME variable in response file
dba	sysdba	All database privileges: start up, shut down, alter database, create and drop database, toggle archivelog mode, back up, and recover database	DBA_GROUP variable in response file or when prompted by OUI graphical installer
oper	sysoper	Start up, shut down, alter database, toggle archivelog mode, back up, and recover database	OPER_GROUP variable in response file or when prompted by OUI graphical installer
asmdba	sysdba for asm	Administrative privileges to Oracle automatic storage management (ASM) instances	n/a
asmoper	sysoper for asm	Starting up and stopping the Oracle ASM instance	n/a
asmadmin	sysasm	Mounting and dismounting of disk groups and other storage administration	n/a

(*continued*)

Table 1-1. (*continued*)

OS Group	Database System Privilege	Authorized Operations	Where Referenced
backupdba	sysbackup	New in 12c; privilege allowing user to start up, shut down, and perform all backup and recovery operations	BACKUPDBA_GROUP in response file or when prompted by OUI graphical installer
dgdba	sysdg	New in 12c; associated with privileges related to managing Data Guard environments	DGDBA_GROUP variable in response file or when prompted by OUI graphical installer
kmdba	syskm	New in 12c; associated with privileges related to encryption management	KMDBA_GROUP variable in response file or when prompted by OUI graphical installer

Table 1-1 contains recommended group names. You don't have to use the group names listed; you can adjust per your requirements. For example, if you have two separate groups using the same server, you may want to create two separate Oracle installations, each managed by different DBAs; the development DBA group might create and install the Oracle binaries with a group named dbadev, whereas a test group using the same box might install a separate set of Oracle binaries managed with a group named dbatest. Each group would have permissions to manipulate only its set of binaries. Or, as mentioned earlier, you may decide to use just one group (dba) for everything. It all depends on your environment.

Once you decide which groups you need, then you need access to the root user to run the groupadd command. As root, add the OS groups that you need. Here, I add the three groups that I foresee will be needed:

```
# groupadd oinstall
# groupadd dba
# groupadd oper
```

If you don't have access to the root account, then you need to get your SA to run the previous commands. You can verify that each group was added successfully by inspecting the contents of the /etc/group file. Here are typical entries created in the /etc/group file:

```
oinstall:x:500:
dba:x:501:
oper:x:502:
```

Now, create the oracle OS user. The following example explicitly sets the group ID to 500 (your company may require use of the same group ID for all installations), establishes the primary group as oinstall, and assigns the dba and oper groups to the newly created oracle user:

```
# useradd -u 500 -g oinstall -G dba,oper oracle
```

You can verify user account information by viewing the /etc/passwd file. Here is what you can expect to see for the oracle user:

```
oracle:x:500:500::/home/oracle:/bin/bash
```

If you need to modify a group, as root, use the groupmod command. If, for any reason, you need to remove a group (as root) use the groupdel command.

If you need to modify a user, as root, use the usermod command. If you need to remove an OS user, use the userdel command. You need root privileges to run the userdel command. This example removes the oracle user from the server:

```
# userdel oracle
```

Step 2. Ensure That the OS Is Adequately Configured

The tasks associated with this step vary somewhat for each database release and OS. You must refer to the Oracle installation manual for the database release and OS vendor to get the exact requirements. To perform this step, you're required to verify and configure OS components such as these:

- Memory and swap space
- System architecture (processor)
- Free disk space (Oracle now takes almost 5GB of space to install)
- Operating system version and kernel
- Operating system software (required packages and patches)

Run the following command to confirm the memory size on a Linux server:

```
$ grep MemTotal /proc/meminfo
```

To verify the amount of memory and swap space, run the following command:

```
$ free -t
```

To verify the amount of space in the /tmp directory, enter this command:

```
$ df -h /tmp
```

To display the amount of free disk space, execute this command:

```
$ df -h
```

To verify the OS version, enter this command:

```
$ cat /proc/version
```

To verify kernel information, run the following command:

```
$ uname -r
```

To determine whether the required packages are installed, execute this query, and provide the required package name:

```
$ rpm -q <package_name>
```

Again, database server requirements vary quite a bit by OS and database version. You can download the specific installation manual from the Documentation page of the Oracle web site (www.oracle.com/documentation).

Note   The OUI displays any deficiencies in OS software and hardware. Running the installer is covered in step 6.

Step 3. Obtain the Oracle Installation Software

Usually, the easiest way to obtain the Oracle software is to download it from the Oracle web site. Navigate to the software download page (www.oracle.com/technology/software), and download the Oracle database version that is appropriate for the type of OS and hardware on which you want to install it (Linux, Solaris, Windows, and so on).

Step 4. Unzip the Files

For previous versions, it was recommended to unzip the files in a standard directory where you can place the Oracle installation media. Now with Oracle 18c, there are different ways that the media is presented, imaged based or by RPM. The image software must now be extracted in the directory of the ORACLE_HOME. The zipped file can be placed in a temporary directory but extracted to the ORACLE_HOME. The runInstaller will run from the ORACLE_HOME directory for installation.

Create the directories for the ORACLE_HOME:

```
$ mkdir -p /u01/app/oracle/product/18.1.0/dbhome_1
$ chown oracle:oinstall /u01/app/oracle/product/18.1.0/dbhome_1
```

The zip files can be downloaded or copied over to a temporary directory such as /tmp or /home/oracle.

Use the unzip command to the newly created ORACLE_HOME directory to the newly created ORACLE_HOME directory:

```
$ cd /u01/app/oracle/product/18.1.0/dbhome_1
$ unzip -q /tmp/db_home.zip
```

RPM can now be used with Oracle 18c to perform the installation for a single database instance. The RPM was used before as a preinstallation check and is now available for installations, even of the Oracle client. This will need to be performed as root.

```
$ yum -y install oracle-database-server-18c-preinstall
$ ls -lt /opt
$ chown -R oracle:oinstall /opt
```

Now go to the directory for the rpm and run the command to perform the RPM-based install. The ORACLE_HOME directory will be created in /opt/oracle/product/18.1.0.0.0-1/dbhome_1.

```
$ cd /tmp/rpm
$ rpm -ivh oracle-ee-db-18.1.0.0.0-1.x86_64.rpm  -- rpm name may vary based
on version
```

Tip   On some installations of previous versions of Oracle, you may find that the distribution file is provided as a compressed `cpio` file. You can uncompress and unbundle the file with one command, as follows: `$ cat 10gr2_db_sol.cpio.gz | gunzip | cpio -idvm`

Step 5. Creating oraInst.loc File

If an `oraInst.loc` file already exists on your server, then you can skip this step. Creating the `oraInst.loc` file only needs to be performed the first time you install binaries on a server, using the silent install method. If you're using the OUI graphical installer, then the `oraInst.loc` file is created automatically for you.

On Linux servers the `oraInst.loc` file is usually located in the `/etc` directory. On other Unix systems (such as Solaris), this file is located in the `/var/opt/oracle` directory. The `oraInst.loc` file contains the following information:

- Oracle inventory directory path

- Name of OS group that has permissions for installing and upgrading Oracle software

The Oracle inventory directory path is the location of files associated with managing Oracle installations and upgrades. Typically, there is one Oracle inventory per host. Within this directory structure is the `inventory.xml` file, which contains a record of where various versions of Oracle have been installed on the server.

The Oracle inventory OS group has the OS permissions required for installing and upgrading Oracle software. Oracle recommends that you name this group `oinstall`. You'll find that sometimes DBAs assign the inventory group to the `dba` group. If your environment doesn't require a separate group (such as `oinstall`), then using the `dba` group is fine.

You can create the `oraInst.loc` file with a utility such as `vi`. Here are some sample entries in the file:

```
inventory_loc=/u01/app/oraInventory
inst_group=oinstall
```

As root, ensure that the response file is owned by the oracle OS user and that it has the proper file access privileges:

```
# chown oracle:oinstall oraInst.loc
# chmod 664 oraInst.loc
```

Step 6. Configure the Response File, and Run the Installer

You can run the OUI in one of two modes: graphical or silent. Typically, DBAs use the graphical installer. However, I strongly prefer using the silent install option for the following reasons:

- Silent installs don't require the availability of X Window System software.

- You avoid performance issues with remote graphical installs, which can be extremely slow when trying to paint screens locally.

- Silent installs can be scripted and automated. This means that every install can be performed with the same, consistent standards, regardless of which team member is performing the install (I even have the SA install the Oracle binaries this way).

The key to performing a silent install is to use a response file.

After unzipping the Oracle software, navigate to the ORACLE_HOME directory; for example,

```
$ cd /u01/app/oracle/product/18.1.0/dbhome_1
```

Next, find the sample response files that Oracle provides:

```
$ find . -name "*.rsp"
```

Depending on the version of Oracle and the OS platform, the names and number of response files that you find may be quite different. The next two sections show two scenarios: an Oracle Database 12c Release 1 silent install and an Oracle Database 18c Release 1 silent install.

Keep in mind that the format of response files can differ quite a bit, depending on the Oracle database version. For example, there are major differences between Oracle Database 11g and 12c even between release 2 of these versions. When you install a new release, you must inspect the response file and determine which parameters must be set. Be sure to modify the appropriate parameters for your environment. If you're unsure what to set the ORACLE_HOME and ORACLE_BASE values to, see the section "Understanding the Optimal Flexible Architecture," earlier in this chapter, for a description of the OFA standard directories.

There are sometimes idiosyncrasies to these parameters that are specific to a release. For instance, if you don't want to specify your My Oracle Support (MOS) login information, then you need to set the following parameter as follows:

```
DECLINE_SECURITY_UPDATES=true
```

If you don't set DECLINE_SECURITY_UPDATES to TRUE, then you will be expected to provide your MOS login information. Failure to do so will cause the installation to fail. After you've configured your response file, you can run the Oracle installer in silent mode. Note that you have to enter the entire directory path for the location of your response file.

Note   On Windows the `setup.exe` command is equivalent to the Linux/Unix `runInstaller` command.

If you encounter errors with the installation process, you can view the associated log file. Each time you attempt to run the installer, it creates a log file with a unique name that includes a timestamp. The log file is located in the oraInventory/logs directory. You can stream the output to your screen as the OUI writes to it:

```
$ tail -f <logfile name>
```

Here is an example of a log file name:

```
installActions2012-04-33 11-42-52AM.log
```

Oracle Database 12c Release 1 Scenario

Navigate to the database directory and issue the find command to locate sample response files. Here are the response files provided with an Oracle Database 12c Release 1 on a Linux server:

```
$ find . -name "*.rsp"
./response/db_install.rsp
./response/netca.rsp
./response/dbca.rsp
```

Copy one of the response files so that you can modify it. This example copies the db_install.rsp file to the current working directory and names the file inst.rsp:

```
$ cp response/db_install.rsp inst.rsp
```

Modify the inst.rsp file. Here is a partial listing of an Oracle Database 12c Release 1 response file (the first two lines are actually a single line of code but have been placed on two lines in order to fit on the page). The lines of code are the only variables that I modified. I removed the comments so that you could more clearly see which variables were modified:

```
oracle.install.responseFileVersion=/oracle/install/rspfmt_dbinstall_
response_schema_v12.1.0
oracle.install.option=INSTALL_DB_SWONLY
ORACLE_HOSTNAME=oraserv1
UNIX_GROUP_NAME=oinstall
INVENTORY_LOCATION=/home/oracle/orainst/12.1.0.1/database/stage/products.xml
SELECTED_LANGUAGES=en
ORACLE_HOME=/u01/app/oracle/product/12.1.0.1/db_1
ORACLE_BASE=/u01/app/oracle
oracle.install.db.InstallEdition=EE
oracle.install.db.DBA_GROUP=dba
oracle.install.db.OPER_GROUP=oper
oracle.install.db.BACKUPDBA_GROUP=dba
oracle.install.db.DGDBA_GROUP=dba
oracle.install.db.KMDBA_GROUP=dba
DECLINE_SECURITY_UPDATES=true
```

Be sure to modify the appropriate parameters for your environment. If you're unsure what to set the ORACLE_HOME and ORACLE_BASE values to, see the section "Understanding the Optimal Flexible Architecture," earlier in this chapter, for a description of the OFA standard directories.

After you've configured your response file, you can run the Oracle installer in silent mode. Note that you have to enter the entire directory path for the location of your response file:

```
$ ./runInstaller -ignoreSysPrereqs -force -silent -responseFile \
  /home/oracle/orainst/12.1.0.1/database/inst.rsp
```

The previous command is entered on two lines. The first line is continued to the second line via the backward slash (\).

If you encounter errors with the installation process, you can view the associated log file. Each time you attempt to run the installer, it creates a log file with a unique name that includes a timestamp. The log file is created in the oraInventory/logs directory. You can stream the output to your screen as the OUI writes to it:

```
$ tail -f <logfile name>
```

Here is an example of a log file name:

```
installActions2012-11-04_02-57-29PM.log
```

If everything runs successfully, in the output you're notified that you need to run the root.sh script as the root user:

```
/u01/app/oracle/product/12.1.0.1/db_1/root.sh
```

Run the root.sh script as the root OS user. Then, you should be able to create an Oracle database (database creation is covered in Chapter 2).

Oracle Database 18c Release 1 Scenario

Navigate to the database directory and issue the find command to locate sample response files. Here are the response files provided with an Oracle Database 18c Release 1 on a Linux server:

```
$ find . -name "*.rsp"
./response/db_install.rsp
./response/netca.rsp
./response/dbca.rsp
```

Copy one of the response files so that you can modify it. This example copies the db_install.rsp file to the current working directory and names the file inst.rsp:

```
$ cp response/db_install.rsp inst.rsp
```

Modify the inst.rsp file. Here is a partial listing of an Oracle Database 18c Release 1 response file (the first two lines are actually a single line of code but have been placed on two lines in order to fit on the page). The lines of code are the only variables that I modified. I removed the comments so that you could more clearly see which variables were modified:

```
oracle.install.responseFileVersion=/oracle/install/rspfmt_dbinstall_
response_schema_v18.0.0
oracle.install.option=INSTALL_DB_SWONLY
ORACLE_HOSTNAME=oraserv1
UNIX_GROUP_NAME=oinstall
INVENTORY_LOCATION=/home/oracle/orainst/18.1.0.1/database/stage/products.xml
SELECTED_LANGUAGES=en
ORACLE_HOME=/u01/app/oracle/product/18.1.0.1/db_1
ORACLE_BASE=/u01/app/oracle
oracle.install.db.InstallEdition=EE
oracle.install.db.DBA_GROUP=dba
oracle.install.db.OPER_GROUP=oper
oracle.install.db.BACKUPDBA_GROUP=dba
oracle.install.db.DGDBA_GROUP=dba
oracle.install.db.KMDBA_GROUP=dba
DECLINE_SECURITY_UPDATES=true
```

Be sure to modify the appropriate parameters for your environment. If you're unsure what to set the ORACLE_HOME and ORACLE_BASE values to, see the section "Understanding the Optimal Flexible Architecture," earlier in this chapter, for a description of the OFA standard directories.

After you've configured your response file, you can run the Oracle installer in silent mode. Note that you have to enter the entire directory path for the location of your response file:

```
$ ./runInstaller -ignoreSysPrereqs -force -silent -responseFile \
  /home/oracle/orainst/18.1.0.1/database/inst.rsp
```

The previous command is entered on two lines. The first line is continued to the second line via the backward slash (\).

If you encounter errors with the installation process, you can view the associated log file. Each time you attempt to run the installer, it creates a log file with a unique name that includes a timestamp. The log file is created in the oraInventory/logs directory. You can stream the output to your screen as the OUI writes to it:

```
$ tail -f <logfile name>
```

Here is an example of a log file name:

```
installActions2017-11-04_02-57-29PM.log
```

If everything runs successfully, in the output you're notified that you need to run the `root.sh` script as the `root` user:

```
/u01/app/oracle/product/18.1.0.1/db_1/root.sh
```

Run the `root.sh` script as the `root` OS user. Then, you should be able to create an Oracle database (database creation is covered in Chapter 2). The configuration assistants can run in the response file or silent mode to run the Net Configuration and Database Configuration Assistant.

Step 7. Troubleshoot Any Issues

If you encounter an error, using a response file, 90 percent of the time it's due to an issue with how you set the variables in the file. Inspect those variables carefully and ensure that they're set correctly. Also, if you don't fully specify the command-line path to the response file, you receive errors such as this:

```
OUI-10203: The specified response file ... is not found.
```

Here is another common error when the path or name of the response file is incorrectly specified:

```
OUI-10202: No response file is specified for this session.
```

Listed next is the error message you receive if you enter a wrong path to your `products.xml` file within the response file's `FROM_LOCATION` variable:

```
OUI-10133: Invalid staging area
```

Also, be sure to provide the correct command-line syntax when running a response file. If you incorrectly specify or misspell an option, you may receive a misleading error message, such as `DISPLAY not set`. When using a response file, you don't need to have your `DISPLAY` variable set. This message is confusing because, in this scenario, the error is caused by an incorrectly specified command-line option and has nothing to do with the `DISPLAY` variable. Check all options entered from the command line and ensure that you haven't misspelled an option.

Problems can also occur when you specify an ORACLE_HOME, and the silent installation "thinks" the given home already exists:

```
Check complete: Failed <<<<
Recommendation: Choose a new Oracle Home for installing this product.
```

Check your inventory.xml file (in the oraInventory/ContentsXML directory), and make sure there isn't a conflict with an already existing Oracle home name.

There are log files that are generated with the installation, along with the files that are part of the inventory. The /tmp directory is going to have log files based on the timestamp of when the installation was performed. Make sure that all log files are examined when trying to troubleshoot; even system logs are useful if there were processes or memory issues hit during the process. When you're troubleshooting issues with Oracle installations, remember that the installer uses two key files to keep track of what software has been installed, and where: oraInst.loc and inventory.xml. Table 1-2 describes the files used by the Oracle installer.

Table 1-2. *Useful Files for Troubleshooting Oracle Installation Issues*

File name	Directory Location	Contents
oraInst.loc	The location of this file varies by OS. On Linux the file is in /etc; on Solaris, it's in /var/opt/oracle.	oraInventory directory location and installation OS group
inst.loc	\\HKEY_LOCAL_MACHINE\\Software\ Oracle (Windows registry)	Inventory information
inventory.xml	oraInventory/ContentsXML/ inventory.xml	Oracle home names and corresponding directory location
.log files	oraInventory/logs	Installation log files, which are extremely useful for troubleshooting

Step 8. Apply Any Additional Patches

As already stated before the first step, the Oracle software is available in the base releases. However, if there are additional releases, patch sets, and security patches available, these should all be applied before rolling out a new set of Oracle binaries. The installation is going to be for a different reason on the server or in the environment, and the installation should be the same as the other environments with a possible exception of security patching.

Sections later in this chapter, "Upgrading Oracle Software" and "Applying Interim Patches," have the details to apply the patches, but it is important to have this step here to get to the latest version of the software before releasing it for use. Right after the install of the binaries is a good time to make sure everything has been updated and ready for the database to be created.

Installing with a Copy of an Existing Installation

DBAs sometimes install Oracle software by using a utility such as tar to copy an existing installation of the Oracle binaries to a different server (or a different location on the same server). This approach is fast and simple (especially compared with downloading and running the Oracle installer). This technique allows DBAs to easily install the Oracle software on multiple servers, while ensuring that each installation is identical.

The new ways of delivering the media files provide ways to unzip in the ORACLE_HOME directory, or just run the rpm package that will run the installation. The advantage of using this method is be able to copy over a patched set of the binaries. There cannot be any databases running during this time or Oracle processes during this time of copying the files to provide a static copy of the files.

Installing Oracle with an existing copy of the binaries is a two-part process:

1. Copy the binaries, using an OS utility.

2. Attach the Oracle home.

These steps are detailed in the next two sections.

Tip   See MOS note 300062.1 for instructions on how to clone an existing Oracle installation.

Step 1. Copy the Binaries, Using an OS Utility

You can use any OS copy utility to perform this step. The Linux/Unix tar, scp, and rsync utilities are commonly used by DBAs to copy files. This example shows how to use the

Linux/Unix tar utility to replicate an existing set of Oracle binaries to a different server. First, locate the target Oracle home binaries that you want to copy:

```
$ echo $ORACLE_HOME
/ora01/app/oracle/product/18.1.0.1/db_1
```

In this example the tar utility copies every file and subdirectory in or below the db_1 directory:

```
$ cd $ORACLE_HOME
$ cd ..
$ tar -cvf orahome.tar db_1
```

Now, copy the orahome.tar file to the server on which you want to install the Oracle software. In this example, the tar file is copied to the /u01/app/oracle/product/18.1.0.1 directory on a different server. The tar file is extracted there and creates a db_1 directory as part of the extract:

```
$ cd /u01/app/oracle/product/18.1.0.1
```

Make sure you have plenty of disk space available to extract the files. A typical Oracle installation can consume at least 3–4GB of space. Use the Linux/Unix df command to verify that you have enough space:

```
$ df -h | sort
```

Next, extract the files:

```
$ tar -xvf orahome.tar
```

When the tar commanddb_1 directory beneath the /u01/app/oracle/product/18.1.0.1 directory. directory.

Tip Use the tar -tvf <tarfile_name> command to preview which directories and files are restored without restoring them.

Listed next is a powerful one-line combination of commands that allows you to bundle the Oracle files, copy them to a remote server, and have them extracted remotely:

```
$ tar -cvf - <locDir> | ssh <remoteNode> "cd <remoteDir>; tar -xvf -"
```

For instance, the following command copies everything in the dev_1 directory to the remote ora03 server /home/oracle directory:

```
$ tar -cvf - dev_1 | ssh ora03 "cd /home/oracle; tar -xvf -"
```

ABSOLUTE PATHS VS. RELATIVE PATHS

Some older, non-GNU versions of tar use absolute paths when extracting files. The next line of code shows an example of specifying the absolute path when creating an archive file:

```
$ tar -cvf orahome.tar /home/oracle
```

Specifying an absolute path with non-GNU versions of tar can be dangerous. These older versions of tar restore the contents with the same directories and file names from which they were copied. This means that any directories and file names that previously existed on disk are overwritten.

When using older versions of tar, it's much safer to use a relative pathname. This example first changes to the /home directory and then creates an archive of the oracle directory (relative to the current working directory):

```
$ cd /home
$ tar -cvf orahome.tar oracle
```

The previous example uses the relative pathname.

You don't have to worry about absolute vs. relative paths on most Linux systems. This is because these systems use the GNU version of tar. This version strips off the forward slash (/) and restores files relative to where your current working directory is located.

Use the man tar command if you're not sure whether you have a GNU version of the tar utility. You can also use the tar -tvf <tarfile name> command to preview which directories and files are restored to what locations.

Step 2. Attach the Oracle Home

One issue with using a copy of an existing installation to install the Oracle software is that if you later attempt to upgrade the software, the upgrade process will throw an error and abort. This is because a copied installation isn't registered in oraInventory. Before you upgrade a set of binaries installed via a copy, you must first register the Oracle home so that it appears in the `inventory.xml` file. This is called attaching an Oracle home.

To attach an Oracle home, you need to know the location of your `oraInst.loc` file on your server. On Linux servers this file is usually located in the `/etc` directory. On Solaris this file can generally be found in the `/var/opt/oracle` directory.

After you've located your `oraInst.loc` file, navigate to the `ORACLE_HOME/oui/bin` directory (on the server on which you installed the Oracle binaries from a copy):

```
$ cd $ORACLE_HOME/oui/bin
```

Now, attach the Oracle home by running the `runInstaller` utility, as shown:

```
$ ./runInstaller -silent -attachHome -invPtrLoc /etc/oraInst.loc \
ORACLE_HOME="/u01/app/oracle/product/18.1.0.1/db_1" ORACLE_HOME_NAME="ONEW"
```

You should see this as the last message in the output, if successful:

```
'AttachHome' was successful.
```

You can also examine the contents of your `oraInventory/ContentsXML/inventory.xml` file. Here is a snippet of the line inserted into the `inventory.xml` file as a result of running the `runInstaller` utility with the `attachHome` option:

```
<HOME NAME="ONEW" LOC="/u01/app/oracle/product/18.1.0.1/db_1" TYPE="O"
IDX="2"/>
```

Installing Read-Only Oracle Home

A new feature of Oracle 18c is to have a read-only Oracle Home for the binaries. The database tools and processes will be under the ORACLE_BASE path instead of ORACLE_HOME path. The ORACLE_HOME directory will have the database configurations and logs for the databases created.

A read-only Oracle binary home will separate the software from the database information and allows for sharing the software across different deployments. This enables seamless patching and updating of the binaries to minimize database downtime and allows for applying patches to one image in order to distribute to several servers. This separation also simplifies the provisioning because the focus can be on the database configuration.

There are now additional environment variables that will contain the directory path for the Oracle Home, ORACLE_BASE_HOME, ORACLE_BASE_CONFIG.

To enable a read-only Oracle home, the software needs to be install as described with the binaries only and not the configuration assistants. Then run the following:

```
$ cd /u01/app/oracle/product/18.1.0.1/dbhome18c/bin
$ roohctl -enable
```

After enabling the read-only home, the DBCA can be run to create databases. There is a check to know if the database is in a read-only home:

```
$ cd $ORACLE_HOME/bin
$ ./orabasehome
```

If a directory is returned, the Oracle home is in read-only.

Upgrading Oracle Software

You can also upgrade a version of the Oracle software, using the silent installation method. Begin by downloading the upgrade version from the MOS web site (http://support.oracle.com) (you need a valid support contract to do this). Read the upgrade documentation that comes with the new software. The upgrade procedure can vary quite a bit, depending on what version of Oracle you're using.

For the most recent upgrades that I've performed, the procedure was much like installing a new set of Oracle binaries. You can use the OUI in either graphical or silent mode to install the software. See the section "Installing Oracle," earlier in this chapter, for information on using the silent mode installation method.

Database migrations to new version are successful using the Database Upgrade Assistant (DBUA). This will perform a migration to the latest version of the database and upgrade the services. New with 18c the services must be upgraded with this method, install the latest version of the software and then to complete the migration run the DBUA.

Note   Upgrading the Oracle software isn't the same as upgrading an Oracle database. This section only deals with using the silent install method for upgrading the Oracle software. Additional steps are involved for upgrading a database. See MOS note 730365.1 for instructions on how to upgrade a database.

Depending on the version being upgraded, you may be presented with two different scenarios. Here is scenario A:

1. Shut down any databases using the Oracle home to be upgraded.

2. Upgrade the Oracle home binaries.

3. Start up the database and run any required upgrade scripts.

Here are the steps for the scenario B approach to an upgrade:

1. Leave the existing Oracle home as it is—don't upgrade it.

2. Install a new Oracle home that is the same version as the old Oracle home.

3. Upgrade the new Oracle home to the desired version.

4. When you're ready, shut down the database using the old Oracle home; set the OS variables to point to the new, upgraded Oracle home; start up the database; and run any required upgrade scripts.

Which of the two previous scenarios is better? Scenario B has the advantage of leaving the old Oracle home as it is; therefore, if, for any reason, you need to switch back to the old Oracle home, you have those binaries available. Scenario B has the disadvantage of requiring extra disk space to contain two installations of Oracle home. This usually isn't an issue, because after the upgrade is complete, you can delete the old Oracle home when it's convenient.

Databases can also be upgraded to a new container database in a multitenant environment. This will be discussed more in Chapter 22, but the pluggable databases can be moved to a container database that has already been upgraded.

Tip   Consider using the Database Upgrade Assistant (DBUA) to upgrade an Oracle database.

Reinstalling After Failed Installation

You may run into a situation in which you're attempting to install Oracle, and for some reason the installation fails. You correct the issue and attempt to rerun the Oracle installer. However, you receive this message:

```
CAUSE: The chosen installation conflicted with software already
       installed in the given Oracle home.
ACTION: Install into a different Oracle home.
```

In this situation, Oracle thinks that the software has already been installed, for a couple of reasons:

- Files in the ORACLE_HOME directory are specified in the response file.

- An existing Oracle home and location in your oraInventory/ ContentsXML/inventory.xml file match what you have specified in the response file.

Oracle doesn't allow you to install a new set of binaries over an existing Oracle home. If you're sure you don't need any of the files in the ORACLE_HOME directory, you can remove them (be very careful—ensure that you absolutely want to do this). This example navigates to ORACLE_HOME and then removes the db_1 directory and its contents:

```
$ cd $ORACLE_HOME
$ cd ..
$ rm -rf db_1
```

Also, even if there are no files in the ORACLE_HOME directory, the installer inspects the inventory.xml file for previous Oracle home names and locations. In the inventory.xml file, you must remove the entry corresponding to the Oracle home location that matches the Oracle home you're trying to install to. To remove the entry, first, locate your oraInst.loc file, which contains the directory of your oraInventory. Next, navigate to the oraInventory/ ContentsXML directory. Make a copy of inventory.xml before you modify it:

```
$ cp inventory.xml inventory.xml.old
```

Then, edit the inventory.xml file with an OS utility (such as vi), and remove the line that contains the Oracle home information of your previously failed installation. You can now attempt to execute the runInstaller utility again.

Applying Interim Patches

Sometimes, you're required to apply a patch to resolve a database issue or eradicate a bug. You can usually obtain patches from the MOS web site and install them with the opatch utility. Here are the basic steps for applying a patch:

1. Obtain the patch from MOS (requires a valid support contract).

2. Unzip the patch file.

3. Carefully read the README.txt file for special instructions.

4. Shut down any databases and processes using the Oracle home to which the patch is being applied.

5. Apply the patch.

6. Verify that the patch was installed successfully.

A brief example will help illustrate the process of applying a patch. Here, the patch number 14390252 is applied to an 11.2.0.3 database on a Solaris box. First, download the p14390252_112030_SOLARIS64.zip file from MOS (https://support.oracle.com). Next, unzip the file on the server to which the patch is being applied:

```
$ unzip p14390252_112030_SOLARIS64.zip
```

The README.txt instructs you to change the directory, as follows:

```
$ cd 14390252
```

Make sure you follow the instructions included in the README.txt, such as shutting down any databases that use the Oracle home to which the patch is being applied:

```
$ sqlplus / as sysdba
SQL> shutdown immediate;
```

Next, apply the patch. Ensure that you perform this step as the owner of the Oracle software (usually the oracle OS account). Also make sure your ORACLE_HOME variable is set to point to the Oracle home to which you're applying the patch. In this example, because the opatch utility isn't in a path included in the PATH directory, you specify the entire path:

```
$ $ORACLE_HOME/OPatch/opatch napply -skip_subset -skip_duplicate
```

Finally, verify that the patch was applied by listing the inventory of patches:

```
$ $ORACLE_HOME/OPatch/opatch lsinventory
```

Here is some sample output for this example:

```
Patch  13742433    : applied on Sun Nov 04 13:49:07 MST 2012
Unique Patch ID:  15427576
```

Tip   See MOS note 242993.1 for more information regarding the `opatch` utility.

Installing Remotely with the Graphical Installer

The installation can be performed once using the GUI for a Read-Only Oracle Home. In today's global environment, DBAs often find themselves tasked with installing Oracle software on remote Linux/Unix servers. In these situations, I strongly suggest that you use the silent installation mode with a response file (as mentioned earlier). However, if you want to install Oracle on a remote server via the graphical installer, this section of the chapter describes the required steps.

Note   If you're in a Windows-based environment, use the Remote Desktop Connection or Virtual Network Computing (VNC) to install software remotely.

One issue that frequently arises is how to run the Oracle installer on a remote server and have the graphical output displayed to your local computer. Figure 1-2 shows the basic components and utilities required to run the Oracle graphical installer remotely.

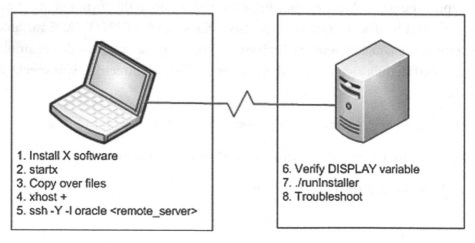

Figure 1-2. *Components needed for a remote Oracle graphical installation*

Listed next are the steps for setting up your environment to display the graphical screens on your local computer while remotely running the Oracle installer:

1. Install software on the local computer that allows for X Window System emulation and secure networking.

2. Start an X session on the local computer and issue the `startx` command.

3. Copy the Oracle installation files to the remote server.

4. Run the `xhost` command.

5. Log in to the remote computer from an X terminal.

6. Ensure that the `DISPLAY` variable is set correctly on the remote computer.

7. Execute the `runInstaller` utility on the remote server.

8. Troubleshoot.

These steps are explained in the following sections.

Step 1. Install X Software and Networking Utilities on the Local PC

If you're installing Oracle on a remote server, and you're using your home personal computer (PC), then you first need to install software on your PC that allows you to run X Window System software and to run commands such as `ssh` (secure shell) and `scp` (secure copy). Several free tools are available that provide this functionality. One such tool is Cygwin, which you can download from the Cygwin web site (`http://x.cygwin.com`). Be sure to install the packages that provide the X emulation and secure networking utilities, such as `ssh` and `scp`.

Step 2. Start an X Session on the Local Computer

After you install on your local computer the software that allows you to run X Window System software, you can open an X terminal window and start the X server via the `startx` command:

```
$ startx
```

Here is a snippet of the output:

```
xauth:  creating new authority file /home/test/.serverauth.3012
waiting for X server to begin accepting connections.
```

When the X software has started, run a utility such as xeyes to determine whether X is working properly:

```
$ xeyes
```

Figure 1-3 shows what a local terminal session looks like, using the Cygwin X terminal session tool.

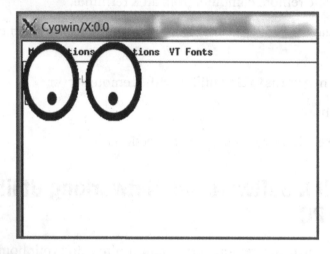

Figure 1-3. *Running xeyes utility on a local computer*

If you can't get a utility such as xeyes to execute, stop at this step until you get it working. You must have correctly functioning X software before you can remotely install Oracle, using the graphical installer.

Step 3. Copy the Oracle Installation Media to the Remote Server

From the X terminal, run the scp command to copy the Oracle installation media to the remote server. Here is the basic syntax for using scp:

```
$ scp <localfile> <username>@<remote_server>:<remote_directory>
```

The next line of code copies the Oracle installation media to a remote Oracle OS user on a remote server in the home directory oracle:

```
$ scp linux_18cR1_database_1of2.zip oracle@shrek2:.
```

Step 4. Run the xhost Command

From the X screen, enable access to the remote host via the xhost command. This command must be run from your local computer:

```
$ xhost +
access control disabled, clients can connect from any host.
```

The prior command allows any client to connect to the local X server. If you want to enable remote access specifically for the remote computer on which you're installing the software, provide an Internet protocol (IP) address or hostname (of the remote server). In this example, the remote hostname is tst-z1.central.sun.com:

```
$ xhost +tst-z1.central.sun.com
tst-z1.central.sun.com being added to access control list
```

Step 5. Log In to the Remote Computer from X

From your local X terminal, use the ssh utility to log in to the remote server on which you want to install the Oracle software:

```
$ ssh -Y -l oracle <hostname>
```

Step 6. Ensure that the DISPLAY Variable Is Set Correctly on the Remote Computer

When you've logged in to the remote box, verify that your DISPLAY variable has been set:

```
$ echo $DISPLAY
```

You should see something similar to this:

```
localhost:10.0
```

If your DISPLAY variable is set to localhost:10.0, then proceed to the next step. Otherwise, follow the next set of recommendations.

If your DISPLAY variable isn't set, you must ensure that it's set to a value that reflects your local home computer location. From your local home computer, you can use the ping or arp utility to determine the IP address that identifies your local computer. Run the following command on your home computer:

```
C:\> ping <local_computer>
```

Tip   If you don't know your local home computer name, on Windows you can look in the Control Panel, then System, then reference the Computer name.

Now, from the remote server, execute this command to set the DISPLAY variable to contain the IP address of the local computer:

```
$ export DISPLAY=129.151.31.147:0.0
```

Note that you must append the :0.0 to the end of the IP address. If you're using the C shell, use the setenv command to set the DISPLAY variable:

```
$ setenv DISPLAY 129.151.31.147:0.0
```

If you're unsure which shell you're using, use the echo command to display the SHELL variable:

```
$ echo $SHELL
```

Step 7. Execute the runInstaller Utility

Navigate to the directory where you copied and unzipped the Oracle software on the remote server. Locate the runInstaller utility, and run it, as shown:

```
$ ./runInstaller
```

If everything goes well, you should see a screen appear in order to walk through the steps of the installation.

From here, you can point and click your way through an Oracle installation of the software. Many DBAs are more comfortable installing the software through a graphical screen. This is a particularly good method if you aren't familiar with Oracle's installation process and want to be prompted for input and presented with reasonable default values.

Step 8. Troubleshoot

Most issues with remote installations occur in steps 4, 5, and 6. Make sure you've properly enabled remote-client access to your local X server (running on your home computer) via the xhost command. The xhost command must be run on the local computer on which you want the graphical display presented. Using the + (plus sign) with the remote hostname adds a host to the local access list. This enables the remote server to display an X window on the local host. If you type the xhost command by itself (with no parameters), it displays all remote hosts that can display X sessions on the local computer:

```
$ xhost
access control disabled, clients can connect from any host
```

Setting the DISPLAY OS variable on the remote server is also crucial. This allows you to log in to another host remotely and display an X application back to your local computer. The DISPLAY variable must be set on the remote database server to contain information that points it to the local computer on which you want the graphical screen displayed.

Installation in the Cloud

Oracle 18c is a database released for the cloud first. Oracle 18c for server installation became available several months after the use in the cloud and being able to perform installs in the cloud. Oracle provides a couple of different options for databases in the cloud, and a common one is Infrastructure as a Service (IaaS). IaaS provides the infrastructure, server, OS, and users that are needed to be able to install your own software and then create databases. Database provisioning is another option, Platform as a Service (PaaS) can provide the Oracle binaries, and just the databases will need to be created on that cloud service.

Since we have been discussing the software installation on a server and existing OS, this will be an install on IaaS in the cloud. The database binaries would walk through the same steps as described throughout this chapter. Configuration of the cloud service provided would be based on the amount of storage, CPU, and memory requested. There is flexibility of numbers of CPUs and memory that can be requested and then expanded for future needs quickly and efficiently in the cloud.

Oracle is also available in AWS where it can be selected as an AMI from the store and installed. Along with this option in other platforms, Oracle can be installed as part of an IaaS. IaaS is available in the different cloud offerings, AWS, and others, but some of the server configurations are going to be optimized on the Oracle Cloud and different options of the licensing might be available. These are discussions with the Oracle sales team to get licenses and requirements planned, but a decision to go to the cloud needs to be discussed with the business and decide if the flexible resources and the time to deployment are going to be of value.

In the Oracle Cloud, the database deployment is chosen, with an available Domain and shape of the bare-metal machines based on the CPU and other resources for the IaaS server. The software edition is the next choice, which is also the same with non-cloud installations of the binary. Using IaaS in the cloud, their ssh keys, root access, and other access such as SYS that is just for the customer and not accessible by the Oracle cloud provider. This is just for the server that has been requested. The configuration assistants can be run later after the binary install or select to run immediately after the binaries are installed.

After these basic choices, the installation happens in the cloud. The server is then ready for use to create databases and set up for management and monitoring. These steps will be discussed later in the following chapters to include how to also manage the databases in the cloud.

Summary

This chapter detailed techniques for efficiently installing the Oracle binaries. Oracle 18c provides new ways to deploy the Oracle binaries including a Read-Only Oracle Home. These methods are especially useful if you work in environments in which you are geographically separated from the database servers. The Oracle silent installation method is efficient because it doesn't require graphical software and uses a response file that helps enforce consistency from one installation to the next. When working in chaotic and constantly changing environments, you should benefit from the installation tips and procedures described here.

The Oracle binaries are installed in cloud environments when using Infrastructure as a Service (IaaS), and this makes provisioning of servers and databases very efficient. IaaS allow for the DBAs to have full access of the provisioned server to perform database creation, but the installation of the database binaries is simplified and similar to a response file install. Many DBAs feel more comfortable using Oracle's graphical installer for installing the database software. However, the graphical installer can be troublesome when the server is in a remote location or embedded deeply within a secure network. A slow network or a security feature can greatly impede the graphical installation process. In these situations, make sure you correctly configure the required X software and OS variables (such as DISPLAY).

It's critical as a DBA to be an expert in Oracle installation procedures. If the Oracle installation software isn't correctly installed, you won't be able to successfully create a database. Once you have properly installed Oracle, you can go on to the next step of starting the background processes and creating a database. The topics of starting Oracle and issuing and creating a database are discussed next, in Chapter 2.

CHAPTER 2

Creating a Database

Chapter 1 detailed how to efficiently install the Oracle binaries. After you've installed the Oracle software, the next logical task is creating a database. There are a few standard ways for creating Oracle databases:

- Use the Database Configuration Assistant (dbca) utility.

- Run a CREATE DATABASE statement from SQL*Plus.

- Clone a database from an existing database.

Oracle's dbca utility has a graphical interface from which you can configure and create databases. This visual tool is easy to use and has a very intuitive interface. If you need to create a development database and get going quickly, then this tool is more than adequate. Having said that, I normally don't use the dbca utility to create databases. In Linux/Unix environments, the dbca tool depends on X software and an appropriate setting for the OS DISPLAY variable. The dbca utility therefore requires some setup and can perform poorly if you're installing on remote servers when the network throughput is slow.

The dbca utility also allows you to create a database in silent mode, without the graphical component. Using dbca in silent mode with a response file is an efficient way to create databases in a consistent and repeatable manner. The dbca tool can run in silent mode after the binary installation or launched separately. This approach also works well when you're installing on remote servers, which could have a slow network connection or not have the appropriate X software installed.

When you're creating databases on remote servers, it's usually easier and more efficient to use SQL*Plus. The SQL*Plus approach is simple and inherently scriptable. In addition, SQL*Plus works no matter how slow the network connection is, and it isn't dependent on a graphical component. However, the dbca utility allows for new features to be adopted quickly in the databases being created. This chapter starts by showing you how to quickly create a database using SQL*Plus, and also how to make your database

© Michelle Malcher and Darl Kuhn 2019
M. Malcher and D. Kuhn, *Pro Oracle Database 18c Administration*,
https://doi.org/10.1007/978-1-4842-4424-1_2

remotely available by enabling a listener process. Later, the chapter demonstrates how to use the dbca utility in silent mode with a response file to create a database.

Setting OS Variables

Before creating a database, you need to know a bit about OS variables, often called environment variables. Before you run SQL*Plus (or any other Oracle utility), you must set several OS variables:

- ORACLE_HOME

- ORACLE_SID

- LD_LIBRARY_PATH

- PATH

The ORACLE_HOME variable defines the starting point directory for the default location for the initialization file, which is ORACLE_HOME/dbs on Linux/Unix. On Windows this directory is usually ORACLE_HOME\database. The ORACLE_HOME variable is also important because it defines the starting point directory for locating the Oracle binary files (such as sqlplus, dbca, netca, rman, and so on) that are in ORACLE_HOME/bin.

The ORACLE_SID variable defines the default name of the database you're attempting to create. ORACLE_SID is also used as the default name for the parameter file, which is init<ORACLE_SID>.ora or spfile<ORACLE_SID>.ora.

The LD_LIBRARY_PATH variable is important because it specifies where to search for libraries on Linux/Unix boxes. The value of this variable is typically set to include ORACLE_HOME/lib.

The PATH variable specifies which directories are looked in by default when you type a command from the OS prompt. In almost all situations, ORACLE_HOME/bin (the location of the Oracle binaries) must be included in your PATH variable.

You can take several different approaches to setting the prior variables. This chapter discusses three, beginning with a hard-coded manual approach and ending with the approach that I personally prefer: leveraging the oratab file. Why discuss different approaches? Because it is important to understand that environments are configured differently. Understanding that these steps are needed to connect to the database will help with troubleshooting and verify that the binaries are installed and available. There are also different tools that are available because of policies and server configurations, such as doing silent installs compared to using the UI.

A Manually Intensive Approach

In Linux/Unix, when you're using the Bourne, Bash, or Korn shell, you can set OS variables manually from the OS command line with the export command:

```
$ export ORACLE_HOME=/u01/app/oracle/product/18.0.0.0/db_1
$ export ORACLE_SID=o12c
$ export LD_LIBRARY_PATH=/usr/lib:$ORACLE_HOME/lib
$ export PATH=$ORACLE_HOME/bin:$PATH
```

For the C or tcsh shell, use the setenv command to set variables:

```
$ setenv ORACLE_HOME <path>
$ setenv ORACLE_SID <sid>
$ setenv LD_LIBRARY_PATH <path>
$ setenv PATH <path>
```

Another way that DBAs set these variables is by placing the previous export or setenv commands into a Linux/Unix startup file, such as . bash_profile, . bashrc, or . profile. That way, the variables are automatically set upon login. This is accomplished by just editing the startup file or profile files to inserting the variables. Even with the other options, it is still good to have a default ORACLE_HOME set in the startup files.

However, manually setting OS variables (either from the command line or by hard-coding values into a startup file) isn't the optimal way to instantiate these variables. For example, if you have multiple databases with multiple Oracle homes on a box, manually setting these variables quickly becomes unwieldy and not very maintainable.

Oracle's Approach to Setting OS Variables

A much better method for setting OS variables is use of a script that uses a file that contains the names of all Oracle databases on a server and their associated Oracle homes. This approach is flexible and maintainable. For instance, if a database's ORACLE_HOME changes (e.g., after an upgrade), you only have to modify one file on the server and not hunt down where the ORACLE_HOME variables may be hard-coded into scripts.

Oracle provides a mechanism for automatically setting the required OS variables. Oracle's approach relies on two files: oratab and oraenv.

Understanding oratab

You can think of the entries in the `oratab` file as a registry of what databases are installed on a box and their corresponding Oracle home directories. The `oratab` file is automatically created for you when you install the Oracle software. On Linux boxes, `oratab` is usually placed in the `/etc` directory. On Solaris servers, the `oratab` file is placed in the `/var/opt/oracle` directory. If, for some reason, the `oratab` file isn't automatically created, you can manually create the directory and file.

The `oratab` file is used in Linux/Unix environments for the following purposes:

- Automating the sourcing of required OS variables

- Automating the start and stop of Oracle databases on the server

The `oratab` file has three columns with this format:

```
<database_sid>:<oracle_home_dir>:Y|N
```

The Y or N indicates whether you want Oracle to restart automatically on reboot of the box; Y indicates yes, and N indicates no. Automating the startup and shutdown of your database is covered in detail in Chapter 20. Oracle srvctl also has management policies that are set for automatic restart of the databases that don't use the oratab.

Comments in the `oratab` file start with a pound sign (#). Here is a typical `oratab` file entry:

```
o12c:/u01/app/oracle/product/18.0.0.0/db_1:N
rcat:/u01/app/oracle/product/18.0.0.0/db_1:N
```

The names of the databases on the previous lines are `o12c` and `rcat`. The path of each database's ORACLE_HOME directory is next on the line (separated from the database name by a colon [`:`]).

Several Oracle-supplied utilities use the `oratab` file:

- `oraenv` uses `oratab` to set the OS variables.

- `dbstart` uses it to start the database automatically on server reboots (if the third field in `oratab` is Y).

- `dbshut` uses it to stop the database automatically on server reboots (if the third field in `oratab` is Y).

The `oraenv` tool is discussed in the following section.

Using oraenv

If you don't properly set the required OS variables for an Oracle environment, then utilities such as SQL*Plus, Oracle Recovery Manager (RMAN), Data Pump, and so on won't work correctly. The oraenv utility automates the setting of required OS variables (such as ORACLE_HOME, ORACLE_SID, and PATH) on an Oracle database server. This utility is used in Bash, Korn, and Bourne shell environments (if you're in a C shell environment, there is a corresponding coraenv utility).

The oraenv utility is located in the O RACLE_HOME/bin directory. You can run it manually, like this:

```
$ . oraenv
```

Note that the syntax to run this from the command line requires a space between the dot (.) and the oraenv tool. You're prompted for ORACLE_SID and if the ORACLE_SID is not in the oratab file, it will prompt for the ORACLE_HOME values:

```
ORACLE_SID = [oracle] ?
ORACLE_HOME = [/home/oracle] ?
```

You can also run the oraenv utility in a noninteractive way by setting OS variables before you run it. This is useful for scripting when you don't want to be prompted for input:

```
$ export ORACLE_SID=o18c
$ export ORAENV_ASK=NO
$ . oraenv
```

Keep in mind that if you set your ORACLE_SID to a value that isn't found with the oratab file, then you may be prompted for values such as ORACLE_HOME.

My Approach to Setting OS Variables

I don't use Oracle's oraenv file to set the OS variables (see the previous section, "Using oraenv," for details of Oracle's approach). Instead, I use a script named oraset. The oraset script depends on the oratab file's being in the correct directory and expected format:

```
<database_sid>:<oracle_home_dir>:Y|N
```

As mentioned in the previous section, the Oracle installer should create an `oratab` file for you in the correct directory. If it doesn't, then you can manually create and populate the file. In Linux, the `oratab` file is usually created in the `/etc` directory. On Solaris servers, the `oratab` file is located in the `/var/opt/oracle` directory.

Next, use a script that reads the `oratab` file and sets the OS variables. Here is an example of an `oraset` script that reads the `oratab` file and presents a menu of choices (based on the database names in the `oratab` file):

```bash
#!/bin/bash
# Sets Oracle environment variables.
# Setup: 1. Put oraset file in /etc (Linux), in /var/opt/oracle (Solaris)
#        2. Ensure /etc or /var/opt/oracle is in $PATH
# Usage: batch mode: . oraset <SID>
#        menu mode:  . oraset
#=====================================================
if [ -f /etc/oratab ]; then
  OTAB=/etc/oratab
elif [ -f /var/opt/oracle/oratab ]; then
  OTAB=/var/opt/oracle/oratab
else
      echo 'oratab file not found.'
      exit
fi
#
if [ -z $1 ]; then
  SIDLIST=$(egrep -v '#|\*' ${OTAB} | cut -f1 -d:)
  # PS3 indicates the prompt to be used for the Bash select command.
  PS3='SID? '
  select sid in ${SIDLIST}; do
    if [ -n $sid ]; then
      HOLD_SID=$sid
      break
    fi
  done
else
  if egrep -v '#|\*' ${OTAB} | grep -w "${1}:">/dev/null; then
```

```
  HOLD_SID=$1
 else
   echo "SID: $1 not found in $OTAB"
 fi
 shift
fi
#
export ORACLE_SID=$HOLD_SID
export ORACLE_HOME=$(egrep -v '#|\*' $OTAB|grep -w $ORACLE_SID:|cut -f2 -d:)
export ORACLE_BASE=${ORACLE_HOME%%/product*}
export TNS_ADMIN=$ORACLE_HOME/network/admin
export ADR_BASE=$ORACLE_BASE/diag
export PATH=$ORACLE_HOME/bin:/usr/ccs/bin:/opt/SENSsshc/bin/\
:/bin:/usr/bin:.:/var/opt/oracle:/usr/sbin
export LD_LIBRARY_PATH=/usr/lib:$ORACLE_HOME/lib
```

You can run the oraset script either from the command line or from a startup file (such as .profile, .bash_profile, or .bashrc). To run oraset from the command line, place the oraset file in a standard location, such as /var/opt/oracle (Solaris) or /etc (Linux), and run, as follows:

```
$ . /etc/oraset
```

Note that the syntax to run this from the command line requires a space between the dot (.) and the rest of the command. When you run oraset from the command line, you should be presented with a menu such as this:

```
1) o18c
2) rcat
SID?
```

In this example you can now enter 1 or 2 to set the OS variables required for whichever database you want to use. This allows you to set up OS variables interactively, regardless of the number of database installations on the server.

You can also call the oraset file from an OS startup file. Here is a sample entry in the . bashrc file:

```
. /etc/oraset
```

Now, every time you log in to the server, you're presented with a menu of choices that you can use to indicate the database for which you want the OS variables set. If you want the OS variables automatically set to a particular database, then put an entry such as this in the .bashrc file:

```
. /etc/oraset o18c
```

The prior line will run the oraset file for the o18c database and set the OS variables appropriately.

Creating a Database

This section explains how to create an Oracle database manually with the SQL*Plus CREATE DATABASE statement. These are the steps required to create a database:

1. Set the OS variables.

2. Configure the initialization file.

3. Create the required directories.

4. Create the database.

5. Create a data dictionary.

Each of these steps is covered in the following sections.

Step 1. Set the OS Variables

As mentioned previously, before you run SQL*Plus (or any other Oracle utility), you must set several OS variables. You can either manually set these variables or use a combination of files and scripts to set the variables. Here's an example of setting these variables manually:

```
$ export ORACLE_HOME=/u01/app/oracle/product/18.0.0.0/db_1
$ export ORACLE_SID=o18c
$ export LD_LIBRARY_PATH=/usr/lib:$ORACLE_HOME/lib
$ export PATH=$ORACLE_HOME/bin:$PATH
```

See the section "Setting OS Variables," earlier in this chapter, for a complete description of these variables and techniques for setting them.

Step 2. Configure the Initialization File

Oracle requires that you have an initialization file in place before you attempt to start the instance. The initialization file is used to configure features such as memory and to control file locations. You can use two types of initialization files:

- Server parameter binary file (spfile)

- init.ora text file

Oracle recommends that you use a spfile for reasons such as these:

- You can modify the contents of the spfile with the SQL ALTER SYSTEM statement.

- You can use remote-client SQL sessions to start the database without requiring a local (client) initialization file.

- There are more dynamic parameters that can be set using the spfile without any downtown.

These are good reasons to use an spfile. However, some shops still use the traditional init.ora file. The init.ora file also has advantages:

- You can directly edit it with an OS text editor.

- You can place comments in it that detail a history of modifications.

When I first create a database, I find it easier to use an init.ora file. This file can be easily converted later to a spfile if required (via the CREATE SPFILE FROM PFILE statement). In this example, my database name is o18c, so I place the following contents in a file named inito18c.ora and put the file in the ORACLE_HOME/dbs directory:

```
db_name=o18c
db_block_size=8192
memory_target=300M
memory_max_target=300M
processes=200
control_files=(/u01/dbfile/o18c/control01.ctl,/u02/dbfile/o18c/control02.ctl)
job_queue_processes=10
```

```
open_cursors=500
fast_start_mttr_target=500
undo_management=AUTO
undo_tablespace=UNDOTBS1
remote_login_passwordfile=EXCLUSIVE
```

Ensure that the initialization file is named correctly and located in the appropriate directory. This is critical because when starting your instance, Oracle first looks in the ORACLE_HOME/dbs directory for parameter files with specific formats, in this order:

- spfile<SID>.ora

- spfile.ora

- init<SID>.ora

In other words, Oracle first looks for a file named spfile<SID>.ora. If found, the instance is started; if not, Oracle looks for spfile.ora and then init<SID>.ora. If one of these files is not found, Oracle throws an error.

This may cause some confusion if you're not aware of the files that Oracle looks for, and in what order. For example, you may make a change to an init<SID>.ora file and expect the parameter to be instantiated after stopping and starting your instance. If there is a spfile<SID>.ora in place, the init<SID>.ora is completely ignored.

Note   You can manually instruct Oracle to look for a text parameter file in a directory, using the pfile=<directory/filename> clause with the startup command; under normal circumstances, you shouldn't need to do this. You want the default behavior, which is for Oracle to find a parameter file in the ORACLE_ HOME/dbs directory (for Linux/Unix). The default directory on Windows is ORACLE_ HOME/database.

Table 2-1 lists best practices to consider when configuring an Oracle initialization file.

Table 2-1. *Initialization File Best Practices*

Best Practice	Reasoning
Oracle recommends that you use a binary server parameter file (spfile).	Spfile allows for dynamic changes to parameters. If there is an acceptable maintenance window, then using the init.ora file would be fine to use.
In general, don't set initialization parameters if you're not sure of their intended purpose. When in doubt, use the default.	Setting initialization parameters can have far-reaching consequences in terms of database performance. Only modify parameters if you know what the resulting behavior will be.
For 11g and higher, set the memory_target and memory_max_target initialization parameters.	Doing this allows Oracle to manage all memory components for you.
For 10g, set the sga_target and sga_target_max initialization parameters.	Doing this lets Oracle manage most memory components for you.
For 10g, set pga_aggregate_target and workarea_size_policy.	Doing this allows Oracle to manage the memory used for the sort space.
Starting with 10g, use the automatic UNDO feature. This is set using the undo_management and undo_tablespace parameters.	Doing this allows Oracle to manage most features of the UNDO tablespace.
Set open_cursors to a higher value than the default. I typically set it to 500. Active online transaction processing (OLTP) databases may need a much higher value.	The default value of 50 is almost never enough. Even a small, one-user application can exceed the default value of 50 open cursors.
Name the control files with the pattern /<mount_point>/dbfile/<database_name>/controlON.ctl.	This deviates slightly from the OFA standard. I find this location easier to navigate to, as opposed to being located under ORACLE_BASE.
Use at least two control files, preferably in different locations, using different disks.	If one control file becomes corrupt, it's always a good idea to have at least one other control file available.

Step 3. Create the Required Directories

Any OS directories referenced in the parameter file or CREATE DATABASE statement must be created on the server before you attempt to create a database. For instance, in the previous section's initialization file, the control files are defined as

```
control_files=(/u01/dbfile/o18c/control01.ctl,/u02/dbfile/o18c/control02.ctl)
```

From the previous line, ensure that you've created the directories / u01/dbfile/ o18c and / u02/dbfile/o18c (modify this according to your environment). In Linux/ Unix you can create directories, including any parent directories required, by using the m kdir command with the p switch:

```
$ mkdir -p /u01/dbfile/o18c
$ mkdir -p /u02/dbfile/o18c
```

Also make sure you create any directories required for data files and online redo logs referenced in the CREATE DATABASE statement (see step 4). For this example, here are the additional directories required:

```
$ mkdir -p /u01/oraredo/o18c
$ mkdir -p /u02/oraredo/o18c
```

If you create the previous directories as the root user, ensure that the oracle user and dba groups are properly set to own the directories, subdirectories, and files. This example recursively changes the owner and group of the following directories:

```
# chown -R oracle:dba /u01
# chown -R oracle:dba /u02
```

Step 4. Create the Database

After you've established OS variables, configured an initialization file, and created any required directories, you can now create a database. This step explains how to use the CREATE DATABASE statement to create a database.

Before you can run the CREATE DATABASE statement, you must start the background processes and allocate memory via the STARTUP NOMOUNT statement:

```
$ sqlplus / as sysdba
SQL> startup nomount;
```

When you issue a STARTUP NOMOUNT statement, SQL*Plus attempts to read the initialization file in the ORACLE_HOME/dbs directory (see step 2). The STARTUP NOMOUNT statement instantiates the background processes and memory areas used by Oracle. At this point, you have an Oracle instance, but you have no database.

Note   An Oracle instance is defined as the background processes and memory areas. The Oracle database is defined as the physical files (data files, control files, online redo logs) on disk.

Listed next is a typical Oracle CREATE DATABASE statement:

```
CREATE DATABASE o18c
    MAXLOGFILES 16
    MAXLOGMEMBERS 4
    MAXDATAFILES 1024
    MAXINSTANCES 1
    MAXLOGHISTORY 680
    CHARACTER SET AL32UTF8
DATAFILE
'/u01/dbfile/o18c/system01.dbf'
    SIZE 500M REUSE
    EXTENT MANAGEMENT LOCAL
UNDO TABLESPACE undotbs1 DATAFILE
'/u01/dbfile/o18c/undotbs01.dbf'
    SIZE 800M
SYSAUX DATAFILE
'/u01/dbfile/o18c/sysaux01.dbf'
    SIZE 500M
DEFAULT TEMPORARY TABLESPACE TEMP TEMPFILE
'/u01/dbfile/o18c/temp01.dbf'
    SIZE 500M
DEFAULT TABLESPACE USERS DATAFILE
'/u01/dbfile/o18c/users01.dbf'
    SIZE 20M
LOGFILE GROUP 1
```

```
      ('/u01/oraredo/o18c/redo01a.rdo',
       '/u02/oraredo/o18c/redo01b.rdo') SIZE 50M,
      GROUP 2
      ('/u01/oraredo/o18c/redo02a.rdo',
       '/u02/oraredo/o18c/redo02b.rdo') SIZE 50M,
      GROUP 3
      ('/u01/oraredo/o18c/redo03a.rdo',
       '/u02/oraredo/o18c/redo03b.rdo') SIZE 50M
USER sys     IDENTIFIED BY foo
USER system IDENTIFIED BY foo;
```

In this example the script is placed in a file named credb.sql and is run from the SQL*Plus prompt as the SYS user:

```
SQL> @credb.sql
```

If it's successful, you should see the following message:

```
Database created.
```

Note   See Chapter 22 for details on creating a pluggable database.

If any errors are thrown while the CREATE DATABASE statement is running, check the alert log file. Typically, errors occur when required directories don't exist, the memory allocation isn't sufficient, or an OS limit has been exceeded. If you're unsure of the location of your alert log, issue the following query:

```
SQL> select value from v$diag_info where name = 'Diag Trace';
```

The prior query should work even when your database is in the nomount state. Another way to quickly find the alert log file is from the OS:

```
$ cd $ORACLE_BASE
$ find . -name "alert*.log"
```

Tip   The default format for the name of the alert log file is alert_<SID>.log.

There are few key things to point out about the prior CREATE DATABASE statement example. Note that the SYSTEM data file is defined as locally managed. This means that any tablespace created in this database must be locally managed (as opposed to dictionary managed). Oracle throws an error if you attempt to create a dictionary-managed tablespace in this database. This is the desired behavior.

A dictionary-managed tablespace uses the Oracle data dictionary to manage extents and free space, whereas a locally managed tablespace uses a bitmap in each data file to manage its extents and free space. Locally managed tablespaces have these advantages:

- Performance is increased.

- No coalescing is required.

- Contention for resources in the data dictionary is reduced.

- Recursive space management is reduced.

Also note that the TEMP tablespace is defined as the default temporary tablespace. This means that any user created in the database automatically has the TEMP tablespace assigned to him or her as the default temporary tablespace. After you create the data dictionary (see step 5), you can verify the default temporary tablespace with this query:

```
select *
from database_properties
where property_name = 'DEFAULT_TEMP_TABLESPACE';
```

Finally, note that the USERS tablespace is defined as the default permanent tablespace for any users created that don't have a default tablespace defined in a CREATE USER statement. After you create the data dictionary (see step 5), you can run this query to determine the default tablespace:

```
select *
from database_properties
where property_name = 'DEFAULT_PERMANENT_TABLESPACE';
```

Table 2-2 lists best practices to consider when you are creating an Oracle database.

Table 2-2. *Best Practices for Creating an Oracle Database*

Best Practice	Reasoning
Use the REUSE clause with caution. Normally, you should use it only when you're re-creating a database.	The REUSE clause instructs Oracle to overwrite existing files, regardless of whether they are in use or not. This is dangerous.
Create a default temporary tablespace with TEMP somewhere in the name.	Every user should be assigned a temporary tablespace of the type TEMP, including the SYS user. If you don't specify a default temporary tablespace, then the SYSTEM tablespace is used. You never want a user to be assigned a temporary tablespace of SYSTEM. If your database doesn't have a default temporary tablespace, use the ALTER DATABASE DEFAULT TEMPORARY TABLESPACE statement to assign one.
Create a default permanent tablespace named USERS.	This ensures that users are assigned a default permanent tablespace other than SYSTEM. If your database doesn't have a default permanent tablespace, use the ALTER DATABASE DEFAULT TABLESPACE statement to assign one.
Use the USER SYS and USER SYSTEM clauses to specify nondefault passwords.	Doing this creates the database with nondefault passwords for database accounts that are usually the first targets for hackers.
Create at least three redo log groups, with two members each.	At least three redo log groups provide time for the archive process to write out archive redo logs between switches. Two members mirror the online redo log members, providing some fault tolerance.
Give the redo logs a name such as redoNA.rdo.	This deviates slightly from the OFA standard, but I've had files with the extension .log accidentally deleted more than once (it shouldn't ever happen, but it has).

(*continued*)

Table 2-2. (*continued*)

Best Practice	Reasoning
Make the database name somewhat intelligent, such as PAPRD, PADEV1, or PATST1.	This helps you determine what database you're operating in and whether it's a production, development, or test environment.
Use the ? variable when you're creating the data dictionary (see step 5). Don't hard-code the directory path.	SQL*Plus interprets the ? as the directory contained in the OS ORACLE_HOME variable. This prevents you from accidentally running scripts from the wrong version of ORACLE_HOME.

Tip   Many of these settings in the CREATE DATABASE are done for you using the dbca. The tablespaces can be set up or defaults can be used along with making sure the users are not going to be creating objects in the SYSTEM tablespaces and no default passwords are used. Using dbca will take new features and security options as part of the database creation.

Note that the CREATE DATABASE statement used in this step deviates slightly from the OFA standard in terms of the directory structure. I prefer not to place the Oracle data files, online redo logs, and control files under ORACLE_BASE (as specified by the OFA standard). I instead directly place files under directories named /<mount point>/<file_type>/<database_name>, because the path names are much shorter. The shorter path names make command-line navigation to directories easier, and the names fit more cleanly in the output of SQL SELECT statements. Figure 2-1 displays this deviation from the OFA standard.

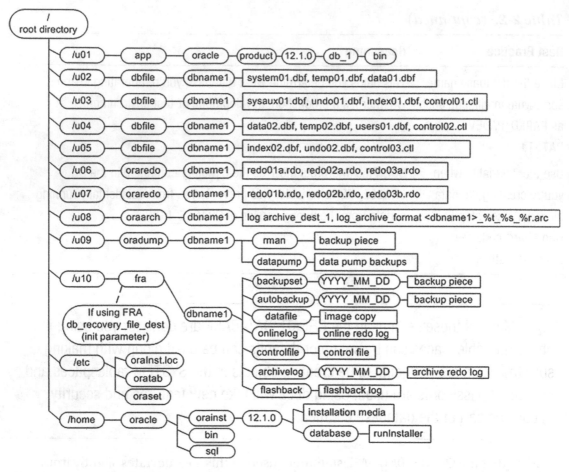

Figure 2-1. *A slight deviation from the OFA standard for laying out database files*

It's not my intention to have you use nonstandard OFA structures. Rather, do what makes sense for your environment and requirements. Apply reasonable standards that foster manageability, maintainability, and scalability.

Step 5. Create a Data Dictionary

After your database is successfully created, you can instantiate the data dictionary by running two scripts. These scripts are created when you install the Oracle binaries. You must run these scripts as the SYS schema:

```
SQL> show user
USER is "SYS"
```

Before I create the data dictionary, I like to spool an output file that I can inspect in the event of unexpected errors:

```
SQL> spool create_dd.lis
```

Now, create the data dictionary:

```
SQL> @?/rdbms/admin/catalog.sql
SQL> @?/rdbms/admin/catproc.sql
```

After you successfully create the data dictionary, as the SYSTEM schema, create the product user profile tables:

```
SQL> connect system/<password>
SQL> @?/sqlplus/admin/pupbld
```

These tables allow SQL*Plus to disable commands on a user-by-user basis. If the pupbld.sql script isn't run, then all non-sys users see the following warning when logging in to SQL*Plus:

```
Error accessing PRODUCT_USER_PROFILE
Warning: Product user profile information not loaded!
You may need to run PUPBLD.SQL as SYSTEM
```

These errors can be ignored. If you don't want to see them when logging in to SQL*Plus, make sure you run the pupbld.sql script.

At this point, you should have a fully functional database. You next need to configure and implement your listener to enable remote connectivity and, optionally, set up a password file. These tasks are described in the next two sections.

Configuring and Implementing the Listener

After you've installed binaries and created a database, you need to make the database accessible to remote-client connections. You do this by configuring and starting the Oracle listener. Appropriately named, the listener is the process on the database server that "listens" for connection requests from remote clients. If you don't have a listener started on the database server, then you can't connect from a remote client.

The listener can be included as part of the database home or part of the grid home. The listener only needs to be there once as there only can be one active grid home and the possibility of multiple database homes. This is one place to manage and maintain the listener. Having the listener as part of the grid environment allows for patching separate from the databases and with the grid as part of an infrastructure patching process. Also keep in mind when maintaining the listener to have the proper ORACLE_HOME set to keep the listener running in the desired home. The next two methods show the listener being configured in the database, but it can be easily followed for the grid home.

There are two methods for setting up a listener: the Oracle Net Configuration Assistant (netca) or manually configuring the listener.ora file.

Implementing a Listener with the Net Configuration Assistant

The netca utility assists you with all aspects of implementing a listener. You can run the netca tool in either graphical or silent mode. Using the netca in graphical mode is easy and intuitive. To use the netca in graphical mode, ensure that you have the proper X software installed, then issue the xhost + command, and check that your DISPLAY variable is set; for example,

```
$ xhost +
$ echo $DISPLAY
:0.0
```

You can now run the netca utility:

```
$ netca
```

Next, you will be guided through several screens from which you can choose options such as name of the listener, desired port, and so on.

You can also run the netca utility in silent mode with a response file. This mode allows you to script the process and ensure repeatability when creating and implementing listeners. First, find the default listener response file within the directory structure that contains the Oracle install media:

```
$  find . -name "netca.rsp"
./18.0.0.0/database/response/netca.rsp
```

Now, make a copy of the file so that you can modify it:

```
$ cp 18.0.0.0/database/response/netca.rsp mynet.rsp
```

If you want to change the default name or other attributes, then edit the mynet.rsp file with an OS utility such as vi:

```
$ vi mynet.rsp
```

For this example, I haven't modified any values within the mynet.rsp file. In other words, I'm using all the default values already contained within the response file. Next, the netca utility is run in silent mode:

```
$ netca -silent -responsefile /home/oracle/orainst/mynet.rsp
```

The utility creates a listener.ora and sqlnet.ora file in the ORACLE_HOME/network/admin directory and starts a default listener.

Manually Configuring a Listener

When you're setting up a new environment, manually configuring the listener is a two-step process:

1. Configure the listener.ora file.

2. Start the listener.

The listener.ora file is located by default in the ORACLE_HOME/network/admin directory. This is the same directory that the TNS_ADMIN OS variable should be set to. When manually configuring the listener and updating the listener.ora file, be aware of parentheses and any special characters, and a misconfigured listener.ora will result in not being able to start, and along with another listener on the same port is the first place to look.

Here is a sample listener.ora file that contains network configuration information for one database:

```
LISTENER =
  (DESCRIPTION_LIST =
    (DESCRIPTION =
      (ADDRESS_LIST =
        (ADDRESS = (PROTOCOL = TCP)(HOST = oracle18c)(PORT = 1521))
      )
    )
  )
```

```
SID_LIST_LISTENER =
  (SID_LIST =
    (SID_DESC =
      (GLOBAL_DBNAME = o18c)
      (ORACLE_HOME = /u01/app/oracle/product/18.0.0.0/db_1)
      (SID_NAME = o18c)
    )
  )
```

This code listing has two sections. The first defines the listener name and service; in this example the listener name is LISTENER. The second defines the list of SIDs for which the listener is listening for incoming connections (to the database). The format of the SID list name is SID_LIST_<name of listener>. The name of the listener must appear in the SID list name. The SID list name in this example is SID_LIST_LISTENER.

Also, you don't have to explicitly specify the SID_LIST_LISTENER section (the second section) in the prior code listing. This is because the process monitor (PMON) background process will automatically register any running databases as a service with the listener; this is known as dynamic registration. However, some DBAs prefer to explicitly list which databases should be registered with the listener and therefore include the second section; this is known as static registration.

After you have a listener.ora file in place, you can start the listener background process with the lsnrctl utility:

```
$ lsnrctl start
```

You should see informational messages, such as the following:

```
Listening Endpoints Summary...
  (DESCRIPTION=(ADDRESS=(PROTOCOL=tcp)(HOST=oracle18c)(PORT=1521)))
Services Summary...
Service "o18c" has 1 instance(s).
```

You can verify the services for which a listener is listening via

```
$ lsnrctl services
```

You can check the status of the listener with the following query:

```
$ lsnrctl status
```

For a complete listing of listener commands, issue this command:

```
$ lsnrctl help
```

Tip   Use the Linux/Unix `ps -ef | grep tns` command to view any listener processes running on a server.

Connecting to a Database through the Network

Once the listener has been configured and started, you can test remote connectivity from a SQL*Plus client, as follows:

```
$ sqlplus user/pass@'server:port/service_name'
```

In the next line of code, the user and password are `system/foo`, connecting the `oracle18c` server, port 1521, to a database named o18c:

```
$ sqlplus system/foo@'oracle18c:1521/o18c'
```

This example demonstrates what is known as the easy connect naming method of connecting to a database. It's easy because it doesn't rely on any setup files or utilities. The only information you need to know is username, password, server, port, and service name (SID).

Another common connection method is local naming. This method relies on connection information in the `ORACLE_HOME/network/admin /tnsnames.ora` file. In this example the `tnsnames.ora` file is edited, and the following Transparent Network Substrate (TNS) (Oracle's network architecture) entry is added:

```
o18c =
  (DESCRIPTION =
    (ADDRESS = (PROTOCOL = TCP)(HOST = oracle18c)(PORT = 1521))
    (CONNECT_DATA = (SERVICE_NAME = o18c)))
```

Now, from the OS command line, you establish a connection by referencing the o18c TNS information that was placed in the `tnsnames.ora` file:

```
$ sqlplus system/foo@o18c
```

This connection method is local because it relies on a local client copy of the tnsnames.ora file to determine the Oracle Net connection details. By default, SQL*Plus inspects the directory defined by the TNS_ADMIN variable for a file named tnsnames.ora. If not found, then the directory defined by ORACLE_HOME/network/admin is searched. If the tnsnames.ora file is found, and if it contains the alias specified in the SQL*Plus connection string (in this example, o18c), then the connection details are derived from the entry in the tnsnames.ora file.

The other connection-naming methods that Oracle uses are external naming and directory naming. See the *Oracle Net Services Administrator's Guide*, which can be freely downloaded from the Technology Network area of the Oracle web site (http://otn. oracle.com), for further details.

Tip   You can use the netca utility to create a tnsnames.ora file. Start the utility and choose the Local Net Service Name Configuration option. You will be prompted for input, such as the SID, hostname, and port.

Creating a Password File

Creating a password file is optional. There are some good reasons for requiring a password file:

- You want to assign non-sys users sys* privileges (sysdba, sysoper, sysbackup, and so on).

- You want to connect remotely to your database via Oracle Net with sys* privileges.

Oracle Data Guard setup and needing password files on the standby servers.

- An Oracle feature or utility requires the use of a password file.

Perform the following steps to implement a password file:

1. Create the password file with the orapwd utility.

2. Set the initialization parameter REMOTE_LOGIN_PASSWORDFILE to EXCLUSIVE.

In a Linux/Unix environment, use the orapwd utility to create a password file, as follows:

```
$ cd $ORACLE_HOME/dbs
$ orapwd file=orapw<ORACLE_SID> password=<sys password>
```

In a Linux/Unix environment, the password file is usually stored in ORACLE_HOME/ dbs; in Windows it's typically placed in the ORACLE_HOME\database directory.

The format of the filename that you specify in the previous command may vary by OS. For instance, in Windows the format is PWD<ORACLE_SID>.ora. The following example shows the syntax in a Windows environment:

```
c:\> cd %ORACLE_HOME%\database
c:\> orapwd file=PWD<ORACLE_SID>.ora password=<sys password>
```

To enable the use of the password file, set the initialization parameter REMOTE_ LOGIN_PASSWORDFILE to EXCLUSIVE (this is the default value). If the parameter is not set to EXCLUSIVE, then you'll have to modify your parameter file:

```
SQL> alter system set remote_login_passwordfile='EXCLUSIVE' scope=spfile;
```

You need to stop and start the instance to instantiate the prior setting.

You can add users to the password file via the GRANT <any SYS privilege> statement. You want to be careful with these privileges and use of the password file for secure configurations. Only the accounts that need these privileges should be granted along with access to the password file. The following example grants SYSDBA privileges to the heera user (and thus adds heera to the password file):

```
 VSQL> grant sysdba to heera;
Grant succeeded.
```

Enabling a password file also allows you to connect to your database remotely with SYS*-level privileges via an Oracle Net connection. This example shows the syntax for a remote connection with SYSDBA-level privileges:

```
$ sqlplus <username>/<password>@<database connection string> as sysdba
```

This allows you to do remote maintenance with sys* privileges (sysdba, sysoper, sysbackup, and so on) that would otherwise require your logging in to the database server physically. You can verify which users have sys* privileges by querying the V$PWFILE_USERS view:

```
SQL> select * from v$pwfile_users;
```

Here is some sample output:

```
USERNAME                       SYSDB SYSOP SYSAS SYSBA SYSDG SYSKM     CON_ID
------------------------       ----- ----- ----- ----- ----- ----- ----------
SYS                            TRUE  TRUE  FALSE FALSE FALSE FALSE          0
```

The concept of a privileged user is also important to RMAN backup and recovery. Like SQL*Plus, RMAN uses OS authentication and password files to allow privileged users to connect to the database. Only a privileged account is allowed to back up, restore, and recover a database.

Starting and Stopping the Database

Before you can start and stop an Oracle instance, you must set the proper OS variables (previously covered in this chapter). You also need access to either a privileged OS account or a privileged database user account. Connecting as a privileged user allows you to perform administrative tasks, such as starting, stopping, and creating databases. You can use either OS authentication or a password file to connect to your database as a privileged user.

Understanding OS Authentication

OS authentication means that if you can log in to a database server via an authorized OS account, you're allowed to connect to your database without the requirement of an additional password. A simple example demonstrates this concept. First, the `id` command is used to display the OS groups to which the `oracle` user belongs:

```
$ id
uid=500(oracle) gid=506(oinstall) groups=506(oinstall),507(dba),508(oper)
```

Next, a connection to the database is made with SYSDBA privileges, purposely using a bad (invalid) username and password:

```
$ sqlplus bad/notgood as sysdba
```

I can now verify that the connection as SYS was established:

```
SYS@o18c> show user
USER is "SYS"
```

How is it possible to connect to the database with an incorrect username and password? Actually, it is not a bad thing (as you might initially think). The prior connection works because Oracle ignores the username/password provided, as the user was first verified via OS authentication. In that example the `oracle` OS user belongs to the `dba` OS group and is therefore allowed to make a local connection to the database with SYSDBA privileges without having to provide a correct username and password.

See Table 1-1, in Chapter 1, for a complete description of OS groups and the mapping to corresponding database privileges. Typical groups include `dba` and `oper`; these groups correspond to `sysdba` and `sysoper` database privileges, respectively. The `sysdba` and `sysoper` privileges allow you to perform administrative tasks, such as starting and stopping your database.

In a Windows environment, an OS group is automatically created (typically named `ora_dba`) and assigned to the OS user that installs the Oracle software. You can verify which OS users belong to the `ora_dba` group as follows: select Start ➤ Control Panel ➤ Administrative Tools ➤ Computer Management ➤ Local Users and Groups ➤ Groups. You should see a group with a name such as `ora_dba`. You can click that group and view which OS users are assigned to it. In addition, for OS authentication to work in Windows environments, you must have the following entry in your `sqlnet.ora` file:

```
SQLNET.AUTHENTICATION_SERVICES=(NTS)
```

The `sqlnet.ora` file is usually located in the `ORACLE_HOME/network/admin` directory.

Starting the Database

Starting and stopping your database is a task that you perform frequently. To start/stop your database, connect with a `sysdba`- or `sysoper`-privileged user account, and issue the `startup` and `shutdown` statements. The following example uses OS authentication to connect to the database:

```
$ sqlplus / as sysdba
```

After you're connected as a privileged account, you can start your database, as follows:

```
SQL> startup;
```

For the prior command to work, you need either a `spfile` or `init.ora` file in the `ORACLE_HOME/dbs` directory. See the section "Step 2: Configure the Initialization File," earlier in this chapter, for details.

Note   Stopping and restarting your database in quick succession is known colloquially in the DBA world as bouncing your database.

When your instance starts successfully, you should see messages from Oracle indicating that the system global area (SGA) has been allocated. The database is mounted and then opened:

```
ORACLE instance started.

Total System Global Area   313159680 bytes
Fixed Size                   2259912 bytes
Variable Size              230687800 bytes
Database Buffers            75497472 bytes
Redo Buffers                4714496 bytes
Database mounted.
Database opened.
```

From the prior output, the database startup operation goes through three distinct phases in opening an Oracle database:

1. Starting the instance

2. Mounting the database

3. Opening the database

You can step through these one at a time when you start your database. First, start the Oracle instance (background processes and memory structures):

```
SQL> startup nomount;
```

Next, mount the database. At this point, Oracle reads the control files:

```
SQL> alter database mount;
```

Finally, open the data files and online redo log files:

```
SQL> alter database open;
```

This startup process is depicted graphically in Figure 2-2.

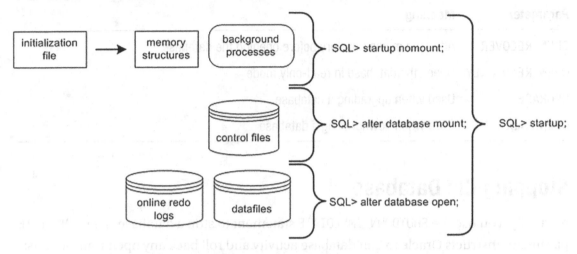

Figure 2-2. *Phases of Oracle startup*

When you issue a STARTUP statement without any parameters, Oracle automatically steps through the three startup phases (nomount, mount, open). In most cases, you will issue a STARTUP statement with no parameters to start your database. Table 2-3 describes the meanings of parameters that you can use with the database STARTUP statement.

Table 2-3. *Parameters Available with the* startup *Command*

Parameter	Meaning
FORCE	Shuts down the instance with ABORT before restarting it; useful for troubleshooting startup issues; not normally used
RESTRICT	Only allows users with the RESTRICTED SESSION privilege to connect to the database
PFILE	Specifies the client parameter file to be used when starting the instance
QUIET	Suppresses the display of SGA information when starting the instance
NOMOUNT	Starts background processes and allocates memory; doesn't read control files
MOUNT	Starts background processes, allocates memory, and reads control files
OPEN	Starts background processes, allocates memory, reads control files, and opens online redo logs and data files

(continued)

Table 2-3. (*continued*)

Parameter	Meaning
OPEN RECOVER	Attempts media recovery before opening the database
OPEN READ ONLY	Opens the database in read-only mode
UPGRADE	Used when upgrading a database
DOWNGRADE	Used when downgrading a database

Stopping the Database

Normally, you use the SHUTDOWN IMMEDIATE statement to stop a database. The IMMEDIATE parameter instructs Oracle to halt database activity and roll back any open transactions:

```
SQL> shutdown immediate;
Database closed.
Database dismounted.
ORACLE instance shut down.
```

Table 2-4 provides a detailed definition of the parameters available with the SHUTDOWN statement. In most cases, SHUTDOWN IMMEDIATE is an acceptable method of shutting down your database. If you issue the SHUTDOWN command with no parameters, it's equivalent to issuing SHUTDOWN NORMAL.

Table 2-4. *Parameters Available with the SHUTDOWN Command*

Parameter	Meaning
NORMAL	Wait for users to log out of active sessions before shutting down.
TRANSACTIONAL	Wait for transactions to finish, and then terminate the session.
TRANSACTIONAL LOCAL	Perform a transactional shutdown for local instance only.
IMMEDIATE	Terminate active sessions immediately. Open transactions are rolled back.
ABORT	Terminate the instance immediately. Transactions are terminated and aren't rolled back.

Starting and stopping your database is a fairly simple process. If the environment is set up correctly, you should be able to connect to your database and issue the appropriate STARTUP and SHUTDOWN statements.

Tip   If you experience any issues with starting or stopping your database, look in the alert log for details. The alert log usually has a pertinent message regarding any problems.

You should rarely need to use the SHUTDOWN ABORT statement. Usually, SHUTDOWN IMMEDIATE is sufficient. Having said that, there is nothing wrong with using SHUTDOWN ABORT. If SHUTDOWN IMMEDIATE isn't working for any reason, then use SHUTDOWN ABORT. Also remember on startup after a SHUTDOWN ABORT command, the database is going to need to recover media files and might take a significant amount of time to run through the files.

On a few, rare occasions the SHUTDOWN ABORT will fail to work. In those situations, you can use ps -ef | grep smon to locate the Oracle system-monitor process and then use the Linux/Unix k ill command to terminate the instance. When you kill a required Oracle background process, this causes the instance to abort. Obviously, you should use an OS kill command only as a last resort.

DATABASE VS. INSTANCE

Although DBAs often use the terms *database* and *instance* synonymously, these two terms refer to very different architectural components. In Oracle the term *database* denotes the physical files that make up a database: the data files, online redo log files, and control files. The term *instance* denotes the background processes and memory structures.

For example, you can create an instance without having a database present. Before a database is physically created, you must start the instance with the STARTUP NOMOUNT statement. In this state you have background processes and memory structures without any associated data files, online redo logs, or control files. The database files aren't created until you issue the CREATE DATABASE statement.

Another important point to remember is that an instance can only be associated with one database, whereas a database can be associated with many different instances (as with Oracle Real Application Clusters [RAC]). An instance can mount and open a database one time

---

only. Each time you stop and start a database, a new instance is associated with it. Previously created background processes and memory structures are never associated with a database.

To demonstrate this concept, close a database with the ALTER DATABASE CLOSE statement:

```
SQL> alter database close;
```

If you attempt to restart the database, you receive an error:

```
SQL> alter database open;
ERROR at line 1:
ORA-16196: database has been previously opened and closed
```

This is because an instance can only ever mount and open one database. You must stop and start a new instance before you can mount and open the database.

Using the dbca to Create a Database

You can also use the dbca utility to create a database. This utility works in two modes: graphical and silent. To use the dbca in graphical mode, ensure you have the proper X software installed, then issue the xhost + command, and make certain your DISPLAY variable is set; for example,

```
$ xhost +
$ echo $DISPLAY
:0.0
```

To run the dbca in graphical mode, type in dbca from the OS command line:

```
$ dbca
```

The graphical mode is very intuitive and will walk you through all aspects of creating a database. You may prefer to use this mode if you are new to Oracle and want to be explicitly prompted with choices.

You can also run the dbca in silent mode with a response file. In some situations, using dbca in graphical mode isn't feasible. This may be due to slow networks or the unavailability of X software. To create a database, using dbca in silent mode, perform the following steps:

1. Locate the d bca.rsp file.

2. Make a copy of the d bca.rsp file.

3. Modify the copy of the d bca.rsp file for your environment.

4. Run the dbca utility in silent mode.

First, navigate to the location in which you copied the Oracle database installation software, and use the find command to locate dbca.rsp:

```
$ find . -name dbca.rsp
./18.0.0.0/database/response/dbca.rsp
```

Copy the file so that you're not modifying the original (in this way, you'll always have a good, original file):

```
$ cp dbca.rsp mydb.rsp
```

Now, edit the mydb.rsp file. Minimally, you need to modify the following parameters: GDBNAME, SID, SYSPASSWORD, SYSTEMPASSWORD, SYSMANPASSWORD, DBSNMPPASSWORD, DATAFILEDESTINATION, STORAGETYPE, CHARACTERSET, and NATIONALCHARACTERSET. Following is an example of modified values in the mydb.rsp file:

```
[CREATEDATABASE]
GDBNAME = "O18DEV"
SID = "O18DEV"
TEMPLATENAME = "General_Purpose.dbc"
SYSPASSWORD = "foo"
SYSTEMPASSWORD = "foo"
SYSMANPASSWORD = "foo"
DBSNMPPASSWORD = "foo"
DATAFILEDESTINATION ="/u01/dbfile"
STORAGETYPE="FS"
CHARACTERSET = "AL32UTF8"
NATIONALCHARACTERSET= "UTF8"
```

Next, run the dbca utility in silent mode, using a response file:

```
$ dbca -silent -responseFile /home/oracle/orainst/mydb.rsp
```

You should see output such as

```
Copying database files
1% complete
...
```

```
Creating and starting Oracle instance
...
62% complete
Completing Database Creation
...
100% complete
Look at the log file ... for further details.
```

If you look in the log files, note that the dbca utility uses the rman utility to restore the data files used for the database. Then, it creates the instance and performs postinstallation steps. On a Linux server you should also have an entry in the /etc/oratab file for your new database.

Many DBAs launch dbca and configure databases in the graphical mode, but a few exploit the options available to them using the response file. With effective utilization of the response file, you can consistently automate the database creation process. You can modify the response file to build databases on ASM and even create RAC databases. In addition, you can control just about every aspect of the response file, similar to launching the dbca in graphical mode.

Tip   You can view all options of the dbca via the help parameter: dbca -help

---

USING DBCA TO GENERATE A CREATE DATABASE STATEMENT

You can use the dbca utility to generate a CREATE DATABASE statement. You can perform this either interactively with the graphical interface or via silent mode. The key is to choose the "custom database template" and also specify the option to "generate database creation scripts." This example uses the silent mode to generate a script that contains a CREATE DATABASE statement:

```
$ dbca -silent -generateScripts -customCreate -templateName New_Database.dbt \
  -gdbName DKDEV
```

The prior line of code instructs the dbca to create a script named CreateDB.sql and place it in the ORACLE_BASE/admin/DKDEV/scripts directory. The CreateDB.sql file contains a CREATE DATABASE statement within it. Also created is an init.ora file for initializing your instance.

In this example, the scripts required to create a database are generated for you. No database is created until you manually run the scripts.

This technique gives you an automated method for generating a CREATE DATABASE statement. This is especially useful if you are new to Oracle and are unsure of how to construct a CREATE DATABASE statement or if you are using a new version of the database and want a valid CREATE DATABASE statement generated by an Oracle utility.

Dropping a Database

If you have an unused database that you need to drop, you can use the DROP DATABASE statement to accomplish this. Doing so removes all data files, control files, and online redo logs associated with the database.

Needless to say, use extreme caution when dropping a database. Before you drop a database, ensure that you're on the correct server and are connected to the correct database. On a Linux/Unix system, issue the following OS command from the OS prompt:

```
$ uname -a
```

Next, connect to SQL*Plus, and be sure you're connected to the database you want to drop:

```
SQL> select name from v$database;
```

After you've verified that you're in the correct database environment, issue the following SQL commands from a SYSDBA-privileged account:

```
SQ> shutdown immediate;
SQL> startup mount exclusive restrict;
SQL> drop database;
```

Caution   Obviously, you should be careful when dropping a database. You aren't prompted when dropping the database and, as of this writing, there is no UNDROP ACCIDENTALLY DROPPED DATABASE command. Use extreme caution when dropping a database, because this operation removes data files, control files, and online redo log files.

The DROP DATABASE command is useful when you have a database that needs to be removed. It may be a test database or an old database that is no longer used. The DROP DATABASE command doesn't remove old archive redo log files. You must manually remove those files with an OS command (such as rm, in Linux/Unix, or del, at the Windows command prompt). You can also instruct RMAN to remove archive redo log files.

How Many Databases on One Server?

Sometimes, when you're creating new databases, this question arises: How many databases should you put on one server? One extreme is to have only one database running on each database server. This architecture is illustrated in Figure 2-3, which shows two different database servers, each with its own installation of the Oracle binaries. This type of setup is profitable for the hardware vendor but in many environments isn't an economical use of resources.

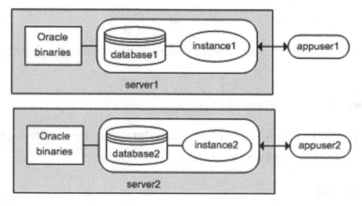

Figure 2-3. *Architecture with one server per database*

If you have enough memory, central processing unit (CPU), and disk resources, then you should consider creating multiple databases on one server. You can create a new installation of the Oracle binaries for each database or have multiple databases share one set of Oracle binaries. Figure 2-4 shows a configuration using one set of Oracle binaries that's shared by multiple databases on one server. Of course, if you have requirements for different versions of the Oracle binaries, you must have multiple Oracle homes to house those installations.

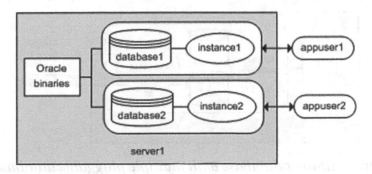

Figure 2-4. *Multiple databases sharing one set of Oracle binaries on a server*

If you don't have the CPU, memory, or disk resources to create multiple databases on one server, consider using one database to host multiple applications and users, as shown in Figure 2-5. In environments such as this, be careful not to use public synonyms, because there may be collisions between applications. It's typical to create different schemas and tablespaces to be used by different applications in such environments.

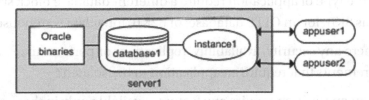

Figure 2-5. *One database used by multiple applications and users*

With Oracle Database 18c you have the option of using the pluggable database feature. This technology allows you to house several pluggable databases within one container database. The pluggable databases share the instance, background processes, undo, and Oracle binaries but function as completely separate databases. Each pluggable database has its own set of tablespaces (including SYSTEM) that are not visible to any other pluggable databases within the container database. This allows you to securely implement an isolated database that shares resources with other databases. Figure 2-6 depicts this architecture (see Chapter 23 for details on how to implement a pluggable database).

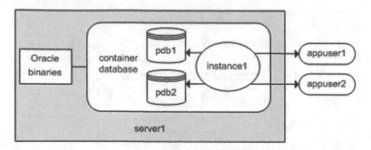

Figure 2-6. *One container database with multiple pluggable databases*

You must consider several architectural aspects when determining whether to use one database to host multiple applications and users:

- Do the applications generate vastly different amounts of redo, which may necessitate differently sized online redo logs?

- Are the queries used by applications dissimilar enough to require different amounts of undo, sorting space, and memory?

- Does the type of application require a different database block size, such as 8KB, for an OLTP database; or 32KB, for a data warehouse?

- Are there any security, availability, replication, or performance requirements that require an application to be isolated?

- Does an application require any features available only in the Enterprise Edition of Oracle?

- Does an application require the use of any special Oracle features, such as Data Guard, partitioning, Streams, or RAC?

- What are the backup and recovery requirements for each application? Does one application require online backups and the other application doesn't? Does one application require tape backups?

- Is any application dependent on an Oracle database version? Will there be different database upgrade schedules and requirements?

Table 2-5 describes the advantages and disadvantages of these architectural considerations regarding how to use Oracle databases and applications. This is just looking at the database instances without using multitenancy with container and pluggable databases. We will revisit these disadvantages when leveraging containers as this allows you to consolidate on fewer servers. This will be discussed in Chapter 22.

Table 2-5. *Oracle Database Configuration Advantages and Disadvantages*

Configuration	Advantages	Disadvantages
One database per server	Dedicated resources for the application using the database; completely isolates applications from each other;	Most expensive; requires more hardware
Multiple databases and Oracle homes per server	requires fewer servers	Multiple databases competing for disk, memory, and CPU resources
Multiple databases and one installation of Oracle binaries on the server	Requires fewer servers; doesn't require multiple installations of the Oracle binaries	Multiple databases competing for disk, memory, and CPU resources
One database and one Oracle home serving multiple applications	Only requires one server and one database; inexpensive	Multiple databases competing for disk, memory, and CPU resources; multiple applications dependent on one database; one single point of failure
Container database containing multiple pluggable databases	Least expensive; allows multiple pluggable databases to use the infrastructure of one parent container database securely	Multiple databases competing for disk, memory, and CPU resources; multiple applications dependent on one database; one single point of failure

Understanding Oracle Architecture

This chapter introduced concepts such as database (data files, online redo log files, control files), instance (background processes and memory structures), parameter file, password file, and listener. Now is a good time to present an Oracle architecture diagram that shows the various files and processes that constitute a database and instance. Some of the concepts depicted in Figure 2-7 have already been covered in detail: for example, database vs. instance. Other aspects of Figure 2-7 will be covered in future chapters. However, it's appropriate to include a high-level diagram such as this in order to represent visually the concepts already discussed and to lay the foundation for understanding upcoming topics in this book.

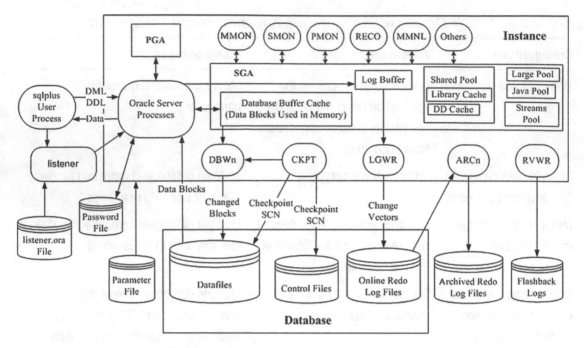

Figure 2-7. *Oracle database architecture*

There are several aspects to note about Figure 2-7. Communication with the database is initiated through a `sqlplus` user process. Typically, the user process connects to the database over the network. This requires that you configure and start a listener process. The listener process hands off incoming connection requests to an Oracle server process, which handles all subsequent communication with the client process. If a remote connection is initiated as a `sys*`-level user, then a password file is required. A password file is also required for local `sys*` connections that don't use OS authentication.

The instance consists of memory structures and background processes. When the instance starts, it reads the parameter file, which helps establish the size of the memory processes and other characteristics of the instance. When starting a database, the instance goes through three phases: nomount (instance started), mount (control files opened), and open (data files and online redo logs opened).

The number of background processes varies by database version (more than 30 in the latest version of Oracle). You can view the names and descriptions of the processes via this query:

```
SQL> select name, description from v$bgprocess;
```

The major background processes include

> DBWn: The database writer writes blocks from the database buffer cache to the data files.

> CKPT: The checkpoint process writes checkpoint information to the control files and data file headers.

> LGWR: The log writer writes redo information from the log buffer to the online redo logs.

> ARCn: The archiver copies the content of online redo logs to archive redo log files.

> RVWR: The recovery writer maintains before images of blocks in the fast recovery area.

> MMON: The manageability monitor process gathers automatic workload repository statistics.

> MMNL: The manageability monitor lite process writes statistics from the active session history buffer to disk.

> SMON: The system monitor performs system level clean-up operations, including instance recovery in the event of a failed instance, coalescing free space, and cleaning up temporary space.

> PMON: The process monitor cleans up abnormally terminated database connections and also automatically registers a database instance with the listener process.

> RECO: The recoverer process automatically resolves failed distributed transactions.

The structure of the SGA varies by Oracle release. You can view details for each component via this query:

```
SQL> select pool, name from v$sgastat;
```

The major SGA memory structures include

> SGA: The SGA is the main read/write memory area and is composed of several buffers, such as the database buffer cache, redo log buffer, shared pool, large pool, java pool, and streams pool.

> Database buffer cache: The buffer cache stores copies of blocks read from data files.

> Log buffer: The log buffer stores changes to modified data blocks.

> Shared pool: The shared pool contains library cache information regarding recently executed SQL and PL/SQL code. The shared pool also houses the data dictionary cache, which contains structural information about the database, objects, and users.

Finally, the program global area (PGA) is a memory area separate from the SGA. The PGA is a process-specific memory area that contains session-variable information.

Summary

After you've installed the Oracle binaries, you can create a database. Before creating a database, make sure you've correctly set the required OS variables. You also need an initialization file and to pre-create any necessary directories. You should carefully think about which initialization parameters should be set to a nondefault value. In general, I try to use as many default values as possible and only change an initialization parameter when there is a good reason. If performing too many manual processes and steps, the process needs to be reexamined. With the latest version of the database, many of the environment variables are set; directories will be created when using the configuration assists, dbca, and netca. Using response files is another way to automate the processes for creation.

This chapter focused on using SQL*Plus to create databases. This is an efficient and repeatable method for creating a database. When you're crafting a CREATE DATABASE statement, consider the size of the data files and online redo logs for placement and storage needs of the database. The internal parameters and sizing should be understood as part of the internal knowledge of the databases for later troubleshooting and other configurations. Using the new features of the latest release is going to increase the efficiencies of the databases. Some environments might be using previous versions, which makes it even more important to understand the internals of what is needed to create the database.

I've worked in some environments in which management dictated the requirement of one database per server; unless this is a container database with multiple pluggable databases, there are unutilized resources on the server. A fast server with large memory areas and many CPUs should be capable of hosting several different databases. You must determine what architecture meets your business requirements when deciding how many databases to place on one box.

After you've created a database, the next step is to configure the environment so that you can efficiently navigate, operate, and monitor the database. These tasks are described in the next chapter.

CHAPTER 3

Configuring an Efficient Environment

After you install the Oracle binaries and create a database, you should configure your environment to enable you to operate efficiently. Regardless of the functionality of graphical database administration tools, DBAs still need to perform many tasks from the OS command line and manually execute SQL statements. A DBA who takes advantage of the OS and SQL has a clear advantage over a DBA who doesn't.

In any database environment (Oracle, MySQL, and so on), an effective DBA uses advanced OS features to allow you to quickly navigate the directory, locate files, repeat commands, display system bottlenecks, and so forth. To achieve this efficiency, you must be knowledgeable about the OS that houses the database.

In addition to being proficient with the OS, you must also be skillful with the SQL interface into the database. Although you can glean much diagnostic information from graphical interfaces, SQL enables you to take a deeper dive into the internals to do advanced troubleshooting and derive database intelligence.

This chapter lays the foundation for efficient use of the OS and SQL to manage your databases. You can use the following OS and database features to configure your environment for effectiveness:

- OS variables

- Shell aliases

- Shell functions

- Shell scripts

- SQL scripts

© Michelle Malcher and Darl Kuhn 2019
M. Malcher and D. Kuhn, *Pro Oracle Database 18c Administration*,
https://doi.org/10.1007/978-1-4842-4424-1_3

When you're in a stressful situation, it's paramount to have an environment in which you can quickly discern where you are and what accounts you're using and to have tools that help you quickly identify problems. The techniques described in this chapter are like levers: they provide leverage for doing large amounts of work fast. These tools let you focus on the issues you may be facing instead of verifying your location or worrying about command syntax.

This chapter begins by detailing OS techniques for enabling maximum efficiency. Later sections show how you can use these tools to display environment details automatically, navigate the file system, monitor the database proactively, and triage.

Tip   Consistently use one OS shell when working on your database servers. I recommend that you use the Bash shell; it contains all the most useful features from the other shells (Korn and C), plus it has additional features that add to its ease of use.

Customizing Your OS Command Prompt

Typically, DBAs work with multiple servers and multiple databases. In these situations, you may have numerous terminals' sessions open on your screen. You can run the following types of commands to identify your current working environment:

```
$ hostname -a
$ id
$ who am i
$ echo $ORACLE_SID
$ pwd
```

To avoid confusion about which server you're working on, it's often desirable to configure your command prompt to display information regarding its environment, such as the machine name and database SID. In this example, the command prompt name is customized to include the hostname, user, and Oracle SID:

```
$ PS1='[\h:\u:${ORACLE_SID}]$ '
```

The \h specifies the hostname. The \u specifies the current OS user. $ORACLE_SID contains the current setting for your Oracle instance identifier. Here is the command prompt for this example:

```
[oracle18c:oracle:o18c]$
```

The command prompt contains three pieces of important information about the environment: server name, OS username, and database name. When you're navigating among multiple environments, setting the command prompt can be an invaluable tool for keeping track of where you are and what environment you're in.

If you want the OS prompt automatically configured when you log in, then you need to set it in a startup file. In a Bash shell environment, you typically use the . bashrc file. This file is normally located in your HOME directory. Place the following line of code in . bashrc:

```
PS1='[\h:\u:${ORACLE_SID}]$ '
```

When you place this line of code in the startup file, then any time you log in to the server, your OS prompt is set automatically for you. In other shells, such as the Korn shell, the . profile file is the startup file.

Depending on your personal preference, you may want to modify the command prompt for your particular needs. For example, many DBAs like the current working directory displayed in the command prompt. To display the current working directory information, add the \ w variable:

```
$ PS1='[\h:\u:\w:${ORACLE_SID}]$ '
```

As you can imagine, a wide variety of options are available for the information shown in the command prompt. Here is another popular format:

```
$ PS1='|\u@${ORACLE_SID}@\h:\W]$ '
```

Table 3-1 lists many of the Bash shell variables you can use to customize the OS command prompt.

Table 3-1. *Bash Shell Backslash-Escaped Variables Used for Customizing the Command Prompt*

Variable	Description
\ a	ASCII bell character
\ d	Date in "weekday month day-of-month" format
\ h	Hostname
\ e	ASCII escape character
\ j	Number of jobs managed by the shell
\ l	Base name of the shell's terminal device
\ n	Newline
\ r	Carriage return
\ s	Name of the shell
\ t	Time in 24-hour HH:MM:SS format
\ T	Time in 12-hour HH:MM:SS format
\ @	Time in 12-hour AM/PM format
\ A	Time in 24-hour HH:MM format
\ u	Current shell
\ v	Version of the Bash shell
\ V	Release of the Bash shell
\ w	Current working directory
\ W	Base name of the current working directory (not the full path)
\ !	History number of command
\ $	If the effective user identifier (UID) is 0, then displays #; otherwise, displays $

The variables available for use with your command prompt vary somewhat by OS and shell. For example, in a Korn shell environment, the hostname variable displays the server name in the OS prompt:

```
$ export PS1="[`hostname`]$ "
```

If you want to include the `ORACLE_SID` variable within that string, then set it as follows:

```
$ export PS1=[`hostname`':"${ORACLE_SID}"]$ '
```

Try not to go overboard in terms of how much information you display in the OS prompt. Too much information limits your ability to type in and view commands on one line. As a rule of thumb, minimally you should include the server name and database name displayed in the OS prompt. Having that information readily available will save you from making the mistake of thinking that you're in one environment when you're really in another.

Customizing Your SQL Prompt

DBAs frequently use SQL*Plus to perform daily administrative tasks. Often, you'll work on servers that contain multiple databases. Obviously, each database contains multiple user accounts. When connected to a database, you can run the following commands to verify information such as your username, database connection, and hostname:

```
SQL> show user;
SQL> select name from v$database;
```

This is very useful to verify development versus production accounts, in order to keep them separate. Using a SQLPROMPT for a quick visual besides querying the database will make sure the right environment is being used for any queries, changes, etc.

A more efficient way to determine your username and SID is to set your SQL prompt to display that information; for example,

```
SQL> SET SQLPROMPT '&_USER.@&_CONNECT_IDENTIFIER.> '
```

An even more efficient way to configure your SQL prompt is to have it automatically run the `SET SQLPROMPT` command when you log in to SQL*Plus. Follow these steps to fully automate this:

1. Create a file named `login.sql`, and place in it the `SET SQLPROMPT` command.

2. Set your SQLPATH OS variable to include the directory location of login.sql. In this example, the SQLPATH OS variable is set in the .bashrc OS file, which is executed each time a new shell is logged in to or started. Here is the entry:

```
export SQLPATH=$HOME/scripts
```

3. Create a file named login.sql in the HOME/scripts directory. Place the following line in the file:

```
SET SQLPROMPT '&_USER.@&_CONNECT_IDENTIFIER.> '
```

4. To see the result, you can either log out and log back in to your server or source the .bashrc file directly:

```
$ . ./.bashrc
```

Now, log in to SQL. Here is an example of the SQL*Plus prompt:

```
SYS@devdb1>
```

If you connect to a different user, this should be reflected in the prompt:

```
SQL> conn system/foo
```

The SQL*Plus prompt now displays

```
SYSTEM@devdb1
```

Setting your SQL prompt is an easy way to remind yourself which environment and user you're currently connected as. This will help prevent you from accidentally running an SQL statement in the wrong environment. The last thing you want is to think you're in a development environment and then discover that you've run a script to delete objects while connected in a production environment.

Table 3-2 contains a complete list of SQL*Plus variables that you can use to customize your prompt.

Table 3-2. *Predefined SQL*Plus Variables*

Variable	Description
_ CONNECT_IDENTIFIER	Connection identifier, such as the Oracle SID
_ DATE	Current date
_ EDITOR	Editor used by the SQL EDIT command
_ O_VERSION	Oracle version
_ O_RELEASE	Oracle release
_ PRIVILEGE	Privilege level of the current connected session
_ SQLPLUS_RELEASE	SQL*Plus release number
_ USER	Current connected user

Creating Shortcuts for Frequently Used Commands

In Linux/Unix environments, you can use two common methods to create shortcuts to other commands: create aliases for often repeated commands and use functions to form shortcuts for groups of commands. The following sections describe ways in which you can deploy these two techniques.

Using Aliases

An alias is a simple mechanism for creating a short piece of text that will execute other shell commands. Here is the general syntax:

```
$ alias <alias_name>='<shell command>'
```

For instance, when faced with database problems, it's often useful to create an alias that runs a cd command that places you in the directory containing the database alert log. This example creates an alias (named bdump) that changes the current working directory to where the alert log is located:

```
$ alias bdump='cd /u01/app/oracle/diag/rdbms/o18c/o18c/trace'
```

Now, instead of having to type the `cd` command, along with a lengthy (and easily forgettable) directory path, you can simply type in `bdump`, and they are placed in the specified directory:

```
$ bdump
$ pwd
/u01/app/oracle/diag/rdbms/o18c/o18c/trace
```

The prior technique allows you to navigate to the directory of interest efficiently and accurately. This is especially handy when you manage many different databases on different servers. You simply have to set up a standard set of aliases that allow you to navigate and work more efficiently.

To show all aliases that have been defined, use the `alias` command, with no arguments:

```
$ alias
```

Listed next are some common examples of alias definitions you can use:

```
alias l.='ls -d .*'
alias ll='ls -l'
alias lsd='ls -altr | grep ^d'
alias sqlp='sqlplus "/ as sysdba"'
alias shutdb='echo "shutdown immediate;" | sqlp'
alias startdb='echo "startup;" | sqlp'
```

If you want to remove an alias definition from your current environment, use the `unalias` command. The following example removes the alias for `lsd`:

```
$ unalias lsd
```

LOCATING THE ALERT LOG

In Oracle Database 11g and higher, the alert log directory path has this structure:

```
ORACLE_BASE/diag/rdbms/LOWER(<db_unique_name>)/<instance_name>/trace
```

Usually (but not always) the db_unique_name is the same as the instance_name. In Data Guard environments the db_unique_name will often not be the same as the instance_name. You can verify the directory path with this query:

```
SQL> select value from v$diag_info where name = 'Diag Trace';
```

The name of the alert log follows this format:

```
alert_<ORACLE_SID>.log
```

You can also locate the alert log from the OS (whether the database is started or not) via these OS commands:

```
$ cd $ORACLE_BASE
$ find . -name alert_<ORACLE_SID>.log
```

In the prior find command, you'll need to replace the <ORACLE_SID> value with the name of your database.

Using a Function

Much like an alias, you can also use a function to form command shortcuts. A function is defined with this general syntax:

```
$ function <function_name> {
  shell commands
}
```

For example, the following line of code creates a simple function (named bdump) that allows you to change the current working directory, dependent on the name of the database passed in:

```
function bdump {
if [ "$1" = "engdev" ]; then
  cd /orahome/app/oracle/diag/rdbms/engdev/ENGDEV/trace
elif [ "$1" = "stage" ]; then
  cd /orahome/app/oracle/diag/rdbms/stage/STAGE/trace
fi
echo "Changing directories to $1 Diag Trace directory"
pwd
}
```

You can now type bdump, followed by a database name at the command line, to change your working directory to the Oracle background dump directory:

```
$ bdump stage
Changing directories to stage Diag Trace directory
/orahome/app/oracle/diag/rdbms/stage/STAGE/trace
```

Using functions is usually preferable to using aliases. Functions are more powerful than aliases because of features such as the ability to operate on parameters passed in on the command line and allowing for multiple lines of code and therefore more complex coding.

DBAs commonly establish functions by setting them in the H OME/.bashrc file. A better way to manage functions is to create a file that stores only function code and call that file from the . bashrc file. It's also better to store special purpose files in directories that you've created for these files. For instance, create a directory named bin under HOME. Then, in the bin directory, create a file named dba_fcns, and place in it your function code. Now, call the dba_fcns file from the . bashrc file. Here is an example of an entry in a .bashrc file:

```
. $HOME/bin/dba_fcns
```

Listed next is a small sample of some of the types of functions you can use:

```
# show environment variables in sorted list
  function envs {
    if test -z "$1"
      then /bin/env | /bin/sort
      else /bin/env | /bin/sort | /bin/grep -i $1
    fi
  } # envs
#------------------------------------------------------------#
# find largest files below this point
function flf {
  find . -ls | sort -nrk7 | head -10
}
#------------------------------------------------------------#
```

```
# find largest directories consuming space below this point
function fld {
  du -S . | sort -nr | head -10
}
#-------------------------------------------------------------#
function bdump {
  if [ $ORACLE_SID = "o18c" ]; then
    cd /u01/app/oracle/diag/rdbms/o18c/o18c/trace
  elif [ $ORACLE_SID = "CDB1" ]; then
    cd /u01/app/oracle/diag/rdbms/cdb1/CDB1/trace
  elif [ $ORACLE_SID = "rcat" ]; then
    cd /u01/app/oracle/diag/rdbms/rcat/rcat/trace
  fi
  pwd
} # bdump
```

If you ever wonder whether a shortcut is an alias or a function, use the type command to verify a command's origin. This example verifies that bdump is a function:

```
$ type bdump
```

Rerunning Commands Quickly

When there are problems with a database server, you need to be able to quickly run commands from the OS prompt. You may be having some sort of performance issue and want to run commands that navigate you to directories that contain log files, or you may want to display the top-consuming processes from time to time. In these situations, you don't want to waste time having to retype command sequences.

One time-saving feature of the Bash shell is that it has several methods for editing and rerunning previously executed commands. The following list highlights several options available for manipulating previously typed commands:

- Scrolling with the up (↑) and down (↓) arrow keys

- Using Ctrl+P and Ctrl+N

- Listing the command history

- Searching in reverse

- Setting the command editor

Each of these techniques is described briefly in the following sections.

Scrolling with the Up and Down Arrow Keys

You can use the up arrow to scroll up through your recent command history. As you scroll through previously run commands, you can rerun a desired command by pressing the Enter or Return key.

If you want to edit a command, use the Backspace key to erase characters, or use the left arrow to navigate to the desired location in the command text. After you've scrolled up through the command stack, use the down arrow to scroll back down through previously viewed commands.

Note   If you're familiar with Windows, scrolling through the command stack is similar to using the DOSKEY utility.

Using Ctrl+P and Ctrl+N

The Ctrl+P keystroke (pressing the Ctrl and P keys at the same time) displays your previously entered command. If you've pressed Ctrl+P several times, you can scroll back down the command stack by pressing Ctrl+N (pressing the Ctrl and N keys at the same time).

Listing the Command History

You can use the history command to display commands that the user previously entered:

```
$ history
```

Depending on how many commands have previously been executed, you may see a lengthy stack. You can limit the output to the last n number of commands by providing a number with the command. For example, the following query lists the last five commands that were run:

```
$ history 5
```

Here is some sample output:

```
273  cd -
274  grep -i ora alert.log
275  ssh -Y -l oracle 65.217.177.98
276  pwd
277  history 5
```

To run a previously listed command in the output, use an exclamation point (!) (sometimes called the bang) followed by the history number. In this example, to run the p wd command on line 276, use !, as follows:

```
$ !276
```

To run the last command you ran, use !!, as shown here:

```
$ !!
```

Searching in Reverse

Press Ctrl+R, and you're presented with the Bash shell reverse-search utility:

```
$ (reverse-i-search)`':
```

From the reverse-i-search prompt, as you type each letter, the tool automatically searches through previously run commands that have text similar to the string you entered. As soon as you're presented with the desired command match, you can rerun the command by pressing the Enter or Return key. To view all commands that match a string, press Ctrl+R repeatedly. To exit the reverse search, press Ctrl+C.

Setting the Command Editor

You can use the set - o command to make your command-line editor be either vi or emacs. This example sets the command-line editor to be vi:

```
$ set -o vi
```

Now, when you press Esc+K, you're placed in a mode in which you can use vi commands to search through the stack of previously entered commands.

For example, if you want to scroll up the command stack, you can use the K key; similarly, you can scroll down using the J key. When in this mode you can use the slash (/) key and then type a string to be searched for in the entire command stack.

Tip   Before you attempt to use the command editor feature, be sure you're thoroughly familiar with either the vi or emacs editor.

A short example will illustrate the power of this feature. Say you know that you ran the ls - altr command about an hour ago. You want to run it again, but this time without the r (reverse-sort) option. To enter the command stack, press Esc+K:

```
$ Esc+K
```

You should now see the last command you executed. To search the command stack for the ls command, type /ls, and then press Enter or Return:

```
$ /ls
```

The most recently executed ls command appears at the prompt:

```
$ ls -altr
```

To remove the r option, use the right arrow key to place the prompt over the r on the screen, and press X to remove the r from the end of the command. After you've edited the command, press the Enter or Return key to execute it.

Developing Standard Scripts

I've worked in shops where the database administration team developed hundreds of scripts and utilities to help manage an environment. One company had a small squad of DBAs whose job function was to maintain the environmental scripts. I think that's overkill. I tend to use a small set of focused scripts, with each script usually less than 50 lines long. If you develop a script that another DBA can't understand or maintain, then it loses its effectiveness. Also, if you have to execute a command more than a couple of times, a script should be created to execute it. If it is something that is now a standard, regular check, or job, the script can be used to automate the process.

These scripts are handy to put into jobs that will be automatically run or during a time of troubleshooting since it needs to be completed quickly. There are other tools that also maintain database and provide proactive alerts and monitoring of multiple databases instead of a script being run against one database at a time.

Note All the scripts in this chapter are available for download from the Source Code/Download area of the Apress web site (`www.apress.com`).

This section contains several short shell functions, shell scripts, and SQL scripts that can help you manage a database environment. This is by no means a complete list of scripts—rather, it provides a starting point from which you can build. Each subsection heading is the name of a script.

Note Before you attempt to run a shell script, ensure that it's executable. Use the chmod command to achieve this: `chmod 750 <script>`

---

dba_setup

Usually, you'll establish a common set of OS variables and aliases in the same manner for every database server. When navigating among servers, you should set these variables and aliases in a consistent and repeatable manner. Doing so helps you (or your team) operate efficiently in every environment. For example, it's extremely useful to have the OS prompt set in a consistent way when you work with dozens of different servers. This helps you quickly identify what box you're on, which OS user you're logged in as, and so on.

One technique is to store these standard settings in a script and then have that script executed automatically when you log in to a server. I usually create a script named dba_setup to set these OS variables and aliases. You can place this script in a directory such as HOME/bin and automatically execute the script via a startup script (see the section "Organizing Scripts" later in this chapter). Here are the contents of a typical dba_setup script:

```
# set prompt
PS1='[\h:\u:${ORACLE_SID}]$ '
```

```
#
export EDITOR=vi
export VISUAL=$EDITOR
export SQLPATH=$HOME/scripts
set -o vi
#
# list directories only
alias lsd="ls -p | grep /"
# show top cpu consuming processes
alias topc="ps -e -o pcpu,pid,user,tty,args | sort -n -k 1 -r | head"
# show top memory consuming processes
alias topm="ps -e -o pmem,pid,user,tty,args | sort -n -k 1 -r | head"
#
alias sqlp='sqlplus "/ as sysdba"'
alias shutdb='echo "shutdown immediate;" | sqlp'
alias startdb='echo "startup;" | sqlp'
```

dba_fcns

Use this script to store OS functions that help you navigate and operate in your database environment. Functions tend to have more functionality than do aliases. You can be quite creative with the number and complexity of functions you use. The idea is that you want a consistent and standard set of functions that you can call, no matter which database server you're logged in to.

Place this script in a directory such as HOME/bin. Usually, you'll have this script automatically called when you log in to a server via a startup script (see the section "Organizing Scripts" later in this chapter). Here are some typical functions you can use:

```
#------------------------------------------------------------#
# show environment variables in sorted list
  function envs {
    if test -z "$1"
      then /bin/env | /bin/sort
      else /bin/env | /bin/sort | /bin/grep -i $1
    fi
  } # envs
```

```
#-------------------------------------------------------------#
# login to sqlplus
  function sp {
    time sqlplus "/ as sysdba"
  } # sp
#-------------------------------------------------------------#
# find largest files below this point
function flf {
  find . -ls | sort -nrk7 | head -10
}
#-------------------------------------------------------------#
# find largest directories consuming space below this point
function fld {
  du -S . | sort -nr | head -10
}
#-------------------------------------------------------------#
# change directories to directory containing alert log file
function bdump {
    cd /u01/app/oracle/diag/rdbms/o18c/o18c/trace
  } # bdump
#-------------------------------------------------------------#
```

tbsp_chk.bsh

This script checks to see if any tablespaces are surpassing a certain fullness threshold. Store this script in a directory such as HOME/bin. Make sure you modify the script to contain the correct username, password, and e-mail address for your environment.

You also need to establish the required OS variables, such as ORACLE_SID and ORACLE_HOME. You can either hard-code those variables into the script or call a script that sources the variables for you. The next script calls a script (named oraset) that sets the OS variables (see Chapter 2 for the details of this script). You don't have to use this script—the idea is to have a consistent and repeatable way of establishing OS variables for your environment.

You can run this script from the command line. In this example I passed it the database name (o18c) and wanted to see what tablespaces had less than 20 percent space left:

```
$ tbsp_chk.bsh o18c 20
```

The output indicates that two tablespaces for this database have less than 20 percent space left:

```
space not okay
0 % free UNDOTBS1, 17 % free SYSAUX,
```

Here are the contents of the tbsp_chk.bsh script:

```
#!/bin/bash
#
if [ $# -ne 2 ]; then
  echo "Usage: $0 SID threshold"
  exit 1
fi
# either hard code OS variables or source them from a script.
# see Chapter 2 for details on using oraset to source oracle OS variables
. /var/opt/oracle/oraset $1
#
crit_var=$(
sqlplus -s <<EOF
system/foo
SET HEAD OFF TERM OFF FEED OFF VERIFY OFF
COL pct_free FORMAT 999
SELECT (f.bytes/a.bytes)*100 pct_free,'% free',a.tablespace_name||','
FROM
(SELECT NVL(SUM(bytes),0) bytes, x.tablespace_name
FROM dba_free_space y, dba_tablespaces x
WHERE x.tablespace_name = y.tablespace_name(+)
AND x.contents != 'TEMPORARY' AND x.status != 'READ ONLY'
AND x.tablespace_name  NOT LIKE 'UNDO%'
GROUP BY x.tablespace_name) f,
(SELECT SUM(bytes) bytes, tablespace_name
```

```
FROM dba_data_files
GROUP BY tablespace_name) a
WHERE a.tablespace_name = f.tablespace_name
AND   (f.bytes/a.bytes)*100 <= $2
ORDER BY 1;
EXIT;
EOF)
if [ "$crit_var" = "" ]; then
  echo "space okay"
else
  echo "space not okay"
  echo $crit_var
  echo $crit_var | mailx -s "tbsp getting full on $1" dkuhn@gmail.com
fi
exit 0
```

Usually, you run a script such as this automatically, on a periodic basis, from a scheduling utility, such as cron. Here is a typical cron entry that runs the script once an hour:

```
# Tablespace check
2 * * * * /orahome/bin/tbsp_chk.bsh INVPRD 10 1>/orahome/bin/log/tbsp_chk.
log 2>&1
```

This cron entry runs the job and stores any informational output in the tbsp_chk. log file.

When running tbsp_chk.bsh in an Oracle Database 12c pluggable database environment from the root container, you'll need to reference the CDD_* views rather than the DBA_* views for the script to properly report on space regarding all pluggable databases (within the container database). You should also consider adding the NAME and CON_ID to the query so that you can view which pluggable database is potentially having space issues; for example,

```
SELECT a.name, (f.bytes/a.bytes)*100 pct_free,'% free',a.tablespace_name||','
FROM
(SELECT c.name, NVL(SUM(bytes),0) bytes, x.tablespace_name
FROM cdb_free_space y, cdb_tablespaces x, v$containers c
```

```
WHERE x.tablespace_name = y.tablespace_name(+)
AND x.contents != 'TEMPORARY' AND x.status != 'READ ONLY'
AND x.tablespace_name  NOT LIKE 'UNDO%'
AND x.con_id = y.con_id
AND x.con_id = c.con_id
GROUP BY c.name, x.tablespace_name) f,
(SELECT c.name, SUM(d.bytes) bytes, d.tablespace_name
FROM cdb_data_files d, v$containers c
WHERE d.con_id = c.con_id
GROUP BY c.name, tablespace_name) a
WHERE a.tablespace_name = f.tablespace_name
AND  (f.bytes/a.bytes)*100 <= 50
AND   a.name NOT IN ('PDB$SEED')
AND   a.name = f.name
ORDER BY 1;
```

conn.bsh

You need to be alerted if there are issues with connecting to databases. This script checks to see if a connection can be established to the database. If a connection can't be established, an e-mail is sent. Place this script in a directory such as HOME/bin. Make sure you modify the script to contain the correct username, password, and e-mail address for your environment.

You also need to establish the required OS variables, such as ORACLE_SID and ORACLE_HOME. You can either hard-code those variables into the script or call a script that sources the variables for you. Like the previous script, this script calls a script (named oraset) that sets the OS variables (see Chapter 2).

The script requires that the ORACLE_SID be passed to it; for example,

```
$ conn.bsh INVPRD
```

If the script can establish a connection to the database, the following message is displayed:

```
success
db ok
```

Here are the contents of the conn.bsh script:

```
#!/bin/bash
if [ $# -ne 1 ]; then
  echo "Usage: $0 SID"
  exit 1
fi
# either hard code OS variables or source them from a script.
# see Chapter 2 for details on oraset script to source OS variables
. /etc/oraset $1
#
echo "select 'success' from dual;" | sqlplus -s system/foo@o18c | grep success
if [[ $? -ne 0 ]]; then
  echo "problem with $1" | mailx -s "db problem" dkuhn@gmail.com
else
  echo "db ok"
fi
#
exit 0
```

This script is usually automated via a utility such as cron. Here is a typical cron entry:

```
# Check to connect to db.
18 * * * * /home/oracle/bin/conn.bsh o18c 1>/home/oracle/bin/log/conn.log 2>&1
```

This cron entry runs the script once per hour. Depending on your availability requirements, you may want to run a script such as this on a more frequent basis.

filesp.bsh

Use the following script to check for an operating mount point that is filling up. Place the script in a directory such as HOME/bin. You need to modify the script so that the mntlist variable contains a list of mount points that exist on your database server. Because this script isn't running any Oracle utilities, there is no reason to set the Oracle-related OS variables (as with the previous shell scripts):

```
#!/bin/bash
mntlist="/orahome /ora01 /ora02 /ora03"
```

```
for ml in $mntlist
do
echo $ml
usedSpc=$(df -h $ml | awk '{print $5}' | grep -v capacity | cut -d "%" -f1 -)
BOX=$(uname -a | awk '{print $2}')
#
case $usedSpc in
[0-9])
arcStat="relax, lots of disk space: $usedSpc"
;;
[1-7][0-9])
arcStat="disk space okay: $usedSpc"
;;
[8][0-9])
arcStat="space getting low: $usedSpc"
echo $arcStat | mailx -s "space on: $BOX" dkuhn@gmail.com
;;
[9][0-9])
arcStat="warning, running out of space: $usedSpc"
echo $arcStat | mailx -s "space on: $BOX" dkuhn@gmail.com
;;
[1][0][0])
arcStat="update resume, no space left: $usedSpc"
echo $arcStat | mailx -s "space on: $BOX" dkuhn@gmail.com
;;
*)
arcStat="huh?: $usedSpc"
esac
#
BOX=$(uname -a | awk '{print $2}')
echo $arcStat
#
done
#
exit 0
```

You can run this script manually from the command line, like this:

```
$ filesp.bsh
```

Here is the output for this database server:

```
/orahome
disk space okay: 79
/ora01
space getting low: 84
/ora02
disk space okay: 41
/ora03
relax, lots of disk space: 9
```

This is the type of script you should run on an automated basis from a scheduling utility such as cron. Here is a typical cron entry:

```
# Filesystem check
7 * * * * /orahome/bin/filesp.bsh 1>/orahome/bin/log/filesp.log 2>&1
```

Keep in mind that the shell script used in this section (filesp.bsh) may require modification for your environment. The shell script is dependent on the output of the df -h command, which does vary by OS and version. For instance, on a Solaris box the output of df -h appears as follows:

```
$ df -h
Filesystem              size    used   avail  capacity   Mounted on
/ora01                   50G     42G    8.2G     84%      /ora01
/ora02                   50G     20G     30G     41%      /ora02
/ora03                   50G    4.5G     46G      9%      /ora03
/orahome                 30G     24G    6.5G     79%      /orahome
```

This line in the shell script selectively reports on the "capacity" in the output of the df -h command:

```
usedSpc=$(df -h $ml | awk '{print $5}' | grep -v capacity | cut -d "%" -f1 -)
```

For your environment, you'll have to modify the prior line to correctly extract the information related to disk space remaining per mount point. For example, say you're on a Linux box and issue a df -h command, and you observe the following output:

```
Filesystem              Size  Used Avail Use% Mounted on
/dev/mapper/VolGroup00-LogVol00
                        222G  162G   49G  77% /
```

There's only one mount point, and the disk space percentage is associated with the "Use%" column. Therefore, to extract the pertinent information, you'll need to modify the code associated with usedSpc within the shell script; for example,

```
df -h / | grep % | grep -v Use | awk '{print $4}' | cut -d "%" -f1 -
```

The shell script will thus need to have the following lines modified, as shown:

```
mntlist="/"
for ml in $mntlist
do
echo $ml
usedSpc=$(df -h / | grep % | grep -v Use | awk '{print $4}' | cut -d "%" -f1 -)
```

login.sql

Use this script to customize aspects of your SQL*Plus environment. When logging in to SQL*Plus in Linux/Unix, the login.sql script is automatically executed if it exists in a directory contained within the SQLPATH variable. If the SQLPATH variable hasn't been defined, then SQL*Plus looks for login.sql in the current working directory from which SQL*Plus was invoked. For instance, here is how the SQLPATH variable is defined in my environment:

```
$ echo $SQLPATH
/home/oracle/scripts
```

I created the login.sql script in the / home/oracle/scripts directory. It contains the following lines:

```
-- set SQL prompt
SET SQLPROMPT '&_USER.@&_CONNECT_IDENTIFIER.> '
```

Now, when I log in to SQL*Plus, my prompt is automatically set:

```
$ sqlplus / as sysdba
SYS@o12c>
```

top.sql

The following script lists the top CPU-consuming SQL processes. It's useful for identifying problem SQL statements. Place this script in a directory such as HOME/ scripts:

```
select * from(
select
 sql_text
,buffer_gets
,disk_reads
,sorts
,cpu_time/1000000 cpu_sec
,executions
,rows_processed
from v$sqlstats
order by cpu_time DESC)
where rownum < 11;
```

This is how you execute this script:

```
SQL> @top
```

Here is a snippet of the output, showing an SQL statement that is consuming a large amount of database resources:

```
INSERT INTO "REP_MV"."GEM_COMPANY_MV"
SELECT   CASE GROUPING_ID(trim(upper(nvl(ad.organization_name,u.company))))
WHEN O THEN
trim(upper(nvl(ad.organization_name,u.company)))

11004839    20937562          136    21823.59          17        12926019
```

lock.sql

This script displays sessions that have locks on tables that are preventing other sessions from completing work. The script shows details about the blocking and waiting sessions. You should place this script in a directory such as HOME/scripts. Here are the contents of lock.sql:

```
SET LINES 83 PAGES 30
COL blkg_user    FORM a10
COL blkg_machine FORM a10
COL blkg_sid     FORM 99999999
COL wait_user    FORM a10
COL wait_machine FORM a10
COL wait_sid     FORM 9999999
COL obj_own      FORM a10
COL obj_name     FORM a10
--
SELECT
 s1.username      blkg_user
,s1.machine       blkg_machine
,s1.sid           blkg_sid
,s1.serial#       blkg_serialnum
,s1.sid || ',' || s1.serial# kill_string
,s2.username      wait_user
,s2.machine       wait_machine
,s2.sid           wait_sid
,s2.serial#       wait_serialnum
,lo.object_id     blkd_obj_id
,do.owner         obj_own
,do.object_name   obj_name
FROM v$lock l1
    ,v$session s1
    ,v$lock l2
    ,v$session s2
    ,v$locked_object lo
    ,dba_objects do
```

```
WHERE  s1.sid = l1.sid
AND    s2.sid = l2.sid
AND    l1.id1 = l2.id1
AND    s1.sid = lo.session_id
AND    lo.object_id = do.object_id
AND    l1.block = 1
AND    l2.request > 0;
```

The lock.sql script is useful for determining what session has a lock on an object and also for showing the blocked session. You can run this script from SQL*Plus, as follows:

```
SQL> @lock.sql
```

Here is a partial listing of the output (truncated so that it fits on one page):

```
BLKG_USER  BLKG_MACHI  BLKG_SID BLKG_SERIALNUM
---------- ----------  -------- --------------
KILL_STRING
--------------------------------------------------------------------------
WAIT_USER  WAIT_MACHI WAIT_SID WAIT_SERIALNUM BLKD_OBJ_ID OBJ_OWN    OBJ_NAME
---------- ---------- -------- -------------- ----------- ---------- ----------
MV_MAINT   speed            24             11
24,11
MV_MAINT   speed            87              7       19095 MV_MAINT   INV
```

When running lock.sql in an Oracle Database 18c pluggable database environment from the root container, you'll need to change DBA_OBJECTS to CDB_OBJECTS for the script to properly report locks throughout the entire database. You should also consider adding the NAME and CON_ID to the query so that you can view the container in which the lock is occurring. Here's a snippet of the modified query (you'll need to replace the "..." with columns you want to report on):

```
SELECT
 u.name
,s1.username     blkg_user
...
,do.object_name obj_name
```

```
FROM v$lock l1
    ,v$session s1
    ,v$lock l2
    ,v$session s2
    ,v$locked_object lo
    ,cdb_objects do
    ,v$containers u
WHERE s1.sid = l1.sid
AND    s2.sid = l2.sid
AND    l1.id1 = l2.id1
AND    s1.sid = lo.session_id
AND    lo.object_id = do.object_id
AND    l1.block = 1
AND    l2.request > 0
AND    do.con_id = u.con_id;
```

users.sql

This script displays information about when users were created and whether their account is locked. The script is useful when you're troubleshooting connectivity issues. Place the script in a directory such as HOME/scripts. Here is a typical users.sql script for displaying user account information:

```
SELECT
  username
 ,account_status
 ,lock_date
 ,created
FROM dba_users
ORDER BY username;
```

You can execute this script from SQL*Plus, as follows:

```
SQL> @users.sql
```

Here is some sample output:

```
USERNAME          ACCOUNT_ST LOCK_DATE     CREATED
--------------    ---------- ------------  ------------
SYS               OPEN                     09-NOV-12
SYSBACKUP         OPEN                     09-NOV-12
SYSDG             OPEN                     09-NOV-12
```

When running users.sql in an Oracle Database 18c pluggable database environment from the root container, you'll nccd to change DBA_USERS to CDB_USERS and add the NAME and CON_ID columns to report on all users in all pluggable databases; for example,

```
SELECT
  c.name
 ,u.username
 ,u.account_status
 ,u.lock_date
 ,u.created
FROM cdb_users   u
    ,v$containers c
WHERE u.con_id = c.con_id
ORDER BY c.name, u.username;
```

Organizing Scripts

When you have a set of scripts and utilities, you should organize them such that they're consistently implemented for each database server. They should become part of your steps for post installation of the Oracle binaries. These scripts will not only be able to be consistently deployed as part of this process but can also be used to test the installation and setup of databases. Follow these steps to implement the preceding DBA utilities for each database server in your environment:

1. Create OS directories in which to store the scripts.

2. Copy your scripts and utilities to the directories created in step 1.

3. Configure your startup file to initialize the environment.

These steps are detailed in the following sections.

Step 1. Create Directories

Create a standard set of directories on each database server to store your custom scripts. A directory beneath the HOME directory of the oracle user is usually a good location. I generally create the following three directories:

- HOME/bin. Standard location for shell scripts that are run in an automated fashion (such as from cron).

- HOME/bin/log. Standard location for log files generated from the scheduled shell scripts.

- HOME/scripts. Standard location for storing SQL scripts.

You can use the mkdir command to create the previous directories, as follows:

```
$ mkdir -p $HOME/bin/log
$ mkdir $HOME/scripts
```

It doesn't matter where you place the scripts or what you name the directories, as long as you have a standard location so that when you navigate from server to server, you always find the same files in the same locations. In other words, it doesn't matter what the standard is, only that you have a standard.

Step 2. Copy Files to Directories

Place your utilities and scripts in the appropriate directories. Copy the following files to the HOME/bin directory:

```
dba_setup
dba_fcns
tbsp_chk.bsh
conn.bsh
filesp.bsh
```

Place the following SQL scripts in the HOME/scripts directory:

```
login.sql
top.sql
lock.sql
users.sql
```

Step 3. Configure the Startup File

Place the following code in the .bashrc file or the equivalent startup file for the shell you use (.profile for the Korn shell). Here is an example of how to configure the . bashrc file:

```
# Source global definitions
if [ -f /etc/bashrc ]; then
        . /etc/bashrc
fi
#
# source oracle OS variables
. /etc/oraset <default_database>
#
# User specific aliases and functions
. $HOME/bin/dba_setup
. $HOME/bin/dba_fcns
```

Now, each time you log in to an environment, you have full access to all the OS variables, aliases, and functions established in the dba_setup and dba_fcns files. If you don't want to log off and back in, then run the file manually, using the dot (.) command. This command executes the lines contained within a file. The following example runs the . bashrc file:

```
$ . $HOME/.bashrc
```

The dot instructs the shell to source the script. Sourcing tells the shell process you're currently logged in to, to inherit any variables set with an export command in an executed script. If you don't use the dot notation, then the variables set within the script are visible only in the context of the subshell that is spawned when the script is executed.

Note   In the Bash shell, the source command is equivalent to the dot (.) command.

Automating Scripts

Having these scripts in your arsenal allows for quick resolution of issues or perform tasks. It also provides a standard process for running these things against the database instead of having different SQL or tasks running. It is a first step to automating the work against the database.

The object is to have a database that can provide information and perform the needed tasks to address these issues. It might seem that talking about these scripts in this chapter does not make any sense now; however, having these scripts can provide the basis for the automation or tools can. Understanding what needs to be monitored and alerted assist in setting up the environment that is proactive and does not require a DBA running scripts manually at all hours of the day and night.

Most of these scripts fit nicely with an Oracle Enterprise Management tool as they can be inserted into scheduled jobs and run at different level of permissions. The scripts are also good to deploy for the initial testing of the database environments when they are provisioned by a more automated response file or cloud control. These tests can validate that the creation steps are still properly set up and working with each version.

Summary

This chapter described how to configure an efficient environment. This is especially important for DBAs who manage multiple databases on multiple servers. Regular maintenance and troubleshooting activities require you to log in directly to the database server. To promote efficiency and sanity, you should develop a standard set of OS tools and SQL scripts that help you maintain multiple environments. You can use standard features of the OS to assist with navigating, repeating commands, showing system bottlenecks, quickly finding critical files, and so on.

The techniques for configuring a standard OS are especially useful when you're working on multiple servers with multiple databases. When you have multiple terminal sessions running simultaneously, it's easy to lose your bearings and forget which session is associated with a particular server and database. With just a small amount of setup, you can make certain that your OS prompt always shows information such as the host and database. Likewise, you can always set your SQL prompt to show the username and database connection. These techniques help ensure that you don't accidentally run a command or script in the wrong environment.

Anything that needs to be run against the database a few times is a perfect candidate for automation. These scripts can be used to start to configure scheduled jobs and be leveraged to develop proactive monitoring around the multiple databases.

After you have installed the Oracle binaries, created a database, and configured your environment, you are ready to perform additional database administration tasks, such as creating tablespaces for the applications. The topic of tablespace creation and maintenance is discussed in the next chapter.

CHAPTER 4

Tablespaces and Data Files

The term *tablespace* is something of a misnomer, in that it's not just a space for tables. Rather, a tablespace is a logical container that allows you to manage groups of data files, the physical files on disk that consume space. Once a tablespace is created, you can then create database objects (tables and indexes) within tablespaces, which results in space allocated on disk in the associated data files.

A tablespace is logical in the sense that it is only visible through data dictionary views (such as DBA_TABLESPACES); you manage tablespaces through SQL*Plus or graphical tools (such as Enterprise Manager), or both. Tablespaces only exist while the database is up and running.

Data files can also be viewed through data dictionary views DBA_DATA_FILES) but additionally have a physical presence, as they can be viewed outside the database through OS utilities (such as the command ls to list the files). Data files persist whether the database is open, or closed.files persist whether the database is open or closed.

Oracle databases typically contain several tablespaces. A tablespace can have one or more data files associated with it, but a data file can be associated with only one tablespace. In other words, a data file can't be shared between two (or more) tablespaces.

Objects (such as tables and indexes) are owned by users and created within tablespaces. An object is logically instantiated as a segment. A segment consists of extents of space within the tablespace. An extent consists of a set of database blocks. Figure 4-1 shows the relationships between these logical and physical constructs used to manage space within an Oracle database.

© Michelle Malcher and Darl Kuhn 2019
M. Malcher and D. Kuhn, *Pro Oracle Database 18c Administration*,
https://doi.org/10.1007/978-1-4842-4424-1_4

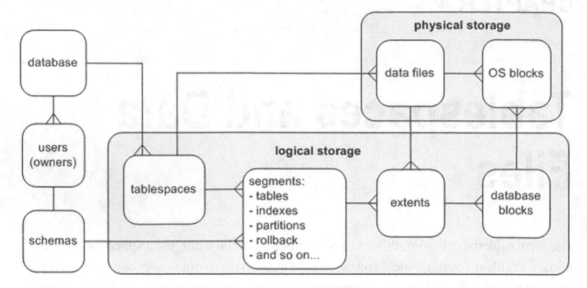

Figure 4-1. *Relationships of logical storage objects and physical storage*

As you saw in Chapter 2, when you create a database, typically five tablespaces are created when you execute the CREATE DATABASE statement:

- SYSTEM

- SYSAUX

- UNDO

- TEMP

- USERS

These five tablespaces are the minimal set of storage containers you need to operate a database (one could argue, however, that you don't need the USERS tablespace; more on that in the next section). SYSTEM and SYSAUX are actually the only required tablespaces, since UNDO and TEMP can be named differently. In a container database, PDBs have the user tablespaces associated with it. In PDB creation, the tablespace is part of the configuration. As you open a database for use, you should quickly create additional tablespaces for storing application data. This chapter discusses the purpose of the standard set of tablespaces, the need for additional tablespaces, and how to manage these critical database storage containers. The chapter focuses on the most common and critical tasks associated with creating and maintaining tablespaces and data files, progressing to more advanced topics, such as moving and renaming data files.

Understanding the First Five

The SYSTEM tablespace provides storage for the Oracle data dictionary objects. This tablespace is where all objects owned by the SYS user are stored. The SYS user should be the only user that owns objects created in the SYSTEM tablespace.

The SYSAUX (system auxiliary) tablespace is created when you create the database. This is an auxiliary tablespace used as a data repository for Oracle database tools, such as Enterprise Manager, Statspack, LogMiner, Logical Standby, and so on. Audit logs are collected in the SYSAUX tablespace by default but should be configured to use another tablespace created for audit records. Even some of these other tools can be configured to use additional tablespaces depending on retention and separation rules and keep the data outside of the default system tablespaces.

The UNDO tablespace stores the information required to undo the effects of a transaction (insert, update, delete, or merge). This information is required in the event a transaction is purposely rolled back (via a ROLLBACK statement). The undo information is also used by Oracle to recover from unexpected instance crashes and to provide read consistency for SQL statements. Additionally, some database features, such as Flashback Query, use the undo information.

Some Oracle SQL statements require a sort area, either in memory or on disk. For example, the results of a query may need to be sorted before being returned to the user. Oracle first uses memory to sort the query results, and when there is no longer sufficient memory, the TEMP tablespaceextra temporary storage may also be required when creating or rebuilding indexes. The space is only used for transient data for the session, and no permanent objects can be stored in a TEMP tablespace. If temporary objects are needed for a process outside of one session, the object should be stored in a permanent user tablespace. When you create a database, typically you create the TEMP tablespace and specify it to be the default temporary tablespace for any users you create. There can be multiple temporary tablespaces, with different names, that can be assigned to different groups of users or applications to avoid conflicts between temp space usage.

The USERS tablespace is not absolutely required but is often used as a default permanent tablespace for table and index data for users. As shown in Chapter 2, you can create a default permanent tablespace for users when you create your database. This means that when a user attempts to create a table or index, if no tablespace is specified during object creation, by default the object is created in the default permanent tablespace.

Understanding the Need for More

Although you could put every database user's data in the USERS tablespace, this usually isn't scalable or maintainable for any type of serious database application. Instead, it's more efficient to create additional tablespaces for application users. You typically create at least two tablespaces specific to each application using the database: one for the application table data and one for the application index data. For example, for the APP user APP_DATA and APP_INDEX for table and index data, respectively.

DBAs used to separate table and index data for performance reasons. The thinking was that separating table data from index data would reduce input/ouput (I/O) contention. This is because the data files (for each tablespace) could be placed on different disks, with separate controllers.

With modern storage configurations, which have multiple layers of abstraction between the application and the underlying physical storage devices, it's debatable whether you can realize any performance gains by creating multiple separate tablespaces. But, there still are valid reasons for creating multiple tablespaces for table and index data:

- Backup and recovery requirements may be different for the tables and indexes.

- The indexes may have storage requirements different from those of the table data.

- Simplify management of objects by logically grouping tables and indexes separately.

In addition to separate tablespaces for data and indexes, you sometimes create separate tablespaces for objects of different sizes. For instance, if an application has very large tables, you can create an APP_DATA_LARGE tablespace that has a large extent size and a separate APP_DATA_SMALL tablespace that has a smaller extent size. This concept also extends to binary large object (LOB) data types. You may want to separate a LOB column in its own tablespace because you want to manage the LOB tablespace storage characteristics differently from those of the regular table data. Automatic Segment Space Management (ASSM) will be allocated extent size and based on information of the objects stored. Even if not setting the large and smaller extents manually and using ASSM, the grouping of the objects in this way will assist in the management of the objects as well as the automated space management.

Note   The separation of objects by type and extent size is becoming less important because of the physical storage devices and memory. The advances in the storage technology will help databases perform better even without the object configuration. Depending on your requirements, you should consider creating separate tablespaces for each application using the database. There are now application containers and PDBs for this separation of tablespaces. Even though this will be discussed more in Chapter 22, Figure 4-2 shows the different tablespaces in CDBs and PDBs.

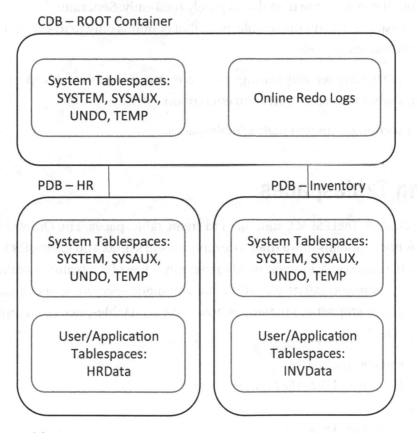

Figure 4-2. *Tablespaces in CDBs and PDBs*

However, to look at a separate tablespace example, for an inventory application INV_ DATA and INV_INDEX; for a human resources application create HR_DATA and HR_INDEX. Here are some reasons to consider creating separate tablespaces for each application using the database:

- Applications may have different availability requirements. Separate tablespaces let you take tablespaces offline for one application without affecting another application.

- Applications may have different backup and recovery requirements. Separate tablespaces let tablespaces be backed up and recovered independently.

- Applications may have different storage requirements. Separate tablespaces allow for different settings for space quotas, extent sizes, and segment management.

- You may have some data that is purely read-only. Separate tablespaces let you put a tablespace that contains only read-only data into read-only mode.

- You may have security settings such as encryption of the tablespace and other tablespaces without encryption.

The next section discusses creating tablespaces.

Creating Tablespaces

You use the CREATE TABLESPACE statement to create tablespaces. The *Oracle SQL Reference Manual* contains more than a dozen pages of syntax and examples for creating tablespaces. In most scenarios, you need to use only a few of the features available, namely, locally managed extent allocation and automatic segment space management. The following code snippet demonstrates how to create a tablespace that employs the most common features:

```
create tablespace tools
  datafile '/u01/dbfile/o18c/tools01.dbf'
  size 100m
  extent management local
  uniform size 128k
  segment space management auto;
```

You need to modify this script for your environment. For example, the directory path, data file size, and uniform extent size should be changed per environment requirements.

You create tablespaces as locally managed by using the EXTENT MANAGEMENT LOCAL clause. A locally managed tablespace uses a bitmap in the data file to efficiently determine whether an extent is in use. The storage parameters NEXT, PCTINCREASE, MINEXTENTS, MAXEXTENTS, and DEFAULT are not valid for extent options in locally managed tablespaces.

Note   A locally managed tablespace with uniform extents must be minimally sized for at least five database blocks per extent.

As you add data to objects in tablespaces, Oracle automatically allocates more extents to an associated tablespace data file as needed to accommodate the growth. You can instruct Oracle to allocate a uniform size for each extent via the UNIFORM SIZE [size] clause. If you don't specify a size, then the default uniform extent size is 1MB.

The uniform extent size that you use varies, depending on the storage requirements of your tables and indexes. In some scenarios, I create several tablespaces for a given application. For instance, you can create a tablespace for small objects that has a uniform extent size of 512KB, a tablespace for medium-sized objects that has a uniform extent size of 4MB, a tablespace for large objects with a uniform extent size of 16MB, and so on.

Alternatively, you can specify that Oracle determine the extent size via the AUTOALLOCATE clause. Oracle allocates extent sizes of 64KB, 1MB, 8MB, or 64MB. Using AUTOALLOCATE is appropriate when you think objects in one tablespace will be of varying sizes.

The SEGMENT SPACE MANAGEMENT AUTO clause instructs Oracle to manage the space within the block. When you use this clause, there is no need to specify parameters, such as PCTUSED, FREELISTS, and FREELIST GROUPS. The alternative to AUTO space management is MANUAL. When you use MANUAL, you can adjust the parameters to the requirements of your application. I recommend that you use AUTO and not MANUAL. Using AUTO vastly reduces the number of parameters you need to configure and manage.

When a data file fills up, you can instruct Oracle to increase the size of the data file automatically, with the AUTOEXTEND feature. Using AUTOEXTEND allows for processes to run without needing DBA intervention when getting close to running out of space. However, you must monitor tablespace growth and plan for additional space. This includes watching for processes that might load a large amount of data. Manually adding space might limit having a runaway SQL process that accidentally grows a tablespace

123

until it has consumed all the space on a mount point, but a load process that is larger one month over another might be rolled back if it fails on additional space requirements. Using the parameter RESUMABLE in the database, you will be allowed to set a time to be able to respond to tablespace issues. If you inadvertently fill up a mount point that contains a control file or the Oracle binaries, you can hang your database. The use of Automatic Storage Management (ASM) will also help here to be able to add another disk to the diskgroup to avoid filling up a mount point and, used with RESUMABLE, provides the time to manage. Monitoring and planning for storage and growth are still the best methods for managing the tablespaces sizing to be able to proactively add the needed space.

If you do use the AUTOEXTEND feature, I suggest that you always specify a corresponding MAXSIZE so that a runaway SQL process doesn't accidentally fill up a tablespace that in turn fills up a mount point. Here is an example of creating an autoextending tablespace with a cap on its maximum size:

```
create tablespace tools
  datafile '/u01/dbfile/o18c/tools01.dbf'
  size 100m
  autoextend on maxsize 1000m
  extent management local
  uniform size 128k
  segment space management auto;
```

For security, tablepaces can be transparently encrypted. Transparent means that the application does not need to change to use the encrypted tablespaces. This will allow for data at rest in the data files to be encrypted, and when the database is open, the tablespace is decrypted using the encryption key in the database wallet to be able to see the data through queries. Using encryption makes it so that the data files cannot be viewed in plain text, which is the same for backups of the data files. As already stated, there are many options for creating tablespaces, and this security option does require management of the encryption key, which can be centrally located or locally with the database. The create tablespace command is simple enough:

```
create tablespace HRDATA encryption using 'AES256' default
storage(encrypt);
```

When you are using CREATE TABLESPACE scripts in different environments, it's useful to be able to parameterize portions of the script. For instance, in development you may size the data files at 100MB, whereas in production the data files may be 100GB. Use ampersand (&) variables to make CREATE TABLESPACE scripts more portable among environments.

The next listing defines ampersand variables at the top of the script, and those variables determine the sizes of data files created for the tablespaces:

```
define tbsp_large=5G
define tbsp_med=500M
--
create tablespace reg_data
  datafile '/u01/dbfile/o18c/reg_data01.dbf'
  size &&tbsp_large
  extent management local
  uniform size 128k
  segment space management auto;
--
create tablespace reg_index
  datafile '/u01/dbfile/o18c/reg_index01.dbf'
  size &&tbsp_med
  extent management local
  uniform size 128k
  segment space management auto;
```

Using ampersand variables allows you to modify the script once and have the variables reused throughout the script. You can parameterize all aspects of the script, including data file mount points and extent sizes.

You can also pass the values of the ampersand variables in to the CREATE TABLESPACE script from the SQL*Plus command line. This lets you avoid hard-coding a specific size in the script and instead provide the sizes at runtime. To accomplish this, first define at the top of the script the ampersand variables to accept the values being passed in:

```
define tbsp_large=&1
define tbsp_med=&2
--
create tablespace reg_data
  datafile '/u01/dbfile/o12c/reg_data01.dbf'
  size &&tbsp_large
  extent management local
```

125

```
  uniform size 128k
  segment space management auto;
--
create tablespace reg_index
  datafile '/u01/dbfile/o12c/reg_index01.dbf'
  size &&tbsp_med
  extent management local
  uniform size 128k
  segment space management auto;
```

Now, you can pass variables in to the script from the SQL*Plus command line. The following example executes a script named cretbsp.sql and passes in two values that set the ampersand variables to 5G and 500M, respectively:

```
SQL> @cretbsp  5G  500M
```

Automatic Storage Management (ASM) also simplifies the creation of the tablespace because it will take the defaults of the DiskGroup and parameters that are set to use ASM. This will be discussed later in this chapter, but here is a quick example:

```
SQL> create tablespace HRDATA;
```

Table 4-1 summarizes the best practices for creating and managing tablespaces.

Table 4-1. *Best Practices for Creating and Managing Tablespaces*

Best Practice	Reasoning
Create separate tablespaces for different applications using the same database.	If a tablespace needs to be taken offline, it affects only one application.
For an application, separate table data from index data in different tablespaces.	Table and index data may have different storage requirements and simplify object management.
With AUTOEXTEND, specify a maximum size.	Specifying a maximum size prevents a runaway SQL statement from filling up a storage device.

(continued)

Table 4-1. (*continued*)

Best Practice	Reasoning
Create tablespaces as locally managed. You shouldn't create a tablespace as dictionary managed.	This provides better performance and manageability.
For a tablespace's data file naming convention, use a name that contains the tablespace name followed by a two-digit number that's unique within data files for that tablespace.	Doing this makes it easy to identify which data files are associated with which tablespaces.
Try to minimize the number of data files associated with a tablespace.	You have fewer data files to manage.
In tablespace CREATE scripts, use ampersand variables to define aspects such as storage characteristics.	This makes scripts more reusable among various environments.

If you ever need to verify the SQL required to re-create an existing tablespace, you can do so with the DBMS_METADATA package. First, set the LONG variable to a large value:

```
SQL> set long 1000000
```

Next, use the DBMS_METADATA package to display the CREATE TABLESPACE data definition language (DDL) for all tablespaces within the database:

```
select dbms_metadata.get_ddl('TABLESPACE',tablespace_name)
from dba_tablespaces;
```

Tip   You can also use Data Pump to extract the DDL of database objects. See Chapter 13 for details.

Renaming a Tablespace

Sometimes you need to rename a tablespace. You may want to do this because a tablespace was initially erroneously named, or you may want the tablespace name to better conform to your database naming standards. Use the ALTER TABLESPACE statement to rename a tablespace. This example renames a tablespace from TOOLS to TOOLS_DEV:

```
SQL> alter tablespace tools rename to tools_dev;
```

When you rename a tablespace, Oracle updates the name of the tablespace in the data dictionary, control files, and data file headers. Keep in mind that renaming a tablespace doesn't rename any associated data files. See the section "Renaming or Relocating a Data File," later in this chapter, for information on renaming data files.

Note   You can't rename the S YSTEM tablespace or the S YSAUX tablespace.

Changing a Tablespace's Write Mode

In environments such as data warehouses, you may need to load data into tables and then never modify the data again. To enforce that no objects in a tablespace can be modified, you can alter the tablespace to be read-only. To do this, use the ALTER TABLESPACE statement:

```
SQL> alter tablespace inv_mgmt_rep read only;
```

One advantage of a read-only tablespace is that you only have to back it up once. You should be able to restore the data files from a read-only tablespace no matter how long ago the backup was made.

If you need to modify the tablespace out of read-only mode, you do so as follows:

```
SQL> alter tablespace inv_mgmt_rep read write;
```

Make sure you re-enable backups of a tablespace after you place it in read/write mode.

Note   You can't make a tablespace that contains active rollback segments read-only. For this reason, the SYSTEM tablespace can't be made read-only because it contains the SYSTEM rollback segment.

Be aware that individual tables can be modified to be read-only. This allows you to control the read-only at a much more granular level (than at the tablespace level); for example,

```
SQL> alter table my_tab read only;
```

While in read-only mode, you can't issue any insert, update, or delete statements against the table. Making individual tables read/write can be advantageous when you're doing maintenance (such as a data migration) and you want to ensure that users don't update the data.

This example modifies a table back to read/write mode:

```
SQL> alter table my_tab read write;
```

Dropping a Tablespace

If you have a tablespace that is unused, it is best to drop it so it does not clutter your database, consume unnecessary resources, and potentially confuse DBAs who are not familiar with the database. Before dropping a tablespace, it is a good practice to first take it offline:

```
SQL> alter tablespace inv_data offline;
```

You may want to wait to see if anybody screams that an application is broken because it can no longer write to a table or index in the tablespace to be dropped. Depending on the reason for dropping a tablespace, objects can be moved to another tablespace first before dropping. When you are sure the tablespace is not required, drop it, and delete its data files:

```
SQL> drop tablespace inv_data including contents and datafiles;
```

Tip   You can drop a tablespace whether it is online or offline. The exception to this is the SYSTEM and SYSAUX tablespaces, which cannot be dropped. It's always a good idea to take a tablespace offline before you drop it. By doing so, you can better determine if an application is using any objects in the tablespace. If you attempt to query a table in an offline tablespace, you receive this error: ORA-00376: file can't be read at this time.

Dropping a tablespace using INCLUDING CONTENTS AND DATAFILES permanently removes the tablespace and any of its data files. Make certain the tablespace does not contain any data you want to keep before you drop it.

If you attempt to drop a tablespace that contains a primary key that is referenced by a foreign key associated with a table in a tablespace different from the one you are trying to drop, you receive this error:

ORA-02449: unique/primary keys in table referenced by foreign keys

Run this query first to determine whether any foreign key constraints will be affected:

```
select p.owner,
       p.table_name,
       p.constraint_name,
       f.table_name referencing_table,
       f.constraint_name foreign_key_name,
       f.status fk_status
from   dba_constraints p,
       dba_constraints f,
       dba_tables      t
where  p.constraint_name = f.r_constraint_name
and    f.constraint_type = 'R'
and    p.table_name = t.table_name
and    t.tablespace_name = UPPER('&tablespace_name')
order by 1,2,3,4,5;
```

If there are referenced constraints, you need to first drop the constraints or use the CASCADE CONSTRAINTS clause of the DROP TABLESPACE statement. This statement uses CASCADE CONSTRAINTS to drop any affected constraints automatically:

```
SQL> drop tablespace inv_data including contents and data files cascade
constraints;
```

This statement drops any referential integrity constraints from tables outside the tablespace being dropped that reference tables within the dropped tablespace.

If you drop a tablespace that has required objects in a production system, the results can be catastrophic. You must perform some sort of recovery to get the tablespace and its objects back. Needless to say, be very careful when dropping a tablespace. Table 4-2 lists recommendations to consider when you do this.

Table 4-2. *Best Practices for Dropping Tablespaces*

Best Practice	Reasoning

Before dropping a tablespace, run a script such as this to determine if any objects exist in the tablespace:
`select owner, segment_name,`
`segment_type`
`from dba_segments`
`where`
`tablespace_name=upper('&&tbsp_name');`
	Doing this ensures that no tables or indexes exist in the tablespace before you drop it.

Consider renaming tables in a tablespace before you drop it.	If any applications are using tables within the tablespace to be dropped, the application throws an error when a required table is renamed.
If there are no objects in the tablespace, resize the associated data files to a very small number, such as 10MB.	Reducing the size of the data files to a miniscule amount of space quickly shows whether any applications are trying to access objects that require space in a tablespace.
Make a backup of your database before dropping a tablespace.	This ensures that you have a way to recover objects that are discovered to be in use after you drop the tablespace.
Take the tablespace and data files offline before you drop the tablespace. Use the `ALTER TABLESPACE` statement to take the tablespace offline.	This helps determine if any applications or users are using objects in the tablespace. They can't access the objects if the tablespace and data files are offline.
When you are sure a tablespace is not in use, use the `DROP TABLESPACE ... INCLUDING CONTENTS AND DATAFILES` statement.	This removes the tablespace and physically removes any data files associated with it. Some DBAs don't like this approach, but you should be fine if you've taken the necessary precautions.

Using Oracle Managed Files

The Oracle Managed File (OMF) feature automates many aspects of tablespace management, such as file placement, naming, and sizing. You control OMF by setting the following initialization parameters:

- `DB_CREATE_FILE_DEST`

- `DB_CREATE_ONLINE_LOG_DEST_N`

- `DB_RECOVERY_FILE_DEST`

If you set these parameters before you create the database, Oracle uses them for the placement of the data files, control files, and online redo logs. You can also enable OMF after your database has been created. Oracle uses the values of the initialization parameters for the locations of any newly added files. Oracle also determines the name of the newly added file. These parameters are set as part input in dbca for the creation of a database.

The advantage of using OMF is that creating tablespaces is simplified. For example, the `CREATE TABLESPACE` statement does not need to specify anything other than the tablespace name. First, enable the OMF feature by setting the `DB_CREATE_FILE_DEST` parameter:

```
SQL> alter system set db_create_file_dest='/u01';
```

Now, issue the `CREATE TABLESPACE` statement:

```
SQL> create tablespace inv1;
```

This statement creates a tablespace named INV1, with a default data file size of 100MB. Keep in mind that you can override the default size of 100MB by specifying a size:

```
SQL> create tablespace inv2 datafile size 20m;
```

To view the details of the associated data files, query the `V$DATAFILE` view, and note that Oracle has created subdirectories beneath the /u01 directory and named the file with the OMF format:

```
SQL> select name from v$datafile where name like '%inv%';
NAME
-------------------------------------------------------------
/u01/O18C/datafile/o1_mf_inv1_8b5l63q6_.dbf
/u01/O18C/datafile/o1_mf_inv2_8b5lflfc_.dbf
```

One limitation of OMF is that you're limited to one directory for the placement of data files. If you want to add data files to a different directory, you can alter the location dynamically:

```
SQL> alter system set db_create_file_dest='/u02';
```

Creating a Bigfile Tablespace

The bigfile feature allows you to create a tablespace with a very large data file assigned to it. The advantage of using the bigfile feature is this potential to create very large files. With an 8KB block size, you can create a data file as large as 32TB. With a 32KB block size, you can create a data file up to 128TB.

Use the BIGFILE clause to create a bigfile tablespace:

```
create bigfile tablespace inv_big_data
  datafile '/u01/dbfile/o18c/inv_big_data01.dbf'
  size 10g
  extent management local
  uniform size 128k
  segment space management auto;
```

As long as you have plenty of space associated with the filesystem supporting the bigfile tablespace data file, you can store massive amounts of data in a tablespace.

One potential disadvantage of using a bigfile tablespace is that if, for any reason, you run out of space on a filesystem that supports the data file associated with the bigfile, you can't expand the size of the tablespace (unless you can add space to the filesystem). You can't add more data files to a bigfile tablespace if they're placed on separate mount points. A bigfile tablespace allows only one data file to be associated with it.

You can make the bigfile tablespace the default type of tablespace for a database, using the ALTER DATABASE SET DEFAULT BIGFILE TABLESPACE statement. However, it is not recommend to be doing that. You could potentially create a tablespace, not knowing it was a bigfile tablespace, and when you discovered that you needed more space, you would not know that you could not add another data file on a different mount point for this tablespace. Using ASM is less of an issue because a new disk can be dynamically added to a DISKGROUP for this tablespace.

Enabling Default Table Compression Within a Tablespace Tablespace

When working with large databases, you may want to consider compressing the data. Compressed data results in less disk space, less memory, and fewer I/O operations. Queries reading compressed data potentially execute faster because fewer blocks are required to satisfy the result of the query. But compression does have a cost; it requires more CPU resources, as the data are compressed and uncompressed while reading and writing.

When creating a tablespace, you can enable data compression features. Doing so does not compress the tablespace. Rather, any tables you create within the tablespace inherit the compression characteristics of the tablespace. This example creates a tablespace with ROW STORE COMPRESS ADVANCED:

```
CREATE TABLESPACE tools_comp
  DATAFILE '/u01/dbfile/o18c/tools_comp01.dbf'
  SIZE 100m
  EXTENT MANAGEMENT LOCAL
  UNIFORM SIZE 512k
  SEGMENT SPACE MANAGEMENT AUTO
  DEFAULT ROW STORE COMPRESS ADVANCED;
```

Note   If you're using Oracle Database 11g, then use the COMPRESS FOR OLTP clause instead of ROW STORE COMPRESS ADVANCED.

Now when a table is created within this tablespace, it will automatically be created with the ROW STORE COMPRESS ADVANCED feature. You can verify the compression characteristics of a tablespace via this query:

```
select tablespace_name, def_tab_compression, compress_for
from dba_tablespaces;
```

Tip   See Chapter 7 for full details on table compression.

If a tablespace is already created, you can alter its compression characters, as follows:

```
SQL> alter tablespace tools_comp default row store compress advanced;
```

Here's an example that alters a tablespace's default compress to BASIC:

```
SQL> alter tablespace tools_comp default compress basic;
```

You can disable tablespace compression via the NOCOMPRESS clause:

```
SQL> alter tablespace tools_comp default nocompress;
```

Note   Most compression features require the Enterprise Edition of Oracle and the Advanced Compression option (for a fee). Using compression ratios and amount of data existing, growth and retention can show the value of this option.

Displaying Tablespace Size

DBAs often use monitoring scripts to alert them when they need to increase the space allocated to a tablespace. Depending on whether or not you are in a multitenant, container database environment, your SQL for determining space usage will vary. For a regular database (non-container), you can use the DBA-level views to determine space usage. The following script displays the percentage of free space left in a tablespace and data file:

```
SET PAGESIZE 100 LINES 132 ECHO OFF VERIFY OFF FEEDB OFF SPACE 1 TRIMSP ON
COMPUTE SUM OF a_byt t_byt f_byt ON REPORT
BREAK ON REPORT ON tablespace_name ON pf
COL tablespace_name FOR A17    TRU HEAD 'Tablespace|Name'
COL file_name       FOR A40    TRU HEAD 'Filename'
COL a_byt           FOR 9,990.999 HEAD 'Allocated|GB'
COL t_byt           FOR 9,990.999 HEAD 'Current|Used GB'
COL f_byt           FOR 9,990.999 HEAD 'Current|Free GB'
COL pct_free        FOR 990.0    HEAD 'File %|Free'
COL pf              FOR 990.0    HEAD 'Tbsp %|Free'
```

```
COL seq NOPRINT
DEFINE b_div=1073741824
--
SELECT 1 seq, b.tablespace_name, nvl(x.fs,0)/y.ap*100 pf, b.file_name
file_name,
  b.bytes/&&b_div a_byt, NVL((b.bytes-SUM(f.bytes))/&&b_div,b.bytes/&&b_div)
t_byt,
  NVL(SUM(f.bytes)/&&b_div,0) f_byt, NVL(SUM(f.bytes)/b.bytes*100,0) pct_free
FROM dba_free_space f, dba_data_files b
 ,(SELECT y.tablespace_name, SUM(y.bytes) fs
    FROM dba_free_space y GROUP BY y.tablespace_name) x
 ,(SELECT x.tablespace_name, SUM(x.bytes) ap
    FROM dba_data_files x GROUP BY x.tablespace_name) y
WHERE f.file_id(+) = b.file_id
AND    x.tablespace_name(+) = y.tablespace_name
and    y.tablespace_name =  b.tablespace_name
AND    f.tablespace_name(+) = b.tablespace_name
GROUP BY b.tablespace_name, nvl(x.fs,0)/y.ap*100, b.file_name, b.bytes
UNION
SELECT 2 seq, tablespace_name,
  j.bf/k.bb*100 pf, b.name file_name, b.bytes/&&b_div a_byt,
  a.bytes_used/&&b_div t_byt, a.bytes_free/&&b_div f_byt,
  a.bytes_free/b.bytes*100 pct_free
FROM v$temp_space_header a, v$tempfile b
 ,(SELECT SUM(bytes_free) bf FROM v$temp_space_header) j
 ,(SELECT SUM(bytes) bb FROM v$tempfile) k
WHERE a.file_id = b.file#
ORDER BY 1,2,4,3;
```

If you don't have any monitoring in place, you are alerted via the SQL statement that is attempting to perform an insert or update operation that the tablespace requires more space but isn't able to allocate more. At that point, an ORA-01653 error is thrown, indicating the object can't extend.

After you determine that a tablespace needs more space, you need to either increase the size of a data file or add a data file to the tablespace. See the section "Altering Tablespace Size," later in this chapter, for a discussion of these topics.

Tip   See Chapter 22 for full details on reporting on space within a pluggable database environment using the container database (CDB)-level views.

DISPLAYING ORACLE ERROR MESSAGES AND ACTIONS

You can use the oerr utility to quickly display the cause of an error and simple instructions on what actions to take; for example,

```
$ oerr ora 01653
```

Here is the output for this example:

```
01653, 00000, "unable to extend table %s.%s by %s in tablespace %s"
// *Cause:  Failed to allocate an extent of the required number of blocks for
//          a table segment in the tablespace indicated.
// *Action: Use ALTER TABLESPACE ADD DATAFILE statement to add one or more
//          files to the tablespace indicated.
```

The oerr utility's output gives you a fast and easy way to triage problems. If the information provided isn't enough, then Google is a good second option.

Altering Tablespace Size

When you've determined which data file you want to resize, first make sure you have enough disk space to increase the size of the data file on the mount point on which the data file exists:

```
$ df -h | sort
```

Use the ALTER DATABASE DATAFILE ... RESIZE command to increase the data file's size. This example resizes the data file to 1GB:

```
SQL> alter database datafile '/u01/dbfile/o18c/users01.dbf' resize 1g;
```

If you don't have space on an existing mount point to increase the size of a data file, then you must add a data file. To add a data file to an existing tablespace, use the ALTER TABLESPACE ... ADD DATAFILE statement:

```
SQL> alter tablespace users
     add datafile '/u02/dbfile/o18c/users02.dbf' size 100m;
```

With bigfile tablespaces, you have the option of using the ALTER TABLESPACE statement to resize the data file. This works because only one data file can be associated with a bigfile tablespace:

```
SQL> alter tablespace inv_big_data resize 1P;
```

Resizing data files can be a daily task when you're managing databases with heavy transaction loads. Increasing the size of an existing data file allows you to add space to a tablespace without adding more data files. If there isn't enough disk space left on the storage device that contains an existing data file, you can add a data file in a different location to an existing tablespace.

To add space to a temporary tablespace, first query the V $TEMPFILE view to verify the current size and location of temporary data files:

```
SQL> select name, bytes from v$tempfile;
```

Then, use the TEMPFILE option of the ALTER DATABASE statement:

```
SQL> alter database tempfile '/u01/dbfile/o18c/temp01.dbf' resize 500m;
```

You can also add a file to a temporary tablespace via the ALTER TABLESPACE statement:

```
SQL> alter tablespace temp add tempfile '/u01/dbfile/o18c/temp02.dbf'
size 5000m;
```

Toggling Data Files Offline and Online

Sometimes when you are performing maintenance operations (such as renaming data files), you may need to first take a data file offline. You can use either the ALTER TABLESPACE or the ALTER DATABASE DATAFILE statement to toggle data files offline and online.

Tip   As of Oracle Database 12c, you can move and rename data files while they are online and open for use. See "Renaming or Relocating a Data File," later in this chapter, for a discussion of this.

Use the ALTER TABLESPACE ... OFFLINE NORMAL statement files offline. You do not need to specify NORMAL, because it's the default:

```
SQL> alter tablespace users offline;
```

When you place a tablespace offline in normal mode, Oracle performs a checkpoint on the data files associated with the tablespace. This ensures that all modified blocks in memory that are associated with the tablespace are flushed and written to the data files. You will not need to perform media recovery when you bring the tablespace and its associated data files back online.

You cannot use the ALTER TABLESPACE statement to place tablespaces offline when the database is in mount mode. If you attempt to take a tablespace offline while the database is mounted (but not open), you receive the following error:

```
ORA-01109: database not open
```

Note When in mount mode, you must use the ALTER DATABASE DATAFILE statement to take a data file offline It might not be necessary, but there might be more than one data file for the tablespace, and each file will need to be taken offline.

When taking a tablespace offline, you can also specify ALTER TABLESPACE ... OFFLINE TEMPORARY. In this scenario, Oracle initiates a checkpoint on all data files associated with the tablespace that are online. Oracle does not initiate a checkpoint on offline data files associated with the tablespace.

You can specify ALTER TABLESPACE ... OFFLINE IMMEDIATE when taking a tablespace offline. Your database must be in archivelog mode in this situation, or the following error is thrown:

```
ORA-01145: offline immediate disallowed unless media recovery enabled
```

When using OFFLINE IMMEDIATE, Oracle does not issue a checkpoint on the data files. You must perform media recovery on the tablespace before bringing it back online.

Note You cannot take the SYSTEM or UNDO tablespace offline while the database is open. SYSAUX can be taken offline, however; some functions might not be available, or errors might appear.

You can also use the ALTER DATABASE DATAFILE statement to take a data file offline. If your database is open for use, then it must be in archivelog mode in order for you to take a data file offline with the ALTER DATABASE DATAFILE statement. If you attempt to take a data file offline using the ALTER DATABASE DATAFILE statement, and your database is not in archivelog mode, the ORA-01145 error is thrown.

If your database is not in archivelog mode, you must specify ALTER DATABASE DATAFILE ... OFFLINE FOR DROP when taking a data file offline. You can specify the entire file name or provide the file number. In this example, data file 6 is taken offline:

```
SQL> alter database datafile 4 offline for drop;
```

Now, if you attempt to bring online the offline data file, you receive the following error:

```
SQL> alter database datafile 4 online;
ORA-01113: file 4 needs media recovery
```

When you use the OFFLINE FOR DROP clause, no checkpoint is taken on the data file. This means you need to perform media recovery on the data file before bringing it online. Performing media recovery applies any changes to the data file that are recorded in the online redo logs that aren't in the data files themselves. Before you can bring online a data file that was taken offline with the OFFLINE FOR DROP clause, you must perform media recovery on it. You can specify either the entire file name or the file number:

```
SQL> recover datafile 4;
```

If the redo information that Oracle needs is contained in the online redo logs, you should see this message:

```
Media recovery complete.
```

If your database is not in archivelog mode, and if Oracle needs redo information not contained in the online redo logs to recover the data file, then you cannot recover the data file and place it back online.

If your database is in archivelog mode, you can take it offline without the FOR DROP clause. In this scenario, Oracle overlooks the FOR DROP clause. Even when your database is in archivelog mode, you need to perform media recovery on a data file that has been taken offline with the ALTER DATABASE DATAFILE statement. Table 4-3 summarizes the options you must consider when taking a tablespace/data files offline.

Note   While the database is in mount mode (and not open), you can use the ALTER DATABASE DATAFILE command to take any data file offline, including SYSTEM and UNDO.

Table 4-3. *Options for Taking Tablespaces/Data Files Offline*

Statement	Archivelog Mode Required?	Media Recovery Required When Toggling Online?	Works in Mount Mode?
ALTER TABLESPACE ... OFFLINE NORMAL	No	No	No
ALTER TABLESPACE ... OFFLINE TEMPORARY	No	Maybe: Depends on whether any data files already have offline status	No
ALTER TABLESPACE ... OFFLINE IMMEDIATE	No	Yes	No
ALTER DATABASE DATAFILE ... OFFLINE	Yes	Yes	Yes
ALTER DATABASE DATAFILE ... OFFLINE FOR DROP	No	Yes	Yes

These steps to offline data files and tablespaces provide opportunities to practice media recovery and walk through these scenarios with new databases or test databases. This practice is useful for taking notes, documenting the error messages, and gathering notes on what happened and results for availability in a pressure situation when these errors appear.

Renaming or Relocating a Data File

You may occasionally need to move or rename a data file. For example, you may need to move data files because of changes in the storage devices or because the files were created in the wrong location or with a nonstandard name. As of Oracle Database 12c, you have the option of renaming or moving data files, or both, while they are online. Otherwise, you will have to take data files offline for maintenance operations.

Performing Online Data File Operations

New in Oracle Database 12c is the ALTER DATABASE MOVE DATAFILE command. This command allows you to rename or move data files without any downtime. This vastly simplifies the task of moving or renaming a data file, as there is no need to manually place data files offline/online and use OS commands to physically move the files. This once manually intensive (and error-prone) operation has now been simplified to a single SQL command.

A data file must be online for the online move or rename to work. Here is an example of renaming an online data file:

```
SQL> alter database move datafile '/u01/dbfile/o18c/users01.dbf' to
    '/u01/dbfile/o18c/users_dev01.dbf';
```

Here is an example of moving a data file to a new mount point:

```
SQL> alter database move datafile '/u01/dbfile/o18c/hrdata01.dbf' to
    '/u02/dbfile/o18c/hrdata01.dbf';
```

You can also specify the data file number when renaming or moving a data file; for example,

```
SQL> alter database move datafile 2 to '/u02/dbfile/o18c/sysuax01.dbf';
```

In the previous example, you are specifying that data file 2 be moved.

If you're moving a data file and, for any reason, want to keep a copy of the original file, you can use the KEEP option:

```
SQL> alter database move datafile 4 to '/u02/dbfile/o18c/users01.dbf' keep;
```

You can specify the REUSE clause to overwrite an existing file:

```
SQL> alter database move datafile 4 to '/u01/dbfile/o18c/users01.dbf' reuse;
```

Oracle will not allow you to overwrite (reuse) a data file that is currently being used by the database. That is a good thing.

Performing Offline Data File Operations

Previous to 12c to rename or move a data file, you must take the data file offline. There are two somewhat different approaches to moving and renaming offline data files:

- Use a combination of SQL commands and OS commands.

- Use a combination of re-creating the control file and OS commands.

Because these are offline functions, I have normally planned these steps to happen before or after a patch or upgrade maintenance activity that requires some downtime as well. Unless it is an emergency step to move off of a disk or mount point, this normally can happen during that time. If these types of activities become a regular occurrence, it will be worth the time and effort to looking into using ASM since that provides other options for moving files around. These two techniques are discussed in the next two sections.

Using SQL and OS Commands

Here are the steps for renaming a data file using SQL commands and OS commands:

1. Use the following query to determine the names of existing data files:

   ```
   SQL> select name from v$datafile;
   ```

2. Take the data file offline, using either the ALTER TABLESPACE or ALTER DATABASE DATAFILE statement (see the previous section, "Performing Offline Data File Operations," for details on how to do this). You can also shut down your database and then start it in mount mode; the data files can be moved while in this mode because they aren't open for use.

3. Physically move the data file to the new location, using either an OS command (like mv or cp) or the COPY_FILE procedure of the DBMS_FILE_TRANSFER built-in PL/SQL package.

4. Use either the A LTER TABLESPACE ... RENAME DATAFILE ... TO statement or the A LTER DATABASE RENAME FILE ... TO statement to update the control file with the new data file name.

5. Alter the data file online.

Note   If you need to rename data files associated with the SYSTEM or UNDO tablespace, you must shut down your database and start it in mount mode. When your database is in mount mode, you can rename these data files via the ALTER DATABASE RENAME FILE statement.

The following example demonstrates how to move the data files associated with a single tablespace. First, take the data files offline with the ALTER TABLESPACE statement:

```
SQL> alter tablespace users offline;
```

Now, from the OS prompt, move the data files to a new location, using the Linux/Unix m v command:

```
$ mv /u01/dbfile/o18c/users01.dbf /u02/dbfile/o18c/users01.dbf
```

Update the control file with the ALTER TABLESPACE statement:

```
alter tablespace users
rename datafile
'/u01/dbfile/o18c/users01.dbf'
to
'/u02/dbfile/o18c/users01.dbf';
```

Finally, bring the data files within the tablespace back online:

```
SQL> alter tablespace users online;
```

If you want to rename data files from multiple tablespaces in one operation, you can use the ALTER DATABASE RENAME FILE statement (instead of the ALTER TABLESPACE... RENAME DATAFILE statement). The following example renames several data files in the database. Because the SYSTEM and UNDO tablespaces' data files are being moved, you must shut down the database first and then place it in mount mode:

```
SQL> conn / as sysdba
SQL> shutdown immediate;
SQL> startup mount;
```

Because the database is in mount mode, the data files are not open for use, and thus there is no need to take the data files offline. Next, physically move the files via the Linux mv command:

```
$ mv /u01/dbfile/o18c/system01.dbf /u02/dbfile/o18c/system01.dbf
$ mv /u01/dbfile/o18c/sysaux01.dbf /u02/dbfile/o18c/sysaux01.dbf
$ mv /u01/dbfile/o18c/undotbs01.dbf /u02/dbfile/o18c/undotbs01.dbf
```

Note   You must move the files before you update the control file. The ALTER
DATABASE RENAME FILE command expects the file to be in the renamed
location. If the file is not there, an error is thrown: ORA-27037: unable to
obtain file status.

Now, you can update the control file to be aware of the new file name:

```
alter database rename file
'/u01/dbfile/o18c/system01.dbf',
'/u01/dbfile/o18c/sysaux01.dbf',
'/u01/dbfile/o18c/undotbs01.dbf'
to
'/u02/dbfile/o18c/system01.dbf',
'/u02/dbfile/o18c/sysaux01.dbf',
'/u02/dbfile/o18c/undotbs01.dbf';
```

You should be able to open your database:

```
SQL> alter database open;
```

Re-creating the Control File and OS Commands

Another way you can relocate all data files in a database is to use a combination of a
re-created control file and OS commands. The steps for this operation are as follows:

1. Create a trace file that contains a CREATE CONTROLFILE statement.

2. Modify the trace file to display the new location of the data files.

3. Shut down the database.

4. Physically move the data files, using an OS command.

5. Start the database in nomount mode.

6. Run the CREATE CONTROLFILE command.

Note   When you re-create a control file, be aware that any RMAN information that was contained in the file will be lost. If you are not using a recovery catalog, you can repopulate the control file with RMAN backup information, using the RMAN CATALOG command.

The following example walks through the previous steps. First, you write a CREATE CONTROLFILE statement to a trace file via an ALTER DATABASE BACKUP CONTROLFILE TO TRACE statement:

```
SQL> alter database backup controlfile to trace as '/tmp/mvctrlfile.sql'
noresetlogs;
```

There are a couple of items to note about the prior statement. First, a file named mvctrlfile.sql is created in the /tmp directory; this file contains a CREATE CONTROLFILE statement. Second, the prior statement uses the NORESETLOGS clause; this instructs Oracle to write only one SQL statement to the trace file. If you do not specify NORESETLOGS, Oracle writes two SQL statements to the trace file: one to re-create the control file with the NORESETLOGS option and one to re-create the control file with RESETLOGS. Normally, you know whether you want to reset the online redo logs as part of re-creating the control file. In this case, you know that you do not need to reset the online redo logs when you re-create the control file (because the online redo logs have not been damaged and are still in the normal location for the database).

Next, edit the /tmp/mvctrlfile.sql file, and change the names of the directory paths to the new locations. Here is a CREATE CONTROLFILE statement for this example:

```
CREATE CONTROLFILE REUSE DATABASE "O18C" NORESETLOGS  NOARCHIVELOG
    MAXLOGFILES 16
    MAXLOGMEMBERS 4
    MAXDATAFILES 1024
    MAXINSTANCES 1
    MAXLOGHISTORY 876
LOGFILE
  GROUP 1 (
    '/u01/oraredo/o18c/redo01a.rdo',
    '/u02/oraredo/o18c/redo01b.rdo'
  ) SIZE 50M BLOCKSIZE 512,
```

```
  GROUP 2 (
    '/u01/oraredo/o18c/redo02a.rdo',
    '/u02/oraredo/o18c/redo02b.rdo'
  ) SIZE 50M BLOCKSIZE 512,
  GROUP 3 (
    '/u01/oraredo/o18c/redo03a.rdo',
    '/u02/oraredo/o18c/redo03b.rdo'
  ) SIZE 50M BLOCKSIZE 512
DATAFILE
  '/u01/dbfile/o18c/system01.dbf',
  '/u01/dbfile/o18c/sysaux01.dbf',
  '/u01/dbfile/o18c/undotbs01.dbf',
  '/u01/dbfile/o18c/users01.dbf'
CHARACTER SET AL32UTF8;
```

Now, shut down the database:

```
SQL> shutdown immediate;
```

Physically move the files from the OS prompt. This example uses the Linux mv command to move the files:

```
$ mv /u02/dbfile/o18c/system01.dbf /u01/dbfile/o18c/system01.dbf
$ mv /u02/dbfile/o18c/sysaux01.dbf /u01/dbfile/o18c/sysaux01.dbf
$ mv /u02/dbfile/o18c/undotbs01.dbf /u01/dbfile/o18c/undotbs01.dbf
$ mv /u02/dbfile/o18c/users01.dbf /u01/dbfile/o18c/users01.dbf
```

Start up the database in nomount mode:

```
SQL> startup nomount;
```

Then, execute the file that contains the CREATE CONTROLFILE statement (in this example, mvctrlfile.sql):

```
SQL> @/tmp/mvctrlfile.sql
```

If the statement is successful, you see the following message:

```
Control file created.
```

Finally, alter your database open:

```
SQL> alter database open;
```

Using ASM for Tablespaces

ASM is a way to manage the physical disk and storage allocation to the Oracle database and files system. Adding storage becomes adding disks to a disk group and allows for additional space to be dynamically available to the tablespaces. With storage hardware advances, there are also ways to add disks to mount points as well. It just depends how the databases and environments are being managed and configured if ASM is part of the environment.

There are plenty of advantages for using ASM from shared storage, ease of disk management to data file repairs, and verification specific for the database. ASM, normally named +ASM, is another instance that needs to be available for the database to be able to use the disk groups. This is a way to share storage for several databases, rebalance workloads, and provide higher availability for the database storage.

The parameters for using a default storage space have already been discussed and instead of naming mount points that can change as databases grow or move, the database using +ASM can use a disk group without having to worry about names for mount points. A disk group `oradata` is created to be used for the database storage. The parameters for file destinations are set using the following command:

```
SQL> alter system set DB_CREATE_FILE_DEST = '+oradata';
```

To create the tablespace:

```
SQL> create tablespace hrdata;
```

This will create a tablespace hrdata on the oradata diskgroup. The file names are generated by +ASM and, to create aliases by default, a template for file names in +ASM. If a template is used, the DB_CREATE_FILE_DEST parameter will point to that template along with the disk group.

```
SQL> alter system set DB_CREATE_FILE_DEST = '+oradata(datatemplate)';
```

The data files and tablespace views are still available to see what tablespaces are created and the data files that are part of the database. The view `v$datafile` and `dba_data_files` will show the files starting with the diskgroup +oradata.

The dba_tablespaces view will still show the hrdata tablespace as with non-ASM databases. There are also additional views that will show the files in the disk groups. To see the ASM disks in a disk group view, v$asm_disk should be queried. The files in the disk group are seen in the v$asm_file and v$asm_alias views.

From v$asm_file the file number, type, and space information are available and v$asm_alias brings in the data file name:

```
SQL> select file.file_number, alias.name, file.type
From v$asm_file file, v$asm_alias alias
Where file.group_number=alias.group_number and file.file_number=alias.
file_number;
```

The Oracle cloud uses the ASM and ASM Cluster File System (ACFS) to present the storage. It does simplify and automate storage management. There is not a need for another volume or file manager tool. Again, there are advantages to use the storage management tools that come with the Oracle database. There are plenty of reference materials to show how to create disk groups, add or drop disks, perform maintenance, and manage the ASM storage and file systems.

Summary

This chapter discussed managing tablespace and data files. Tablespaces are logical containers for a group of data files. Data files are the physical files on disk that contain data. You should plan carefully when creating tablespaces and the corresponding data files.

Tablespaces allow you to separate the data of different applications. You can also separate tables from indexes. These allow you to customize storage characteristics of the tablespace for each application. Furthermore, tablespaces provide a way to better manage applications that have different availability and backup and recovery requirements. Even though there are many options that are possible to configure with tablespaces, the storage technology advances to handle many of the needs to separate data files, extents, and autoextend. Using the storage features and tools such as ASM will help manage the disk and performance of the storage needed for the database. The tablespace options are simplified by these steps. Planning for storage is then in the area of growth of the data and monitoring for space usage to proactively increase the allocation of space for the tablespace.

Security options allow for transparent encryption for the data at rest in the tablespace. The tablespace is created with the encryption option, and the wallet and keys are open with the database to allow for viewing of the data in the database but not through the files on the server.

As a DBA you must be proficient in managing tablespaces and data files. In any type of environment, you have to add, rename, relocate, and drop these storage containers. These are ideal tests that can be done when first creating a database or in a test environment to practice the commands and restoring data files. The commands, errors, and issues can be logged for future reference to use in a pressure situation for data file corruption and recovery.

Oracle requires three types of files for a database to operate: data files, control files, and online redo log files. The next chapter focuses on control file and online redo log file management.

## CHAPTER 5

Managing Control Files, Online Redo Logs, and Archivelogs

An Oracle database consists of three types of mandatory files: data files, control files, and online redo logs. Chapter 4 focused on tablespaces and data files. This chapter looks at managing control files and online redo logs and implementing archivelogs. The first part of the chapter discusses typical control file maintenance tasks, such as adding, moving, and removing control files. The middle part of the chapter examines DBA activities related to online redo log files, such as renaming, adding, dropping, and relocating these critical files. Finally, the architectural aspects of enabling and implementing archiving are covered.

Managing Control Files

A control file is a small binary file that stores the following types of information:

- Database name
- Names and locations of data files
- Names and locations of online redo log files
- Current online redo log sequence number
- Checkpoint information
- Names and locations of RMAN backup files

© Michelle Malcher and Darl Kuhn 2019
M. Malcher and D. Kuhn, *Pro Oracle Database 18c Administration*,
https://doi.org/10.1007/978-1-4842-4424-1_5

You can query much of the information stored in the control file from data dictionary views. This example displays the types of information stored in the control file by querying v$controlfile_record_section:

```
SQL> select distinct type from v$controlfile_record_section;
```

Here is a partial listing of the output:

```
TYPE
---------------------------
FILENAME
TABLESPACE
RMAN CONFIGURATION
BACKUP CORRUPTION
PROXY COPY
FLASHBACK LOG
REMOVABLE RECOVERY FILES
AUXILIARY DATAFILE COPY
DATAFILE
```

You can view database-related information stored in the control file via the v$database view. The v$ views are based on x$ tables or views, and the v$database is based on an x$database, which is just a read of the control file:

```
SQL> select name, open_mode, created, current_scn from v$database;
```

Here is the output for this example:

```
NAME       OPEN_MODE             CREATED   CURRENT_SCN
---------  --------------------  --------- -----------
O18C       READ WRITE            28-SEP-12   2573820
```

Every Oracle database must have at least one control file. When you start your database in nomount mode, the instance is aware of the location of the control files from the CONTROL_FILES initialization parameter in the spfile or init.ora file. When you issue a STARTUP NOMOUNT command, Oracle reads the parameter file and starts the background processes and allocates memory structures:

```
-- locations of control files are known to the instance
SQL> startup nomount;
```

At this point, the control files have not been touched by any processes. When you alter your database into mount mode, the control files are read and opened for use:

```
-- control files opened
SQL> alter database mount;
```

If any of the control files listed in the CONTROL_FILES initialization parameter are not available, then you cannot mount your database.

When you successfully mount your database, the instance is aware of the locations of the data files and online redo logs but has not yet opened them. After you alter your database into open mode, the data files and online redo logs are opened:

```
-- datafiles and online redo logs opened
SQL> alter database open;
```

Note   Keep in mind that when you issue the STARTUP command (with no options), the previously described three phases are automatically performed in this order: nomount, mount, open. When you issue a SHUTDOWN command, the phases are reversed: close the database, unmount the control file, stop the instance.

The control file is created when the database is created. As you saw in Chapter 2, you should create at least two control files when you create your database (to avoid a single point of failure). Previously, you should have multiple control files stored on separate storage devices controlled by separate controllers, but because of storage devices it might be difficult to know if it is a separate device, so it is important to have fault-tolerant devices with mirroring. The control file is a very important part of the database and needs to be available or very quickly restored if needed.

Control files can also be on ASM disk groups. This allows for one control file in the +ORADATA disk group and another file in +FRA disk group. Managing the control files and details inside remain the same as on the file system except that the control files are just using ASM disk groups.

After the database has been opened, Oracle will frequently write information to the control files, such as when you make any physical modifications (e.g., creating a tablespace, adding/removing/resizing a data file). Oracle writes to all control files specified by the CONTROL_FILES initialization parameter. If Oracle cannot write to one of the control files, an error is thrown:

```
ORA-00210: cannot open the specified control file
```

153

If one of your control files becomes unavailable, shut down your database, and resolve the issue before restarting (see Chapter 19 for using RMAN to restore a control file). Fixing the problem may mean resolving a storage-device failure or modifying the CONTROL_FILES initialization parameter to remove the control file entry for the control file that is not available.

DISPLAYING THE CONTENTS OF A CONTROL FILE

You can use the ALTER SESSION statement to display the physical contents of the control file; for example,

```
SQL> oradebug setmypid
SQL> oradebug unlimit
SQL> alter session set events 'immediate trace name controlf level 9';
SQL> oradebug tracefile_name
```

The prior line of code displays the following name of the trace file:

```
/ora01/app/oracle/diag/rdbms/o18c/o18c/trace/o18c_ora_4153.trc
```

The trace file is written to the $ ADR_HOME/trace directory. You can also view the trace directory name via this query:

```
SQL> select value from v$diag_info where name='Diag Trace';
```

Here is a partial listing of the contents of the trace file:

```
***************************************************************************
DATABASE ENTRY
***************************************************************************
 (size = 316, compat size = 316, section max = 1, section in-use = 1,
  last-recid= 0, old-recno = 0, last-recno = 0)
 (extent = 1, blkno = 1, numrecs = 1)
 09/28/2012 16:04:54
 DB Name "O18C"
 Database flags = 0x00404001 0x00001200
 Controlfile Creation Timestamp  09/28/2012 16:04:57
 Incmplt recovery scn: 0x0000.00000000
```

You can inspect the contents of the control file when troubleshooting or when trying to gain a better understanding of Oracle internals.

Viewing Control File Names and Locations

If your database is in a nomount state, a mounted state, or an open state, you can view the names and locations of the control files, as follows:

```
SQL> show parameter control_files
```

You can also view control file location and name information by querying the V$CONTROLFILE view. This query works while your database is mounted or open:

```
SQL> select name from v$controlfile;
```

If, for some reason, you cannot start your database at all, and you need to know the names and locations of the control files, you can inspect the contents of the initialization (parameter) file to see where they are located. If you are using a spfile, even though it is a binary file, you can still open it with a text editor. The safest approach is to make a copy of the spfile and then inspect its contents with an OS editor:

```
$ cp $ORACLE_HOME/dbs/spfileo18c.ora $ORACLE_HOME/dbs/spfileo18c.copy
$ vi $ORACLE_HOME/dbs/spfileo18c.copy
```

You can also use the strings command to search for values in a binary file:

```
$ strings spfileo18c.ora | grep -i control_files
```

If you are using a text-based initialization file, you can view the file directly, with an OS editor, or use the g rep command:

```
$ grep -i control_files $ORACLE_HOME/dbs/inito18c.ora
```

Adding a Control File

Adding a control file means copying an existing control file and making your database aware of the copy by modifying your CONTROL_FILES parameter. This task must be done while your database is shut down. This procedure only works when you have a good existing control file that can be copied. Adding a control file isn't the same thing as creating or restoring a control file.

Tip   See Chapter 4 for an example of re-creating a control file for the purpose of renaming and moving data files. See Chapter 19 for an example of re-creating a control file for the purpose of renaming a database.

If your database uses only one control file, and that control file becomes damaged, you need to either restore a control file from a backup (if available) and perform a recovery or re-create the control file. If you are using two or more control files, and one becomes damaged, you can use the remaining good control file(s) to quickly get your database into an operating state.

If a database is using only one control file, the basic procedure for adding a control file is as follows:

1. Alter the initialization file CONTROL_FILES parameter to include the new location and name of the control file.

2. Shut down your database.

3. Use an OS command to copy an existing control file to the new location and name.

4. Restart your database.

Depending on whether you use a spfile or an init.ora file, the previous steps vary slightly. The next two sections detail these different scenarios.

Spfile Scenario

If your database is open, you can quickly determine whether you are using a spfile with the following SQL statement:

```
SQL> show parameter spfile
```

Here is some sample output:

```
NAME                            TYPE        VALUE
------------------------------  ----------  -----------------------------
spfile                          string      /ora01/app/oracle/product/18.1
                                            .0.1/db_1/dbs/spfileo18c.ora
```

When you have determined that you are using a spfile, use the following steps to add a control file:

1. Determine the CONTROL_FILES parameter's current value:

   ```
   SQL> show parameter control_files
   ```

The output shows that this database is using only one control file:

```
NAME                                TYPE        VALUE
----------------------------------- ----------- -------------------------------
control_files                       string      /u01/dbfile/o18c/control01.ctl
```

2. Alter your CONTROL_FILES parameter to include the new control file that you want to add, but limit the scope of the operation to the spfile (you cannot modify this parameter in memory). Make sure you also include any control files listed in step 1:

   ```
   SQL> alter system set control_files='/u01/dbfile/o18c/control01.ctl',
   '/u01/dbfile/o18c/control02.ctl' scope=spfile;
   ```

3. Shut down your database:

   ```
   SQL> shutdown immediate;
   ```

4. Copy an existing control file to the new location and name. In this example, a new control file named control02.ctl is created via the OS cp command:

   ```
   $ cp /u01/dbfile/o18c/control01.ctl /u01/dbfile/o18c/control02.ctl
   ```

5. Start up your database:

   ```
   SQL> startup;
   ```

You can verify that the new control file is being used by displaying the CONTROL_FILES parameter:

```
SQL> show parameter control_files
```

Here is the output for this example:

```
NAME                          TYPE          VALUE
--------------------          -----------   -------------------------------
control_files                 string        /u01/dbfile/o18c/control01.ctl
                                            ,/u01/dbfile/o18c/control02.ctl
```

Init.ora Scenario

Run the following statement to verify that you are using an init.ora file. If you are not using a spfile, the VALUE column is blank:

```
SQL> show parameter spfile
NAME                              TYPE          VALUE
-------------------------------   -----------   -------------------------------
spfile                            string
```

To add a control file when using a text init.ora file, perform the following steps:

1. Shut down your database:

   ```
   SQL> shutdown immediate;
   ```

2. Edit your init.ora file with an OS utility (such as vi), and add the new control file location and name to the CONTROL_FILES parameter. This example opens the init.ora file, using vi, and adds control02.ctl to the CONTROL_FILES parameter:

   ```
   $ vi $ORACLE_HOME/dbs/inito18c.ora
   ```

   Listed next is the CONTROL_FILES parameter after control02.ctl is added:

   ```
   control_files='/u01/dbfile/o18c/control01.ctl',
                  '/u01/dbfile/o18c/control02.ctl'
   ```

3. From the OS, copy the existing control file to the location and name of the control file being added:

   ```
   $ cp /u01/dbfile/o18c/control01.ctl /u01/dbfile/o18c/control02.ctl
   ```

4. Start up your database:

   ```
   SQL> startup;
   ```

You can view the control files in use by displaying the CONTROL_FILES parameter:

```
SQL> show parameter control_files
```

For this example, here is the output:

```
NAME                          TYPE         VALUE
--------------------------    ----------   ------------------------------
control_files                 string       /u01/dbfile/o18c/control01.ctl
                                           ,/u01/dbfile/o18c/control02.ctl
```

Moving a Control File

You may occasionally need to move a control file from one location to another. For example, if new storage is added to the database server, you may want to move an existing control file to the newly available location.

The procedure for moving a control file is very similar to adding a control file. The only difference is that you rename the control file instead of copying it. This example shows how to move a control file when you are using a spfile:

1. Determine the CONTROL_FILES parameter's current value:

   ```
   SQL> show parameter control_files
   ```

The output shows that this database is using only one control file:

```
NAME                            TYPE         VALUE
------------------------------  ----------   ------------------------------
control_files                   string       /u01/dbfile/o18c/control01.ctl
```

2. Alter your CONTROL_FILES parameter to reflect that you are moving a control file. In this example, the control file is currently in this location:

   ```
   /u01/dbfile/o18c/control01.ctl
   ```

You are moving the control file to this location:

```
/u02/dbfile/o18c/control01.ctl
```

Alter the spfile to reflect the new location for the control file. You have to specify SCOPE=SPFILE because the CONTROL_FILES parameter cannot be modified in memory:

```
SQL> alter system set
     control_files='/u02/dbfile/o18c/control01.ctl' scope=spfile;
```

3. Shut down your database:

```
SQL> shutdown immediate;
```

4. At the OS prompt, move the control file to the new location. This example uses the OS mv command:

```
$ mv /u01/dbfile/o18c/control01.ctl /u02/dbfile/o18c/control01.ctl
```

5. Start up your database:

```
SQL> startup;
```

You can verify that the new control file is being used by displaying the CONTROL_FILES parameter:

```
SQL> show parameter control_files
```

Here is the output for this example:

```
NAME                                 TYPE        VALUE
------------------------------------ ----------- --------------------------------
control_files                        string      /u02/dbfile/o18c/control01.ctl
```

Removing a Control File

You may run into a situation in which you experience a media failure with a storage device that contains one of your multiplexed control files:

```
ORA-00205: error in identifying control file, check alert log for more info
```

In this scenario, you still have at least one good control file. To remove a control file, follow these steps:

1. Identify which control file has experienced media failure by inspecting the `alert.log` for information:

    ```
    ORA-00210: cannot open the specified control file
    ORA-00202: control file: '/u01/dbfile/o18c/control02.ctl'
    ```

2. Remove the unavailable control file name from the `CONTROL_FILES` parameter. If you are using an `init.ora` file, modify the file directly with an OS editor (such as `vi`). If you are using a spfile, modify the `CONTROL_FILES` parameter with the `ALTER SYSTEM` statement. In this spfile example the `control02.ctl` control file is removed from the `CONTROL_FILES` parameter:

    ```
    SQL> alter system set control_files='/u01/dbfile/o18c/control01.ctl'
         scope=spfile;
    ```

This database now has only one control file associated with it. You should never run a production database with just one control file. See the section "Adding a Control File," earlier in this chapter, for details on how to add more control files to your database.

3. Stop and start your database:

    ```
    SQL> shutdown immediate;
    SQL> startup;
    ```

Note   If SHUTDOWN IMMEDIATE does not work, use SHUTDOWN ABORT to shut down your database. There is nothing wrong with using SHUTDOWN ABORT to quickly close a database when SHUTDOWN IMMEDIATE hangs; however, remember that the database is rolling back changes and might not be hanging. Depending on the transactions that are in a rollback state, the startup might take some time or hinder performance.

Control files can be in an ASM diskgroup. This will allow for you to move the back-end disk and storage around without having to move datafiles or control files. If the ASM layer is used, the storage devices and disks become transparent to the database files. This does not protect from a possible recovery from corruption of a file or if a file is removed, but it does prevent having to move files because of location and disk being used. The files will be of type CONTROLFILE in the ASM views to know the location of the files.

Online Redo Logs

Online redo logs store a record of transactions that have occurred in your database. These logs serve the following purposes:

- Provide a mechanism for recording changes to the database so that in the event of a media failure, you have a method of recovering transactions.

- Ensure that in the event of total instance failure, committed transactions can be recovered (crash recovery) even if committed data changes have not yet been written to the data files.

- Allow administrators to inspect historical database transactions through the Oracle LogMiner utility.

- They are read by Oracle tools such as GoldenGate or Streams to replicate data.

You are required to have at least two online redo log groups in your database. Each online redo log group must contain at least one online redo log `member`. The `member` is the `physical file` that exists on disk. You can create multiple members in each redo log group, which is known as multiplexing your online redo log group.

Tip   I highly recommend that you multiplex your online redo log groups and, if possible, have each member on a separate physical device governed by a separate controller.

The log-writer log buffer (in the SGA) to the online redo log files (on disk). The redo record has a system change number (SCN) assigned to it in order to identify the transaction redo information. There are committed and uncommitted records written to the redo logs. The log writer flushes the contents of the redo log buffer when any of the following are true:

- A `COMMIT` is issued.

- A log switch occurs.

- Three seconds go by.

- The redo log buffer is one-third full.

Since this is a database process, the container database (CDB) will manage the redo logs. PDBs do not have their own redo logs, which also means that planning for space and sizing of the redo logs is at the CDB level and includes all of the PDB transactions. This architecture will be discussed more in Chapter 22, but the transaction sizing is based on all of the PDBs for a CDB.

The online redo log group that the log writer is actively writing to is the current online redo log group. The log writer writes simultaneously to all members of a redo log group. The log writer needs to successfully write to only one member in order for the database to continue operating. The database ceases operating if the log writer cannot write successfully to at least one member of the current group.

When the current online redo log group fills up, a log switch occurs, and the log writer starts writing to the next online redo log group. A log sequence number is assigned to each redo log when a switch occurs to be used for archiving. The log writer writes to the online redo log groups in a round-robin fashion. Because you have a finite number of online redo log groups, eventually the contents of each online redo log group are overwritten. If you want to save a history of the transaction information, you must place your database in archivelog mode (see the section "Implementing Archivelog Mode" later in this chapter).

When your database is in archivelog mode, after every log switch the archiver background process copies the contents of the online redo log file to an archived redo log file. In the event of a failure, the archived redo log files allow you to restore the complete history of transactions that have occurred since your last database backup.

Figure 5-1 displays a typical setup for the online redo log files. This figure shows three online redo log groups, each containing two members. The database is in archivelog mode. In the figure, group 2 has recently been filled with transactions, a log switch has occurred, and the log writer is now writing to group 3. The archiver process is copying the contents of group 2 to an archived redo log file. When group 3 fills up, another log switch will occur, and the log writer will begin writing to group 1. At the same time, the archiver process will copy the contents of group 3 to archive log sequence 3 (and so forth).

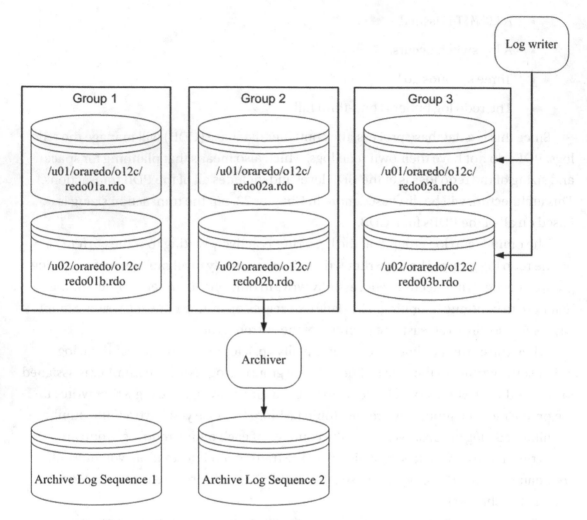

Figure 5-1. *Online redo log configuration*

The online redo log files are not intended to be backed up. These files contain only the most recent redo transaction information generated by the database. When you enable archiving, the archived redo log files are the mechanism for protecting your database transaction history.

The contents of the current online redo log files are not archived until a log switch occurs. This means that if you lose all members of the current online redo log file, you lose transactions. Listed next are several mechanisms log files:log files:

- Multiplex the groups.

- Consider setting the ARCHIVE_LAG_TARGET initialization parameter to ensure that the online redo logs are switched at regular intervals.

- If possible, never allow two members of the same group to share the same physical disk.

- Ensure that OS file permissions are set appropriately (restrictive, that only the owner of the Oracle binaries has permissions to write and read).

- Use physical storage devices that are redundant (i.e., RAID [redundant array of inexpensive disks]).

- Appropriately size the log files, so that they switch and are archived at regular intervals.

Note   The only tool provided by Oracle that can protect you and preserve all committed transactions in the event that you lose all members of the current online redo log group is Oracle Data Guard, implemented in maximum protection mode. See MOS note 239100.1 for more details regarding Oracle Data Guard protection modes.

Flash is another option for redo logs. Since the logs are written out to archivelogs and require fast writes, flash drives are a way to improve performance of redo logs. If flash is not available, the options are to place redo logs on physical disks and based on the previous list to minimize failures. Solid state disks might not provide faster writes, which does not make them the ideal choice for redo logs.

The online redo log files are never backed up by an RMAN backup or by a user-managed hot backup. If you did back up the online redo log files, it would be meaningless to restore them. The online redo log files contain the latest redo generated by the database. You would not want to overwrite them from a backup with old redo information. For a database in archivelog mode, the online redo log files contain the most recently generated transactions that are required to perform a complete recovery. The redo log files should also be excluded from other system backup (non-database) along with other data files.

Displaying Online Redo Log Information

Use the V$LOG and V$LOGFILE views to display information about online redo log groups and corresponding members:

```
COL group#     FORM 99999
COL thread#    FORM 99999
COL grp_status FORM a10
COL member     FORM a30
COL mem_status FORM a10
COL mbytes     FORM 999999
--
SELECT
 a.group#
,a.thread#
,a.status grp_status
,b.member member
,b.status mem_status
,a.bytes/1024/1024 mbytes
FROM v$log      a,
     v$logfile b
WHERE a.group# = b.group#
ORDER BY a.group#, b.member;
```

Here is some sample output:

```
GROUP# THREAD# GRP_STATUS MEMBER                          MEM_STATUS  MBYTES
------ ------- ---------- ------------------------------- ---------- -------
     1       1 INACTIVE   /u01/oraredo/o18c/redo01a.rdo                   50
     1       1 INACTIVE   /u02/oraredo/o18c/redo01b.rdo                   50
     2       1 CURRENT    /u01/oraredo/o18c/redo02a.rdo                   50
     2       1 CURRENT    /u02/oraredo/o18c/redo02b.rdo                   50
```

When you are diagnosing online redo log issues, the V$LOG and V$LOGFILE views are particularly helpful. You can query these views while the database is mounted or open. Table 5-1 briefly describes each view.

Table 5-1. *Useful Views Related to Online Redo Logs*

View	Description
V$LOG	Displays the online redo log group information stored in the control file
V$LOGFILE	Displays online redo log file member information

The STATUS column of the V$LOG view is especially useful when you are working with online redo log groups. Table 5-2 describes each status and its meaning for the V$LOG view.

Table 5-2. *Status for Online Redo Log Groups in the V$LOG View*

Status	Meaning
CURRENT	The log group is currently being written to by the log writer.
ACTIVE	The log group is required for crash recovery and may or may not have been archived.
CLEARING	The log group is being cleared out by an ALTER DATABASE CLEAR LOGFILE command.
CLEARING_CURRENT	The current log group is being cleared of a closed thread.
INACTIVE	The log group is not required for crash recovery and may or may not have been archived.
UNUSED	The log group has never been written to; it was recently created.

The STATUS column of the V$LOGFILE view also contains useful information. This view offers information about each physical online redo log file member of a log group. Table 5-3 provides descriptions of each status and its meaning for each log file member.

Table 5-3. *Status for Online Redo Log File Members in the V$LOGFILE View*

Status	Meaning
INVALID	The log file member is inaccessible or has been recently created.
DELETED	The log file member is no longer in use.
STALE	The log file member's contents are not complete.
NULL	The log file member is being used by the database.

It is important to differentiate between the STATUS column in V$LOG and the STATUS column in V$LOGFILE. The STATUS column in V$LOG reflects the status of the log group. The STATUS column in V$LOGFILE reports the status of the physical online redo log file member. Refer to these tables when diagnosing issues with your online redo logs.

Determining the Optimal Size of Online Redo Log Groups

Try to size the online redo logs so that they switch anywhere from two to six times per hour. The V$LOG_HISTORY contains a history of how frequently the online redo logs have switched. Execute this query to view the number of log switches per hour:

```
select count(*)
,to_char(first_time,'YYYY:MM:DD:HH24')
from v$log_history
group by to_char(first_time,'YYYY:MM:DD:HH24')
order by 2;
```

Here is a snippet of the output:

```
 COUNT(*) TO_CHAR(FIRST
---------- -------------
        1 2012:10:23:23
        3 2012:10:24:03
       28 2012:10:24:04
       23 2012:10:24:05
       68 2012:10:24:06
       84 2012:10:24:07
       15 2012:10:24:08
```

From the previous output, you can see that a great deal of log switch activity occurred from approximately 4:00 AM to 7:00 AM This could be due to a nightly batch job or users in different time zones updating data. For this database the size of the online redo logs should be increased. You should try to size the online redo logs to accommodate peak transaction loads on the database.

The V$LOG_HISTORYsystem change number (SCN). As stated, a general rule of thumb is that you should size your online redo log files so that they switch approximately two to six times per hour. You do not want them switching too often because there is overhead with the log switch; however, leaving transaction information in the redo log without archiving will create issues with recovery. If a disaster causes a media failure in your current online redo log, you can lose those transactions that haven't been archived. If a disaster causes a media failure in your current online redo log, you can lose those transactions that haven't been archived.

Oracle initiates a checkpoint as part of a log switch. During a checkpoint, the database-writer background process writes modified (also called dirty) blocks to disk, which is resource intensive. Checkpoint messages in the alert log will also be a way of looking at how fast logs are switching or if there are waits associated with archiving.

Tip   Use the ARCHIVE_LAG_TARGET initialization parameter to set a maximum amount of time (in seconds) between log switches. A typical setting for this parameter is 1,800 seconds (30 minutes). A value of 0 (default) disables this feature. This parameter is commonly used in Oracle Data Guard environments to force log switches after the specified amount of time elapses.

You can also query the OPTIMAL_LOGFILE_SIZE column from the V$INSTANCE_RECOVERY view to determine if your online redo log files have been sized correctly:

```
SQL> select optimal_logfile_size from v$instance_recovery;
```

Here is some sample output:

```
OPTIMAL_LOGFILE_SIZE
--------------------
349
```

This column reports the redo log file size (in megabytes) that is considered optimal, based on the initialization parameter setting of FAST_START_MTTR_TARGET. Oracle recommends that you configure all online redo logs to be at least the value of OPTIMAL_LOGFILE_SIZE. However, when sizing your online redo logs, you must take into consideration information about your environment (such as the frequency of the switches).

Determining the Optimal Number of Redo Log Groups

Oracle requires at least two redo log groups in order to function. But, having just two groups sometimes isn't enough. To understand why this is so, remember that every time a log switch occurs, it initiates a checkpoint. As part of a checkpoint the database writer writes all modified (dirty) blocks from the SGA to the data files on disk. Also recall that the online redo logs are written to in a round-robin fashion, and that eventually the information in a given log is overwritten. Before the log writer can begin to overwrite information in an online redo log, all modified blocks in the SGA associated with the redo log must first be written to a data file. If not, all modified blocks have been written to the data files, you see this message in the alert.log file:

```
Thread 1 cannot allocate new log, sequence <sequence number>
Checkpoint not complete
```

Another way to explain this issue is that Oracle needs to store in the online redo logs any information that would be required to perform a crash recovery. To help you visualize this, see Figure 5-2.

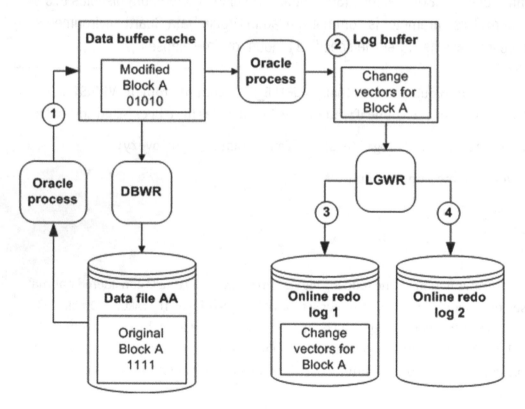

Figure 5-2. *Redo protected until the modified (dirty) buffer is written to disk*

At time 1, Block A is read from Data File AA into the buffer cache and modified. At time 2 the redo-change vector information (how the block changed) is written to the log buffer. At time 3 the log-writer process writes the Block A change-vector information

170

to online redo log 1. At time 4 a log switch occurs, and online redo log 2 becomes the current online redo log.

Now, suppose that online redo log 2 fills up quickly and another log switch occurs, at which point the log-writer attempts to write to online redo log 1. The log writer isn't allowed to overwrite information in online redo log 1 until the database writer writes Block A to Data File AA. Until Block A is written to Data File AA, Oracle needs information in the online redo logs to recover this block in the event of a power failure or shutdown abort. Before Oracle overwrites information in the online redo logs, it ensures that blocks protected by redo have been written to disk. If these modified blocks haven't been written to disk, Oracle temporarily suspends processing until this occurs. There are a few ways to resolve this issue:

- Add more redo log groups.

- Lower the value of FAST_START_MTTR_TARGET. Doing so causes the database-writer process to write older modified blocks to disk in a shorter time frame.

- Tune the database-writer process (modify DB_WRITER_PROCESSES).

If you notice that the Checkpoint not complete message is occurring often (say, several times a day), I recommend that you add one or more log groups to resolve the issue. Adding an extra redo log gives the database writer more time to write modified blocks in the database buffer cache to the data files before the associated redo with a block is overwritten. There is little downside to adding more redo log groups. The main concern is that you could bump up against the MAXLOGFILES value that was used when you created the database. If you need to add more groups and have exceeded the value of MAXLOGFILES, then you must re-create your control file and specify a high value for this parameter.

If adding more redo log groups doesn't resolve the issue, you should carefully consider lowering the value of FAST_START_MTTR_TARGET. When you lower this value, you can potentially see more I/O because the database-writer process is more actively writing modified blocks to data files. Ideally, it would be nice to verify the impact of modifying FAST_START_MTTR_TARGET in a test environment before making the change in production. You can modify this parameter while your instance is up; this means you can quickly modify it back to its original setting if there are unforeseen side effects.

Finally, consider increasing the value of the DB_WRITER_PROCESSES parameter. Carefully analyze the impact of modifying this parameter in a test environment before you apply it to production. This value requires that you stop and start your database; therefore, if there are adverse effects, downtime is required to change this value back to the original setting.

Adding Online Redo Log Groups

If you determine that you need to add an online redo log group, use the ADD LOGFILE GROUP statement. In this example, the database already contains two online redo log groups that are sized at 50M each. An additional log group is added that has two members and is sized at 50MB:

```
alter database add logfile group 3
('/u01/oraredo/o18c/redo03a.rdo',
 '/u02/oraredo/o18c/redo03b.rdo') SIZE 50M;
```

In this scenario I highly recommend that the log group you add be the same size and have the same number of members as the existing online redo logs. If the newly added group doesn't have the same physical characteristics as the existing groups, it's harder to accurately determine performance issues. If a larger size is preferred, the new group can be added at the larger size, then the other groups can be dropped and re-created with the larger size value in order to keep the size of the redo logs the same (an example of this is in the next section).

For example, if you have two log groups sized at 50MB, and you add a new log group sized at 500MB, this is very likely to produce the Checkpoint not complete issue described in the previous section. This is because flushing all modified blocks from the SGA that are protected by the redo in a 500MB log file can potentially take much longer than flushing modified blocks from the SGA that are protected by a 50MB log file.

Resizing and Dropping Online Redo Log Groups

You may need to change the size of your online redo logs (see the section "Determining the Optimal Size of Online Redo Log Groups" earlier in this chapter). You cannot directly modify the size of an existing online redo log (as you can a data file). To resize an online redo log, you have to first add online redo log groups that are the size you want, and then drop the online redo logs that are the old size.

Say you want to resize the online redo logs to be 200MB each. First, you add new groups that are 200MB, using the A DD LOGFILE GROUP statement. The following example adds log group 4, with two members sized at 200MB:

```
alter database add logfile group 4
('/u01/oraredo/o18c/redo04a.rdo',
 '/u02/oraredo/o18c/redo04b.rdo') SIZE 200M;
```

Note   You can specify the size of the log file in bytes, kilobytes, megabytes, or gigabytes.

After you've added the log files with the new size, you can drop the old online redo logs. A log group must have an INACTIVE status before you can drop it. You can check the status of the log group, as shown here:

```
SQL> select group#, status, archived, thread#, sequence# from v$log;
```

You can drop an inactive log group with the ALTER DATABASE DROP LOGFILE GROUP statement:

```
SQL> alter database drop logfile group <group #>;
```

If you attempt to drop the current online log group, Oracle returns an ORA-01623 error, stating that you cannot drop the current group. Use the ALTER SYSTEM SWITCH LOGFILE statement to switch the logs and make the next group the current group:

```
SQL> alter system switch logfile;
```

After a log switch the log group that was previously the current group retains an active status as long as it contains redo that Oracle requires to perform crash recovery. If you attempt to drop a log group with an active status, Oracle throws an ORA-01624 error, indicating that the log group is required for crash recovery. Issue an ALTER SYSTEM CHECKPOINT command to make the log group inactive:

```
SQL> alter system checkpoint;
```

Additionally, you cannot drop an online redo log group if doing so leaves your database with only one log group. If you attempt to do this, Oracle throws an ORA-01567 error and informs you that dropping the log group is not permitted because it would leave you with fewer than two log groups for your database (as mentioned earlier, Oracle requires at least two redo log groups in order to function).

Dropping an online redo log group does not remove the log files from the OS. You have to use an OS command to do this (such as the rm Linux/Unix command). Before you remove a file from the OS, ensure that it is not in use and that you do not remove a live online redo log file. For every database on the server, issue this query to view which online redo log files are in use:

```
SQL> select member from v$logfile;
```

Before you physically remove a log file, first switch the online redo logs enough times that all online redo log groups have recently been switched; doing so causes the OS to write to the file and thus give it a new timestamp. For example, if you have three groups, make sure you perform at least three log switches:

```
SQL> alter system switch logfile;
SQL> /
SQL> /
```

Tip   These steps of adding and removing redo logs is another exercise to perform before turning over a new database or a regularly scheduled testing period for practice and testing scripts to perform in production databases.

Now, verify at the OS prompt that the log file you intend to remove does not have a new timestamp. First, go to the directory containing the online redo log files:

```
$ cd  /u01/oraredo/o18c
```

Then, list the files to view the latest modification date:

```
$ ls -altr
```

When you are absolutely sure the file is not in use, you can remove it. The danger in removing a file is that if it happens to be an in-use online redo log, and the only member of a group, you can cause serious damage to your database. Ensure that you have a good backup of your database and that the file you are removing is not used by any databases on the server.

Adding Online Redo Log Files to a Group

You may occasionally need to add a log file to an existing group. For example, if you have an online redo log group that contains only one member, you should consider adding a log file (to provide a higher level of protection against a single-log file member failure). Use the ALTER DATABASE ADD LOGFILE MEMBER statement to add a member file to an existing online redo log group. You need to specify the new member file location, name, and group to which you want to add the file:

```
SQL> alter database add logfile member '/u02/oraredo/o18c/redo01b.rdo'
    to group 1;
```

Make certain you follow standards with regard to the location and names of any newly added redo log files.

Removing Online Redo Log Files from a Group

Occasionally, you may need to remove a log file from a group. For example, your database may have experienced a failure with one member of a multiplexed group, and you want to remove the apostate member. First, make sure the log file you want to drop is not in the current group:

```
SELECT a.group#, a.member, b.status, b.archived, SUM(b.bytes)/1024/1024
mbytes
FROM v$logfile a, v$log b
WHERE a.group# = b.group#
GROUP BY a.group#, a.member, b.status, b.archived
ORDER BY 1, 2;
```

If you attempt to drop a log file that is in the group with the CURRENT status, you receive the following error:

```
ORA-01623: log 2 is current log for instance o18c (thread 1) - cannot drop
```

If you are attempting to drop a member from the current online redo log group, then force a switch, as follows:

```
SQL> alter system switch logfile;
```

Use the `ALTER DATABASE DROP LOGFILE MEMBER` statement log group. You do not need to specify the group number because you are removing a specific file:

```
SQL> alter database drop logfile member '/u01/oraredo/o18c/redo04a.rdo';
```

You also cannot drop the last remaining log file of a group. A group must contain at least one log file. If you attempt to drop the last remaining log file of a group, you receive the following error:

```
ORA-00361: cannot remove last log member ...
```

Moving or Renaming Redo Log Files

Sometimes you need to move or rename online redo log files. For example, you may have added some new mount points to the system, and you want to move the online redo logs to the new storage. You can use two methods to accomplish this task:

- Add the new log files in the new location and drop the old log files.

- Physically rename the files from the OS.

If you cannot afford any downtime, consider adding new log files in the new location and then dropping the old log files. See the section "Adding Online Redo Log Groups," earlier in this chapter, for details on how to add a log group. See also the section "Resizing and Dropping Online Redo Log Groups," earlier in this chapter, for details on how to drop a log group.

Alternatively, you can physically move the files from the OS. You can do this with the database open or closed. If your database is open, ensure that the files you move are not part of the current online redo log group (because those are actively written to by the log-writer background process). It is dangerous to try to do this task while your database is open because on an active system, the online redo logs may be switching at a rapid rate, which creates the possibility of attempting to move a file while it is being switched to be the current online redo log. Therefore, I recommend that you only try to do this while your database is closed.

The next example shows how to move the online redo log files with the database shut down. Here are the steps:

1. Shut down your database:

    ```
    SQL> shutdown immediate;
    ```

2. From the OS prompt, move the files. This example uses the mv command to accomplish this task:

```
$ mv /u02/oraredo/o18c/redo02b.rdo /u01/oraredo/o18c/redo02b.rdo
```

3. Start up your database in mount mode:

```
SQL> startup mount;
```

4. Update the control file with the new file locations and names:

```
SQL> alter database rename file '/u02/oraredo/o18c/redo02b.rdo'
        to '/u01/oraredo/o18c/redo02b.rdo';
```

5. Open your database:

```
SQL> alter database open;
```

You can verify that your online redo logs are in the new locations by querying the V$LOGFILE view. I recommend as well that you switch your online redo logs several times and then verify from the OS that the files have recent timestamps. Also check the alert.log file for any pertinent errors.

Controlling the Generation of Redo

For some types of applications, you may know beforehand that you can easily re-create the data. An example might be a data warehouse environment in which you perform direct path inserts or use SQL*Loader to load data. In these scenarios you can turn off the generation of redo for direct path loading. You use the N OLOGGING clause to do this:

```
create tablespace inv_mgmt_data
  datafile '/u01/dbfile/o12c/inv_mgmt_data01.dbf' size 100m
  extent management local
  uniform size 128k
  segment space management auto
  nologging;
```

If you have an existing tablespace and want to alter its logging mode, use the ALTER TABLESPACE statement:

```
SQL> alter tablespace inv_mgmt_data nologging;
```

You can confirm the tablespace logging mode by querying the DBA_TABLESPACES view:

```
SQL> select tablespace_name, logging from dba_tablespaces;
```

The generation of redo logging cannot be suppressed for regular INSERT, UPDATE, and DELETE statements. For regular data manipulation language (DML) statements, the NOLOGGING clause is ignored. The NOLOGGING clause does apply, however, to the following types of DML:

- Direct path INSERT statements

- Direct path SQL*Loader

The NOLOGGING clause also applies to the following types of DDL statements:

- CREATE TABLE ... AS SELECT (NOLOGGING only affects the initial create, not subsequent regular DML, statements against the table)

- ALTER TABLE ... MOVE

- ALTER TABLE ... ADD/MERGE/SPLIT/MOVE/MODIFY PARTITION

- CREATE INDEX

- ALTER INDEX ... REBUILD

- CREATE MATERIALIZED VIEW

- ALTER MATERIALIZED VIEW ... MOVE

- CREATE MATERIALIZED VIEW LOG

- ALTER MATERIALIZED VIEW LOG ... MOVE

Be aware that if redo isn't logged for a table or index, and you have a media failure before the object is backed up, then you cannot recover the data; you receive an ORA-01578 error, indicating that there is logical corruption of the data.

Note   You can also override the tablespace level of logging at the object level. For example, even if a tablespace is specified as NOLOGGING, you can create a table with the LOGGING clause.

Implementing Archivelog Mode

Recall from the discussion earlier in this chapter that archive redo logs are created only if your database is in archivelog mode. If you want to preserve your database transaction history to facilitate point-in-time and other types of recovery, you need to enable that mode.

In normal operation, changes to your data generate entries in the database redo log files. As each online redo log group fills up, a log switch is initiated. When a log switch occurs, the log-writer process stops writing to the most recently filled online redo log group and starts writing to a new online redo log group. The online redo log groups are written to in a round-robin fashion—meaning the contents of any given online redo log group will eventually be overwritten. Archivelog mode preserves redo data for the long term by employing an archiver background process to copy the contents of a filled online redo log to what is termed an *archive redo log file*. The trail of archive redo log files is crucial to your ability to recover the database with all changes intact, right up to the precise point of failure.

Making Architectural Decisions

When you implement archivelog mode, you also need a strategy for managing the archived log files. The archive redo logs consume disk space. If left unattended, these files will eventually use up all the space allocated for them. If this happens, the archiver cannot write a new archive redo log file to disk, and your database will stop processing transactions. At that point, you have a hung database. You then need to intervene manually by creating space for the archiver to resume work. For these reasons, there are several architectural decisions you must carefully consider before you enable archiving:

- Where to place the archive redo logs and whether to use the fast recovery area to store them

- How to name the archive redo logs

- How much space to allocate to the archive redo log location

- How often to back up the archive redo logs

- When it's okay to permanently remove archive redo logs from disk

- How to remove archive redo logs (e.g., have RMAN remove the logs, based on a retention policy)

- Whether multiple archive redo log locations should be enabled

- When to schedule the small amount of downtime that is required (if a production database)

As a general rule of thumb, you should have enough space in your primary archive redo location to hold at least a day's worth of archive redo logs. This lets you back them up on a daily basis and then remove them from disk after they have been backed up.

If you decide to use a fast recovery area (FRA) for your archive redo log location, you must ensure that it contains sufficient space to hold the number of archive redo logs generated between backups. Keep in mind that the FRA typically contains other types of files, such as RMAN backup files, flashback logs, and so on. If you use an FRA, be aware that the generation of other types of files can potentially impact the space required by the archive redo log files. There are parameters that can be set to manage the FRA and provide a way to resize the space for recovery in order for the database to continue instead of having to increase space on the file system.

The parameters DB_RECOVERY_FILE_DEST and DB_RECOVERY_FILE_DEST_SIZE set the file location for the FRA and the size of the space to be used by the database. These can also prevent one database filling up the space for other databases that might be on the same server. The ASM diskgroup FRA can be created to manage the space using ASM. `DB_RECOVERY_FILE_DEST = +FRA`, will allow the area to use the FRA diskgroup. Again, there are advantages of managing space behind the scene in a scenario that fills up space. Using these parameters along with ASM removes specific file systems and allows for more options to quickly address issues with archive logs and using the recovery areas. FRA is recommended for this since the parameters are dynamic and can will allow for changes to occur to prevent the database hanging. This should be included in the planning and architecting of the archive mode of the database.

You need a strategy for automating the backup and removal of archive redo log files. For user-managed backups, this can be implemented with a shell script that periodically copies the archive redo logs to a backup location and then removes them from the primary location. As you will see in later chapters, RMAN automates the backup and removal of archive redo log files.

If your business requirements are such that you must have a certain degree of high availability and redundancy, then you should consider writing your archive redo logs to more than one location. Some shops set up jobs to copy the archive redo logs periodically to a different location on disk or even to a different server.

Setting the Archive Redo File Location

Before you set your database mode to archiving, you should specifically instruct Oracle where you want the archive redo logs to be placed. You can set the archive redo log file destination with the following techniques:

- Set the LOG_ARCHIVE_DEST_N database initialization parameter.

- Implement FRA.

These two approaches are discussed in detail in the following sections.

Tip   If you do not specifically set the archive redo log location via an initialization parameter or by enabling the FRA, then the archive redo logs are written to a default location. For Linux/Unix, the default location is ORACLE_HOME/dbs. For Windows, the default location is ORACLE_HOME\database. For active production database systems, the default archive redo log location is rarely appropriate.

Setting the Archive Location to a User-Defined Disk Location (non-FRA)

If you are using an init<SID>.ora file, modify the file with an OS utility (such as vi). In this example the archive redo log location is set to /u01/oraarch/o18c:

```
log_archive_dest_1='location=/u01/oraarch/o18c'
log_archive_format='o12c_%t_%s_%r.arc'
```

In the prior line of code, my standard for naming archive redo log files includes the ORACLE_SID (in this example, o18c to start the string); the mandatory parameters %t, %s, and %r; and the string .arc, to end. I like to embed the name of the ORACLE_SID in the string to avoid confusion when multiple databases are housed on one server. I like to use the extension .arc to differentiate the files from other types of database files.

Tip   If you do not specify a value for LOG_ARCHIVE_FORMAT, Oracle uses a default, such as %t_%s_%r.dbf. One aspect of the default format that I do not like is that it ends with the extension .dbf, which is widely used for data files. This can cause confusion about whether a particular file can be safely removed because it is an old archive redo log file or should not be touched because it is a live data file. Most DBAs are reluctant to issue commands such as rm *.dbf for fear of accidentally removing live data files.

If you are using a spfile, use ALTER SYSTEM to modify the appropriate initialization variables:

```
SQL> alter system set log_archive_dest_1='location=/u01/oraarch/o18c'
scope=both;
SQL> alter system set log_archive_format='o12c_%t_%s_%r.arc' scope=spfile;
```

You can dynamically change the LOG_ARCHIVE_DEST_n parameters while your database is open. However, you have to stop and start your database for the LOG_ARCHIVE_FORMAT parameter to take effect.

RECOVERING FROM SETTING A BAD SPFILE PARAMETER

Take care not to set the LOG_ARCHIVE_FORMAT to an invalid value; for example,

```
SQL> alter system set log_archive_format='%r_%y_%dk.arc' scope=spfile;
```

If you do so, when you attempt to stop and start your database, you won't even get to the nomount phase (because the spfile contains an invalid parameter):

```
SQL> startup nomount;
ORA-19905: log_archive_format must contain %s, %t and %r
```

In this situation, if you are using a spfile, you cannot start your instance. You have a couple of options here. If you are using RMAN and are backing up the spfile, then restore the spfile from a backup.

If you are not using RMAN, you can also try to edit the spfile directly with an OS editor (such as vi), but Oracle doesn't recommend or support this.

The alternative is to create an init.ora file manually from the contents of the spfile. First, rename the spfile that contains a bad value:

```
$ cd $ORACLE_HOME/dbs
$ mv spfile<SID>.ora spfile<SID>.old
```

In SQLPlus create the init.ora file from the spfile.

```
SQL> create pfile=inito18c.ora from spfile;
```

Then, open the pfile with a text editor, such as vi:

```
$ vi inito18c.ora
```

Modify the bad parameter to contain a valid value. Exit out of the pfile. You should now be able to start up your database using the pfile. Then you can copy the pfile into a new spf

```
SQL> create spfile from pfile;
```

Then you can start up the database using the fixed spfile.

When you specify LOG_ARCHIVE_FORMAT, you must include %t (or %T), %s (or %S), and d% in the format string. Table 5-4 lists the valid variables you can use with the LOG_ARCHIVE_FORMAT initialization parameter.

Table 5-4. *Valid Variables for the Log Archive Format String*

Format String	Meaning
%s	Log sequence number
%S	Log sequence number padded to the left with zeros
%t	Thread number
%T	Thread number padded to the left with zeros
%a	Activation ID
%d	Database ID
%r	Resetlogs ID required to ensure uniqueness across multiple incarnations of the database

You can view the value of the LOG_ARCHIVE_DEST_N parameter by running the following:

```
SQL> show parameter log_archive_dest
```

Here is a partial listing of the output:

```
NAME                                TYPE         VALUE
--------------------------------    ----------   --------------------------
log_archive_dest                    string
log_archive_dest_1                  string       location=/u01/oraarch/o18c
log_archive_dest_10                 string
```

You can enable up to 31 different locations for the archive redo log file destination. For most production systems, one archive redo log destination location is usually sufficient. If you need a higher degree of protection, you can enable multiple destinations. Keep in mind that when you use multiple destinations, the archiver must be able to write to at least one location successfully. If you enable multiple mandatory locations and set LOG_ARCHIVE_MIN_SUCCEED_DEST to be higher than 1, then your database may hang if the archiver cannot write to all mandatory locations.

You can check the details regarding the status of archive redo log locations via this query:

```
select
 dest_name
,destination
,status
,binding
from v$archive_dest;
```

Here is a small sample of the output:

```
DEST_NAME           DESTINATION                       STATUS     BINDING
------------------- -------------------------------   ---------  ---------
LOG_ARCHIVE_DEST_1  /u01/oraarch/o18c                 VALID      OPTIONAL
LOG_ARCHIVE_DEST_2                                     INACTIVE   OPTIONAL
```

Using the FRA for Archive Log Files

The FRA is an area on disk—specified via database initialization parameters—that can be used to store files, such as archive redo logs, RMAN backup files, flashback logs, and multiplexed control files and online redo logs. To enable the use of FRA, you must set two initialization parameters (in this order):

- DB_RECOVERY_FILE_DEST_SIZE specifies the maximum space to be used for all files that are stored in the FRA for a database.

- DB_RECOVERY_FILE_DEST specifies the base directory for the FRA.

When you create an FRA, you are not really creating anything—you are telling Oracle which directory to use when storing files that go in the FRA. For example, say 200GB of space are reserved on a mount point, and you want the base directory for the FRA to be /u01/fra. To enable the FRA, first set DB_RECOVERY_FILE_DEST_SIZE:

```
SQL> alter system set db_recovery_file_dest_size=200g scope=both;
```

Next, set the DB_RECOVERY_FILE_DEST parameter:

```
SQL> alter system set db_recovery_file_dest='/u01/fra' scope=both;
```

If you are using an init.ora file, modify it with an OS utility (such as vi) with the appropriate entries.

After you enable FRA, by default, Oracle writes archive redo logs to subdirectories in the FRA.

Note   If you've set the LOG_ARCHIVE_DEST_N parameter to be a location on disk, archive redo logs are not written to the FRA.

You can verify that the archive location is using FRA:

```
SQL> archive log list;
```

If archive files are being written to the FRA, you should see output like this:

```
Database log mode              Archive Mode
Automatic archival             Enabled
Archive destination            USE_DB_RECOVERY_FILE_DEST
```

You can display the directory associated with the FRA like this:

```
SQL> show parameter db_recovery_file_dest
```

When you first implement FRA, there are no subdirectories beneath the base FRA directory (specified with DB_RECOVERY_FILE_DEST). The first time Oracle needs to write a file to the FRA, it creates any required directories beneath the base directory. For example, after you implement FRA, if archiving for your database is enabled, then the first time a log switch occurs, Oracle creates the following directories beneath the base FRA directory:

```
<SID>/archivelog/<YYYY_MM_DD>
```

Each day that archive redo logs are generated results in a new directory's being created in the FRA, using the directory name format YYYY_MM_DD. Archive redo logs written to the FRA use the OMF format naming convention (regardless of whether you've set the LOG_ARCHIVE_FORMAT parameter).

If you want archive redo logs written to both FRA and a non-FRA location, you can enable that, as follows:

```
SQL> alter system set log_archive_dest_1='location=/u01/oraarch/o18c';
SQL> alter system set log_archive_dest_2='location=USE_DB_RECOVERY_FILE_DEST';
```

Enabling Archivelog Mode

After you have set the location for your archive redo log files, you can enableSYS (or a user with the SYSDBA privilege) and do the following:

```
$ sqlplus / as sysdba
SQL> shutdown immediate;
SQL> startup mount;
SQL> alter database archivelog;
SQL> alter database open;
```

You can confirm archivelog mode with this query:

```
SQL> archive log list;
```

You can also confirm it as follows:

```
SQL> select log_mode from v$database;

LOG_MODE
------------
ARCHIVELOG
```

Disabling Archivelog Mode

Usually, you don't disable archivelog mode for a production database. However, you may be doing a big data load and want to reduce any overhead associated with the archiving process, and so you want to turn off archivelog mode before the load begins and then re-enable it after the load. If you do this, be sure you make a backup as soon as possible after re-enabling archiving.

To disable archiving, do the following as SYS (or a user with the SYSDBA privilege):

```
$ sqlplus / as sysdba
SQL> shutdown immediate;
SQL> startup mount;
SQL> alter database noarchivelog;
SQL> alter database open;
```

You can confirm archivelog mode with this query:

```
SQL> archive log list;
```

You can also confirm the log mode, as follows:

```
SQL> select log_mode from v$database;

LOG_MODE
------------
NOARCHIVELOG
```

Reacting to a Lack of Disk Space in Your Archive Log Destination

The archiver background process writes archive redo logs to a location that you specify. If, for any reason, the archiver process cannot write to the archive location, your database hangs. Any users attempting to connect receive this error:

```
ORA-00257: archiver error. Connect internal only, until freed.
```

As a production-support DBA, you never want to let your database get into that state. Sometimes, unpredictable events happen, and you have to deal with unforeseen issues.

Note   DBAs who support production databases have a mindset completely different from that of architect DBAs. Getting new ideas or learning about new technologies is a perfect time to work together and communicate what might work or not work in your environment. Set up time outside of troubleshooting with production DBAs and architects to plan and set strategies for the environment.

In this situation your database is as good as down and completely unavailable. To fix the issue, you have to act quickly:

- Move files to a different location.

- Compress old files in the archive redo log location.

- Permanently remove old files.

- Switch the archive redo log destination to a different location (this can be changed dynamically, while the database is up and running).

- If using FRA, increase the space allocation for DB_RECOVERY_FILE_DEST_SIZE.

- If using FRA, change the destination to different location in the parameter DB_RECOVERY_FILE_DEST.

- RMAN backup and delete the archive log files.

- Remove expired files from the directory using RMAN.

Moving files is usually the quickest and safest way to resolve the archiver error along with increasing the allocation or directory with the DB_RECOVERY_FILE_DEST parameters. You can use an OS utility such as mv to move old archive redo logs to a different location. If they are needed for a subsequent restore and recovery, you can let the recovery process know about the new location. Be careful not to move an archive redo log that is currently being written to. If an archived redo log file appears in V$ARCHIVED_LOG, that means it has been completely archived.

You can use an OS utility such as gzip to compress archive redo log files in the current archive destination. If you do this, you have to remember to uncompress any files that may be later needed for a restore and recovery. Be careful not to compress an archive redo log that is currently being written to.

Another option is to use an OS utility such as rm to remove archive redo logs from the disk permanently. This approach is dangerous because you may need those archive redo logs for a subsequent recovery. If you do remove archive redo log files, and you don't have a backup of them, you should make a full backup of your database as soon as possible. Using RMAN to back up and delete the files is a much safer approach and assures that recovery is possible until another backup is performed. Again, this approach is risky and should only be done as a last resort; if you delete archive redo logs that haven't been backed up, then you chance not being able to perform a complete recovery.

If another location on your server has plenty of space, you can consider changing the location to which the archive redo logs are being written. You can perform this operation while the database is up and running; for example,

```
SQL> alter system set log_archive_dest_1='location=/u02/oraarch/o18c';
```

After you've resolved the issue with the primary location, you can switch back the original location.

Note   When a log switch occurs, the archiver determines where to write the archive redo logs, based on the current FRA setting or a LOG_ARCHIVE_DEST_N parameter. It doesn't matter to the archiver if the destination has recently changed.

When the archive redo log file destination is full, you have to scramble to resolve it. This is why a good deal of thought should precede enabling archiving for 24-7 production databases.

For most databases, writing the archive redo logs to one location is sufficient. However, if you have any type of disaster recovery or high-availability requirement, then you should write to multiple locations. Sometimes, DBAs set up a job to back up the archive redo logs every hour and copy them to an alternate location or even to an alternate server.

Backing Up Archive Redo Log Files

Depending on your business requirements, you may need a strategy for backing up archive redo log files. Minimally, you should back up any archive redo logs generated during a backup of a database in archivelog mode. Additional strategies may include the following:

- Periodically copying archive redo logs to an alternate location and then removing them from the primary destination

- Copying the archive redo logs to tape and then deleting them from disk

- Using two archive redo log locations

- Using Data Guard for a robust disaster recovery solution

Keep in mind that you need all archive redo logs generated since the begin time of the last good backup to ensure that you can completely recover your database. Only after you are sure you have a good backup of your database should you consider removing archive redo logs that were generated prior to the backup.

If you are using RMAN as a backup and recovery strategy, then you should use RMAN to back up the archive redo logs. Additionally, you should specify an RMAN retention policy for these files and have RMAN remove the archive redo logs only after the retention policy requirements are met (e.g., back up files at least once before removing from disk) (see Chapter 18 for details on using RMAN) .

Summary

This chapter described how to configure and manage control files and online redo log files and enable archiving. Control files and online redo logs are critical database files; a normally operating database cannot function without them.

Control files are small binary files that contain information about the structure of the database. Any control files specified in the parameter file must be available in order for you to mount the database. If a control file becomes unavailable, then your database will cease operating with the next log switch or needed write to the control file until you resolve the issue. I highly recommend that you configure your database with at least three control files. If one control file becomes unavailable, you can replace it with a copy of a good existing control file. It is critical that you know how to configure, add, and remove these files.

Online redo logs are crucial files that record the database's transaction history. If you have multiple instances connected to one database, then each instance generates its own redo thread. Each database must be created with two or more online redo log groups. You can operate a database with each group's having just one online redo log member. However, I highly recommend that you create your online redo log groups with two members in each group. If an online redo log has at least one member that can be written to, your database will continue to function. If all members of an online redo log group are unavailable, then your database will cease to operate. As a DBA you must be extremely proficient in creating, adding, moving, and dropping these critical database files. Using storage options such as flash will allow for faster writes to the redo logs. Solid state disks might not provide faster writes, which does not make them the ideal choice for redo logs.

Archiving is the mechanism for ensuring you have all the transactions required to recover the database. Once enabled, the archiver needs to successfully copy the online redo log after a log switch occurs. If the archiver cannot write to the primary archive destination, then your database will hang. Therefore, you need to map out carefully the amount of disk space required and how often to back up and subsequently remove these files.

Using Fast Recovery Area (FRA) provides additional ways to manage the archive logs and allows for some flexibility in planning for growth and sizing of the disk needed for the archive logs.

The chapters up to this point in the book have covered tasks such as installing the Oracle software; creating databases; and managing tablespaces, data files, control files, online redo log files, and archiving. The next several chapters concentrate on how to configure a database for application use and include topics such as creating users and database objects.

CHAPTER 6

Users and Basic Security

After you have installed the binaries, implemented a database, and created tablespaces, the next logical task is to secure your database and begin creating new users. When you create a database, several default user accounts are created by default. As a DBA, you must be aware of these accounts and how to manage them. The default accounts are frequently the first place a hacker will look to gain access to a database; therefore, you must take precautions to secure these users. Depending on what options you install and which version of the database you implement, there could be 20 or more default accounts.

As applications and users need access to the database, you'll need to create and manage new accounts. This includes choosing an appropriate authentication method, implementing password security, and allocating privileges to users. These topics are discussed in detail in this chapter.

Managing Default Users

As stated, when you create a database, Oracle creates several default database users. In earlier releases, these default users would either set a default password or take input from database creation. With Oracle 18c, all of the default accounts are locked on installation except for SYS and SYSTEM. Passwords can be set for each one or unlocked on a custom basis; however, it would be recommended only to unlock the accounts that are absolutely needed. As one of the steps of the dbca, all of the accounts are listed and available to be changed instead of just the SYS and SYSTEM accounts, seen in Figure 6-1.

193

© Michelle Malcher and Darl Kuhn 2019
M. Malcher and D. Kuhn, *Pro Oracle Database 18c Administration*,
https://doi.org/10.1007/978-1-4842-4424-1_6

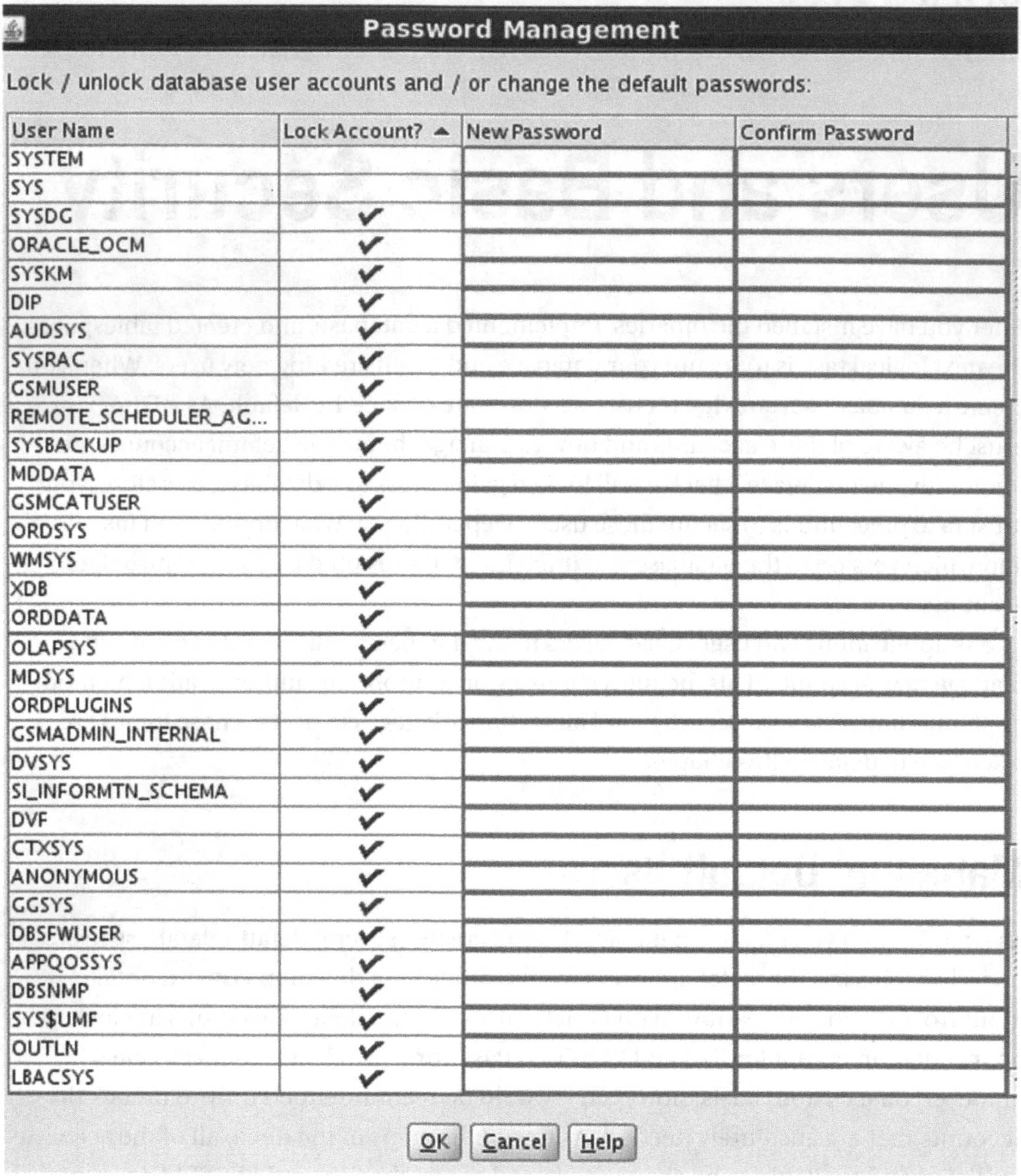

	Password Management		
Lock / unlock database user accounts and / or change the default passwords:			
User Name	**Lock Account? ▲**	**New Password**	**Confirm Password**
SYSTEM			
SYS			
SYSDG	✔		
ORACLE_OCM	✔		
SYSKM	✔		
DIP	✔		
AUDSYS	✔		
SYSRAC	✔		
GSMUSER	✔		
REMOTE_SCHEDULER_AG...	✔		
SYSBACKUP	✔		
MDDATA	✔		
GSMCATUSER	✔		
ORDSYS	✔		
WMSYS	✔		
XDB	✔		
ORDDATA	✔		
OLAPSYS	✔		
MDSYS	✔		
ORDPLUGINS	✔		
GSMADMIN_INTERNAL	✔		
DVSYS	✔		
SI_INFORMTN_SCHEMA	✔		
DVF	✔		
CTXSYS	✔		
ANONYMOUS	✔		
GGSYS	✔		
DBSFWUSER	✔		
APPQOSSYS	✔		
DBSNMP	✔		
SYS$UMF	✔		
OUTLN	✔		
LBACSYS	✔		

OK   Cancel   Help

Figure 6-1. Default accounts and password management

The specific users that are created vary by database version. If you have just created your database, you can view the default user accounts, as follows:

```
SQL> select username from dba_users order by 1;
```

Here is a partial listing of some default database user accounts:

```
USERNAME
--------------------------------------------------------------------------
ANONYMOUS
APPQOSSYS
AUDSYS
DBSNMP
DIP
GSMADMIN_INTERNAL
GSMCATUSER
GSMUSER
ORACLE_OCM
OUTLN
SYS
SYSTEM
...
```

What DBAs find frustrating about the prior list is that it is hard to keep track of what the default accounts are and if they're really required. Some DBAs may be tempted to drop default accounts so as not to clutter up the database. I would not advise that. It is safer to change passwords and lock these accounts (as shown in the next section). If you drop an account, it can be difficult to figure out exactly how it was originally created, whereas if you lock an account, you can simply unlock it to reactivate it.

Note   If you are working in a pluggable database environment, you can view all users while connected as a privileged account to the root container by querying CDB_USERS. Unless otherwise noted in this chapter, the queries assume that you are not working in a pluggable environment (and that you are therefore using the DBA-level views). If you are in a pluggable environment, to view information across all pluggable databases, you'll need to use the CDB level views while connected to the root container.

SYS VS. SYSTEM

Oracle novices sometimes ask, "What's the difference between the SYS and SYSTEM schemas?" The SYS schema is the superuser of the database; owns all internal data dictionary objects; and is used for tasks such as creating a database, starting or stopping the instance, backup and recovery, and adding or moving data files. These types of tasks typically require the SYSDBA or SYSOPER role. Security for these roles is often controlled through access to the OS account owner of the Oracle software. Additionally, security for these roles can be administered via a password file, which allows remote client/server access. Starting with 12c the SYS account could also be locked in some databases. Locking the account prevented unauthorized access from the server and another OS account but SYSDBA will need to be granted to an authorized user first. Even though locking the SYS account will prevent a shared default account from being used, there are some options or systems that might require SYS to remained unlocked. The password should be managed appropriately and locked down, as with other highly privileged accounts.

In contrast, the SYSTEMaccount is not very special. It is just an account that has been granted the DBA role. Many shops lock the SYSTEM schema after database creation and never use it because it is often the first schema a hacker will try to access when attempting to break into a database.

Rather than risking an easily guessable entry point to the database, privileged users should be granted the role directly or as part of their security group. Another account might be used for automated jobs and granted the DBA role for administrative tasks. Tasks such as creating users, changing passwords, and granting database privileges are available through other APIs to manage privileges instead of having these highly privileged accounts in the database. It is normally a requirement that auditing shows which DBA logged on and when, then create a separate privileged account for each DBA on the team (and, in turn, on database auditing). I have normally had one account for regular use and a separate privileged account that was granted the privileges needed to perform tasks as the DBA.

Locking Accounts and Expiring Passwords

To begin securing your database, you should minimally change the password for every default account and then lock any accounts that you are not using. As already discussed, this happens now by default in the database, but when performing upgrades there might be other default accounts that come with older versions and should be locked after changing passwords. Locking an account means that a user won't be able to access it unless a DBA explicitly unlocks it. Also consider having policies that change the password for each account. Expiring the password means that when a user first attempts to access an account, that user will be forced to change the password, but it does not require the current password, so it is better to change passwords and lock the accounts.

After creating a database, I usually lock every default account and change their passwords; I unlock default users only as they are needed. The following script generates the SQL statements:

```
SQL> alter user <username> identified by <new password>;
SQL> select
  'alter user ' || username || ' account lock;'
from dba_users;
```

A locked user can only be accessed by altering the user to an unlocked state; for example,

```
SQL> alter user outln account unlock;
```

A user with an expired password is prompted for a new password when first connecting to the database as that user. When connecting to a user, Oracle checks to see if the current password is expired and, if so, prompts the user, as follows:

```
ORA-28001: the password has expired
Changing password for ...
New password:
```

After entering the new password, the user is prompted to enter it again:

```
Retype new password:
Password changed
Connected.
```

Using a password vault would allow you to change the passwords first and then lock the accounts. If you need to use one of the default accounts, the account can be unlocked and the password pulled from the password vault or changed again by the security administrator.

Note   You can lock the SYS account, but this has no influence on your ability to connect as the SYS user through OS authentication or when using a password file.

There is no `alter user <user_name> password unexpire` command. To unexpire a password, you simply need to change it. The user can change the password (as demonstrated in the prior bits of code), or, as a DBA, you can change the password for a user:

```
SQL> alter user <username> identified by <new password>;
```

Identifying DBA-Created Accounts

If you have inherited a database from another DBA, then sometimes it is useful to determine whether the DBA created a user or if a user is a default account created by Oracle. As mentioned earlier, usually several user accounts are created for you when you create a database. The number of accounts varies somewhat by database version and options installed. Run this query to display users that have been created by another DBA versus those created by Oracle (such as those created by default when the database is created):

```
select distinct u.username
,case when d.user_name is null then 'DBA created account'
 else 'Oracle created account'
 end
from dba_users     u
    ,default_pwd$ d
where u.username=d.user_name(+);
```

For default users, there should be a record in the DEFAULT_PWD$ view. So, if a user doesn't exist in DEFAULT_PWD$, then you can assume it is not a default account. Given that logic, another way to identify just the default users would be this:

```
select distinct(user_name)
from default_pwd$
where user_name in (select username from dba_users);
```

The prior queries are not 100 percent accurate, as there are users that exist in DEFAULT_PWD$ that can be created manually by a DBA (e.g., FOO). For example, in Oracle 18c, AUDSYS is a default account and does not have a row in DEFAULT_PWD$. Having said that, the prior queries do provide a starting point for separating the default accounts from ones created by you (or another DBA).

Note   The DEFAULT_PWD$ view is available starting with Oracle Database 11g. See MOS note 227010.1 for more details about guidelines on checking for default passwords. The current versions of Oracle require a different password to be used and no longer uses the default ones. New installations are not a problem, but upgrades might still have users with default passwords, and the upgrade is an optimal time to change the passwords and lock the accounts.

Checking Default Passwords

You should also check your database to determine whether any accounts are using default passwords. If you are using an Oracle Database 11g or higher, you can check the DBA_USERS_WITH_DEFPWD view whether any Oracle-created user accounts are still set to the default password:

```
SQL> select * from dba_users_with_defpwd;
```

If you are not using Oracle Database 11g or higher, then you have to check the passwords manually or use a script. Listed next is a simple shell script that attempts to connect to the database, using default passwords:

```
#!/bin/bash
if [ $# -ne 1 ]; then
  echo "Usage: $0 SID"
  exit 1
fi
# Source oracle OS variables via oraset script.
# See chapter 2 for more details on setting OS variables.
. /etc/oraset $1
#
userlist="system sys dbsnmp dip oracle_ocm outln"
for u1 in $userlist
do
#
case $u1 in
system)
pwd=manager
```

```
cdb=$1
;;
sys)
pwd="change_on_install"
cdb="$1 as sysdba"
;;
*)
pwd=$u1
cdb=$1
esac
#
echo "select 'default' from dual;" | \
  sqlplus -s $u1/$pwd@$cdb | grep default >/dev/null
if [[ $? -eq 0 ]]; then
  echo "ALERT: $u1/$pwd@$cdb default password"
  echo "def pwd $u1 on $cdb" | mailx -s "$u1 pwd default" dkuhn@gmail.com
else
  echo "cannot connect to $u1 with default password."
fi
done
exit 0
```

If the script detects a default password, an e-mail is sent to the appropriate DBA. This script is just a simple example, the point being that you need some sort of mechanism for detecting default passwords. You can create your own script or modify the previous script to suit your requirements.

Creating Users

When you are creating a user, you need to consider the following factors:

- Username and authentication method

- Basic privileges

- Default permanent tablespace and space quotas

- Default temporary tablespace

These aspects of creating a user are discussed in the following sections.

Note   New in Oracle Database 12c, pluggable database environments have common users and local users. Common users span all pluggable databases within a container database. Local users exist within one pluggable database. See Chapter 22 for details on managing common users and local users.

Choosing a Username and Authentication Method

Pick a username that gives you an idea as to what application the user will be using. For example, if you have an inventory management application, a good choice for a username is INV_MGMT. Choosing a meaningful username helps identify the purpose of a user. This can be especially useful if a system is not documented properly.

Authentication is the method used to confirm that the user is authorized to use the account. Oracle supports a robust set of authentication methods:

- Database authentication (username and password stored in database)

- OS authentication

- Network authentication

- Global user authentication and authorization

- External service authentication

A simple, easy, and reliable form of authentication is through the database. In this form of authentication, the username and password are stored within the database. The password is not stored in plain text; it is stored in a secure, encrypted format. When connecting to the database, the user provides a username and password. The database checks the entered username and password against information stored in the database, and if there's a match, the user is allowed to connect to the database with the privileges associated with the account.

Another commonly implemented authentication method is through the OS. OS authentication means that if you can successfully log in to a server, then it is possible to establish a connection to a local database without providing username and password details. In other words, you can associate database privileges with an OS account or and associated OS group, or both. With 18c you can centrally manage your users in the Active Directory and integrate as user or global users in the database.

Examples of database and OS authentication and global users are discussed in the next two sections. If you have more sophisticated authentication requirements, then you should investigate network, global, or external service authentication. See the Oracle Database Security Guide and the Oracle Database Advanced Security Administrator's Guide, which can be freely downloaded from the Technology Network area of the Oracle web site (http://otn.oracle.com), for more details regarding these methods.

Creating a User with Database Authentication

Database authentication is established with the CREATE USER SQL statement. Creating users as a DBA, your account must have the CREATE USER system privilege. This example creates a user named HEERA with the password CHAYA and assigns the default permanent tablespace USERS, default temporary tablespace TEMP, and unlimited space quota on the USERS tablespace: USERS tablespace:

```
create user heera identified by chaya
default tablespace users
temporary tablespace temp
quota unlimited on users;
```

This creates a bare-bones schema that has no privileges to do anything in the database. To make the user useful, you must minimally grant it the CREATE SESSION system privilege:

```
SQL> grant create session to heera;
```

If the new schema needs to be able to create tables, you need to grant it additional privileges, such as CREATE TABLE:

```
SQL> grant create table to heera;
```

You can also use the GRANT...IDENTIFIED BY statement to create a user; for example,

```
grant create table, create session
to heera identified by chaya;
```

If the user doesn't exist, the account is created by the prior statement. If the user does exist, the password is changed to the one specified by the IDENTIFIED BY clause (and any specified grants are also applied).

> **Note**   Sometimes, when DBAs create a user, they'll assign default roles to a schema, such as CONNECT and RESOURCE. These roles contain system privileges, such as CREATE SESSION and CREATE TABLE (and several other privileges, which vary by database release). I recommend against doing this, because Oracle has stated that those roles may not be available in future releases. There are security and audit reasons to create specific roles that are needed and only grant those roles to users in the database.

Creating a User with OS Authentication

OS authentication assumes that if the user can log in to the database server, then database privileges can be associated with and derived from the OS user account. There are two types of OS authentication:

- Authentication through assigning specific OS roles to users (allows database privileges to be mapped to users)

- Authentication for regular database users via the IDENTIFIED EXTERNALLY clause

Authentication through OS roles is detailed in Chapter 2. This type of authentication is used by DBAs and allows them to connect to an OS account, such as oracle, and then connect to the database with SYSDBA privileges without having to specify a username and password.

After logging in to the database server, users created with the IDENTIFIED EXTERNALLY clause can connect to the database without having to specify a username or password. This type of authentication has some interesting advantages:

- Users with access to the server don't have to maintain a database username and password.

- Scripts that log in to the database don't have to use hard-coded passwords if executed by OS-authenticated users.

- Another database user can't hack into a user by trying to guess the username and password connection string. The only way to log in to an OS-authenticated user is from the OS.

When using OS authentication, Oracle prefixes the value contained in OS_AUTHENT_ PREFIX database initialization parameter to the OS user connecting to the database. The default value for this parameter is OPS$. Oracle strongly recommends that you set the OS_AUTHENT_PREFIX parameter to a null string; for example,

```
SQL> alter system set os_authent_prefix=" scope=spfile;
```

You have to stop and start your database for this modification to take effect. After you have set the OS_AUTHENT_PREFIX parameter, you can create an externally authenticated user. For instance, say you have an OS user named jsmith, and you want anybody with access to this OS user to be able to log in to the database without supplying a password. Use the CREATE EXTERNALLY statement to do this:

```
SQL> create user jsmith identified externally;
SQL> grant create session to jsmith;
```

Now, when jsmith logs in to the database server, this user can connect to SQL*Plus, as follows:

```
$ sqlplus /
```

No username or password is required, because the user has already been authenticated by the OS.

Configuring a Centrally Managed User

A centrally managed user is considered to be a user in one place, such as Active Directory or another LDAP service. The user can be managed for authentication and authorizations centrally, such that a user in Active Directory will have authentication managed via password or another type of key, and with the use of security groups, has the authorizations managed. If a user changes security groups, the authorization will change, and if the user is inactive in Active Directory, the user cannot authenticate to other applications or databases.

A user can be created in the database as a global user, which means that the database will reach out to Active Directory to get details about the user, first just to authenticate the password and then to verify the groups for authorization. The database is configured with a user to Active Directory and the ldap.ora file is updated with the information to use to authenticate against the Active Directory. Once this is configured, a user can be created with the following syntax:

```
SQL> create user jsmithdba identified globally as
'cn=jsmithdba group,ou=dbateam,dc=example,dc=com';
```

This allows Oracle database to recognize the user jsmithdba, which is in Active Directory, as a user that is allowed to access this database. The password is the same as the one in Active Directory, and the group can be used to map to a database role for permissions.

Identity management is important for an enterprise, and this allows a person to have roles and tasks based on their functions in the enterprise, and as those functions may change or no longer with the company, the account is then centrally managed instead of in each database. The Oracle cloud has an Identity Management that will configure roles and allow for users to be added, and they are managed as part of the Identity Management service and not in each database.

Note   Users can be imported into the Oracle Cloud so that each individual account does not have to be entered. Even if not importing all of the enterprise users, working in this way will allow for some consideration of which users should be migrated over and then verify the roles.

Understanding Schemas vs. Users

A schema is a collection of database objects (such as tables and indexes). A is not usually important, but there are some subtle differences.

When you log in to an Oracle database, you connect using a username and password. In this example, the user is INV_MGMT, and the password is f00bar:

```
SQL> connect inv_mgmt/f00bar
```

When you connect as a user, by default you can manipulate objects in the schema owned by the user with which you connected to the database. For example, when you attempt to describe a table, Oracle by default accesses the current user's schema. Therefore, there is no reason to preface the table name with the currently connected user (owner). Suppose the currently connected user is INV_MGMT. Consider the following DESCRIBE command:

```
SQL> describe inventory;
```

The prior statement is identical in function to the following statement:

```
SQL> desc inv_mgmt.inventory;
```

You can alter your current user's session to point at a different schema via the ALTER SESSION statement:

```
SQL> alter session set current_schema = hr;
```

This statement does not grant the current user (in this example, INV_MGMT) any extra privileges. The statement does instruct Oracle to use the schema qualifier HR for any subsequent SQL statements that reference database objects. If the appropriate privileges have been granted, the INV_MGMT user can access the HR user's objects without having to prefix the schema name to the object name.

Just as describe and desc are identical functions, describing the table EMPLOYEES is the same as using HR.EMPLOYEES.

```
SQL>  desc HR.EMPLOYEES
If alter session is set to HR, the results are the same:
SQL> desc EMPLOYEES
```

Note   Oracle does have a CREATE SCHEMA statement. Ironically, CREATE SCHEMA does not create a schema or a user. Rather, this statement provides a method for creating several objects (tables, views, grants) in a schema as one transaction. I have rarely seen the CREATE SCHEMA statement used, but it is something to be aware of in case you are in a shop that does use it.

Assigning Default Permanent and Temporary Tablespaces

Ensuring that users have a correct default permanent tablespace and temporary tablespace helps prevent issues of inadvertently filling up the SYSTEM or SYSAUX tablespaces, which could cause the database to become unavailable as well as engendering performance problems. The concern is that when you don't define a default permanent and temporary tablespace for your database, when you create a user, by default the SYSTEM tablespace is used. This is never a good thing.

As outlined in Chapter 2, you should establish a default permanent tablespace and temporary tablespace when creating the database. Also shown in Chapter 2 were the SQL statements for identifying and altering the default permanent tablespace and temporary tablespace. This ensures that when you create a user and don't specify default permanent and temporary tablespaces, the database defaults will be applied. The SYSTEM tablespace will therefore never be used for the default permanent and temporary tablespaces.

Having said that, the reality is that you'll most likely encounter databases that were not set up this way. When maintaining a database, you should verify the default permanent and temporary tablespace settings to make certain they meet your database standards. You can look at user information by selecting from the DBA_USERS view:

```
select
 username
,password
,default_tablespace
,temporary_tablespace
from dba_users;
```

Here is a small sample of the output:

USERNAME	PASSWORD	DEFAULT_TABLESPACE	TEMPORARY_TABLESPACE
JSMITH	EXTERNAL	USERS	TEMP
MV_MAINT		USERS	TEMP
AUDSYS		USERS	TEMP
GSMUSER		USERS	TEMP
XS$NULL		USERS	TEMP

None of your users, other than the SYS user, should have a default permanent tablespace of SYSTEM. You don't want any users other than SYS creating objects in the SYSTEM tablespace. The SYSTEM tablespace should be reserved for the SYS user's objects. If other users' objects existed in the SYSTEM tablespace, you would run the risk of filling up that tablespace and compromising the availability of your database. This also means if you are logging in with the SYS account, caution should be used to specific tablespaces when creating tables and other objects.

All your users should be assigned a temporary tablespace that has been created as type temporary. Usually, this tablespace is named TEMP (see Chapter 4 for more details).

If you find any users with inappropriate default tablespace settings, you can modify them with the ALTER USER statement:

```
SQL> alter user inv_mgmt default tablespace users temporary tablespace temp;
```

You never want any users with a temporary tablespace of SYSTEM. If a user has a temporary tablespace of SYSTEM, then any sort area for which the user requires temporary disk storage acquires extents in the SYSTEM tablespace. This can lead to the SYSTEM tablespace's filling up. You don't want this ever to occur, because a SYS schema's inability to acquire more space as its objects grow can lead to a nonfunctioning database. To check for users that have a temporary tablespace of SYSTEM, run this script:

```
SQL> select username from dba_users where temporary_tablespace='SYSTEM';
```

Typically, I use the script name creuser.sql when creating a user. This script uses variables that define the usernames, passwords, default tablespace name, and so on. For each environment in which the script is executed (development, test, quality assurance (QA), beta, production), you can change the ampersand variables, as required. For instance, you can use a different password and different tablespaces for each separate environment.

Here's an example creuser.sql script:

```
DEFINE cre_user=inv_mgmt
DEFINE cre_user_pwd=inv_mgmt_pwd
DEFINE def_tbsp=inv_data
DEFINE idx_tbsp=inv_index
DEFINE def_temp_tbsp=temp
DEFINE smk_ttbl=zzzzzzz
--
CREATE USER &&cre_user IDENTIFIED BY &&cre_user_pwd
DEFAULT TABLESPACE &&def_tbsp
TEMPORARY TABLESPACE &&def_temp_tbsp;
--
GRANT CREATE SESSION TO &&cre_user;
GRANT CREATE TABLE   TO &&cre_user;
--
ALTER USER &&cre_user QUOTA UNLIMITED ON &&def_tbsp;
ALTER USER &&cre_user QUOTA UNLIMITED ON &&idx_tbsp;
```

```
--
-- Smoke test
CONN &&cre_user/&&cre_user_pwd
CREATE TABLE &&smk_ttbl(test_id NUMBER) TABLESPACE &&def_tbsp;
CREATE INDEX &&smk_ttbl._idx1 ON &&smk_ttbl(test_id) TABLESPACE &&idx_tbsp;
INSERT INTO &&smk_ttbl VALUES(1);
DROP TABLE &&smk_ttbl;
```

SMOKE TEST

Smoke test is a term used in occupations such as plumbing, electronics, and software development. The term refers to the first check done after initial assembly or repairs in order to provide some level of assurance that the system works properly.

In plumbing, a smoke test forces smoke through the drainage pipes. The forced smoke helps quickly identify cracks or leaks in the system. In electronics, a smoke test occurs when power is first connected to a circuit. This sometimes produces smoke if the wiring is faulty.

In software development, a smoke test is a simple test of the system to ensure that it has some level of workability. Many managers have reportedly been seen to have smoke coming out their ears when the smoke test fails.

Modifying Passwords

Use the ALTER USER command to modify an existing user's password. This example changes the HEERA user's password to FOOBAR:

```
SQL> alter user HEERA identified by FOOBAR;
```

You can change the password of another account only if you have the ALTER USER privilege granted to your user. This privilege is granted to the DBA role. After you change a password for a user, any subsequent connection to the database by that user requires the password indicated by the ALTER USER statement.

In Oracle Database 11g or higher, when you modify a password, it is case sensitive. If you are using Oracle Database 10g or lower, the password is not case sensitive. The behavior with the case is set with a parameter SEC_CASE_SENSITIVE_LOGON and by default is TRUE. This is a parameter that should be checked that it was not changed to make sure that case-sensitive passwords are used unless needed for legacy applications that would be allowed until the password could be adjusted.

SQL*PLUS PASSWORD COMMAND

You can change the password for a user with the SQL*Plus PASSWORD command. After issuing the command, you are prompted for a new password: prompted for a new password:

```
SQL> passw heera
Changing password for heera
New password:
Retype new password:
Password changed
```

This method has the advantage of changing a password for a user without displaying the new password on the screen.

Schema Only Account

Previously without a schema only account, a DBA would have to log in as a different user to perform some create table scripts and issue grants. With 18c there are new Schema Only Accounts that can be created without passwords. This is for application schemas and holds all of the objects, so changes to these objects can be done if granted the privilege to access these accounts. These accounts have no privilege to log in directly to the database. So even without a password, there is no possibility to log in, and an error will occur.

```
SQL> create user app1 NO AUTHENTICATION;
```

In the dba_users table, this user will have an AUTHENTICATION_TYPE=NONE, and the password column will also be NULL. Schema only accounts can have privileges granted to create table and other objects; however, it cannot have any of the administrative privileges assigned to it. Even granting CONNECT SESSION to the schema only account will not allow you to log in to this schema account directly.

```
SQL> grant create session to app1;
Grant succeeded.
```

```
SQL> connect app1
Enter password:
ERROR:
ORA-01005: null password given; logon denied

Warning: You are no longer connected to ORACLE.
SQL> connect app1
Enter password:
ERROR:
ORA-01017: invalid username/password; logon denied
```

In order to perform the DDL statements in other accounts including the schema only accounts, a proxy connection can be made. Even before 18c, using a proxy connection was possible, and with the schema only account, it continues to be possible in order to perform any necessary code as the schema. Here is an example using jsmithdba as our account as we log in to the database, and the schema only account is app1.

```
SQL> alter user app1 grant connect through jsmithdba;
SQL> connect jsmithdba/password1
SQL> select sys_context('USERENV','SESSION_USER') as session_user,
     sys_context('USERENV','SESSION_SCHEMA') as session_schema,
     sys_context('USERENV','PROXY_USER') as proxy_id,
     user
        from dual;

SESSION_USER SESSION_SCHEMA      PROXY_ID       USER
---------------------- ------------------------------------- -------------
APP1         APP1                JSMITHDBA      APP1
```

This schema without a password can simply be used to application schemas and allow privileges to be granted to the objects or become this schema to run code. This is something to consider for application schemas; and, as we will see in the upcoming section on "Managing Privileges," grants and permissions can still be handled by roles for these objects.

Modifying Users

Sometimes you need to modify existing users for the following types of reasons:

- Change a user's password

- Lock or unlock a user

- Change the default permanent or temporary tablespace, or both

- Change a profile or role

- Change system or object privileges

- Modify quotas on tablespaces

Use the ALTER USER statement to modify users. Listed next are several SQL statements that modify a user. This example changes a user's password, using the IDENTIFIED BY clause:

```
SQL> alter user inv_mgmt identified by i2jy22a;
```

If you don't set a default permanent tablespace and temporary tablespace when you initially create the user, you can modify them after creation, as shown here:

```
SQL> alter user inv_mgmt default tablespace users temporary tablespace
temp;
```

This example locks a user account:

```
SQL> alter user inv_mgmt account lock;
```

And, this example alters the user's quota on the USERS tablespace:

```
SQL> alter user inv_mgmt quota 500m on users;
```

Note   Since ALTER USER is a highly privileged command and there are many reasons for using it, it might now fall in the hands of a security team to execute. There are other commands and procedures that can be written around this, and then the permissions are given to those to execute. Also, a database vault limits the ability to alter users and allows for the security teams to perform these actions.

Dropping Users

Before you drop a user, I recommend that you first lock the user. Locking the user prevents others from connecting to a locked database account. This allows you to better determine whether someone is using the account before it is dropped. Here is an example of locking a user:

```
SQL> alter user heera account lock;
```

Any user or application attempting to connect to this user now receives the following error:

```
ORA-28000: the account is locked
```

To view the users and lock dates in your database, issue this query:

```
SQL> select username, lock_date from dba_users;
```

To unlock an account, issue this command:

```
SQL> alter user heera account unlock;
```

Locking users is a very handy technique for securing your database and discovering which users are active.

Be aware that by locking a user, you are not locking access to a user's objects. For instance, if a USER_A has select, insert, update, and delete privileges on tables owned by USER_B, if you lock the USER_B account, USER_A can still issue DML statements against the objects owned by USER_B. To determine whether the objects are being used, see the auditing section of Chapter 20.

Tip   If a user's objects don't consume inordinate amounts of disk space, then before you drop the user, it is prudent to make a quick backup. See Chapter 13 for details on using Data Pump to back up a single user.

After you are sure that a user and its objects are not needed, use the DROP USER statement to remove a database account. This example drops the user HEERA:

```
SQL> drop user heera;
```

The prior command won't work if the user owns any database objects. Use the CASCADE clause to remove a user and have its objects dropped:

```
SQL> drop user heera cascade;
```

Note   The DROP USER statement may take a great deal of time to execute if the user being dropped owns a vast number of database objects. In these situations, you may want to consider dropping the user's objects before dropping the user.

---

schemas are also dropped. Oracle invalidates but doesn't drop any views, synonyms, procedures, functions, or packages that are dependent on the dropped user's objects. This is why it is important that application objects are put in a different schema instead of creating all of the objects under an individual account. If an application is being decommissioned, then backups and retention policies should also be considered. This is why it is important that application objects are put in a different schema instead of creating all of the objects under an individual account. If an application is being decommissioned, then backups and retention policies should also be considered.

Enforcing Password Security and Resource Limits

When you are creating users, sometimes requirements call for passwords to adhere to a set of security rules: for example, necessitating that the password be of a certain length and contain numeric characters. Also, when you set up database users, you may want to ensure that a certain user is not capable of consuming inordinate amounts of CPU resources.

You can use a database profile to meet these types of requirements. An Oracle profile is a database object that serves two purposes:

- Enforces password security settings
- Limits system resources that a user consumes

These topics are discussed in the next several sections.

Tip   Don't confuse a database profile with a SQL profile. A database profile is an object assigned to a user that enforces password security and constrains database resource usage, whereas a SQL profile is associated with a SQL statement and contains corrections to statistics that help the optimizer generate a more efficient execution plan.

Basic Password Security

When you create a user, if no profile is specified, the DEFAULT profile is assigned to the newly created user. To view the current settings for a profile, issue the following SQL:

```
select profile, resource_name, resource_type, limit
from dba_profiles
order by profile, resource_type;
```

Here is a partial listing of the output:

PROFILE	RESOURCE_NAME	RESOURCE_TYPE	LIMIT
DEFAULT	CONNECT_TIME	KERNEL	UNLIMITED
DEFAULT	PRIVATE_SGA	KERNEL	UNLIMITED
DEFAULT	COMPOSITE_LIMIT	KERNEL	UNLIMITED
DEFAULT	SESSIONS_PER_USER	KERNEL	UNLIMITED
DEFAULT	LOGICAL_READS_PER_SESSION	KERNEL	UNLIMITED
DEFAULT	CPU_PER_CALL	KERNEL	UNLIMITED
DEFAULT	IDLE_TIME	KERNEL	UNLIMITED
DEFAULT	LOGICAL_READS_PER_CALL	KERNEL	UNLIMITED
DEFAULT	CPU_PER_SESSION	KERNEL	UNLIMITED
DEFAULT	PASSWORD_LIFE_TIME	PASSWORD	180
DEFAULT	PASSWORD_GRACE_TIME	PASSWORD	7
DEFAULT	PASSWORD_REUSE_TIME	PASSWORD	UNLIMITED
DEFAULT	PASSWORD_REUSE_MAX	PASSWORD	UNLIMITED
DEFAULT	PASSWORD_LOCK_TIME	PASSWORD	1
DEFAULT	FAILED_LOGIN_ATTEMPTS	PASSWORD	10
DEFAULT	PASSWORD_VERIFY_FUNCTION	PASSWORD	NULL
DEFAULT	INACTIVE_ACCOUNT_TIME	PASSWORD	UNLIMITED

ORA_STIG_PROFILE	CONNECT_TIME	KERNEL	DEFAULT
ORA_STIG_PROFILE	IDLE_TIME	KERNEL	15
ORA_STIG_PROFILE	LOGICAL_READS_PER_CALL	KERNEL	DEFAULT
ORA_STIG_PROFILE	CPU_PER_CALL	KERNEL	DEFAULT
ORA_STIG_PROFILE	PASSWORD_GRACE_TIME	PASSWORD	5
ORA_STIG_PROFILE	PASSWORD_LOCK_TIME	PASSWORD	UNLIMITED
ORA_STIG_PROFILE	PASSWORD_VERIFY_FUNCTION	PASSWORD	ORA12C_STIG_VERIFY_FUNCTION
ORA_STIG_PROFILE	PASSWORD_REUSE_MAX	PASSWORD	10
ORA_STIG_PROFILE	PASSWORD_REUSE_TIME	PASSWORD	365
ORA_STIG_PROFILE	PASSWORD_LIFE_TIME	PASSWORD	60
ORA_STIG_PROFILE	FAILED_LOGIN_ATTEMPTS	PASSWORD	3
ORA_STIG_PROFILE	INACTIVE_ACCOUNT_TIME	PASSWORD	35

A profile's password restrictions are in effect as soon as the profile is assigned to a user. For example, from the previous output, if you have assigned the DEFAULT profile to a user, that user is allowed only ten consecutive failed login attempts before the user account is automatically locked by Oracle. See Table 6-1 for a description of the password profile security settings.

Tip   See MOS note 454635.1 for details on Oracle Database DEFAULT profile changes.

You can alter the DEFAULT profile to customize it for your environment. For instance, say you want to enforce a cap on the maximum number of days a password can be used. The next line of code sets the PASSWORD_LIFE_TIME of the DEFAULT profile to 300 days:

```
SQL> alter profile default limit password_life_time 300;
```

Table 6-1. *Password Security Settings*

Password Setting	Description	Default
FAILED_LOGIN_ATTEMPTS	Number of failed login attempts before the schema is locked	10 attempts
PASSWORD_GRACE_TIME	Number of days after a password expires that the owner can log in with an old password	7 days
PASSWORD_LIFE_TIME	Number of days a password is valid	180 days
PASSWORD_LOCK_TIME	Number of days an account is locked after FAILED_LOGIN_ATTEMPTS has been reached	1 day
PASSWORD_REUSE_MAX	Number of days before a password can be reused	Unlimited
PASSWORD_REUSE_TIME	Number of times a password must change before a password can be reused	Unlimited
PASSWORD_VERIFY_FUNCTION	Database function used to verify the password	Null
INACTIVE_ACCOUNT_TIME	Number of days a user who has not logged in to the account, and then will lock the account	Unlimited

The PASSWORD_REUSE_TIME and PASSWORD_REUSE_MAX settings must be used in conjunction. If you specify an integer for one parameter (it doesn't matter which one) and UNLIMITED for the other parameter, the then current password can never be reused.

If you want to specify that the DEFAULT profile password must be changed 10 times within 100 days before it can be reused, use a line of code similar to this:

```
SQL> alter profile default limit password_reuse_time 100 password_reuse_max 10;
```

Although using the DEFAULT profile is sufficient for many environments, you may need tighter security management. I recommend that you create custom security profiles and assign them to users, as required. For example, create a profile specifically for application users:

```
CREATE PROFILE SECURE_APP LIMIT
PASSWORD_LIFE_TIME 200
PASSWORD_GRACE_TIME 10
PASSWORD_REUSE_TIME 1
PASSWORD_REUSE_MAX 1
```

```
FAILED_LOGIN_ATTEMPTS 3
PASSWORD_LOCK_TIME 1
INACTIVE_ACCOUNT_TIME 60;
```

After you create the profile, you can assign it to users, as appropriate. The following SQL generates a SQL script, named `alt_prof_dyn.sql`, that you can use to assign the newly created profile to users:

```
set head off;
spo alt_prof_dyn.sql
select 'alter user ' || username || ' profile secure_app;'
from dba_users where username like '%APP%';
spo off;
```

Be careful when assigning profiles to application accounts that use the database. If you want to enforce that a password changes at a regular frequency, be sure you understand the impact on production systems. Passwords tend to get hard-coded into response files and code. Enforcing password changes in these environments can wreak havoc, as you try to chase down all the places where the password is referenced. If you don't want to enforce the periodic changing of the password, you can set `PASSWORD_LIFE_TIME` to a high value such as 10,000 or unlimited.

HAS THE PASSWORD EVER CHANGED?

When you are determining if a password is secure, it is useful to check to see whether the password for a user has ever been changed. If the password for a user has never been changed, this may be viewed as a security risk. This example performs such a check:

```
select
 name
,to_char(ctime,'dd-mon-yy hh24:mi:ss')
,to_char(ptime,'dd-mon-yy hh24:mi:ss')
,length(password)
from user$
where password is not null
and password not in ('GLOBAL','EXTERNAL')
and ctime=ptime;
```

In this script the CTIME column contains the timestamp of when the user was created. The PTIME column contains the timestamp of when the password was changed. If the CTIME and PTIME are identical, then the password has never changed.

Password Strength

A password that cannot be easily guessed is considered a strong password. The strength of a password can be quantified in terms of length, use of upper/lowercase, nondictionary-based words, numeric characters, and so on. For example, a password of L5K0ta890g would be considered strong, whereas a password of pass would be considered weak. There are a couple schools of thought on enforcing password strength:

- Use easily remembered passwords so that you don't have them written down or recorded in a file somewhere. Because the passwords are not sophisticated, they are not very secure.

- Enforce a level of sophistication (strength) for passwords. Such passwords are not easily remembered and thus must be recorded somewhere, which is not secure.

You may choose to enforce a degree of password strength because you think it is the most secure option. Or you may be required to enforce password security sophistication by your corporate security team (and thus have no choice in the matter). This section is not about debating which of the prior methods is preferable. Should you choose to impose a degree of strength for a password, this section describes how to enforce the rules.

You can enforce a minimum standard of password complexity by assigning a password verification function to a user's profile. Oracle supplies a default password verification function that you create by running the following script as the SYS schema:

```
SQL> @?/rdbms/admin/utlpwdmg
```

The prior script creates the following password verification functions:

- ora12c_verify_function (Oracle Database 12c and 18c)

- ora12c_strong_verify_function (very secure Oracle Database 12c and 18c)

- verify_function_11G (Oracle Database 11g)

- verify_function (Oracle Database 10g)

Once the password verify function has been created, you can use the ALTER PROFILE command to associate the password verify function with all users to which a given profile is assigned. There is no new password function for 18c, so the password complexity function is the same one that is used for 12c. For instance, in Oracle Database 18c, to set the password verify function of the DEFAULT profile, issue this command:

```
SQL> alter profile default limit PASSWORD_VERIFY_FUNCTION
ora12c_verify_function;
```

If, for any reason, you need to back out of the new security modifications, run this statement to disable the password function:

```
SQL> alter profile default limit PASSWORD_VERIFY_FUNCTION null;
```

When enabled, the password verification function ensures that users are correctly creating or modifying their passwords. The utlpwdmgsql script creates a function that checks a password to make certain it meets basic security standards, such as minimum password length and password not the same as username. You can verify that the new security function is in effect by attempting to change the password of a user to which the DEFAULT profile has been assigned. This example tries to change the password to less than the minimum length:

```
SQL> password
Changing password for HEERA
Old password:
New password:
Retype new password:
ERROR:
ORA-28003: password verification for the specified password failed
ORA-20001: Password length less than 8
```

Note   For Oracle Database 18c, 12c, and 11g, when using the standard password verify function, the minimum password length is eight characters. For Oracle Database 10g, the minimum length is four characters.

Keep in mind that it is possible to modify the code used to create the password verification function. For example, you can open and modify the script used to create this function:

```
$ vi $ORACLE_HOME/rdbms/admin/utlpwdmg.sql
```

If you feel that the Oracle-supplied verification function is too strong or overly restrictive, you can create your own function and assign the appropriate database profiles to it.

Note   As of Oracle Database 12g, the SEC_CASE_SENSITIVE_LOGON parameter has been deprecated. Setting this initialization parameter to FALSE allows you to make passwords case insensitive.

Limiting Database Resource Usage

As mentioned earlier, the password profile settings take effect as soon as you assign the profile to a user. Unlike password settings, kernel resource profile restrictions don't take effect until you set the RESOURCE_LIMIT initialization parameter to TRUE for your database; for example,

```
SQL> alter system set resource_limit=true scope=both;
```

To view the current setting of the RESOURCE_LIMIT parameter, issue this query:

```
SQL> select name, value from v$parameter where name='resource_limit';
```

When you create a user, if you don't specify a profile, then the DEFAULT profile is assigned to the user. You can modify the DEFAULT profile with the ALTER PROFILE statement. The next example modifies the DEFAULT profile to limit CPU_PER_SESSION to 240,000 (in hundredths of seconds):

```
SQL> alter profile default limit cpu_per_session 240000;
```

This limits any user with the DEFAULT profile to 2,400 seconds of CPU use. You can set various limits in a profile. Table 6-2 describes the database resource settings you can limit via a profile.

Table 6-2. *Database Resource Profile Settings*

Profile Resource	Meaning
COMPOSITE_LIMIT	Limit, based on a weighted-sum algorithm for these resources: CPU_PER_SESSION, CONNECT_TIME, LOGICAL_READS_PER_SESSION, and PRIVATE_SGA
CONNECT_TIME	Connect time, in minutes
CPU_PER_CALL	CPU time limit per call, in hundredths of seconds
CPU_PER_SESSION	CPU time limit per session, in hundredths of seconds
IDLE_TIME	Idle time, in minutes
LOGICAL_READS_PER_CALL	Blocks read per call
LOGICAL_READS_PER_SESSION	Blocks read per session
PRIVATE_SGA	Amount of space consumed in the shared pool
SESSIONS_PER_USER	Number of concurrent sessions

You can also create a custom profile and assign it to users via the CREATE PROFILE statement. You can then assign that profile to any existing database users. The following SQL statement creates a profile that limits resources, such as the amount of CPU an individual session can consume:

```
create profile user_profile_limit
limit
sessions_per_user 20
cpu_per_session 240000
logical_reads_per_session 1000000
connect_time 480
idle_time 120;
```

After you create a profile, you can assign it to a user. In the next example, the user HEERA is assigned USER_PROFILE_LIMIT:

```
SQL> alter user heera profile user_profile_limit;
```

Note   Oracle recommends that you use Database Resource Manager to manage database resource limits. However, for basic resource management needs, I find database profiles (implemented via SQL) to be an effective and easy mechanism for managing resource usage. If you have more sophisticated resource management requirements, investigate the Database Resource Manager feature.

As part of the CREATE USER statement, you can specify a profile other than DEFAULT:

```
SQL> create user heera identified by foo profile user_profile_limit;
```

When should you use database profiles? You should always take advantage of the password security settings of the DEFAULT profile. You can easily modify the default settings of this profile, as required by your business rules.

A profile's kernel resource limits are useful when you have power users who need to connect directly to the database and run queries. For example, you can use the kernel resource settings to limit the amount of CPU time a user consumes, which is handy when a user writes a bad query that inadvertently consumes excessive database resources.

Note   You can only assign one database profile to a user, so if you need to manage both password security and resource limits, make certain you set both within the same profile.

Managing Privileges

A database user must be granted privileges before the user can perform any tasks in the database. In Oracle, you assign privileges either by granting a specific privilege to a user or by granting the privilege to a role and then granting the role that contains the privilege to a user. There are two types of privileges: system privileges and object privileges. The following sections discuss these privileges in detail.

Assigning Database System Privileges

Database system privileges allow you to do tasks such as connecting to the database and creating and modifying objects. There are hundreds of different system privileges. You can view system privileges by querying the DBA_SYS_PRIVS view:

```
SQL> select distinct privilege from dba_sys_privs;
```

You can grant privileges to other users or roles. To be able to grant privileges, a user needs the GRANT ANY PRIVILEGE privilege or must have been granted a system privilege with ADMIN OPTION.

Use the GRANT statement to assign a system privilege to a user. For instance, minimally a user needs CREATE SESSION to be able to connect to the database. You grant this system privilege as shown:

```
SQL> grant create session to inv_mgmt;
```

Usually, a user needs to do more than just connect to the database. For instance, a user may need to create tables and other types of database objects. This example grants a user the CREATE TABLE and CREATE DATABASE LINK system privileges:

```
SQL> grant create table, create database link to inv_mgmt;
```

Same for the schema only account:

```
SQL> grant create table, create database link to app1;
```

If you need to take away privileges, use the REVOKE statement:

```
SQL> revoke create table from inv_mgmt;
```

Oracle has a feature that allows you to grant a system privilege to a user and also give that user the ability to administer a privilege. You do this with the WITH ADMIN OPTION clause:

```
SQL> grant create table to inv_mgmt with admin option;
```

I rarely use WITH ADMIN OPTION when granting privileges. Usually, a user with the DBA role is used to grant privileges, and that privilege is not generally meted out to non-DBA users in the database. This is because it would be hard to keep track of who assigned what system privileges, for what reason, and when. In a production environment, this would be untenable.

You can also grant system privileges to the PUBLIC user group (I don't recommend doing this). For example, you could grant CREATE SESSION to all users that ever need to connect to the database, as follows:

```
SQL> grant create session to public;
```

Now, every user that is created can automatically connect to the database. Granting system privileges to the PUBLIC user group is almost always a bad idea. As a DBA, one of your main priorities is to ensure that the data in the database are safe and secure. Granting privileges to the PUBLIC role is a sure way of not being able to manage who is authorized to perform specific actions within the database. In other words, do not grant system privileges to public.

Assigning Database Object Privileges

Database object privileges allow you to access and manipulate other users' objects. The types of database objects to which you can grant privileges include tables, views, materialized views, sequences, packages, functions, procedures, user-defined types, and directories. To be able to grant object privileges, one of the following must be true:

- You own the object.
- You have been granted the object privilege with GRANT OPTION.
- You have the GRANT ANY OBJECT PRIVILEGE system privilege.

This example grants object privileges (as the object owner) to the INV_MGMT_APP user:

```
SQL> grant insert, update, delete, select on registrations to inv_mgmt_app;
```

The GRANT ALL statement is equivalent to granting INSERT, UPDATE, DELETE, and SELECT to an object. The next statement is equivalent to the prior statement:

```
SQL> grant all on registrations to inv_mgmt_app;
```

You can also grant INSERT and UPDATE privileges to tables, at the column level. The next example grants INSERT privileges to specific columns in the INVENTORY table:

```
SQL> grant insert (inv_id, inv_name, inv_desc) on inventory to inv_mgmt_app;
```

If you want a user that is being granted object privileges to be able to subsequently grant those same object privileges to other users, then use the WITH GRANT OPTION clause:

```
SQL> grant insert on registrations to inv_mgmt_app with grant option;
```

Now, the INV_MGMT_APP user can grant insert privileges on the REGISTRATIONS table to other users.

I rarely use the WITH GRANT OPTION when granting object privileges. Allowing other users to propagate object privileges to users makes it hard to keep track of who assigned what object privileges, for what reason, when, and so on. In a production environment, this would be untenable. When you are managing a production environment, when problems arise, you need to know what changed, when, and for what reason.

You can also grant object privileges to the PUBLIC user group (I don't recommend doing this). For example, you could grant select privileges on a table to PUBLIC:

```
SQL> grant select on registrations to public;
```

Now, every user can select from the REGISTRATIONS table. Granting object privileges to the PUBLIC role is almost always a bad idea. As a DBA, one of your main priorities is to ensure that the data in the database are safe and secure. Granting object privileges to the PUBLIC role is a sure way of not being able to manage who can access what data in the database. Again, DO NOT grant object privileges to PUBLIC.

If you need to take away object privileges, use the REVOKE statement. This example revokes DML privileges from the INV_MGMT_APP user:

```
SQL> revoke insert, update, delete, select on registrations from inv_mgmt_app;
```

Grouping and Assigning Privileges

A role is a database object that allows you to group together system or object privileges, or both, in a logical manner so that you can assign those privileges in one operation to a user. Roles help you manage aspects of database security in that they provide a central object that has privileges assigned to it. You can subsequently assign the role to multiple users or other roles.

To create a role, connect to the database as a user that has the CREATE ROLE system privilege. Next, create a role and assign to it the system or object privileges that you

want to group together. This example uses the CREATE ROLE statement to create the
JR_DBA role:

```
SQL> create role jr_dba;
```

The next several lines of SQL grant system privileges to the newly created role:

```
SQL> grant select any table to jr_dba;
SQL> grant create any table to jr_dba;
SQL> grant create any view to jr_dba;
SQL> grant create synonym to jr_dba;
SQL> grant create database link to jr_dba;
```

Next, grant the role to any schema you want to possess those privileges:

```
SQL> grant jr_dba to lellison;
SQL> grant jr_dba to mhurd;
```

The users LELLISON and MHURD can now perform tasks such as creating synonyms
and views. To see the users to which a role is assigned, query the DBA_ROLE_PRIVS view:

```
SQL> select grantee, granted_role from dba_role_privs order by 1;
```

To see roles granted to your currently connected user, query from the USER_ROLE_
PRIVS view:

```
SQL> select * from user_role_privs;
```

To revoke a privilege from a role, use the REVOKE command:

```
SQL> revoke create database link from jr_dba;
```

Similarly, use the REVOKE command to remove a role from a user:

```
SQL> revoke jr_dba from lellison;
```

Note   Unlike other database objects, roles don't have owners. A role is defined by
the privileges assigned to it.

PL/SQL AND ROLES

If you work with PL/SQL, sometimes you get this error when attempting to compile a procedure or a function:

```
PL/SQL: ORA-00942: table or view does not exist
```

What's confusing is that you can describe the table:

```
SQL> desc app_table;
```

Why doesn't PL/SQL seem to be able to recognize the table? It is because PL/SQL requires that the owner of the package, procedure, or function be explicitly granted privileges to any objects referenced in the code. The owner of the PL/SQL code can't have obtained the grants through a role.

When confronted with this issue, try this as the owner of the PL/SQL code:

```
SQL> set role none;
```

Now, try to run a SQL statement that accesses the table in question:

```
SQL> select count(*) from app_table;
```

If you can no longer access the table, then you have been granted access through a role. To resolve the issue, explicitly grant access to any tables to the owner of the PL/SQL code (as the owner of the table):

```
SQL> connect owner/pass
SQL> grant select on app_table to proc_owner;
```

You should be able to connect as the owner of the PL/SQL code and successfully compile your code.

Roles are going to provide a way to grant the needed privileges for a function or tasks for the user to perform. As the user maps to security groups, the roles are the best way to manage the privileges. Role-based access to the different objects and system privileges are going to allow simple auditing to know who has a role and verify that there are not individual privileges being granted.

Summary

After you create a database, one of your first tasks is to secure any default user accounts. Default accounts are locked after database creation, and a valid approach is to open them only as they are required. Other approaches include changing or expiring the password, or both. After the default users' accounts have been secured, you are responsible for creating users that need access to the database. This often includes application users, DBAs, and developers.

You should consider using a secure profile for any users you create. Additionally, think about password security when creating users. Oracle provides a password function that enforces a certain level of password strength. I recommend that you use a combination of profiles and a password function as a first step in creating a secure database.

Schema only accounts and managing privileges in roles will tighten up the user security in the database and provide efficient ways to audit and verify that users are receiving the appropriate privileges.

As the databases ages, you need to maintain the user accounts. Usually, the requirements for database accounts change over time. You are responsible for ensuring that the correct system and object privileges are maintained for each account. With any legacy system, you'll eventually need to lock and drop users. Dropping unused accounts helps ensure that your environment is more secure and maintainable. Using centrally managed users simplifies these steps as the accounts have passwords changed and set to inactive in one directory instead of in every database. Also, the security groups serve as mappings to the database roles for privileges that match their job functions.

The next logical step after creating users is to create database objects. Chapter 7 deals with concepts related to table creation.

CHAPTER 7

Tables and Constraints

The previous chapters in this book covered topics that prepare you for the next logical step in creating database objects. For example, you need to install the Oracle binaries and create a database, tablespaces, and users before you start creating tables. Usually, the first objects created for an application are the tables, constraints, and indexes. This chapter focuses on the management of tables and constraints. The administration of indexes is covered in Chapter 8.

A table is the basic storage container for data in a database. You create and modify the table structure via DDL statements, such as CREATE TABLE and ALTER TABLE. You access and manipulate table data via DML statements (INSERT, UPDATE, DELETE, MERGE, SELECT).

Tip One important difference between DDL and DML statements is that with DML statements, you must explicitly issue a COMMIT or ROLLBACK to end the transaction.

A constraint is a mechanism for enforcing that data adhere to business rules. For example, you may have a business requirement that all customer IDs be unique within a table. In this scenario, you can use a primary key constraint to guarantee that all customer IDs inserted or updated in a CUSTOMER table are unique. Constraints inspect data as they're inserted, updated, and deleted to ensure that no business rules are violated.

This chapter deals with common techniques for creating and maintaining tables and constraints. Almost always, when you create a table, the table needs one or more constraints defined; therefore, it makes sense to cover constraint management along with tables. The first part of the chapter focuses on common table creation and maintenance tasks. The latter part of the chapter details constraint management.

© Michelle Malcher and Darl Kuhn 2019
M. Malcher and D. Kuhn, *Pro Oracle Database 18c Administration*,
https://doi.org/10.1007/978-1-4842-4424-1_7

Understanding Table Types

The Oracle database supports a vast and robust variety of table types. These various types are described in Table 7-1.

Table 7-1. *Oracle Table Type Descriptions*

Table Type	Description	Typical Use
Heap organized	The default table type and the most commonly used	Table type to use unless you have a specific reason to use a different type
Temporary	Session private data, stored for the duration of a session or transaction; space allocated in temporary segments	Program needs a temporary table structure to store and sort data; table is not required after program ends
Index organized	Data stored in a B-tree (balanced tree) index structure sorted by primary key	Table is queried mainly on primary key columns; provides fast random access
Partitioned	A logical table that consists of separate physical segments	Type used with large tables with millions of rows
External	Tables that use data stored in OS files outside the database	Type lets you efficiently access data in a file outside the database (such as a CSV file)
In-Memory External	Data that is not needed to load into Oracle storage and used for scanning as part of big data sets	Data that can be scanned for both RDBMS and Hadoop in-memory
Clustered	A group of tables that share the same data blocks	Type used to reduce I/O for tables that are often joined on the same columns
Hash clustered	A table with data that is stored and retrieved using a hash function	Reduces the I/O for tables that are mostly static (not growing after initially loaded)
Nested	A table with a column with a data type that is another table	Rarely used
Object	A table with a column with a data type that is an object type	Rarely used

This chapter focuses on the table types that are most often used: in particular, heap organized, index organized, and temporary tables. Partitioned tables are used extensively in data warehouse environments and are covered separately, in Chapter 12.

External tables are covered in Chapter 14. For details on table types not covered in this book, see the SQL Language Reference Guide, which is available for download from the Oracle Technology Network web site (http://otn.oracle.com).

Understanding Data Types

When creating a table, you must specify the columns names and corresponding data types. As a DBA you should understand the appropriate use of each data type. I've seen many application issues (performance and accuracy of data) caused by the wrong choice of data type. For instance, if a character string is used when a date data type should have been used, this causes needless conversions and headaches when attempting to do date math and reporting. Compounding the problem, after an incorrect data type is implemented in a production environment, it can be very difficult to modify data types, as this introduces a change that might possibly break existing code. Once you go wrong, it is extremely tough to recant and backtrack and choose the right course. It is more likely you will end up with hack upon hack as you attempt to find ways to force the ill-chosen data type to do the job that it was never intended to do.

Having said that, Oracle supports the following groups of data types:

- Character
- Numeric
- Date/Time
- RAW
- ROWID
- LOB
- JSON

A brief description and usage recommendation are provided in the following sections.

Note   Specialized data types, any types, spatial types, media types, and user-defined types, are not covered in this book. For more details regarding these data types, see the SQL Language Reference Guide available from the Oracle Technology Network web site (http://otn.oracle.com). JSON will be briefly covered as new features and enhancements as part of Oracle 18c.

Character

Use a character data type to store characters and string data. The following character data types are available in Oracle:

- VARCHAR2
- CHAR
- NVARCHAR2 and NCHAR

VARCHAR2

The VARCHAR2 data type is what you should use in most scenarios to hold character/string data. A VARCHAR2 only allocates space based on the number of characters in the string. If you insert a one-character string into a column defined to be VARCHAR2(30), Oracle will only consume space for the one character. The following example verifies this behavior:

```
SQL> create table d(d varchar2(30));
insert into d values ('a');
select dump(d) from d;
```

Here is a snippet of the output, verifying that only 1B has been allocated:

```
DUMP(D)
----------------
Typ=1 Len=1
```

Note   Oracle does have another data type, the VARCHAR (without the "2"). I only mention this because you are bound to encounter this data type at some point in your Oracle DBA career. Oracle currently defines VARCHAR as synonymous with VARCHAR2. Oracle strongly recommends that you use VARCHAR2 (and not VARCHAR), as Oracle's documentation states that VARCHAR might serve a different purpose in the future.

When you define a VARCHAR2 column, you must specify a length. There are two ways to do this: BYTE and CHAR. BYTE specifies the maximum length of the string in bytes, whereas CHAR specifies the maximum number of characters. For example, to specify a string that contains at the most 30B, you define it as follows:

```
varchar2(30 byte)
```

To specify a character string that can contain at most 30 characters, you define it as follows:

```
varchar2(30 char)
```

Many DBAs do not realize that if you do not specify either BYTE or CHAR, then the default length is calculated in bytes. In other words, VARCHAR2(30) is the same as VARCHAR2(30 byte).

In almost all situations, you are safer specifying the length using CHAR. When working with multibyte character sets, if you specified the length to be VARCHAR2(30 byte), you may not get predictable results, because some characters require more than 1 byte of storage. In contrast, if you specify VARCHAR2(30 char), you can always store 30 characters in the string, regardless of whether some characters require more than 1 byte.

CHAR

In almost every scenario, a VARCHAR2 is preferable to a CHAR. The VARCHAR2 data type is more flexible and space efficient than CHAR. This is because a CHAR is a fixed-length character field. If you define a CHAR(30) and insert a string that consists of only one character, Oracle will allocate 30B of space. This can be an inefficient use of space. If using CHAR, it does make sense to only use it if the size of the value will not change and is absolutely static. I have normally only used CHAR if the length was under 8, and the size was absolutely fixed. The following example verifies this behavior:

```
SQL> create table d(d char(30));
insert into d values ('a');
select dump(d) from d;
```

Here is a snippet of the output, verifying that 30B have been consumed:

```
DUMP(D)
----------------
Typ=96 Len=30
```

NVARCHAR2 and NCHAR

The NVARCHAR2 and NCHAR data types are useful if you have a database that was originally created with a single-byte, fixed-width character set, but sometime later you need to store multibyte character set data in the same database. You can use the NVARCHAR2 and NCHAR data types to support this requirement.

It is simpler to standardize with use of VARCHAR2 and provide enough length to handle the multibyte characters or use the length in character instead of using NVARCHAR2 and NCHAR.

Note   For Oracle Database 11g and lower, 4,000 was the largest size allowed for a VARCHAR2 or NVARCHAR2 data type. In Oracle Database 12c and higher, you can specify up to 32,767 characters in a VARCHAR2 or NVARCHAR2 data type. Prior to 12c, if you wanted to store character data larger greater than 4,000 characters, the logical choice was a CLOB (see the section "LOB," later in this chapter, for more details).

Numeric

Use a numeric data type to store data that you will potentially need to use with mathematic functions, such as SUM, AVG, MAX, and MIN. Never store numeric information in a character data type. When you use a VARCHAR2 to store data that are inherently numeric, you are introducing future failures into your system. Eventually, you will want to report or run calculations on numeric data, and if they're not a numeric data type, you will get unpredictable and oftentimes wrong results.

Oracle supports three numeric data types:

- NUMBER

- BINARY_DOUBLE

- BINARY_FLOAT

For most situations, you will use the NUMBER data type for any type of number data. Its syntax is NUMBER(scale, precision) where scale is the total number of digits, and precision is the number of digits to the right of the decimal point. So, with a number defined as NUMBER(5, 2) you can store values +/–999.99. That is a total of five digits, with two used for precision to the right of the decimal point. If defined as NUMBER(5) the values can be to the right or left of the decimal with a total of five digits, this value will fit, 2.4563 as would 55,555.

Tip   Oracle allows a maximum of 38 digits for a NUMBER data type. This is almost always sufficient for any type of numeric application.

What sometimes confuses DBAs is that you can create a table with columns defined as INT, INTEGER, REAL, DECIMAL, and so on. These data types are all implemented by Oracle with a NUMBER data type. For example, a column specified as INTEGER is implemented as a NUMBER(38).

The BINARY_DOUBLE and BINARY_FLOAT data types are used for scientific calculations. These map to the DOUBLE and FLOAT Java data types. Unless your application is performing rocket science calculations, then use the NUMBER data type for all your numeric requirements.

Date/Time

When capturing and reporting on date-related information, you should always use a DATE or TIMESTAMP data type (and not VARCHAR2). Using the correct date-related data type allows you to perform accurate Oracle date calculations and aggregations and dependable sorting for reporting. If you use a VARCHAR2 for a field that contains date information, you are guaranteeing future reporting inconsistencies and needless conversion functions (such as TO_DATE and TO_CHAR).

Oracle supports three date-related data types:

- DATE

- TIMESTAMP

- INTERVAL

The DATE data type contains a date component as well as a time component that is granular to the second. By default, if you do not specify a time component when inserting data, then the time value defaults to midnight (0 hour at the 0 second). If you need to track time at a more granular level than the second, then use TIMESTAMP; otherwise, feel free to use DATE.

The TIMESTAMP data type contains a date component and a time component that is granular to fractions of a second. When you define a TIMESTAMP, you can specify the fractional second precision component. For instance, if you wanted five digits of fractional precision to the right of the decimal point, you would specify that as

TIMESTAMP(5)

The maximum fractional precision is 9; the default is 6. If you specify 0 fractional precision, then you have the equivalent of the DATE data type.

The TIMESTAMP data type comes in two additional variations: TIMESTAMP WITH TIME ZONE and TIMESTAMP WITH LOCAL TIME ZONE. These are time zone–aware data types, meaning that when the user selects the data, the time value is adjusted to the time zone of the user's session.

Oracle also provides an INTERVAL data type. This is meant to store a duration, or interval, of time. There are two types: INTERVAL YEAR TO MONTH and INTERVAL DAY TO SECOND. Use the former when precision to the year and month is required. Use the latter when you need to store interval data granular to the day and second.

CHOOSING YOUR INTERVAL TYPE

When choosing an interval type, let your choice be driven by the level of granularity you desire in your results. For example, you can use INTERVAL DAY TO SECOND to store intervals several years in length—it is just that you will express such intervals in terms of days, perhaps of several hundreds of days. If you record only a number of years and months, then you can never actually get to the correct number of days, because the number of days represented by a year or a month depends on which specific year and month are under discussion.

Similarly, if you need granularity in terms of months, you can't back into the correct number of months based on the number of days. So, choose the type to match the granularity needed in your application.

RAW

The RAW data type allows you to store binary data in a column. This type of data is sometimes used for storing globally unique identifiers or small amounts of encrypted data.

Note   Prior to Oracle Database 12c, the maximum size for a RAW column was 2,000 bytes. As of Oracle Database 12c, you can declare a RAW to have a maximum size of 32,767 bytes. If you have large amounts of binary data to store, then use a BLOB.

If you select data from a RAW column, SQL*Plus implicitly applies the built-in RAWTOHEX function to the data retrieved. The data are displayed in hexadecimal format, using characters 0–9 and A–F. When inserting data into a RAW column, the built-in HEXTORAW is implicitly applied.

This is important because if you create an index on a RAW column, the optimizer may ignore the index, as SQL*Plus is implicitly applying functions where the RAW column is referenced in the SQL. A normal index may be of no use, whereas a function-based index using RAWTOHEX may result in a substantial performance improvement.

ROWID

When DBAs hear the word ROWID (row identifier), they often think of a pseudocolumn provided with every table row that contains the physical location of the row on disk; that is correct. However, many DBAs do not realize that Oracle supports an actual ROWID data type, meaning that you can create a table with a column defined as the type ROWID.

There are a few practical uses for the ROWID data type. One valid application would be if you are having problems when trying to enable a referential integrity constraint and want to capture the ROWID of rows that violate a constraint. In this scenario, you could create a table with a column of the type ROWID and store in it the ROWIDs of offending records within the table. This affords you an efficient way to capture and resolve issues with the offending data (see the section "Enabling Constraints," later in this chapter, for more details).

Tip   Never be tempted to use a ROWID data type and the associated ROWID of a row within the table for the primary key value. This is because the ROWID of a row in a table can change. For example, an ALTER TABLE...MOVE command will potentially change every ROWID within a table. Normally, the primary key values of rows within a table should never change. For this reason, instead of using ROWID for a primary key value, use a sequence-generated nonmeaningful number (see the section "Creating a Table with an Autoincrementing (Identity) Column," later in this chapter, for further discussion).

LOB

Oracle supports storing large amounts of data in a column via a LOB data type. Oracle supports the following types of LOBs:

- CLOB
- NCLOB
- BLOB
- BFILE

Tip   The LONG and LONG RAW data types are deprecated and should not be used.

If you have textual data that do not fit within the confines of a VARCHAR2, then you should use a CLOB to store these data. A CLOB is useful for storing large amounts of character data, such as log files. An NCLOB is similar to a CLOB but allows for information encoded in the nation character set of the database.

BLOBs are large amounts of binary data that usually are not meant to be human readable. Typical BLOB data include images, audio, and video files.

CLOBs, NCLOBs, and BLOBs are known as internal LOBs. This is because they are stored inside the Oracle database. These data types reside within data files associated with the database.

BFILEs are known as external LOBs. BFILE columns store a pointer to a file on the OS that is outside the database. When it is not feasible to store a large binary file within the database, then use a BFILE. BFILEs do not participate in database transactions and are not covered by Oracle security or backup and recovery. If you need those features, then use a BLOB and not a BFILE.

Tip   See Chapter 11 for a full discussion of LOBs.

JSON

Previous versions of Oracle had procedures to be able to convert table data into JSON or read JSON into the database. The JSON can be put into the database tables with JSON columns. The schema or any other details about the JSON data does not need to be known, and it can be stored in the table with other data and queried using SQL.

Here is an example to create a table with a JSON column:

```
SQL> CREATE TABLE dept
(deptno      NUMBER(10)
,dname       VARCHAR2(14 CHAR)
,dprojects      VARCHAR2(32767)
CONSTRAINT ensure_json CHECK (dprojects is JSON));
```

JSON can be inserted into the column with the other columns using an SQL INSERT statement, and the JSON data can be queried also using SQL.

```
SELECT dept.deptno, dept.dprojects.projectID, dept.dprojects.projectName
from dept;
```

This will pull out of the JSON data the projectID and projectName for each of the projects contained in the data. There is definitely more to working with JSON, and there are packages to make handling the data in the database simplified. It allows for data APIs in JSON to be pulled and put into the database. Storing the JSON data in a column will allow for simple queries to be run against the database to work with other data columns.

Creating a Table

The number of table features expands with each new version of Oracle. Consider this: the 12c version of the *Oracle SQL Language Reference Guide* presents more than 80 pages of syntax associated with the CREATE TABLE statement. Moreover, the ALTER TABLE statement takes up another 90-plus pages of details related to table maintenance. For most situations, you typically need to use only a fraction of the table options available.

Listed next are the general factors that you should consider when creating a table:

- Type of table (heap organized, temporary, index organized, partitioned, and so on)

- Naming conventions

- Column data types and sizes

- Constraints (primary key, foreign keys, and so on)

- Index requirements (see Chapter 8 for details)

- Initial storage requirements

- Special features (virtual columns, read-only, parallel, compression, no logging, invisible columns, and so on)

- Growth requirements

- Tablespace(s) for the table and its indexes

Before you run a CREATE TABLE statement, you need to give some thought to each item in the previous list. To that end, DBAs often use data modeling tools to help manage the creation of DDL scripts that are used to make database objects. Data modeling tools allow you to define visually tables and relationships and the underlying database features.

Creating a Heap-Organized Table

You use the CREATE TABLE statement(s), and data types and lengths associated with the columns. The Oracle default table type is heap organized. The term *heap* means that the data are not stored in a specific order in the table (instead, they're a heap of data). Here is a simple example of creating a heap-organized table:

```
SQL> CREATE TABLE dept
(deptno      NUMBER(10)
,dname       VARCHAR2(14 CHAR)
,loc         VARCHAR2(14 CHAR));
```

If you do not specify a tablespace, then the table is created in the default permanent tablespace of the user that creates the table. Allowing the table to be created in the default permanent tablespace is fine for a few small test tables. For anything more sophisticated, you should explicitly specify the tablespace in which you want tables created. For reference (in future examples), here are the creation scripts for two sample tablespaces: HR_DATA and HR_INDEX:

```
SQL> CREATE TABLESPACE hr_data
  DATAFILE '/u01/dbfile/O18C/hr_data01.dbf' SIZE 1000m
  EXTENT MANAGEMENT LOCAL
```

```
  UNIFORM SIZE 512k SEGMENT SPACE MANAGEMENT AUTO;
--
SQL> CREATE TABLESPACE hr_index
  DATAFILE '/u01/dbfile/O18C/hr_index01.dbf' SIZE 100m
  EXTENT MANAGEMENT LOCAL
  UNIFORM SIZE 512k SEGMENT SPACE MANAGEMENT AUTO;
```

Usually, when you create a table, you should also specify constraints, such as the primary key. The following code shows the most common features you use when creating a table. This DDL defines primary keys, foreign keys, tablespace information, and comments:

```
SQL> CREATE TABLE dept
(deptno      NUMBER(10)
,dname       VARCHAR2(14 CHAR)
,loc         VARCHAR2(14 CHAR)
,CONSTRAINT dept_pk PRIMARY KEY (deptno)
 USING INDEX TABLESPACE hr_index
) TABLESPACE hr_data;
--
SQL> COMMENT ON TABLE dept IS 'Department table';
--
SQL> CREATE UNIQUE INDEX dept_uk1 ON dept(dname)
TABLESPACE hr_index;
--
SQL> CREATE TABLE emp
(empno       NUMBER(10)
,ename       VARCHAR2(10 CHAR)
,job         VARCHAR2(9 CHAR)
,mgr         NUMBER(4)
,hiredate    DATE
,sal         NUMBER(7,2)
,comm        NUMBER(7,2)
,deptno      NUMBER(10)
,CONSTRAINT emp_pk PRIMARY KEY (empno)
 USING INDEX TABLESPACE hr_index
) TABLESPACE hr_data;
```

```
--
SQL> COMMENT ON TABLE emp IS 'Employee table';
--
SQL> ALTER TABLE emp ADD CONSTRAINT emp_fk1
FOREIGN KEY (deptno)
REFERENCES dept(deptno);
--
SQL> CREATE INDEX emp_fk1 ON emp(deptno)
TABLESPACE hr_index;
```

When creating a table, I usually do not specify table-level physical space properties. The table inherits its space properties from the tablespace in which it is created. This simplifies administration and maintenance. If you have tables that require different physical space properties, then you can create separate tablespaces to hold tables with differing needs. For instance, you might create a HR_DATA_LARGE tablespace with extent sizes of 16MB and a HR_DATA_SMALL tablespace with extent sizes of 128KB and choose where a table is created based on its storage requirements. See Chapter 4 for details regarding the creation of tablespaces.

Table 7-2 lists some guidelines that are not hard-and-fast rules; adapt them as needed for your environment. Some of these guidelines may seem like obvious suggestions. However, after inheriting many databases over the years, I have seen each of these recommendations violated in some way that makes database maintenance difficult and unwieldy.

Table 7-2. *Guidelines to Consider When Creating Tables*

Recommendation	Reasoning
Use standards when naming tables, columns, constraints, triggers, indexes, and so on.	Helps document the application and simplifies maintenance.
If a column always contains numeric data, make it a number data type.	Enforces a business rule and allows for the greatest flexibility, performance, and consistency when using Oracle SQL math functions (which may behave differently for a "01" character versus a "1" number).

(*continued*)

Table 7-2. (*continued*)

Recommendation	Reasoning
If you have a business rule that defines the length and precision of a number field, then enforce it; for example, NUMBER(7,2). If you do not have a business rule, make it NUMBER(38).	Enforces a business rule and keeps the data cleaner.
For character data that are of variable length, use VARCHAR2 (and not VARCHAR).	Follows Oracle's recommendation of using VARCHAR2 for character data (instead of VARCHAR). The Oracle documentation states that in the future, VARCHAR will be redefined as a separate data type.
For character data, specify the size in CHAR; for example, VARCHAR2(30 CHAR).	When working with multibyte data, you will get more predictable results, as multibyte characters are usually stored in more than1B.
If you have a business rule that specifies the maximum length of a column, then use that length, as opposed to making all columns VARCHAR2(4000).	Enforces a business rule and keeps the data cleaner.
Use DATE and TIMESTAMP data types appropriately.	Enforces a business rule, ensures that the data are of the appropriate format, and allows for the greatest flexibility when using SQL date functions.
Specify a separate tablespace for the table and indexes. Let the table and indexes inherit storage attributes from the tablespaces.	Simplifies administration and maintenance.
Most tables should be created with a primary key.	Enforces a business rule and allows you to uniquely identify each row.
Create a numeric surrogate key to be the primary key for each table. Use the identity column for the surrogate key or a sequence to populate.	Makes joins easier and more efficient.

(*continued*)

Table 7-2. (*continued*)

Recommendation	Reasoning
Create primary key constraints out of line.	Allows you more flexibility when creating the primary key, especially if you have a situation in which the primary key consists of multiple columns.
Create a unique key for the logical user—a recognizable combination of columns that makes a row one of a kind.	Enforces a business rule and keeps the data cleaner.
Create comments for the tables and columns.	Helps document the application and eases maintenance.
Avoid LOB data types if possible.	Prevents maintenance issues associated with LOB columns, such as unexpected growth and performance issues when copying.
If a column should always have a value, then enforce it with a NOT NULL constraint.	Enforces a business rule and keeps the data cleaner.
Create audit-type columns, such as CREATE_DTT and UPDATE_DTT, which are automatically populated with default values or triggers, or both.	Helps with maintenance and determining when data were inserted or updated, or both. Other types of audit columns to consider include the users that inserted and updated the row.
Use check constraints where appropriate.	Enforces a business rule and keeps the data cleaner.
Define foreign keys where appropriate.	Enforces a business rule and keeps the data cleaner.

Implementing Virtual Columns

With Oracle Database 11g and higher, you can create a virtual column as part of your table definition. A virtual column is based on one or more existing columns from the same table or a combination of constants, SQL functions, and user-defined PL/SQL functions, or both. Virtual columns are not stored on disk; they are evaluated at runtime, when the SQL query executes. Virtual columns can be indexed and have stored statistics.

Prior to Oracle Database 11g, you could simulate a virtual column via a SELECT statement or in a view definition. For example, this next SQL SELECT statement generates a virtual value when the query is executed:

```
SQL> select inv_id, inv_count,
  case when inv_count <= 100 then 'GETTING LOW'
       when inv_count > 100 then 'OKAY'
  end
from inv;
```

Why use a virtual column? The advantages of doing so are as follows:

- You can create an index on a virtual column; internally, Oracle creates a function-based index.

- You can store statistics in a virtual column that can be used by the cost-based optimizer (CBO).

- Virtual columns can be referenced in WHERE clauses.

- Virtual columns are permanently defined in the database; there is one central definition of such a column.

Here is an example of creating a table with a virtual column:

```
SQL> create table inv(
 inv_id number
,inv_count number
,inv_status generated always as (
  case when inv_count <= 100 then 'GETTING LOW'
       when inv_count > 100 then 'OKAY'
  end)
);
```

In the prior code listing, specifying GENERATED ALWAYS is optional. For example, this listing is equivalent to the previous one:

```
SQL> create table inv(
 inv_id number
,inv_count number
,inv_status as (
```

```
  case when inv_count <= 100 then 'GETTING LOW'
     when inv_count > 100 then 'OKAY'
  end)
);
```

I prefer to add GENERATED ALWAYS because it reinforces in my mind that the column is always virtual. The GENERATED ALWAYS helps document inline what you've done. This aids in maintenance for other DBAs who come along long after you.

To view values generated by virtual columns, first insert some data into the table:

```
SQL> insert into inv (inv_id, inv_count) values (1,100);
```

Next, select from the table to view the generated value:

```
SQL> select * from inv;
```

Here is some sample output:

```
  INV_ID  INV_COUNT INV_STATUS
---------- ---------- -----------
         1        100 GETTING LOW
```

Note   If you insert data into the table, nothing is stored in a column set to GENERATED ALWAYS AS. The virtual value is generated when you select from the table.

You can also alter a table to contain a virtual column:

```
SQL> alter table inv add(
inv_comm generated always as(inv_count * 0.1) virtual
);
```

And, you can change the definition of an existing virtual column:

```
SQL> alter table inv modify inv_status generated always as(
case when inv_count <= 50 then 'NEED MORE'
     when inv_count >50 and inv_count <=200 then 'GETTING LOW'
     when inv_count > 200 then 'OKAY'
end);
```

You can access virtual columns in SQL queries (DML or DDL). For instance, suppose you want to update a permanent column based on the value in a virtual column:

```
SQL> update inv set inv_count=100 where inv_status='OKAY';
```

A virtual column itself can't be updated via the SET clause of an UPDATE statement. However, you can reference a virtual column in the WHERE clause of an UPDATE or DELETE statement.

Optionally, you can specify the data type of a virtual column. If you omit the data type, Oracle derives it from the expression you use to define the virtual column.

Several caveats are associated with virtual columns:

- You can only define a virtual column on a regular, heap-organized table. You cannot define a virtual column on an index-organized table, an external table, a temporary table, object tables, or cluster tables.

- Virtual columns cannot reference other virtual columns.

- Virtual columns can only reference columns from the table in which the virtual column is defined.

- The output of a virtual column must be a scalar value (i.e., a single value, not a set of values).

To view the definition of a virtual column, use the DBMS_METADATA package to see the DDL associated with the table. If you are selecting from SQL*Plus, you need to set the LONG variable to a value large enough to show all data returned:

```
SQL> set long 10000;
SQL> select dbms_metadata.get_ddl('TABLE','INV') from dual;
```

Here is a snippet of the output:

```
  SQL> CREATE TABLE "INV_MGMT"."INV"
    (    "INV_ID" NUMBER,
 "INV_COUNT" NUMBER,
 "INV_STATUS" VARCHAR2(11) GENERATED ALWAYS AS (CASE  WHEN "INV_COUNT"<=50
THEN
'NEED MORE' WHEN ("INV_COUNT">50 AND "INV_COUNT"<=200) THEN 'GETTING LOW'
WHEN "
INV_COUNT">200 THEN 'OKAY' END) VIRTUAL ...
```

Implementing Invisible Columns

Starting with Oracle Database 12c, you can create invisible columns. When a column is invisible, it cannot be viewed via

- DESCRIBE command
- SELECT * (to access all of a table's columns)
- %ROWTYPE (in PL/SQL)
- Describes within an Oracle Call Interface (OCI)

However, the column can be accessed if explicitly specified in a SELECT clause or referenced directly in a DML statement (INSERT, UPDATE, DELETE, or MERGE). Invisible columns can also be indexed (just like visible columns).

The main use for an invisible column is to ensure that adding a column to a table will not disrupt any of the existing application code. If the application code does not explicitly access the invisible column, then it appears to the application as if the column does not exist.

A table can be created with invisible columns, or a column can be added or altered so as to be invisible. A column that is defined as invisible can also be altered so as to be visible. Here is an example of creating a table with an invisible column:

```
SQL> create table inv
(inv_id     number
,inv_desc   varchar2(30 char)
,inv_profit number invisible);
```

Now, when the table is described, note that the invisible column is not displayed:

```
SQL> desc inv
```

Name	Null?	Type
INV_ID		NUMBER
INV_DESC		VARCHAR2(30 CHAR)

A column that has been defined as invisible is still accessible if you specify it directly in a SELECT statement or any DML operations. For example, when selecting from a table, you can view the invisible column by specifying it in the SELECT clause:

```
SQL> select inv_id, inv_desc, inv_profit from inv;
```

Note   When you create a table that has invisible columns, at least one column must be visible.

Making Read-Only Tables

You can place individual tables in read-only mode. Doing so prevents any INSERT, UPDATE, or DELETE statements from running against a table. An alternate way to do this is to make the tablespace read-only and use this table for the tables that are static for read-only.

There are several reasons why you may require the read-only feature at the table level:

- The data in the table are historical and should never be updated in normal circumstances.

- You are performing some maintenance on the table and want to ensure that it does not change while it is being updated.

- You want to drop the table, but before you do, you want to better determine if any users are attempting to update the table.

Use the ALTER TABLE statement to place a table in read-only mode:

```
SQL> alter table inv read only;
```

You can verify the status of a read-only table by issuing the following query:

```
SQL> select table_name, read_only from user_tables where read_only='YES';
```

To modify a read-only table to read/write, issue the following SQL:

```
SQL> alter table inv read write;
```

Note   The read-only table feature requires that the database initialization COMPATIBLE parameter be set to 11.1.0 or higher.

Understanding Deferred-Segment Creation

Starting with Oracle Database 11g Release 2, when you create a table, the creation of the associated segment is deferred until the first row is inserted into the table. This feature has some interesting implications. For instance, if you have thousands of objects that you are initially creating for an application (such as when you first install it), no space is consumed by any of the tables (or associated indexes) until data are inserted into the application tables. This means that the initial DDL runs more quickly when you create a table, but the first INSERT statement runs slightly slower.

To illustrate the concept of deferred segments, first create a table:

```
SQL> create table inv(inv_id number, inv_desc varchar2(30 CHAR));
```

You can verify that the table has been created by inspecting USER_TABLES:

```
SQL> select
  table_name
,segment_created
from user_tables
where table_name='INV';
```

Here is some sample output:

```
TABLE_NAME                      SEG
------------------------------- ---
INV                             NO
```

Next, query USER_SEGMENTS to verify that a segment has not yet been allocated for the table:

```
SQL> select
  segment_name
,segment_type
,bytes
from user_segments
where segment_name='INV'
and segment_type='TABLE';
```

Here is the corresponding output for this example:

```
no rows selected
```

Now, insert a row into a table:

```
SQL> insert into inv values(1,'BOOK');
```

Rerun the query, selecting from USER_SEGMENTS, and note that a segment has been created:

```
SEGMENT_NAME      SEGMENT_TYPE              BYTES
---------------   -------------------   ----------
INV               TABLE                      65536
```

If you are used to working with older versions of Oracle, the deferred-segment creation feature can cause confusion. For example, if you have space-related monitoring reports that query DBA_SEGMENTS or DBA_EXTENTS, be aware that these views are not populated for a table or any indexes associated with a table until the first row is inserted into the table.

Note   You can disable the deferred-segment creation feature by setting the database initialization parameter DEFERRED_SEGMENT_CREATION to FALSE. The default for this parameter is TRUE.

Creating a Table with an Autoincrementing (Identity) Column

Starting with Oracle Database 12c, you can define a column that is automatically populated and incremented when inserting data. This feature is ideal for automatically populating primary key columns.

Tip   Prior to Oracle Database 12c, you would have to create a sequence manually and then access the sequence when inserting into the table. Sometimes, DBAs would create triggers on tables to simulate an autoincrementing column based on a sequence (see Chapter 9 for details).

You define an autoincrementing (identity) column with the GENERATED AS IDENTITY clause. This example creates a table with primary key column that will be automatically populated and incremented:

```
SQL> create table inv(
 inv_id number generated as identity
,inv_desc varchar2(30 char));
--
SQL> alter table inv add constraint inv_pk primary key (inv_id);
```

Now, you can populate the table without having to specify the primary key value:

```
SQL> insert into inv (inv_desc) values ('Book');
SQL> insert into inv (inv_desc) values ('Table');
```

Selecting from the table shows that the INV_ID column has been automatically populated:

```
SQL> select * from inv;
```

Here is some sample output:

```
  INV_ID INV_DESC
---------- ------------------------------
       1 Book
       2 Table
```

When you create an identity column, Oracle automatically creates a sequence and associates the sequence with the column. You can view the sequence information in USER_SEQUENCES:

```
SQL> select sequence_name, min_value, increment_by from user_sequences;
```

Here is some sample output for this example:

```
SEQUENCE_NAME          MIN_VALUE INCREMENT_BY
-------------------- ----------- ------------
ISEQ$$_43216                   1            1
```

You can identify identity columns via this query:

```
SQL> select table_name, identity_column
from user_tab_columns
where identity_column='YES';
```

When creating a table with an identity column (such as in the prior example), you can't directly specify a value for the identity column; for example, if you try this:

```
SQL> insert into inv values(3,'Chair');
```

you will receive an error:

```
ORA-32795: cannot insert into a generated always identity column
```

If, for some reason, you need to occasionally insert values into an identity column, then use the following syntax when creating:

```
SQL> create table inv(
 inv_id number generated by default on null as identity
,inv_desc varchar2(30 char));
```

Because the underlying mechanism for populating an identity column is a sequence, you have some control over how the sequence is created (just like you would if you manually created a sequence). For instance, you can specify at what number to start the sequence and by how much the sequence increments each time. This example specifies that the underlying sequence starts at the number 50 and increments by two each time:

```
SQL> create table inv(
 inv_id number generated as identity (start with 50 increment by 2)
,inv_desc varchar2(30 char));
```

There are some caveats to be aware of when using autoincrementing (identity) columns:

- Only one per table is allowed.

- They must be numeric.

- They cannot have default values.

- NOT NULL and NOT DEFERRABLE constraints are implicitly applied.

- CREATE TABLE ... AS SELECT will not inherit identity column properties.

Also keep in mind that after inserting into a column that is autoincremented, if you issue a rollback, the transaction is rolled back, but not the autoincremented values from the sequence. This is the expected behavior of a sequence. You can roll back such an insert, but the sequence values are used and gone.

Tip   See Chapter 9 for details on how to manage a sequence.

Allowing for Default Parallel SQL Execution

If you work with large tables, you may want to consider creating your tables as PARALLEL. This instructs Oracle to set the degree of parallelism for queries and any subsequent INSERT, UPDATE, DELETE, MERGE, and query statements. This example creates a table with a PARALLEL clause of 2:

```
SQL> create table inv
(inv_id      number,
 inv_desc    varchar2(30 char),
 create_dtt date default sysdate)
parallel 2;
```

You can specify PARALLEL, NOPARALLEL, or PARALLEL N. If you do not specify N, Oracle sets the degree of parallelism based on the PARALLEL_THREADS_PER_CPU initialization parameter. You can verify the degree of parallelism with this query:

```
SQL> select table_name, degree from user_tables;
```

The main issue to be aware of here is that if a table has been created with a default degree of parallelism, any subsequent queries will execute with parallel threads. You may wonder why a query or a DML statement is executing in parallel (without explicitly invoking a parallel operation).

WHERE ARE ALL THE P_0 PROCESSES COMING FROM?

I once got a call from a production support person who reported that nobody could connect to the database because of an ORA-00020 maximum number of processes error. I logged into the box and noted that there were hundreds of ora_p parallel query processes running.

I had to kill some of the processes manually so that I could connect to the database. Upon further inspection, I traced the parallel query sessions to an SQL statement and table. The table, in this case, had been created with a default parallel degree of 64 (do not ask me why), which in turn spawned hundreds of processes and sessions when the table was queried.

This maxed out the number of allowed connections to the database and caused the issue. This can be resolved with setting the parallel to NOPARALLEL or to 1. Also, the resource manager will limit the number of connections allowed.

You can also alter a table to modify its default degree of parallelism:

```
SQL> alter table inv parallel 1;
```

With Oracle 18c, the resource parameter PQ_TIMEOUT_ACTION is available to timeout parallel queries that are inactive. This will allow parallel queries with high priority to have the needed resources to execute. There is also a simpler way to cancel the runaway SQL without having to manually kill the processes using ALTER SYSTEM CANCEL SQL statement.

Tip   Keep in mind that PARALLEL_THREADS_PER_CPU is platform dependent and can vary from a development environment to a production environment. Therefore, if you do not specify the degree of parallelism, the behavior of parallel operations can vary, depending on the environment.

Compressing Table Data

As your database grows, you may want to consider table level compression. Compressed data have the benefit of using less disk space and less memory and reduced I/O. Queries that read compressed data potentially run faster because there are fewer blocks to process. However, CPU usage increases as the data are compressed and uncompressed as writes and reads occur, so there is a tradeoff.

Starting with Oracle Database 12c, there are four types of compression available:

- Basic compression

- Advanced row compression (previously referred to as OLTP compression)

- Warehouse compression (hybrid columnar compression)

- Archive compression (hybrid columnar compression)

Basic compression is enabled with the COMPRESS or COMPRESS BASIC clause (they are synonymous). This example creates a table with basic compression:

```
SQL> create table inv
(inv_id      number,
 inv_desc    varchar2(300 char),
 create_dtt  timestamp)
compress basic;
```

Basic compression provides compression as data are direct-path inserted into the table. By default, tables created with COMPRESS BASIC have a PCTFREE setting of 0. You can override this by specifying PCTFREE when creating the table.

Note Basic compression requires the Oracle Enterprise Edition, but it does not require an extra license. Other types of compression are additional license options for the database. As with options of the database, evaluation needs to be done for storage cost and compression ratio to provide the right cost analysis of this option.

Advanced row compression is enabled with the ROW STORE COMPRESS ADVANCED clause:

```
SQL> create table inv
(inv_id      number,
 inv_desc    varchar2(300 char),
 create_dtt  timestamp)
row store compress advanced;
```

Advanced row compression provides compression when initially inserting data into the table as well as in any subsequent DML operations. You can verify the compression for a table via the following SELECT statement:

```
SQL> select table_name, compression, compress_for
from user_tables
where table_name='INV';
```

Here is some sample output:

```
TABLE_NAME              COMPRESS COMPRESS_FOR
--------------------    -------- ------------------------------
INV                     ENABLED  ADVANCED
```

> **Note**   OLTP table compression is a feature of the Oracle Advanced Compression option. This option requires an additional license from Oracle and is only available with the Oracle Enterprise Edition.

You can also create a tablespace with the compression clause. Any table created in that tablespace will inherit the tablespace compression settings. For example, here is how to set the default level of compression for a tablespace:

```
SQL> CREATE TABLESPACE hr_data
  DEFAULT ROW STORE COMPRESS ADVANCED
  DATAFILE '/u01/dbfile/O12C/hr_data01.dbf' SIZE 100m
  EXTENT MANAGEMENT LOCAL
  UNIFORM SIZE 512k SEGMENT SPACE MANAGEMENT AUTO;
```

If you have a table that already exists, you can alter it to allow compression (either basic or advanced):

```
SQL> alter table inv row store compress advanced;
```

> **Note**   Oracle does not support compression for tables with more than 255 columns.

Altering to allow compression does not compress the existing data in the table. You will need to rebuild the table with Data Pump or move the table to compress the data that were in it prior to enabling compression:

```
SQL> alter table inv move;
```

Note   If you move the table, then you will also need to rebuild any associated indexes.

You can disable compression via the NOCOMPRESS clause. This does not affect existing data within the table. Rather, it affects future inserts (basic and advanced row compression) and future DML (advanced row compression); for example,

```
SQL> alter table inv nocompress;
```

Oracle also has a warehouse and archive hybrid columnar compression feature that is available when using certain types of storage (such as Exadata). This type of compression is enabled with the COLUMN STORE COMPRESS FOR QUERY LOW|HIGH or COLUMN STORE COMPRESS FOR ARCHIVE LOW|HIGH clause. For more details regarding this type of compression, see the Oracle Technology Network web site (http://otn.oracle.com).

Avoiding Redo Creation

When you are creating a table, you have the option of specifying the NOLOGGING clause. The NOLOGGING feature can greatly reduce the amount of redo generation for certain types of operations. Sometimes, when you are working with large amounts of data, it is desirable, for performance reasons, to reduce the redo generation when you initially create and insert data into a table.

The downside to eliminating redo generation is that you cannot recover the data created via NOLOGGING in the event a failure occurs after the data are loaded (and before you can back up the table). If you can tolerate some risk of data loss, then use NOLOGGING, but back up the table soon after the data are loaded. If your data are critical, then do not use NOLOGGING. If your data can be easily re-created, then NOLOGGING is desirable when you are trying to improve performance of large data loads.

One perception is that NOLOGGING eliminates redo generation for the table for all DML operations. That is not correct. The NOLOGGING feature never affects redo generation for normal DML statements (regular INSERT, UPDATE, and DELETE).

The NOLOGGING feature can significantly reduce redo generation for the following types of operations:

- SQL*Loader direct-path load

- Direct-path INSERT /*+ append */

- CREATE TABLE AS SELECT

- ALTER TABLE MOVE

- Creating or rebuilding an index

You need to be aware of some quirks (features) when using NOLOGGING. If your database is in FORCE LOGGING mode, then redo is generated for all operations, regardless of whether you specify NOLOGGING. Likewise, when you are loading a table, if the table has a referential foreign key constraint defined, then redo is generated regardless of whether you specify NOLOGGING.

You can specify NOLOGGING at one of the following levels:

- Statement

- CREATE TABLE or ALTER TABLE

- CREATE TABLESPACE or ALTER TABLESPACE

I prefer to specify the NOLOGGING clause at the statement or table level. In these scenarios, it is obvious to the DBA executing the statement or DDL that NOLOGGING is used. If you specify NOLOGGING at the tablespace level, then each DBA who creates objects within that tablespace must be aware of this tablespace-level setting. In teams with multiple DBAs, it is easy for one DBA to be unaware that another DBA has created a tablespace with NOLOGGING.

This example first creates a table with the NOLOGGING option:

```
SQL> create table inv(inv_id number)
tablespace users
nologging;
```

Next, do a direct-path insert with some test data, and commit the data:

```
SQL> insert /*+ append */ into inv select level from dual
connect by level <= 10000;
--
SQL> commit;
```

What happens if you have a media failure after you have populated a table in NOLOGGING mode (and before you have made a backup of the table)? After a restore and recovery operation, it will appear that the table has been restored:

```
SQL> desc inv
Name                                 Null?     Type
----------------------------------   --------  ----------------------------
INV_ID                                         NUMBER
```

However, try to execute a query that scans every block in the table:

```
SQL> select * from inv;
```

Here, an error is thrown, indicating that there is logical corruption in the data file:

```
ORA-01578: ORACLE data block corrupted (file # 5, block # 203)
ORA-01110: data file 5: '/u01/dbfile/O18C/users01.dbf'
ORA-26040: Data block was loaded using the NOLOGGING option
```

In other words, the data are unrecoverable because the redo does not exist to restore them. Again, the NOLOGGING option is suitable for large batch loading of data that can easily be reproduced in the event a failure occurs before a backup of the database can be taken after a NOLOGGING operation.

If you specify a logging clause at the statement level, it overrides any table or tablespace setting. If you specify a logging clause at the table level, it sets the default mode for any statements that do not specify a logging clause and overrides the logging setting at the tablespace. If you specify a logging clause at the tablespace level, it sets the default logging for any CREATE TABLE statements that do not specify a logging clause.

You verify the logging mode of the database as follows:

```
SQL> select name, log_mode, force_logging from v$database;
```

The next statement verifies the logging mode of a tablespace:

```
SQL> select tablespace_name, logging from dba_tablespaces;
```

And, this example verifies the logging mode of a table:

```
SQL> select owner, table_name, logging from dba_tables where logging = 'NO';
```

You can view the effects of NOLOGGING in a few different ways. One way is to enable autotracing with statistics and view the redo size:

```
SQL> set autotrace trace statistics;
```

Then, run a direct-path INSERT statement, and view the redo size statistic:

```
insert /*+ append */ into inv select level from dual
connect by level <= 10000;
```

Here is a snippet of the output:

```
Statistics
-------------------------------------------------------------
      13772  redo size
```

With logging disabled, for direct-path operations, you should see a much smaller redo size number than with a regular INSERT statement, such as,

```
SQL> insert into inv select level from dual
connect by level <= 10000;
```

Here is the partial output, indicating that the redo size is much greater:

```
Statistics
-------------------------------------------------------------
     159152  redo size
```

Another method for determining the effects of NOLOGGING is to measure the amount of redo generated for an operation with logging enabled versus operating in NOLOGGING mode. If you have a development environment that you can test in, you can monitor how often the redo logs switch while the operation is taking place. Another simple test is to time how long the operation takes with and without logging. The operation performed in NOLOGGING mode should be faster (because a minimal amount of redo is being generated).

Creating a Table from a Query

Sometimes. it is convenient to create a table based on the definition of an existing table. For instance, say you want to create a quick backup of a table before you modify the table's structure or data. Use the CREATE TABLE AS SELECT statement (CTAS) this; for example,

```
create table inv_backup
as select * from inv;
```

The previous statement creates an identical table, complete with data. If you do not want the data included—you just want the structure of the table replicated—then provide a WHERE clause that always evaluates to false (in this example, 1 will never equal 2):

```
SQL> create table inv_empty
as select * from inv
where 1=2;
```

You can also specify that no redo be logged when a CTAS table is created. For large data sets, this can reduce the amount of time required to create the table:

```
SQL> create table inv_backup
nologging
as select * from inv;
```

Be aware that using the CTAS technique with the NOLOGGING clause creates the table as NOLOGGING and does not generate the redo required to recover the data that populate the table as the result of the SELECT statement. Also, if the tablespace (in which the CTAS table is being created) is defined as NOLOGGING, then no redo is generated. In these scenarios, you can't restore and recover your table in the event a failure occurs before you are able to back up the table. If your data are critical, then do not use the NOLOGGING clause.

You can also specify parallelism and storage parameters. Depending on the number of CPUs, you may see some performance gains:

```
SQL> create table inv_backup
nologging
tablespace hr_data
parallel 2
as select * from inv;
```

Note   The CTAS technique does not create any indexes, constraints, or triggers. You have to create indexes and triggers separately if you need those objects from the original table.

ENABLING DDL LOGGING

Oracle allows you to enable the logging of DDL statements to a log file. This type of logging is switched on with the ENABLE_DDL_LOGGING parameter (the default is FALSE). You can set this at the session or system level. This feature provides you with an audit trail regarding which DDL statements have been issued and when they were run. Here is an example of setting this parameter at the system level:

```
SQL> alter system set enable_ddl_logging=true scope=both;
```

After this parameter is set to TRUE, DDL statements will be logged to a log file. Oracle does not log every type of DDL statement, only the most common ones to a log file. The exact location of the DDL logging file and number of files vary by database version. The location (directory path) of this file can be determined via this query:

```
SQL> select value from v$diag_info where name='Diag Alert';
VALUE
--------------------------------------------------
/ora01/app/oracle/diag/rdbms/o18c/O18C/alert
```

Depending on the type of auditing, there are multiple files that capture DDL logging. To find these files, first determine the location of your diagnostic home directory:

```
SQL> select value from v$diag_info where name='ADR Home';
VALUE
--------------------------------------
/ora01/app/oracle/diag/rdbms/o18c/O18C
```

Now, change your current working directory to the prior directory and the subdirectory of log; for example,

```
$ cd /ora01/app/oracle/diag/rdbms/o18c/O18C/log
```

Within this directory, there will be a file with the format ddl_<SID>.log. This contains a log of DDL statements that have been issued after DDL logging has been enabled. You can also view DDL logging in the log.xml file. This file is located in the ddl subdirectory beneath the previously mentioned log directory; for example,

```
$ cd /ora01/app/oracle/diag/rdbms/o18c/O18C/log/ddl
```

Once you navigate to the prior directory, you can view the log.xml file with an OS utility such as vi.

Modifying a Table

Altering a table is a common task. New requirements frequently mean that you need to rename, add, drop, or change column data types. In development environments, changing a table can be a trivial task: you do not often have large quantities of data or hundreds of users simultaneously accessing a table. However, for active production systems, you need to understand the ramifications of trying to change tables that are currently being accessed or that are already populated with data, or both.

Obtaining the Needed Lock

When you modify a table, you must have an exclusive lock on the table. One issue is that if a DML transaction has a lock on the table, you cannot alter it. In this situation, you receive this error:

```
ORA-00054: resource busy and acquire with NOWAIT specified or timeout expired
```

The prior error message is somewhat confusing in that it leads you to believe that you can resolve the problem by acquiring a lock with NOWAIT. However, this is a generic message that is generated when the DDL you are issuing cannot obtain an exclusive lock on the table. In this situation, you have a few options:

- After issuing the DDL command and receiving the ORA-00054 error, rapidly press the forward slash (/) key repeatedly in hopes of modifying the table between transactions.

- Wait for a maintenance window to schedule the change the table to not lock user out of the table. Shut down the database and start it in restricted mode, modify the table, and then open the database for normal use.

- Set the DDL_LOCK_TIMEOUT parameter.

The last item in the previous list instructs Oracle to repeatedly attempt to run a DDL statement until it obtains the required lock on the table. You can set the DDL_LOCK_TIMEOUT parameter at the system or session level. This next example instructs Oracle to repeatedly try to obtain a lock for 100 seconds:

```
SQL> alter session set ddl_lock_timeout=100;
```

The default value for the system-level DDL_LOCK_TIMEOUT initialization parameter is 0. If you want to modify the default behavior for every session in the system, issue an ALTER SYSTEM SET statement. The following command sets the default time-out value to 10 seconds for the system:

```
SQL> alter system set ddl_lock_timeout=10 scope=both;
```

Note   There are online table operations with the DBMS_REDEFINITION package that will allow for table changes from column types, name, size, etc., to renaming tables. Using this package will also allow for online operations without disruption of the database users for implementing other options. This is also a good way to validate new procedures and table changes before making the switch.

Renaming a Table

There are a couple of reasons for renaming a table:

- Make the table conform to standards

- Better determine whether the table is being used before you drop it

This example renames a table, from INV to INV_OLD:

```
SQL> rename inv to inv_old;
```

If successful, you should see this message:

```
Table renamed.
```

Adding a Column

Use the ALTER TABLE ... ADD statement to add a column to a table. This example adds a column to the INV table:

```
SQL> alter table inv add(inv_count number);
```

If successful, you should see this message:

```
Table altered.
```

Altering a Column

Occasionally, you need to alter a column to adjust its size or change its data type. Use the ALTER TABLE ... MODIFY statement to adjust the size of a column. This example changes the size of a column to 256 characters:

```
SQL> alter table inv modify inv_desc varchar2(256 char);
```

If you decrease the size of a column, first ensure that no values exist that are greater than the decreased size value:

```
SQL> select max(length(<column_name>)) from <table_name>;
```

When you change a column to NOT NULL, there must be a valid value for each column. First, verify that there are no NULL values:

```
SQL> select <column_name> from <table_name> where <column_name> is null;
```

If any rows have a NULL value for the column you are modifying to NOT NULL, then you must first update the column to contain a value. Here is an example of modifying a column to NOT NULL:

```
SQL> alter table inv modify(inv_desc not null);
```

You can also alter the column to have a default value. The default value is used any time a record is inserted into the table, but no value is provided for a column:

```
SQL> alter table inv modify(inv_desc default 'No Desc');
```

If you want to remove the default value of a column, then set it to NULL:

```
SQL> alter table inv modify(inv_desc default NULL);
```

Sometimes, you need to change a table's data type; for example, a column that was originally incorrectly defined as a VARCHAR2 needs to be changed to a NUMBER. Before you change a column's data type, first verify that all values for an existing column are valid numeric values. Here is a simple PL/SQL script to do this:

```
SQL> create or replace function isnum(v_in varchar2)
  return varchar is
  val_err exception;
  pragma exception_init(val_err, -6502); -- char to num conv. error
```

```
  scrub_num number;
begin
  scrub_num := to_number(v_in);
  return 'Y';
  exception when val_err then
  return 'N';
end;
/
```

You can use the ISNUM function to detect whether data in a column are numeric. The function defines a PL/SQL pragma exception for the ORA-06502 character-to-number conversion error. When this error is encountered, the exception handler captures it and returns an N. If the value passed in to the ISNUM function is a number, then a Y is returned. If the value can't be converted to a number, then an N is returned. Here is a simple example illustrating the prior concepts:

```
SQL> create table stage(hold_col varchar2(30));
SQL> insert into stage values(1);
SQL> insert into stage values('x');
SQL> select hold_col from stage where isnum(hold_col)='N';

HOLD_COL
------------------------------
x
```

Similarly, when you modify a character column to a DATE or TIMESTAMP data type, it is prudent to check first to see whether the data can be successfully converted. Here is a function that does that:

```
SQL> create or replace function isdate(p_in varchar2, f_in varchar2)
return varchar is
scrub_dt date;
begin
scrub_dt := to_date(p_in, f_in);
return 'Y';
exception when others then
return 'N';
end;
/
```

When you call the ISDATE function, you need to pass it a valid date-format mask, such as YYYYMMDD. Here is a simple example to demonstrate the prior concept:

```
SQL> create table stage2 (hold_col varchar2(30));
SQL> insert into stage2 values('20130103');
SQL> insert into stage2 values('03-JAN-13');
SQL> select hold_col from stage2 where isdate(hold_col,'YYYYMMDD')='N';

HOLD_COL
------------------------------
03-JAN-13
```

Renaming a Column

There are a couple of reasons to rename a column:

- Sometimes, requirements change, and you may want to modify the column name to better reflect what the column is used for.

- If you are planning to drop a column, it does not hurt to rename the column first to better determine whether any users or applications are accessing it.

Use the ALTER TABLE ... RENAME statement to rename a column:

```
SQL> alter table inv rename column inv_count to inv_amt;
```

Dropping a Column

Tables sometimes end up having columns that are never used. This may be because the initial requirements changed or were inaccurate. If you have a table that contains an unused column, you should consider dropping it. If you leave an unused column in a table, you may run into issues with future DBAs not knowing what the column is used for, and the column can potentially consume space unnecessarily.

Before you drop a column, I recommend that you first rename it. Doing so gives you an opportunity to determine whether any users or applications are using the column. After you are confident the column is not being used, first make a backup of the table, using Data Pump export, and then drop the column. These strategies provide you with options if you drop a column and then subsequently realize that it is needed.

To drop a column, use the ALTER TABLE ... DROP statement:

```
SQL> alter table inv drop (inv_name);
```

Be aware that the DROP operation may take some time if the table from which you are removing the column contains a large amount of data. This time lag may result in the delay of transactions while the table is being modified (because the ALTER TABLE statement locks the table). In scenarios such as this, you may want to first mark the column unused and then later drop it, when you have a maintenance window:

```
SQL> alter table inv set unused (inv_name);
```

When you mark a column unused, it no longer shows up in the table description. The SET UNUSED clause does not incur the overhead associated with dropping the column. This technique allows you to quickly stop the column from being seen or used by SQL queries or applications. Any query that attempts to access an unused column receives the following error:

```
ORA-00904: ... invalid identifier
```

You can later drop any unused columns when you've scheduled some downtime for the application. Use the DROP UNUSED clause to remove any columns marked UNUSED.

```
SQL> alter table inv drop unused columns;
```

Displaying Table DDL

Sometimes, DBAs do a poor job of documenting what DDL is used when creating or modifying a table. Normally, you should maintain the database DDL code in a source control repository or in some sort of modeling tool. If your shop does not have the DDL source code, there are a few ways that you can manually reproduce DDL:

- Query the data dictionary.
- Use Data Pump.
- Use the DBMS_METADATA package.

Back in the olden days, say, version 7 and earlier, DBAs often wrote SQL that queried the data dictionary in an attempt to extract the DDL required to re-create objects. Although this method was better than nothing, it was often prone to errors because the SQL didn't account for every object creation feature.

The Data Pump utility is an excellent method for generating the DDL used to create database objects. Using Data Pump to generate DDL is covered in detail in Chapter 13.

The GET_DDL function of the DBMS_METADATA package is usually the quickest way to display the DDL required to create an object. This example shows how to generate the DDL for a table named INV:

```
SQL> set long 10000
SQL> select dbms_metadata.get_ddl('TABLE','INV') from dual;
```

Here is some sample output:

```
DBMS_METADATA.GET_DDL('TABLE','INV')
--------------------------------------

 SQL>   CREATE TABLE "MV_MAINT"."INV"
   (    "INV_ID" NUMBER,
        "INV_DESC" VARCHAR2(30 CHAR),
        "INV_COUNT" NUMBER
   ) SEGMENT CREATION DEFERRED
  PCTFREE 10 PCTUSED 40 INITRANS 1 MAXTRANS 255
NOCOMPRESS LOGGING
  TABLESPACE "USERS";
```

The following SQL statement displays all the DDL for the tables in a schema:

```
SQL> select
dbms_metadata.get_ddl('TABLE',table_name)
from user_tables;
```

If you want to display the DDL for a table owned by another user, add the SCHEMA parameter to the GET_DDL procedure:

```
SQL> select
dbms_metadata.get_ddl(object_type=>'TABLE', name=>'INV', schema=>'INV_APP')
from dual;
```

> **Note** You can display the DDL for almost any database object type, such as INDEX, FUNCTION, ROLE, PACKAGE, MATERIALIZED VIEW, PROFILE, CONSTRAINT, SEQUENCE, and SYNONYM.

Dropping a Table

If you want to remove an object, such as a table, from a user, use the DROP TABLE statement. This example drops a table named INV:

```
SQL> drop table inv;
```

You should see the following confirmation:

```
Table dropped.
```

If you attempt to drop a parent table that has either a primary key or unique key referenced as a foreign key in a child table, you see an error such as

```
ORA-02449: unique/primary keys in table referenced by foreign keys
```

You need to either drop the referenced foreign key constraint(s) or use the CASCADE CONSTRAINTS option when dropping the parent table:

```
SQL> drop table inv cascade constraints;
```

You must be the owner of the table or have the DROP ANY TABLE system privilege to drop a table. If you have the DROP ANY TABLE privilege, you can drop a table in a different schema by prepending the schema name to the table name:

```
SQL> drop table inv_mgmt.inv;
```

If you do not prepend the table name to a user name, Oracle assumes you are dropping a table in your current schema.

> **Tip** If flashback query or flashback database is enabled, keep in mind that you can flash back a table to before drop for an accidentally dropped table.

Undropping a Table

Suppose you accidentally drop a table, and you want to restore it. First, verify that the table you want to restore is in the recycle bin:

```
SQL> show recyclebin;
```

Here is some sample output:

```
ORIGINAL NAME   RECYCLEBIN NAME                    OBJECT TYPE       DROP TIME
-------------   ---------------                    -----------    ----------------
INV             BIN$0F27WtJGbXngQ4TQTwq5Hw==$0 TABLE             2012-12-08:12:56:45
```

Next, use the FLASHBACK TABLE...TO BEFORE DROP statement to recover the dropped table:

```
SQL> flashback table inv to before drop;
```

Note You cannot use the FLASHBACK TABLE...TO BEFORE DROP statement for a table created in the SYSTEM tablespace.

When you issue a DROP TABLE statement (without PURGE), the table is actually renamed (to a name that starts with BIN$) and placed in the recycle bin. The recycle bin is a mechanism that allows you to view some of the metadata associated with a dropped object. You can view complete metadata regarding renamed objects by querying DBA_SEGMENTS:

```
SQL> select
  owner
,segment_name
,segment_type
,tablespace_name
from dba_segments
where segment_name like 'BIN$%';
```

The FLASHBACK TABLE statement simply renames the table its original name. By default, the RECYCLEBIN feature is enabled. You can change the default by setting the RECYCLEBIN initialization parameter to OFF.

I recommend that you not disable the RECYCLEBIN feature. It is safer to leave this feature enabled and purge the RECYCLEBIN to remove objects that you want permanently deleted. This means that the space associated with a dropped table is not released until you purge your RECYCLEBIN. If you want to purge the entire contents of the currently connected user's recycle bin, use the PURGE RECYCLEBIN statement:

```
SQL> purge recyclebin;
```

If you want to purge the recycle bin for all users in the database, then do the following, as a DBA-privileged user:

```
SQL> purge dba_recyclebin;
```

If you want to bypass the RECYCLEBIN feature and permanently drop a table, use the PURGE option of the DROP TABLE statement:

```
SQL> drop table inv purge;
```

You cannot use the FLASHBACK TABLE statement to retrieve a table dropped with the PURGE option. All space used by the table is released, and any associated indexes and triggers are also dropped.

Removing Data from a Table

You can use either the DELETE statement or the TRUNCATE statement to remove records from a table. You need to be aware of some important differences between these two approaches. Table 7-3 summarizes the attributes of the DELETE and TRUNCATE statements.

Table 7-3. *Features of DELETE and TRUNCATE*

	DELETE	TRUNCATE
Choice of COMMIT or ROLLBACK	YES	NO
Generates undo	YES	NO
Resets the high-water mark to 0	NO	YES
Affected by foreign key constraints	NO	YES
Performs well with large amounts of data	NO	YES

Using DELETE

One big difference is that the DELETE statement can be either committed or rolled back. Committing a DELETE statement makes the changes permanent:

```
SQL> delete from inv;
SQL> commit;
```

If you issue a ROLLBACK statement instead of COMMIT, the table contains data as they were before the DELETE was issued.

Using TRUNCATE

TRUNCATE is a DDL statement. This means that Oracle automatically commits the statement (and the current transaction) after it runs, so there is no way to roll back a TRUNCATE statement. If you need the option of choosing to roll back (instead of committing) when removing data, then you should use the DELETE statement. However, the DELETE statement has the disadvantage of generating a great deal of undo and redo information. Thus, for large tables, a TRUNCATE statement is usually the most efficient way to remove data.

Note   It might be possible to run flashback query with a CTAS statement to query the table before the truncate and restore that data into another table. You would CREATE TABLE tableflashback as SELECT * from table as of TIMESTAMP.... This depends on UNDO size and retention, but is something to look into before pulling from a backup.

This example uses a TRUNCATE statement to remove all data from the COMPUTER_ SYSTEMS table:

```
SQL> truncate table computer_systems;
```

By default, Oracle deallocates all space used for the table, except the space defined by the MINEXTENTS table-storage parameter. If you do not want the TRUNCATE statement to deallocate the extents, use the REUSE STORAGE parameter:

```
SQL> truncate table computer_systems reuse storage;
```

The TRUNCATE statement sets the high-water mark of a table back to 0. When you use a DELETE statement to remove data from a table, the high-water mark does not change. One advantage of using a TRUNCATE statement and resetting the high-water mark is that full-table scans only search for rows in blocks below the high-water mark. This can have significant performance implications.

You can't truncate a table that has a primary key defined that is referenced by an enabled foreign key constraint in a child table—even if the child table contains zero rows. Oracle prevents you from doing this because in a multiuser system, there is the possibility that another session can populate the child table with rows in between the time you truncate the child table and the time you subsequently truncate the parent table. In this scenario, you must temporarily disable the referenced foreign key constraints, issue the TRUNCATE statement, and then re-enable the constraints.

Because a TRUNCATE statement is DDL, you can't truncate two separate tables as one transaction. Compare this behavior with that of DELETE. Oracle does allow you to use the DELETE statement to remove rows from a parent table while the constraints are enabled that reference a child table. This is because DELETE generates undo, is read consistent, and can be rolled back.

Note   Another way to remove data from a table is to drop and re-create the table. However, this means that you also have to re-create any indexes, constraints, grants, and triggers that belong to the table. Additionally, when you drop a table, it is unavailable until you re-create it and reissue any required grants. Usually, dropping and re-creating a table are acceptable only in a development or test environment.

Viewing and Adjusting the High-Water Mark

Oracle defines the high-water mark of a table as the boundary between used and unused space in a segment. When you create a table, Oracle allocates a number of extents to the table, defined by the MINEXTENTS table-storage parameter. Each extent contains a number of blocks. Before data are inserted into the table, none of the blocks have been used, and the high-water mark is 0.

As data are inserted into a table, and extents are allocated, the high-water mark boundary is raised. A DELETE statement does not reset the high-water mark.

You need to be aware of a couple of performance-related issues regarding the high-water mark:

- SQL query full-table scans

- Direct-path load-space usage

Oracle sometimes needs to scan every block of a table (under the high-water mark) when performing a query. This is known as a full-table scan. If a significant amount of data have been deleted from a table, a full-table scan can take a long time to complete, even for a table with zero rows.

Also, when doing direct-path loads, Oracle inserts data above the high-water mark line. Potentially, you can end up with a large amount of unused space in a table that is regularly deleted from and that is also loaded via a direct-path mechanism.

There are several methods for detecting space below the high-water mark:

- Autotrace tool

- DBMS_SPACE package

- Selecting from the data dictionary extents view

The autotrace tool offers a simple method for detecting high-water mark issues. Autotrace is advantageous because it is easy to use, and the output is simple to interpret.

You can use the DBMS_SPACE package to determine the high-water mark of objects created in tablespaces that use autospace segment management. The DBMS_SPACE package allows you to check for high-water mark problems programmatically. The downside to this approach is that the output is somewhat cryptic and difficult to derive concrete answers from.

Selecting from DBA/ALL/USER_EXTENTS provides you with information such as the number of extents and bytes consumed. This is a quick and easy way to detect high-water mark issues.

Tracing to Detect Space Below the High-Water Mark

You can run this simple test to detect whether you have an issue with unused space below the high-water mark:

1. SQL> set autotrace trace statistics.

2. Run the query that performs the full-table scan.

3. Compare the number of rows processed with the number of logical I/Os (memory and disk accesses).

If the number of rows processed is low, but the number of logical I/Os is high, you may have an issue with the number of free blocks below the high-water mark. Here is a simple example to illustrate this technique:

```
SQL> set autotrace trace statistics
```

The next query generates a full-table scan on the INV table:

```
SQL> select * from inv;
```

Here is a snippet of the output from AUTOTRACE:

```
no rows selected

Statistics
-------------------------------------------------------------
         4  recursive calls
         0  db block gets
      7371  consistent gets
      2311  physical reads
```

The number of rows returned is zero, yet there are 7,371 consistent gets (memory accesses) and 2,311 physical reads from disk, indicating free space beneath the high-water mark.

Next, truncate the table, and run the query again:

```
SQL> truncate table inv;
SQL> select * from inv;
```

Here is a partial listing from the output of AUTOTRACE:

```
no rows selected

Statistics
-----------------------------------------------------------
        6  recursive calls
        0  db block gets
       12  consistent gets
        0  physical reads
```

Note that the number of memory accesses and physical reads are now quite small.

Using DBMS_SPACE to Detect Space Below the High-Water Mark

You can use the DBMS_SPACE package to detect free blocks beneath the high-water mark. Here is an anonymous block of PL/SQL that you can call from SQL*Plus:

```
SQL> set serverout on size 1000000
SQL> declare
  p_fs1_bytes number;
  p_fs2_bytes number;
  p_fs3_bytes number;
  p_fs4_bytes number;
  p_fs1_blocks number;
  p_fs2_blocks number;
  p_fs3_blocks number;
  p_fs4_blocks number;
  p_full_bytes number;
```

```
    p_full_blocks number;
    p_unformatted_bytes number;
    p_unformatted_blocks number;
begin
    dbms_space.space_usage(
        segment_owner       => user,
        segment_name        => 'INV',
        segment_type        => 'TABLE',
        fs1_bytes           => p_fs1_bytes,
        fs1_blocks          => p_fs1_blocks,
        fs2_bytes           => p_fs2_bytes,
        fs2_blocks          => p_fs2_blocks,
        fs3_bytes           => p_fs3_bytes,
        fs3_blocks          => p_fs3_blocks,
        fs4_bytes           => p_fs4_bytes,
        fs4_blocks          => p_fs4_blocks,
        full_bytes          => p_full_bytes,
        full_blocks         => p_full_blocks,
        unformatted_blocks  => p_unformatted_blocks,
        unformatted_bytes   => p_unformatted_bytes
    );
    dbms_output.put_line('FS1: blocks = '||p_fs1_blocks);
    dbms_output.put_line('FS2: blocks = '||p_fs2_blocks);
    dbms_output.put_line('FS3: blocks = '||p_fs3_blocks);
    dbms_output.put_line('FS4: blocks = '||p_fs4_blocks);
    dbms_output.put_line('Full blocks = '||p_full_blocks);
end;
/
```

In this scenario, you want to check the INV table for free space below the high-water mark. Here is the output of the previous PL/SQL:

```
FS1: blocks = 0
FS2: blocks = 0
FS3: blocks = 0
FS4: blocks = 3646
Full blocks = 0
```

In the prior output the FS1 parameter shows that 0 blocks have 0 to 25 percent free space. The FS2 parameter shows that 0 blocks have 25 to 50 percent free space. The FS3 parameter shows that 0 blocks have 50 to 75 percent free space. The FS4 parameter shows there are 3,646 blocks with 75 to 100 percent free space. Finally, there are 0 full blocks. Because there are no full blocks, and a large number of blocks are mostly empty, you can see that free space exists below the high-water mark.

Selecting from Data Dictionary Extents View

You can also detect tables with high-water mark issues by selecting from DBA/ALL/USER_ EXTENTS views. If a table has a large number of extents allocated to it but has zero rows, that is an indication that an extensive amount of data has been deleted from the table; for example,

```
SQL> select count(*) from user_extents where segment_name='INV';

  COUNT(*)
----------
        44
```

Now, inspect the number of rows in the table:

```
SQL> select count(*) from inv;

  COUNT(*)
----------
         0
```

The prior table most likely has had data inserted into it, which resulted in extents being allocated. And, subsequently, data were deleted, and the extents remained.

Lowering the High-Water Mark

How can you reduce a table's high-water mark? You can use several techniques to set the high-water mark back to 0:

- A TRUNCATE statement

- ALTER TABLE ... SHRINK SPACE

- ALTER TABLE ... MOVE

Using the TRUNCATE statement was discussed earlier in this chapter (see the section "Using TRUNCATE"). Shrinking a table and moving a table are discussed in the following sections.

Shrinking a Table

To readjust the high-water mark, you must enable row movement for the table and then use the ALTER TABLE...SHRINK SPACE statement. The tablespace in which the table is created must have been built with automatic segment space management enabled. You can determine the tablespace segment space management type via this query:

```
SQL> select tablespace_name, segment_space_management from dba_tablespaces;
```

The SEGMENT_SPACE_MANAGEMENT value must be AUTO for the tablespace in which the table is created. Next, you need to enable row movement for the table to be shrunk. This example enables row movement for the INV table:

```
SQL> alter table inv enable row movement;
```

Now, you can shrink the space used by the table:

```
SQL> alter table inv shrink space;
```

You can also shrink the space associated with any index segments via the CASCADE clause:

```
SQL> alter table inv shrink space cascade;
```

Moving a Table

Moving a table means either rebuilding the table in its current tablespace or building it in a different tablespace. You may want to move a table because its current tablespace has disk space storage issues or because you want to lower the table's high-water mark.

Use the ALTER TABLE ... MOVE statement to move a table from one tablespace to another. This example moves the INV table to the USERS tablespace:

```
SQL> alter table inv move tablespace users;
```

You can verify that the table has been moved by querying USER_TABLES:

```
SQL> select table_name, tablespace_name from user_tables where table_
name='INV';
```

```
TABLE_NAME              TABLESPACE_NAME
--------------------    -------------------------------
INV                     USERS
```

Note   The ALTER TABLE ... MOVE statement does not allow DML to execute while it is running. There are some restrictions, but there is an ALTER TABLE ... ONLINE MOVE that will not restrict access to the table or using DBMS_REDEFINITION package.

You can also specify NOLOGGING when you move a table:

```
SQL> alter table inv move tablespace users nologging;
```

Moving a table with NOLOGGING eliminates most of the redo that would normally be generated when the table is relocated. The downside to using NOLOGGING is that if a failure occurs immediately after the table is moved (and hence, you do not have a backup of the table after it is moved), then you can't restore the contents of the table. If the data in the table are critical, then do not use NOLOGGING when moving them.

When you move a table, all its indexes are rendered unusable. This is because a table's index includes the ROWID as part of the structure. The table ROWID contains information about the physical location. Given that the ROWID of a table changes when the table moves from one tablespace to another (because the table rows are now physically located in different data files), any indexes on the table contain incorrect information. To rebuild the index, use the ALTER INDEX ... REBUILD command.

ORACLE ROWID

Every row in every table has an address. The address of a row is determined from a combination of the following:

```
Datafile number
Block number
Location of the row within the block
Object number
```

You can display the address of a row in a table by querying the ROWID pseudocolumn; for example,

```
SQL> select rowid, emp_id from emp;
```

Here is some sample output:

```
ROWID               EMP_ID
------------------ ----------
AAAFJAAAFAAAAJfAAA         1
```

The ROWID pseudocolumn value is not physically stored in the database. Oracle calculates Its value when you query it. The ROWID contents are displayed as base 64 values that can contain the characters A–Z, a–z, 0–9, +, and /. You can translate the ROWID value into meaningful information via the DMBS_ROWID package. For instance, to display the relative file number in which a row is stored, issue this statement:

```
SQL> select dbms_rowid.rowid_relative_fno(rowid), emp_id from emp;
```

Here is some sample output:

```
DBMS_ROWID.ROWID_RELATIVE_FNO(ROWID)     EMP_ID
------------------------------------- ----------
                                  5          1
```

You can use the ROWID value in the SELECT and WHERE clauses of an SQL statement. In most cases, the ROWID uniquely identifies a row. However, it is possible to have rows in different tables that are stored in the same cluster and that therefore contain rows with the same ROWID.

Creating a Temporary Table

Use the `CREATE GLOBAL TEMPORARY TABLE` statement to create a table that stores data only provisionally. You can specify that the temporary table retain the data for a session or until a transaction commits. Use `ON COMMIT PRESERVE ROWS` to specify that the data be deleted at the end of the user's session. In this example, the rows will be retained until the user either explicitly deletes the data or terminates the session:

```
SQL> create global temporary table today_regs
on commit preserve rows
as select * from f_registrations
where create_dtt > sysdate - 1;
```

Specify `ON COMMIT DELETE ROWS` to indicate that the data should be deleted at the end of the transaction. The following example creates a temporary table named `TEMP_OUTPUT` and specifies that records should be deleted at the end of each committed transaction:

```
create global temporary table temp_output(
  temp_row varchar2(30))
on commit delete rows;
```

Note   If you do not specify a commit method for a global temporary table, then the default is `ON COMMIT DELETE ROWS`.

You can create a temporary table and grant other users access to it. However, a session can only view the data that it inserts into a table. In other words, if two sessions are using the same temporary table, a session cannot select any data inserted into the temporary table by a different session.

A global temporary table is useful for applications that need to briefly store data in a table structure. After you create a temporary table, it exists until you drop it. In other words, the definition of the temporary table is "permanent"—it is the data that are short-lived (in this sense, the term temporary table can be misleading).

You can view whether a table is temporary by querying the `TEMPORARY` column of `DBA/ALL/USER_TABLES`:

```
SQL> select table_name, temporary from user_tables;
```

Temporary tables are designated with a Y in the TEMPORARY column. Regular tables contain an N in the TEMPORARY column.

When you create records in a temporary table, space is allocated in your default temporary tablespace. You can verify this by running the following SQL:

```
SQL> select username, contents, segtype from v$sort_usage;
```

If you are working with a large number of rows and need better performance for selectively retrieving rows, you may want to consider creating an index on the appropriate columns in your temporary table:

```
SQL> create index temp_index on temp_output(temp_row);
```

Use the DROP TABLE command to drop a temporary table:

```
SQL> drop table temp_output;
```

TEMPORARY TABLE REDO

No redo data are generated for changes to blocks of a global temporary table. However, rollback (undo) data are generated for a transaction against a temporary table. Because the rollback data generate redo, some redo data are associated with a transaction for a temporary table. You can verify this by turning on statistics tracing and viewing the redo size as you insert records into a temporary table:

```
SQL> set autotrace on
```

Next, insert a few records into the temporary table:

```
SQL> insert into temp_output values(1);
```

Here is a snippet of the output (only showing the redo size):

```
140 redo size
```

The redo load is less for temporary tables than normal tables because the redo generated is only associated with the rollback (undo) data for a temporary table transaction.

Additionally, starting with Oracle Database 12c, the undo for temporary objects is stored in the temporary tablespace, not the undo tablespace.

Creating an Index-Organized Table

Index-organized tables (IOTs) are efficient objects when the table data are typically accessed through querying on the primary key. Use the `ORGANIZATION INDEX` clause to create an IOT:

```
SQL> create table prod_sku
(prod_sku_id number,
sku varchar2(256),
create_dtt timestamp(5),
constraint prod_sku_pk primary key(prod_sku_id)
)
organization index
including sku
pctthreshold 30
tablespace inv_data
overflow
tablespace inv_data;
```

An IOT stores the entire contents of the table's row in a B-tree index structure. IOTs provide fast access for queries that have exact matches or range searches, or both, on the primary key.

All columns specified, up to and including the column specified in the `INCLUDING` clause, are stored in the same block as the `PROD_SKU_ID` primary key column. In other words, the `INCLUDING` clause specifies the last column to keep in the table segment. Columns listed after the column specified in the `INCLUDING` clause are stored in the overflow data segment. In the previous example, the `CREATE_DTT` column is stored in the overflow segment.

`PCTTHRESHOLD` specifies the percentage of space reserved in the index block for the IOT row. This value can be from 1 to 50 and defaults to 50 if no value is specified. There must be enough space in the index block to store the primary key.

The `OVERFLOW` clause details which tablespace should be used to store overflow data segments. Note that `DBA/ALL/USER_TABLES` includes an entry for the table name used when creating an IOT. Additionally, `DBA/ALL/USER_INDEXES` contains a record with the name of the primary key constraint specified. The `INDEX_TYPE` column contains a value of `IOT - TOP` for IOTs:

```
SQL> select index_name,table_name,index_type from user_indexes;
```

Managing Constraints

The next several sections in this chapter deal with constraints. Constraints provide a mechanism for ensuring that data conform to certain business rules. You must be aware of what types of constraints are available and when it is appropriate to use them. Oracle offers several types of constraints:

- Primary key
- Unique key
- Foreign key
- Check
- NOT NULL

Implementing and managing these constraints are discussed in the following sections.

Creating Primary Key Constraints

When you implement a database, most tables you create require a primary key constraint to guarantee that every record in the table can be uniquely identified. There are multiple techniques for adding a primary key constraint to a table. The first example creates the primary key inline with the column definition:

```
SQL> create table dept(
 dept_id number primary key
,dept_desc varchar2(30));
```

If you select the CONSTRAINT_NAME from USER_CONSTRAINTS, note that Oracle generates a cryptic name for the constraint (such as SYS_C003682). Use the following syntax to explicitly give a name to a primary key constraint:

```
SQL> create table dept(
dept_id number constraint dept_pk primary key using index tablespace users,
dept_desc varchar2(30));
```

Note   When you create a primary key constraint, Oracle also creates a unique index with the same name as the constraint. You can control which tablespace the unique index is placed in via the USING INDEX TABLESPACE clause.

You can also specify the primary key constraint definition after the columns have been defined. The advantage of doing this is that you can define the constraint on multiple columns. The next example creates the primary key when the table is created, but not inline with the column definition:

```
SQL> create table dept(
dept_id number,
dept_desc varchar2(30),
constraint dept_pk primary key (dept_id)
using index tablespace users);
```

If the table has already been created, and you want to add a primary key constraint, use the ALTER TABLE statement. This example places a primary key constraint on the DEPT_ID column of the DEPT table:

```
SQL> alter table dept
add constraint dept_pk primary key (dept_id)
using index tablespace users;
```

When a primary key constraint is enabled, Oracle automatically creates a unique index associated with the primary key constraint. Some DBAs prefer to first create a non-unique index on the primary key column and then define the primary key constraint:

```
SQL> create index dept_pk on dept(dept_id) tablespace users;
SQL> alter table dept add constraint dept_pk primary key (dept_id);
```

The advantage of this approach is that you can drop or disable the primary key constraint independently of the index. When you are working with large data sets, you may want that sort of flexibility. If you do not create the index before creating the primary key constraint, then whenever you drop or disable the primary key constraint, the index is automatically dropped.

Confused about which method to use to create a primary key? All the methods are valid and have their merits. Table 7-4 summarizes the primary key and unique key constraint creation methods. I've used all these methods to create primary key constraints. Usually, I use the ALTER TABLE statement, which adds the constraint after the table has been created.

Table 7-4. *Primary Key and Unique Key Constraint Creation Methods*

Constraint Creation Method	Advantages	Disadvantages
Inline, no name	Very simple	Oracle-generated name makes troubleshooting harder; less control over storage attributes; only applied to a single column
Inline, with name	Simple; user-defined name makes troubleshooting easier	Requires more thought than inline without name
Inline, with name and tablespace definition	User-defined name and tablespace; makes troubleshooting easier	Less simple
After column definition (out of line)	User-defined name and tablespace; can operate on multiple columns	Less simple
ALTER TABLE add just constraint	Lets you manage constraints in statements (and files) separate from table creation scripts; can operate on multiple columns	More complicated
CREATE INDEX, ALTER TABLE add constraint	Separates the index and constraint, so you can drop/disable constraints without affecting the index; can operate on multiple columns	Most complicated: more to maintain, more moving parts

Enforcing Unique Key Values

In addition to creating a primary key constraint, you should create unique constraints on any combinations of columns that should always be unique within a table. For example, for the primary key for a table, it is common to use a numeric key (sometimes called a surrogate key) that is populated via a sequence. Besides the surrogate primary key, sometimes users have a column (or columns) that the business uses to uniquely identify a record (also called a logical key). Using both a surrogate key and a logical key does the following:

- Lets you efficiently join parent and child tables on a single numeric column

- Allows updates to logical key columns without changing the surrogate key

A unique key guarantees uniqueness on the defined column(s) within a table. There are some subtle differences between primary key and unique key constraints. For example, you can define only one primary key per table, but there can be several unique keys. Also, a primary key does not allow a NULL value in any of its columns, whereas a unique key allows NULL values.

As with the primary key constraint, you can use several methods to create a unique column constraint. This method uses the UNIQUE keyword inline with the column:

```
SQL> create table dept(
 dept_id number
,dept_desc varchar2(30) unique);
```

If you want to explicitly name the constraint, use the CONSTRAINT keyword:

```
SQL> create table dept(
 dept_id number
,dept_desc varchar2(30) constraint dept_desc_uk1 unique);
```

As with primary keys, Oracle automatically creates an index associated with the unique key constraint. You can specify inline the tablespace information to be used for the associated unique index:

```
SQL> create table dept(
 dept_id number
,dept_desc varchar2(30) constraint dept_desc_uk1
   unique using index tablespace users);
```

You can also alter a table to include a unique constraint:

```
SQL> alter table dept
add constraint dept_desc_uk1 unique (dept_desc)
using index tablespace users;
```

And you can create an index on the columns of interest before you define a unique key constraint:

```
SQL> create index dept_desc_uk1 on dept(dept_desc) tablespace users;
SQL> alter table dept add constraint dept_desc_uk1 unique(dept_desc);
```

This can be helpful when you are working with large data sets, and you want to be able to disable or drop the unique constraint without dropping the associated index.

Tip   You can also enforce a unique key constraint with a unique index. See Chapter 8 for details on using unique indexes to enforce unique constraints.

Creating Foreign Key Constraints

Foreign key constraints are used to ensure that a column value is contained within a defined list of values. Using a foreign key constraint is an efficient way of enforcing that data be a predefined value before an insert or update is allowed. This technique works well for the following scenarios:

- The list of values contains many entries.

- Other information about the lookup value needs to be stored.

- It is easy to select, insert, update, or delete values via SQL.

For example, suppose the EMP table is created with a DEPT_ID column. To ensure that each employee is assigned a valid department, you can create a foreign key constraint that enforces the rule that each DEPT_ID in the EMP table must exist in the DEPT table.

Tip   If the condition you want to check for consists of a small list that does not change very often, consider using a check constraint instead of a foreign key constraint. For instance, if you have a column that will always be defined as containing either a 0 or a 1, a check constraint is an efficient solution.

For reference, here's how the parent table DEPT table was created for these examples:

```
SQL> create table dept(
dept_id number primary key,
dept_desc varchar2(30));
```

A foreign key must reference a column in the parent table that has a primary key or a unique key defined on it. DEPT is the parent table and has a primary key defined on DEPT_ID.

You can use several methods to create a foreign key constraint. The following example creates a foreign key constraint on the DEPT_ID column in the EMP table:

```
SQL> create table emp(
emp_id number,
name varchar2(30),
dept_id constraint emp_dept_fk references dept(dept_id));
```

Note that the DEPT_ID data type is not explicitly defined. The foreign key constraint derives the data type from the referenced DEPT_ID column of the DEPT table. You can also explicitly specify the data type when you define a column (regardless of the foreign key definition):

```
SQL> create table emp(
emp_id number,
name varchar2(30),
dept_id number constraint emp_dept_fk references dept(dept_id));
```

You can also specify the foreign key definition out of line from the column definition in the CREATE TABLE statement:

```
SQL> create table emp(
emp_id number,
name varchar2(30),
dept_id number,
constraint emp_dept_fk foreign key (dept_id) references dept(dept_id)
);
```

And, you can alter an existing table to add a foreign key constraint:

```
SQL> alter table emp
add constraint emp_dept_fk foreign key (dept_id)
references dept(dept_id);
```

Note Unlike with primary key and unique key constraints, Oracle does not automatically add an index to foreign key columns; you must explicitly create indexes on them. See Chapter 8 for a discussion on why it is important to create indexes on foreign key columns and how to detect foreign key columns that do not have associated indexes.

Checking for Specific Data Conditions

A check constraint works well for lookups when you have a short list of fairly static values, such as a column that can be either Y or N. In this situation the list of values most likely won't change, and no information needs to be stored other than Y or N, so a check constraint is the appropriate solution. If you have a long list of values that needs to be periodically updated, then a table and a foreign key constraint are a better solution.

Also, a check constraint works well for a business rule that must always be enforced and that can be written with a simple SQL expression. If you have sophisticated business logic that must be validated, then the application code is more appropriate.

You can define a check constraint when you create a table. The following enforces the ST_FLG column to contain either a 0 or 1:

```
SQL> create table emp(
emp_id number,
emp_name varchar2(30),
st_flg number(1) CHECK (st_flg in (0,1))
);
```

A slightly better method is to give the check constraint a name:

```
SQL> create table emp(
emp_id number,
emp_name varchar2(30),
st_flg number(1) constraint st_flg_chk CHECK (st_flg in (0,1))
);
```

A more descriptive way to name the constraint is to embed information in the constraint name that describes the condition that was violated; for example,

```
SQL> create table emp(
emp_id number,
emp_name varchar2(30),
st_flg number(1) constraint "st_flg must be 0 or 1" check (st_flg in (0,1))
);
```

You can also alter an existing column to include a constraint. The column must not contain any values that violate the constraint being enabled:

```
SQL> alter table emp add constraint
    "st_flg must be 0 or 1" check (st_flg in (0,1));
```

Note   The check constraint must evaluate to a true or unknown (NULL) value in the row being inserted or updated. You cannot use subqueries or sequences in a check constraint. Also, you can't reference the SQL functions UID, USER, SYSDATE, or USERENV or the pseudocolumns LEVEL or ROWNUM.

Enforcing Not Null Conditions

Another common condition to check for is whether a column is null; you use the NOT NULL constraint to do this. The NOT NULL constraint can be defined in several ways. The simplest technique is shown here:

```
SQL> create table emp(
emp_id number,
emp_name varchar2(30) not null);
```

A slightly better approach is to give the NOT NULL constraint a name that makes sense to you. Naming the constraint will allow you to see what the constraint is for instead of a system-generated constraint, which might be confused with a primary or foreign key constraint:

```
SQL> create table emp(
emp_id number,
emp_name varchar2(30) constraint emp_name_nn not null);
```

Use the ALTER TABLE command if you need to modify a column for an existing table. For the following command to work, there must not be any NULL values in the column being defined as NOT NULL:

```
SQL> alter table emp modify(emp_name not null);
```

Note   If there are currently NULL values in a column that is being defined as NOT NULL, you must first update the table so that the column has a value in every row.

Disabling Constraints

One nice feature of Oracle is that you can disable and enable constraints without dropping and re-creating them. This means that you avoid having to know the DDL statements that would be required to re-create the dropped constraints.

Occasionally, you need to disable constraints. For example, you may be trying to truncate a table but receive the following error message:

ORA-02266: unique/primary keys in table referenced by enabled foreign keys

Oracle does not allow a truncate operation on a parent table with a primary key that is referenced by an enabled foreign key in a child table. If you need to truncate a parent table, you first have to disable all the enabled foreign key constraints that reference the parent table's primary key. Run this query to determine the names of the constraints that need to be disabled:

```
SQL> col primary_key_table form a18
SQL> col primary_key_constraint form a18
SQL> col fk_child_table form a18
SQL> col fk_child_table_constraint form a18
--
SQL> select
 b.table_name primary_key_table
,b.constraint_name primary_key_constraint
,a.table_name fk_child_table
,a.constraint_name fk_child_table_constraint
from dba_constraints a
,dba_constraints b
where a.r_constraint_name = b.constraint_name
and a.r_owner = b.owner
and a.constraint_type = 'R'
and b.owner = upper('&table_owner')
and b.table_name = upper('&pk_table_name');
```

For this example, there is only one foreign key dependency:

```
PRIMARY_KEY_TAB PRIMARY_KEY_CON FK_CHILD_TABLE  FK_CHILD_TABLE_
--------------- --------------- --------------- ---------------
DEPT            DEPT_PK         EMP             EMP_DEPT_FK
```

Use the ALTER TABLE statement to disable constraints on a table. In this case, there is only one foreign key to disable:

```
SQL> alter table emp disable constraint emp_dept_fk;
```

You can now truncate the parent table:

```
SQL> truncate table dept;
```

Do not forget to reenable the foreign key constraints after the truncate operation has completed, like this:

```
SQL> alter table emp enable constraint emp_dept_fk;
```

You can disable a primary key and all dependent foreign key constraints with the CASCADE option of the DISABLE clause. For example, the next line of code disables all foreign key constraints related to the primary key constraint:

```
SQL> alter table dept disable constraint dept_pk cascade;
```

This statement does not cascade through all levels of dependencies; it only disables the foreign key constraints directly dependent on DEPT_PK. Also keep in mind that there is no ENABLE...CASCADE statement. To re-enable the constraints, you have to query the data dictionary to determine which constraints have been disabled and then re-enable them individually.

Sometimes, you run into situations, when loading data, in which it is convenient to disable all the foreign keys before loading the data. In these situations, the imp utility imports the tables in alphabetical order and does not ensure that child tables are imported before parent tables. You may also want to run several import jobs in parallel to take advantage of parallel hardware. In such scenarios, you can disable the foreign keys, perform the import, and then re-enable the foreign keys.

Here is a script that uses SQL to generate SQL to disable all foreign key constraints for a user:

```
SQL> set lines 132 trimsp on head off feed off verify off echo off pagesize 0
SQL> spo dis_dyn.sql
SQL> select 'alter table ' || a.table_name
|| ' disable constraint ' || a.constraint_name || ';'
from dba_constraints a
,dba_constraints b
where a.r_constraint_name = b.constraint_name
and a.r_owner = b.owner
and a.constraint_type = 'R'
and b.owner = upper('&table_owner');
SQL> spo off;
```

This script generates a file, named `dis_dyn.sql`, which contains the SQL statements to disable all the foreign key constraints for a user.

EnablingConstraints

This section contains a few scripts to help you enable constraints that you've disabled. Listed next is a script that creates a file with the SQL statements required to re-enable any foreign key constraints for tables owned by a specified user:

```
SQL> set lines 132 trimsp on head off feed off verify off echo off pagesize 0
SQL> spo enable_dyn.sql
SQL> select 'alter table ' || a.table_name
|| ' enable constraint ' || a.constraint_name || ';'
from dba_constraints a
,dba_constraints b
where a.r_constraint_name = b.constraint_name
and a.r_owner = b.owner
and a.constraint_type = 'R'
and b.owner = upper('&table_owner');
SQL> spo off;
```

When enabling constraints, by default, Oracle checks to ensure that the data do not violate the constraint definition. If you are fairly certain that the data integrity is fine and that you do not need to incur the performance hit by revalidating the constraint, you can use the NOVALIDATE clause when re-enabling the constraints. Here is an example:

```
SQL> select 'alter table ' || a.table_name
|| ' modify constraint ' || a.constraint_name || ' enable novalidate;'
from dba_constraints a
,dba_constraints b
where a.r_constraint_name = b.constraint_name
and a.r_owner = b.owner
and a.constraint_type = 'R'
and b.owner = upper('&table_owner');
```

The NOVALIDATE clause instructs Oracle not to validate the constraints being enabled, but it does enforce that any new DML activities adhere to the constraint definition.

In multiuser systems the possibility exists that another session has inserted data into the child table while the foreign key constraint was disabled. If that happens, you see the following error when you attempt to re-enable the foreign key:

```
ORA-02298: cannot validate (<owner>.<constraint>) - parent keys not found
```

In this scenario, you can use the ENABLE NOVALIDATE clause:

```
SQL> alter table emp enable novalidate constraint emp_dept_fk;
```

To clean up the rows that violate the constraint, first ensure that you have an EXCEPTIONS table created in your currently connected schema. If you do not have an EXCEPTIONS table, use this script to create one:

```
SQL> @?/rdbms/admin/utlexcpt.sql
```

Next, populate the EXCEPTIONS table with the rows that violate the constraint, using the EXCEPTIONS INTO clause:

```
SQL> alter table emp modify constraint emp_dept_fk validate
exceptions into exceptions;
```

This statement still throws the ORA-02298 error as long as there are rows that violate the constraint. The statement also inserts records into the EXCEPTIONS table for any bad rows. You can now use the ROW_ID column of the EXCEPTIONS table to remove any records that violate the constraint.

Here, you see that one row needs to be removed from the EMP table:

```
SQL> select * from exceptions;
```

Here is some sample output:

```
ROW_ID              OWNER     TABLE_NAME CONSTRAINT
------------------- --------- ---------- --------------------
AAAFKQAABAAAK8JAAB MV_MAINT  EMP        EMP_DEPT_FK
```

To remove the offending record, issue a DELETE statement:

```
SQL> delete from emp where rowid = 'AAAFKQAABAAAK8JAAB';
```

If the EXCEPTIONS table contains many records, you can run a query such as the following to delete by OWNER and TABLE_NAME:

```
SQL> delete from emp where rowid in
(select row_id
from exceptions
where owner=upper('&owner') and table_name = upper('&table_name'));
```

You may also run into situations in which you need to disable primary key or unique key constraints, or both. For instance, you may want to perform a large data load and for performance reasons want to disable the primary key and unique key constraints. You do not want to incur the overhead of having every row checked as it is inserted.

The same general techniques used for disabling foreign keys are applicable for disabling primary and unique keys. Run this query to display the primary key and unique key constraints for a user:

```
SQL> select
a.table_name
,a.constraint_name
,a.constraint_type
from dba_constraints a
where a.owner = upper('&table_owner')
and a.constraint_type in ('P','U')
order by a.table_name;
```

When the table name and constraint name are identified, use the ALTER TABLE statement to disable the constraint:

```
SQL> alter table dept disable constraint dept_pk;
```

Note   Oracle does not let you disable a primary key or unique key constraint that is referenced in an enabled foreign key constraint. You first have to disable the foreign key constraint.

Summary

This chapter focused on basic activities related to creating and maintaining tables. Tables are the containers that store the data within the database. Key table management tasks include modifying, moving, deleting from, shrinking, and dropping. You must also be familiar with how to implement and use special table types, such as temporary, IOT, and read-only.

Oracle also provides various constraints to help you manage the data within tables. Constraints form the bedrock of data integrity. In most cases, each table should include a primary key constraint that ensures that every row is uniquely identifiable. Additionally, any parent–child relationships should be enforced with foreign key constraints. You can use unique constraints to implement business rules that require a column or combination of columns to be unique. Check and NOT NULL constraints ensure that columns contain business-specified data requirements.

Modifying tables can be done online with DBMS_REDEFINITION packages and scripts can be generated to prepare for table changes. It is something to test through the development environments in order to have all of the pieces such as indexes and enabling constraints as a script to run together so not to forget to enable or create keys and indexes.

After you create tables, the next logical activity is to create indexes where appropriate. Indexes are optional database objects that help improve performance. Index creation and maintenance tasks are covered in the next chapter.

CHAPTER 8

Indexes

An index is an optionally created database object used primarily to increase query performance. Indexes can also limit the amount of data that is returned in the results without having to retrieve all of data columns of a table. This can help keep results in memory and bring back results faster. The purpose of a database index is similar to that of an index in the back of a book. A book index associates a topic with a page number. When you are locating information in a book, it is usually much faster to examine the index first, find the topic of interest, and identify associated page numbers. With this information, you can navigate directly to specific page numbers in the book.

If a topic only appears on a few pages within the book, then the number of pages to read is minimal. In this manner, the usefulness of the index decreases with an increase in the number of times a topic appears in a book. In other words, if a subject entry appears on every page of the book, there would be no benefit to creating an index on it. In this scenario, regardless of the presence of an index, it would be more efficient for the reader to scan every page of the book.

Note   In database parlance, searching all blocks of a table is known as a full-table scan. Full-table scans occur when there is no available index or when the query optimizer determines a full-table scan is a more efficient access path than using an existing index.

Similar to a book index (topic and page number), a database index stores the column value of interest, along with its row identifier (ROWID). The ROWID contains the physical location of the table row on disk that stores the column value. With the ROWID in hand, Oracle can efficiently retrieve table data with a minimum of disk reads. In this way, indexes function as a shortcut to the table data. If there is no available index, then Oracle reads each row in the table to determine if the row contains the desired information.

© Michelle Malcher and Darl Kuhn 2019
M. Malcher and D. Kuhn, *Pro Oracle Database 18c Administration*,
https://doi.org/10.1007/978-1-4842-4424-1_8

Note   In addition to improving performance, Oracle uses indexes to help enforce enabled primary key and unique key constraints. Additionally, Oracle can better manage certain table-locking scenarios when indexes are placed on foreign key columns.

Whereas it is possible to build a database application devoid of indexes, without them or too many of them, you are almost guaranteeing poor performance. Indexes allow for excellent scalability, even with very large data sets. If indexes are so important to database performance, why not place them on all tables and column combinations? The answer is short: indexes are not free. They consume disk space and system resources. As column values are modified, any corresponding indexes must also be updated. In this way, indexes use storage, I/O, CPU, and memory resources. A poor choice of indexes leads to wasted disk usage and excessive consumption of system resources. This results in a decrease in database performance and greater cost for DML statements.

Automation and proactively tuning database applications are ever-growing areas of the database. Indexes, statistics, and overall database configuration play into developing the strategies to tune. Oracle 18c provides enhanced statistics and collection of information about indexes being used. These tools can be utilized as part of the index planning and design for the database tables and indexes.

For these reasons, when you design and build an Oracle database application, consideration must be given to your indexing strategy. As an application architect, you must understand the physical properties of an index, what types of indexes are available, and strategies for choosing which table and column combinations to index. A correct indexing methodology is central to achieving maximum performance for your database.

Deciding When to Create an Index

There are usually two different situations in which DBAs and developers decide to create indexes:

- Proactively, when first deploying an application; the DBAs/ developers make an educated guess as to which tables and columns to index.

- Reactively, when application performance bogs down, and users complain of poor performance; then, the DBAs/developers attempt to identify slow-executing SQL queries and how indexes might be a solution.

The prior two topics are discussed in the next two sections.

Proactively Creating Indexes

When creating a new database application, part of the process involves identifying primary keys, unique keys, and foreign keys. The columns associated with those keys are usually candidates for indexes. Here are some guidelines:

- Define a primary key constraint for each table. This results in an index automatically being created on the columns specified in the primary key.

- Create unique key constraints on columns that are required to be unique and that are different from the primary key columns. Each unique key constraint results in an index automatically being created on the columns specified in the constraint.

- Manually create indexes on foreign key columns. This is done for better performance, to avoid certain locking issues.

In other words, some of the decision process on what tables and columns to index is automatically done for you when determining the table constraints. When creating primary and unique key constraints, Oracle automatically creates indexes for you. There is some debate about whether or not to create indexes on foreign key columns. See the section "Indexing Foreign Key Columns," later in this chapter, for further discussion.

These indexes can be automated to run with table creation or as part of the object builds in the database. Also, if foreign keys are newly created, an index can be generated as part of the code to make sure that the indexes are be created as changes are made and instead of manually checking all of the constraints, indexes, and keys, DDL can be generated based on new objects and added as part of proactively creating indexes.

In addition to creating indexes related to constraints, if you have enough knowledge of the SQL contained within the application, you can create indexes related to tables and columns referenced in SELECT, FROM, and WHERE clauses. In my experience, DBAs and developers are not adept at proactively identifying such indexes. Rather, these indexing requirements are usually identified reactively.

Reactively Creating Indexes

Rarely do DBAs and developers accurately create the right mix of indexes when first deploying an application. And, that is not a bad thing or unexpected; it is hard to predict everything that occurs in a large database system. Furthermore, as the application matures, changes are introduced to the database (new tables, new columns, new constraints, database upgrades that add new features/behaviors, and so on). The reality is that you will have to react to unforeseen situations in your database that warrant adding indexes to improve performance.

Index strategies also have to be revisited for major database releases or system resource changes. For example, more memory on the server will allow for a table scan to perform better and maybe eliminate a need for an index. Or for an index that was beneficial because of how the optimizer was calculating cost, upgrades might validate a different query plan for better performance.

Note   Index strategies are not just about creating indexes but also about cleaning up indexes that are no longer in use because of better statistics and optimizer query plans without the index.

Here is a typical process for reactively identifying poorly performing SQL statements and improving performance with indexes:

1. A poorly performing SQL statement is identified (a user complains about a specific statement, the DBA runs automatic database diagnostic monitor (ADDM), or automatic workload repository (AWR) reports to identify resource-consuming SQL, and so on).

2. DBA checks the table and index statistics to ensure that out-of-date statistics are not causing the optimizer to make bad choices.

3. DBA/developer determines that the query cannot be rewritten in a way that alleviates performance issues.

4. DBA/developer examines the SQL statement and determines which tables and columns are being accessed, by inspecting the SELECT, FROM, and WHERE clauses.

5. DBA/developer performs testing and recommends that an index be created, based on a table and one or more columns.

Once you have identified a poorly performing SQL query, consider creating indexes for the following situations:

- Create indexes on columns used often as predicates in the WHERE clause; when multiple columns from a table are used in the WHERE clause, consider using a concatenated (multicolumn) index.

- Create a covering index (i.e., an index on all columns) in the SELECT clause.

- Create indexes on columns used in the ORDER BY, GROUP BY, UNION, and DISTINCT clauses.

Oracle allows you to create an index that contains more than one column. Multicolumn indexes are known as concatenated indexes (also called composite indexes). These indexes are especially effective when you often use multiple columns in the WHERE clause when accessing a table. Concatenated indexes are, in many instances, more efficient in this situation than creating separate, single-column indexes (See the section "Creating Concatenated Indexes," later in this chapter, for more details).

Columns included in the SELECT and WHERE clauses are also potential candidates for indexes. Sometimes, a covering index in a SELECT clause results in Oracle using the index structure itself (and not the table) to satisfy the results of the query. Also, if the column values are selective enough, Oracle can use an index on columns referenced in the WHERE clause to improve query performance.

Also consider creating indexes on columns used in the ORDER BY, GROUP BY, UNION, and DISTINCT clauses. This may result in greater efficiency for queries that frequently use these SQL constructs.

It is okay to have multiple indexes per table. However, the more indexes you place on a table, the slower the DML statements. Do not fall into the trap of randomly adding indexes to a table until you stumble upon the right combination of indexed columns. Rather, verify the performance of an index before you create it in a production environment. Oracle 18c has improved how it reviews index usage, and these statistics can be taken into consideration when deciding to keep indexes or if a different index is needed.

Also keep in mind that it is possible to add an index that increases the performance of one statement, while hurting the performance of others. You must be sure that the statements that are improved warrant the penalty being applied to other statements. You should only add an index when you are certain it will improve performance.

Planning for Robustness

After you have decided that you need to create an index, it is prudent to make a few foundational decisions that will affect maintainability and availability. Oracle provides a wide assortment of indexing features and options. As a DBA or a developer, you need to be aware of the various features and how to use them. If you choose the wrong type of index or use a feature incorrectly, there may be serious, detrimental performance implications. Listed next are manageability features to consider before you create an index:

- Type of index

- Initial space required and growth

- Temporary tablespace usage while the index is being created (for large indexes)

- Tablespace placement

- Naming conventions

- Which column(s) to include

- Whether to use a single column or a combination of columns

- Special features, such as the PARALLEL clause, NOLOGGING, compression, and invisible indexes

- Uniqueness

- Impact on performance of SELECT statements (improvement)

- Impact on performance of INSERT, UPDATE, and DELETE statements

These topics are discussed in subsequent sections in this chapter.

Determining Which Type of Index to Use

Oracle provides a wide range of index types and features. The correct use of indexes results in a well-performing and scalable database application. Conversely, if you incorrectly or unwisely implement a feature, there may be detrimental performance implications. Table 8-1 summarizes the various Oracle index types available. At first glance, this is a long list and may be somewhat overwhelming to somebody new to Oracle. However, deciding which index type to use is not as daunting as it might initially seem. For most applications, you should simply use the default B-tree index type.

Note   Several of the index types listed in Table 8-1 are actually just variations on the B-tree index. A reverse-key index, for example, is merely a B-tree index optimized for evenly spreading I/O when the index value is sequentially generated and inserted with similar values.

Table 8-1. *Oracle Index Type and Usage Descriptions*

Index Type	Usage
B-tree	Default index; good for columns with high cardinality (i.e., high degree of distinct values). Use a normal B-tree index unless you have a concrete reason to use a different index type or feature.
IOT	This index is efficient when most of the column values are included in the primary key. You access the index as if it were a table. The data are stored in a B-tree-like structure. See Chapter 7 for details on this type of index.
Unique	A form of B-tree index; used to enforce uniqueness in column values; often used with primary key and unique key constraints but can be created independently of constraints.
Reverse key	A form of B-tree index; useful for balancing I/O in an index that has many sequential inserts.
Key compressed	Good for concatenated indexes in which the leading column is often repeated; compresses leaf block entries; applies to B-tree and IOT indexes.
Descending	A form of B-tree index; used with indexes in which corresponding column values are sorted in a descending order (the default order is ascending). You cannot specify descending for a reverse-key index, and Oracle ignores descending if the index type is bitmap.
Bitmap	Excellent in data warehouse environments with low cardinality (i.e., low degree of distinct values) columns and SQL statements using many AND or OR operators in the WHERE clause. Bitmap indexes are not appropriate for OLTP databases in which rows are frequently updated. You cannot create a unique bitmap index.

(continued)

Table 8-1. (*continued*)

Index Type	Usage
Bitmap join	Useful in data warehouse environments for queries that use star schema structures that join fact and dimension tables.
Function based	Good for columns that have SQL functions applied to them; can be used with either a B-tree or bitmap index.
Indexed virtual column	An index defined on a virtual column (of a table); useful for columns that have SQL functions applied to them; a viable alternative to a function-based index.
Virtual	Allows you to create an index with no physical segment or extents via the NOSEGMENT clause of CREATE INDEX; useful in tuning SQL without consuming resources required to build the physical index. Any index type can be created as virtual.
Invisible	The index is not visible to the query optimizer. However, the structure of the index is maintained as table data are modified. Useful for testing an index before making it visible to the application. Any index type can be created as invisible.
Global partitioned	Global index across all partitions in a partitioned or regular table; can be a B-tree index type and cannot be a bitmap index type.
Local partitioned	Local index based on individual partitions in a partitioned table; can be either a B-tree or bitmap index type.
Domain	Specific for an application or cartridge.
B-tree cluster	Used with clustered tables.
Hash cluster	Used with hash clusters.

This chapter focuses on the most commonly used indexes and features—B-tree, function based, unique, bitmap, reverse key, and key compressed—and the most used options. IOTs are covered in Chapter 7, and partitioned indexes are covered in Chapter 12. If you need more information about index types or features, see the Oracle SQL Reference Guide, which is available for download from the Technology Network area of the Oracle web site (http://otn.oracle.com).

Estimating the Size of an Index Before Creation

If you do not work with large databases, then you do not need to worry about estimating the amount of space an index will initially consume. However, for large databases, you absolutely need an estimate on how much space it will take to create an index. If you have a large table in a data warehouse environment, a corresponding index could easily be hundreds of gigabytes in size. In this situation, you need to ensure that the database has adequate disk space available.

The best way to predict the size of an index is to create it in a test environment that has a representative set of production data. If you cannot build a complete replica of production data, a subset of data can often be used to extrapolate the size required in production. If you do not have the luxury of using a cut of production data, you can also estimate the size of an index using the DBMS_SPACE.CREATE_INDEX_COST procedure.

Note   I have seen tables that are several hundred gigabytes in size, but the index space is twice the amount of the tablespace. It is not because the index has more columns but because it has so many different indexes. Having three or more indexes for each very large table starts to add up quickly.

For reference, here is the table creation script that the index used in the subsequent examples is based on:

```
SQL> CREATE TABLE cust
(cust_id    NUMBER
,last_name  VARCHAR2(30)
,first_name VARCHAR2(30)
) TABLESPACE users;
```

Next, several thousand records are inserted into the prior table. Here is a snippet of the insert statements:

```
SQL> insert into cust values(7,'ACER','SCOTT');
SQL> insert into cust values(5,'STARK','JIM');
SQL> insert into cust values(3,'GREY','BOB');
SQL> insert into cust values(11,'KAHN','BRAD');
SQL> insert into cust values(21,'DEAN','ANN');
...
```

Now, suppose you want to create an index on the CUST table like this:

```
SQL> create index cust_idx1 on cust(last_name);
```

Here is the procedure for estimating the amount of space the index will initially consume:

```
SQL> set serverout on
SQL> exec dbms_stats.gather_table_stats(user,'CUST');
SQL> variable used_bytes number
SQL> variable alloc_bytes number
SQL> exec dbms_space.create_index_cost( 'create index cust_idx1 on
cust(last_name)', -
                :used_bytes, :alloc_bytes );
SQL> print :used_bytes
```

Here is some sample output for this example:

```
USED_BYTES
----------
  19800000

SQL> print :alloc_bytes


ALLOC_BYTES
----------
  33554432
```

The used_bytes variable gives you an estimate of how much room is required for the index data. The alloc_bytes variable provides an estimate of how much space will be allocated within the tablespace.

Next, go ahead and create the index.

```
SQL> create index cust_idx1 on cust(last_name);
```

The actual amount of space consumed is shown by this query:

```
SQL> select bytes from user_segments where segment_name='CUST_IDX1';
```

The output indicates that the estimated number of allocated bytes is in the ballpark of the amount of space actually consumed:

```
BYTES
----------
34603008
```

Your results may vary, depending on the number of records, the number of columns, the data types, and the accuracy of statistics.

In addition to the initial sizing, keep in mind that the index will grow as records are inserted into the table. You will have to monitor the space consumed by the index and ensure that there is enough disk space to accommodate future growth requirements.

CREATING INDEXES AND TEMPORARY TABLESPACE SPACE

Related to space usage, sometimes DBAs forget that Oracle often requires space in either memory or disk to sort an index as it is created. If the available memory area is consumed, then Oracle allocates disk space as required within the default temporary tablespace. If you are creating a large index, you may need to increase the size of your temporary tablespace.

Another approach is to create an additional temporary tablespace and then assign it to be the default temporary tablespace of the user creating the index. After the index is created, you can drop the temporary tablespace (that was created just for the new index) and reassign the user's default temporary tablespace back to the original temporary tablespace.

Creating Separate Tablespaces for Indexes

For critical applications, you must give some thought to how much space tables and indexes will consume and how fast they grow. Space consumption and object growth have a direct impact on database availability. If you run out of space, your database will become unavailable. The best way to manage space in the database is by creating tablespaces tailored to space requirements and then creating objects in specified tablespaces that you have designed for those objects. With that in mind, I recommend that you separate tables and indexes into different tablespaces. Consider the following reasons:

- Doing so allows for differing backup and recovery requirements. You may want the flexibility of backing up the indexes at a different frequency than the tables. Or, you may choose not to back up indexes because you know that you can re-create them.

- If you let the table or index inherit its storage characteristics from the tablespace, when using separate tablespaces, you can tailor storage attributes for objects created within the tablespace. Tables and indexes often have different storage requirements (such as extent size and logging).

- When running maintenance reports, it is sometimes easier to manage tables and indexes when the reports have sections separated by tablespace.

If these reasons are valid for your environment, it is probably worth the extra effort to employ different tablespaces for tables and indexes. If you do not have any of the prior needs, then it is fine to put tables and indexes together in the same tablespace.

I should point out that DBAs often consider placing indexes in separate tablespaces for performance reasons. If you have the luxury of creating a storage system from scratch and can set up mount points that have their own sets of disks and controllers, you may see some I/O benefits from separating tables and indexes into different tablespaces. Nowadays, storage administrators often give you a large slice of storage in a storage area network (SAN), and there is no way to guarantee that data and indexes will be stored physically, on separate disks (and controllers). Thus, you typically do not gain any performance benefits by separating tables and indexes into different tablespaces.

The following code shows an example of building separate tablespaces for tables and indexes. It creates locally managed tablespaces, using a fixed extent size and automatic segment space management:

```
SQL> CREATE TABLESPACE reporting_data
  DATAFILE '/u01/dbfile/O18C/reporting_data01.dbf' SIZE 1G
  EXTENT MANAGEMENT LOCAL
  UNIFORM SIZE 1M
  SEGMENT SPACE MANAGEMENT AUTO;
--
SQL> CREATE TABLESPACE reporting_index
  DATAFILE '/u01/dbfile/O18C/reporting_index01.dbf' SIZE 500M
  EXTENT MANAGEMENT LOCAL
  UNIFORM SIZE 128K
  SEGMENT SPACE MANAGEMENT AUTO;
```

I prefer to use uniform extent sizes because that ensures that all extents within the tablespace will be of the same size, which reduces fragmentation as objects are created and dropped. The automatic segment space management feature allows Oracle to manage automatically many storage attributes that previously had to be monitored and maintained by the DBA manually.

Inheriting Storage Parameters from the Tablespace

When creating a table or an index, there are a few tablespace-related technical details to be aware of. For instance, if you do not specify storage parameters when creating tables and indexes, then they inherit storage parameters from the tablespace. This is the desired behavior in most circumstances; it saves you from having to specify these parameters manually. If you need to create an object with storage parameters different from those of its tablespace, then you can do so within the CREATE TABLE/INDEX statement.

Also keep in mind that if you do not explicitly specify a tablespace, by default, indexes are created in the default permanent tablespace for the user. This is acceptable for development and test environments. For production environments, you should consider explicitly naming tablespaces in the CREATE TABLE/INDEX statement.

Placing Indexes in Tablespaces, Based on Extent Size

If you know how large an index may initially be or what its growth requirements are, consider placing the index in a tablespace that is appropriate in terms of the size of the tablespace and the size of the extents. I'll sometimes create two or more index tablespaces per application. Here is an example:

```
SQL> create tablespace inv_idx_small
  datafile '/u01/dbfile/O18C/inv_idx_small01.dbf' size 100m
  extent management local
  uniform size 128k
  segment space management auto;
--
SQL> create tablespace inv_idx_med
  datafile '/u01/dbfile/O18C/inv_idx_med01.dbf' size 1000m
  extent management local
  uniform size 4m
  segment space management auto;
```

Indexes that have small space and growth requirements are placed in the INV_IDX_ SMALL tablespace, and indexes that have medium storage requirements would be created in INV_IDX_MED. If you discover that an index is growing at an unpredicted rate, consider dropping the index and re-creating it in a different tablespace or rebuilding the index in a more appropriate tablespace.

Creating Portable Scripts

I oftentimes find myself working in multiple database environments, such as development, testing, and production. Typically, I will create a tablespace first in development, then later in testing, and finally in production. Frequently, there are aspects of the script that need to change as it is promoted through the environments. For instance, development may need only 100MB of space, but production may need 10GB.

In these situations, it is handy to use ampersand variables to make the scripts somewhat portable among environments. For example, this next script uses an ampersand variable at the top of the script to define the tablespace size. The ampersand variable is then referenced within the CREATE TABLESPACE statement:

```
SQL> define reporting_index_size=100m
--
SQL> create tablespace reporting_index
  datafile '/u01/dbfile/O18C/reporting_index01.dbf' size &&reporting_index_
size
  extent management local
  uniform size 128k
  segment space management auto;
```

If you are only working with one tablespace, then there is not much to gain from using the prior technique. But, if you are creating dozens of tablespaces within numerous environments, then it pays to build in the reusability. Keep in mind that you can use ampersand variables anywhere within the script for any values you think may differ from one environment to the next.

Establishing Naming Standards

When you are creating and managing indexes, it is highly desirable to develop some standards regarding naming. Consider the following motives:

- Diagnosing issues is simplified when error messages contain information that indicates the table, index type, and so on.

- Reports that display index information are more easily grouped and therefore are more readable, making it easier to spot patterns and issues.

Given those needs, here are some sample index-naming guidelines:

- Primary key index names should contain the table name and a suffix such as _PK.

- Unique key index names should contain the table name and a suffix such as _UKN, where N is a number.

- Indexes on foreign key columns should contain the foreign key table and a suffix such as _FKN, where N is a number.

- Indexes that are not used for constraints should contain the table name and a suffix such as _IDXN, where N is a number.

- Function-based index names should contain the table name and a suffix such as _FNXN, where N is a number.

- Bitmap index names should contain the table name and a suffix such as _BMXN, where N is a number.

Some shops use prefixes when naming indexes. For example, a primary key index would be named PK_CUST (instead of CUST_PK). All these various naming standards are valid.

Tip   It does not matter what the standard is, as long as everybody on the team follows the same standard.

Creating Indexes

As described previously, when you think about creating tables, you must think about the corresponding index architecture. Creating the appropriate indexes and using the correct index features will usually result in dramatic performance improvements. Conversely, creating indexes on the wrong columns or using features in the wrong situations can cause dramatic performance degradation.

Having said that, after giving some thought to what kind of index you need, the next logical step is to create the index. Creating indexes and implementing specific features are discussed in the next several sections.

Creating B-tree Indexes

The default index type in Oracle is a B-tree index. To create a B-tree index on an existing table, use the CREATE INDEX statement. This example creates an index on the CUST table, specifying LAST_NAME as the column:

```
SQL> CREATE INDEX cust_idx1 ON cust(last_name);
```

By default, Oracle will create an index in your default permanent tablespace. Sometimes, that may be the desired behavior. But often, for manageability reasons, you want to create the index in a specific tablespace. Use the following syntax to instruct Oracle to build an index in a specific tablespace:

```
SQL> CREATE INDEX cust_idx1 ON cust(last_name) TABLESPACE reporting_index;
```

Tip   If you do not specify any physical storage properties for an index, the index inherits its properties from the tablespace in which it is created. This is usually an acceptable method for managing index storage.

Because B-tree indexes are the default type and are used extensively with Oracle applications, it is worth taking some time to explain how this particular type of index works. A good way to understand the workings of an index is to show its conceptual structure, along with its relationship with a table (an index cannot exist without a table).

Take a look at Figure 8-1; the top section illustrates the CUST table, with some data. The table data are stored in two separate data files, and each data file contains two blocks. The bottom part of the diagram shows a balanced, treelike structure of a B-tree index named CUST_IDX1, created on a LAST_NAME of the CUST table. The index is stored in one data file and consists of four blocks.

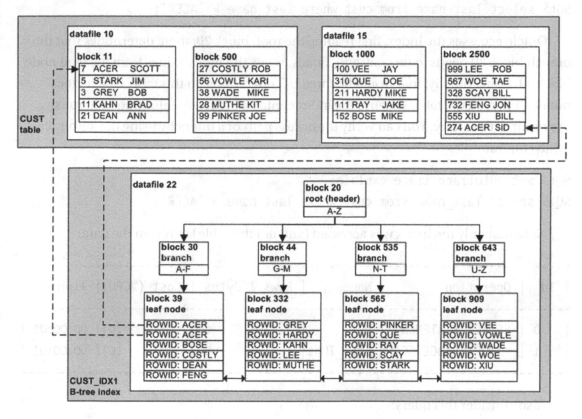

Figure 8-1. *Oracle B-tree hierarchical index structure and associated table*

The index definition is associated with a table and column(s). The index structure stores a mapping of the table's ROWID and the column data on which the index is built. A ROWID usually uniquely identifies a row within a database and contains information to physically locate a row (data file, block, and row position within block). The two dotted lines in Figure 8-1 depict how the ROWID (in the index structure) points to the physical row in the table for the column values of ACER.

The B-tree index has a hierarchical tree structure. When Oracle accesses the index, it starts with the top node, called the root (or header) block. Oracle uses this block to determine which second-level block (also called a branch block) to read next.

The second-level block points to several third-level blocks (leaf nodes), which contain a ROWID and the name value. In this structure, it will take three I/O operations to find the ROWID. Once the ROWID is determined, Oracle will use it to read the table block that contains the ROWID.

A couple of examples will help illustrate how an index works. Consider this query:

```
SQL> select last_name from cust where last_name = 'ACER';
```

Oracle accesses the index, first reading the root, block 20; then, determines that the branch block 30 needs to be read; and, finally, reads the index values from the lead node block 39. Conceptually, that would be three I/O operations. In this case, Oracle does not need to read the table because the index contains sufficient information to satisfy the result of the query. You can verify the access path of a query by using the autotrace utility; for example,

```
SQL> set autotrace trace explain;
SQL> select last_name from cust where last_name = 'ACER';
```

Note that only the index was accessed (and not the table) to return the data:

```
----------------------------------------------------------------------------
| Id | Operation          | Name     | Rows | Bytes | Cost (%CPU)| Time     |
----------------------------------------------------------------------------
|  0 | SELECT STATEMENT   |          |   1  |    6  |   1    (0)| 00:00:01 |
|* 1 |  INDEX RANGE SCAN  | CUST_IDX1|   1  |    6  |   1    (0)| 00:00:01 |
----------------------------------------------------------------------------
```

Also consider this query:

```
SQL> select first_name, last_name from cust where last_name = 'ACER';
```

Here, Oracle would follow the same index access path by reading blocks 20, 30, and 39. However, because the index structure does not contain the FIRST_NAME value, Oracle must also use the ROWID to read the appropriate rows in the CUST table (blocks 11 and 2500). Here is a snippet of the output from autotrace, indicating that the table has also been accessed:

```
------------------------------------------------------------------------
| Id  | Operation                          | Name      | Rows | Bytes |Cost
------------------------------------------------------------------------
|   0 | SELECT STATEMENT                   |           |    1 |    44 |   2
|   1 |   TABLE ACCESS BY INDEX ROWID BATCHED| CUST    |    1 |    44 |   2
|*  2 |     INDEX RANGE SCAN               | CUST_IDX1 |    1 |       |   1
------------------------------------------------------------------------
```

Also note at the bottom of Figure 8-1 the bidirectional arrows between the leaf nodes. This illustrates that the leaf nodes are connected via a doubly linked list, thus making index range scans possible. For instance, suppose you have this query:

```
SQL> select last_name from cust where last_name >= 'A' and last_name <= 'J';
```

To determine where to start the range scan, Oracle would read the root, block 20; then, the branch block 30; and, finally, the leaf node block 39. Because the leaf node blocks are linked, Oracle can navigate forward as needed to find all required blocks (and does not have to navigate up and down through branch blocks). This is a very efficient traversal mechanism for range scans.

ARBORISTIC VIEWS

Oracle provides two types of views containing details about the structure of B-tree indexes:

- INDEX_STATS

- DBA/ALL/USER_INDEXES

The INDEX_STATS view contains information regarding the HEIGHT (number of blocks from root to leaf blocks), LF_ROWS (number of index entries), and so on. The INDEX_STATS view is only populated after you analyze the structure of the index; for example,

```
SQL> analyze index cust_idx1 validate structure;
```

The DBA/ALL/USER_INDEXES views contain statistics, such as BLEVEL (number of blocks from root to branch blocks; this equals HEIGHT − 1); LEAF_BLOCKS (number of leaf blocks); and so on. The DBA/ALL/USER_INDEXES views are populated automatically when the index is created and refreshed via the DBMS_STATS package.

Creating Concatenated Indexes

Oracle allows you to create an index that contains more than one column. Multicolumn indexes are known as concatenated indexes. These indexes are especially effective when you often use multiple columns in the WHERE clause when accessing a table.

Suppose you have this scenario, in which two columns from the same table are used in the WHERE clause:

```
SQL> select first_name, last_name
from cust
where first_name = 'JIM'
and last_name = 'STARK';
```

Because both FIRST_NAME and LAST_NAME are often used in WHERE clauses for retrieving data, it may be efficient to create a concatenated index on the two columns:

```
SQL> create index cust_idx2 on cust(first_name, last_name);
```

Often, it is not clear whether a concatenated index is more efficient than a single-column index. For the previous SQL statement, you may wonder whether it is more efficient to create two single-column indexes on FIRST_NAME and LAST_NAME, such as

```
SQL> create index cust_idx3 on cust(first_name);
SQL> create index cust_idx4 on cust(last_name);
```

In this scenario, if you are consistently using the combination of columns that appear in the WHERE clause, then the optimizer will most likely use the concatenated index and not the single-column indexes. Using a concatenated index, in these situations, is usually much more efficient. You can verify that the optimizer chooses the concatenated index by generating an explain plan; for example:

```
SQL> set autotrace trace explain;
```

Then, run this query:

```
SQL> select first_name, last_name
from cust
where first_name = 'JIM'
and last_name = 'STARK';
```

Here is some sample output, indicating that the optimizer uses the concatenated index on CUST_IDX2 to retrieve data:

```
--------------------------------------------------------------------------------
| Id  | Operation         | Name      | Rows  | Bytes | Cost (%CPU)| Time     |
--------------------------------------------------------------------------------
|   0 | SELECT STATEMENT  |           |     1 |    44 |     1  (0)| 00:00:01 |
|*  1 |   INDEX RANGE SCAN| CUST_IDX2 |     1 |    44 |     1  (0)| 00:00:01 |
--------------------------------------------------------------------------------
```

In older versions of Oracle (circa version 8)if the leading-edge column (or columns) appeared in the WHERE clause. In modern versions the optimizer can use a concatenated index even if the leading-edge column (or columns) is not present in the WHERE clause. This ability to use an index without reference to leading-edge columns is known as the skip-scan feature.

A concatenated index that is used for skip scanning can, in certain situations, be more efficient than a full-table scan. However, you should try to create concatenated indexes that use the leading column. If you are consistently using only a lagging-edge column of a concatenated index, then consider creating a single-column index on the lagging column.

CREATING MULTIPLE INDEXES ON THE SAME SET OF COLUMNS

Prior to Oracle Database 12c, you could not have multiple indexes defined on the exact same combination of columns in one table. This has changed in 12c. You can now have multiple indexes on the same set of columns. However, you can only do this if there is something physically different about the indexes, for example, one index is created as a B-tree index, and the second, as a bitmap index.

Also, there can be only one visible index for the same combination of columns. Any other indexes created on that same set of columns must be declared invisible; for example,

```
SQL> create index cust_idx2 on cust(first_name, last_name);
SQL> create bitmap index cust_bmx1 on cust(first_name, last_name) invisible;
```

Prior to Oracle Database 12c, if you attempted the previous operation, the second creation statement would throw an error such as ORA-01408: such column list already indexed.

Why would you want two indexes defined on the same set of columns? You might want to do this if you originally implemented B-tree indexes and now wanted to change them to bitmap—the idea being, you create the new indexes as invisible, then drop the original indexes and make the new indexes visible. In a large database environment, this would enable you to make the change quickly. See the section on "Implementing Invisible Indexes" for more information.

Implementing Function-Based Indexes

Function-based indexes are created with SQL functions or expressions in their definitions. Sometimes, function-based indexes are required when queries use SQL functions. For example, consider the following query, which uses an SQL UPPER function:

```
SQL> select first_name from cust where UPPER(first_name) = 'JIM';
```

In this scenario there may be a normal B-tree index on the FIRST_NAME column, but Oracle will not use a regular index that exists on a column when a function is applied to it.

In this situation, you can create a function-based index to improve performance of queries that use an SQL function in the WHERE clause. This example creates a function-based index:

```
SQL> create index cust_fnx1 on cust(upper(first_name));
```

Function-based indexes allow index lookups on columns referenced by functions in the WHERE clause of an SQL query. The index can be as simple as the preceding example, or it can be based on complex logic stored in a PL/SQL function.

Note   Any user-created SQL functions must be declared deterministic before they can be used in a function-based index. *Deterministic* means that for a given set of inputs, the function always returns the same results. You must use the keyword DETERMINISTIC when creating a user-defined function that you want to use in a function-based index.

If you want to see the definition of a function-based index, select from the DBA/ALL/USER_IND_EXPRESSIONS view to display the SQL associated with the index. If you are using SQL*Plus, be sure to issue a SET LONG command first; for example,

```
SQL> SET LONG 500
SQL> select index_name, column_expression from user_ind_expressions;
```

The SET LONG command in this example tells SQL*Plus to display up to 500 characters from the COLUMN_EXPRESSION column, which is of type LONG.

Creating Unique Indexes

When you create a B-tree index, you can also specify that the index be unique. Doing so ensures that non-NULL values are unique when you insert or update columns in a table.

Suppose you have identified a column (or combination of columns) in the table (outside the primary key) that is used heavily in the WHERE clause. In addition, this column (or combination of columns) has the requirement that it be unique within a table. This is a good scenario in which to use a unique index. Use the UNIQUE clause to create a unique index:

```
SQL> create unique index cust_uk1 on cust(first_name, last_name);
```

Note   The unique index does not enforce uniqueness for NULL values inserted into the table. In other words, you can insert the value NULL into the indexed column for multiple rows.

You must be aware of some interesting nuances regarding unique indexes, primary key constraints, and unique key constraints (see Chapter 7 for a detailed discussion of primary key constraints and unique key constraints). When you create a primary key constraint or a unique key constraint, Oracle automatically creates a unique index and a corresponding constraint that is visible in DBA/ALL/USER_CONSTRAINTS.

When you only create a unique index explicitly (as in the example in this section), Oracle creates a unique index but does not add an entry for a constraint in DBA/ALL/USER_CONSTRAINTS. Why does this matter? Consider this scenario:

```
SQL> create unique index cust_uk1 on cust(first_name, last_name);
SQL> insert into cust values(500,'JOHN','DEERE');
SQL> insert into cust values(501,'JOHN','DEERE');
```

Here is the corresponding error message that is thrown:

```
ERROR at line 1:
ORA-00001: unique constraint (MV_MAINT.CUST_UK1) violated
```

If you are asked to troubleshoot this issue, the first place you look is in DBA_CONSTRAINTS for a constraint named CUST_IDX1. However, there is no information:

```
SQL> select constraint_name
from dba_constraints
where constraint_name='CUST_UK1';
```

Here is the output:

```
no rows selected
```

The no rows selected message can be confusing: the error message thrown when you insert into the table indicates that a unique constraint has been violated, yet there is no information in the constraint-related data dictionary views. In this situation, you have to look at DBA_INDEXES and DBA_IND_COLUMNS to view the details of the unique index that has been created:

```
SQL> select a.owner, a.index_name, a.uniqueness, b.column_name
from dba_indexes a, dba_ind_columns b
where a.index_name='CUST_UK1'
and    a.table_owner = b.table_owner
and    a.index_name = b.index_name;
```

If you want to have information related to the constraint in the DBA/ALL/USER_CONSTRAINTS views, you can explicitly associate a constraint after the index has been created:

```
SQL> alter table cust add constraint cust_idx1 unique(first_name, last_name);
```

In this situation, you can enable and disable the constraint independent of the index. However, because the index was created as unique, the index still enforces uniqueness regardless of whether the constraint has been disabled.

When should you explicitly create a unique index versus creating a constraint and having Oracle automatically create the index? There are no hard-and-fast rules. I prefer creating a unique key constraint and letting Oracle automatically create the unique index, because then I get information in both the DBA/ALL/USER_CONSTRAINTS and DBA/ALL/USER_INDEXES views.

But, Oracle's documentation recommends that if you have a scenario in which you are strictly using a unique constraint to improve query performance, it is preferable to create only the unique index. This is appropriate. If you take this approach, just be aware that you may not find any information in the constraint-related data dictionary views.

Implementing Bitmap Indexes

Bitmap indexes are recommended for columns with a relatively low degree of distinct values (low cardinality). You should not use bitmap indexes in OLTP databases with high INSERT/UPDATE/DELETE activities, owing to locking issues; the structure of the bitmap index results in many rows potentially being locked during DML operations, which causes locking problems for high-transaction OLTP systems.

Bitmap indexes are commonly used in data warehouse environments. A typical star schema structure consists of a large fact table and many small dimension (lookup) tables. In these scenarios, it is common to create bitmap indexes on fact table foreign key columns. The fact tables are typically inserted into on a daily basis and usually are not updated or deleted from.

Listed next is a simple example that demonstrates the creation and structure of a bitmap index. First, create a LOCATIONS table:

```
SQL> create table locations(
 location_id number
,region       varchar2(10));
```

Now, insert the following rows into the table:

```
SQL> insert into locations values(1,'NORTH');
SQL> insert into locations values(2,'EAST');
SQL> insert into locations values(3,'NORTH');
SQL> insert into locations values(4,'WEST');
SQL> insert into locations values(5,'EAST');
SQL> insert into locations values(6,'NORTH');
SQL> insert into locations values(7,'NORTH');
```

You use the BITMAP keyword to create a bitmap index. The next line of code creates a bitmap index on the REGION column of the LOCATIONS table:

```
SQL> create bitmap index locations_bmx1 on locations(region);
```

Bitmap indexes are effective at retrieving rows when multiple AND and OR conditions appear in the WHERE clause. For example, to perform the task find all rows with a region of EAST or WEST, a Boolean algebra OR operation is performed on the EAST and WEST bitmaps to quickly return rows 2, 4, and 5. The last row of Table 8-2 shows the OR operation on the EAST and WEST bitmap.

Table 8-2. *Results of an OR Operation*

Value/Row	Row 1	Row 2	Row 3	Row 4	Row 5	Row 6	Row 7
EAST	0	1	0	0	1	0	0
WEST	0	0	0	1	0	0	0
Boolean OR on EAST and WEST	0	1	0	1	1	0	0

Note   Bitmap indexes and bitmap join indexes are available only with the Oracle Enterprise Edition of the database. Also, you cannot create a unique bitmap index.

Creating Bitmap Join Indexes

Bitmap join indexes store the results of a join between two tables in an index. Bitmap join indexes are beneficial because they avoid joining tables to retrieve results. The syntax for a bitmap join index differs from that of a regular bitmap index in that it contains FROM and WHERE clauses. Here is the basic syntax for creating a bitmap join index:

```
SQL> create bitmap index <index_name>
on <fact_table> (<dimension_table.dimension_column>)
from <fact_table>, <dimension_table>
where <fact_table>.<foreign_key_column> = <dimension_table>.<primary_key_column>;
```

Bitmap join indexes are appropriate in situations in which you are joining two tables, using the foreign key column (or columns) in one table relating to the primary key column (or columns) in the other table. For example, suppose you typically retrieve the FIRST_NAME and LAST_NAME from the CUST dimension table while joining to a large

F_SHIPMENTS fact table. This next example creates a bitmap join index between the
F_SHIPMENTS and CUST tables:

```
SQL> create bitmap index f_shipments_bmx1
on f_shipments(cust.first_name, cust.last_name)
from f_shipments, cust
where f_shipments.cust_id = cust.cust_id;
```

Now, consider a query such as this:

```
SQL> select c.first_name, c.last_name
from f_shipments s, cust c
where s.cust_id = c.cust_id
and c.first_name = 'JIM'
and c.last_name = 'STARK';
```

The optimizer can choose to use the bitmap join index, thus avoiding the expense of
having to join the tables. For small amounts of data, the optimizer will most likely choose
not to use the bitmap join index, but as the data in the table grow, using the bitmap join
index becomes more cost-effective than full-table scans or using other indexes.

Implementing Reverse-Key Indexes

Reverse-key indexes are similar to B-tree indexes, except that the bytes of the index key
are reversed when an index entry is created. For example, if the index values are 201, 202,
and 203, the reverse-key index values are 102, 202, and 302:

Index value	Reverse key value
201	102
202	202
203	302

Reverse-key indexes can perform better in scenarios in which you need a way to
evenly distribute index data that would otherwise have similar values clustered together.
Thus, when using a reverse-key index, you avoid having I/O concentrated in one
physical disk location within the index during large inserts of sequential values.

Use the REVERSE clause to create a reverse-key index:

```
SQL> create index cust_idx1 on cust(cust_id) reverse;
```

You can verify that an index is reverse key by running the following query:

```
SQL> select index_name, index_type from user_indexes;
```

Here is some sample output, showing that the CUST_IDX1 index is reverse key:

```
INDEX_NAME           INDEX_TYPE
-------------------- ----------------------------
CUST_IDX1            NORMAL/REV
```

Note   You cannot specify REVERSE for a bitmap index or an IOT.

Creating Key-Compressed Indexes

Index compression is useful for indexes that contain multiple columns in which the leading index column value is often repeated. Compressed indexes, in these situations, have the following advantages:

- Reduced storage

- More rows stored in leaf blocks, which can result in less I/O when accessing a compressed index

Suppose you have a table defined as follows:

```
SQL> create table users(
 last_name  varchar2(30)
,first_name varchar2(30)
,address_id number);
```

You want to create a concatenated index on the LAST_NAME and FIRST_NAME columns. You know from examining the data that there is duplication in the LAST_NAME column. Use the COMPRESS N clause to create a compressed index:

```
SQL> create index users_idx1 on users(last_name, first_name) compress 2;
```

The prior line of code instructs Oracle to create a compressed index on two columns. You can verify that an index is compressed as follows: select index_name, compression

```
from user_indexes
where index_name like 'USERS%';
```

Here is some sample output, indicating that compression is enabled for the index:

```
INDEX_NAME                           COMPRESS
----------------------------------   --------
USERS_IDX1                           ENABLED
```

Note   You cannot create a key-compressed index on a bitmap index.

Parallelizing Index Creation

In large database environments in which you are attempting to create an index on a table that is populated with many rows, you may be able to greatly increase the index creation speed by using the PARALLEL clause:

```
SQL> create index cust_idx1 on cust(cust_id)
parallel 2
tablespace reporting_index;
```

If you do not specify a degree of parallelism, Oracle selects a degree, based on the number of CPUs on the box times the value of PARALLEL_THREADS_PER_CPU.

You can run this query to verify the degree of parallelism associated with an index:

```
SQL> select index_name, degree from user_indexes;
```

Avoiding Redo Generation When Creating an Index

You can optionally create an index with the NOLOGGING clause. Doing so has these implications:

- The redo is not generated that would be required to recover the index in the event of a media failure.

- Subsequent direct-path operations also will not generate the redo
  required to recover the index information in the event of a media failure.

Here is an example of creating an index with the NOLOGGING clause:

```
SQL> create index cust_idx1 on cust(cust_id)
nologging
tablespace users;
```

The main advantage of NOLOGGING is that when you create the index, a minimal amount of redo information is generated, which can have significant performance implications for a large index. The disadvantage is that if you experience a media failure soon after the index is created (or have records inserted via a direct-path operation), and you restore and recover the database from a backup that was taken prior to the index creation, you will see this error when the index is accessed:

```
ORA-01578: ORACLE data block corrupted (file # 4, block # 1044)
ORA-01110: data file 4: '/u01/dbfile/O18C/users01.dbf'
ORA-26040: Data block was loaded using the NOLOGGING option
```

This error indicates that the index is logically corrupt. In this scenario, you must re-create the index before it is usable. In most scenarios it is acceptable to use the NOLOGGING clause when creating an index, because the index can be recreated without affecting the table on which the index is based.

You can run this query to view whether an index has been created with NOLOGGING:

```
SQL> select index_name, logging from user_indexes;
```

Implementing Invisible Indexes

As discussed in creating an index on the same columns with only one visible, you have the option of making an index invisible to the optimizer. Oracle still maintains an invisible index (as DML occurs on the table) but does not make it available for use by the optimizer. You can use the OPTIMIZER_USE_INVISIBLE_INDEXES database parameter to make an invisible index visible to the optimizer.

Invisible indexes have a couple of interesting uses:

- Altering an index to be invisible before dropping it allows you to quickly recover if you later determine that the index is required.

- You may be able to add an invisible index to a third-party application without affecting existing code or support agreements.

These two scenarios are discussed in the following sections.

Making an Existing Index Invisible

Suppose you have identified an index that is not being used and are considering dropping it. In earlier releases of Oracle, you could mark the index UNUSABLE and then later drop indexes that you were certain weren't being used. If you later determined that you needed an unusable index, the only way to re-enable the index was to rebuild it. For large indexes this could take a great amount of time and database resources.

Making an index invisible has the advantage of telling only the optimizer not to use the index. The invisible index is still maintained as the underlying table has records inserted, updated, and deleted. If you decide that you later need the index, there is no need to rebuild it; you simply make it visible again.

You can create an index as invisible or alter an existing index to be invisible; for example,

```
SQL> create index cust_idx2 on cust(first_name) invisible;
SQL> alter index cust_idx1 invisible;
```

You can verify the visibility of an index via this query:

```
SQL> select index_name, status, visibility from user_indexes;
```

Here is some sample output:

```
INDEX_NAME            STATUS    VISIBILITY
--------------------  --------  ----------
CUST_IDX1             VALID     INVISIBLE
CUST_IDX2             VALID     INVISIBLE
USERS_IDX1            VALID     VISIBLE
```

Use the VISIBLE clause to make an invisible index visible to the optimizer again:

```
SQL> alter index cust_idx1 visible;
```

Caution   If you have a B-tree index on a foreign key column, and you decide to make it invisible, Oracle can still use the index to prevent certain locking issues. Before you drop an index on a column associated with a foreign key constraint, ensure that it is not used by Oracle to prevent locking issues. See the section "Indexing Foreign Key Columns," later in this chapter, for details.

Guaranteeing Application Behavior Is Unchanged When You Add an Index

You can also use an invisible index when you are working with third-party applications. Often, third-party vendors do not support customers adding their own indexes to an application. However, there may be a scenario in which you are certain you can increase a query's performance without affecting other queries in the application.

You can create the index as invisible and then use the OPTIMIZER_USE_INVISIBLE_ INDEXES parameter to instruct the optimizer to consider invisible indexes. This parameter can be set at the system or session level. Here is an example:

```
SQL> create index cust_idx1 on cust(cust_id) invisible;
```

Now, set the OPTIMIZER_USE_INVISIBLE_INDEXES database parameter to TRUE. This instructs the optimizer to consider invisible indexes for the currently connected session:

```
SQL> alter session set optimizer_use_invisible_indexes=true;
```

You can verify that the index is being used by setting AUTOTRACE to on and running the SELECT statement:

```
SQL> set autotrace trace explain;
SQL> select cust_id from cust where cust_id = 3;
```

Here is some sample output, indicating that the optimizer chose to use the invisible index:

```
-------------------------------------------------------------------------
| Id  | Operation        | Name      | Rows  | Bytes | Cost (%CPU)| Time     |
-------------------------------------------------------------------------
|   0 | SELECT STATEMENT |           |     1 |     5 |     1  (0)| 00:00:01 |
|*  1 |   INDEX RANGE SCAN| CUST_IDX1 |     1 |     5 |     1  (0)| 00:00:01 |
-------------------------------------------------------------------------
```

Keep in mind that *invisible index* simply means an index the optimizer cannot see. Just like any other index, an invisible index consumes space and resources during DML statements.

Maintaining Indexes

As applications age, you invariably have to perform some maintenance activities on existing indexes. You may need to rename an index to conform to newly implemented standards, or you may need to rebuild a large index to move it to a different tablespace that better suits the index's storage requirements. The following list shows common tasks associated with index maintenance:

- Renaming an index
- Displaying the DDL for an index
- Rebuilding an index
- Setting indexes to unusable
- Monitoring an index
- Dropping an index

Each of these items is discussed in the following sections.

Renaming an Index

Sometimes you need to rename an index. The index may have been erroneously named when it was created, or perhaps you want a name that better conforms to naming standards. Use the ALTER INDEX ... RENAME TO statement to rename an index:

```
SQL> alter index cust_idx1 rename to cust_index1;
```

You can verify that the index was renamed by querying the data dictionary:

```
SQL> select
  table_name
 ,index_name
 ,index_type
 ,tablespace_name
 ,status
from user_indexes
order by table_name, index_name;
```

Displaying Code to Re-create an Index

You may be performing routine maintenance activities, such as moving an index to a different tablespace, and before you do so, you want to verify the current storage settings. You can use the DBMS_METADATA package to display the DDL required to re-create an index. If you are using SQL*PlusLONG variable to a value large enough to display all the output. Here is an example:

```
SQL> set long 10000
SQL> select dbms_metadata.get_ddl('INDEX','CUST_IDX1') from dual;
```

Here is a partial listing of the output:

```
SQL> CREATE INDEX "MV_MAINT"."CUST_IDX1" ON "MV_MAINT"."CUST" ("CUST_ID")
  PCTFREE 10 INITRANS 2 MAXTRANS 255 INVISIBLE COMPUTE STATISTICS
```

To show all index DDL for a user, run this query:

```
SQL> select dbms_metadata.get_ddl('INDEX',index_name) from user_indexes;
```

You can also display the DDL for a particular user. You must provide as input to the GET_DDL function the object type, object name, and schema; example,

```
SQL> select
dbms_metadata.get_ddl(object_type=>'INDEX', name=>'CUST_IDX1',
schema=>'INV')
from dual;
```

Rebuilding an Index

There are a couple of good reasons to rebuild an index:

- Modifying storage characteristics, such as changing the tablespace
- Rebuilding an index that was previously marked unusable to make it usable again

Use the REBUILD clause to rebuild an index. This example rebuilds an index named CUST_IDX1:

```
SQL> alter index cust_idx1 rebuild;
```

Oracle attempts to acquire a lock on the table and rebuild the index online. If there are any active transactions that haven't committed, Oracle will not be able to obtain a lock, and the following error will be thrown:

```
ORA-00054: resource busy and acquire with NOWAIT specified or timeout
expired
```

In this scenario, you can either wait until there is little activity in the database or try setting the DDL_LOCK_TIMEOUT parameter:

```
SQL> alter session set ddl_lock_timeout=15;
```

The DDL_LOCK_TIMEOUT initialization parameter instructs Oracle to repeatedly attempt to obtain a lock (for 15 seconds, in this case).

If no tablespace is specified, Oracle rebuilds the index in the tablespace in which the index currently exists. Specify a tablespace if you want the index rebuilt in a different tablespace:

```
SQL> alter index cust_idx1 rebuild tablespace reporting_index;
```

If you are working with a large index, you may want to consider using features such as NOLOGGING or PARALLEL, or both. This next example rebuilds an index in parallel, while generating a minimal amount of redo:

```
SQL> alter index cust_idx1 rebuild parallel nologging;
```

Note   See the sections "Avoiding Redo Generation When Creating an Index" and "Parallelizing Index Creation," earlier in this chapter, for details on using these features with indexes.

REBUILDING FOR PERFORMANCE REASONS

In the olden days (version 7 or so), in the name of performance, DBAs religiously rebuilt indexes on a regular basis. Every DBA and his (or her) dog had a script similar to the one listed next, which uses SQL to generate the SQL required to rebuild indexes for a schema:

```
SPO ind_build_dyn.sql
SET HEAD OFF PAGESIZE 0 FEEDBACK OFF;
SELECT 'ALTER INDEX ' || index_name || ' REBUILD;'
FROM user_indexes;
SPO OFF;
SET FEEDBACK ON;
```

However, it is debatable whether rebuilding an index with the newer versions of Oracle achieves any performance gain. Usually, the only valid reason for rebuilding an index is that the index has become corrupt or unusable or that you want to modify storage characteristics (such as the tablespace).

Making Indexes Unusable

If you have identified an index that is no longer being used, you can mark it UNUSABLE. From that point forward, Oracle will not maintain the index, nor will the optimizer consider the index for use in SELECT statements. The advantage of marking the index UNUSABLE (rather than dropping it) is that if you later determine that the index is being used, you can alter it to a USABLE state and rebuild it without needing the DDL on hand to re-create it.

Here is an example of marking an index UNUSABLE:

```
SQL> alter index cust_idx1 unusable;
```

You can verify that it is unusable via this query:

```
SQL> select index_name, status from user_indexes;
```

The index has an UNUSABLE status:

```
INDEX_NAME           STATUS
-------------------- --------
CUST_IDX1            UNUSABLE
```

If you determine that the index is needed (before you drop it), then it must be rebuilt to become usable again:

```
SQL> alter index cust_idx1 rebuild;
```

Another common scenario for marking indexes UNUSABLE is that you are performing a large data load. When you want to maximize table-loading performance, you can mark the indexes UNUSABLE before performing the load. After you have loaded the table, you must rebuild the indexes to make them usable again.

Note   The alternative to setting an index to UNUSABLE is to drop and re-create it. This approach requires the CREATE INDEX DDL.

Monitoring Index Usage

You may have inherited a database, and as part of getting to know the database and application, you want to determine which indexes are being used (or not). The idea is that you can identify indexes that are not being used and drop them, thus eliminating the extra overhead and storage required.

Use the ALTER INDEX...MONITORING USAGE statement to enable basic index monitoring. The following example enables monitoring an index:

```
SQL> alter index cust_idx1 monitoring usage;
```

The first time the index is accessed, Oracle records this; you can view whether an index has been accessed via the v$index_usage_info or DBA_INDEX_USAGE view. To report which indexes are being monitored and have been used, run this query:

```
SQL> select * from dba_index_usage;
```

Most likely, you will not monitor only one index. Rather, you will want to monitor all indexes for a user. In this situation, use SQL to generate SQL to create a script you that can run to turn on monitoring for all indexes. Here is such a script:

```
SQL> select
  'alter index ' || index_name || ' monitoring usage;'
from user_indexes;
```

The DBA_OBJECT_USAGE view only shows information for the currently connected user. If you inspect the TEXT column of DBA_VIEWS, note the following line:

```
where io.owner# = userenv('SCHEMAID')
```

If you are logged in as a DBA-privileged user and want to view the status of all indexes that have monitoring enabled (regardless of the user), execute this query:

```
SQL> select io.name, t.name,
        decode(bitand(i.flags, 65536), 0, 'NO', 'YES'),
        decode(bitand(ou.flags, 1), 0, 'NO', 'YES'),
        ou.start_monitoring,
        ou.end_monitoring
from sys.obj$ io, sys.obj$ t, sys.ind$ i, sys.object_usage ou
  where i.obj# = ou.obj#
  and io.obj# = ou.obj#
  and t.obj# = i.bo#;
```

The prior query removes the line from the query that restricts the currently logged-in user. This provides you with a convenient way to view all monitored indexes.

> **Caution**   Keep in mind that Oracle can use an index defined on a foreign key column to prevent certain locking issues (see the sections "Determining if Foreign Key Columns Are Indexed" and "Implementing an Index on a Foreign Key Column," later in this chapter, for further discussion). Oracle's internal use of the index is not recorded in DBA_INDEX_USAGE or V$INDEX_USAGE_INFO. Be very careful before dropping an index defined on a foreign key column.

Dropping an Index

If you have determined that an index is not being used, then it is a good idea to drop it. Unused indexes take up space and can potentially slow down DML statements (because the index must be maintained as part of those DML operations). Use the DROP INDEX statement to drop an index:

```
SQL> drop index cust_idx1;
```

Dropping an index is a permanent DDL operation; there is no way to undo an index drop other than to rebuild the index. Before you drop an index, it does not hurt to quickly capture the DDL required to rebuild the index. Doing so will allow you to re-create the index in the event you subsequently discover that you did need it after all.

Indexing Foreign Key Columns

Foreign key constraints ensure that when inserting into a child table, a corresponding parent table record exists. This is the mechanism for guaranteeing that data conform to parent–child business relationship rules. Foreign keys are also known as referential integrity constraints.

Unlike primary key and unique key constraints, Oracle does not automatically create indexes on foreign key columns. Therefore, you must create a foreign key index manually, based on the columns defined as the foreign key constraint. In most scenarios, you should create indexes on columns associated with a foreign key. Here are two good reasons:

- Oracle can often make use of an index on foreign key columns to improve the performance of queries that join a parent table and child table (using the foreign key columns).

- If no B-tree index exists on the foreign key columns, when you insert
  or delete a record from a child table, all rows in the parent table are
  locked. For applications that actively modify both the parent and
  child tables, this will cause locking and deadlock issues (see the
  section "Determining if Foreign Key Columns Are Indexed," later in
  this chapter, for an example of this locking issue).

One could argue that if you know your application well enough and can predict
that queries will not be issued that join tables on foreign key columns and that certain
update/delete scenarios will never be encountered (that result in entire tables being
locked), then, by all means, do not place an index on foreign key columns. In my
experience, however, this is seldom the case: developers rarely think about how the
"black box database" might lock tables; some DBAs are equally unaware of common
causes of locking; teams experience high turnover rates, and the DBA de jour is left
holding the bag for issues of poor database performance and hung sessions. Considering
the time and resources spent chasing down locking and performance issues, it does not
cost that much to put an index on each foreign key column in your application. I know
some purists will argue against this, but I tend to avoid pain, and an unindexed foreign
key column is a ticking bomb.

Having made my recommendation, I'll first cover creating a B-tree index on a foreign
key column. Then, I'll show you some techniques for detecting unindexed foreign key
columns.

Implementing an Index on a Foreign Key Column

Say you have a requirement that every record in the ADDRESS table be assigned a
corresponding CUST_ID column from the CUST table. To enforce this relationship, you
create the ADDRESS table and a foreign key constraint, as follows:

```
SQL> create table address(address_id number
,cust_address varchar2(2000)
,cust_id number);
--
SQL> alter table address add constraint addr_fk1
foreign key (cust_id) references cust(cust_id);
```

Note   A foreign key column must reference a column in the parent table that has a primary key or unique key constraint defined on it. Otherwise, you will receive the error ORA-02270: no matching unique or primary key for this column-list.

You realize that the foreign key column is used extensively when joining the CUST and ADDRESS tables and that an index on the foreign key column will increase performance. In this situation, you have to create an index manually. For instance, a regular B-tree index is created on the foreign key column of CUST_ID in the ADDRESS table.

```
SQL> create index addr_fk1
on address(cust_id);
```

You do not have to name the index the same name as the foreign key (as I did in these lines of code). It is a personal preference as to whether you do that. I feel it is easier to maintain environments when the constraint and corresponding index have the same name.

When creating an index, if you do not specify the tablespace name, Oracle places the index in the user's default tablespace. It is usually a good idea to explicitly specify which tablespace the index should be placed in; for example,

```
SQL> create index addr_fk1
on address(cust_id)
tablespace reporting_index;
```

Note   An index on foreign key columns does not have to be of the type B-tree. In data warehouse environments, it is common to use bitmap indexes on foreign key columns in star schema fact tables. Unlike B-tree indexes, bitmap indexes on foreign key columns do not resolve parent–child table-locking issues. Applications that use star schemas typically are not deleting or modifying the child record from fact tables; therefore, locking is less of an issue, in this situation, regardless of the use bitmap indexes on foreign key columns.

Determining if Foreign Key Columns Are Indexed

If you are creating an application from scratch, it is fairly easy to create the code and ensure that each foreign key constraint has a corresponding index. However, if you have inherited a database, it is prudent to check if the foreign key columns are indexed.

You can use data dictionary views to verify if all columns of a foreign key constraint have a corresponding index. The task is not as simple as it might first seem. For example, here is a query that gets you started in the right direction:

```
SQL> SELECT DISTINCT
  a.owner                              owner
 ,a.constraint_name                   cons_name
 ,a.table_name                        tab_name
 ,b.column_name                       cons_column
 ,NVL(c.column_name,'***Check index****') ind_column
FROM dba_constraints  a
    ,dba_cons_columns b
    ,dba_ind_columns  c
WHERE constraint_type = 'R'
AND a.owner            = UPPER('&&user_name')
AND a.owner            = b.owner
AND a.constraint_name = b.constraint_name
AND b.column_name      = c.column_name(+)
AND b.table_name       = c.table_name(+)
AND b.position         = c.column_position(+)
ORDER BY tab_name, ind_column;
```

This query, while simple and easy to understand, does not correctly report on unindexed foreign keys for all situations. For example, in the case of multicolumn foreign keys, it does not matter if the constraint is defined in an order different from that of the index columns, as long as the columns defined in the constraint are in the leading edge of the index. In other words, if the constraint is defined as COL1 and then COL2, then it is okay to have a B-tree index defined on leading-edge COL2 and then COL1.

Another issue is that a B-tree index protects you from locking issues, but a bitmap index does not. In this situation, the query should also check the index type.

In these scenarios, you will need a more sophisticated query to detect indexing issues related to foreign key columns. The following example is a more complex query that uses the LISTAGG analytical function to compare columns (returned as a string in one row) in a foreign key constraint with corresponding indexed columns:

```
SQL> SELECT
 CASE WHEN ind.index_name IS NOT NULL THEN
   CASE WHEN ind.index_type IN ('BITMAP') THEN
     '** Bitmp idx **'
   ELSE
     'indexed'
   END
 ELSE
   '** Check idx **'
 END checker
,ind.index_type
,cons.owner, cons.table_name, ind.index_name, cons.constraint_name, cons.cols
FROM (SELECT
        c.owner, c.table_name, c.constraint_name
        ,LISTAGG(cc.column_name, ',' ) WITHIN GROUP (ORDER BY cc.column_
        name) cols
     FROM dba_constraints  c
        ,dba_cons_columns cc
     WHERE c.owner              = cc.owner
     AND   c.owner = UPPER('&&schema')
     AND   c.constraint_name = cc.constraint_name
     AND   c.constraint_type = 'R'
     GROUP BY c.owner, c.table_name, c.constraint_name) cons
LEFT OUTER JOIN
(SELECT
 table_owner, table_name, index_name, index_type, cbr
,LISTAGG(column_name, ',' ) WITHIN GROUP (ORDER BY column_name) cols
 FROM (SELECT
        ic.table_owner, ic.table_name, ic.index_name
        ,ic.column_name, ic.column_position, i.index_type
        ,CONNECT_BY_ROOT(ic.column_name) cbr
```

```
      FROM dba_ind_columns ic
          ,dba_indexes      i
      WHERE ic.table_owner = UPPER('&&schema')
      AND   ic.table_owner = i.table_owner
      AND   ic.table_name  = i.table_name
      AND   ic.index_name  = i.index_name
      CONNECT BY PRIOR ic.column_position-1 = ic.column_position
      AND PRIOR ic.index_name = ic.index_name)
   GROUP BY table_owner, table_name, index_name, index_type, cbr) ind
ON   cons.cols       = ind.cols
AND cons.table_name = ind.table_name
AND cons.owner       = ind.table_owner
ORDER BY checker, cons.owner, cons.table_name;
```

This query will prompt you for a schema name and then will display foreign key constraints that do not have corresponding indexes. This query also checks for the index type; as previously stated, bitmap indexes may exist on foreign key columns but do not prevent locking issues.

TABLE LOCKS AND FOREIGN KEYS

Here is a simple example that demonstrates the locking issue when foreign key columns are not indexed. First, create two tables (DEPT and EMP), and associate them with a foreign key constraint:

```
SQL> create table emp(emp_id number primary key, dept_id number);
SQL> create table dept(dept_id number primary key);
SQL> alter table emp add constraint emp_fk1 foreign key (dept_id) references
dept(dept_id);
```

Next, insert some data:

```
SQL> insert into dept values(10);
SQL> insert into dept values(20);
SQL> insert into dept values(30);
SQL> insert into emp values(1,10);
SQL> insert into emp values(2,20);
```

```
SQL> insert into emp values(3,10);
SQL> commit;
```

Open two terminal sessions. From one, delete one record from the child table (do not commit):

```
SQL> delete from emp where dept_id = 10;
```

Then, attempt to delete from the parent table some data not affected by the child table delete:

```
SQL> delete from dept where dept_id = 30;
```

The delete from the parent table hangs until the child table transaction is committed. Without a regular B-tree index on the foreign key column in the child table, any time you attempt to insert or delete in the child table, a table-wide lock is placed on the parent table; this prevents deletes or updates in the parent table until the child table transaction completes.

Now, run the prior experiment, except this time, additionally create an index on the foreign key column of the child table:

```
SQL> create index emp_fk1 on emp(dept_id);
```

You should be able to run the prior two delete statements independently. When you have a B-tree index on the foreign key columns, if deleting from the child table, Oracle will not excessively lock all rows in the parent table.

Summary

Indexes are critical objects separate from tables; they vastly increase the performance of a database application. Your index architecture should be well planned, implemented, and maintained. Carefully choose which tables and columns are indexed. Although they dramatically increase the speed of queries, indexes can slow down DML statements, because the index has to be maintained as the table data changes. Indexes also consume disk space. Thus, indexes should be created only when required.

New versions of Oracle and more resources bring improvements to how index or table scans perform. With upgrades and changes to the database system, old indexes should be reviewed if they are still needed. SQL Tuning steps to verify the indexes are very important, and using tools such as making an index invisible will help to validate if an index is needed before being dropped.

Oracle's B-tree index is the default index type and is sufficient for most applications. However, you should be aware of other index types and their uses. Specific features, such as bitmap and function-based indexes, should be implemented where applicable. This chapter has discussed various aspects of implementing and maintaining indexes. Table 8-3 summarizes the guidelines and techniques covered in this chapter.

Table 8-3. *Summary of Guidelines for Creating Indexes*

Guideline	Reasoning
Create as many indexes as you need, but try to keep the number to a minimum. Add indexes judiciously. Test first to determine quantifiable performance gains.	Indexes increase performance, but also consume disk space and processing resources and time for DML statements. Do not add indexes unnecessarily.
The required performance of queries you execute against a table should form the basis of your indexing strategy.	Indexing columns used in SQL queries will help performance the most.
Consider using the SQL Tuning Advisor or the SQL Access Advisor for indexing recommendations.	These tools provide recommendations and a second set of "eyes" on your indexing decisions.
Create primary key constraints for all tables.	This will automatically create a B-tree index (if the columns in the primary key are not already indexed).
Create unique key constraints where appropriate.	This will automatically create a B-tree index (if the columns in the unique key are not already indexed).
Create indexes on foreign key columns.	Foreign key columns are usually included in the WHERE clause when joining tables and thus improve performance of SQL SELECT statements. Creating a B-tree index on foreign key columns also reduces locking issues when updating and inserting into child tables.
Carefully select and test indexes on small tables (small being fewer than a few thousand rows).	Even on small tables, indexes can sometimes perform better than full-table scans.

(continued)

Table 8-3 (*continued*)

Guideline	Reasoning
Use the correct type of index.	Correct index usage maximizes performance. See Table 8-1 for more details.
Use the basic B-tree index type if you do not have a verifiable performance gain from using a different index type.	B-tree indexes are suitable for most applications in which you have high-cardinality column values.
Consider using bitmap indexes in data warehouse environments.	These indexes are ideal for low-cardinality columns in which the values are not updated often. Bitmap indexes work well on foreign key columns on star schema fact tables in which you often run queries that use AND and OR join conditions.
Consider using a separate tablespace for indexes (i.e., separate from tables).	Table and index data may have different storage or backup and recovery requirements, or both. Using separate tablespaces lets you manage indexes separately from tables.
Let the index inherit its storage properties from the tablespace.	This makes it easier to manage and maintain index storage.
Use consistent naming standards.	This makes maintenance and troubleshooting easier.
Do not rebuild indexes unless you have a solid reason to do so.	Rebuilding indexes is generally unnecessary unless an index is corrupt or unusable, or you want to move an index to different tablespace.
Monitor your indexes, and drop those that are not used.	Doing this frees up physical space and improves the performance of DML statements.
Before dropping an index, consider marking it `invisible`.	This allows you to better determine if there are any performance issues before you drop the index. These options let you rebuild or re-enable the index without requiring the DDL creation statement.

Refer to these guidelines as you create and manage indexes in your databases. These recommendations are intended to help you correctly use index technology.

Using automated tuning procedures and statistics from the Oracle database will provide information about the need and use of indexes. Along with understanding the strategies for using indexes, these tools will be helpful in managing the objects and using indexes to help with query performance.

After you build a database and users and configure the database with tables and indexes, the next step is to create additional objects needed by the application and users. Besides tables and indexes, typical objects include views, synonyms, and sequences. Building these database objects is detailed in the next chapter.

CHAPTER 9

Views, Synonyms, and Sequences

This chapter focuses on views, synonyms, and sequences. Views are used extensively in reporting applications and also to present subsets of data to users. Synonyms provide a method of transparently allowing users to display and use other users' objects. Sequences are often utilized to generate unique integers that are used to populate primary key and foreign key values.

Note Although views, synonyms, and sequences may not seem as important as tables and indexes, the truth of the matter is that they are almost equally important to understand. An application with any level of sophistication will encompass what's discussed in this chapter.

Implementing Views

In one sense, you can think of a view as an SQL statement stored in the database. Conceptually, when you select from a view, Oracle looks up the view definition in the data dictionary, executes the query the view is based on, and returns the results.

In addition to selecting from a view, in some scenarios it is possible to execute INSERT, UPDATE, and DELETE statements against the view, which results in modifications to the underlying table data. So, in this sense, instead of simply describing a view as a stored SQL statement, it is more accurate to conceptualize a view as a logical table built on other tables or views, or both.

Having said that, listed next are the common uses for views:

- Create an efficient method of storing an SQL query for reuse.

- Provide an interface layer between an application and physical tables.

- Hide the complexity of an SQL query from an application.

- Report to a user only a subset of columns or rows, or both.

With all this in mind, the next step is to create a view and observe some of its characteristics.

Creating a View

You can create views on tables, materialized views, or other views. To create a view, your user account must have the CREATE VIEW system privilege. If you want to create a view in another user's schema, then you must have the CREATE ANY VIEW privilege.

For reference, the view creation example in this section depends on the following base table:

```
SQL> create table sales(
 sales_id number primary key
,amnt     number
,state    varchar2(2)
,sales_person_id number);
```

Also assume that the table has the following data initially inserted into it:

```
SQL> insert into sales values(1, 222, 'CO', 8773);
SQL> insert into sales values(20, 827, 'FL', 9222);
```

Then, the CREATE VIEW statement is used to create a view. The following code creates a view (or replaces it if the view already exists) that selects a subset of columns and rows from the SALES table:

```
SQL> create or replace view sales_rockies as
select sales_id, amnt, state
from sales
where state in ('CO','UT','WY','ID','AZ');
```

Note   If you do not want to accidentally replace an existing view definition, then use `CREATE VIEW view`, and not `CREATE OR REPLACE VIEW view`. The `CREATE VIEW <view>` statement will throw an ORA-00955 error if the view already exists, whereas the `CREATE OR REPLACE VIEW view` overwrites the existing definition.

Now, when you select from `SALES_ROCKIES`, it executes the view query and returns data from the `SALES` table as appropriate:

```
SQL> select * from sales_rockies;
```

Given the view query, it is intuitive that the output shows only the following columns and one row:

```
SALES_ID        AMNT ST
---------- ---------- --
         1         222 CO
```

What is not as apparent is that you can also issue `UPDATE`, `INSERT`, and `DELETE` statements against a view, which results in modification of the underlying table data. For example, the following insert statement against the view results in the insertion of a record in the `SALES` table:

```
SQL> insert into sales_rockies(
 sales_id, amnt, state)
values
(2,100,'CO');
```

Additionally, as the owner of the table and view (or as a DBA), you can grant DML privileges to other users on the view. For instance, you can grant `SELECT`, `INSERT`, `UPDATE`, and `DELETE` privileges on the view to another user, which will allow the user to select and modify data referencing the view. However, having privileges on the view does not give the user direct SQL access to the underlying table(s).

Thus, any users granted privileges on the view will be able to manipulate data through the view but not issue SQL against the objects the view is based on.

Note that you can insert a value into the view that results in a row in the underlying table that is not selectable by the view:

```
SQL> insert into sales_rockies(
 sales_id, amnt, state)
values (3,123,'CA');

SQL> select * from sales_rockies;

  SALES_ID      AMNT ST
---------- ---------- --
         1       222 CO
         2       100 CO
```

In contrast, the query on the underlying table shows that rows exist that are not returned by the view:

```
SQL> select * from sales;

  SALES_ID      AMNT ST SALES_PERSON_ID
---------- ---------- -- ---------------
         1       222 CO            8773
        20       827 FL            9222
         2       100 CO
         3       123 CA
```

If you want the view to only allow insert and update statements that result in data modifications that are selectable by the view statement, then use the WITH CHECK OPTION (see the next section, "Checking Updates").

Checking Updates

You can specify that a view should allow modifications to the underlying table data only if those data are selectable by the view. This behavior is enabled with the WITH CHECK OPTION:

```
SQL> create or replace view sales_rockies as
select sales_id, amnt, state
from sales
where state in ('CO','UT','WY','ID','AZ')
with check option;
```

Using the WITH CHECK OPTION means that you can only insert or update rows that would be returned by the view query. For example, this UPDATE statement works because the statement is not changing the underlying data in a way would result in the row's not being returned by the view query:

```
SQL> update sales_rockies set state='ID' where sales_id=1;
```

However, this next update statement fails because it attempts to update the STATE column to a value that is not selectable by the query on which the view is based:

```
SQL> update sales_rockies set state='CA' where sales_id=1;
```

In this example, the following error is thrown:

```
ORA-01402: view WITH CHECK OPTION where-clause violation
```

I have rarely seen the WITH CHECK OPTION used. Having said that, if your business requirements mandate that updatable views only have the ability to update data selectable by the view query, then, by all means, use this feature.

Creating Read-Only Views

If you do not want a user to be able to perform INSERT, UPDATE, or DELETE operations on a view, then do not grant those object privileges on the view to that user. Furthermore, you should also create a view with the WITH READ ONLY clause for any views for which you do not want the underlying tables to be modified. The default behavior is that a view is updatable (assuming the object privileges exist).

This example creates a view with the WITH READ ONLY clause:

```
SQL> create or replace view sales_rockies as
select sales_id, amnt, state
from sales
where state in ('CO','UT','WY','ID','AZ')
with read only;
```

Even if a user (including the owner) has privileges to delete, insert, or update the view, if such an operation is attempted, the following error is thrown:

```
ORA-42399: cannot perform a DML operation on a read-only view
```

If you use views for reporting and never intend for the views to be used as a mechanism for modifying the underlying table's data, then you should always create the views with the WITH READ ONLY clause. Doing so prevents accidental modifications to the underlying tables through a view that was never intended to be used to modify data.

Updatable Join Views

If you have multiple tables defined in the FROM clause of the SQL query on which the view is based, it is still possible to update the underlying tables. This is known as an updatable join view.

For reference purposes, here are the CREATE TABLE statements for the two tables used in the examples in this section:

```
SQL> create table emp(
 emp_id number primary key
,emp_name varchar2(15)
,dept_id number);
--
SQL> create table dept(
 dept_id number primary key
,dept_name varchar2(15),
 constraint emp_dept_fk
 foreign key(dept_id) references dept(dept_id));
```

And, here are some seed data for the two tables:

```
SQL> insert into dept values(1,'HR');
SQL> insert into dept values(2,'IT');
SQL> insert into dept values(3,'SALES');
SQL> insert into emp values(10,'John',2);
SQL> insert into emp values(20,'Bob',1);
SQL> insert into emp values(30,'Craig',2);
SQL> insert into emp values(40,'Joe',3);
SQL> insert into emp values(50,'Jane',1);
SQL> insert into emp values(60,'Mark',2);
```

Here is an example of an updatable join view, based on the two prior base tables:

```
SQL> create or replace view emp_dept_v
as
select a.emp_id, a.emp_name, b.dept_name, b.dept_id
from emp a, dept b
where a.dept_id = b.dept_id;
```

There are some restrictions regarding the columns on which DML operations are permitted. For instance, columns in the underlying tables can be updated only if the following conditions are true:

- The DML statement must modify only one underlying table.

- The view must be created without the READ ONLY clause.

- The column being updated belongs to the key-preserved table in the join view (there is only one key-preserved table in a join view).

An underlying table in a view is key preserved if the table's primary key can also be used to uniquely identify rows returned by the view. An example with data will help illustrate whether an underlying table is key preserved. In this scenario, the primary key of the EMP table is the EMP_ID column; the primary key of the DEPT table is the DEPT_ID column. Here are some sample data returned by querying the view listed previously in this section:

```
EMP_ID EMP_NAME         DEPT_NAME        DEPT_ID
---------- ---------------- ---------------- ----------
    10 John             IT                    2
    20 Bob              HR                    1
    30 Craig            IT                    2
    40 Joe              SALES                 3
    50 Jane             HR                    1
    60 Mark             IT                    2
```

As you can see from the output of the view, the EMP_ID column is always unique. Therefore, the EMP table is key preserved (and its columns can be updated). In contrast, the view's output shows that it is possible for the DEPT_ID column to be not unique. Therefore, the DEPT table is not key preserved (and its columns can't be updated).

When you update the view, any modifications that result in columns that map to the underlying EMP table should be allowed because the EMP table is key preserved in this view. For example, this UPDATE statement is successful:

```
SQL> update emp_dept_v set emp_name = 'Jon' where emp_name = 'John';
```

However, statements that result in updating the DEPT table's columns are not allowed. The next statement attempts to update a column in the view that maps to the DEPT table:

```
SQL> update emp_dept_v set dept_name = 'HR West' where dept_name = 'HR';
```

Here is the resulting error message that's thrown:

```
ORA-01779: cannot modify a column which maps to a non key-preserved table
```

To summarize, an updatable join view can select from many tables, but only one of the tables in the join view is key preserved. The primary key and foreign key relationships of the tables in the query determine which table is key preserved.

Creating an INSTEAD OF Trigger

For views that are not read-only, when you issue a DML statement against a view, Oracle attempts to modify the data in the table that the view is based on. It is also possible to instruct Oracle to ignore the DML statement and instead execute a block of PL/SQL. This feature is known as an INSTEAD OF trigger. It allows you to modify the underlying base tables in ways that you can't with regular join views.

I am not a huge fan of INSTEAD OF triggers. In my opinion, if you are considering using them, you should rethink how you are issuing DML statements to modify base tables. Maybe you should allow the application to issue INSERT, UPDATE, and DELETE statements directly against the base tables instead of trying to build PL/SQL INSTEAD OF triggers on a view.

Think about how you will maintain and troubleshoot issues with INSTEAD OF triggers. Will it be difficult for the next DBA to figure out how the base tables are being modified? Will it be easy for the next DBA or developer to make modifications to the INSTEAD OF triggers? When an INSTEAD OF trigger throws an error, will it be obvious what code is throwing the error and how to resolve the problem?

Having said that, if you determine that you require an INSTEAD OF trigger on a view, use the INSTEAD OF clause to create it, and embed within it the required PL/SQL. This example creates an INSTEAD OF trigger on the EMP_DEPT_V view:

```
SQL> create or replace trigger emp_dept_v_updt
instead of update on emp_dept_v
for each row
begin
  update emp set emp_name=UPPER(:new.emp_name)
  where emp_id=:old.emp_id;
end;
/
```

Now, when an update is issued against EMP_DEPT_V, instead of the DML being executed, Oracle intercepts the statement and runs the INSTEAD OF PL/SQL code; for example,

```
SQL> update emp_dept_v set emp_name='Jonathan' where emp_id = 10;
1 row updated.
```

Then, you can verify that the trigger correctly updated the table by selecting the data:

```
SQL> select * from emp_dept_v;

    EMP_ID EMP_NAME         DEPT_NAME           DEPT_ID
---------- ---------------- ---------------- ----------
        10 JONATHAN         IT                        2
        20 Bob              HR                        1
        30 Craig            IT                        2
        40 Joe              SALES                     3
        50 Jane             HR                        1
        60 Mark             IT                        2
```

This code is a simple example, but it illustrates that you can have PL/SQL execute instead of the DML that was run on the view. Again, be careful when using INSTEAD OF triggers; be sure you are confident that you can efficiently diagnose and resolve any related issues that may arise.

Implementing an Invisible Column

Starting with Oracle Database 12c, you can create or modify a column in a table or view to be invisible (see Chapter 7 for details on adding an invisible column to a table). One good use for an invisible column is to ensure that adding a column to a table or view will not disrupt any of the existing application code. If the application code does not explicitly access the invisible column, then it appears to the application as if the column does not exist.

A small example will demonstrate the usefulness of an invisible column. Suppose you have a table created and populated with some data as follows:

```
SQL> create table sales(
 sales_id number primary key
,amnt    number
,state   varchar2(2)
,sales_person_id number);
--
SQL> insert into sales values(1, 222, 'CO', 8773);
SQL> insert into sales values(20, 827, 'FL', 9222);
```

And, furthermore, you have a view based on the prior table, created as shown:

```
SQL> create or replace view sales_co as
select sales_id, amnt, state
from sales where state = 'CO';
```

For the purpose of this example, suppose you also have a reporting table such as this:

```
SQL> create table rep_co(
 sales_id number
,amnt    number
,state   varchar2(2));
```

And, it is populated with this insert statement, which uses SELECT *:

```
SQL> insert into rep_co select * from sales_co;
```

Sometime later, a new column is added to the view:

```
SQL> create or replace view sales_co as
select sales_id, amnt, state, sales_person_id
from sales where state = 'CO';
```

Now, consider what happens to the statement that is inserted into REP_CO. Because it uses a SELECT *, it breaks because there hasn't been a corresponding column added to the REP_CO table:

```
SQL> insert into rep_co select * from sales_co;

ORA-00913: too many values
```

The prior insert statement no longer is able to populate the REP_CO table because the statement does not account for the additional column that has been added to the view.

Now, consider the same scenario, but with the column added to the SALES_CO view with an invisible column:

```
SQL> create or replace view sales_co
(sales_id, amnt, state, sales_person_id invisible)
as
select
 sales_id, amnt, state, sales_person_id
from sales
where state = 'CO';
```

When a view column is defined as invisible, this means that the column will not show up when describing the view or in the output of SELECT *. This ensures that the insert statement based on a SELECT * will continue to work.

One could successfully argue that you should never create an insert statement based on a SELECT * and that you therefore would never encounter this issue. Or, one could argue that the REP_CO table in this example should also have a column added to it to avoid the problem. However, when working with third-party applications, you oftentimes have no control over poorly written code. In this scenario, you can add an invisible column to a view without fear of breaking any existing code.

Having said that, the invisible column is not entirely invisible. If you know the name of an invisible column, you can select from it directly; for example,

```
SQL> select sales_id, amnt, state, sales_person_id from sales_co;
```

In this sense, the invisible column is only unseen to poorly written application code or to users that do not know the column exists.

Modifying a View Definition

If you need to modify the SQL query on which a view is based, then either drop and re-create the view, or use the CREATE OR REPLACE syntax, as in the previous examples. For instance, say you add a REGION column to the SALES table:

```
SQL> alter table sales add (region varchar2(30));
```

Now, to add the REGION column to the SALES_ROCKIES view, run the following command to replace the existing view definition:

```
SQL> create or replace view sales_rockies as
select sales_id, amnt, state, region
from sales
where state in ('CO','UT','WY','ID','AZ')
with read only;
```

The advantage of using the CREATE OR REPLACE method is that you do not have to reestablish access to the view for users with previously granted permissions. The alternative to CREATE OR REPLACE is to drop and re-create the view with the new definition. If you drop and re-create the view, you must regrant privileges to any users or roles that were previously granted access to the dropped and re-created object. For this reason, I almost never use the drop-and-re-create method when altering the structure of a view.

What happens if you remove a column from a table, and there is a corresponding view that references the removed column? For example,

```
SQL> alter table sales drop (region);
```

If you attempt to select from the view, you will receive an ORA-04063 error. When modifying underlying tables, you can check to see if a view is affected by the table change by compiling the view; for example,

```
SQL> alter view sales_rockies compile;
```

```
Warning: View altered with compilation errors.
```

In this way, you can proactively determine whether or not a table change affects dependent views. In this situation, you should re-create the view sans the dropped table column:

```
SQL> create or replace view sales_rockies as
select sales_id, amnt, state
from sales
where state in ('CO','UT','WY','ID','AZ')
with read only;
```

Displaying the SQL Used to Create a View

Sometimes, when you are troubleshooting issues with the information a view returns, you need to see the SQL query on which the view is based. The view definition is stored in the TEXT column of the DBA/USER/ALL_VIEWS views. Note that the TEXT column of the DBA/USER/ALL_VIEWS views is a LONG data type and that, by default, SQL*Plus only shows 80 characters of this type. You can set it longer, as follows:

```
SQL> set long 5000
```

Now, use the following script to display the text associated with a particular view for a user:

```
SQL> select view_name, text
from dba_views
where owner = upper('&owner')
and view_name like upper('&view_name');
```

You can also query ALL_VIEWS for the text of any view you have access to:

```
SQL> select text
from all_views
where owner='MV_MAINT'
and view_name='SALES_ROCKIES';
```

If you want to display the view text that exists within your schema, use USER_VIEWS:

```
SQL> select text
from user_views
where view_name=upper('&view_name');
```

Note   The TEXT column of DBA/ALL/USER_VIEWS does not hide information regarding columns that were defined as invisible.

You can also use the DBMS_METADATA package's GET_DDL function to display a view's code. The data type returned from GET_DDL is a CLOB; therefore, if you run it from SQL*Plus, make sure you first set your LONG variable to a sufficient size to display all the text. For example, here is how to set LONG to 5,000 characters:

```
SQL> set long 5000
```

Now, you can display the view definition by invoking DBMS_METADATA.GET_DDL with a SELECT statement, as follows:

```
SQL> select dbms_metadata.get_ddl('VIEW','SALES_ROCKIES') from dual;
```

If you want to display the DDL for all views for the currently connected user, run this SQL:

```
SQL> select dbms_metadata.get_ddl('VIEW', view_name) from user_views;
```

Renaming a View

There are a couple of good reasons to rename a view. You may want to change the name so that it better conforms to a standard one, or you may want to rename a view before dropping it so that you can better determine whether it is in use. Use the RENAME statement to change the name of a view. This example renames a view:

```
SQL> rename sales_rockies to sales_rockies_old;
```

You should see this message:

```
Table renamed.
```

The prior message would make more sense if it said, "View renamed"; just be aware that the message, in this case, does not exactly match the operation.

Dropping a View

Before you drop a view, consider renaming it. If you are certain that a view is not being used anymore, then it makes sense to keep your schema as clean as possible and drop any unused objects. Use the DROP VIEW statement to drop a view:

```
SQL> drop view sales_rockies_old;
```

Keep in mind that when you drop a view, any dependent views, materialized views, and synonyms become invalid. Additionally, any grants associated with the dropped view are also removed.

Managing Synonyms

Synonyms provide a mechanism for creating an alternate name or alias for an object. For example, say USER1 is the currently connected user, and USER1 has select access to USER2's EMP table. Without a synonym, USER1 must select from USER2's EMP table, as follows:

```
SQL> select * from user2.emp;
```

Assuming it has the CREATE SYNONYM system privilege, USER1 can do the following:

```
SQL> create synonym emp for user2.emp;
```

Now, USER1 can transparently select from USER2's EMP table:

```
SQL> select * from emp;
```

You can create synonyms for the following types of database objects:

- Tables

- Views, object views

- Other synonyms

- Remote objects via a database link

- PL/SQL packages, procedures, and functions

- Materialized views

- Sequences

- Java class schema object

- User-defined object types

Creating a synonym that points to another object eliminates the need to specify the schema owner and also allows you to specify a name for the synonym that does not match the object name. This lets you create a layer of abstraction between an object and the user, often referred to as object transparency. Synonyms allow you to manage objects transparently and separately from the users that access the objects. You can also seamlessly relocate objects to different schemas or even different databases. The application code that references the sequences does not need to change—only the definition of the synonym. Now with schema only accounts, the synonyms are going to allow for referencing the objects since there is not an account logging into these schemas.

Tip   You can use synonyms to set up multiple application environments within one database. Each environment has its own synonyms that point to a different user's objects, allowing you to run the same code against several different schemas within one database. You may do this because you can't afford to build a separate box or database for development, testing, quality assurance, production, and so on.

Creating a Synonym

A user must be granted the CREATE SYNONYM system privilege before creating a synonym. Once that privilege is granted, use the CREATE SYNONYM command to create an alias for another database object. You can specify CREATE OR REPLACE SYNONYM if you want the statement to create the synonym, if it does not exist, or replace the synonym definition, if it does. This is usually acceptable behavior.

In this example, a synonym will be created that provides access to a view. First, the owner of the view must grant select access to the view. Here, the owner of the view is MV_MAINT:

```
SQL> show user;
USER is "MV_MAINT"

SQL> grant select on sales_rockies to app_user;
```

Next, connect to the database as the user that will create the synonym.

```
SQL> conn app_user/foo
```

While connected as APP_USER, a synonym is created that points to a view named SALES_ROCKIES, owned by MV_MAINT:

```
SQL> create or replace synonym sales_rockies for mv_maint.sales_rockies;
```

Now, the APP_USER can directly reference the SALES_ROCKIES view:

```
SQL> select * from sales_rockies;
```

With the CREATE SYNONYM command, if you do not specify OR REPLACE (as shown in the example), and the synonym already exists, then an ORA-00955 error is thrown. If it is okay to overwrite any prior existing synonym definitions, then specify the OR REPLACE clause.

The creation of the synonym does not also create the privilege to access an object. Such privileges must be granted separately, usually before you create the synonym (as shown in the example).

By default, when you create a synonym, it is a private synonym. This means that it is owned by the user that created the synonym and that other users can't access it unless they are granted the appropriate object privileges.

Creating Public Synonyms

You can also define a synonym as public (see the previous section, "Creating a Synonym," for a discussion of private synonyms), which means that any user in the database has access to the synonym. Sometimes, an inexperienced DBA does the following:

```
SQL> grant all on sales to public;
SQL> create public synonym sales for mv_maint.sales;
```

Now, any user that can connect to the database can perform any INSERT, UPDATE, DELETE, or SELECT operation on the SALES table that exists in the MV_MAINT schema. You may be tempted to do this so that you do not have to bother setting up individual grants and synonyms for each schema that needs access. This is almost always a bad idea. There are a few issues with using public synonyms:

- Troubleshooting can be problematic if you are not aware of globally defined (public) synonyms; DBAs tend to forget or are unaware that public synonyms were created.

- Applications that share one database can have collisions on object names if multiple applications use public synonyms that are not unique within the database.

- Security should be administered as needed, not on a wholesale basis.

I usually try to avoid using public synonyms. However, there may be scenarios that warrant their use. For example, when Oracle creates the data dictionary, public synonyms are used to simplify the administration of access to internal database objects. To display any public synonyms in your database, run this query:

```
SQL> select owner, synonym_name
from dba_synonyms
where owner='PUBLIC';
```

Dynamically Generating Synonyms

Sometimes, it is useful to dynamically generate synonyms for all tables or views for a schema that needs private synonyms. The following script uses SQL*Plus commands to format and capture the output of an SQL script that generates synonyms for all tables within a schema:

```
SQL> CONNECT &&master_user/&&master_pwd
--
SQL> SET LINESIZE 132 PAGESIZE 0 ECHO OFF FEEDBACK OFF
SQL> SET VERIFY OFF HEAD OFF TERM OFF TRIMSPOOL ON
--
SQL> SPO gen_syns_dyn.sql
--
SQL> select 'create or replace synonym ' || table_name ||
       ' for ' || '&&master_user..' ||
  table_name || ';'
from user_tables;
--
SQL> SPO OFF;
--
SQL> SET ECHO ON FEEDBACK ON VERIFY ON HEAD ON TERM ON;
```

Look at the &master_user variable with the two dots appended to it in the SELECT statement: What is the purpose of double-dot syntax? A single dot at the end of an ampersand variable instructs SQL*Plus to concatenate anything after the single dot to the ampersand variable. When you place two dots together, that tells SQL*Plus to concatenate a single dot to the string contained in the ampersand variable.

Displaying Synonym Metadata

The DBA/ALL/USER_SYNONYMS views contain information about synonyms in the database. Use the following SQL to view synonym metadata for the currently connected user:

```
SQL> select synonym_name, table_owner, table_name, db_link
from user_synonyms
order by 1;
```

The ALL_SYNONYMS view displays all private synonyms, all public synonyms, and any private synonyms owned by different users for which your currently connected user has select access to the underlying base table. You can display information for all private and public synonyms in your database by querying the DBA_SYNONYMS view.

The TABLE_NAME column in the DBA/ALL/USER_SYNONYMS views is a bit of a misnomer because TABLE_NAME can reference many types of database objects, such as another synonym, view, package, function, procedure, or materialized view. Similarly, TABLE_OWNER refers to the owner of the object (and that object may not necessarily be a table).

When you are diagnosing data integrity issues, sometimes you first want to identify what table or object is being accessed. You can select from what appears to be a table, but in reality, it may be a synonym that points to a view that selects from a synonym, which in turn points to a table in a different database.

The following query is often a starting point for figuring out whether an object is a synonym, a view, or a table:

```
SQL> select owner, object_name, object_type, status
from dba_objects
where object_name like upper('&object_name%');
```

Note that using the wildcard character the percentage sign (%) in this query allows you to enter the object's partial name. Therefore, the query has the potential to return information regarding any object that partially matches the text string you enter.

You can also use the GET_DDL function of the DBMS_METADATA package to display synonym metadata. If you want to display the DDL for all synonyms for the currently connected user, run this SQL:

```
SQL> set long 5000
SQL> select dbms_metadata.get_ddl('SYNONYM', synonym_name) from
user_synonyms;
```

You can also display the DDL for a particular user. You must provide as input to the GET_DDL function the object type, object name, and schema:

```
SQL> select dbms_metadata.get_ddl(object_type=>'SYNONYM',
          name=>'SALES_ROCKIES', schema=>'APP_USER') from dual;
```

Renaming a Synonym

You may want to rename a synonym so that it conforms to naming standards or in order to determine whether it is being used. Use the RENAME statement to change the name of a synonym:

```
SQL> rename inv_s to inv_st;
```

Note that the output displays this message:

```
Table renamed.
```

The prior message is somewhat misleading. It indicates that a table has been renamed when, in this scenario, it was a synonym.

Dropping a Synonym

If you are certain that you no longer need a synonym, then you can drop it. Unused synonyms can be confusing to others called on to enhance or debug existing applications. Use the DROP SYNONYM statement to drop a private synonym:

```
SQL> drop synonym inv;
```

If it is a public synonym, then you need to specify PUBLIC when you drop it:

```
SQL> drop public synonym inv_pub;
```

If successful, you should see this message:

```
Synonym dropped.
```

Managing Sequences

A sequence is a database object that users can access to select unique integers. Sequences are typically used to generate integers for populating primary key and foreign key columns. You increment a sequence by accessing it via a SELECT, INSERT, or UPDATE statement. Oracle guarantees that a sequence number is unique when selected; no two user sessions can choose the same sequence number.

There is no way to guarantee that occasional gaps will not occur in the numbers generated by a sequence. Usually, some number of sequence values are cached in memory, and in the event of an instance failure (power failure, shutdown abort), any unused values still in memory are lost. Even if you do not cache the sequence, nothing stops a user from acquiring a sequence as part of a transaction and then rolling back that transaction (the transaction is rolled back, but not the sequence). For most applications, it is acceptable to have a mostly gap-free, unique integer generator. Just be aware that gaps can exist.

Creating a Sequence

For many applications, creating a sequence can be as simple as this:

```
SQL> create sequence inv_seq;
```

By default, the starting number is 1, the increment is 1, the default number of sequences cached in memory is 20, and the maximum value is 10^{27}. You can verify the default values via this query:

```
SQL> select sequence_name, min_value, increment_by, cache_size, max_value
from user_sequences;
```

You have a great deal of latitude in changing aspects of a sequence when creating it. For example, this command creates a sequence with a starting value of 1,000 and a maximum value of 1,000,000:

```
SQL> create sequence inv_seq2 start with 10000 maxvalue 1000000;
```

Table 9-1 lists the various options available when you are creating a sequence.

Table 9-1. *Sequence Creation Options*

Option	Description
INCREMENT BY	Specifies the interval between sequence numbers
START WITH	Specifies the first sequence number generated
MAXVALUE	Specifies the maximum value of the sequence
NOMAXVALUE	Sets the maximum value of a sequence to a really big number (10^{28} -1)
MINVALUE	Specifies the minimum value of sequence
NOMINVALUE	Sets the minimum value to 1 for an ascending sequence; sets the value to $-(10^{28}-1)$ for a descending sequence
CYCLE	Specifies that when the sequence hits a maximum or minimum value, it should start generating numbers from the minimum value for an ascending sequence and from the maximum value for a descending sequence
NOCYCLE	Tells the sequence to stop generating numbers after a maximum or minimum value is reached
CACHE	Specifies how many sequence numbers to preallocate and keep in memory. If CACHE and NOCACHE are not specified, the default is CACHE 20.
NOCACHE	Specifies that sequence numbers are not to be cached
ORDER	Guarantees that the numbers are generated in the order of request
NOORDER	Used if it is not necessary to guarantee that sequence numbers are generated in the order of request. This is usually acceptable and is the default.
SCALE	Enable sequence scalability by using a numeric offset that removes all duplicates. It is recommended not to use ORDER when using SCALE.
EXTEND	Default value is 6 and is the value of the scalable offset
NOEXTEND	Default setting for the SCALE clause. Sequences can then only be as wide as the maximum number of digits in the sequence.
NOSCALE	Disables sequence scalability

Using Sequence Pseudocolumns

After a sequence is created, you can use two pseudocolumns to access the sequence's value:

- NEXTVAL

- CURRVAL

You can reference these pseudocolumns in any SELECT, INSERT, or UPDATE statements. To retrieve a value from the INV_SEQ sequence, access the NEXTVAL value, as shown:

```
SQL> select inv_seq.nextval from dual;
```

Now that a sequence number has been retrieved for this session, you can use it multiple times by accessing the CURRVAL value:

```
SQL> select inv_seq.currval from dual;
```

The following example uses a sequence to populate the primary key value of a parent table and then uses the same sequence to populate the corresponding foreign key values in a child table. The sequence can be accessed directly in the INSERT statement. The first time you access the sequence, use the NEXTVAL pseudocolumn.

```
SQL> insert into inv(inv_id, inv_desc) values (inv_seq.nextval, 'Book');
```

If you want to reuse the same sequence value, you can reference it via the CURRVAL pseudocolumn. Next, a record is inserted into a child table that uses the same value for the foreign key column as its parent primary key value:

```
SQL> insert into inv_lines
    (inv_line_id,inv_id,inv_item_desc)
      values
    (1, inv_seq.currval, 'Tome1');
--
SQL> insert into inv_lines
    (inv_line_id,inv_id,inv_item_desc)
      values
    (2, inv_seq.currval, 'Tome2');
```

Autoincrementing Columns

Tip   Starting with Oracle Database 12c, you can create a table with identity columns that are automatically populated with sequence values. See Chapter 7 for details.

If you are not able to use the identity column, then you can simulate this automatic incrementing functionality by using triggers. For instance, say you create a table and sequence, as follows:

```
SQL> create table inv(inv_id number, inv_desc varchar2(30));
SQL> create sequence inv_seq;
```

Next, create a trigger on the INV table that automatically populates the INV_ID column from the sequence:

```
SQL> create or replace trigger inv_bu_tr
before insert on inv
for each row
begin
  select inv_seq.nextval into :new.inv_id from dual;
end;
/
```

Now, insert a couple of records into the INV table:

```
SQL> insert into inv (inv_desc) values( 'Book');
SQL> insert into inv (inv_desc) values( 'Pen');
```

Select from the table to verify that the INV_ID column is indeed populated automatically by the sequence:

```
SQL> select * from inv;
    INV_ID INV_DESC
---------- ------------------------------
         1 Book
         2 Pen
```

I generally do not like using this technique. Yes, it makes it easier for the developers, in that they do not have to worry about populating the key columns. However, it is more work for the DBA to generate the code required to maintain the columns to be automatically populated. Because I'm the DBA, and I like to keep the database code that I maintain as simple as possible, I usually tell the developers that we are not using this autoincrementing column approach and that we'll instead use the technique of directly calling the sequence in the DML statements (as shown in the previous section, "Using Sequence Pseudocolumns").

Scalable Sequences

A new feature is the scalable sequence that allows for prefixing a sequence with a unique numeric offset. Like the reverse key index discussed in Chapter 8, this helps with hotspots and having every server using the same offset and having numbers together. The scalable sequence uses the options of SCALE, EXTEND, NOEXTEND, and NOSCALE.

SQL> create sequence inv_seq scale;

Information about options used for scale are in the sequence dictionary columns, SCALE_FLAG and EXTEND_FLAG.

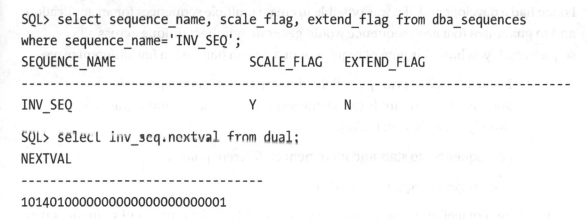

```
SQL> select sequence_name, scale_flag, extend_flag from dba_sequences
where sequence_name='INV_SEQ';
SEQUENCE_NAME                    SCALE_FLAG    EXTEND_FLAG
--------------------------------------------------------------------------
INV_SEQ                          Y             N

SQL> select inv_seq.nextval from dual;
NEXTVAL
----------------------------------
10140100000000000000000000000001
```

The first three numeric values are based on an instance, the next three are based on a session, and then the last number is the next value of the sequence.

GAP-FREE SEQUENCES

People sometimes worry unduly about ensuring that not a single sequence value is lost as rows are inserted into a table. In a few cases, I have seen applications fail because of gaps in sequence values. I have two thoughts on these issues:

- If you are worried about gaps, you are not thinking correctly about the problem you are solving.

- If your application fails because of gaps, you are doing it wrong.

My words are strong, I know, but few, if any, applications need gap-free sequences. If you really and truly need gap-free sequences, then using Oracle sequence objects is the wrong approach. You must instead implement your own sequence generator. You will need to go through agonizing contortions to make sure no gaps exist. Those contortions will impair your code's performance. And, in the end, you will probably fail.

Implementing Multiple Sequences That Generate Unique Values

I once had a developer ask if it was possible to create multiple sequences for an application and to guarantee that each sequence would generate numbers unique across all sequences. If you have this type of requirement, you can handle it a few different ways:

- If you are feeling grumpy, tell the developer that it is not possible and that the standard is to use one sequence per application (this is usually the approach I take).

- Set sequences to start and increment at different points.

- Use ranges of sequence numbers.

If you are not feeling grumpy, you can set up a small, finite number of sequences that always generate unique values by specifying an odd or even starting number and then incrementing the sequence by two. For example, you can set up two odd and two even sequence generators; for example,

```
SQL> create sequence inv_seq_odd start with 1 increment by 2;
SQL> create sequence inv_seq_even start with 2 increment by 2;
```

```
SQL> create sequence inv_seq_odd_dwn start with -1 increment by -2;
SQL> create sequence inv_seq_even_dwn start with -2 increment by -2;
```

The numbers generated by these four sequences should never intersect. However, this approach is limited by its ability to use only four sequences.

If you need more than four unique sequences, you can use ranges of numbers; for example,

```
SQL> create sequence inv_seq_low start with 1 increment by 1 maxvalue
10000000;
SQL> create sequence inv_seq_ml  start with 10000001 increment by 1 maxvalue
20000000;
SQL> create sequence inv_seq_mh  start with 20000001 increment by 1 maxvalue
30000000;
SQL> create sequence inv_seq_high start with 30000001 increment by 1 maxvalue
40000000;
```

With this technique, you can set up numerous different ranges of numbers to be used by each sequence. The downside is that you are limited by the number of unique values that can be generated by each sequence.

Creating One Sequence or Many

Say you have an application with 20 tables. One question that comes up is whether you should use 20 different sequences to populate the primary key and foreign key columns for each table or just 1 sequence.

I recommend using just 1 sequence; 1 sequence is easier to manage than multiple sequences, and it means less DDL code to manage and fewer places to investigate when there are issues.

Sometimes, developers raise issues such as

- Performance problems with only 1 sequence

- Sequence numbers that become too high

If you cache the sequence values, usually there are no performance issues with accessing sequences. The maximum number for a sequence is $10^{28}-1$, so if the sequence is incrementing by one, you will never reach the maximum value (at least, not in this lifetime).

However, in scenarios in which you are generating surrogate keys for the primary and child tables, it is sometimes convenient to use more than 1 sequence. In these situations, multiple sequences per application may be warranted. When you use this approach, you must remember to add a sequence when tables are added and potentially drop sequences as tables are removed. This is not a big deal, but it means a little more maintenance for the DBA, and the developers must ensure that they use the correct sequence for each table.

Viewing Sequence Metadata

If you have DBA privileges, you can query the DBA_SEQUENCES view to display information about all sequences in the database. To view sequences that your schema owns, query the USER_SEQUENCES view:

```
SQL> select sequence_name, min_value, max_value, increment_by
from user_sequences;
```

To view the DDL code required to re-create a sequence, access the DBMS_METADATA view. If you are using SQL*Plus to execute DBMS_METADATA, first ensure that you set the LONG variable:

```
SQL> set long 5000
```

This example extracts the DDL for INV_SEQ:

```
SQL> select dbms_metadata.get_ddl('SEQUENCE','INV_SEQ') from dual;
```

If you want to display the DDL for all sequences for the currently connected user, run this SQL:

```
SQL> select dbms_metadata.get_ddl('SEQUENCE',sequence_name) from user_sequences;
```

You can also generate the DDL for a sequence owned by a particular user by providing the SCHEMA parameter:

```
SQL> select
dbms_metadata.get_ddl(object_type=>'SEQUENCE', name=>'INV_SEQ',
schema=>'INV_APP')
from dual;
```

Renaming a Sequence

Occasionally, you may need to rename a sequence. For instance, a sequence may have been created with an erroneous name, or you may want to rename the sequence before dropping it from the database. Use the RENAME statement to do this. This example renames INV_SEQ to INV_SEQ_OLD:

```
SQL> rename inv_seq to inv_seq_old;
```

You should see the following message:

```
Table renamed.
```

In this case, even though the message says, "Table renamed," it was the sequence that was renamed.

Dropping a Sequence

Usually, you want a drop a sequence either because it is not used or you want to re-create it with a new starting number. To drop a sequence, use the DROP SEQUENCE statement:

```
SQL> drop sequence inv_seq;
```

When an object is dropped, all the associated grants on the object are dropped as well. So, if you need to re-create the sequence, then remember to reissue select grants to other users that may need to use the sequence.

Tip   See the next section, "Resetting a Sequence," for an alternative approach to dropping and re-creating a sequence.

Resetting a Sequence

You may occasionally be required to change the current value of a sequence number. For example, you may work in a test environment in which the developers periodically want the database reset to a previous state. A typical scenario is one in which the developers have scripts that truncate the tables and reseed them with test data and, as part of that exercise, want a sequence set back to a value such as 1.

Oracle's documentation states, "to restart a sequence at a different number, you must drop and re-create it." That's not entirely accurate. In most cases, you should avoid dropping a sequence because you must regrant permissions on the object to users that currently have select permissions on the sequence. This can lead to temporary downtime for your application while you track down those users.

The following technique demonstrates how to set the current value to a higher or lower value, using the ALTER SEQUENCE statement. The basic procedure is as follows:

1. Alter INCREMENT BY to a large number.

2. Select from the sequence to increment it by the large positive or negative value.

3. Set INCREMENT BY back to its original value (usually 1).

This example sets the next value of a sequence number to 1,000 integers higher than the current value:

```
SQL> alter sequence myseq increment by 1000;
SQL> select myseq.nextval from dual;
SQL> alter sequence myseq increment by 1;
```

Verify that the sequence is set to the value you desire:

```
SQL> select myseq.nextval from dual;
```

You can also use this technique to set the sequence number to a much lower number than the current value. The difference is that the INCREMENT BY setting is a large negative number. For example, this example sets the sequence back 1,000 integers:

```
SQL> alter sequence myseq increment by -1000;
SQL> select myseq.nextval from dual;
SQL> alter sequence myseq increment by 1;
```

Verify that the sequence is set to the value you desire:

```
SQL> select myseq.nextval from dual;
```

Additionally, you can automate the task of resetting a sequence number back to a value via an SQL script. This technique is shown in the next several lines of SQL code. The code will prompt you for the sequence name and the value you want the sequence set back to:

```
SQL> UNDEFINE seq_name
SQL> UNDEFINE reset_to
SQL> PROMPT "sequence name" ACCEPT '&&seq_name'
SQL> PROMPT "reset to value" ACCEPT &&reset_to
SQL> COL seq_id NEW_VALUE hold_seq_id
SQL> COL min_id NEW_VALUE hold_min_id
--
SQL> SELECT &&reset_to - &&seq_name..nextval - 1 seq_id
FROM dual;
--
SQL> SELECT &&hold_seq_id - 1 min_id FROM dual;
--
SQL> ALTER SEQUENCE &&seq_name INCREMENT BY &hold_seq_id MINVALUE &hold_min_id;
--
SQL> SELECT &&seq_name..nextval FROM dual;
--
SQL> ALTER SEQUENCE &&seq_name INCREMENT BY 1;
```

To ensure that the sequence has been set to the value you want, select the NEXTVAL from it:

```
SQL> select &&seq_name..nextval from dual;
```

This approach can be quite useful when you are moving applications through various development, test, and production environments. It allows you to reset the sequence without having to reissue object grants.

Summary

Views, synonyms, and sequences are used extensively in Oracle database applications. These objects (along with tables and indexes) afford the technology for creating sophisticated applications.

Views offer a way to create and store complex multitable join queries that can then be used by database users and applications. Views can be used to update the underlying base tables or can be created read-only for reporting requirements.

Synonyms (along with appropriate privileges) provide a mechanism for transparently allowing a user to access objects that are owned by a separate schema. The user accessing a synonym needs to know only the synonym name, regardless of the underlying object type and owner. This lets the application designer seamlessly separate the owner of the objects from the users that access the objects.

Sequences generate unique integers that are often used by applications to populate primary key and foreign key columns. Oracle guarantees that when a sequence is accessed, it will always return a unique value to the selecting user.

After installing the Oracle binaries and creating a database and tablespaces, usually you create an application that consists of the owning user and corresponding tables, constraints, indexes, views, synonyms, and sequences. Metadata regarding these objects are stored internally in the data dictionary. The data dictionary is used extensively for monitoring, troubleshooting, and diagnosing issues. You must be thoroughly fluent with retrieving information from the data dictionary. Retrieving and analyzing data dictionary information is the topic of the next chapter.

CHAPTER 10

Data Dictionary Fundamentals

The previous chapters in this book focused on topics such as creating a database, strategically implementing tablespaces, managing users, basic security, tables, indexes, and constraints. In those chapters, you were presented with several SQL queries, which accessed the data dictionary views in order to

- Show what users are in the database and if any of their passwords expired

- Display the owners of each table and associated privileges

- Show the settings of various database parameters

- Determine which columns have foreign key constraints defined on them

- Display tablespaces and associated data files and space usage

In this regard, Oracle's data dictionary is vast and robust. Almost every conceivable piece of information about your database is available for retrieval. The data dictionary stores critical information about the physical characteristics of the database, users, objects, and dynamic performance metrics. A senior-level DBA must possess an expert knowledge of the data dictionary.

This chapter is a turning point in the book, dividing it between basic DBA tasks and more advanced topics. It is appropriate at this time to dive into the details of the inner workings of the data dictionary. Knowledge of these workings will provide a foundation for understanding your environment, extracting pertinent information, and doing your job.

The first few sections of this chapter detail the architecture of the data dictionary and how it is created. Also shown are the relationships between logical objects and physical structures and how they relate to specific data dictionary views. These understandings will serve as a basis for writing SQL queries to extract the information that you will need to be a more efficient and effective DBA. Finally, several examples are presented, illustrating how DBAs use the data dictionary.

Data Dictionary Architecture

If you inherit a database and are asked to maintain and manage it, typically you will inspect the contents of the data dictionary to determine the physical structure of the database and see what events are currently transacting. Toward this end, Oracle provides two general categories of read-only data dictionary views:

- The contents of your database, such as users, tables, indexes, constraints, and privileges. These are sometimes referred to as the static CDB/DBA/ALL/USER data dictionary views, and they are based on internal tables stored in the SYSTEM tablespace. The term *static*, in this sense, means that the information within these views only changes as you make changes to your database, such as adding a user, creating a table, or modifying a column.

- A real-time view of activity in the database, such as users connected to the database, SQL currently executing, memory usage, locks, and I/O statistics. These views are based on virtual memory tables and are referred to as the dynamic performance views. The information in these views is continuously updated by Oracle as events take place within the database. The views are also sometimes called the V$ or GV$ views.

These types of data dictionary views are described in further detail in the next two sections.

Static Views

Oracle refers to a subset of the data dictionary views as static. These views are based on physical tables maintained internally by Oracle. Oracle's documentation states that these views are static in the sense that the data they contain do not change at a rapid rate (at least, not compared with the dynamic V$ and GV$ views).

The term *static* can sometimes be a misnomer. For example, the DBA_SEGMENTS and DBA_EXTENTS views change dynamically as the amount of data in your database grows and shrinks. Regardless, Oracle has made the distinction between static and dynamic, and it is important to understand this architectural nuance when querying the data dictionary. Prior to Oracle Database 12c, there were only three levels of static views:

- USER

- ALL

- DBA

Starting with Oracle Database 12c, there is a fourth level that is applicable when using the container/pluggable database feature:

- CDB

The USER views contain information available to the current user. For example, the USER_TABLES view contains information about tables owned by the current user. No special privileges are required to select from the USER-level views.

At the next level are the ALL static views. The ALL views show you all object information the current user has access to. For example, the ALL_TABLES view displays all database tables on which the current user can perform any type of DML operation. No special privileges are required to query from the ALL-level views.

Next are the DBA static views. The DBA views contain metadata describing all objects in the database (regardless of ownership or access privilege). To access the DBA views, a DBA role or SELECT_CATALOG_ROLE must be granted to the current user.

The CDB-level views are only applicable if you are using the pluggable database feature. This level provides information about all pluggable databases within a container database (hence the acronym CDB). You will notice that many of the static data dictionary and dynamic performance views have a new column, CON_ID. This column uniquely identifies each pluggable database within a container database.

Tip   See Chapter 22 for a full discussion of pluggable databases. Unless otherwise noted, this chapter focuses on the DBA/ALL/USER-level views. Just keep in mind that if you are working pluggable databases, you may need to access the CDB-level views when reporting on all pluggable databases within a container database.

The static views are based on internal Oracle tables, such as USER$, TAB$, and IND$. If you have access to the SYS schema, you can view underlying tables directly via SQL. For most situations, you only need to access the static views that are based on the underlying internal tables.

The data dictionary tables (such as USER$, TAB$, IND$) are created during the execution of the CREATE DATABASE command. As part of creating a database, the sql.bsq file is executed, which builds these internal data dictionary tables. The sql.bsq file is generally located in the ORACLE_HOME/rdbms/admin directory; you can view it via an OS editing utility (such as vi, in Linux/Unix, or Notepad, in Windows).

The static views are created when you run the catalog.sql script (usually, you run this script once the CREATE DATABASE operation succeeds). The catalog.sql script is located in the ORACLE_HOME/rdbms/admin directory. Figure 10-1 shows the process of creating the static data dictionary views.

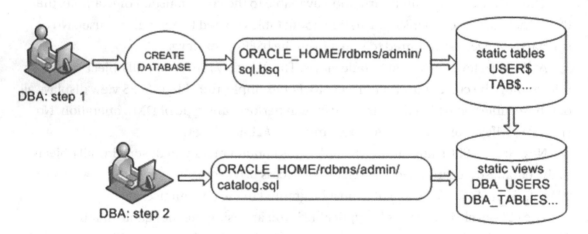

Figure 10-1. *Creating the static data dictionary views*

You can view the creation scripts of the static views by querying the TEXT column of DBA_VIEWS; for example,

```
SQL> set long 5000
SQL> select text from dba_views where view_name='DBA_VIEWS';
```

Here is the output:

```
SQL> select u.name, o.name, v.textlength, v.text, t.typetextlength, t.typetext,
         t.oidtextlength, t.oidtext, t.typeowner, t.typename,
```

```
     decode(bitand(v.property, 134217728), 134217728,
            (select sv.name from superobj$ h, "_CURRENT_EDITION_OBJ" sv
             where h.subobj# = o.obj# and h.superobj# = sv.obj#), null),
     decode(bitand(v.property, 32), 32, 'Y', 'N'),
     decode(bitand(v.property, 16384), 16384, 'Y', 'N'),
     decode(bitand(v.property/4294967296, 134217728), 134217728, 'Y', 'N'),
     decode(bitand(o.flags,8),8,'CURRENT_USER','DEFINER')
from sys."_CURRENT_EDITION_OBJ" o, sys.view$ v, sys.user$ u, sys.typed_view$ t
where o.obj# = v.obj#
  and o.obj# = t.obj#(+)
  and o.owner# = u.user#
```

Note If you manually create a database (not using the dbca utility), you must be connected as the SYS schema when you run the catalog.sql and catproc. sql scripts. The SYS schema is the owner of all objects in the data dictionary.

Dynamic Performance Views

The dynamic performance data dictionary views are colloquially referred to as the V$ and GV$ views. These views are constantly updated by Oracle and reflect the current condition of the instance and database. Dynamic views are critical for diagnosing real-time performance issues.

The V$ and GV$ views are indirectly based on underlying X$ tables, which are internal memory structures that are instantiated when you start your Oracle instance. Some of the V$ views are available the moment the Oracle instance is started. For example, V$PARAMETER contains meaningful data after the STARTUP NOMOUNT command has been issued, and does not require the database to be mounted or open. Other dynamic views (such as V$CONTROLFILE) depend on information in the control file and therefore contain significant information only after the database has been mounted. Some V$ views (such as V$BH) provide kernel-processing information and thus have useful results only after the database has been opened.

At the top layer, the V$ views are actually synonyms that point to underlying SYS.V_$ views. At the next layer down, the SYS.V_$ objects are views created on top of another layer of SYS.V$ views. The SYS.V$ views in turn are based on the SYS.GV$ views. At the bottom layer, the SYS.GV$ views are based on the X$ memory structures.

The top-level V$ synonyms and SYS.V_$ views are created when you run the catalog.sql script, which you usually do after the database is initially created. Figure 10-2 shows the process for creating the V$ dynamic performance views.

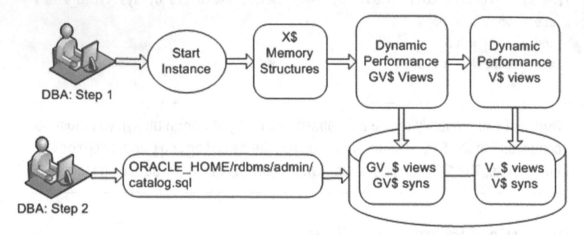

Figure 10-2. *Creating the V$ dynamic performance data dictionary views*

Accessing the V$ views through the topmost synonyms is usually adequate for dynamic performance information needs. On rare occasions, you will want to query internal information that may not be available through the V$ views. In these situations, it is critical to understand the X$ underpinnings.

If you work with Oracle RAC, you should be familiar with the GV$ global views. These views provide global dynamic performance information regarding all instances in a cluster (whereas the V$ views are instance specific). The GV$ views contain an INST_ID column for identifying specific instances in a clustered environment.

You can display the V$ and GV$ view definitions by querying the VIEW_DEFINITION column of the V$FIXED_VIEW_DEFINITION view. For instance, this query displays the definition of the V$CONTROLFILE:

```
SQL> select view_definition
from v$fixed_view_definition
where view_name='V$CONTROLFILE';
```

Here is the output:

```
select STATUS, NAME, IS_RECOVERY_DEST_FILE, BLOCK_SIZE, FILE_SIZE_BLKS,
CON_ID from GV$CONTROLFILE where inst_id = USERENV('Instance')
```

A Different View of Metadata

DBAs commonly face the following types of database issues:

- An insert into a table fails because a tablespace cannot extend.

- The database is refusing connections because the maximum number of sessions is exceeded.

- An application is hung, apparently because of some sort of locking issue.

- A PL/SQL statement is failing, with a memory error.

- RMAN backups have not succeeded for two days.

- A user is trying to update a record, but a unique key constraint violation is thrown.

- An SQL statement has been running for hours longer than normal.

- Application users have reported that performance seems sluggish and that something must be wrong with the database.

The prior list is a small sample of the typical issues a DBA encounters on a daily basis. A certain amount of knowledge is required to be able to efficiently diagnose and handle these types of problems. A fundamental piece of that knowledge is an understanding of Oracle's physical structures and corresponding logical components.

For example, if a table cannot extend because a tablespace is full, what knowledge do you rely on to solve this problem? You need to understand that when a database is created, it contains multiple logical space containers called tablespaces. Each tablespace consists of one or more physical data files. Each data file consists of many OS blocks. Each table consists of a segment, and every segment contains one or more extents. As a segment needs space, it allocates additional extents within a physical data file.

Once you understand the logical and physical concepts involved, you intuitively look in data dictionary views such as DBA_TABLES, DBA_SEGMENTS, DBA_TABLESPACES, and DBA_DATA_FILES to pinpoint the issue and add space as required. In a wide variety of troubleshooting scenarios, your understanding of the relationships of various logical and physical constructs will allow you to focus on querying views that will help you quickly resolve the problem at hand. To that end, inspect Figure 10-3. This diagram describes the relationships between logical and physical structures in an Oracle database. The rounded rectangle shapes represent logical constructs, and the sharp-cornered rectangles are physical files.

Tip   Logical objects are only viewable from SQL after the database has been started. In contrast, physical objects can be viewed via OS utilities even if the instance is not started.

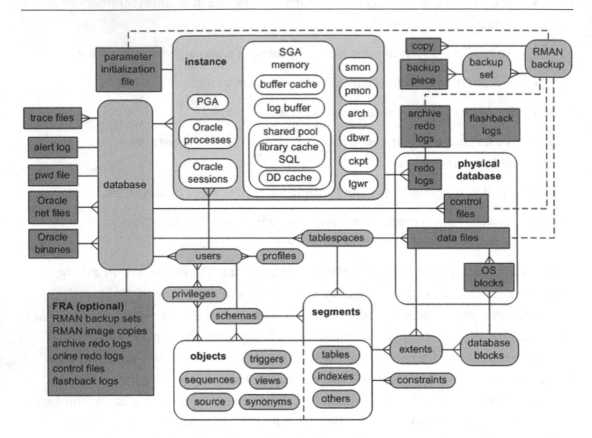

Figure 10-3. *Oracle database logical and physical structure relationships*

Figure 10-3 does not show all the relationships of all logical and physical aspects of an Oracle database. Rather, it focuses on components that you are most likely to encounter on a daily basis. This base relational diagram forms a foundation for leveraging of Oracle's data dictionary infrastructure.

Keep an image of Figure 10-3 open in your mind; now, juxtapose it with Figure 10-4.

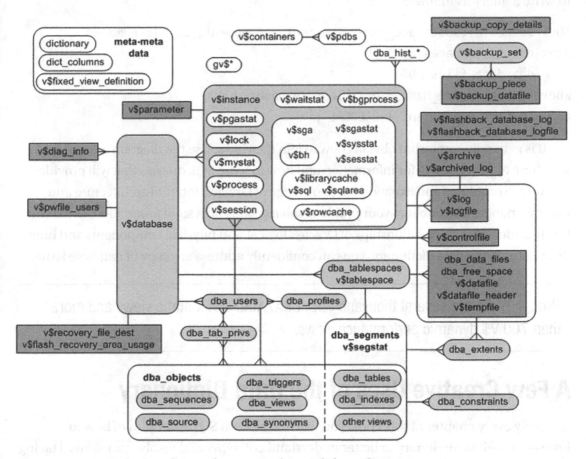

Figure 10-4. *Relationships of commonly used data dictionary views*

Voilà, these data dictionary views map very closely to almost all the logical and physical elements of an Oracle database. Figure 10-4 does not show every data dictionary view. Indeed, the figure barely scratches the surface. However, this diagram does provide you with a secure foundation on which to build your understanding of how to leverage the data dictionary views to get the data you need to do your job.

The diagram does show relationships between views, but it does not specify which columns to use when joining views together. You will have to describe the tables and make an educated guess as to how the views should be joined. For example, suppose you want to display the data files associated with tablespaces that are not locally managed. That requires joining DBA_TABLESPACES to DBA_DATA_FILES. If you inspect those two views, you will notice that each contains a TABLESPACE_NAME column, which allows you to write a query as follows:

```
SQL> select a.tablespace_name, a.extent_management, b.file_name
from dba_tablespaces a,
     dba_data_files  b
where a.tablespace_name = b.tablespace_name
and a.extent_management != 'LOCAL';
```

It is generally somewhat obvious how to join the views. Use the diagram as a guide for where to start looking for information and how to write SQL queries that will provide answers to problems and expand your knowledge of Oracle's internal architecture and inner workings. This anchors your problem-solving skills on a solid foundation. Once you firmly understand the relationships of Oracle's logical and physical components and how this relates to the data dictionary, you can confidently address any type of database issue.

Note   There are several thousand CDB/DBA/ALL/USER static views and more than 700 V$ dynamic performance views.

A Few Creative Uses of the Data Dictionary

In nearly every chapter of this book, you will find several SQL examples of how to leverage the data dictionary to better understand concepts and resolve problems. Having said that, it is worth showing a few offbeat examples of how DBAs leverage the data dictionary. The next few sections do just that. Keep in mind that this is just the tip of the iceberg: there are an endless number of queries and techniques that DBAs employ to extract and use data dictionary information.

Derivable Documentation

Sometimes, if you are troubleshooting an issue and are under pressure, you need to quickly extract information from the data dictionary to help resolve the problem. However, you may not know the exact name of a data dictionary view or its associated columns. If you are like me, it is impossible to keep all the data dictionary view names and column names in your head. Additionally, I work with databases from versions 8 through 12c, and it is difficult to keep track of which particular view may be available with a given release of Oracle.

Books and posters can provide this information, but if you cannot find exactly what you are looking for, you can use the documentation contained in the data dictionary itself. You can query from three views, in particular:

- DBA_OBJECTS

- DICTIONARY

- DICT_COLUMNS

If you know roughly the name of the view from which you want to select information, you can first query from DBA_OBJECTS. For instance, if you are troubleshooting an issue regarding materialized views, and you cannot remember the exact names of the data dictionary views associated with materialized views, you can do this:

```
SQL> select object_name
from dba_objects
where object_name like '%MV%'
and owner='SYS';
```

That may be enough to get you in the ballpark. But often you need more information about each view. This is when the DICTIONARY and DICT_COLUMNS views can be invaluable. The DICTIONARY view stores the names of the data dictionary views. It has two columns:

```
SQL> desc dictionary
```

Name	Null?	Type
TABLE_NAME		VARCHAR2(30)
COMMENTS		VARCHAR2(4000)

For example, say you are troubleshooting an issue with materialized views, and you want to determine the names of data dictionary views related to the materialized view feature. You can run a query such as this:

```
SQL> select table_name, comments
from dictionary
where table_name like '%MV%';
```

Here is a snippet of the output:

```
TABLE_NAME              COMMENTS
------------------------------------------------------------------------------
DBA_MVIEW_LOGS          All materialized view logs in the database
DBA_MVIEWS              All materialized views in the database
DBA_MVIEW_ANALYSIS      Description of the materialized views accessible to dba
DBA_MVIEW_COMMENTS      Comments on all materialized views in the database
```

In this manner, you can quickly determine which view you need to access. If you want further information about the view, you can describe it; for example,

```
SQL> desc dba_mviews
```

If that does not give you enough information regarding the column names, you can query the DICT_COLUMNS view. This view provides comments about the columns of a data dictionary view; for example,

```
SQL> select column_name, comments
from dict_columns
where table_name='DBA_MVIEWS';
```

Here is a fraction of the output:

```
COLUMN_NAME             COMMENTS
--------------------    ---------------------------------------------
OWNER                   Owner of the materialized view
MVIEW_NAME              Name of the materialized view
CONTAINER_NAME          Name of the materialized view container table
QUERY                   The defining query that the materialized view
                        instantiates
```

In this way, you can generate and view documentation regarding most data dictionary objects. The technique allows you to quickly identify appropriate views and the columns that may help you in a troubleshooting situation.

Displaying User Information

You may find yourself in an environment that contains hundreds of databases located on dozens of different servers. In such a scenario, you want to ensure that you do not run the wrong commands or connect to the wrong database, or both. When performing DBA tasks, it is prudent to verify that you are connected as the appropriate account and to the correct database. You can run the following types of SQL commands to verify the currently connected user and database information:

```
SQL> show user;
SQL> select * from user_users;
SQL> select name from v$database;
SQL> select instance_name, host_name from v$instance;
```

As shown in Chapter 3, an efficient way of staying aware of your environment is to set your SQL*Plus prompt automatically, via the login.sql script, to display user and instance information. This example manually sets the SQL prompt:

```
SQL> set sqlprompt '&_USER.@&_CONNECT_IDENTIFIER.> '
```

Here is what the SQL prompt now looks like:

```
SYS@018C>
```

You can also use the SYS_CONTEXT built-in SQL function to extract information from the data dictionary regarding details about your currently connected session. The general syntax for this function is as follows:

```
SYS_CONTEXT('<namespace>','<parameter>',[length])
```

This example displays the user, authentication method, host, and instance:

```
SYS@018C> select
 sys_context('USERENV','CURRENT_USER') usr
,sys_context('USERENV','AUTHENTICATION_METHOD') auth_mth
,sys_context('USERENV','HOST') host
,sys_context('USERENV','INSTANCE_NAME') inst
from dual;
```

USERENV is a built-in Oracle namespace. More than 50 parameters are available when you use the USERENV namespace with the SYS_CONTEXT function. Table 10-1 describes some of the more useful parameters. See the Oracle SQL Language Reference Guide, which can be freely downloaded from the Technology Network area of the Oracle web site (http://otn.oracle.com), for a complete list of parameters.

Table 10-1. *Useful USERENV Parameters Available with SYS_CONTEXT*

Parameter Name	Description
AUTHENTICATED_IDENTITY	Identity used in authentication
AUTHENTICATION_METHOD	Method of authentication
CDB_NAME	Returns the name of the CDB; otherwise returns null
CLIENT_IDENTIFIER	Returns an identifier that is set by the application
CLIENT_INFO	User session information
CON_ID	Container identifier
CON_NAME	Container name
CURRENT_USER	Username for the currently active session
DB_NAME	Name specified by the DB_NAME initialization parameter
DB_UNIQUE_NAME	Name specified by the DB_UNIQUE_NAME initialization parameter
HOST	Hostname for the machine on which the client initiated the database connection
INSTANCE_NAME	Instance name
IP_ADDRESS	IP address of the machine on which the client initiated the database connection
ISDBA	TRUE if the user authenticated with DBA privileges through the OS or password file
NLS_DATE_FORMAT	Date format for the session
OS_USER	OS user from the machine on which the client initiated the database connection
SERVER_HOST	Hostname of the machine on which the database instance is running
SERVICE_NAME	Service name for the connection
SID	Session identifier
TERMINAL	OS identifier for the client terminal

DETERMINING YOUR ENVIRONMENT'S DETAILS

Sometimes, when deploying code through various development, test, beta, and production environments, it is handy to be prompted as to whether you are in the correct environment. The technique for accomplishing this requires two files: answer_yes.sql and answer_no.sql. Here are the contents of answer_yes.sql:

```
-- answer_yes.sql
PROMPT
PROMPT Continuing...
```

And here is answer_no.sql:

```
-- answer_no.sql
PROMPT
PROMPT Quitting and discarding changes...
ROLLBACK;
EXIT;
```

Now, you can insert the following code into the first part of your deployment script; the code will prompt you as to whether you are in the right environment and if you want to continue:

```
WHENEVER SQLERROR EXIT FAILURE ROLLBACK;
WHENEVER OSERROR EXIT FAILURE ROLLBACK;
select host_name from v$instance;
select name as db_name from v$database;
SHOW user;
SET ECHO OFF;
PROMPT
ACCEPT answer PROMPT 'Correct environment? Enter yes to continue: '
@@answer_&answer..sql
```

If you type in yes, then the answer_yes.sql script will execute, and you will continue to run any other scripts you call. If you type in no, then the answer_no.sql script will run, and you will exit from SQL*Plus and end up at the OS prompt. If you press the Enter key without typing either, you will also exit and return to the OS prompt.

Displaying Table Row Counts

When you are investigating performance or space issues, it is useful to display each table's row count. To calculate row counts manually, you would write a query such as this for each table that you own:

```
SQL> select count(*) from <table_name>;
```

Manually crafting the SQL is time consuming and error prone. In this situation, it is more efficient to use SQL to generate the SQL required to solve the problem. To that end, this next example dynamically selects the required text, based on information in the DBA_TABLES view. An output file is spooled that contains the dynamically generated SQL. Run the following SQL code as a DBA-privileged schema. Note that this script contains SQL*Plus-specific commands, such as UNDEFINE and SPOOL. The script prompts you each time for a username:

```
UNDEFINE user
SPOOL tabcount_&&user..sql
SET LINESIZE 132 PAGESIZE 0 TRIMSPO OFF VERIFY OFF FEED OFF TERM OFF
SELECT
  'SELECT RPAD(' || "" || table_name || "" ||',30)'
  || ',' || ' COUNT(*) FROM &&user..' || table_name || ';'
FROM dba_tables
WHERE owner = UPPER('&&user')
ORDER BY 1;
SPO OFF;
SET TERM ON
@@tabcount_&&user..sql
SET VERIFY ON FEED ON
```

This code generates a file, named tabcount_<user>.sql, which contains the SQL statements that select row counts from all tables in the specified schema. If the username you provide to the script is INVUSER, then you can manually run the generated script as follows:

```
SQL> @tabcount_invuser.sql
```

Keep in mind that if the table row counts are high, this script can take a long time to run (several minutes).

Developers and DBAs often use SQL to generate SQL statements. This is a useful technique when you need to apply the same SQL process (repetitively) to many different objects, such as all tables in a schema. If you do not have access to DBA-level views, you can query the USER_TABLES view; for example,

```
SPO tabcount.sql
SET LINESIZE 132 PAGESIZE 0 TRIMSPO OFF VERIFY OFF FEED OFF TERM OFF
SELECT
   'SELECT RPAD(' || "" || table_name || "" ||',30)'
   || ',' || ' COUNT(*) FROM ' || table_name || ';'
FROM user_tables
ORDER BY 1;
SPO OFF;
SET TERM ON
@@tabcount.sql
SET VERIFY ON FEED ON
```

If you have accurate statistics, you can query the NUM_ROWS column of the CDB/DBA/ALL/USER_TABLES views. This column normally has a close row count if statistics are generated on a regular basis. The following query selects NUM_ROWS from the USER_TABLES view:

```
SQL> select table_name, num_rows from user_tables;
```

One final note: if you have partitioned tables and want to show row counts by partition, use the next few lines of SQL and PL/SQL code to generate the SQL required:

```
SQL> UNDEFINE user
SQL> SET SERVEROUT ON SIZE 1000000 VERIFY OFF
SQL> SPO part_count_&&user..txt
SQL> DECLARE
  counter  NUMBER;
  sql_stmt VARCHAR2(1000);
  CURSOR c1 IS
  SELECT table_name, partition_name
  FROM dba_tab_partitions
  WHERE table_owner = UPPER('&&user');
```

```
BEGIN
  FOR r1 IN c1 LOOP
    sql_stmt := 'SELECT COUNT(*) FROM &&user..' || r1.table_name
       ||' PARTITION ( '||r1.partition_name ||' )';
    EXECUTE IMMEDIATE sql_stmt INTO counter;
    DBMS_OUTPUT.PUT_LINE(RPAD(r1.table_name
       ||'('||r1.partition_name||')',30) ||' '||TO_CHAR(counter));
  END LOOP;
END;
/
SPO OFF
```

MANUALLY GENERATING STATISTICS

If you want to generate statistics for a table, use the DBMS_STATS package. This example generates statistics for a user and a table:

```
SQL> exec dbms_stats.gather_table_stats(ownname=>'MV_MAINT',-
        tabname=>'F_SALES',-
        cascade=>true,estimate_percent=>20,degree=>4);
```

You can generate statistics for all objects for a user with the following code:

```
SQL> exec dbms_stats.gather_schema_stats(ownname => 'MV_MAINT',-
        estimate_percent => DBMS_STATS.AUTO_SAMPLE_SIZE,-
        degree => DBMS_STATS.AUTO_DEGREE,-
        cascade => true);
```

The prior code instructs Oracle to estimate the percentage of the table to be sampled with the ESTIMATE_PERCENT parameter, using DBMS_STATS.AUTO_SAMPLE_SIZE. Oracle also chooses the appropriate degree of parallelism with the DEGREE parameter setting of DBMS_STATS.AUTO_DEGREE. The CASCADE parameter instructs Oracle to generate statistics for indexes.

Keep in mind that it is possible that Oracle would not choose the optimal auto sample size. Oracle may choose 10 percent, but you may have experience with setting a low percentage, such as 5 percent, and know that is an acceptable number. In these situations, do not use the AUTO_SAMPLE_SIZE; explicitly provide a number instead.

Showing Primary Key and Foreign Key Relationships

Sometimes when you are diagnosing constraint issues, it is useful to display data dictionary information regarding what primary key constraint is associated with a foreign key constraint. For example, perhaps you are attempting to insert into a child table, and an error is thrown indicating that the parent key does not exist, and you want to display more information about the parent key constraint.

The following script queries the DBA_CONSTRAINTS data dictionary view to determine the parent primary key constraints that are related to child foreign key constraints. You need to provide as input to the script the owner of the table and the child table for which you wish to display primary key constraints:

```
SQL> select
 a.constraint_type cons_type
,a.table_name      child_table
,a.constraint_name child_cons
,b.table_name      parent_table
,b.constraint_name parent_cons
,b.constraint_type cons_type
from dba_constraints a
    ,dba_constraints b
where a.owner     = upper('&owner')
and a.table_name = upper('&table_name')
and a.constraint_type = 'R'
and a.r_owner = b.owner
and a.r_constraint_name = b.constraint_name;
```

The preceding script prompts you for two SQL*Plus ampersand variables (OWNER, TABLE_NAME); if you are not using SQL*Plus, then you may need to modify the script with the appropriate values before you run it.

The following output shows that there are two foreign key constraints. It also shows the parent table primary key constraints:

```
C CHILD_TABLE      CHILD_CONS           PARENT_TABLE    PARENT_CONS          C
- --------------- -------------------- --------------- -------------------- -
R REG_COMPANIES    REG_COMPANIES_FK2    D_COMPANIES     D_COMPANIES_PK       P
R REG_COMPANIES    REG_COMPANIES_FK1    CLUSTER_BUCKETS CLUSTER_BUCKETS_PK   P
```

When the CONSTRAINT_TYPE column (of DBA/ALL/USER_CONSTRAINTS) contains an R value, this indicates that the row describes a referential integrity constraint, which means that the child table constraint references a primary key constraint. You use the technique of joining to the same table twice to retrieve the primary key constraint information. The child constraint columns (R_OWNER, R_CONSTRAINT_NAME) match with another row in the DBA_CONSTRAINTS view that contains the primary key information.

You can also do the reverse of the prior query in this section; for a primary key constraint, you want to find the foreign key columns (if any) that correlate to it. The next script takes the primary key record and looks to see if it has any child records with a constraint type of R. When you run this script, you are prompted for the primary key table owner and name:

```
SQL> select
  b.table_name        primary_key_table
 ,a.table_name        fk_child_table
 ,a.constraint_name   fk_child_table_constraint
from dba_constraints a
    ,dba_constraints b
where a.r_constraint_name = b.constraint_name
and   a.r_owner           = b.owner
and   a.constraint_type   = 'R'
and   b.owner             = upper('&table_owner')
and   b.table_name        = upper('&table_name');
```

Here is some sample output:

```
PRIMARY_KEY_TABLE     FK_CHILD_TABLE       FK_CHILD_TABLE_CONSTRAINT
--------------------  -------------------- ------------------------------
CLUSTER_BUCKETS       CB_AD_ASSOC          CB_AD_ASSOC_FK1
CLUSTER_BUCKETS       CLUSTER_CONTACTS     CLUSTER_CONTACTS_FK1
CLUSTER_BUCKETS       CLUSTER_NOTES        CLUSTER_NOTES_FK1
```

Displaying Object Dependencies

Say you need to drop a table, but before you drop it, you want to display any objects that are dependent on it. For example, you may have a table that has synonyms, views, materialized views, functions, procedures, and triggers that rely on it. Before making the change, you want to review what other objects are dependent on the table. You can use the DBA_DEPENDENCIES data dictionary view to display object dependencies. The following query prompts you for a username and an object name:

```
SQL> select '+' || lpad(' ',level+2) || type || ' ' || owner || '.' || name   dep_tree
from dba_dependencies
connect by prior owner = referenced_owner and prior name = referenced_name
and prior type = referenced_type
start with referenced_owner = upper('&object_owner')
and referenced_name = upper('&object_name')
and owner is not null;
```

In the output each object listed has a dependency on the object you entered. Lines are indented to show the dependency of an object on the object in the preceding line:

```
DEP_TREE
--------------------------------------------------------------
+   TRIGGER STAR2.D_COMPANIES_BU_TR1
+   MATERIALIZED VIEW CIA.CB_RAD_COUNTS
+   SYNONYM STAR1.D_COMPANIES
+    SYNONYM CIA.D_COMPANIES
+     MATERIALIZED VIEW CIA.CB_RAD_COUNTS
```

In this example, the object being analyzed is a table named D_COMPANIES. Several synonyms, materialized views, and one trigger are dependent on this table. For instance, the materialized view CB_RAD_COUNTS, owned by CIA, is dependent on the synonym D_COMPANIES, owned by CIA, which in turn is dependent on the D_COMPANIES synonym, owned by STAR1.

The DBA_DEPENDENCIES view contains a hierarchical relationship between the OWNER, NAME, and TYPE columns and their referenced column names of REFERENCED_OWNER, REFERENCED_NAME, and REFERENCED_TYPE. Oracle provides a number of constructs to perform hierarchical queries. For instance, START WITH and CONNECT BY allow you to identify a starting point in a tree and walk either up or down the hierarchical relationship.

The previous SQL query in this section operates on only one object. If you want to inspect every object in a schema, you can use SQL to generate SQL to create scripts that display all dependencies for a schema's objects. The piece of code in the next example does that. For formatting and output, the code uses some constructs specific to SQL*Plus, such as setting the page sizes and line size and spooling the output:

```
SQL> UNDEFINE owner
SQL> SET LINESIZE 132 PAGESIZE 0 VERIFY OFF FEEDBACK OFF TIMING OFF
SQL> SPO dep_dyn_&&owner..sql
SQL> SELECT 'SPO dep_dyn_&&owner..txt' FROM DUAL;
--
SELECT
'PROMPT ' || '_____'|| CHR(10) ||
'PROMPT ' || object_type || ': ' || object_name || CHR(10) ||
'SELECT ' || "" || '+' || "" || ' ' || ' '|| LPAD(' || "" || ' '
|| "" || ',level+3)' || CHR(10) || ' || type || ' || "" || ' ' || "" ||
' || owner || ' || "" || '.' || "" || ' || name' || CHR(10) ||
' FROM dba_dependencies ' || CHR(10) ||
' CONNECT BY PRIOR owner = referenced_owner AND prior name = referenced_name '
|| CHR(10) ||
' AND prior type = referenced_type ' || CHR(10) ||
' START WITH referenced_owner = ' || "" || UPPER('&&owner') || "" || CHR(10) ||
' AND referenced_name = ' || "" || object_name || "" || CHR(10) ||
' AND owner IS NOT NULL;'
FROM dba_objects
WHERE owner = UPPER('&&owner')
AND object_type NOT IN ('INDEX','INDEX PARTITION','TABLE PARTITION');
--
SELECT 'SPO OFF' FROM dual;
SPO OFF
SET VERIFY ON LINESIZE 80 FEEDBACK ON
```

You should now have a script named dep_dyn_<owner>.sql, created in the same directory from which you ran the script. This script contains all the SQL required to display dependencies on objects in the owner you entered. Run the script to display object dependencies. In this example, the owner is CIA:

```
SQL> @dep_dyn_cia.sql
```

When the script runs, it spools a file with the format dep_dyn_<owner>.txt. You can open that text file with an OS editor to view its contents. Here is a sample of the output from this example:

```
TABLE: DOMAIN_NAMES
+    FUNCTION STAR2.GET_DERIVED_COMPANY
+    TRIGGER STAR2.DOMAIN_NAMES_BU_TR1
+    SYNONYM CIA_APP.DOMAIN_NAMES
```

This output shows that the table DOMAIN_NAMES has three objects that are dependent on it: a function, a trigger, and a synonym.

THE DUAL TABLE

The DUAL table is part of the data dictionary. This table contains one row and one column and is useful when you want to return exactly one row, and you do not have to retrieve data from a particular table. In other words, you just want to return a value. For example, you can perform arithmetic operations, as follows:

```
SQL> select 34*.15 from dual;
    34*.15
----------
      5.1
```

Other common uses are selecting from DUAL to show the current date or to display some text within an SQL script.

Summary

Sometimes, you are handed an old database that has been running for years, and it is up to you to manage and maintain it. In some scenarios, you are not given any documentation regarding the users and objects in the database. Even if you have documentation, it may not be accurate or up-to-date. In these situations, the data dictionary quickly becomes your source of documentation. You can use it to extract user information, the physical structure of the database, security information, objects and owners, currently connected users, and so on.

Oracle provides static and dynamic views in the data dictionary. The static views contain information about the objects in the database. You can use these views to determine which tables are consuming the most space, contain the most rows, have the most extents allocated, and so on. The dynamic performance views offer a real-time window into events currently transacting in the database. These views provide information about currently connected users, SQL executing, where resources are being consumed, and so on. DBAs use these views extensively to monitor and troubleshoot performance issues.

The book now turns its attention toward specialized Oracle features, such as large objects, partitioning, Data Pump, and external tables. These topics are covered in the next several chapters.

CHAPTER 11

Large Objects

Organizations often deal with substantial files that need to be stored and viewed by business users. Generally, LOBs are a data type that is suited to storing large and unstructured data, such as text, log, image, video, sound, and spatial data. Oracle supports the following types of LOBs:

- Character large object (CLOB)

- National character large object (NCLOB)

- Binary large object (BLOB)

- Binary file (BFILE)

Prior to Oracle 8, the LONG and LONG RAW data types were your only options for storing large amounts of data in a column. You should no longer use these data types. The only reason I mention LONG and LONG RAW is because many legacy applications (e.g., Oracle's data dictionary) still use them. You should otherwise use a CLOB instead of LONG and a BLOB instead of LONG RAW.

Also, do not confuse a RAW data type with a LONG RAW. The RAW data type stores small amounts of binary data. The LONG RAW data type has been deprecated for more than a decade.

Another caveat: do not unnecessarily use a LOB data type. For example, for character data, if your application requires fewer than 32,000 single byte characters, use a VARCHAR2 data type CLOB). For binary data, if you are dealing with fewer than 32,000 bytes of binary data, use a RAW data type (and not a BLOB). If you are still not sure which data type your application needs, see Chapter 7 for a description of appropriate uses of Oracle data types.

Before lobbing you into the details of implementing LOBs, it is prudent to review each LOB data type and its appropriate use. After that, examples are provided of creating and working with LOBs and relevant features that you should understand.

© Michelle Malcher and Darl Kuhn 2019
M. Malcher and D. Kuhn, *Pro Oracle Database 18c Administration*,
https://doi.org/10.1007/978-1-4842-4424-1_11

Describing LOB Types

Since the earlier versions of Oracle, the ability to store large files in the database vastly improved with the CLOB, NCLOB, BLOB, and BFILE data types. These additional LOB data types let you store much more data, with greater functionality. Table 11-1 summarizes the types of Oracle LOBs available and their descriptions.

A CLOB such as json, XML, text, and log files. An NCLOB is treated the same as a CLOB but can contain characters in the multibyte national character set for a database.

BLOBsare not human readable. Typical uses for a BLOB are spreadsheets, word-processing documents, images, and audio and video data.

CLOBs, NCLOBs, and BLOBs are known as internal LOBs. This is because these data types are stored inside the Oracle database in data files. Internal LOBs participate in transactions and are covered by Oracle's database security as well as its backup and recovery features.

BFILEs are known as external LOBs. BFILE columns store a pointer to a file on the OS that is outside the database. You can think of a BFILE as a mechanism for providing read-only access to large binary files outside the database on the OS filesystem.

Sometimes, the question arises as to whether you should use a BLOB or a BFILE. BLOBs participate in database transactions and can be backed up, restored, and recovered by Oracle. BFILEs do not participate in database transactions, are read-only, and are not covered by any Oracle security, backup and recovery, replication, or disaster recovery mechanisms. BFILEs are more appropriate for large binary files that are read-only and that do not change while an application is running. For instance, you may have large binary video files that are referenced by a database application. In this scenario, the business determines that you do not need to create and maintain a 500TB database when all the application really needs is a pointer (stored in the database) to the locations of the large files on disk.

Table 11-1. Oracle Large Object Data Types

Data Type	Description	Maximum Size
CLOB	Character large object for storing character documents, such as big text files, log files, XML files, and so on	(4GB–1)* block size
NCLOB	National character large object; stores data in national character set format; supports characters with varying widths	(4GB–1) * block size
BLOB	Binary large object for storing unstructured bitstream data (images, video, and so on)	(4GB–1) * block size
BFILE	Binary file large object stored on the filesystem outside of database; read-only	2^64–1 bytes (OS may impose a size limit that is less than this)

Illustrating LOB Locators, Indexes, and Chunks

Internal LOBs (CLOB, NCLOB, BLOB) store data in pieces called chunks. A chunk is the smallest unit of allocation for a LOB and is made up of one or more database blocks. LOB locators are stored in rows containing a LOB column. The LOB locator points to a LOB index. The LOB index stores information regarding the location of LOB chunks. When a table is queried, the database uses the LOB locator and associated LOB index to locate the appropriate LOB chunks. Figure 11-1 shows the relationship between a table, a row, a LOB locator, and a LOB locator's associated index and chunks.

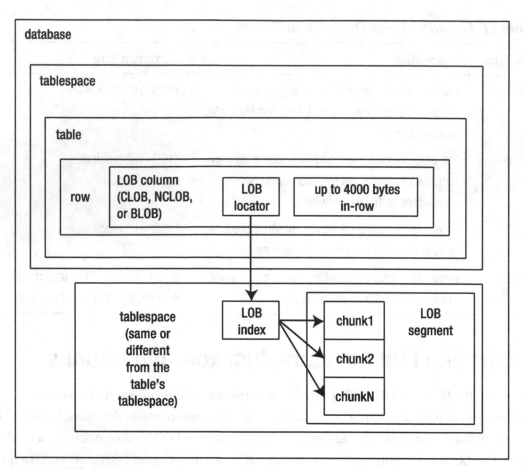

Figure 11-1. *Relationship of table, row, LOB locator, LOB index, and LOB segment*

The LOB locator for a BFILE stores the directory path and file name on the OS. Figure 11-2 shows a BFILE LOB locator that references a file on the OS.

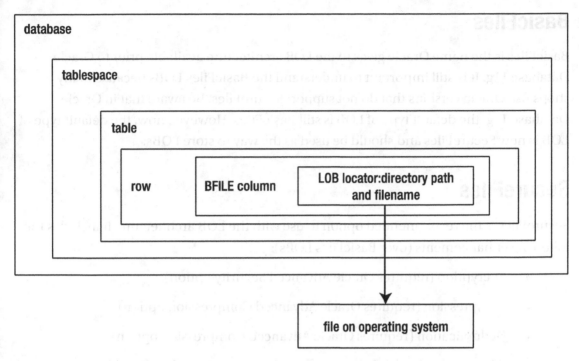

Figure 11-2. *The BFILE LOB locator contains information for locating a file on the OS*

Note   The DBMS_LOB package performs operations on LOBs through the LOB locator.

Distinguishing Between BasicFiles and SecureFiles

Several significant improvements were made to LOBs. Oracle now distinguishes between two different types of underlying LOB architecture:

- BasicFiles
- SecureFiles

These two LOB architectures are discussed in the following sections.

BasicFiles

BasicFiles is the name Oracle gives to the LOB architecture available prior to Oracle Database 11g. It is still important to understand the BasicFiles LOBs because many shops use Oracle versions that do not support SecureFiles. Be aware that in Oracle Database 11g, the default type of LOB is still BasicFiles. However, now, the default type of LOB is now SecureFiles and should be used as the way to store LOBs.

SecureFiles

SecureFiles is the recommended option to use with the LOB architecture. It includes the following enhancements (over BasicFiles LOBs):

- Encryption (requires Oracle Advanced Security option)

- Compression (requires Oracle Advanced Compression option)

- Deduplication (requires Oracle Advanced Compression option)

SecureFiles encryption lets you transparently encrypt LOB data (just like other data types). The compression feature allows for significant space savings. The deduplication feature eliminates duplicate LOBs that otherwise would be stored multiple times.

You need to do a small amount of planning before using SecureFiles. Specifically, use of SecureFiles requires the following:

- A SecureFiles LOB must be stored in a tablespace, using ASSM.

- The DB_SECUREFILE initialization parameter controls whether a SecureFiles file can be used and also defines the default LOB architecture for your database.

A SecureFiles LOB must be created within a tablespace using ASSM. To create an ASSM-enabled tablespace, specify the SEGMENT SPACE MANAGEMENT AUTO clause; for example,

```
SQL> create tablespace lob_data
  datafile '/u01/dbfile/o18c/lob_data01.dbf'
  size 1000m
  extent management local
  uniform size 1m
  segment space management auto;
```

If you have existing tablespaces, you can verify the use of ASSM by querying the DBA_
TABLESPACES view. The SEGMENT_SPACE_MANAGEMENT column should have a value of AUTO
for any tablespaces that you want to use with SecureFiles:

```
select tablespace_name, segment_space_management
from dba_tablespaces;
```

Also, SecureFiles usage is governed by the DB_SECUREFILE database parameter. You
can use either ALTER SYSTEM or ALTER SESSION to modify the value of DB_SECUREFILE.
Table 11-2 describes the valid values for DB_SECUREFILE.

Table 11-2. *Description of DB_SECUREFILE Settings*

DB_SECUREFILE Setting	Description
NEVER	Creates the LOB as a BasicFiles type, regardless of whether the SECUREFILE option is specified
PERMITTED	Allows creation of SecureFiles LOBs
PREFERRED	Default value; specifies that all LOBs are created as a SecureFiles type, unless otherwise stated
ALWAYS	Creates the LOB as a SecureFiles type, unless the underlying tablespace is not using ASSM
IGNORE	Ignores the SecureFiles option, along with any SecureFiles settings

Creating a Table with a LOB Column

The default underlying LOB architecture is SecureFiles. It is recommended to create a
LOB as a SecureFiles. As discussed previously, SecureFiles allows you to use features
such as compression and encryption.

Creating a BasicFiles LOB Column

To create a LOB column, you have to specify a LOB data type. It is best to explicitly
specify the STORE AS BASICFILE clause in order to avoid confusion as to which LOB
architecture is implemented. Listed next is such an example:

```
SQL> create table patchmain(
 patch_id   number
,patch_desc clob)
tablespace users
lob(patch_desc) store as basicfile;
```

When you create a table with a LOB column, you must be aware of some technical underpinnings. Review the following list, and be sure you understand each point:

- Prior to Oracle Database 12c, LOBs, by default, are created as the BasicFiles type.

- Oracle creates a LOB segment and a LOB index for each LOB column.

- The LOB segment has a name of this format: SYS_LOB<string>.

- The LOB index has a name of this format: SYS_IL<string>.

- The <string> is the same for each LOB segment and its associated index.

- The LOB segment and index are created in the same tablespace as the table, unless you specify a different tablespace.

- A LOB segment and a LOB index are not created until a record is inserted into the table (the so-called deferred segment creation feature). This means that DBA/ALL/USER_SEGMENTS and DBA/ALL/USER_EXTENTS have no information in them until a row is inserted into the table.

Oracle creates a LOB segment and a LOB index for each LOB column. The LOB segment stores the data. The LOB index keeps track of where the chunks of LOB data are physically stored and in what order they should be accessed.

You can query the DBA/ALL/USER_LOBS view to display the LOB segment and LOB index names:

```
SQL> select table_name, segment_name, index_name, securefile, in_row
from user_lobs;
```

Here is the output for this example:

```
TABLE_NAME    SEGMENT_NAME                 INDEX_NAME                   SEC IN_
------------  ---------------------------  ---------------------------  --- ---
PATCHMAIN     SYS_LOB0000022332C00002$$    SYS_IL0000022332C00002$$     NO  YES
```

You can also query DBA/USER/ALL_SEGMENTS to view information regarding LOB segments. As mentioned earlier, an initial segment is not created until you insert a row into the table (deferred segment creation). This can be confusing because you may expect a row to be present in DBA/ALL/USER_SEGMENTS immediately after you create the table:

```
SQL> select segment_name, segment_type, segment_subtype, bytes/1024/1024
meg_bytes
from user_segments
where segment_name IN ('&&table_just_created',
                       '&&lob_segment_just_created',
                       '&&lob_index_just_created');
```

The prior query prompts for the segment names. The output shows no rows:

```
no rows selected
```

Next, insert a record into the table that contains the LOB column:

```
SQL> insert into patchmain values(1,'clob text');
```

Rerunning the query against USER_SEGMENTS shows that three segments have been created—one for the table, one for the LOB segment, and one for the LOB index:

```
SEGMENT_NAME               SEGMENT_TYPE       SEGMENT_SU  MEG_BYTES
-------------------------  -----------------  ----------  ----------
PATCHMAIN                  TABLE              ASSM             .0625
SYS_IL0000022332C00002$$   LOBINDEX           ASSM             .0625
SYS_LOB0000022332C00002$$  LOBSEGMENT         ASSM             .0625
```

Implementing a LOB in a Specific Tablespace

By default, the LOB segment is stored in the same tablespace as its table. You can specify a separate tablespace for a LOB segment by using the LOB...STORE AS clause of the CREATE TABLE statement. The next table creation script creates the table in a tablespace and creates separate tablespaces for the CLOB and BLOB columns:

```
SQL> create table patchmain
(patch_id    number
,patch_desc clob
```

```
,patch        blob
) tablespace users
 lob (patch_desc) store as (tablespace lob_data)
,lob (patch)      store as (tablespace lob_data);
```

The following query verifies the associated tablespaces for this table:

```
SQL> select table_name, tablespace_name, 'N/A' column_name
from user_tables
where table_name='PATCHMAIN'
union
select table_name, tablespace_name, column_name
from user_lobs
where table_name='PATCHMAIN';
```

Here is the output:

```
TABLE_NAME            TABLESPACE_NAME         COLUMN_NAME
--------------------  --------------------    --------------------

PATCHMAIN             LOB_DATA                PATCH
PATCHMAIN             LOB_DATA                PATCH_DESC
PATCHMAIN             USERS                   N/A
```

If you think the LOB segment will require different storage characteristics (such as size and growth patterns), then I recommend that you create the LOB in a tablespace separate from that of the table data. This allows you to manage the LOB column storage separately from the regular table data storage.

Creating a SecureFiles LOB Column

As discussed previously, the default LOB architecture is SecureFiles. Having said that, I recommend that you explicitly state which LOB architecture to implement in order to avoid any confusion. As mentioned earlier, the tablespace that contains the SecureFile LOB must be ASSM managed. Here is an example that creates a SecureFiles LOB:

```
SQL> create table patchmain(
 patch_id   number
,patch_desc clob)
lob(patch_desc) store as securefile (tablespace lob_data);
```

Before viewing the data dictionary details regarding the LOB column, insert a record into the table to ensure that segment information is available (owing to the deferred segment allocation feature in Oracle Database 11g Release 2 and higher); for example,

```
SQL> insert into patchmain values(1,'clob text');
```

You can now verify a LOB's architecture by querying the USER_SEGMENTS view:

```
SQL> select segment_name, segment_type, segment_subtype
from user_segments;
```

Here is some sample output, indicating that a LOB segment is a SecureFiles type:

```
SEGMENT_NAME                     SEGMENT_TYPE        SEGMENT_SU
-------------------------        ----------------    ----------
PATCHMAIN                        TABLE               ASSM
SYS_IL0000022340C00002$$  LOBINDEX            ASSM
SYS_LOB0000022340C00002$$ LOBSEGMENT          SECUREFILE
```

You can also query the USER_LOBS view to verify the SecureFiles LOB architecture:

```
SQL> select table_name, segment_name, index_name, securefile, in_row
from user_lobs;
```

Here is the output:

```
TABLE_NAME    SEGMENT_NAME                  INDEX_NAME                      SEC IN_
------------  -------------------------     -------------------------       --- ---
PATCHMAIN     SYS_LOB0000022340C00002$$ SYS_IL0000022340C00002$$  YES YES
```

Note   With the SecureFiles architecture, you no longer need to specify the following options: CHUNK, PCTVERSION, FREEPOOLS, FREELIST, and FREELIST GROUPS.

Implementing a Partitioned LOB

You can create a partitioned table that has a LOB column. Doing so lets you spread a LOB across multiple tablespaces. Such partitioning helps with balancing I/O, maintenance, and backup and recovery operations.

You can partition LOBs by RANGE, LIST, or HASH. The next example creates a LIST-partitioned table in which LOB column data are stored in tablespaces separate from those of the table data:

```
SQL> CREATE TABLE patchmain(
 patch_id   NUMBER
,region     VARCHAR2(16)
,patch_desc CLOB)
LOB(patch_desc) STORE AS (TABLESPACE patch1)
PARTITION BY LIST (REGION) (
PARTITION p1 VALUES ('EAST')
LOB(patch_desc) STORE AS SECUREFILE
(TABLESPACE patch1 COMPRESS HIGH)
TABLESPACE inv_data1
,
PARTITION p2 VALUES ('WEST')
LOB(patch_desc) STORE AS SECUREFILE
(TABLESPACE patch2 DEDUPLICATE NOCOMPRESS)
TABLESPACE inv_data2
,
PARTITION p3 VALUES (DEFAULT)
LOB(patch_desc) STORE AS SECUREFILE
(TABLESPACE patch3 COMPRESS LOW)
TABLESPACE inv_data3
);
```

Note that each LOB partition is created with its own storage options (see the section "Implementing SecureFiles Advanced Features," later in this chapter, for details on SecureFiles features). You can view the details about the LOB partitions as shown:

```
SQL> select table_name, column_name, partition_name, tablespace_name
,compression, deduplication
from user_lob_partitions;
```

Here is some sample output:

```
TABLE_NAME     COLUMN_NAME     PARTITION_ TABLESPACE_NAME COMPRE DEDUPLICATION
-------------- --------------- ---------- --------------- ------ -------------
PATCHMAIN      PATCH_DESC      P1         PATCH1          HIGH   NO
PATCHMAIN      PATCH_DESC      P2         PATCH2          NO     LOB
PATCHMAIN      PATCH_DESC      P3         PATCH3          LOW    NO
```

Tip   You can also view DBA/ALL_USER_PART_LOBS for information about partitioned LOBs.

You can change the storage characteristics of a partitioned LOB column after it is created. To do so, use the ALTER TABLE ... MODIFY PARTITION statement. This example alters a LOB partition to have a high degree of compression:

```
SQL> alter table patchmain modify partition p2
lob (patch_desc) (compress high);
```

The next example modifies a partitioned LOB not to keep duplicate values (via the DEDUPLICATE clause):

```
SQL> alter table patchmain modify partition p3
lob (patch_desc) (deduplicate lob);
```

Note   Partitioning and Advanced Compression, which have been discussed in this chapter, are extra cost options that are available only with the Oracle Enterprise Edition.

Maintaining LOB Columns

The following sections describe some common maintenance tasks that are performed on LOB columns or that otherwise involve LOB columns, including moving columns between tablespaces and adding new LOB columns to a table.

Moving a LOB Column

As mentioned previously, if you create a table with a LOB column and do not specify a tablespace, then, by default, the LOB is created in the same tablespace as its table. This happens sometimes in environments in which the DBAs do not plan ahead very well; only after the LOB column has consumed large amounts of disk space does the DBA wonder why the table has grown so big.

You can use the ALTER TABLE...MOVE...STORE AS statement to move a LOB column to a tablespace separate from that of the table. Here is the basic syntax:

```
SQL> alter table <table_name> move lob(<lob_name>) store as (tablespace
<new_tablespace);
```

The next example moves the LOB column to the LOB_DATA tablespace:

```
SQL> alter table patchmain
move lob(patch_desc)
store as securefile (tablespace lob_data);
```

You can verify that the LOB was moved by querying USER_LOBS:

```
SQL> select table_name, column_name, tablespace_name from user_lobs;
```

To summarize, if the LOB column is populated with large amounts of data, you almost always want to store the LOB in a tablespace separate from that of the rest of the table data. In these scenarios, the LOB data have different growth and storage requirements and are best maintained in their own tablespace.

Adding a LOB Column

If you have an existing table to which you want to add a LOB column, use the ALTER TABLE...ADD statement. The next statement adds the INV_IMAGE column to a table:

```
SQL> alter table patchmain add(inv_image blob);
```

This statement is fine for quickly adding a LOB column to a development environment. For anything else, you should specify the storage characteristics. For instance, this command specifies that a SecureFiles LOB be created in the LOB_DATA tablespace:

```
SQL> alter table patchmain add(inv_image blob)
lob(inv_image) store as securefile(tablespace lob_data);
```

Removing a LOB Column

You may have a scenario in which your business requirements change, and you no longer need a column. Before you remove a column, consider renaming it so that you can better identify whether any applications or users are still accessing it:

```
SQL> alter table patchmain rename column patch_desc to patch_desc_old;
```

After you determine that nobody is using the column, use the ALTER TABLE...DROP statement to drop it:

```
SQL> alter table patchmain drop(patch_desc_old);
```

You can also remove a LOB column by dropping and re-creating a table (without the LOB column). This, of course, permanently removes any data as well.

Also keep in mind that if your recycle bin is enabled, then when you do not drop a table with the PURGE clause, space is still consumed by the dropped table. If you want to remove the space associated with the table, use the PURGE clause, or purge the recycle bin after dropping the table.

Caching LOBs

By default, when reading and writing LOB columns, Oracle does not cache LOBs in memory. You can change the default behavior by setting the cache-related storage options. This example specifies that Oracle should cache a LOB column in memory:

```
SQL> create table patchmain(
 patch_id number
,patch_desc clob)
lob(patch_desc) store as (tablespace lob_data cache);
```

You can verify the LOB caching with this query:

```
SQL> select table_name, column_name, cache from user_lobs;
```

Here is some sample output:

```
TABLE_NAME          COLUMN_NAME          CACHE
------------------- -------------------- ----------
PATCHMAIN           PATCH_DESC           YES
```

Table 11-3 describes the memory cache settings related to LOBs. If you have LOBs that are frequently read and written to, consider using the CACHE option. If your LOB column is read frequently but rarely written to, then the CACHE READS setting is more appropriate. If the LOB column is infrequently read or written to, then the NOCACHE setting is suitable.

Table 11-3. *Cache Descriptions Regarding LOB Columns*

Cache Setting	Meaning
CACHE	Oracle should place LOB data in the buffer cache for faster access.
CACHE READS	Oracle should place LOB data in the buffer cache for reads but not writes.
NOCACHE	LOB data shouldn't be placed in the buffer cache. This is the default for both SecureFiles and BasicFiles LOBs.

Storing LOBs In- and Out of Line

By default, up to approximately 4,000 characters of a LOB column are stored inline with the table row. If the LOB is more than 4,000 characters, then Oracle automatically stores it outside the row data. The main advantage of storing a LOB in row is that small LOBs (fewer than 4,000 characters) require less I/O, because Oracle does not have to search out of row for the LOB data.

However, storing LOB data in row is not always desirable. The disadvantage of storing LOBs in row is that the table row sizes are potentially longer. This can affect the performance of full-table scans, range scans, and updates to columns other than the LOB column. In these situations, you may want to disable storage in the row. For example, you explicitly instruct Oracle to store the LOB outside the row with the DISABLE STORAGE IN ROW clause:

```
SQL> create table patchmain(
 patch_id number
,patch_desc clob
,log_file   blob)
lob(patch_desc, log_file)
store as (
tablespace lob_data
disable storage in row);
```

If you want to store up to 4,000 characters of a LOB in the table row, use the ENABLE STORAGE IN ROW clause when creating the table:

```
SQL> create table patchmain(
 patch_id number
,patch_desc clob
,log_file   blob)
lob(patch_desc, log_file)
store as (
tablespace lob_data
enable storage in row);
```

Note   The LOB locator is always stored inline with the row.

You cannot modify the LOB storage in a row after the table has been created. The only ways to alter storage in row are to move the LOB column or drop and re-create the table. This example alters the storage in row by moving the LOB column:

```
SQL> alter table patchmain
move lob(patch_desc)
store as (enable storage in row);
```

You can verify the in-row storage via the IN_ROW column of USER_LOBS:

```
SQL> select table_name, column_name, tablespace_name, in_row
from user_lobs;
```

A value of YES indicates that the LOB is stored in row:

TABLE_NAME	COLUMN_NAME	TABLESPACE_NAME	IN_ROW
PATCHMAIN	LOG_FILE	LOB_DATA	YES
PATCHMAIN	PATCH_DESC	LOB_DATA	YES

Implementing SecureFiles Advanced Features

As mentioned earlier, the SecureFiles LOB architecture allows you to compress LOB columns, eliminate duplicates, and transparently encrypt LOB data. These features provide high performance and manageability of LOB. The next few sections cover features specific to SecureFiles.

Compressing LOBs

If you are using SecureFiles LOBs, then you can specify a degree of compression. The benefit is that the LOBs consume much less space in the database. The downside is that reading and writing the LOBs may take longer. See Table 11-4 for a description of the compression values.

This example creates a CLOB column with a low degree of compression:

```
SQL> CREATE TABLE patchmain(
 patch_id   NUMBER
,patch_desc CLOB)
LOB(patch_desc) STORE AS SECUREFILE
(COMPRESS LOW)
TABLESPACE lob_data;
```

Table 11-4. *Degrees of Compression Available with SecureFiles LOBs*

Compression Type	Description
HIGH	Highest degree of compression; incurs higher latency when reading and writing the LOB
MEDIUM	Medium level of compression; default value if compression is specified, but with no degree
LOW	Lowest level of compression; provides the lowest latency when reading and writing the LOB

If a LOB has been created as a SecureFiles type, you can alter its compression level. For instance, this command changes the compression to HIGH:

```
SQL> alter table patchmain modify lob(patch_desc) (compress high);
```

If you create a LOB with compression but decide that you do not want to use the feature, you can alter the LOB to have no compression via the NOCOMPRESS clause:

```
SQL> alter table patchmain modify lob(patch_desc) (nocompress);
```

> **Tip**   Try to enable compression, deduplication, and encryption through a CREATE TABLE statement. If you use an ALTER TABLE statement, the table is locked while the LOB is modified.

Deduplicating LOBs

If you have an application in which identical LOBs are associated with two or more rows, you should consider using the SecureFiles deduplication feature. When enabled, this instructs Oracle to check when a new LOB is inserted into a table to see whether that LOB is already stored in another row (for the same LOB column). If the LOB is already stored, then Oracle stores a pointer to the existing identical LOB. This can potentially mean huge space savings for your application.

> **Note**   Deduplication requires the Oracle Advanced Compression option with Enterprise Edition of the Database.

This example creates a LOB column, using the deduplication feature:

```
SQL> CREATE TABLE patchmain(
 patch_id    NUMBER
,patch_desc CLOB)
LOB(patch_desc) STORE AS SECUREFILE
(DEDUPLICATE)
 TABLESPACE lob_data;
```

To verify that the deduplication feature is in effect, run this query:

```
SQL> select table_name, column_name, deduplication
from user_lobs;
```

Here is some sample output:

```
TABLE_NAME        COLUMN_NAME       DEDUPLICATION
---------------   ---------------   ---------------
PATCHMAIN         PATCH_DESC        LOB
```

If an existing table has a SecureFiles LOB, then you can alter the column to enable deduplication:

```
SQL> alter table patchmain
modify lob(patch_desc) (deduplicate);
```

Here is another example that modifies a partitioned LOB to enable deduplication:

```
SQL> alter table patchmain modify partition p2
lob (patch_desc) (deduplicate lob);
```

If you decide that you do not want deduplication enabled, use the KEEP_DUPLICATES clause:

```
SQL> alter table patchmain
modify lob(patch_desc) (keep_duplicates);
```

Encrypting LOBs

You can transparently encrypt a SecureFiles LOB column (just like any other column). Before you use encryption features, you must set up an encryption wallet. I've included a sidebar at the end of this section that details how to set up a wallet.

Note   The SecureFiles encryption feature requires a license for the Oracle Advanced Security option with the Enterprise Edition of the database.

The ENCRYPT clause enables SecureFiles encryption, using Oracle Transparent Data Encryption (TDE). Traditional LOBS, when not using secure files, can be encrypted by using the utility of DBMS_CRYPTO. The following example enables encryption for the PATCH_DESC LOB column:

```
SQL> CREATE TABLE patchmain(
 patch_id number
```

```
,patch_desc clob)
LOB(patch_desc) STORE AS SECUREFILE (encrypt)
tablespace lob_data;
```

When you describe the table, the LOB column now shows that encryption is in effect:

```
SQL> desc patchmain;
Name                                         Null?       Type
------------------------------------------- --------- -----------------------
PATCH_ID                                                 NUMBER
PATCH_DESC                                               CLOB ENCRYPT
```

Here is a slightly different example that specifies the ENCRYPT keyword inline with the LOB column:

```
SQL> CREATE TABLE patchmain(
 patch_id    number
,patch_desc clob encrypt)
LOB (patch_desc) STORE AS SECUREFILE;
```

You can verify the encryption details by querying the DBA_ENCRYPTED_COLUMNS view:

```
SQL> select table_name, column_name, encryption_alg
from dba_encrypted_columns;
```

Here is the output for this example:

```
TABLE_NAME          COLUMN_NAME            ENCRYPTION_ALG
------------------- ---------------------- ------------------
PATCHMAIN           PATCH_DESC             AES 192 bits key
```

If you have already created the table, you can alter a column to enable encryption:

```
SQL> alter table patchmain modify
(patch_desc clob encrypt);
```

You can also specify an encryption algorithm; for example,

```
SQL> alter table patchmain modify
(patch_desc clob encrypt using '3DES168');
```

You can disable encryption for a SecureFiles LOB column via the DECRYPT clause:

```
SQL> alter table patchmain modify
(patch_desc clob decrypt);
```

ENABLING AN ORACLE WALLET

An Oracle wallet is the mechanism Oracle uses to enable encryption. The wallet is an OS file that contains encryption keys. The wallet is enabled via the following steps:

1. Modify the SQLNET.ORA file to contain the location of the wallet:

   ```
   ENCRYPTION_WALLET_LOCATION=
     (SOURCE=(METHOD=FILE) (METHOD_DATA=
         (DIRECTORY=/ora01/app/oracle/product/18.1.0.0/db_1/network/admin)))
   ```

2. Create the wallet file (ewallet.p18) with the ALTER SYSTEM command:

   ```
   SQL> alter system set encryption key identified by foo;
   ```

3. Enable encryption:

   ```
   SQL> alter system set encryption wallet open identified by foo;
   ```

See the Oracle Advanced Security Administrator's Guide, which can be freely downloaded from the Technology Network area of the Oracle web site (http://otn.oracle.com), for full details on implementing encryption.

Migrating BasicFiles to SecureFiles

You can migrate BasicFiles LOB data to SecureFiles via one of the following methods:

- Create a new table, load the data from the old table, and rename the tables

- Move the table

- Redefine the table online

Each of these techniques is described in the following sections.

Creating a New Table

Here is a brief example of creating a new table and loading data from the old table. In this example, PATCHMAIN_NEW is the new table being created with a SecureFiles LOB.

```
SQL> create table patchmain_new(
 patch_id number
,patch_desc clob)
lob(patch_desc) store as securefile (tablespace lob_data);
```

Next, load the newly created table with data from the old table:

```
SQL> insert into patchmain_new select * from patchmain;
```

Now, rename the tables:

```
SQL> rename patchmain to patchmain_old;
SQL> rename patchmain_new to patchmain;
```

When using this technique, be sure any grants that were pointing to the old table are reissued for the new table.

Moving a Table to SecureFiles Architecture

You can also use the ALTER TABLE...MOVE statement to redefine the storage of a LOB as a SecureFiles type; for example,

```
SQL> alter table patchmain
move lob(patch_desc)
store as securefile (tablespace lob_data);
```

You can verify that the column is now a SecureFiles type via this query:

```
SQL> select table_name, column_name, securefile from user_lobs;
```

The SECUREFILE column now has a value of YES:

```
TABLE_NAME      COLUMN_NAME      SEC
--------------- ---------------- ---
PATCHMAIN       PATCH_DESC       YES
```

Migrating with Online Redefinition

You can also redefine a table while it is online via the DBMS_REDEFINITION package. Use the following steps to do an online redefinition:

1. Ensure that the table has a primary key. If the table does not have a primary key, then create one:

    ```
    SQL> alter table patchmain
    add constraint patchmain_pk
    primary key (patch_id);
    ```

2. Create a new table that defines the LOB column(s) as a SecureFiles type:

    ```
    SQL> create table patchmain_new(
     patch_id number
    ,patch_desc clob)
    lob(patch_desc)
    store as securefile (tablespace lob_data);
    ```

3. Map the columns, and copy the data from the original table to the new table (this can take a long time if there are many rows):

    ```
    SQL> declare
      l_col_map varchar2(2000);
    begin
      l_col_map := 'patch_id patch_id, patch_desc patch_desc';
      dbms_redefinition.start_redef_table(
        'MV_MAINT','PATCHMAIN','PATCHMAIN_NEW',l_col_map
        );
    end;
    /
    ```

4. Clone dependent objects of the table being redefined (grants, triggers, constraints, and so on):

    ```
    SQL> set serverout on size 1000000
    SQL> declare
      l_err_cnt integer :=0;
    ```

```
begin
  dbms_redefinition.copy_table_dependents(
    'MV_MAINT','PATCHMAIN','PATCHMAIN_NEW',1,TRUE, TRUE, TRUE,
    FALSE, l_err_cnt
  );
  dbms_output.put_line('Num Errors: ' || l_err_cnt);
end;
/
```

5. Finish the redefinition:

```
SQL> begin
  dbms_redefinition.finish_redef_table('MV_
MAINT','PATCHMAIN','PATCHMAIN_NEW');
end;
/
```

You can confirm that the table has been redefined via this query:

```
SQL> select table_name, column_name, securefile from user_lobs;
```

Here is the output for this example:

```
TABLE_NAME              COLUMN_NAME             SECUREFILE
--------------------    --------------------    --------------------
PATCHMAIN_NEW           PATCH_DESC              NO
PATCHMAIN               PATCH_DESC              YES
```

VIEWING LOB METADATA

You can use any of the DBA/ALL/USER_LOBS views to display information about LOBs in your database:

```
SQL> select table_name, column_name, index_name, tablespace_name
from all_lobs
order by table_name;
```

Also keep in mind that a LOB segment has a corresponding index segment.

```
SQL> select segment_name, segment_type, tablespace_name
from user_segments
where segment_name like 'SYS_LOB%'
or    segment_name like 'SYS_IL%';
```

In this way, you can query both the segment and the index in the DBA/ALL/USER_SEGMENTS views for LOB information.

Loading LOBs

Loading LOB data is not typically the DBA's job, but you should be familiar with techniques used to populate LOB columns. Developers may come to you for help with troubleshooting, performance, or space-related issues.

Loading a CLOB

First, create an Oracle database directory object that points to the OS directory in which the CLOB file is stored. This directory object is used when loading the CLOB. In this example the Oracle directory object is named LOAD_LOB, and the OS directory is /orahome/oracle/lob:

```
SQL> create or replace directory load_lob as '/orahome/oracle/lob';
```

For reference, listed next is the DDL used to create the table in which the CLOB file is loaded:

```
SQL> create table patchmain(
 patch_id number primary key
,patch_desc clob
,patch_file blob)
lob(patch_desc, patch_file)
store as securefile (compress low) tablespace lob_data;
```

This example also uses a sequence named PATCH_SEQ. Here is the sequence creation script:

```
SQL> create sequence patch_seq;
```

The following bit of code uses the DBMS_LOB package to load a text file (patch.txt) into a CLOB column. In this example the table name is PATCHMAIN, and the CLOB column is PATCH_DESC:

```
SQL> declare
  src_clb bfile; -- point to source CLOB on file system
  dst_clb clob;  -- destination CLOB in table
  src_doc_name varchar2(300) := 'patch.txt';
  src_offset integer := 1; -- where to start in the source CLOB
  dst_offset integer := 1;  -- where to start in the target CLOB
  lang_ctx integer := dbms_lob.default_lang_ctx;
  warning_msg number; -- returns warning value if bad chars
begin
  src_clb := bfilename('LOAD_LOB',src_doc_name); -- assign pointer to file
  --
  insert into patchmain(patch_id, patch_desc) -- create LOB placeholder
  values(patch_seq.nextval, empty_clob())
  returning patch_desc into dst_clb;
  --
  dbms_lob.open(src_clb, dbms_lob.lob_readonly); -- open file
  --
  -- load the file into the LOB
  dbms_lob.loadclobfromfile(
  dest_lob => dst_clb,
  src_bfile => src_clb,
  amount => dbms_lob.lobmaxsize,
  dest_offset => dst_offset,
  src_offset => src_offset,
  bfile_csid => dbms_lob.default_csid,
  lang_context => lang_ctx,
  warning => warning_msg
  );
  dbms_lob.close(src_clb); -- close file
  --
  dbms_output.put_line('Wrote CLOB: ' || src_doc_name);
end;
/
```

You can place this code in a file and execute it from the SQL command prompt. In this example, the file that contains the code is named `clob.sql`:

```
SQL> set serverout on size 1000000
SQL> @clob.sql
```

Here is the expected output:

```
Wrote CLOB: patch.txt
PL/SQL procedure successfully completed.
```

Loading a BLOB

Loading a BLOB is similar to loading a CLOB. This example uses the directory object, table, and sequence from the previous example (which loaded a CLOB). Loading a BLOB is simpler than loading a CLOB because you do not have to specify character set information.

This example loads a file named `patch.zip` into the `PATCH_FILE` BLOB column:

```
SQL> declare
  src_blb bfile; -- point to source BLOB on file system
  dst_blb blob;  -- destination BLOB in table
  src_doc_name varchar2(300) := 'patch.zip';
  src_offset integer := 1; -- where to start in the source BLOB
  dst_offset integer := 1;  -- where to start in the target BLOB
begin
  src_blb := bfilename('LOAD_LOB',src_doc_name); -- assign pointer to file
  --
  insert into patchmain(patch_id, patch_file)
  values(patch_seq.nextval, empty_blob())
  returning patch_file into dst_blb; -- create LOB placeholder column first
  dbms_lob.open(src_blb, dbms_lob.lob_readonly);
  --
  dbms_lob.loadblobfromfile(
  dest_lob => dst_blb,
  src_bfile => src_blb,
  amount => dbms_lob.lobmaxsize,
```

```
    dest_offset => dst_offset,
    src_offset => src_offset
    );
    dbms_lob.close(src_blb);
    dbms_output.put_line('Wrote BLOB: ' || src_doc_name);
end;
/
```

You can place this code in a file and run it from the SQL command prompt. Here, the file that contains the code is named blob.sql:

```
SQL> set serverout on size 1000000
SQL> @blob.sql
```

Here is the expected output:

```
Wrote BLOB: patch.zip
PL/SQL procedure successfully completed.
```

Measuring LOB Space Consumed

As discussed previously, a LOB consists of an in-row lob locator, a LOB index, and a LOB segment that is made up of one or more chunks. The space used by the LOB index is usually negligible compared with the space used by the LOB segment. You can view the space consumed by a segment by querying the BYTES column of DBA/ALL/USER_SEGMENTS (just like any other segment in the database). Here is a sample query:

```
SQL> select segment_name, segment_type, segment_subtype,
    bytes/1024/1024 meg_bytes
from user_segments;
```

You can modify the query to report on only LOBs by joining to the USER_LOBS view:

```
SQL> select a.table_name, a.column_name, a.segment_name, a.index_name
,b.bytes/1024/1024 meg_bytes
from user_lobs a, user_segments b
where a.segment_name = b.segment_name;
```

You can also use the DBMS_SPACE.SPACE_USAGE package and procedure to report on the blocks being used by a LOB. This package only works on objects that have been created in an ASSM-managed tablespace. There are two different forms of the SPACE_USAGE procedure: one form reports on BasicFiles LOBs, and the other reports on SecureFiles LOBs.

BasicFiles Space Used

Here is an example of how to call DBMS_SPACE.SPACE_USAGE for a BasicFiles LOB:

```
SQL> declare
    p_fs1_bytes number;
    p_fs2_bytes number;
    p_fs3_bytes number;
    p_fs4_bytes number;
    p_fs1_blocks number;
    p_fs2_blocks number;
    p_fs3_blocks number;
    p_fs4_blocks number;
    p_full_bytes number;
    p_full_blocks number;
    p_unformatted_bytes number;
    p_unformatted_blocks number;
begin
    dbms_space.space_usage(
        segment_owner       => user,
        segment_name        => 'SYS_LOB0000024082C00002$$',
        segment_type        => 'LOB',
        fs1_bytes           => p_fs1_bytes,
        fs1_blocks          => p_fs1_blocks,
        fs2_bytes           => p_fs2_bytes,
        fs2_blocks          => p_fs2_blocks,
        fs3_bytes           => p_fs3_bytes,
        fs3_blocks          => p_fs3_blocks,
        fs4_bytes           => p_fs4_bytes,
        fs4_blocks          => p_fs4_blocks,
```

```
      full_bytes            => p_full_bytes,
      full_blocks           => p_full_blocks,
      unformatted_blocks => p_unformatted_blocks,
      unformatted_bytes  => p_unformatted_bytes
  );
  dbms_output.put_line('Full bytes  = '||p_full_bytes);
  dbms_output.put_line('Full blocks = '||p_full_blocks);
  dbms_output.put_line('UF bytes    = '||p_unformatted_bytes);
  dbms_output.put_line('UF blocks   = '||p_unformatted_blocks);
end;
/
```

In this PL/SQL, you need to modify the code so that it reports on the LOB segment in your environment.

SecureFiles Space Used

Here is an example of how to call DBMS_SPACE.SPACE_USAGE for a SecureFiles LOB:

```
SQL> DECLARE
  l_segment_owner        varchar2(40);
  l_table_name           varchar2(40);
  l_segment_name         varchar2(40);
  l_segment_size_blocks  number;
  l_segment_size_bytes   number;
  l_used_blocks          number;
  l_used_bytes           number;
  l_expired_blocks       number;
  l_expired_bytes        number;
  l_unexpired_blocks     number;
  l_unexpired_bytes      number;
  --
CURSOR c1 IS
SELECT owner, table_name, segment_name
FROM dba_lobs
WHERE table_name = 'PATCHMAIN';
```

```
BEGIN
  FOR r1 IN c1 LOOP
    l_segment_owner := r1.owner;
    l_table_name := r1.table_name;
    l_segment_name := r1.segment_name;
    --
    dbms_output.put_line('------------------------------');
    dbms_output.put_line('Table Name         : ' || l_table_name);
    dbms_output.put_line('Segment Name       : ' || l_segment_name);
    --
    dbms_space.space_usage(
        segment_owner          => l_segment_owner,
        segment_name           => l_segment_name,
        segment_type           => 'LOB',
        partition_name         => NULL,
        segment_size_blocks    => l_segment_size_blocks,
        segment_size_bytes     => l_segment_size_bytes,
        used_blocks            => l_used_blocks,
        used_bytes             => l_used_bytes,
        expired_blocks         => l_expired_blocks,
        expired_bytes          => l_expired_bytes,
        unexpired_blocks       => l_unexpired_blocks,
        unexpired_bytes        => l_unexpired_bytes
    );
    --
    dbms_output.put_line('segment_size_blocks: '|| l_segment_size_blocks);
    dbms_output.put_line('segment_size_bytes : '|| l_segment_size_bytes);
    dbms_output.put_line('used_blocks        : '|| l_used_blocks);
    dbms_output.put_line('used_bytes         : '|| l_used_bytes);
    dbms_output.put_line('expired_blocks     : '|| l_expired_blocks);
    dbms_output.put_line('expired_bytes      : '|| l_expired_bytes);
    dbms_output.put_line('unexpired_blocks   : '|| l_unexpired_blocks);
    dbms_output.put_line('unexpired_bytes    : '|| l_unexpired_bytes);
  END LOOP;
END;
/
```

Again, in this PL/SQL, you need to modify the code so that it reports on the table with the LOB segment in your environment.

Reading BFILEs

As discussed previously, a BFILE data type is simply a column in a table that stores a pointer to an OS file. A BFILE provides you with read-only access to a binary file on disk. To access a BFILE, you must first create a directory object. This is a database object that stores the location of an OS directory. The directory object makes Oracle aware of the BFILE location on disk.

This example first creates a directory object, creates a table with a BFILE column, and then uses the DBMS_LOB package to access a binary file:

```
SQL> create or replace directory load_lob as '/orahome/oracle/lob';
```

Next, a table is created that contains a BFILE data type:

```
SQL> create table patchmain
(patch_id    number
,patch_file bfile);
```

For this example, a file named patch.zip is located in the aforementioned directory. You make Oracle aware of the binary file by inserting a record into the table using the directory object and the file name:

```
SQL> insert into patchmain values(1, bfilename('LOAD_LOB','patch.zip'));
```

Now, you can access the BFILE via the DBMS_LOB package. For \ instance, if you want to verify that the file exists or display the length of the LOB, you can do so as follows:

```
SQL> select dbms_lob.fileexists(bfilename('LOAD_LOB','patch.zip')) from dual;
SQL> select dbms_lob.getlength(patch_file) from patchmain;
```

In this manner, the binary file behaves like a BLOB. The big difference is that the binary file is not stored within the database.

Tip   See the Oracle Database PL/SQL Packages and Types Reference guide for full details on using the DBMS_LOB package. This guide is available on http://otn.oracle.com.

Summary

Oracle lets you store large objects in databases via various LOB data types. LOBs facilitate the storage, management, and retrieval of video clips, images, movies, word-processing documents, large text files, and so on. Oracle can store these files in the database and thus provide backup and recovery and security protection (just as it does for any other data type). BLOBs are used to store binary files, such as images (JPEG, MPEG), movie files, sound files, and so on. If it is not feasible to store the file in the database, you can use a `BFILE` LOB.

Oracle provides two underlying architectures for LOBS: BasicFiles and SecureFiles. BasicFiles is the LOB architecture that has been available since Oracle version 8. The SecureFiles feature was introduced in Oracle Database 11g and is now the default value for LOBs. SecureFiles has many advanced options, such as compression, deduplication, and encryption (these specific features require an extra license from Oracle).

LOBs provide a way to manage very large files. Oracle has another feature—partitioning—which allows you to manage very large tables and indexes. Partitioning is covered in detail in the next chapter.

CHAPTER 12

Partitioning: Divide and Conquer

Oracle provides two key scalability features that enable good performance, even with massively large databases: parallelism and partitioning. Parallelism allows Oracle to start more than one thread of execution to take advantage of multiple hardware resources. Partitioning allows subsets of a table or index to be managed independently (Oracle's "divide and conquer" approach). The focus of this chapter is partitioning strategies.

Partitioning lets you create a logical table or index that consists of separate segments that can each be accessed and worked on by separate threads of execution. Each partition of a table or index has the same logical structure, such as the column definitions, but can reside in separate containers. In other words, you can store each partition in its own tablespace and associated data files. This allows you to manage one large logical object as a group of smaller, more maintainable pieces. The main benefits realized from partitioning are the following:

- Better performance; in some circumstances, SQL queries can operate on a single partition or subset of partitions, which allows for faster execution times.

- Higher availability; the availability of data in one partition is not affected by the unavailability of data in another partition.

- Easier maintenance; inserting, updating, deleting, truncating, rebuilding, and reorganizing data by partition allows for efficient loading and archiving operations that would otherwise be difficult and time consuming.

- Management of partitions; modifying strategies and managing partitions can be online and automated activities.

© Michelle Malcher and Darl Kuhn 2019
M. Malcher and D. Kuhn, *Pro Oracle Database 18c Administration*,
https://doi.org/10.1007/978-1-4842-4424-1_12

Just because you implement partitioning does not mean you will automatically get performance gains, achieve high availability, and ease your administration activities. You need to be aware of how partitioning works and how to leverage various features to reap any benefits. The goal of this chapter is to explain partitioning concepts and how to implement partitioning and to offer guidelines on when to use which features.

Before getting into the details, there are several partitioning terms you should first be familiar with. Table 12-1 describes the meanings of key partitioning terms that are used throughout the chapter.

Table 12-1. *Oracle Partitioning Terminology*

Term	Meaning
Partitioning	Transparently implementing one logical table or index as many separate, smaller segments
Partition key	One or more columns that unambiguously determine which partition a row is stored in
Partition bound	Boundary between partitions
Single-Level partitioning	Partitioning, using a single method
Composite partitioning	Partitioning, using a combination of methods
Subpartition	Partition within a partition
Partition independence	Ability to access partitions separately to perform maintenance operations without affecting the availability of other partitions
Partition pruning	Elimination of unnecessary partitions. Oracle detects which partitions need to be accessed by an SQL statement and removes from consideration any partitions that are not needed.
Partition-wise join	Join executed in partition-sized pieces to improve performance by executing many smaller tasks in parallel rather than one large task in sequence
Local partitioned index	Index that uses the same partition key as its table
Global partitioned index	Index that does not use the same partition key as its table
Global nonpartitioned index	Regular index created on a partitioned table. The index itself is not partitioned.

Also keep in mind, if you work with mainly small OLTP databases, you do not need to create partitioned tables and indexes. However, if you work with very large objects in OLTP databases or in data warehouse environments, you can most likely benefit from partitioning. Partitioning is a key to designing and building scalable, highly available, large database systems.

What Tables Should Be Partitioned?

Following are some rules of thumb for determining whether to partition a table. In general, you should consider partitioning for tables:

- That are greater than 10GB

- That have more than 10 million rows, when SQL operations are getting slower as more data are added

- That you know will grow large (it is better to create a table as partitioned than to rebuild it as partitioned after performance begins to suffer as the table grows)

- That have rows that can be divided in a way that facilitates parallel operations, such as inserting, retrieval, deleting, and backup and recovery

- For which you want to archive the oldest data on a periodic basis or from which you want to drop the oldest partition regularly, as data become stale

One rule is that any table greater than 10GB is a potential candidate for partitioning. Run this query to show the top space-consuming objects in your database:

```
SQL> select * from (
select owner, segment_name, segment_type, partition_name
,sum(bytes)/1024/1024 meg_tot
from dba_segments
group by owner, segment_name, segment_type, partition_name
order by sum(extents) desc)
where rownum <= 10;
```

Here is a snippet of the output from the query:

```
OWNER      SEGMENT_NAME                  SEGMENT_TYPE PARTITION_NAME    MEG_TOT
--------   -------------------------------------- -------------- ----------
MV_MAINT   F_SALES                       TABLE                            15281
MV_MAINT   F_SALES_IDX1                  INDEX                             8075
```

This output shows that a few large objects in this database may benefit from partitioning. For this database, if there are performance issues with these large objects, then partitioning may help.

If you are running the previous query from SQL*Plus, you need to apply some formatting to the columns to reasonably display the output within the limited width of your terminal:

```
set lines 132
col owner form a10
col segment_name form a25
col partition_name form a15
```

In addition to looking at the size of objects, if you can divide your data so that they facilitate operations, such as loading data, querying, backups, archiving, and deleting, you should consider using partitioning. For example, if you work with a table that contains a large number of rows that are often accessed according to a particular time range—such as by day, week, month, or year—it makes sense to consider partitioning. Even data by regions might make sense to partition for loading or accessing because this is how the data is mostly accessed by a list of regions, groups, or categories.

A large table size combined with a good business reason means that you should think about partitioning. Keep in mind that there is more setup work and maintenance when you partition a table. However, as mentioned earlier, it is much easier to partition a table during setup than it is to convert it after it is grown to an unwieldy size. It is also easier to work with the partitions after the table has grown with online maintenance, as partitioning strategies can be modified or partitions can be merged together.

Note Partitioning is an extra cost option that is available only with the Oracle Enterprise Edition. You have to decide, based on your business requirements, whether partitioning is worth the cost. Data warehouses and Very Large Databases (VLDB) should evaluate this option with cost and data access requirements.

Creating Partitioned Tables

Oracle provides a robust set of methods for dividing tables and indexes into smaller subsets. For example, you can divide a table's data by date ranges, such as by month or year. Table 12-2 gives an overview of the partitioning strategies available.

Table 12-2. *Partitioning Strategies*

Partition Type	Description
Range	Allows partitioning based on ranges of dates, numbers, or characters
List	Useful when the partitions fit nicely into a list of values, such as state or region codes
Hash	Allows even distribution of rows when there is no obvious partitioning key
Composite	Allows combinations of other partitioning strategies
Interval	Extends range partitioning by automatically allocating new partitions when new partition key values exceed the existing high range
Reference	Useful for partitioning a child table based on a parent table column
Virtual	Allows partitioning on a virtual column
System	Allows the application inserting the data to determine which partition should be used

The following sections show examples of each partitioning strategy. Additionally, you learn how to place partitions in separate tablespaces; to take advantage of all the benefits of partitioning, you need to understand how to assign a partition to its own tablespace.

Partitioning by Range

Range partitioning is frequently used. This strategy instructs Oracle to place rows in partitions based on ranges of values, such as dates, numbers, or characters. As data are inserted into a range-partitioned table, Oracle determines which partition to place a row in based on the lower and upper bounds of each range partition.

The range-based partition key is defined by the PARTITION BY RANGE clauseCREATE TABLE statement. This determines which column is used to control the partition a row belongs in. You will see some examples shortly.

Each range partition requires a VALUES LESS THAN clause that identifies the non-inclusive value of the upper bound of the range. The first partition defined for a range has no lower bound. Any values less than those set in the first partition's VALUES LESS THAN clause are inserted into the first partition. For partitions other than the first partition, the lower bound of a range is determined by the upper bound of the previous partition.

Optionally, you can create a range-partitioned table's highest partition with the MAXVALUE clause. Any row that does not have a partition key that falls in the lower ranges is inserted into this topmost MAXVALUE partition.

Implementing a NUMBER for the Partition Key Column

Let's look at an example to illustrate the previous concepts. Suppose you are working in a data warehouse environment, in which you typically have a fact table that stores information about an event, such as sales, profits, registrations, and so on. In a fact table, usually one column represents an amount or a count, and another represents a point in time.

Some data warehouse architects choose to represent the point-in-time column with a number that translates into a date—the idea being that a number data type is efficient when joining to multiple dimension tables. For instance, the value 20130101 is used to represent January 1, 2013, and you use that number value (which represents a date) as the column to partition the fact table. This SQL statement creates a table with three partitions based on a range of numbers:

```
SQL> create table f_sales
(sales_amt number
,d_date_id number)
partition by range (d_date_id)(
partition p_2012 values less than (20130101),
partition p_2013 values less than (20140101),
partition p_max  values less than (maxvalue));
```

When creating a range-partitioned table, you do not have to specify a MAXVALUE partition. However, if you do not specify a partition with the MAXVALUE clause, and you attempt to insert a row that does not fall within any other defined ranges, you receive an error such as

ORA-14400: inserted partition key does not map to any partition

When you see that error, you have to add a partition that accommodates the partition key value being inserted or that has the MAXVALUE clause.

Tip   Consider using an interval partitioning strategy, in which partitions are automatically added by Oracle when the high range value is exceeded. See the section "Creating Partitions on Demand" later in this chapter.

You can view information about the partitioned table you just created by running the following query:

```sql
SQL> select table_name, partitioning_type, def_tablespace_name
from user_part_tables
where table_name='F_SALES';
```

Here is a snippet of the output:

```
TABLE_NAME              PARTITION DEF_TABLESPACE_NAME
--------------------    --------- --------------------------------
F_SALES                 RANGE     USERS
```

To view information about the partitions in the table, issue a query as follows:

```sql
SQL> select table_name, partition_name, high_value
from user_tab_partitions
where table_name = 'F_SALES'
order by table_name, partition_name;
```

Here is some sample output:

```
TABLE_NAME              PARTITION_NAME        HIGH_VALUE
--------------------    --------------------  --------------------
F_SALES                 P_2016                20170101
F_SALES                 P_2017                20180101
F_SALES                 P_MAX                 MAXVALUE
```

In this example the D_DATE_ID column is the partitioning key column. The VALUES LESS THAN clauses create the partition boundaries; these define the partition into which a row is inserted. The MAXVALUE parameter creates a partition in which to store rows that do not fit into the other defined partitions (including NULL values).

DETECTING WHEN ADDITIONAL HIGH RANGE IS REQUIRED

When you partition by range without specifying a MAXVALUE partition, you may not accurately predict when a new high partition will need to be added. Additionally, the HIGH_VALUE column in the data dictionary is a LONG data type, which means that you cannot apply the MAX SQL function to return the current high value.

Listed next is a simple shell script that attempts to insert a record that contains a future date to determine if there is an accepting partition. If the record is inserted successfully, the script rolls back the transaction. If the record fails to insert, an error is generated, and the script sends you an e-mail:

```
#!/bin/bash
if [ $# -ne 1 ]; then
  echo "Usage: $0 SID"
  exit 1
fi
export ORACLE_SID=o18c
export ORACLE_HOME=/ora01/app/oracle/product/18.0.0.1/db_1
#
sqlplus -s <<EOF
mv_maint/foo
WHENEVER SQLERROR EXIT FAILURE
COL date_id NEW_VALUE hold_date_id
SELECT to_char(sysdate+30,'yyyymmdd') date_id FROM dual;
--
INSERT INTO mv_maint.f_sales(sales_amt, d_date_id)
VALUES (0, '&hold_date_id');
ROLLBACK;
EOF
```

```
#
if [ $? -ne 0 ]; then
  mailx -s "Partition range issue: f_sales" dkuhn@gmail.com <<EOF
  check f_sales high range.
EOF
else
  echo "f_sales ok"
fi
exit 0
```

Ensure that you do not inadvertently add data to a production table with a script such as this. You have to modify the script carefully to match your table and high-range partition key column.

Implementing a TIMESTAMP for the Partition Key Column

As noted, the example in the previous section created the column D_DATE_ID as a NUMBER data type instead of a DATE data type for the F_SALES table. As opposed to a NUMBER data type, some data warehouse architects would advocate using a DATE or TIMESTAMP data type for the partition key. Here is an example that creates the F_SALES table with a DATE data type for the D_DATE_DTT column:

```
SQL> create table f_sales
(sales_amt   number
,d_date_dtt date
)
partition by range (d_date_dtt)(
 partition p_2016 values less than (to_date('01-01-2017','dd-mm-yyyy')),
 partition p_2017 values less than (to_date('01-01-2018','dd-mm-yyyy')),
 partition p_max  values less than (maxvalue));
```

> **Tip**   Using the date format DD-MM-YYYY may be preferable to one such as 01-MON-YYYY. The DD-MM-YYYY format avoids using character names for the month (JAN, FEB, and so on), which circumvents issues with different character-set languages.

As shown in the prior code, I recommend that you always use TO_DATE to explicitly instruct Oracle on how to interpret the date. Doing so also provides a minimal level of documentation for anybody supporting the database.

Using a DATE data type for the partition key is every bit as valid as using a NUMBER field for the partition key. Just keep in mind that whoever designs the data warehouse tables may have a strong opinion about which technique to use.

Placing Partitions in Tablespaces

Benefits of placing partitions on their own tablespace are now only to recognize the partitions from other tables. There are simplified ways to back up, restore, and place online/offline if each partition has its own tablespace, but online actions and backing up of tables is available even without the partition being in its own tablespace. In certain instances, it might even make sense to put a tablespace and partition in read-only mode, and having their own tablespaces would allow this.

To understand the benefits of using a separate tablespace for each partition, first consider a nonpartitioned table scenario. For reference, here is the CREATE TABLESPACE statement used for this example:

```
SQL> CREATE TABLESPACE p1_tbsp
  DATAFILE '/u01/dbfile/o18c/p1_tbsp01.dbf' SIZE 100m
  EXTENT MANAGEMENT LOCAL
  UNIFORM SIZE 128K
  SEGMENT SPACE MANAGEMENT AUTO;
```

This example creates a partitioned table but does not specify tablespaces for the partitions:

```
SQL> create table f_sales (
 sales_amt number
,d_date_id number)
tablespace p1_tbsp
partition by range(d_date_id)(
 partition y11 values less than (20120101)
,partition y12 values less than (20130101)
,partition y13 values less than (20140101));
```

Figure 12-1 illustrates this approach. Note that in this case, all partitions are stored in the same tablespace.

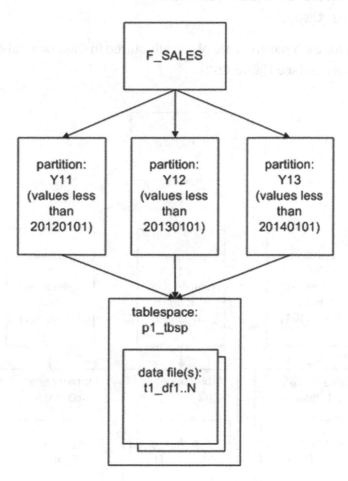

Figure 12-1. *A partitioned table with only one tablespace*

The next example places each partition in a separate tablespace:

```
SQL> create table f_sales (
 sales_amt number
,d_date_id number)
tablespace p1_tbsp
partition by range(d_date_id)(
 partition y11 values less than (20120101)
   tablespace p1_tbsp
```

```
,partition y12 values less than (20130101)
    tablespace p2_tbsp
,partition y13 values less than (20140101)
    tablespace p3_tbsp);
```

Now, the data for each partition are physically stored in their own tablespace and corresponding data files (see Figure 12-2).

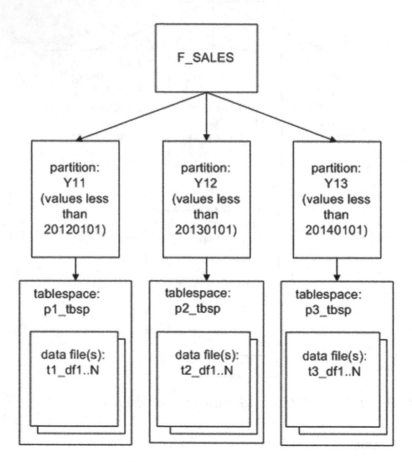

Figure 12-2. *Partitions stored in separate tablespaces*

Partitioning by List

List partitioning works well for partitioning unordered and unrelated sets of data. For example, say you have a large table and want to partition it by state code. To do so, use the PARTITION BY LIST clause Partitioning:table creation:PARTITION BY LIST clause of the CREATE TABLE statement. This example uses state codes to create three list-based partitions:

```
SQL> create table f_sales
 (sales_amt   number
 ,d_date_id   number
 ,state_code varchar2(3))
partition by list (state_code)
 ( partition reg_west values ('AZ','CA','CO','MT','OR','ID','UT','NV')
  ,partition reg_mid  values ('IA','KS','MI','MN','MO','NE','OH','ND')
  ,partition reg_def  values (default));
```

The partition key for a list-partitioned table can be only one column. Use the DEFAULT list to specify a partition for rows that do not match values in the list. If you do not specify a DEFAULT list, then an error is generated when a row is inserted with a value that does not map to the defined partitions. Run this SQL statement to view list values for each partition:

```
SQL> select table_name, partition_name, high_value
from user_tab_partitions
where table_name = 'F_SALES'
order by 1;
```

Here is the output for this example:

```
TABLE_NAME   PARTITION_NAME   HIGH_VALUE
-----------  ---------------- ----------------------------------------------
F_SALES      REG_DEF          default
F_SALES      REG_MID          'IA', 'KS', 'MI', 'MN', 'MO', 'NE', 'OH', 'ND'
F_SALES      REG_WEST         'AZ', 'CA', 'CO', 'MT', 'OR', 'ID', 'UT', 'NV'
```

The HIGH_VALUE column displays the list values defined for each partition. This column is a LONG data type. If you are using SQL*Plus, you may need to set the LONG variable to a value higher than the default (80B), to display the entire contents of the column:

```
SQL> set long 1000
```

Partitioning by Hash

Sometimes a large table does not contain an obvious column by which to partition the table, whether by range or by list. For instance, suppose you use a sequence to populate a surrogate primary key for a table, and you want rows spread evenly across partitions, based on the unique primary key. You may do this because there is not another column to partition, or you may be mainly concerned with the efficiency of inserts.

Hash partitioning maps rows to partitions based on an internal algorithm that spreads data evenly across all defined partitions. You do not have any control over the hashing algorithm or the way Oracle distributes the data. You specify how many partitions you would like, and Oracle divides the data evenly, based on the hash key column.

Tip   Oracle strongly recommends that you use a power of two (2, 4, 8, 16, and so on) for the number of hash partitions. Doing so results in the optimal distribution of rows throughout the partitions.

To create hash-based partitions, use the PARTITION BY HASH clause of the CREATE TABLE statement. This example creates a table that is divided into two partitions; each partition is created in its own tablespace:

```
SQL> create table f_sales(
 sales_id  number primary key
,sales_amt number)
partition by hash(sales_id)
partitions 2 store in(p1_tbsp, p2_tbsp);
```

Of course, you have to modify details, such as the tablespace names, to match those in your environment. Alternatively, you can eliminate the STORE IN clause, and Oracle places all partitions in your default tablespace. If you want to name both the tablespaces and the partitions, you can specify them as follows:

```
SQL> create table f_sales(
 sales_id  number primary key
,sales_amt number)
partition by hash(sales_id)
(partition p1 tablespace p1_tbsp
,partition p2 tablespace p2_tbsp);
```

Hash partitioning has some interesting performance implications. All rows that share the same value for the hash key are inserted into the same partition. This means that inserts are particularly efficient, because the hashing algorithm ensures that the data are distributed uniformly across partitions. Also, if you typically select for a specific key value, Oracle has to access only one partition to retrieve those rows. However, if you search by ranges of values, Oracle will most likely have to search every partition to determine which rows to retrieve. Thus, range searches can perform poorly in hash-partitioned tables.

Blending Different Partitioning Methods

Oracle allows you to partition a table using multiple strategies (composite partitioning). For example, suppose you have a table that you want to partition on a number range, but you also want to subdivide each partition by a list of regions. The following example does just that:

```
SQL> create table f_sales(
  sales_amt   number
 ,state_code varchar2(3)
 ,d_date_id   number)
partition by range(d_date_id)
subpartition by list(state_code)
(partition p2016 values less than (20170101)
  (subpartition p1_north values ('ID','OR')
  ,subpartition p1_south values ('AZ','NM')),
```

```
partition p2017 values less than (20180101)
  (subpartition p2_north values ('ID','OR')
  ,subpartition p2_south values ('AZ','NM')));
```

You can view subpartition information by running the following query:

```
SQL> select table_name, partitioning_type, subpartitioning_type
from user_part_tables
where table_name = 'F_SALES';
```

Here is some sample output:

```
TABLE_NAME   PARTITION SUBPARTIT
-----------  --------- ---------
F_SALES      RANGE     LIST
```

Run the next query to view information about the subpartitions:

```
SQL> select table_name, partition_name, subpartition_name
from user_tab_subpartitions
where table_name = 'F_SALES'
order by table_name, partition_name;
```

Here is a snippet of the output:

```
TABLE_NAME   PARTITION_NAME    SUBPARTITION_NAME
-----------  ----------------  --------------------
F_SALES      P2016             P1_SOUTH
F_SALES      P2016             P1_NORTH
F_SALES      P2017             P2_SOUTH
F_SALES      P2017             P2_NORTH
```

Composite partitioning can be implemented as range-hash (available since version 8i) and range-list (available since version 9i). Now here are the composite partitioning strategies available:

- Range-Hash: Appropriate for ranges that can be subdivided by a somewhat random key, such as a range of D_DATE_ID and then a hash on SALES_ID

- Range-List: Useful when a range can be further partitioned by a list, such as a range of D_DATE_ID and then a list on STATE_CODE

- Range-Range: Appropriate when you have two distinct partition range values, such as D_DATE_ID and SHIP_DATE

- List-Range: Useful when a list can be further subdivided by a range, such as a list on STATE_CODE and then a range of D_DATE_ID

- List-Hash: Useful for further partitioning a list by a somewhat random key, such as a list on STATE_CODE and then a hash on SALES_ID

- List-List: Appropriate when a list can be further delineated by another list, such as COUNTRY_CODE and then STATE_CODE

- Hash-Hash: Useful when a hash can be further subdivided by another unique value, such as SALES_ID and CUSTOMER_ID

- Hash-List: Useful when a hash can be further partitioned by a list, such as a hash on SALES_ID and a list on STATE_CODE

- Hash-Range: Useful when a hash can be further partitioned by a range, such as a hash on SALES_ID and a range of SHIP_DATE

As you can see, composite partitioning gives you a great deal of flexibility in the way you partition your data.

Creating Partitions on Demand

You can instruct Oracle to add partitions to range-partitioned tables automatically. This feature is known as interval partitioning. Oracle dynamically creates a new partition when data inserted exceed the maximum bound of a range-partitioned table. The newly added partition is based on an interval that you specify (hence, the name interval partitioning).

Tip   Think of the interval as a rule you provide, stating how you want future partitions to be created.

Adding Yearly Partitions, Based on Date

Suppose, for instance, you have a range-partitioned table and want Oracle to add a partition automatically when values are inserted above the highest value defined for the highest range. You can use the INTERVAL clause of the CREATE TABLE statement to instruct Oracle to add a partition automatically to the high end of a range-partitioned table. The following example creates a table that initially has one partition, with a high value range of 01-01-2018:

```
SQL> create table f_sales(
 sales_amt  number
,d_date_dtt date)
partition by range (d_date_dtt)
interval(numtoyminterval(1, 'YEAR'))
store in (p1_tbsp, p2_tbsp, p3_tbsp)
(partition p1 values less than (to_date('01-01-2018','dd-mm-yyyy'))
tablespace p1_tbsp);
```

The first partition is created in the P1_TBSP tablespace. As Oracle adds partitions, it assigns a new partition to the tablespaces defined in the STORE IN clause (the program is supposed to store them in a round-robin fashion but is not always consistent).

Note   With interval partitioning, you can specify only a single key column from the table, and it must be either a DATE or a NUMBER data type. This is because the interval is mathematically added to these data types. You cannot use a VARCHAR2, as you cannot add a number to a VARCHAR2 data type.

The interval in this example is one year, specified by the INTERVAL(NUMTOYMINTERVAL(1, 'YEAR')) clause. If a record is inserted into the table with a D_DATE_DTT value greater than or equal to 01-01-2018, Oracle automatically adds a new partition to the high end of the table. You can check the details of the partition by running this SQL statement:

```
SQL> set lines 132
col table_name form a10
col partition_name form a9
col part_pos form 999
col interval form a10
```

```
col tablespace_name form a12
col high_value form a30
--
SQL> select table_name, partition_name, partition_position part_pos
       ,interval, tablespace_name, high_value
from user_tab_partitions
where table_name = 'F_SALES'
order by table_name, partition_position;
```

Here is some sample output (the column headings have been shortened, and the HIGH_VALUE column has been cut short so that the output fits on the page):

```
TABLE_NAME PARTITION   PART_POS INTERVAL   TABLESPACE_N HIGH_VALUE
---------- ----------  -------- ---------  ------------------------------
F_SALES    P1               1 NO    P1_TBSP    TO_DATE(' 2018-01-01 00:00:00'
```

Next, insert data above the high value for the highest partition:

```
SQL> insert into f_sales values(1, sysdate+1000);
```

Here is what the output from selecting from USER_TAB_PARTITIONS now shows:

```
TABLE_NAME PARTITION  PART_POS INTERVAL TABLESPACE_N HIGH_VALUE
---------- ---------- -------- -------- ------------------------------
F_SALES    P1              1 NO          P1_TBSP TO_DATE(' 2018-01-01 00:00:00'
F_SALES    SYS_P3344       2 YES         P1_TBSP TO_DATE(' 2021-01-01 00:00:00'
```

A partition was automatically created with a high value of 2021-01-01. If you do not like the name that Oracle gives the partition, you can rename it:

```
SQL> alter table f_sales rename partition sys_p3344 to p2;
```

Note what happens when a value is inserted that falls into a year interval between the two partitions:

```
SQL> insert into f_sales values(1, sysdate+500);
```

USER_TAB_PARTITIONS view shows that another partition has been created because the value inserted falls into a year interval that is not included in the existing partitions:

TABLE_NAME	PARTITION	PART_POS	INTERVAL	TABLESPACE_N	HIGH_VALUE
F_SALES	P1	1	NO	P1_TBSP	TO_DATE(' 2018-01-01 00:00:00'
F_SALES	SYS_P3345	2	YES	P3_TBSP	TO_DATE(' 2020-01-01 00:00:00'
F_SALES	SYS_P3344	3	YES	P1_TBSP	TO_DATE(' 2021-01-01 00:00:00'

Note   If there is more than one INTERVAL partition with a value of NO, then all but the last one can be dropped. In other words, if there is only one partition with an INTERVAL value of NO, then the partition cannot be dropped. For example, attempting to drop partition P1 from the table in the prior example generates an ORA-14758 error.

Adding Weekly Partitions, Based on Date

You can also have Oracle add partitions by other increments of time, such as a week; for example,

```
SQL> create table f_sales(
 sales_amt  number
,d_date_dtt date)
partition by range (d_date_dtt)
interval(numtodsinterval(7,'day'))
store in (p1_tbsp, p2_tbsp, p3_tbsp)
(partition p1 values less than (to_date('01-01-2018', 'dd-mm-yyyy'))
tablespace p1_tbsp);
```

As data are inserted into future weeks, new weekly partitions will be created automatically; for example,

```
SQL> insert into f_sales values(100, sysdate+7);
SQL> insert into f_sales values(200, sysdate+14);
```

Running this query verifies that partitions have automatically been added:

```
SQL> select table_name, partition_name, partition_position part_pos
      ,interval, tablespace_name, high_value
```

```
from user_tab_partitions
where table_name = 'F_SALES'
order by table_name, partition_position;
```

Here is some sample output:

```
TABLE_NAME PARTITION PART_POS INTERVAL TABLESPACE_N HIGH_VALUE
---------- --------- -------- -------- ------------ ----------------------------
F_SALES    P1               1 NO       P1_TBSP      TO_DATE(' 2018-01-01 00:00:00'
F_SALES    SYS_P3725        2 YES      P3_TBSP      TO_DATE(' 2018-01-15 00:00:00'
F_SALES    SYS_P3726        3 YES      P1_TBSP      TO_DATE(' 2018-01-22 00:00:00'
```

In this way, Oracle automatically manages the addition of weekly partitions to the table.

Adding Daily Partitions, Based on Number

Recall from the section "Partitioning by Range," earlier in this chapter, how a number field (D_DATE_ID) was used as a range-based partition key. Suppose you want to create daily interval partitions in a table with such a partitioning strategy automatically. In this situation, you need to specify an INTERVAL of one. Here is an example:

```
SQL> create table f_sales(
 sales_amt number
,d_date_id number)
partition by range (d_date_id)
interval(1)
(partition p1 values less than (20180101));
```

As long as your application can correctly use a number that represents a valid date, there should not be any issues. As each new day's data are inserted, a new daily partition is created. For example, suppose these data are inserted:

```
SQL> insert into f_sales values(100,20180130);
SQL> insert into f_sales values(50,20180131);
```

Two corresponding partitions are automatically created. This can be verified via this query:

```
select table_name, partition_name, partition_position part_pos
       ,interval, tablespace_name, high_value
from user_tab_partitions
where table_name = 'F_SALES'
order by table_name, partition_position;
```

Here is the corresponding output:

```
TABLE_NAME PARTITION PART_POS INTERVAL   TABLESPACE_N HIGH_VALUE
---------- --------- -------- ---------- ------------ --------------------
F_SALES    P1               1 NO         USERS        20180101
F_SALES    SYS_P3383        2 YES        USERS        20180131
F_SALES    SYS_P3384        3 YES        USERS        20180132
```

Be aware that the HIGH_VALUE column can contain numbers that map to invalid dates. This is to be expected. For instance, when creating a partition with a D_DATE_ID of 20180131, Oracle will calculate the upper boundary to be the value 20180132. The high boundary value is defined as less than (but not equal to) any values inserted into the partition. The only reason I mention this here is because if you attempt to perform date arithmetic on the value in HIGH_VALUE, you will need to account for potential numbers that map to invalid dates. In this specific example, you would have to subtract one from the value in HIGH_VALUE to obtain a valid date.

As previously shown in the section, a daily interval partitioning scheme based on a number works fine. However, such a scheme does not work as well if you want to create interval partitions by month or year. This is because there is no number that consistently represents a month or year. If you need date-based interval functionality, then use a date and not a number-based interval functionality.

Partitioning to Match a Parent Table

You can use the PARTITION BY REFERENCE clause to specify that a child table should be partitioned in the same way as its parent. This allows a child table to inherit the partitioning strategy of its parent table. Any parent table partition maintenance operations are automatically applied to the child record tables.

Note   Before the advent of the partitioning-by-reference feature, you had to physically duplicate and maintain the parent table column in the child table. Doing so not only requires more disk space, but also is a source of error when maintaining the partitions.

For example, say you want to create a parent ORDERS table and a child ORDER_ITEMS table that are related by primary key and foreign key constraints on the ORDER_ID column. The parent ORDERS table will be partitioned on the ORDER_DATE column. Even though it would not contain the ORDER_DATE column, you wonder whether you can partition the child ORDER_ITEMS table so that the records are distributed the same way as in the parent ORDERS table. This example creates a parent table with a primary key constraint on ORDER_ID and range partitions on ORDER_DATE:

```
SQL> create table orders(
 order_id    number
,order_date  date
,constraint order_pk primary key(order_id))
partition by range(order_date)
(partition p16  values less than (to_date('01-01-2017','dd-mm-yyyy'))
,partition p17  values less than (to_date('01-01-2018','dd-mm-yyyy'))
,partition pmax values less than (maxvalue));
```

Next, you create the child ORDER_ITEMS table. It is partitioned by naming the foreign key constraint as the referenced object:

```
SQL> create table order_items(
 line_id   number
,order_id number not null
,sku       number
,quantity number
,constraint order_items_pk  primary key(line_id, order_id)
,constraint order_items_fk1 foreign key (order_id) references orders)
partition by reference (order_items_fk1);
```

Note that the foreign key column ORDER_ID must be defined as NOT NULL The foreign key column must be enabled and enforced.

You can inspect the partition key columns via the following query:

```
SQL> select name, column_name, column_position
from user_part_key_columns
where name in ('ORDERS','ORDER_ITEMS');
```

Here is the output for this example:

NAME	COLUMN_NAME	COLUMN_POSITION
ORDERS	ORDER_DATE	1
ORDER_ITEMS	ORDER_ID	1

Note that the child table is partitioned by the ORDER_ID column. This ensures that the child record is partitioned in the same manner as the parent record (because the child record is related to the parent record via the ORDER_ID key column).

When you create the referenced-partition child table, if you do not explicitly name the child table partitions, by default, Oracle creates partitions for the child table with the same partition names as its parent table. This example explicitly names the child table referenced partitions:

```
SQL> create table order_items(
 line_id  number
,order_id number not null
,sku      number
,quantity number
,constraint order_items_pk  primary key(line_id, order_id)
,constraint order_items_fk1 foreign key (order_id) references orders)
partition by reference (order_items_fk1)
(partition c16
,partition c17
,partition cmax);
```

Starting with Oracle Database 12c, you can also specify an interval-reference partitioning strategy. This allows for partitions to be automatically created for both the parent and child tables. Here is what the table creation scripts look like for this feature:

```
SQL> create table orders(
 order_id    number
,order_date  date
,constraint order_pk primary key(order_id))
partition by range(order_date)
interval(numtoyminterval(1, 'YEAR'))
(partition p1 values less than (to_date('01-01-2018','dd-mm-yyyy')));
--
SQL> create table order_items(
 line_id   number
,order_id number not null
,sku       number
,quantity number
,constraint order_items_pk  primary key(line_id, order_id)
,constraint order_items_fk1 foreign key (order_id) references orders)
partition by reference (order_items_fk1);
```

Inserting some sample data will demonstrate how the partitions are automatically created:

```
SQL> insert into orders values(1,sysdate);
SQL> insert into order_items values(10,1,123,1);
SQL> insert into orders values(2,sysdate+400);
SQL> insert into order_items values(20,2,456,1);
```

Now, run this query to verify the partition details:

```
SQL> select table_name, partition_name, partition_position part_pos
      ,interval, tablespace_name, high_value
from user_tab_partitions
where table_name IN ('ORDERS','ORDER_ITEMS')
order by table_name, partition_position;
```

Here is a snippet of the output:

```
TABLE_NAME   PARTITION PART_POS  INTERVAL   TABLESPACE_N HIGH_VALUE
--------------------------------------------------------------------------------
ORDERS       P1            1 NO       USERS    TO_DATE(' 2018-01-01 00:00:00'
ORDERS       SYS_P3761     2 YES      USERS    TO_DATE(' 2019-01-01 00:00:00'
ORDERS       SYS_P3762     3 YES      USERS    TO_DATE(' 2020-01-01 00:00:00'
ORDER_ITEMS P1             1 NO       USERS
ORDER_ITEMS SYS_P3761      2 YES      USERS
ORDER_ITEMS SYS_P3762      3 YES      USERS
```

Partitioning on a Virtual Column

You can partition on a virtual column. (See Chapter 7 for a discussion of virtual columns). Here is a sample script that creates a table named EMP, with the virtual column COMMISSION and a corresponding range partition for the virtual column:

```
SQL> create table emp (
 emp_id    number
,salary    number
,comm_pct number
,commission generated always as (salary*comm_pct)
)
partition by range(commission)
(partition p1 values less than (1000)
,partition p2 values less than (2000)
,partition p3 values less than (maxvalue));
```

This strategy allows you to partition on a column that is not stored in the table but that is computed dynamically. Virtual column partitioning is appropriate when there is a business requirement to partition on a column that is not physically stored in a table. The expression behind a virtual column can be a complex calculation, return a subset of a column string, combine column values, and so on. The possibilities are endless.

For example, you may have a ten-character-string column in which the first two digits represent a region, and the last eight digits represent a specific location (this is a bad design, but it happens). In this case, it may make sense, from a business perspective, to partition on the first two digits of this column (by region).

Giving an Application Control Over Partitioning

You may have a rare scenario, in which you want the application inserting records into a table to explicitly control which partition it inserts data into. You can use the PARTITION BY SYSTEM clause INSERT statement to specify into which partition to insert data. This next example creates a system-partitioned table with a three partitions: statement to specify into which partition to insert data. This next example creates a system-partitioned table with three partitions:

```
SQL> create table apps
(app_id number
,app_amnt number)
partition by system
(partition p1
,partition p2
,partition p3);
```

When inserting data into this table, you must specify a partition. The next line of code inserts a record into partition P1:

```
SQL> insert into apps partition(p1) values(1,100);
```

When you are updating or deleting, if you do not specify a partition, Oracle scans all partitions of a system-partitioned table to find the relevant rows. Therefore, you should specify a partition when updating and deleting to avoid poor performance.

A system-partitioned table is helpful in the unusual situation of needing to explicitly control which partition a record is inserted into. This allows your application code to manage the distribution of records among the partitions. I recommend that you use this feature only when you cannot use one of Oracle's other partitioning mechanisms to meet your business requirement.

Maintaining Partitions

When using partitions, you will eventually have to perform some sort of maintenance operation. For instance, you may be required to move, exchange, rename, split, merge, or drop partitions. The various partition maintenance tasks are described in this section.

Viewing Partition Metadata

When you are maintaining partitions, it is helpful to view metadata information about the partitioned objects. Oracle provides many data dictionary views that contain information about partitioned tables and indexes. Table 12-3 outlines these views.

Keep in mind that the DBA-level views contain data for all partitioned objects in the database, the ALL level shows partitioning information to which the currently connect user has access, and the USER-level offers information about the partitioned objects owned by the currently connected user.

Table 12-3. *Data Dictionary Views Containing Partitioning Information*

View	Information Contained
DBA/ALL/USER_PART_TABLES	Displays partitioned table information
DBA/ALL/USER_TAB_PARTITIONS	Contains information regarding individual table partitions
DBA/ALL/USER_TAB_SUBPARTITIONS	Shows subpartition-level table information regarding storage and statistics
DBA/ALL/USER_PART_KEY_COLUMNS	Displays partition key columns
DBA/ALL/USER_SUBPART_KEY_COLUMNS	Contains subpartition key columns
DBA/ALL/USER_PART_COL_STATISTICS	Shows column-level statistics
DBA/ALL/USER_SUBPART_COL_STATISTICS	Displays subpartition-level statistics
DBA/ALL/USER_PART_HISTOGRAMS	Contains histogram information for partitions
DBA/ALL/USER_SUBPART_HISTOGRAMS	Shows histogram information for subpartitions
DBA/ALL/USER_PART_INDEXES	Displays partitioned index information
DBA/ALL/USER_IND_PARTITIONS	Contains information regarding individual index partitions
DBA/ALL/USER_IND_SUBPARTITIONS	Shows subpartition-level index information
DBA/ALL/USER_SUBPARTITION_TEMPLATES	Displays subpartition template information

Two views you will use quite often are DBA_PART_TABLES and the DBA_TAB_ PARTITIONS. The DBA_PART_TABLES view contains table-level partitioning information, such as partitioning method and default storage settings. The DBA_TAB_PARTITIONS view provides information about the individual table partitions, such as the partition name and storage settings for individual partitions.information about the individual table partitions, such as the partition name and storage settings for individual partitions.

Moving a Partition

Suppose you create a list-partitioned table, as shown:

```
SQL> create table f_sales
 (sales_amt   number
 ,d_date_id   number
 ,state_code varchar2(20))
partition by list (state_code)
 ( partition reg_west values ('AZ','CA','CO','MT','OR','ID','UT','NV')
  ,partition reg_mid  values ('IA','KS','MI','MN','MO','NE','OH','ND')
  ,partition reg_rest values (default));
```

Also, for this partitioned table, you decide to create a locally partitioned index, as follows:

```
SQL> create index f_sales_lidx1 on f_sales(state_code) local;
```

You decide to create as well a nonpartitioned global index, as follows:

```
SQL> create index f_sales_gidx1 on f_sales(d_date_id) global;
```

And, you create a global partitioned index column:

```
SQL> create index f_sales_gidx2 on f_sales(sales_amt)
global partition by range(sales_amt)
(partition pg1 values less than (25)
,partition pg2 values less than (50)
,partition pg3 values less than (maxvalue));
```

Later, you decide that you want to move a partition to a specific tablespace. In this scenario, you can use the ALTER TABLE...MOVE PARTITION statement to relocate a table partition. This example moves the REG_WEST partition to a new tablespace:

```
SQL> alter table f_sales move partition reg_west tablespace p1_tbsp;
```

Moving a partition to a different tablespace is a fairly simple operation. Whenever you do this, however, make sure you check on the status of any indexes associated with the table:

```
SQL> select b.table_name, a.index_name, a.partition_name
,a.status, b.locality
from user_ind_partitions a
    ,user_part_indexes    b
where a.index_name=b.index_name
and table_name = 'F_SALES';
```

Here is some sample output:

TABLE_NAME	INDEX_NAME	PARTITION	Status	LOCALI
F_SALES	F_SALES_LIDX1	REG_MID	USABLE	LOCAL
F_SALES	F_SALES_LIDX1	REG_REST	USABLE	LOCAL
F_SALES	F_SALES_LIDX1	REG_WEST	UNUSABLE	LOCAL
F_SALES	F_SALES_GIDX2	PG1	UNUSABLE	GLOBAL
F_SALES	F_SALES_GIDX2	PG2	UNUSABLE	GLOBAL
F_SALES	F_SALES_GIDX2	PG3	UNUSABLE	GLOBAL

You must rebuild any unusable indexes. As opposed to rebuilding the indexes manually, when moving a partition, you can specify that the indexes associated with it be rebuilt with the UPDATE INDEXES clause:

```
SQL> alter table f_sales move partition reg_west tablespace p1_tbsp update
indexes;
```

Starting with Oracle Database 12c, when moving a partition, you can specify that all indexes be updated via the ONLINE clause:

```
SQL> alter table f_sales move partition reg_west online tablespace p1_tbsp;
```

The prior line of code tells Oracle to maintain all indexes during the move operation.

Automatically Moving Updated Rows

By default, Oracle does not let you update a row by setting the partition key to a value outside the row's current partition. For example, this statement updates the partition key column (D_DATE_ID) to a value that would result in the row's needing to exist in a different partition:

```
SQL> update f_sales set d_date_id = 20130901 where d_date_id = 20120201;
```

You receive the following error:

```
ORA-14402: updating partition key column would cause a partition change
```

In this scenario, use the ENABLE ROW MOVEMENT clause of the ALTER TABLE statement to allow updates to the partition key that would change the partition in which a value belongs. For this example, the F_SALES table is first modified to enable row movement:

```
SQL> alter table f_sales enable row movement;
```

You should now be able to update the partition key to a value that moves the row to a different segment. You can verify that row movement has been enabled by querying the ROW_MOVEMENT column of the USER_TABLES view:

```
SQL> select row_movement from user_tables where table_name='F_SALES';
```

You should see the value ENABLED:

```
ROW_MOVE
--------
ENABLED
```

To disable row movement, use the DISABLE ROW MOVEMENT clause:

```
SQL> alter table f_sales disable row movement;
```

Partitioning an Existing Table

You may have a nonpartitioned table that has grown quite large and want to partition it. There are several methods for converting a nonpartitioned table to a partitioned table. Table 12-4 lists the pros and cons of various techniques.

Table 12-4. *Methods of Converting a Nonpartitioned Table*

Conversion Method	Advantages	Disadvantages
`ALTER TABLE ... MODIFY PARTITION BY ... ONLINE`	`ONLINE` operation to modify table and add partitions	Additional consideration with indexes; can use update indexes
`CREATE <new_part_tab> AS SELECT * FROM <old_tab>`	Simple; can use NOLOGGING and PARALLEL options; direct path load	Requires space for both old and new tables
`INSERT /*+ APPEND */ INTO <new_part_tab> SELECT * FROM <old_tab>`	Fast; simple; direct path load	Requires space for both old and new tables
Data Pump EXPDP old table; IMPDP new table (or EXP IMP if using older version of Oracle)	Fast; less space required; takes care of grants, privileges, and so on. Loading can be done per partition with filtering conditions.	More complicated because you need to use a utility
Create partitioned new_part_tab>; exchange partitions with old_tab>	Potentially less downtime	Many steps; complicated
Use DBMS_REDEFINITION package	Converts existing table inline	Many steps; complicated
Create CSV file or external table; load new_part_tab> with SQL*Loader	Loading can be done partition by partition.	Many steps; complicated

As shown in Table 12-4, one of the easiest ways to partition an existing table is to use ALTER TABLE; this has been available since Oracle 12c. By performing this modification, indexes will need to be verified either as local or global indexes and possibly created for new strategies, but the table is an ONLINE action that allows for use of the table while the ALTER table is being completed.

To convert a nonpartitioned table into a partitioned one, the partitioning strategy needs to be listed as well as the partitions.

```
SQL> alter table f_sales modify
partition by range (d_date_id)
(partition p2012 values less than(20130101),
 partition p2013 values less than(20140101),
 partition pmax values less than(maxvalue))
online;
```

Another easy method is to create a new table—one that is partitioned—and load it with data from the old table. Listed next are the required steps:

1. If this is a table in an active production database, you should schedule some downtime for the table to ensure that no active transactions are occurring while it is being migrated.

2. Create a new, partitioned table from the old with CREATE TABLE <new table> AS SELECT * FROM <old table>.

3. Drop or rename the old table.

4. Rename the table created in step 2 to the name of the dropped/ renamed table.

For instance, let's assume that the F_SALES table used so far in this chapter was created as a nonpartitioned table. The following statement creates a new table that is partitioned, taking data from the old table, which is not:

```
SQL> create table f_sales_new
partition by range (d_date_id)
(partition p2012 values less than(20130101),
 partition p2013 values less than(20140101),
 partition pmax values less than(maxvalue))
nologging
as select * from f_sales;
```

Now, you can drop (or rename) the old, nonpartitioned table and rename the new, partitioned table the old table's name. Be sure you do not need the old table before you drop it with the PURGE option, as this permanently drops the table:

```
SQL> drop table f_sales purge;
SQL> rename f_sales_new to f_sales;
```

Finally, create any required constraints, grants, indexes, and statistics for the new table. You should now have a partitioned table that replaces the old, nonpartitioned table.

For the last step, if the original table contains many constraints, grants, and indexes, you may want to use Data Pump expd to export the original table without data. Then, after the new table is created, use Data Pump impdp to create the constraints, grants, and indexes for the new table. Also consider generating fresh statistics for the newly created table.

Another thought is if there is any potential for a table to grow very large, it can be created to handle partitioning and then additional partitions can be created as needed. Even when performing the ALTER table command, testing should be done to confirm creating the partitioning with a couple of partitions to add and modify with additional ones as discussed in the next section.

Adding a Partition

Sometimes it is hard to predict how many partitions you should initially establish for a table. A typical example is a range-partitioned table that is created without a MAXVALUE-created partition. You make a partitioned table that contains enough partitions for two years into the future, and then you forget about the table. Sometime in the future, application users report that this message is being thrown:

```
ORA-14400: inserted partition key does not map to any partition
```

Tip   Consider using interval partitioning, which enables Oracle to add range partitions automatically when the upper bound is exceeded.

Range

For a range-partitioned table, if the table's highest bound is not defined with a MAXVALUE, you can use the ALTER TABLE...ADD PARTITION statement to add a partition to the high end of the table. If you are not sure what the current upper bound is, query the data dictionary:

```
SQL> select table_name, partition_name, high_value
from user_tab_partitions
where table_name = UPPER('&&tab_name')
order by table_name, partition_name;
```

This example adds a partition to the high end of a range-partitioned table:

```
SQL> alter table f_sales add
partition p_2018 values less than (20190101) tablespace p18_tbsp;
```

Starting with Oracle Database 12c, you can add multiple partitions at the same time; for example,

```
SQL> alter table f_sales add
 partition p_2018 values less than (20190101) tablespace p18_tbsp
,partition p_2019 values less than (20200101) tablespace p19_tbsp;
```

Note   If you have a range-partitioned table with the high range bounded by MAXVALUE, you cannot add a partition. In this situation, you have to split an existing partition (see the section "Splitting a Partition" later in this chapter).

List

For a list-partitioned table, you can add a new partition only if there is not a DEFAULT partition defined. The next example adds a partition to a list-partitioned table:

```
SQL> alter table f_sales add partition reg_east values('GA');
```

Starting with Oracle Database 12c, you can add multiple partitions with one statement:

```
SQL> alter table f_sales add partition reg_mid_east values('TN'),
                           partition reg_north values('NY');
```

Hash

If you have a hash-partitioned table, use the ADD PARTITION clause, as follows, to add a partition:

```
SQL> alter table f_sales add partition p3 update indexes;
```

Note   When you are adding to a hash-partitioned table, if you do not specify the UPDATE INDEXES clause, any global indexes must be rebuilt. Additionally, you must rebuild any local indexes for the newly added partition.

After adding a partition to a hash-partitioned table, always check the indexes to be sure they all still have a VALID status:

```
SQL> select b.table_name, a.index_name, a.partition_name, a.status,
b.locality
from user_ind_partitions a
    ,user_part_indexes    b
where a.index_name=b.index_name
and table_name = upper('&&part_table');
```

Also check the status of any global nonpartitioned indexes:

```
SQL> select index_name, status
from user_indexes
where table_name = upper('&&part_table');
```

I highly recommend that you always test a maintenance operation in a nonproduction database to determine any unforeseen side effects.

Exchanging a Partition with an Existing Table

Exchanging a partition is a common technique for transparently loading new data into large partitioned tables. The technique involves taking a stand-alone table and swapping it with an existing partition (in an already partitioned table), allowing you to add fully loaded new partitions (and associated indexes) without affecting the availability or performance of operations against the other partitions in the table.

This simple example illustrates the process. Say you have a range-partitioned table, created as follows:

```
SQL> create table f_sales
(sales_amt number
,d_date_id number)
partition by range (d_date_id)
(partition p_2016 values less than (20170101),
 partition p_2017 values less than (20180101),
 partition p_2018 values less than (20190101));
```

You also create a local bitmap index on the D_DATE_ID column:

```
SQL> create bitmap index d_date_id_fk1 on
f_sales(d_date_id) local;
```

Now, add a new partition to the table to store new data:

```
SQL> alter table f_sales add partition p_2019
values less than(20200101);
```

Next, create a staging table, and insert data that fall within the range of values for the newly added partition:

```
SQL> create table workpart(
  sales_amt number
 ,d_date_id number);
--
SQL> insert into workpart values(100,20190201);
SQL> insert into workpart values(120,20190507);
```

Then, create a bitmap index on the WORKPART table that matches the structure of the bitmap index on F_SALES:

```
SQL> create bitmap index d_date_id_fk2
on workpart(d_date_id);
```

Now, exchange the WORKPART table with the P_2019 partition:

```
SQL> alter table f_sales
exchange partition p_2019
```

with table workpart
including indexes without validation;

A quick query of the F_SALES table verifies that the partition was exchanged successfully:

```
SQL> select * from f_sales partition(p_2019);
```

Here is the output:

```
SALES_AMT   D_DATE_ID
---------   ---------
      100    20190201
      120    20190507
```

This query displays that the indexes are all still usable:

```
SQL> select index_name, partition_name, status from user_ind_partitions;
```

You can also verify that a local index segment was created for the new partition:

```
SQL> select segment_name, segment_type, partition_name
from user_segments
where segment_name IN('F_SALES','D_DATE_ID_FK1');
```

The ability to exchange partitions is an extremely powerful feature. It allows you to take a partition in an existing table and make it a stand-alone table, while making a stand-alone table (which can be fully populated before the partition exchange operation) part of a partitioned table. When you exchange a partition, Oracle simple updates the entries in the data dictionary to perform the exchange.

When you exchange a partition with the WITHOUT VALIDATION clause, you instruct Oracle not to validate that the rows in the incoming partition (or subpartition) are valid entries for the defined range. This has the advantage of making the exchange a very quick operation because Oracle is only updating pointers in the data dictionary to perform the exchange operation. You need to make sure your data are accurate if you use WITHOUT VALIDATION.

If a primary key is defined for the partitioned table, the table being exchanged must have the same primary key structure defined. If there is a primary key, the WITHOUT VALIDATION clause does not stop Oracle from enforcing unique constraints.

Renaming a Partition

Sometimes, you may be required to rename a table partition or index partition. For example, you may want to rename a partition before you drop it (to ensure that it is not being used). Also, you may want to rename objects so that they conform to standards. In these scenarios, use the ALTER TABLE or ALTER INDEX statement as appropriate.

This example uses the ALTER TABLE statement to rename a table partition:

```
SQL> alter table f_sales rename partition p_2018 to part_2018;
```

The next line of code uses the ALTER INDEX statement to rename an index partition:

```
SQL> alter index d_date_id_fk1 rename partition p_2018 to part_2018;
```

You can query the data dictionary to verify the information regarding renamed objects. This query shows partitioned table names:

```
SQL> select table_name, partition_name, tablespace_name
from user_tab_partitions;
```

Similarly, this query displays partitioned index information:

```
SQL> select index_name, partition_name, status
,high_value, tablespace_name
from user_ind_partitions;
```

Splitting a Partition

Suppose you have identified a partition that has too many rows, and you want to split it into two partitions. Use the ALTER TABLE...SPLIT PARTITION statement to split an existing partition. The following example splits a partition in a range-partitioned table:

```
SQL> alter table f_sales split partition p_2018 at (20180601)
into (partition p_2018_a, partition p_2018)
update indexes;
```

If you do not specify UPDATE INDEXES, local indexes will become UNUSABLE, and you need to rebuild any local indexes associated with the split partition as well as any global indexes. You can verify the status of partitioned indexes with this SQL:

```
SQL> select index_name, partition_name, status from user_ind_partitions;
```

The next example splits a list partition. First, here is the CREATE TABLE statement, which shows you how the list partitions were originally defined:

```
SQL> create table f_sales
 (sales_amt   number
 ,d_date_id   number
 ,state_code varchar2(3))
partition by list (state_code)
 ( partition reg_west values ('AZ','CA','CO','MT','OR','ID','UT','NV')
  ,partition reg_mid  values ('IA','KS','MI','MN','MO','NE','OH','ND')
  ,partition reg_rest values (default));
```

Next, the REG_MID partition is split:

```
SQL> alter table f_sales split partition reg_mid values
('IA','KS','MI','MN') into
(partition reg_mid_a,
 partition reg_mid_b)
update indexes;
```

The REG_MID_A partition now contains the values IA, KS, MI, and MN, and REG_MID_B is assigned the remaining values, MO, NE, OH, and ND.

The split partition operation allows you to create two new partitions from a single partition. Each new partition has its own segment, physical attributes, and extents. The segment associated with the original partition is deleted.

Merging Partitions

When you create a partition, sometimes it is hard to predict how many rows the partition will eventually contain. You may have two partitions that do not contain enough data to warrant separate partitions. In such a situation, use the ALTER TABLE...MERGE PARTITIONS statement to combine partitions.

The following example merges two partitions into one existing partition:

```
SQL> alter table f_sales merge partitions p_2017, p_2018 into partition
p_2018;
```

In this example, the partitions are organized by a range of dates. The partition into which you are merging is defined as accepting rows with the highest range of the two merged partitions. Any local indexes are also merged into the new, single partition.

You can verify the status of the partitioned indexes by querying the data dictionary:

```
SQL> select index_name, partition_name, tablespace_name, high_value,status
from user_ind_partitions
order by 1,2;
```

With Oracle 18c, the merge operation can now be performed online using the ONLINE clause. This will allow the data to still be available as the merge is being executed, and the UPDATE INDEXES clause should be used to maintain and rebuild any associated indexes at the same time.

```
SQL> alter table f_sales merge partitions p_2017, p_2018 into partition p_2018
tablespace p2_tbsp
update indexes
online;
```

Keep in mind that the merge operation takes longer when you use the UPDATE INDEXES clause. If you want to minimize the length of the merge operation, do not use this clause. Instead, manually rebuild local indexes associated with a merged partition:

```
SQL> alter table f_sales modify partition p_2018 rebuild unusable local indexes;
```

You can rebuild each partition of a global index with the ALTER INDEX...REBUILD PARTITION statement:

```
SQL> alter index f_glo_idx1 rebuild partition sys_p680;
SQL> alter index f_glo_idx1 rebuild partition sys_p681;
SQL> alter index f_glo_idx1 rebuild partition sys_p682;
```

You can merge two or more partitions with the ALTER TABLE...MERGE PARTITIONS statement. The name of the partition into which you are merging can be the name of one of the partitions you are merging or a completely new name.

Before you merge two (or more) partitions, make certain the partition into which you are merging has enough space in its tablespace to accommodate all the merged rows. If there is not enough space, you receive an error that the tablespace cannot extend to the necessary size. extend to the necessary size.

Dropping a Partition

You occasionally need to drop a partition. A common scenario is that you have old data that are not used anymore, meaning that the partition can be dropped.

First, identify the name of the partition you want to drop. Run the following query to list partitions for a particular table for the currently connected user:

```
SQL> select segment_name, segment_type, partition_name
from user_segments
where segment_name = upper('&table_name');
```

Next, use the ALTER TABLE...DROP PARTITION statement to remove a partition from a table. This example drops the P_2018 partition from the F_SALES table:

```
SQL> alter table f_sales drop partition p_2018;
```

When dropping a partition, you will need to rebuild any global indexes. This can be done within the same DDL statement, as the following example shows:

```
SQL> alter table f_sales drop partition p_2018 update global indexes;
```

If you want to drop a subpartition, use the DROP SUBPARTITION clause:

```
SQL> alter table f_sales drop subpartition p2_south;
```

You can query USER_TAB_SUBPARTITIONS to verify that the subpartition has been dropped.

Note   Oracle does not let you drop all subpartitions of a composite-partitioned table. There must be at least one subpartition per partition.

When you drop a partition, there is no undrop operation. Therefore, before you do this, be sure you are in the correct environment and really do need to drop the partition. If you need to preserve the data in a partition to be dropped, merge the partition with another partition instead of dropping it.

You cannot drop a partition from a hash-partitioned table. For hash-partitioned tables, you must coalesce partitions to remove one. And, you cannot explicitly drop a partition from a reference-partitioned table. When a parent table partition is dropped, it is also dropped from corresponding child reference-partitioned tables.

Generating Statistics for a Partition

After you load a large amount of data into a partition, you should generate statistics to reflect the newly inserted data. Use the EXECUTE statement to run the DBMS_STATS package in order to generate statistics for a particular partition. In this example, the owner is STAR, the table is F_SALES, and the partition being analyzed is P_2018:

```
SQL> exec dbms_stats.gather_table_stats(ownname=>'MV_MAINT',-
tabname=>'F_SALES',-
partname=>'P_2018');
```

If you are working with a large partition, you probably want to specify the percentage sampling size and degree of parallelism and also generate statistics for any indexes:

```
SQL> exec dbms_stats.gather_table_stats(ownname=>'MV_MAINT',-
tabname=>'F_SALES',-
partname=>'P_2018',-
estimate_percent=>dbms_stats.auto_sample_size,-
degree=>dbms_stats.auto_degree,-
cascade=>true);
```

For a partitioned table, you can generate statistics on either a single partition or the entire table. I recommend that you generate statistics whenever a significant amount of data change in the partition. You need to understand your tables and data well enough to determine whether generating new statistics is required.

You can instruct Oracle to scan only newly added partitions when generating global statistics. This feature is enabled via the DBMS_STATS package:

```
SQL> exec DBMS_STATS.SET_TABLE_PREFS(user,'F_SALES','INCREMENTAL','TRUE');
```

You can verify the table preferences for the table as follows:

```
SQL> select dbms_stats.get_prefs('INCREMENTAL', tabname=>'F_SALES') from
dual;
```

The incremental global statistics gathering must be used in conjunction with DBMS_STATS.AUTO_SAMPLE_SIZE. This can greatly reduce the time and resources required to gather incremental statistics for partitions newly added to large tables.

Removing Rows from a Partition

You can use several techniques to remove rows from a partition. If the data in the particular partition are no longer required, consider dropping the partition. If you want to remove the data and leave the partition intact, then you can either truncate or delete from it. Truncating a partition quickly and permanently removes the data. If you need the option of rolling back the removal of records, then you should delete (instead of truncate). Both truncating and deleting are described next.

First, identify the name of the partition from which you want to remove records:

```
SQL> select segment_name, segment_type, partition_name
from user_segments
where partition_name is not null;
```

Use the ALTER TABLE...TRUNCATE PARTITION statement to remove all records from a partition. This example truncates a partition from the F_SALES table:

```
SQL> alter table f_sales truncate partition p_2013;
```

The prior command removes data only from the specified partition and not the entire table. Also keep in mind that truncating a partition will invalidate any global indexes. You can update the global indexes while you issue a TRUNCATE as follows:

```
SQL> alter table f_sales truncate partition p_2013 update global indexes;
```

Truncating a partition is an efficient way to remove large amounts of data. When you truncate a partition, however, there is no rollback mechanism. The truncate operation permanently deletes the data from the partition.

If you need the option of rolling back a transaction, use the DELETE statement:

```
SQL> delete from f_sales partition(p_2013);
```

The downside to this approach is that if you have millions of records, the DELETE operation can take a long time to run. Also, for a large number of records, DELETE generates a great deal of rollback information. This can cause performance issues for other SQL statements contending for resources.

Manipulating Data Within a Partition

If you need to select or manipulate data within one partition, specify the partition name as part of the SQL statement. For instance, you can select the rows from a specific partition, as shown:

```
SQL> select * from f_sales partition (p_2013);
```

If you want to select from two (or more) partitions, then use the UNION clause:

```
SQL> select * from f_sales partition (p_2013)
Union all
select * from f_sales partition (p_2014);
```

If you are a developer, and you do not have access to the data dictionary to view which partitions are available, you can use the SELECT...PARTITION FOR <partition_key_value> syntax. With this new syntax, you provide a partition key value, and Oracle determines what partition the key value belongs in and returns the rows from that partition; for example,

```
SQL> select * from f_sales partition for (20130202);
```

You can also update and delete partition rows. This example updates a column in a partition:

```
SQL> update f_sales partition(p_2013) set sales_amt=200;
```

You can use the PARTITION FOR <partition_key_value> syntax for update, delete, and truncate operations; for example,

```
SQL> update f_sales partition for (20130202) set sales_amt=200;
```

Note   See the previous section, "Removing Rows from a Partition," for examples of deleting and truncating a partition.

Partitioning Indexes

In today's large database environments, indexes can grow to unwieldy sizes. Partitioning indexes provides the same benefits as partitioning tables: improved performance, scalability, and maintainability.

You can create an index that uses the partitioning strategy of its table (local), or you can create an index that is partitioned differently from its table (global). Both of these techniques are described in the following sections.

Partitioning an Index to Follow Its Table

When you create an index on a partitioned table, you have the option of making it a LOCAL data type. A local partitioned index is partitioned in the same manner as the partitioned table. Each table partition has a corresponding index that contains ROWID values and index-key values for just that table partition. In other words, the ROWID values in a local partitioned index only point to rows in the corresponding table partition.

The following example illustrates the concept of a locally partitioned index. First, create a table that has only two partitions:

```
SQL> create table f_sales (
 sales_id number
,sales_amt number
,d_date_id number)
tablespace p1_tbsp
partition by range(d_date_id)(
 partition y12 values less than (20130101)
   tablespace p1_tbsp
,partition y13 values less than (20140101)
   tablespace p2_tbsp);
```

And, say five records are inserted into the table, with three records inserted into partition Y12 and two records inserted into partition Y13:

```
SQL> insert into f_sales values(1,20,20120322);
SQL> insert into f_sales values(2,33,20120507);
SQL> insert into f_sales values(3,72,20120101);
SQL> insert into f_sales values(4,12,20130322);
SQL> insert into f_sales values(5,98,20130507);
```

Next, use the LOCAL clause of the CREATE INDEX statement to create a local index on the partitioned table. This example creates a local index on the D_DATE_ID column of the F_SALES table:

```
SQL> create index f_sales_fk1 on f_sales(d_date_id) local;
```

Run the following query to view information about partitioned indexes:

```
SQL> select index_name, table_name, partitioning_type
from user_part_indexes
where table_name = 'F_SALES';
```

Here is some sample output:

```
INDEX_NAME                         TABLE_NAME PARTITION
------------------------------     ---------- ---------
F_SALES_FK1                        F_SALES    RANGE
```

Now, query the USER_IND_PARTITIONS table to view information about the locally partitioned index:

```
SQL> select index_name, partition_name, tablespace_name
from user_ind_partitions
where index_name = 'F_SALES_FK1';
```

Note that an index partition has been created for each partition of the table and that the index is created in the same tablespace as the table partition:

```
INDEX_NAME           PARTITION_NAME         TABLESPACE_NAME
--------------------  --------------------   ----------------
F_SALES_FK1           Y12                    P1_TBSP
F_SALES_FK1           Y13                    P2_TBSP
```

Figure 12-3 conceptually shows how a locally managed index is constructed.

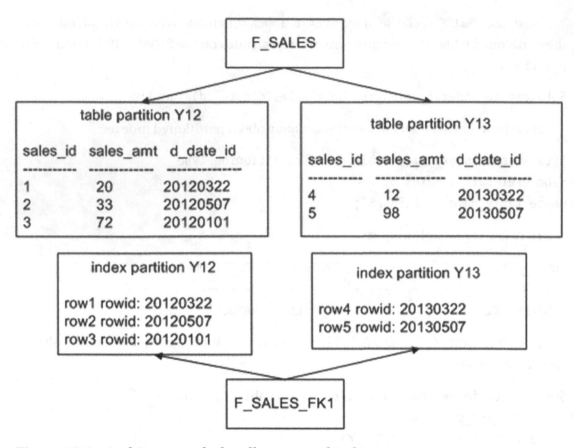

Figure 12-3. *Architecture of a locally managed index*

If you want the local index partitions to be created in a tablespace (or tablespaces) separate from that of the table partitions, specify the tablespace(s) when creating the index:

```
SQL> create index f_sales_fk1 on f_sales(d_date_id) local
(partition y12 tablespace users
,partition y13 tablespace users);
```

Querying USER_IND_PARTITIONS now shows that the index partitions have been created in tablespaces separate from the table partitions' tablespace:

```
INDEX_NAME            PARTITION_NAME        TABLESPACE_NAME
--------------------  --------------------  ----------------

F_SALES_FK1           Y12                   USERS
F_SALES_FK1           Y13                   USERS
```

If you specify the partition information when building a local partitioned index, the number of partitions must match the number of partitions in the table on which the partitioned index is built.

Oracle automatically keeps local index partitions in sync with the table partitions. You cannot explicitly add a partition to or drop a partition from a local index. When you add or drop a table partition, Oracle automatically performs the corresponding work for the local index. Oracle manages the local index partitions, regardless of how the local indexes have been assigned to tablespaces.

Local indexes are common in data warehouse and DSS environments. If you query frequently by using the partitioned column(s), a local index is appropriate. This approach lets Oracle use the appropriate index and table partition to quickly retrieve the data.

There are two types of local indexes: local prefixed and local nonprefixed. A local prefixed index is one in which the leftmost column of the index matches the table partition key. The previous example in this section is a local prefixed index because its leftmost column (D_DATE_ID) is also the partition key for the table.

A local nonprefixed index is one in which the leftmost column does not match the partition key used to partition the corresponding table. For example, this is a local nonprefixed index:

```
SQL> create index f_sales_idx1 on f_sales(sales_id) local;
```

The index is partitioned with the SALES_ID column, which is not the partition key of the table, and is therefore a nonprefixed index. You can verify whether an index is considered prefixed by querying the ALIGNMENT column from USER_PART_INDEXES:

```
SQL> select index_name, table_name, alignment, locality
from user_part_indexes
where table_name = 'F_SALES';
```

Here is some sample output:

```
INDEX_NAME           TABLE_NAME            ALIGNMENT     LOCALI
-------------------- --------------------- ------------- ------
F_SALES_FK1          F_SALES               PREFIXED      LOCAL
F_SALES_IDX1         F_SALES               NON_PREFIXED  LOCAL
```

You may wonder why the distinction exists between prefixed and nonprefixed. A local index that is nonprefixed does not include the partition key as a leading edge of its index definition. This can have performance implications, in that a range scan accessing a nonprefixed index may need to search every index partition. If there are a large number of partitions, this can result in poor performance.

You can choose to create all local indexes as prefixed by including the partition key column in the leading edge of the index. For instance, you can create the F_SALES_IDX2 index as prefixed as follows:

```
SQL> create index f_sales_idx2 on f_sales(d_date_id, sales_id) local;
```

Is a prefixed index preferable to a nonprefixed index? It depends on how you query your tables. You have to generate explain plans for the queries you use and examine whether a prefixed index is better able to take advantage of partition pruning (eliminating partitions to search) than a nonprefixed index. Also keep in mind that a multicolumn local prefixed index consumes more space and resources than a local nonprefixed index.

Partitioning an Index Differently from Its Table

An index that is partitioned differently from its base table is known as a global index. An entry in a global index can point to any of the partitions of its base table. You can create a global index on any type of partitioned table.

You can create either a range-partitioned or a hash-based global index. Use the keyword GLOBAL to specify that the index is built with a partitioning strategy separate from that of its corresponding table. You must always specify a MAXVALUE when creating a range-partitioned global index.

The following example creates a range-based global index:

```
SQL> create index f_sales_gidx1 on f_sales(sales_amt)
global partition by range(sales_amt)
(partition pg1 values less than (25)
,partition pg2 values less than (50)
,partition pg3 values less than (maxvalue));
```

Figure 12-4 shows that with a global index, the partitioning strategy of the index does not accord with the partitioning strategy of the table.

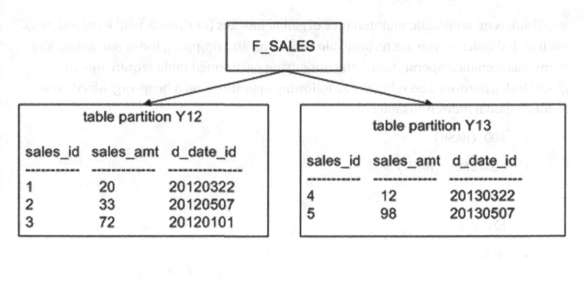

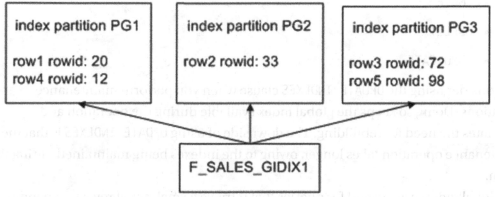

Figure 12-4. *Architecture of a global index*

The other type of global partitioned index is hash based. This example creates a hash-partitioned global index:

```
SQL> create index f_sales_gidx2 on f_sales(sales_id)
global partition by hash(sales_id) partitions 3;
```

In general, global indexes are more difficult to maintain than local indexes. I recommend that you try to avoid using global indexes and use local indexes whenever possible.

There is no automatic maintenance of global indexes (as there is with local indexes). With global indexes, you are responsible for adding and dropping index partitions. Also, many maintenance operations on the underlying partitioned table require that the global index partitions be rebuilt. The following operations on a heap-organized table render a global index unusable:

- ADD (HASH)

- COALESCE (HASH)

- DROP

- EXCHANGE

- MERGE

- MOVE

- SPLIT

- TRUNCATE

Consider using the UPDATE INDEXES clause when you perform maintenance operations. Doing so keeps the global index available during the operation and eliminates the need for rebuilding. The downside of using UPDATE INDEXES is that the maintenance operation takes longer, owing to the indexes being maintained during the action.

Global indexes are useful for queries that retrieve a small set of rows via an index. In these situations, Oracle can eliminate (prune) any unnecessary index partitions and efficiently retrieve the data. For example, global range-partitioned indexes are useful in OLTP environments, where you need quick access to individual records.

Partial Indexes

Starting with Oracle Database 12c, you can specify that index partitions be initially created in an unusable state. You may want to do this if you have pre-created partitions and do not yet have data for range partitions that map to future dates—the idea being that you will build the index after the partitions have been loaded (at some future date).

You control whether a local index is created in a usable state via the INDEXING ON|OFF clause. Here is an example that specifies by default that index partitions will be unusable, unless explicitly turned on:

```
SQL> create table f_sales (
 sales_id number
,sales_amt number
,d_date_id number
)
indexing off
partition by range (d_date_id)
(partition p1 values less than (20170101)  indexing on,
 partition p2 values less than (20180101)  indexing on,
 partition p3 values less than (20190101)  indexing on,
 partition p4 values less than (20200101)  indexing off);
```

Next, a local partitioned index is created on the table, specifying that the partial index functionality should be used:

```
SQL> create index f_sales_lidx1 on f_sales(d_date_id)
local indexing partial;
```

You can verify which partitions are usable (or not) via this query:

```
SQL> select a.index_name, a.partition_name, a.tablespace_name, a.status
from user_ind_partitions a, user_indexes b
where b.table_name = 'F_SALES'
and a.index_name = b.index_name;
```

Here is some sample output for this example:

INDEX_NAME	PARTITION_	TABLESPACE_NAME	STATUS
F_SALES_LIDX1	P1	USERS	USABLE
F_SALES_LIDX1	P2	USERS	USABLE
F_SALES_LIDX1	P3	USERS	USABLE
F_SALES_LIDX1	P4	USERS	UNUSABLE

In this way, you can control whether the index is maintained as data are inserted into the partition. You may not initially want an index partition created in a usable state because it will slow down bulk loads of data. In this situation, you would first load the data and then make the index usable by rebuilding it:

```
SQL> alter index f_sales_lidx1 rebuild partition p4;
```

Partition Pruning

Partition pruningin an SQL query specifically accesses a table on a partition key. Oracle only searches the partitions that contain data the query needs (and does not access any partitions that do not contain such data—pruning them, so to speak).

For example, say a partitioned table is defined as follows:

```
SQL> create table f_sales (
 sales_id   number
,sales_amt number
,d_date_id number)
tablespace p1_tbsp
partition by range(d_date_id)(
 partition y17 values less than (20180101)
    tablespace p1_tbsp
,partition y18 values less than (20190101)
    tablespace p2_tbsp
,partition y19 values less than (20200101)
    tablespace p3_tbsp);
```

Additionally, you create a local index on the partition key column:

```
SQL> create index f_sales_fk1 on f_sales(d_date_id) local;
```

And, say you insert some sample data:

```
SQL> insert into f_sales values(1,100,20170202);
SQL> insert into f_sales values(2,200,20180202);
SQL> insert into f_sales values(3,300,20190202);
```

To illustrate the process of partition pruning, enable the autotrace facility:

```
SQL> set autotrace trace explain;
```

Now, execute an SQL statement that accesses a row based on the partition key:

```
SQL> select sales_amt from f_sales where d_date_id = '20180202';
```

Autotrace displays the explain plan. Some of the columns have been removed in order to fit the output on the page neatly:

```
----------------------------------------------------------------------------
| Id | Operation                   | Name        | Pstart| Pstop |
----------------------------------------------------------------------------
|  0 | SELECT STATEMENT            |             |       |       |
|  1 |   PARTITION RANGE SINGLE    |             |   2 |     2 |
|  2 |    TABLE ACCESS BY LOCAL    |             |       |       |
|    |    INDEX ROWID BATCHED      | F_SALES     |   2 |     2 |
|* 3 |     INDEX RANGE SCAN        | F_SALES_FK1 |   2 |     2 |
----------------------------------------------------------------------------
```

In this output, Pstart shows that the starting partition accessed is partition 2. Pstop shows that the last partition accessed is partition 2. In this example, partition 2 is the only partition used to retrieve data; the other partitions in the table are not accessed at all by the query.

If a query is executed that does not use the partition key, then all partitions are accessed; for example,

```
SQL> select * from f_sales;
```

Here is the corresponding explain plan:

```
---------------------------------------------------------------------
| Id | Operation              | Name    | Rows| Pstart| Pstop|
---------------------------------------------------------------------
|  0 | SELECT STATEMENT       |         |   3 |       |      |
|  1 | PARTITION RANGE ALL    |         |   3 |    1 |    3 |
|  2 | TABLE ACCESS FULL      | F_SALES |   3 |    1 |    3 |
---------------------------------------------------------------------
```

Note in this output that the starting partition is partition 1, and the stopping partition is partition 3. This means that partitions 1 through 3 are accessed by this query, with no pruning of partitions.

This example is simple but demonstrates the concept of partition pruning. When you access the table by the partition key, you can drastically reduce the number of rows Oracle needs to inspect and process. This has huge performance benefits for queries that are able to prune partitions.

Modifying the Partition Strategy

Before Oracle 18c, if you created a partitioned table using a specific strategy such as hash to some other strategy, you would have to re-create the table using one of the methods mentioned to migrate from a nonpartitioned to a partitioned table. Now to a hash-partitioned table to a composite range-hash partitioned table, it is an ALTER table statement that can be performed online or offline. Indexes that are a prefix for the new strategy will be migrated to a local partitioned index or automatically turn into a global index.

```
SQL> create table f_sales(
 sales_id number
, sales_amt  number
 ,state_code varchar2(3)
 ,d_date_id  number)
partition by hash(sales_id);

SQL> alter table f_sales modify
partition by range(d_date_id)
subpartition by hash(sales_id)
subpartitions 8
(partition p2016 values less than (20170101),
partition p2017 values less than (20180101))
ONLINE
UPDATE INDEXES;
```

Summary

Oracle provides a partitioning feature that is critical for implementing large tables and indexes. Partitioning is vital for building highly scalable and maintainable applications. This feature works on the concept of logically creating an object (table or index) but implementing the object as several separate database segments. A partitioned object allows you to build, load, maintain, and query on a partition-by-partition basis. Maintenance operations, such as deleting, archiving, updating, and inserting data are manageable because you are working on only a small subset of the large logical table.

If you work in data warehouse environments or with large databases, you must be highly knowledgeable about partitioning concepts. As a DBA, you are required to create and maintain partitioned objects. You have to make recommendations about table partitioning strategies and where to use local and global indexes. These decisions have a huge impact on the usability and performance of the system. Many of the new features for partitioning allow for online operations, such as merging of partitions and changing from nonpartitioned or changing partitioning strategies. This allows for the object and data to be available while working on these large tables and managing the partitioning strategies as needed.

The book now moves on to utilities used to copy and move users, objects, and data from one environment to another. Oracle's Data Pump and external tables feature are coming up.

CHAPTER 13

Data Pump

Data Pump is often described as an upgraded version of the old exp/imp utilities. It is a bit like calling a modern smartphone a replacement for an old rotary-dial landline. Although the old utilities are dependable and work well, Data Pump encompasses that functionality while adding completely new dimensions to how data can be lifted and moved between environments. This chapter will help explain how Data Pump makes your current data transfer tasks easier and will also show how to move information and solve problems in ways that you did not think were possible.

Data Pump enables you to efficiently back up, replicate, secure, and transform large amounts of data and metadata. You can use Data Pump in a variety of ways:

- Perform point-in-time logical backups of the entire database or subsets of data

- Replicate entire databases or subsets of data for testing or development

- Quickly generate DDL required to re-create objects

- Upgrade a database by exporting from the old version and importing into the new version

Sometimes, DBAs exert an old-fashion-like attachment to the exp/imp utilities because the DBAs are familiar with the syntax of these utilities, and they get the job done quickly. Even if those legacy utilities are easy to use, you should consider using Data Pump going forward. Data Pump contains substantial functionality over the old exp/imp utilities:

- Performance with large data sets, allowing efficient export and import gigabytes of data

- Interactive command-line utility, which lets you disconnect and then later attach to active Data Pump jobs along with monitoring of job progress

© Michelle Malcher and Darl Kuhn 2019
M. Malcher and D. Kuhn, *Pro Oracle Database 18c Administration*,
https://doi.org/10.1007/978-1-4842-4424-1_13

- Ability to export large amounts of data from a remote database and import them directly into a local database without creating a dump file

- Ability to make on-the-fly changes to schemas, tablespaces, data files, and storage settings from export to import

- Sophisticated filtering of objects and data

- Use to perform transportable tablespace export

- Security-controlled (via database) directory objects and data directories

- Advanced features, such as compression and encryption

The focus of this chapter begins with the Data Pump architecture. There are additional ways to move data between databases with cloning and other functionality that will be discussed in later chapters. Basic export and import utilities should no longer be in use. Having data being written to client machines are a high security risk, and the older utilities of export and import will do this, instead of what Data Pump provides to write the files to the server or a secured file share. Security measures need to be in place to prevent data from being placed in a non-secured area.

Data Pump Architecture

Data Pump consists of the following components:

- expdp (Data Pump export utility)

- impdp (Data Pump import utility)

- DBMS_DATAPUMP PL/SQL package (Data Pump application programming interface [API])

- DBMS_METADATA PL/SQL package (Data Pump Metadata API)

The expdp and impdp utilities use the DBMS_DATAPUMP and DBMS_METADATA built-in PL/SQL packages when exporting and importing data and metadata. The DBMS_DATAPUMP package moves entire databases or subsets of data between database environments. The DBMS_METADATA package exports and imports information about database objects.

Note   You can call the DBMS_DATAPUMP and DBMS_METADATA packages independently (outside expdp and impdp) from SQL*Plus. DBMS_DATAPUMP can be used to monitor the Data Pump jobs. DBMS_METADATA is very useful for retrieving DDL statements. See the Oracle Database PL/SQL Packages and Types Reference Guide, which is available for download from the Technology Network area of the Oracle web site (http://otn.oracle.com) for more details.

When you start a Data Pump export or import job, a master OS process is initiated on the database server. This master process name has the format ora_dmNN_<SID>. On Linux/Unix systems, you can view this process from the OS prompt using the ps command:

```
$ ps -ef | grep -v grep | grep ora_dm
oracle    14602      1  4 08:59 ?        00:00:03 ora_dm00_o12c
```

Depending on the degree of parallelism and the work specified, a number of worker processes are also started. If no parallelism is specified, then only one worker process is started. The master process coordinates the work between master and worker processes. The worker process names have the format ora_dwNN_<SID>.

Also, when a user starts an export or import job, a database status table starts the job. This table exists only for the duration of the Data Pump job. The name of the status table is dependent on what type of job you are running. The table is named with the format SYS_<OPERATION>_<JOB_MODE>_NN, where OPERATION is either EXPORT or IMPORT. JOB_MODE can be one of the following types:

- FULL

- SCHEMA

- TABLE

- TABLESPACE

- TRANSPORTABLE

For example, if you are exporting a schema, a table is created in your account with the name SYS_EXPORT_SCHEMA_NN, where NN is a number that makes the table name unique in the user's schema. This status table contains information such as the objects' exported/imported, start time, elapsed time, rows, and error count. The status table has more than 80 columns.

Tip   The Data Pump status table is created in the default permanent tablespace of the user performing the export/import. Therefore, if the user has no privileges to create a table in the default tablespace, the Data Pump job will fail, with an ORA-31633 error.

The status table is dropped by Data Pump upon successful completion of an export or import job. If you use the KILL_JOB interactive command, the master table is also dropped. If you stop a job with the STOP_JOB interactive command, the table isn't removed and is used in the event you restart the job.

If your job terminates abnormally, the master table is retained. You can delete the status table if you do not plan to restart the job.

When Data Pump runs, it uses a database directory object to determine where to write and read dump files and log files. Usually, you specify which directory object you want Data Pump to use. If you do not specify a directory object, a default directory is used. The default directory path is defined by a data directory object named DATA_PUMP_ DIR. This directory object is automatically created when the database is first created. On Linux/Unix systems, this directory object maps to the ORACLE_HOME/rdbms/log directory.

A Data Pump export creates an export file and a log file. The export file contains the objects being exported. The log file contains a record of the job activities. Figure 13-1 shows the architectural components related to a Data Pump export job.

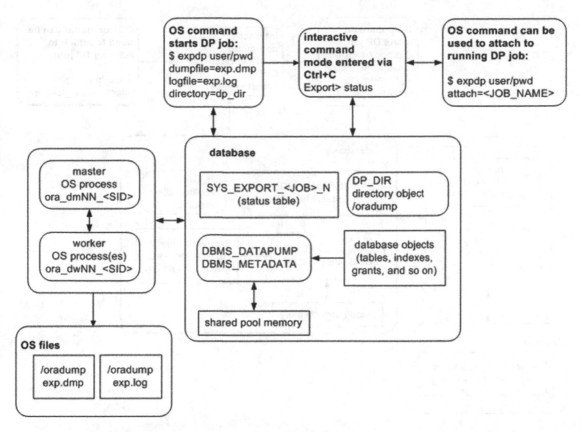

Figure 13-1. *Data Pump export job components*

Similarly, Figure 13-2 displays the architectural components of a Data Pump import job. The main difference between export and import is the direction in which the data flow. Export writes data out of the database, and import brings information into the database. Refer back to these diagrams as you work through Data Pump examples and concepts throughout this chapter.

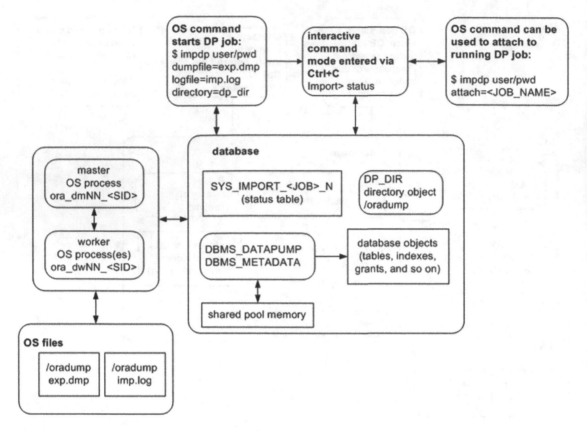

Figure 13-2. *Data Pump import job components*

For each Data Pump job, you must ensure that you have access to a directory object. The basics of exporting and importing are described in the next few sections.

Tip   Because Data Pump internally uses PL/SQL to perform its work, there needs to be some memory available in the shared pool to hold the PL/SQL packages. If there is not enough room in the shared pool, Data Pump will throw an ORA-04031: unable to allocate bytes of shared memory... error and abort. If you receive this error, set the database parameter SHARED_POOL_SIZE to at least 50M. See MOS note 396940.1 for further details.

Getting Started

Now that you have an understanding of the Data Pump architecture, next is a simple example showing the required export setup steps for exporting a table, dropping the table, and then reimporting the table back into the database. This will lay the foundation for all other Data Pump tasks covered in this chapter.

Taking an Export

A small amount of setup is required when you run a Data Pump export job. Here are the steps:

1. Create a database directory object that points to an OS directory that you want to write/read Data Pump files to/from.

2. Grant read and write privileges on the directory object to the database user running the export.

3. From the OS prompt, run the expdp utility.

Step 1. Creating a Database Directory Object

Before you run a Data Pump job, first create a database directory object that corresponds to a physical location on disk. This location will be used to hold the export and log files and should be a location where you know you have plenty of disk space to accommodate the amount of data being exported.

Use the CREATE DIRECTORY command to accomplish this task. This example creates a directory named dp_dir and specifies that it is to map to the /oradump physical location on disk:

```
SQL> create directory dp_dir as '/oradump';
```

To view the details of the newly created directory, issue this query:

```
SQL> select owner, directory_name, directory_path from dba_directories;
```

Here is some sample output:

```
OWNER      DIRECTORY_NAME   DIRECTORY_PATH
---------- ---------------- --------------------
SYS        DP_DIR           /oradump
```

Keep in mind that the directory path specified has to physically exist on the database server. Furthermore, the directory has to be one that the oracle OS user has read/write access to. Finally, the user performing the Data Pump operations needs to be granted read/write access to the directory object (see step 2).

If you do not specify the DIRECTORY parameter when exporting or importing, Data Pump will attempt to use the default database directory object (as previously discussed, this maps to ORACLE_HOME/rdbms/log). This is not recommend using the default directory for two reasons:

- If you are exporting large amounts of data, it is better to have on disk the preferred location, where you know you have enough room to accommodate your disk space requirements. If you use the default directory, you run the risk of inadvertently filling up the mount point associated with ORACLE_HOME and then potentially hanging your database.

- If you grant privileges to non-DBA users to take exports, you do not want them creating large dump files in a location associated with ORACLE_HOME or having access to the ORACLE_HOME directories. Again, you do not want the mount point associated with ORACLE_HOME to become full to the detriment of your database.

Step 2. Granting Access to the Directory

You need to grant permissions on the database directory object to a user that wants to use Data Pump. Use the GRANT statement to allocate the appropriate privileges. If you want a user to be able to read from and write to the directory, you must grant security access. This example grants access to the directory object to a user named MV_MAINT:

```
SQL> grant read, write on directory dp_dir to mv_maint;
```

All directory objects are owned by the SYS user. If you are using a user account that has the DBA role granted to it, then you have the requisite read/write privileges on any directory objects. Permissions can be granted for migrations, data refreshes by developers in test, so granting permissions to a specific directory that might be a file share that is not local on the database server is possible. This also secures the data to the directories that only groups of users can have access to and limits access to other schemas and files.

SECURITY ISSUES WITH THE OLD EXP UTILITY

The idea behind creating directory objects and then granting specific I/O access to the physical storage location is that you can more securely administer which users have the capability to generate read and write activities when normally they would not have permissions. With the legacy exp utility, any user that has access to the tool by default has access to write or read a file to which the owner (usually oracle) of the Oracle binaries has access. It is conceivable that a malicious non-oracle OS user can attempt to run the exp utility to purposely overwrite a critical database file. For example, the following command can be run by any non-oracle OS user with execute access to the exp utility:

```
$ exp heera/foo file=/oradata04/SCRKDV12/users01.dbf
```

However, the user must also have permissions on the file system in order to write the file. Without the permissions on the file system the export will fail.

```
EXP-00028: failed to open /opt/oracle/x.dmp for write
Export file: expdat.dmp >
```

Using another user to run these utilities may allow an unauthorized access to pull data from the database, but the commands will fail if the user does not have write capabilities to the file s

Important note here is not to use the database software directory ORACLE_HOME/bin as a client utility. The execute permissions should be removed from ORACLE_HOME/bin from others so that non-Oracle users will not execute any of the utilities on the database server.

The export utility also allowed users to export directly to the client machine and did not have to be a configured file system with the required privileges. This was mentioned at the beginning of the chapter and a main reason for not allowing these old utilities to be used.

To prevent such issues, with Oracle Data Pump, you first have to create a database object directory that maps to a specific directory and then additionally assign read and write privileges to that directory per user. Thus, Data Pump doesn't have the security problems that exist with the old exp utility.

Step 3. Taking an Export

When the directory object and grants are in place, you can use Data Pump to export information from a database. The simple example in this section shows how to export a table. Later sections in this chapter describe in detail the various ways in which you can export data. The point here is to work through an example that will provide a foundation for understanding more complex topics that follow.

As a non-SYS user, create a table, and populate it with some data:

```
SQL> create table inv(inv_id number);
SQL> insert into inv values (123);
```

Next, as a non-SYS user, export the table. This example uses the previously created directory, named DP_DIR. Data Pump uses the directory path specified by the directory object as the location on disk to which to write the dump file and log file:

```
$ expdp mv_maint/foo directory=dp_dir tables=inv dumpfile=exp.dmp
logfile=exp.log
```

The expdp utility creates a file named exp.dmp in the /oradump directory, containing the information required to re-create the INV table and populate it with data as it was at the time the export was taken. Additionally, a log file named exp.log is created in the /oradump directory, containing logging information associated with this export job.

If you do not specify a dump file name, Data Pump creates a file named expdat.dmp. If a file named expdat.dmp already exists in the directory, then Data Pump throws an error. If you do not specify a log file name, then Data Pump creates one named export.log. If a log file named export.log already exists, then Data Pump overwrites it.

Tip   Although it is possible to execute Data Pump as the SYS user, I do not recommend it for a couple of reasons. First, SYS is required to connect to the database with the AS SYSDBA clause. This requires a Data Pump parameter file with the USERID parameter and quotes around the associated connect string. This is unwieldy. Second, most tables owned by SYS cannot be exported (there are a few exceptions, such as AUD$). If you attempt to export a table owned by SYS, Data Pump will throw an ORA-39166 error and indicate that the table doesn't exist. This is confusing.

FULL export no longer exports the system schemas SYS, ORDSYS or MDSYS, even if exporting using an SYS account.

Importing a Table

One of the key reasons to export data is so that you can re-create database objects. You may want to do this as part of a backup strategy or to replicate data to a different database. Data Pump import uses an export dump file as its input and re-creates database objects contained in the export file. The procedure for importing is similar to exporting:

1. Create a database directory object that points to an OS directory that you want to read/write Data Pump files from.

2. Grant read and write privileges on the directory object to the database user running the export or import.

3. From the OS prompt, run the impdp command.

Steps 1 and 2 were covered in the prior section, "Taking an Export," and therefore will not be repeated here.

Before running the import job, drop the INV table that was created previously.

```
SQL> drop table inv purge;
```

Next, re-create the INV table from the export taken:

```
$ impdp mv_maint/foo directory=dp_dir dumpfile=exp.dmp logfile=imp.log
```

You should now have the INV table re-created and populated with data as it was at the time of the export. Now is a good time to inspect again Figures 13-1 and 13-2. Make sure you understand which files were created by expdb and which files were used by impdp.

Using a Parameter File

Instead of typing commands on the command line, in many situations it is better to store the commands in a file and then reference the file when executing Data Pump export or import. Using parameter files makes tasks more repeatable and less prone to error. You can place the commands in a file once and then reference that file multiple times.

Additionally, some Data Pump commands (such as FLASHBACK_TIME) require the use of quotation marks; in these situations, it is sometimes hard to predict how the OS will interpret these. Whenever a command requires quotation marks, it is highly preferable to use a parameter file.

To use a parameter file, first create an OS text file that contains the commands you want to use to control the behavior of your job. This example uses the Linux/Unix vi command to create a text file named exp.par:

```
$ vi exp.par
```

Now, place the following commands in the exp.par file:

```
userid=mv_maint/foo
directory=dp_dir
dumpfile=exp.dmp
logfile=exp.log
tables=inv
reuse_dumpfiles=y
```

Next, the export operation references the parameter file via the PARFILE command line option:

```
$ expdp parfile=exp.par
```

Data Pump processes the parameters in the file as if they were typed on the command line. If you find yourself repeatedly typing the same commands or using commands that require quotation marks, or both, then consider using a parameter file to increase your efficiency.

Tip   Do not confuse a Data Pump parameter file with the database initialization parameter file. A Data Pump parameter file instructs Data Pump as to which user to connect to the database as, which directory locations to read/write files to and from, what objects to include in the operation, and so on. In contrast, a database parameter file establishes characteristics of the instance upon database startup.

Exporting and Importing with Granularity

Recall from the section "Data Pump Architecture," earlier in this chapter, that there are several different modes in which you can invoke the export/import utilities. For instance, you can instruct Data Pump to export/import in the following modes:

- Entire database

- Schema level

- Table level

- Tablespace level

- Transportable tablespace level

Before diving into the many features of Data Pump, it is useful to discuss these modes and ensure you are aware of how each operates. This will further lay the foundation for understanding concepts introduced later in the chapter.

Exporting and Importing an Entire Database

When you export an entire database, this is sometimes referred to as a full export. In this mode, the resultant export file contains everything required to make a copy of your database. Unless restricted by filtering parameters (see the section "Filtering Data and Objects," later in this chapter), a full export consists of the following:

- All DDL required to re-create tablespaces, users, user tables, indexes, constraints, triggers, sequences, stored PL/SQL, and so on.

- All table data (except the SYS user's tables).

A full export is initiated with the FULL parameter set to Y and must be done with a user that has DBA privileges or that has the DATAPUMP_EXP_FULL_DATABASE role granted to it. Here is an example of taking a full export of a database:

```
$ expdp mv_maint/foo directory=dp_dir dumpfile=full.dmp logfile=full.log full=y
```

As the export is executing, you should see this text in the output, indicating that a full-level export is taking place:

```
Starting "MV_MAINT"."SYS_EXPORT_FULL_01":
```

Be aware that a full export doesn't export everything in the database:

- The contents of the SYS schema are not exported (there are a few exceptions to this, such as the AUD$ table). Consider what would happen if you could export the contents of the SYS schema from one database and import them into another. The SYS schema contents would overwrite internal data dictionary tables/views and thus corrupt the database. Therefore, Data Pump never exports objects owned by SYS.

- Index data are not exported, but rather, the index DDL that contains the SQL required to re-create the indexes during a subsequent import.

Once you have a full export, you can use its contents to either re-create objects in the original database (e.g., in the event a table is accidentally dropped) or replicate the entire database or subsets of users/tables to a different database. This next example assumes that the dump file has been copied **to** a different database server and is now used to import all objects into the destination database:

```
$ impdp mv_maint/foo directory=dp_dir dumpfile=full.dmp logfile=fullimp.log
full=y
```

Tip   To initiate a full database import, you must have DBA privileges or be assigned the DATAPUMP_IMP_FULL_DATABASE role.

In the output displayed on your screen, you should see an indication that a full import is transpiring:

```
Starting "MV_MAINT"."SYS_IMPORT_FULL_01":
```

Running a full-import database job has some implications to be aware of:

- The import job will first attempt to re-create any tablespaces. If a tablespace already exists, or if the directory path a tablespace depends on does not exist, then the tablespace creation statements will fail, and the import job will move on to the next task.

- Next, the import job will alter the SYS and SYSTEM user accounts to contain the same password that was exported. Therefore, after you import from a production system, it is prudent to change the passwords for SYS and SYSTEM, to reflect the new environment.

- Additionally, the import job will then attempt to create any users in the export file. If a user already exists, an error is thrown, and the import job moves on to the next task.

- Users will be imported with the same passwords that were taken from the original database. Depending on your security standards, you may want to change the passwords.

- Tables will be re-created. If a table already exists and contains data, you must specify how you want the import job to handle this. You can have the import job either skip, append, replace, or truncate the table (see the section "Importing When Objects Already Exist" later in this chapter).

- After each table is created and populated, associated indexes are created.

- The import job will also try to import statistics if available. Furthermore, object grants are instantiated.

If everything runs well, the end result will be a database that is logically identical to the source database in terms of tablespaces, users, objects, and so on.

Schema Level

When you initiate an export, unless otherwise specified, Data Pump starts a schema-level export for the user running the export job. User-level exports are frequently used to copy a schema or set of schemas from one environment to another. The following command starts a schema-level export for the MV_MAINT user:

```
$ expdp mv_maint/foo directory=dp_dir dumpfile=mv_maint.dmp
logfile=mv_maint.log
```

In the output displayed on the screen, you should see some text indicating that a schema-level export has been initiated:

```
Starting "MV_MAINT"."SYS_EXPORT_SCHEMA_01"...
```

You can also initiate a schema-level export for users other than the one running the export job with the SCHEMAS parameter. The following command shows a schema-level export for multiple users:

```
$ expdp mv_maint/foo directory=dp_dir dumpfile=user.dmp  schemas=heera,chaya
```

You can initiate a schema-level import by referencing a dump file that was taken with a schema-level export:

```
$ impdp mv_maint/foo directory=dp_dir dumpfile=user.dmp
```

When you initiate a schema-level import, there are some details to be aware of:

- No tablespaces are included in a schema-level export.

- The import job attempts to re-create any users in the dump file. If a user already exists, an error is thrown, and the import job continues.

- The import job will reset the users' passwords, based on the password that was exported.

- Tables owned by the users will be imported and populated. If a table already exists, you must instruct Data Pump on how to handle this with the TABLE_EXISTS_ACTION parameter.

You can also initiate a schema-level import when using a full-export dump file. To do this, specify which schemas you want extracted from the full export:

```
$ impdp mv_maint/foo directory=dp_dir dumpfile=full.dmp schemas=heera,chaya
```

Table Level

You can instruct Data Pump to operate on specific tables via the TABLES parameter. For example, say you want to export

```
$ expdp mv_maint/foo directory=dp_dir dumpfile=tab.dmp \
tables=heera.inv,heera.inv_items
```

You should see some text in the output indicating that a table-level export is transpiring:

```
Starting "MV_MAINT"."SYS_EXPORT_TABLE_01...
```

Similarly, you can initiate a table-level import by specifying a table-level-created dump file:

```
$ impdp mv_maint/foo directory=dp_dir dumpfile=tab.dmp
```

A table-level import only attempts to import the tables and specified data. If a table already exists, an error is thrown, and the import job continues. If a table already exists and contains data, you must specify how you want the export job to handle this. You can have the import job either skip, append, replace, or truncate the table with the TABLE_EXISTS_ACTION parameter.

You can also initiate a table-level import when using a full-export dump file or a schema-level export. To do this, specify which tables you want extracted from the full- or schema-level export:

```
$ impdp mv_maint/foo directory=dp_dir dumpfile=full.dmp tables=heera.inv
```

Tablespace Level

A tablespace-level export/import operates on objects contained within specific tablespaces. This example exports all objects contained in the USERS tablespace:

```
$ expdp mv_maint/foo directory=dp_dir dumpfile=tbsp.dmp tablespaces=users
```

The text displayed in the output should indicate that a tablespace-level export is occurring:

```
Starting "MV_MAINT"."SYS_EXPORT_TABLESPACE_01"...
```

You can initiate a tablespace-level import by specifying an export file that was created with a tablespace-level export:

```
$ impdp mv_maint/foo directory=dp_dir dumpfile=tbsp.dmp
```

You can also initiate a tablespace-level import by using a full export, but specifying the TABLESPACES parameter:

```
$ impdp mv_maint/foo directory=dp_dir dumpfile=full.dmp tablespaces=users
```

A tablespace-level import will attempt to create any tables and indexes within the tablespace. The import doesn't try to re-create the tablespaces themselves. Since a PDB database will have their own tablespaces, this might be an easy level to use for PDB exports.

Note   There is also a transportable tablespace mode export. See the section "Copying Data Files" later in this chapter.

Transferring Data

One of the main uses of Data Pump is the copying of data from one database to another. Often, source and destination databases are located in data centers thousands of miles apart. Data Pump offers several powerful features for efficiently copying data:

- Network link
- Copying data files (transportable tablespaces)
- External tables (see Chapter 14)

Using a network link allows you to take an export and import it into the destination database without having to create a dump file. This is a very efficient way of moving data.

Oracle also provides the transportable tablespace feature, which lets you copy the data files from a source database to the destination and then use Data Pump to transfer the associated metadata. These two techniques are described in the following sections.

Note   See Chapter 14 for a discussion of using external tables to transfer data.

Exporting and Importing Directly Across the Network

Suppose you have two database environments—a production database running on a Solaris box and a test database running on a Linux server. Your boss comes to you with these requirements:

- Make a copy of the production database on the Solaris box.
- Import the copy into the testing database on the Linux server.
- Change the names of the schemas when importing so as to meet the testing database standards for names.

First, consider the steps required to transfer data from one database to another, using the old exp/imp utilities. The steps would look something like this:

1. Export the production database (which creates a dump file on the database server).

2. Copy the dump file to the testing database server.

3. Import the dump file into the testing database.

You can perform those same steps using Data Pump. However, Data Pump provides a much more efficient and transparent method for executing those steps. If you have direct network connectivity between the production and testing database servers, you can take an export and directly import it into your target database without having to create or copy any dump files. Furthermore, you can rename schemas on the fly as you perform the import. Additionally, it does not matter if the source database is running on an OS different from that of the target database.

An example will help illustrate how this works. For this example, the production database users are STAR2, CIA_APP, and CIA_SEL. You want to move these users into a testing database and rename them STAR_JUL, CIA_APP_JUL, and CIA_SEL_JUL. This task requires the following steps:

1. Create users in the test database to be imported into. Here is a sample script that creates the users in the testing database:

```
define star_user=star_jul
define star_user_pwd=star_jul_pwd
define cia_app_user=cia_app_jul
define cia_app_user_pwd=cia_app_jul_pwd
define cia_sel_user=cia_sel_jul
define cia_sel_user_pwd=cia_sel_jul_pwd
--
create user &&star_user identified by &&star_user_pwd;
grant connect,resource to &&star_user;
alter user &&star_user default tablespace dim_data;
--
create user &&cia_app_user identified by &&cia_app_user_pwd;
grant connect,resource to &&cia_app_user;
alter user &&cia_app_user default tablespace cia_data;
```

```
--
create user &&cia_sel_user identified by &&cia_app_user_pwd;
grant connect,resource to &&cia_app_user;
alter user &&cia_sel_user default tablespace cia_data;
```

2. In your testing database, create a database link that points to your production database. The remote user referenced in the CREATE DATABASE LINK statement must have the DBA role granted to it in the production database. Here is a sample CREATE DATABASE LINK script:

```
create database link dk
connect to darl identified by foobar
using 'dwdb1:1522/dwrep1';
```

3. In your testing database, create a directory object that points to the location where you want your log file to go:

```
SQL> create or replace directory engdev as '/orahome/oracle/ddl/engdev';
```

4. Run the import command on the testing box. This command references the remote database via the NETWORK_LINK parameter. The command also instructs Data Pump to map the production database user names to the newly created users in the testing database.

```
$ impdp darl/engdev directory=engdev network_link=dk \
schemas='STAR2,CIA_APP,CIA_SEL' \
remap_schema=STAR2:STAR_JUL,CIA_APP:CIA_APP_JUL,CIA_SEL:CIA_SEL_JUL
```

This technique allows you to move large amounts of data between disparate databases without having to create or copy any dump files or data files. You can also rename schemas on the fly via the REMAP_SCHEMA parameter. This is a very powerful Data Pump feature that lets you transfer data quickly and efficiently.

Tip When replicating entire databases, also consider using the RMAN duplicate database functionality.

DATABASE LINK VS. NETWORK_LINK

Do not confuse exporting while connected to a remote database over a database link with exporting using the NETWORK_LINK parameter. When exporting while connected to a remote database via a database link, the objects being exported exist in the remote database, and the dump file and log file are created on the remote server in the directory specified by the DIRECTORY parameter. For instance, the following command exports objects in the remote database and creates files on the remote server:

```
$ expdp mv_maint/foo@shrek2 directory=dp_dir dumpfile=sales.dmp
```

In contrast, when you export using the NETWORK_LINK parameter, you are creating dump files and log files locally, and the database objects being exported exist in a remote database; for example,

```
$ expdp mv_maint/foo network_link=shrek2 directory=dp_dir dumpfile=sales.dmp
```

Copying Data Files

Oracle provides a mechanism for copying data files from one database to another, in conjunction with using Data Pump to transport the associated metadata. This is known as the transportable tablespace feature. The amount of time this task requires depends on how long it takes you to copy the data files to the destination server. This technique is appropriate for moving data in DSS and data warehouse environments.

Tip   Transporting tablespaces can also be used (in conjunction with the RMAN CONVERT TABLESPACE command) to move tablespaces to a destination server that has a platform different from that of the host.

Follow these steps to transport tablespaces:

1. Ensure that the tablespace is self-contained. These are some common violations of the self-contained rule:

   - An index in one tablespace cannot point to a table in another tablespace that is not in the set of tablespaces being transported.

- A foreign key constraint is defined on a table in a tablespace that references a primary key constraint on a table in a tablespace that isn't in the set of tablespaces being transported.

Run the following check to see if the set of tablespaces being transported violates any of the self-contained rules:

```
SQL> exec dbms_tts.transport_set_check('INV_DATA,INV_INDEX', TRUE);
```

Now, see if Oracle detected any violations:

```
SQL> select * from transport_set_violations;
```

If you do not have any violations, you should see this:

```
no rows selected
```

If you do have violations, such as an index that is built on a table that exists in a tablespace not being transported, then you will have to rebuild the index in a tablespace that is being transported.

2. Make the tablespaces being transported read-only:

```
SQL> alter tablespace inv_data read only;
SQL> alter tablespace inv_index read only;
```

3. Use Data Pump to export the metadata for the tablespaces being transported:

```
$ expdp mv_maint/foo directory=dp_dir dumpfile=trans.dmp \
transport_tablespaces=INV_DATA,INV_INDEX
```

4. Copy the Data Pump export dump file to the destination server.

5. Copy the data file(s) to the destination database. Place the files in the directory where you want them in the destination database server. The file name and directory path must match the import command used in the next step.

6. Import the metadata into the destination database. Use the following parameter file to import the metadata for the data files being transported:

```
userid=mv_maint/foo
directory=dp_dir
dumpfile=trans.dmp
transport_datafiles=/ora01/dbfile/rcat/inv_data01.dbf,
/ora01/dbfile/rcat/inv_index01.dbf
```

If everything goes well, you should see some output indicating success:

```
Job "MV_MAINT"."SYS_IMPORT_TRANSPORTABLE_01" successfully completed...
```

If the data files that are being transported have a block size different from that of the destination database, then you must modify your initialization file (or use an ALTER SYSTEM command) and add a buffer pool that contains the block size of the source database. For example, to add a 16KB buffer cache, place this in the initialization file:

```
db_16k_cache_size=200M
```

You can check a tablespace's block size via this query:

```
SQL> select tablespace_name, block_size from dba_tablespaces;
```

The transportable tablespace mechanism allows you to quickly move data files between databases, even if the databases use different block sizes or have different endian formats. This section does not discuss all the details involved with transportable tablespaces; the focus of this chapter is to show how to use Data Pump to transport data. See the Oracle Database Administrator's Guide, which can be freely downloaded from the Technology Network area of the Oracle Web site (http://otn.oracle.com), for complete details on transportable tablespaces.

Note To generate transportable tablespaces, you must use the Oracle Enterprise Edition. You can use other editions of Oracle to import transportable tablespaces.

Features for Manipulating Storage

Data Pump contains many flexible features for manipulating tablespaces and data files when exporting and importing. The following sections show useful Data Pump techniques when working with these important database objects.

Exporting Tablespace Metadata

Sometimes, you may be required to replicate an environment—say, replicating a production environment into a testing environment. One of the first tasks is to replicate the tablespaces. To this end, you can use Data Pump to pull out just the DDL required to re-create the tablespaces for an environment:

```
$ expdp mv_maint/foo directory=dp_dir dumpfile=inv.dmp \
full=y include=tablespace
```

The FULL parameter instructs Data Pump to export everything in the database. However, when used with INCLUDE, Data Pump exports only the objects specified with that command. In this combination, only metadata regarding tablespaces are exported; no data within the data files are included with the export. You could add the parameter and value of CONTENT=METADATA_ONLY to the INCLUDE command, but this would be redundant.

Now, you can use the SQLFILE parameter to view the DDL associated with the tablespaces that were exported:

```
$ impdp mv_maint/foo directory=dp_dir dumpfile=inv.dmp sqlfile=tbsp.sql
```

When you use the SQLFILE parameter, nothing is imported. In this example the prior command only creates a file named tbsp.sql, containing SQL statements pertaining to tablespaces. You can modify the DDL and run it in the destination database environment; or, if nothing needs to change, you can directly use the dump file by importing tablespaces into the destination database.

Specifying Different Data File Paths and Names

As previously discussed, you can use the combination of the FULL and INCLUDE parameters to export only tablespace metadata information:

```
$ expdp mv_maint/foo directory=dp_dir dumpfile=inv.dmp \
full=y include=tablespace
```

What happens if you want to use the dump file to create tablespaces on a separate database server that has different directory structures? Data Pump allows you to change the data file directory paths and file names in the import step with the REMAP_DATAFILE parameter.

For example, say the source data files existed on a mount point named /ora03, but on the database being imported to, the mount points are named with /ora01. Here is a parameter file that specifies that only tablespaces beginning with the string INV should be imported and that their corresponding data files names be changed to reflect the new environment:

```
userid=mv_maint/foo
directory=dp_dir
dumpfile=inv.dmp
full=y
include=tablespace:"like 'INV%'"
remap_datafile="'/ora03/dbfile/O18C/inv_data01.dbf':'/ora01/dbfile/O18C/
tb1.dbf'"
remap_datafile="'/ora03/dbfile/O18C/inv_index01.dbf':'/ora01/dbfile/O18C/
tb2.dbf'"
```

When Data Pump creates the tablespaces, for any paths that match the first part of the string (to the left of the colon [:]), the string is replaced with the text in the next part of the string (to the right of the colon).

Tip   When working with parameters that require both single and double quotation marks, you will get predictable behavior when using a parameter file. In contrast, if you were to try to enter in the various required quotation marks on the command line, the OS may interpret and pass to Data Pump something other than what you were expecting.

Importing into a Tablespace Different from the Original

You may occasionally be required to export a table and then import it into a different user and a different tablespace. The source database could be different from the destination database, or you could simply be trying to move data between two users within the same database. You can easily handle this requirement with the REMAP_SCHEMA and REMAP_TABLESPACE parameters.

This example remaps the user as well as the tablespace. The original user and tablespaces are HEERA and INV_DATA. This command imports the INV table into the CHAYA user and the DIM_DATA tablespace:

```
$ impdp mv_maint/foo directory=dp_dir dumpfile=inv.dmp
remap_schema=HEERA:CHAYA \
remap_tablespace=INV_DATA:DIM_DATA tables=heera.inv
```

The REMAP_TABLESPACE feature does not re-create tablespaces. It only instructs Data Pump to place objects in tablespaces different from those they were exported from. When importing, if the tablespace that you are placing the object in does not exist, Data Pump throws an error.

Changing the Size of Data Files

You can change the size of the data files when importing by using the TRANSFORM parameter with the PCTSPACE option. Say you have created an export of just the tablespace metadata:

```
$ expdp mv_maint/foo directory=dp_dir dumpfile=inv.dmp full=y
include=tablespace
```

Now, you want to create the tablespaces that contain the string DATA in the tablespace name in a development database, but you do not have enough disk space to create the tablespaces as they were in the source database. In this scenario, you can use the TRANSFORM parameter to specify that the tablespaces be created as a percentage of the original size.

For instance, if you want the tablespaces to be created at 20 percent of the original size, issue the following command:

```
userid=mv_maint/foo
directory=dp_dir
dumpfile=inv.dmp
full=y
include=tablespace:"like '%DATA%'"
transform=pctspace:20
```

The tablespaces are created with data files 20 percent of their original size. The extent allocation sizes are also 20 percent of their original definition. This is important because Data Pump does not check to see if the storage attributes meet the minimum size restrictions for data files. This means that if the calculated smaller size violates an Oracle minimum size (e.g., five blocks for the uniform extent size), an error will be thrown during the import.

This feature is useful when used to export production data and then import it into a smaller database. In these scenarios, you may be filtering out some of the production data via the SAMPLE parameter or QUERY parameters (see the section "Filtering Data and Objects" later in this chapter).

Changing Segment and Storage Attributes

When importing, you can alter the storage attributes of a table by using the TRANSFORM parameter. The general syntax for this parameter is this:

```
TRANSFORM=transform_name:value[:object_type]
```

When you use SEGMENT_ATTRIBUTES:N for the transformation name, you can remove the following segment attributes during an import:

- Physical attributes

- Storage attributes

- Tablespaces

- Logging

You may require this feature when you are importing into a development environment and do not want the tables to come in with all the storage attributes as they were in the production database. For example, in development you may just have one tablespace in which you store all your tables and indexes, whereas in production, you spread the tables and indexes out in multiple tablespaces.

Here is an example that removes the segment attributes:

```
$ impdp mv_maint/foo directory=dp_dir  dumpfile=inv.dmp \
transform=segment_attributes:n
```

You can remove just the storage clause by using `STORAGE:N`:

```
$ impdp mv_maint/foo directory=dp_dir dumpfile=inv.dmp \
transform=storage:n
```

Filtering Data and Objects

Data Pump has a vast array of mechanisms for filtering data and metadata. You can influence what is excluded or included in a Data Pump export or import in the following ways:

- Use the `QUERY` parameter to export or import subsets of data.

- Use the `SAMPLE` parameter to export a percentage of the rows in a table.

- Use the `CONTENT` parameter to exclude or include data and metadata.

- Use the `EXCLUDE` parameter to specifically name items to be excluded.

- Use the `INCLUDE` parameter to name the items to be included (thereby excluding other nondependent items not included in the list).

- Use parameters such as `SCHEMAS` to specify that you only want a subset of the database's objects (those that belong to the specified user or users).

Examples of each of these techniques are described in the following sections.

Note   You cannot use `EXCLUDE` and `INCLUDE` at the same time. These parameters are mutually exclusive.

Specifying a Query

You can use the `QUERY` parameter to instruct Data Pump to write to a dump file only rows that meet a certain criterion. You may want to do this if you're re-creating a test environment and only need subsets of the data. Keep in mind that this technique is unaware of any foreign key constraints that may be in place, so you can't blindly restrict the data sets without considering parent–child relationships.

The QUERY parameter has this general syntax for including a query:

```
QUERY = [schema.][table_name:] query_clause
```

The query clause can be any valid SQL clause. The query must be enclosed by either double or single quotation marks. I recommend using double quotation marks because you may need to have single quotation marks embedded in the query to handle VARCHAR2 data. Also, you should use a parameter file so that there is no confusion about how the OS interprets the quotation marks.

This example uses a parameter file and limits the rows exported for two tables. Here is the parameter file used when exporting:

```
userid=mv_maint/foo
directory=dp_dir
dumpfile=inv.dmp
tables=inv,reg
query=inv:"WHERE inv_desc='Book'"
query=reg:"WHERE reg_id <=20"
```

Say you place the previous lines of code in a file named inv.par. The export job references the parameter file as shown:

```
$ expdp parfile=inv.par
```

The resulting dump file only contains rows filtered by the QUERY parameters. Again, be mindful of any parent–child relationships, and ensure that what gets exported will not violate any constraints on the import.

You can also specify a query when importing data. Here is a parameter file that limits the rows imported into the INV table, based on the INV_ID column:

```
userid=mv_maint/foo
directory=dp_dir
dumpfile=inv.dmp
tables=inv,reg
query=inv:"WHERE inv_id > 10"
```

This text is placed in a file named `inv2.par` and is referenced during the import as follows:

```
$ impdp parfile=inv2.par
```

All the rows from the REG table are imported. Only the rows in the INV table that have an INV_ID greater than 10 are imported.

Exporting a Percentage of the Data

When exporting, the SAMPLE parameter instructs Data Pump to retrieve a certain percentage of rows, based on a number you provide. Data Pump does not keep track of parent–child relationships when exporting. Therefore, this approach does not work well when you have tables linked via foreign key constraints and you are trying to select a percentage of rows randomly.

Here is the general syntax for this parameter:

```
SAMPLE=[[schema_name.]table_name:]sample_percent
```

For example, if you want to export 10 percent of the data in a table, do so as follows:

```
$ expdp mv_maint/foo directory=dp_dir tables=inv sample=10 dumpfile=inv.dmp
```

This next example exports two tables, but only 30 percent of the REG table's data:

```
$ expdp mv_maint/foo directory=dp_dir tables=inv,reg sample=reg:30
dumpfile=inv.dmp
```

Note   The SAMPLE parameter is only valid for exports.

Excluding Objects from the Export File

For export the EXCLUDE parameter instructs Data Pump not to export specified objects (whereas the INCLUDE parameter instructs Data Pump to include only specific objects in the export file). The EXCLUDE parameter has this general syntax:

```
EXCLUDE=object_type[:name_clause] [, ...]
```

The OBJECT_TYPE is a database object, such as TABLE or INDEX. To see which object types can be filtered, view the OBJECT_PATH column of DATABASE_EXPORT_OBJECTS, SCHEMA_EXPORT_OBJECTS, or TABLE_EXPORT_OBJECTS. For example, if you want to view what schema-level objects can be filtered, run this query:

```
SELECT
 object_path
FROM schema_export_objects
WHERE object_path NOT LIKE '%/%';
```

Here is a snippet of the output:

```
OBJECT_PATH
-------------------
STATISTICS
SYNONYM
SYSTEM_GRANT
TABLE
TABLESPACE_QUOTA
TRIGGER
```

The EXCLUDE parameterinstance, for example, says that you are exporting a table but want to exclude the indexes and grants:

```
$ expdp mv_maint/foo directory=dp_dir dumpfile=inv.dmp tables=inv
exclude=index,grant
```

You can filter at a more granular level by using NAME_CLAUSE. The NAME_CLAUSE option of EXCLUDE allows you to specify an SQL filter. To exclude indexes that have names that start with the string "INV," you use the following command:

```
exclude=index:"LIKE 'INV%'"
```

The previous line requires that you use quotation marks; in these scenarios, I recommend that you use a parameter file. Here is a parameter file that contains an EXCLUDE clause:

```
userid=mv_maint/foo
directory=dp_dir
dumpfile=inv.dmp
```

```
tables=inv
exclude=index:"LIKE 'INV%'"
```

A few aspects of the EXCLUDE clause may seem counterintuitive. For example, consider the following export parameter file:

```
userid=mv_maint/foo
directory=dp_dir
dumpfile=sch.dmp
exclude=schema:"='HEERA'"
```

If you attempt to exclude a user in this manner, an error is thrown. This is because the default mode of export is SCHEMA level, and Data Pump cannot exclude and include a schema at the same time. If you want to exclude a user from an export file, specify the FULL mode, and exclude the user:

```
userid=mv_maint/foo
directory=dp_dir
dumpfile=sch.dmp
exclude=schema:"='HEERA'"
full=y
```

Excluding Statistics

By default, when you export a table object, any statistics are also exported. You can prevent statistics from being imported via the EXCLUDE parameter. Here is an example:

```
$ expdp mv_maint/foo directory=dp_dir dumpfile=inv.dmp \
tables=inv exclude=statistics
```

When importing, if you attempt to exclude statistics from a dump file that did not originally include the statistics, then you receive this error:

```
ORA-39168: Object path STATISTICS was not found.
```

You also receive this error if the objects in the exported dump file never had statistics generated for them. If moving to a different environment, it is recommended to regenerate statistics after the import, based on the new home for the data.

Including Only Specific Objects in an Export File

Use the INCLUDE parameter to include only certain database objects in the export file. The following example exports only the procedures and functions that a user owns:

```
$ expdp mv_maint/foo dumpfile=proc.dmp directory=dp_dir
include=procedure,function
```

The proc.dmp file that is created contains only the DDL required to re-create any procedures and functions the user owns.

When using INCLUDE, you can also specify that only specific PL/SQL objects should be exported:

```
$ expdp mv_maint/foo directory=dp_dir dumpfile=ss.dmp \
include=function:\"=\'IS_DATE\'\"
```

Use a parameter file to be able to capture the specifics for PL/SQL exporting. The following example shows the contents of a parameter file that exports specific objects:

```
directory=dp_dir
dumpfile=ss.dmp
include=function:"='ISDATE'",procedure:"='DEPTREE_FILL'"
```

If you specify an object that does not exist, Data Pump throws an error but continues with the export operation:

```
ORA-39168: Object path FUNCTION was not found.
```

Exporting Table, Index, Constraint, and Trigger DDL

Suppose you want to export the DDL associated with tables, indexes, constraints, and triggers in your database. To do this, use the FULL export mode, specify CONTENT=METADATA_ONLY, and only include tables:

```
$ expdp mv_maint/foo directory=dp_dir dumpfile=ddl.dmp \
content=metadata_only full=y include=table
```

When you export an object, Data Pump also exports any dependent objects. So, when you export a table, you also get indexes, constraints, and triggers associated with the table.

Excluding Objects from Import

In general, you can use the same techniques used to filter objects in exports to exclude objects from being imported. Use the EXCLUDE parameter to exclude objects from being imported. For example, to exclude triggers and procedures from being imported, use this command:

```
$ impdp mv_maint/foo dumpfile=inv.dmp directory=dp_dir
exclude=TRIGGER,PROCEDURE
```

You can further refine what is excluded by adding an SQL clause. For example, say you do not want to import triggers that begin with the letter B. Here is what the parameter file looks like:

```
userid=mv_maint/foo
directory=dp_dir
dumpfile=inv.dmp
schemas=HEERA
exclude=trigger:"like 'B%'"
```

Including Objects in Import

You can use the INCLUDE parameter to reduce what is imported. Suppose you have a schema from which you want to import tables that begin with the letter A. Here is the parameter file:

```
userid=mv_maint/foo
directory=dp_dir
dumpfile=inv.dmp
schemas=HEERA
include=table:"like 'A%'"
```

If you place the previous text in a file named h.par, then the parameter file can be invoked as follows:

```
$ impdp parfile=h.par
```

In this example the HEERA schema must already exist. Only tables that start with the letter A are imported.

Common Data Pump Tasks

The following sections describe common features you can use with Data Pump. Many of these features are standard with Data Pump, such as creating a consistent export and taking action when imported objects already exist in the database. Other features, such as compression and encryption, require the Enterprise Edition of Oracle or an extra license, or both. I will point out these requirements (if relevant) for the Data Pump element being covered.

Estimating the Size of Export Jobs

If you are about to export a large amount of data, you can estimate the size of the file that Data Pump creates before you run the export. You may want to do this because you are concerned about the amount of space an export job needs.

To estimate the size, use the `ESTIMATE_ONLY` parameter. This example estimates the size of the export file for an entire database:

```
$ expdp mv_maint/foo estimate_only=y full=y logfile=n
```

Here is a snippet of the output:

```
Estimate in progress using BLOCKS method...
Total estimation using BLOCKS method: 6.75 GB
```

Similarly, you can specify a schema name to get an estimate of the size required to export a user:

```
$ expdp mv_maint/foo estimate_only=y schemas=star2 logfile=n
```

Here is an example of estimating the size required for two tables:

```
$ expdp mv_maint/foo estimate_only=y
tables=star2.f_configs,star2.f_installations \
logfile=n
```

Listing the Contents of Dump Files

Data Pump has a very robust method of creating a file that contains all the SQL that is executed when an import job runs. Data Pump uses the DBMS_METADATA package to create the DDL that you can use to re-create objects in the Data Pump dump file.

Use the SQLFILE option of Data Pump import to list the contents of a Data Pump export file. This example creates a file named expfull.sql, containing the SQL statements that the import process calls (the file is placed in the directory defined by the DPUMP_DIR2 directory object):

```
$ impdp hr/hr DIRECTORY=dpump_dir1 DUMPFILE=expfull.dmp \
SQLFILE=dpump_dir2:expfull.sql
```

If you do not specify a separate directory (such as dpump_dir2, in the previous example), then the SQL file is written to the location specified in the DIRECTORY option.

Tip   You must run the previous command as a user with DBA privileges or the schema that performed the Data Pump export. Otherwise, you get an empty SQL file without the expected SQL statements in it.

When you use the SQLFILE option with an import, the impdp process does not import any data; it only creates a file that contains the SQL commands that would be run by the import process. It is sometimes handy to generate an SQL file for the following reasons:

- Preview and verify the SQL statements before running the import.

- Run the SQL manually to pre-create database objects.

- Capture the SQL that would be required to re-create database objects (users, tables, index, and so on).

In regard to the last bulleted item, sometimes what is checked into the source code control repository does not match what is really been applied to the production database. This procedure can be handy for troubleshooting or documenting the state of the database at a point in time.

Cloning a User

Suppose you need to move a user's objects and data to a new database. As part of the migration, you want to rename the user. First, create a schema-level export file that contains the user you want to clone. In this example the user name is INV:

```
$ expdp mv_maint/foo directory=dp_dir schemas=inv dumpfile=inv.dmp
```

Now, you can use Data Pump import to clone the user. If you want to move the user to a different database, copy the dump file to the remote database, and use the REMAP_ SCHEMA parameter to create a copy of a user. In this example the INV user is cloned to the INV_DW user:

```
$ impdp mv_maint/foo directory=dp_dir remap_schema=inv:inv_dw dumpfile=inv.dmp
```

This command copies all structures and data in the INV user to the INV_DW user. The resulting INV_DW user is identical, in terms of objects, to the INV user. The duplicated schema also contains the same password as the schema from which it was copied.

If you just want to duplicate the metadata from one schema to another, use the CONTENT parameter with the METADATA_ONLY option:

```
$ impdp mv_maint/foo directory=dp_dir remap_schema=inv:inv_dw \
content=metadata_only dumpfile=inv.dmp
```

The REMAP_SCHEMA parameter provides an efficient way to duplicate a schema, with or without the data. During a schema duplication operation, if you want to change the tablespace in which the objects reside, also use the REMAP_TABLESPACE parameter. This allows you to duplicate a schema and also place the objects in a tablespace different from that of the source objects.

You can also duplicate a user from one database to another without first creating a dump file. To do this, use the NETWORK_LINK parameter. See the section "Exporting and Importing Directly Across the Network," earlier in this chapter, for details on copying data directly from one database to another.

Creating a Consistent Export

A consistent export means that all data in the export file are consistent as of a time or an SCN. When you are exporting an active database with many parent–child tables, you should ensure that you get a consistent snapshot of the data.

You create a consistent export by using either the FLASHBACK_SCN or FLASHBACK_TIME parameter. This example uses the FLASHBACK_SCN parameter to take an export. To determine the current value of the SCN of your data set, issue this query:

```
SQL> select current_scn from v$database;
```

Here is some typical output:

```
CURRENT_SCN
-----------
    5715397
```

The following command takes a consistent full export of the database, using the FLASHBACK_SCN parameter:

```
$ expdp mv_maint/foo directory=dp_dir full=y flashback_scn=5715397 \
dumpfile=full.dmp
```

The previous export command ensures that all data exported are consistent with any transactions committed in the database as of the specified SCN.

When you use the FLASHBACK_SCN parameter, Data Pump ensures that the data in the export file are consistent as of the specified SCN. This means that any transactions committed after the specified SCN are not included in the export file.

Note   If you use the NETWORK_LINK parameter in conjunction with FLASHBACK_SCN, then the export is taken with the SCN consistent with the database referenced in the database link.

You can also use FLASHBACK_TIME to specify that the export file should be created with consistent committed transactions as of a specified time. When using FLASHBACK_TIME, Oracle determines the SCN that most closely matches the time specified and uses that to produce an export consistent with that SCN. The syntax for using FLASHBACK_TIME is as follows:

```
FLASHBACK_TIME="TO_TIMESTAMP{<value>}"
```

For some OSs, double quotation marks appearing directly on the command line must be escaped by a backslash (\) because the OS treats them as special characters.

For this reason, it is much more straightforward to use a parameter file. Here are the contents of a parameter file that uses FLASHBACK_TIME:

```
directory=dp_dir
content=metadata_only
dumpfile=inv.dmp
flashback_time="to_timestamp('24-jan-2013 07:03:00','dd-mon-yyyy
hh24:mi:ss')"
```

Depending on your OS, the command-line version of the previous example must be specified as follows:

```
flashback_time=\"to_timestamp\(\'24-jan-2013 07:03:00\',
\'dd-mon-yyyy hh24:mi:ss\'\)\"
```

This line of code should be specified on one line. Here, the code has been placed on two lines in order to fit on the page.

You cannot specify both FLASHBACK_SCN and FLASHBACK_TIME when taking an export; these two parameters are mutually exclusive. If you attempt to use both parameters at the same time, Data Pump throws the following error message and halts the export job:

```
ORA-39050: parameter FLASHBACK_TIME is incompatible with parameter
FLASHBACK_SCN
```

Importing When Objects Already Exist

When exporting and importing data, you often import into schemas in which the objects have been created (tables, indexes, and so on). In this situation, you should import the data but instruct Data Pump to try not to create already existing objects.

You can achieve this with the TABLE_EXISTS_ACTION and CONTENT parameters. The next example instructs Data Pump to append data in any tables that already exist via the TABLE_EXISTS_ACTION=APPEND option. Also used is the CONTENT=DATA_ONLY option, which instructs Data Pump not to run any DDL to create objects (only to load data):

```
$ impdp mv_maint/foo directory=dp_dir dumpfile=inv.dmp \
table_exists_action=append content=data_only
```

Existing objects are not modified in any way, and any new data that exist in the dump file are inserted into any tables.

You may wonder what happens if you just use the TABLE_EXISTS_ACTION option and do not combine it with the CONTENT option:

```
$ impdp mv_maint/foo directory=dp_dir dumpfile=inv.dmp \
table_exists_action=append
```

The only difference is that Data Pump attempts to run DDL commands to create objects if they exist. This does not stop the job from running, but you see an error message in the output, indicating that the object already exists. Here is a snippet of the output for the previous command:

```
Table "MV_MAINT"."INV" exists. Data will be appended ...
```

The default for the TABLE_EXISTS_ACTION parameter is SKIP, unless you also specify the parameter CONTENT=DATA_ONLY. If you use CONTENT=DATA_ONLY, then the default for TABLE_EXISTS_ACTION is APPEND.

The TABLE_EXISTS_ACTION parameter takes the following options:

- SKIP (default if not combined with CONTENT=DATA_ONLY)

- APPEND (default if combined with CONTENT=DATA_ONLY)

- REPLACE

- TRUNCATE

The SKIP option tells Data Pump not to process the object if it exists. The APPEND option instructs Data Pump not to delete existing data, but rather, to add data to the table without modifying any existing data. The REPLACE option instructs Data Pump to drop and re-create objects; this parameter is not valid when the CONTENT parameter is used with the DATA_ONLY option. The TRUNCATE parameter tells Data Pump to delete rows from tables via a TRUNCATE statement.

The CONTENT parameter takes the following options:

- ALL (default)

- DATA_ONLY

- METADATA_ONLY

The ALL option instructs Data Pump to load both data and metadata contained in the dump file; this is the default behavior. The DATA_ONLY option tells Data Pump to load only table data into existing tables; no database objects are created. The METADATA_ONLY option only creates objects; no data are loaded.

Renaming a Table

You have the option of renaming a table during import operations. There are many reasons you may want to rename a table when importing it. For instance, you may have a table in the target schema that has the same name as the table you want to import. You can rename a table when importing by using the REMAP_TABLE parameter. This example imports the table from the HEERA user INV table to the HEERA user INVEN table:

```
$ impdp mv_maint/foo directory=dp_dir dumpfile=inv.dmp tables=heera.inv \
remap_table=heera.inv:inven
```

Here is the general syntax for renaming a table:

```
REMAP_TABLE=[schema.]old_tablename[.partition]:new_tablename
```

Note that this syntax does not allow you to rename a table into a different schema. If you are not careful, you may attempt to do the following (thinking that you're moving a table and renaming it in one operation):

```
$ impdp mv_maint/foo directory=dp_dir dumpfile=inv.dmp tables=heera.inv \
remap_table=heera.inv:scott.inven
```

In the prior example, you end up with a table in the HEERA schema named SCOTT. That can be confusing.

Remapping Data

You can apply a PL/SQL function to alter a column value during either an export or import. For example, you may have an auditor who needs to look at the data, and one requirement is that you apply a simple obfuscation function to sensitive columns. The data do not need to be encrypted; they just need to be changed enough that the auditor cannot readily determine the value of the LAST_NAME column in the CUSTOMERS table.

This example first creates a simple package that is used to obfuscate the data:

```
create or replace package obfus is
  function obf(clear_string varchar2) return varchar2;
  function unobf(obs_string varchar2) return varchar2;
end obfus;
/
--
create or replace package body obfus is
  fromstr varchar2(62) := '0123456789ABCDEFGHIJKLMNOPQRSTUVWXYZ' ||
           'abcdefghijklmnopqrstuvwxyz';
  tostr varchar2(62)    := 'defghijklmnopqrstuvwxyzabc3456789012' ||
            'KLMNOPQRSTUVWXYZABCDEFGHIJ';
--
function obf(clear_string varchar2) return varchar2 is
begin
  return translate(clear_string, fromstr, tostr);
end obf;
--
function unobf(obs_string varchar2) return varchar2 is
begin
  return translate(obs_string, tostr, fromstr);
end unobf;
end obfus;
/
```

Now, when you import the data into the database, you apply the obfuscation
function to the LAST_NAME column of the CUSTOMERS table:

```
$ impdp mv_maint/foo directory=dp_dir dumpfile=cust.dmp tables=customers  \
remap_data=customers.last_name:obfus.obf
```

Selecting LAST_NAME from CUSTOMERS shows that it has been imported in an
obfuscated manner:

```
SQL> select last_name from customers;
LAST_NAME
------------------
```

yYZEJ
tOXXSMU
xERX

You can manually apply the package's UNOBF function to see the real values of the column:

```
SQL> select obfus.unobf(last_name) from customers;
OBFUS.UNOBF(LAST_NAME)
--------------------------
Lopuz
Gennick
Kuhn
```

Suppressing a Log File

By default, Data Pump creates a log file when generating an export or an import. If you know that you do not want a log file generated, you can suppress it by specifying the NOLOGFILE parameter. Here is an example:

```
$ expdp mv_maint/foo directory=dp_dir tables=inv nologfile=y
```

If you choose not to create a log file, Data Pump still displays status messages on the output device. In general, I recommend that you create a log file with every Data Pump operation. This gives you an audit trail of your actions.

Using Parallelism

Use the PARALLEL parameter to parallelize a Data Pump job. For instance, if you know you have four CPUs on a box, and you want to set the degree of parallelism to 4, use PARALLEL as follows:

```
$ expdp mv_maint/foo parallel=4 dumpfile=exp.dmp directory=dp_dir full=y
```

To take full advantage of the parallel feature, ensure that you specify multiple files when exporting. The following example creates one file for each thread of parallelism:

```
$ expdp mv_maint/foo parallel=4 dumpfile=exp1.dmp,exp2.dmp,exp3.dmp,exp4.dmp
```

You can also use the %U substitution variable to instruct Data Pump to create dump files automatically to match the degree of parallelism. The %U variable starts at the value 01 and increments as additional dump files are allocated. This example uses the %U variable:

```
$ expdp mv_maint/foo parallel=4 dumpfile=exp%U.dmp
```

Now, say you need to import from the dump files created from an export. You can either individually specify the dump files or, if the dump files were created with the %U variable, use that on import:

```
$ impdp mv_maint/foo parallel=4 dumpfile=exp%U.dmp
```

In the prior example, the import process starts by looking for a file with the name exp01.dmp, then exp02.dmp, and so on.

Tip   Oracle recommends that the degree of parallelism not be set to more than two times the number of CPUs available on the server. Also, a word of caution using parallelism with a RAC environment: make sure you have CLUSTER=N to avoid parallelism across nodes.

You can also modify the degree of parallelism while the job is running. First, attach in the interactive command mode to the job (see the section "Interactive Command Mode," later in this chapter) for which you want to modify the degree of parallelism. Then, use the PARALLEL option. In this example, the job attached to is SYS_IMPORT_TABLE_01:

```
$ impdp mv_maint/foo attach=sys_import_table_01
Import> parallel=6
```

You can check the degree of parallelism via the STATUS command:

```
Import> status
```

Here is some sample output:

```
Job: SYS_IMPORT_TABLE_01
  Operation: IMPORT
  Mode: TABLE
  State: EXECUTING
  Bytes Processed: 0
  Current Parallelism: 6
```

Note   The PARALLEL feature is only available in the Enterprise Edition of Oracle.

Specifying Additional Dump Files

If you run out of space in the primary data pump location, then you can specify additional data pump locations on the fly. Use the ADD_FILE command from the interactive command prompt. Here is the basic syntax for adding additional files:

```
ADD_FILE=[directory_object:]file_name [,...]
```

This example adds another output file to an already existing Data Pump export job:

```
Export> add_file=alt2.dmp
```

You can also specify a separate database directory object:

```
Export> add_file=alt_dir:alt3.dmp
```

Reusing Output File Names

By default, Data Pump does not overwrite an existing dump file. For example, the first time you run this job, it will run fine because there is no dump file named inv.dmp in the directory being used:

```
$ expdp mv_maint/foo directory=dp_dir dumpfile=inv.dmp
```

If you attempt to run the previous command again with the same directory and the same data pump name, this error is thrown:

```
ORA-31641: unable to create dump file "/oradump/inv.dmp"
```

You can either specify a new data pump name for the export job or use the REUSE_ DUMPFILES parameter to direct Data Pump to overwrite an existing dump file; for example,

```
$ expdp mv_maint/foo directory=dp_dir dumpfile=inv.dmp reuse_dumpfiles=y
```

You should now be able to run the Data Pump export regardless of an existing dump file with the same name in the output directory. When you set REUSE_DUMPFILES to a value of y, if Data Pump finds a dump file with the same name, it overwrites the file.

Note   The default value for REUSE_DUMPFILES is N.

Creating a Daily DDL File

Sometimes, in database environments, changes occur to database objects in unexpected ways. You may have a developer who somehow obtains the production user passwords and decides to make a change on the fly, without telling anybody. Or a DBA may decide not to follow the standard release process and make a change to an object while troubleshooting an issue. These scenarios can be frustrating for production-support DBAs. Whenever there is an issue, the first question raised is, "What changed?"

When you use Data Pump, it is fairly simple to create a file that contains all the DDL to re-create every object in your database. You can instruct Data Pump to export or import just the metadata via the CONTENT=METADATA_ONLY option.

For instance, in a production environment, you can set up a daily job to capture this DDL. If there is ever a question about what changed and when, you can go back and compare the DDL in the daily dump files.

Listed next is a simple shell script that first exports the metadata content from the database and then uses Data Pump import to create a DDL file from that export:

```
#!/bin/bash
# source OS variables, see Chapter 2 for details
. /etc/oraset o18c
#
DAY=$(date +%Y_%m_%d)
SID=DWREP
#-----------------------------------------------------
# First create export dump file with metadata only
expdp mv_maint/foo dumpfile=${SID}.${DAY}.dmp content=metadata_only \
directory=dp_dir full=y logfile=${SID}.${DAY}.log
```

```
#-----------------------------------------------------
# Now create DDL file from the export dump file.
impdp mv_maint/foo directory=dp_dir dumpfile=${SID}.${DAY}.dmp \
SQLFILE=${SID}.${DAY}.sql logfile=${SID}.${DAY}.sql.log
#
exit 0
```

This code listing depends on a database directory object being created that points to where you want the daily dump file to be written. You may also want to set up another job that periodically deletes any files older than a certain amount of time.

Compressing Output

When you use Data Pump to create large files, you should consider compressing the output. As of Oracle Database 11g, the COMPRESSION parameter can be one of the following values: ALL, DATA_ONLY, METADATA_ONLY, or NONE. If you specify ALL, then both data and metadata are compressed in the output. This example exports one table and compresses both the data and metadata in the output file:

```
$ expdp dbauser/foo tables=locations directory=datapump \
dumpfile=compress.dmp compression=all
```

Note   The ALL and DATA_ONLY options of the COMPRESS parameter require a license for the Oracle Advanced Compression option.

New with Oracle Database 12c, you can specify a compression algorithm. The choices are BASIC, LOW, MEDIUM, and HIGH. Here is an example of using MEDIUM compression:

```
$ expdp mv_maint/foo dumpfile=full.dmp directory=dp_dir full=y \
compression=all compression_algorithm=MEDIUM
```

Using the COMPRESSION_ALGORITHM parameter can be especially useful if you are running low on disk space or exporting over a network connection (as it reduces the number of bytes that need to be transferred).

> **Note**   The COMPRESSION_ALGORITHM parameter requires a license for the Oracle Advanced Compression option.

Changing Table Compression Characteristics on Import

Starting with Oracle Database 12c, you can change a table's compression characteristics when importing the table. This example changes the compression characteristics for all tables imported in the job to COMPRESS FOR OLTP. Because the command in this example requires quotation marks, it is placed in a parameter file, as shown:

```
userid=mv_maint/foo
dumpfile=inv.dmp
directory=dp_dir
transform=table_compression_clause:"COMPRESS FOR OLTP"
```

Assume that the parameter file is named imp.par. It can now be invoked as follows:

```
$ impdp parfile=imp.par
```

All tables included in the import job are created as COMPRESS FOR OLTP, and the data are compressed as they are loaded.

> **Note**   Table-level compression (for OLTP) requires a license for the Oracle Advanced Compression option.

Encrypting Data

One potential security issue with Data Pump dump files is that anybody with OS access to the output file can search for strings in the file. On Linux/Unix systems, you can do this with the strings command:

```
$ strings inv.dmp | grep -i secret
```

Here is the output for this particular dump file:

```
Secret Data<
top secret data<
corporate secret data<
```

This command allows you to view the contents of the dump file because the data are in regular text and not encrypted. If you require that the data be secured, you can use Data Pump's encryption features.

This example uses the ENCRYPTION parameter to secure all data and metadata in the output:

```
$ expdp mv_maint/foo encryption=all directory=dp_dir dumpfile=inv.dmp
```

For this command to work, your database must have an encryption wallet in place and open. See the Oracle Advanced Security Administrator's Guide, available for download from the Technology Network area of the Oracle web site (http://otn. oracle.com), for more details on how to create and open a wallet.

Note The Data Pump ENCRYPTION parameter requires that you use the Enterprise Edition of Oracle Database and also requires a license for the Oracle Advanced Security option.

The ENCRYPTION parameter takes the following options:

- ALL
- DATA_ONLY
- ENCRYPTED_COLUMNS_ONLY
- METADATA_ONLY
- NONE

The ALL option enables encryption for both data and metadata. The DATA_ONLY option encrypts just the data. The ENCRYPTED_COLUMNS_ONLY option specifies that only columns encrypted in the database are written to the dump file in an encrypted format. The METADATA_ONLY option encrypts just metadata in the export file.

Exporting Views as Tables

Starting with Oracle Database 12c, you can export a view and later import it as a table. You may want to do this if you need to replicate the data contained in a view to a historical reporting database.

Use the `VIEWS_AS_TABLES` parameter to export a view into a table structure. This parameter has the following syntax:

```
VIEWS_AS_TABLES=[schema_name.]view_name[:template_table_name]
```

Here is an example:

```
$ expdp mv_maint/foo directory=dp_dir dumpfile=v.dmp \
views_as_tables=sales_rockies
```

The dump file can now be used to import a table named `SALES_ROCKIES` into a different schema or database.

```
$ impdp mv_maint/foo directory=dp_dir dumpfile=v.dmp
```

If you just want to import the table (which was created from a view during the export), you can do so as follows:

```
$ impdp mv_maint/foo directory=dp_dir dumpfile=v.dmp tables=sales_rockies
```

The table will have the same columns and data types as per the view definition. The table will additionally contain rows of data that match what would have been selected from the view at the time of the export.

Disabling Logging of Redo on Import

Starting with Oracle Database 12c, you can specify that objects be loaded with nologging of redo. This is achieved via the `DISABLE_ARCHIVE_LOGGING` parameter:

```
$ impdp mv_maint/foo directory=dp_dir dumpfile=inv.dmp \
transform=disable_archive_logging:Y
```

While performing the import, the logging attributes for objects are set to `NO`; after the import the logging attributes are set back to their original values. For operations that Data Pump can perform with direct path (such as inserting into a table), this can reduce the amount of redo generated during an import.

Attaching to a Running Job

One powerful feature of Data Pump is that you can attach to a currently running job and view its progress and status. If you have DBA privileges, you can even attach to a job if you are not the owner. You can attach to either an import or an export job via the ATTACH parameter.

Data Pump is not a job that is run in the foreground like the older utility, exp. Data Pump runs in the background, so that if you press Control-C to break the job, the data pump job continues to run and just the command-line interface is interrupted. Attaching the Data Pump job allows you to perform operations on the job.

Before you attach to a job, you must first determine the Data Pump job name (and owner name, if you're not the owner of the job). Run the following SQL query to display currently running jobs:

```
SQL> select owner_name, operation, job_name, state from dba_datapump_jobs;
```

Here is some sample output:

```
OWNER_NAME OPERATION          JOB_NAME              STATE
---------- ------------------ --------------------- ---------------------
MV_MAINT   EXPORT             SYS_EXPORT_SCHEMA_01  EXECUTING
```

In this example the MV_MAINT user can directly attach to the export job, as shown:

```
$ expdp mv_maint/foo attach=sys_export_schema_01
```

If you are not the owner of the job, you attach to the job by specifying the owner name and the job name:

```
$ expdp system/foobar attach=mv_maint.sys_export_schema_01
```

You should now see the Data Pump command-line prompt:

```
Export>
```

Type STATUS to view the status of the currently attached job:

```
Export> status
```

Stopping and Restarting a Job

If you have a currently running Data Pump job that you want to temporarily stop, you can do so by first attaching to the interactive command mode. You may want to stop a job to resolve space issues or performance issues and then, after resolving the issues, restart the job. This example attaches to an import job:

```
$ impdp mv_maint/foo attach=sys_import_table_01
```

Now, stop the job, using the STOP_JOB parameter:

```
Import> stop_job
```

You should see this output:

```
Are you sure you wish to stop this job ([yes]/no):
```

Type YES to proceed with stopping the job. You can also specify that the job be stopped immediately:

```
Import> stop_job=immediate
```

When you stop a job with the IMMEDIATE option, there may be some incomplete tasks associated with the job. To restart a job, attach to interactive command mode, and issue the START_JOB command:

```
Import> start_job
```

If you want to resume logging job output to your terminal, issue the CONTINUE_CLIENT command:

```
Import> continue_client
```

Terminating a Data Pump Job

You can instruct Data Pump to permanently kill an export or import job. First, attach to the job in interactive command mode, and then issue the KILL_JOB command:

```
Import> kill_job
```

You should be prompted with the following output:

```
Are you sure you wish to stop this job ([yes]/no):
```

Type YES to permanently kill the job. Data Pump unceremoniously kills the job and drops the associated status table from the user running the export or import.

Monitoring Data Pump Jobs

When you have long-running Data Pump jobs, you should occasionally check the status of the job to ensure it has not failed, become suspended, and so on. There are several ways to monitor the status of Data Pump jobs:

- Screen output
- Data Pump log file
- Querying data dictionary views
- Database alert log
- Querying the status table
- Interactive command mode status
- Using the process status (ps) OS utility
- Oracle Enterprise Manager

The most obvious way to monitor a job is to view the status that Data Pump displays on the screen as the job is running. If you have disconnected from the command mode, then the status is no longer displayed on your screen. In this situation, you must use another technique to monitor a Data Pump job.

Data Pump Log File

By default, Data Pump generates a log file for every job. When you start a Data Pump job, it's good practice to name a log file that is specific to that job:

```
$ impdp mv_maint/foo directory=dp_dir dumpfile=archive.dmp logfile=archive.log
```

This job creates a file, named `archive.log`, that is placed in the directory referenced in the database object DP. If you do not explicitly name a log file, Data Pump import creates one named `import.log`, and Data Pump export creates one named `export.log`.

Note The log file contains the same information you see displayed interactively on your screen when running a Data Pump job.

Data Dictionary Views

A quick way to determine whether a Data Pump job is running is to check the DBA_DATAPUMP_JOBS view for anything running with a STATE that has an EXECUTING status:

```
select job_name, operation, job_mode, state
from dba_datapump_jobs;
```

Here is some sample output:

```
JOB_NAME                        OPERATION              JOB_MODE    STATE
------------------------------  ---------------------  ----------  ---------------
SYS_IMPORT_TABLE_04             IMPORT                 TABLE       EXECUTING
SYS_IMPORT_FULL_02              IMPORT                 FULL        NOT RUNNING
```

You can also query the DBA_DATAPUMP_SESSIONS view for session information via the following query:

```
select sid, serial#, username, process, program
from v$session s,
     dba_datapump_sessions d
where s.saddr = d.saddr;
```

Here is some sample output, showing that several Data Pump sessions are in use:

```
      SID     SERIAL#  USERNAME    PROCESS     PROGRAM
----------  ----------  ----------  ----------  ------------------------
     1049        6451  STAGING     11306       oracle@xengdb (DM00)
     1058       33126  STAGING     11338       oracle@xengdb (DW01)
     1048       50508  STAGING     11396       oracle@xengdb (DW02)
```

Database Alert Log

If a job is taking much longer than you expected, look in the database alert log for any messages similar to this:

```
statement in resumable session 'SYS_IMPORT_SCHEMA_02.1' was suspended due to
ORA-01652: unable to extend temp segment by 64 in tablespace REG_TBSP_3
```

This message indicates that a Data Pump import job is suspended and is waiting for space to be added to the REG_TBSP_3 tablespace. After you add space to the tablespace, the Data Pump job automatically resumes processing. By default, a Data Pump job waits 2 hours for space to be added.

Note   In addition to writing to the alert log, for each Data Pump job, Oracle creates a trace file in the ADR_HOME/trace directory. This file contains information such as the session ID and when the job started. The trace file is named with the following format: <SID>_dm00_<process_ID>.trc.

Status Table

Every time you start a Data Pump job, a status table is automatically created in the account of the user running the job. For export jobs the table name depends on what type of export job you are running. The table is named with the format SYS_<OPERATION>_<JOB_MODE>_NN, where OPERATION is either EXPORT or IMPORT. JOB_ MODE can be FULL, SCHEMA, TABLE, TABLESPACE, and so on.

Here is an example of querying the status table for particulars about a currently running job:

```
select name, object_name, total_bytes/1024/1024 t_m_bytes
,job_mode
,state ,to_char(last_update, 'dd-mon-yy hh24:mi')
from SYS_EXPORT_TABLE_01
where state='EXECUTING';
```

Interactive Command Mode Status

A quick way to verify that Data Pump is running a job is to attach in interactive command mode and issue a STATUS command; for example,

```
$ impdp mv_maint/foo attach=SYS_IMPORT_TABLE_04
Import> status
```

Here is some sample output:

```
Job: SYS_IMPORT_TABLE_04
  Operation: IMPORT
  Mode: TABLE
  State: EXECUTING
  Bytes Processed: 0
  Current Parallelism: 4
```

You should see a state of EXECUTING, which indicates that the job is actively running. Other items to inspect in the output are the number of objects and bytes processed. Those numbers should increase as the job progresses.

OS Utilities

You can use the ps OS utility to display jobs running on the server. For example, you can search for master and worker processes, as follows:

```
$ ps -ef | egrep 'ora_dm|ora_dw' | grep -v egrep
```

Here is some sample output:

```
oracle 29871   717   5 08:26:39 ?      11:42 ora_dw01_STAGE
oracle 29848   717   0 08:26:33 ?       0:08 ora_dm00_STAGE
oracle 29979   717   0 08:27:09 ?       0:04 ora_dw02_STAGE
```

If you run this command multiple times, you should see the processing time (seventh column) increase for one or more of the current jobs. This is a good indicator that Data Pump is still executing and doing work.

Summary

Data Pump is an extremely powerful and feature-rich tool. If you have not used Data Pump much, then I recommend that you take some time to reread this chapter and work through the examples. This tool greatly simplifies tasks such as moving users and data from one environment to another. You can export and import subsets of users, filter and remap data via SQL and PL/SQL, rename users and tablespaces, compress, encrypt, and parallelize, all with one command. It really is that powerful.

Data Pump provides the features needed to move data between databases without even storing the data on disk for transport. Data can be filtered or remapped to other schemas and tables with the features of Data Pump. The Data Pump jobs are started and can be monitored, paused, or stopped.

Although Data Pump is an excellent tool for moving database objects and data from one environment to another, sometimes you need to transfer large quantities of data to and from OS flat files. You use external tables to achieve this task. This is the topic of the next chapter in this book.

CHAPTER 14

External Tables

Sometimes, DBAs and developers do not grasp the utility of external tables. The Oracle external table feature enables you to perform a few operations:

- Transparently select information from OS files that has delimited or fixed fields into the database.

- Create platform-independent dump files that can be used to transfer data. You can also create these files as compressed and encrypt them for efficient and secure data transportation.

- Allow SQL to be run inline against the file data without creating an external table in the database.

Tip   Comma Separated files (CSV) files are a type of flat files and may be referred to as just flat files.

One common use of an external table is the selection of data from an OS flat file via SQL*Plus. Simply put, external tables allow for reading data in the database from flat files without having to load the data into a table first. This will allow for transformations to be done against the files while loading the needed data into the database. Using the external table can simplify or enhance ETL processes (Extract Transformation and Loading). When using an external table in this mode, you must specify the type of data in the file and how the data are organized. You can select from an external table but are not permitted to modify the contents (no inserts, updates, or deletes).

You can also use an external table feature that enables you to select data from the database and write that information to a binary dump file. The definition of the external table determines what tables and columns will be used to unload data. Using an external table in this mode provides a method for extracting large amounts of data to a platform-independent file that you can later load into a different database.

© Michelle Malcher and Darl Kuhn 2019
M. Malcher and D. Kuhn, *Pro Oracle Database 18c Administration*,
https://doi.org/10.1007/978-1-4842-4424-1_14

All that is required to enable external tables is to first create a database directory object that specifies the location of the OS file. Then, you use the CREATE TABLE... ORGANIZATION EXTERNAL statement to make the database aware of OS files that can be used as sources or targets of data.

This chapter starts by comparing using SQL*Loader—Oracle's traditional data-loading utility—with external tables for the loading of data into the database. Several examples illustrate the flexibility and power of using external tables as a loading and data-transformation tool. The chapter finishes with an external table example of how to unload data into a dump file.

SQL*Loader vs. External Tables

One general use of an external table is to employ SQL to load data from an OS file into a regular database table. This facilitates the loading of large amounts of data from flat files into the database. In older versions of Oracle, this type of loading was performed via SQL*Loader or through custom Pro*C programs.

Almost anything you can do with SQL*Loader, you can achieve with external tables. An important difference is that SQL*Loader loads data into a table, and external tables do not need to do this. External tables are more flexible and intuitive than SQL*Loader. Additionally, you can obtain very good performance when loading data with external tables by using direct path and parallel features.

A quick comparison of how data are loaded into the database via SQL*Loader and external tables highlights the usage. Listed next are the steps that you use to load and transform data with SQL*Loader:

1. Create a parameter file that SQL*Loader uses to interpret the format of the data in the OS file.

2. Create a regular database table into which SQL*Loader will insert records. The data will be staged here until they can be further processed.

3. Run the SQL*Loader sqlldr utility to load data from the OS file into the database table (created in step 2). When loading data, SQL*Loader has some features that allow you to transform data. This step is sometimes frustrating because it can take several trial-and-error runs to correctly map the parameter file to the table and corresponding columns.

4. Create another table that will contain the completely transformed data.

5. Run SQL to extract the data from the staging table (created in step 2), and then transform and insert the data into the production table (created in step 4).

Compare the previous SQL*Loader list to the following steps for loading and transforming data, using external tables:

1. Execute a `CREATE TABLE...ORGANIZATION EXTERNAL` script that maps the structure of the OS file to table columns. After this script is run, you can directly use SQL to query the contents of the OS file.

2. Create a regular table to hold the completely transformed data.

3. Run SQL statements to load and fully transform the data from the external table (created in step 1) into the table created in step 2.

For many shops, SQL*Loader underpins large data-loading operations. It continues to be a good tool for that task. However, you may want to investigate using external tables. External tables have the following advantages:

-   Loading data with external tables is more straightforward and requires fewer steps.

-   The interface for creating and loading from external tables is SQL*Plus. Many DBAs/developers find SQL*Plus more intuitive and powerful than SQL*Loader's parameter file interface.

-   You can view data (via SQL) in an external table before they're loaded into a database table.

-   You can load, transform, and aggregate the data without an intermediate staging table. For large amounts of data, this can be a huge space savings.

The next several sections contain examples of using external tables to read from OS files.

Loading CSV Files into the Database

You can load small or very large CSV flat files into the database, using external tables and SQL. Figure 14-1 shows the architectural components involved with using an external table to view and load data from an OS file. A directory object is required that specifies the location of the OS file. The CREATE TABLE...ORGANIZATION EXTERNAL statement creates a database object that SQL*Plus can use to directly select from the OS file.

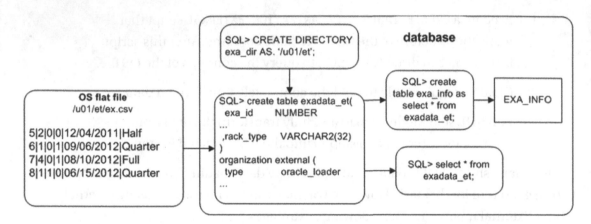

Figure 14-1. *Architectural components of an external table used to read a flat file*

Here are the steps for using an external table to access an OS flat file:

1. Create a database directory object that points to the location of the CSV file.

2. Grant read and write privileges on the directory object to the user creating the external table. (Even though it is easier to use a DBA-privileged account, with various security options, access to the tables and data might not be available to the account. Permissions need to be verified and granted as needed.)

3. Run the CREATE TABLE...ORGANIZATION EXTERNAL statement.

4. Use SQL*Plus to access the contents of the CSV file.

In this example, the flat file is named ex.csv and is located in the /u01/et directory. It contains the following data:

```
5|2|0|0|12/04/2011|Half
6|1|0|1|09/06/2012|Quarter
7|4|0|1|08/10/2012|Full
8|1|1|0|06/15/2012|Quarter
```

Note   Some of the delimited file examples in this chapter are separated by characters other than a comma, such as a pipe (|). The character used depends on the data and the user supplying the flat file. A comma is not always useful as the delimiter, as the data being loaded may contain commas as valid characters within the data. Fixed field length can also be used instead of using a delimiter.

Creating a Directory Object and Granting Access

First, create a directory object that points to the location of the flat file on disk:

```
SQL> create directory exa_dir as '/u01/et';
```

This example uses a database account that has the DBA role granted to it; therefore, you don't need to grant READ and WRITE on the directory object to the user (your account) that is accessing the directory object. If you are not using a DBA account to read from the directory object, then grant these privileges to the account, using this object:

```
SQL> grant read, write on directory exa_dir to reg_user;
```

Creating an External Table

Then, fashion the script that creates the external table that will reference the flat file. The CREATE TABLE...ORGANIZATION EXTERNAL statement provides the database with the following information:

- How to interpret data in the flat file and a mapping of data in file to column definitions in the database

- A DEFAULT DIRECTORY clause that identifies the directory object, which in turn specifies the directory of the flat file on disk

- The LOCATION clause, which identifies the name of the flat file

The next statement creates a database object that looks like a table but that is able to retrieve data directly from the flat file:

```
SQL> create table exadata_et(
  exa_id          NUMBER
 ,machine_count NUMBER
 ,hide_flag       NUMBER
 ,oracle          NUMBER
 ,ship_date       DATE
 ,rack_type       VARCHAR2(32)
)
organization external (
  type                oracle_loader
  default directory exa_dir
  access parameters
  (
    records delimited  by newline
    fields  terminated by '|'
    missing field values are null
    (exa_id
    ,machine_count
    ,hide_flag
    ,oracle
    ,ship_date char date_format date mask "mm/dd/yyyy"
    ,rack_type)
  )
  location ('ex.csv')
)
reject limit unlimited;
```

An external table named EXADATA_ET is created when you execute this script. Now, use SQL*Plus to view the contents of the flat file:

```
SQL> select * from exadata_et;
```

EXA_ID	MACHINE_COUNT	HIDE_FLAG	ORACLE	SHIP_DATE	RACK_TYPE
5	2	0	0	04-DEC-11	Half
6	1	0	1	06-SEP-12	Quarter
7	4	0	1	10-AUG-12	Full
8	1	1	0	15-JUN-12	Quarter

Generating SQL to Create an External Table

If you are currently working with SQL*Loader and want to convert to using external tables, you can use SQL*Loader to generate the SQL required to create the external table, using the EXTERNAL_TABLE option. A small example will help demonstrate this process. Suppose you have the following table DDL:

```
SQL> create table books
(book_id number,
 book_desc varchar2(30));
```

In this situation, you want to load the following data from a CSV file into the BOOKS table. The data are in a file named books.dat and are as follows:

```
1|RMAN Recipes
2|Linux for DBAs
3|SQL Recipes
```

You also have a books.ctl SQL*Loader control file that contains the following data:

```
load data
INFILE 'books.dat'
INTO TABLE books
APPEND
FIELDS TERMINATED BY '|'
(book_id,
 book_desc)
```

You can use SQL*Loader with the EXTERNAL_TABLE=GENERATE_ONLY clause to generate the SQL required to create an external table; for example,

```
$ sqlldr dk/foo control=books.ctl log=books.log external_table=generate_only
```

The prior line of code does not load any data. Rather it creates a file, named books.log, that contains the SQL required to create an external table. Here is a partial listing of the code generated:

```
CREATE TABLE "SYS_SQLLDR_X_EXT_BOOKS"
(
  "BOOK_ID" NUMBER,
  "BOOK_DESC" VARCHAR2(30)
)
ORGANIZATION external
(
  TYPE oracle_loader
  DEFAULT DIRECTORY SYS_SQLLDR_XT_TMPDIR_00000
  ACCESS PARAMETERS
  (
    RECORDS DELIMITED BY NEWLINE CHARACTERSET US7ASCII
    BADFILE 'SYS_SQLLDR_XT_TMPDIR_00000':'books.bad'
    LOGFILE 'books.log_xt'
    READSIZE 1048576
    FIELDS TERMINATED BY "|" LDRTRIM
    REJECT ROWS WITH ALL NULL FIELDS
    (
      "BOOK_ID" CHAR(255)
        TERMINATED BY "|",
      "BOOK_DESC" CHAR(255)
        TERMINATED BY "|"
    )
  )
  location
  (
    'books.dat'
  )
)REJECT LIMIT UNLIMITED;
```

Before you run the prior code, create a directory that points to the location of the books.dat file; for example,

```
SQL> create or replace directory SYS_SQLLDR_XT_TMPDIR_00000
    as '/u01/sqlldr';
```

Now, if you run the SQL code generated by SQL*Loader, you should be able to view the data in the SYS_SQLLDR_X_EXT_BOOKS table:

```
SQL> select * from SYS_SQLLDR_X_EXT_BOOKS;
```

Here is the expected output:

```
BOOK_ID BOOK_DESC
---------- --------------------------------
       1 RMAN Recipes
       2 Linux for DBAs
       3 SQL Recipes
```

This is a powerful technique, especially if you already have existing SQL*Loader control files and want to ensure that you have the correct syntax when converting to external tables.

Viewing External Table Metadata

At this point, you can also view metadata regarding the external table. Query the DBA_EXTERNAL_TABLES view for details:

```
SQL> select
 owner
,table_name
,default_directory_name
,access_parameters
from dba_external_tables;
```

Here is a partial listing of the output:

```
OWNER      TABLE_NAME      DEFAULT_DIRECTORY_NA ACCESS_PARAMETERS
---------- --------------- -------------------- --------------------
SYS        EXADATA_ET      EXA_DIR              records delimited ...
```

Additionally, you can select from the DBA_EXTERNAL_LOCATIONS table for information regarding any flat files referenced in an external table:

```
SQL> select
 owner
,table_name
,location
from dba_external_locations;
```

Here is some sample output:

```
OWNER       TABLE_NAME       LOCATION
----------  ---------------  --------------------
SYS         EXADATA_ET       ex.csv
```

Loading a Regular Table from the External Table

Now, you can load data contained in the external table into a regular database table. When you do this, you can take advantage of Oracle's direct-path loading and parallel features. This example creates a regular database table that will be loaded with data from the external table:

```
SQL> create table exa_info(
  exa_id         NUMBER
 ,machine_count NUMBER
 ,hide_flag     NUMBER
 ,oracle        NUMBER
 ,ship_date     DATE
 ,rack_type     VARCHAR2(32)
) nologging parallel 2;
```

You can direct-path load this regular table (via the APPEND hint) from the contents of the external table, as follows:

```
SQL> insert /*+ APPEND */ into exa_info select * from exadata_et;
```

You can verify that the table was direct-path loaded by attempting to select from it before you commit the data:

```
SQL> select * from exa_info;
```

Here is the expected error:

```
ORA-12838: cannot read/modify an object after modifying it in parallel
```

After you commit the data, you can select from the table:

```
SQL> commit;
SQL> select * from exa_info;
```

Note   Conversion errors may appear when reading or writing data with external tables. Conversion of numbers to dates or to character fields should be recognized, but when receiving these errors, it is possible to explicitly create the conversion in the statements. Using TO_NUMBER, TO_DATE, and TO_CHAR will help to avoid these issues if the conversion is not made implicitly.

The other way to direct-path load a table is to use the CREATE TABLE AS SELECT (CTAS) statement. A CTAS statement automatically attempts to do a direct-path load. In this example, the EXA_INFO table is created and loaded in one statement:

```
SQL> create table exa_info nologging parallel 2 as select * from exadata_et;
```

By using direct-path loading and parallelism, you can achieve loading performance similar to that of SQL*Loader. The advantage of using SQL to create a table from an external table is that you can perform complex data transformations using standard SQL*Plus features when building your regular database table (EXA_INFO, in this example).

Any CTAS statements automatically process with the degree of parallelism that has been defined for the underlying table. However, when you use INSERT AS SELECT statements, you need to enable parallelism for the session:

```
SQL> alter session enable parallel dml;
```

As a last step, you should generate statistics for any table that has been loaded with a large amount of data. Here is an example:

```
SQL> exec dbms_stats.gather_table_stats(-
 ownname=>'SYS',-
 tabname=>'EXA_INFO',-
 estimate_percent => 20, -
 cascade=>true);
```

Performing Advanced Transformations

Oracle provides sophisticated techniques for transforming data. This section details how to use a pipelined function to transform data in an external table. Listed next are the steps for doing this:

1. Create an external table.

2. Create a record type that maps to the columns in the external table.

3. Create a table, based on the record type created in step 2.

4. Create a pipelined function that is used to inspect each row as it is loaded and to transform data, based on business requirements.

5. Use an INSERT statement that selects from the external table and that uses the pipelined function to transform data as they are loaded.

This example uses the same external table and CSV file created in the section, "Loading CSV Files into the Database," earlier in this chapter. Recall that the external table name is EXADATA_ET and that the CSV file name is ex.csv. After you create the external table, then create a record type that maps to the column names in the external table:

```
SQL> create or replace type rec_exa_type is object
(
  exa_id         number
 ,machine_count  number
 ,hide_flag      number
 ,oracle_flag    number
 ,ship_date      date
 ,rack_type      varchar2(32)
);
```

Next, create a table based on the previous record type:

```
SQL> create or replace type table_exa_type is table of rec_exa_type;
```

Oracle PL/SQL allows you to use functions as a row source for SQL operations. This feature is known as pipelining. It lets you use complex transformation logic, combined with the power of SQL*Plus. For this example, you create a pipelined function to transform selected column data as they are loaded. Specifically, this function randomly generates a number for the ORACLE_FLAG column:

```
SQL> create or replace function exa_trans
return table_exa_type pipelined is
begin
for r1 in
   (select rec_exa_type(
      exa_id, machine_count, hide_flag
     ,oracle_flag, ship_date, rack_type
     ) exa_rec
    from exadata_et) loop
  if (r1.exa_rec.hide_flag = 1) then
    r1.exa_rec.oracle_flag := dbms_random.value(low => 1, high => 100);
  end if;
 pipe row (r1.exa_rec);
end loop;
return;
end;
/
```

Now, you can use this function to load data into a regular database table. For reference, here is the CREATE TABLE statement that instantiates the table to be loaded:

```
SQL> create table exa_info(
  exa_id         NUMBER
 ,machine_count NUMBER
 ,hide_flag     NUMBER
 ,oracle_flag   NUMBER
 ,ship_date     DATE
 ,rack_type     VARCHAR2(32)
) nologging parallel 2;
```

Next, use the pipelined function to transform data selected from the external table and insert them into the regular database table, in one step:

```
SQL> insert into exa_info select * from table(exa_trans);
```

Here is the data that are loaded into the EXA_INFO table for this example:

```
SQL> select * from exa_info;
```

Here is some sample output, showing the rows with a random value in the ORACLE_FLAG column:

EXA_ID	MACHINE_COUNT	HIDE_FLAG	ORACLE_FLAG	SHIP_DATE	RACK_TYPE
5	2	1	32	03-JAN-17	Half
6	1	0	0	06-SEP-17	Quarter
7	4	0	0	10-AUG-17	Full
8	1	1	58	15-JUL-17	Quarter

Although the example in this section is simple, you can use the technique to apply any level of transformational logic. This technique allows you to embed the transformation requirements in a pipelined PL/SQL function that modifies data as each row is loaded.

Viewing Text Files from SQL

External tables allow you to use SQL SELECT statements to retrieve information from OS flat files. For example, say you want to report on the contents of the alert log file. First, create a directory object that points to the location of the alert log:

```
SQL> select value from v$diag_info where name = 'Diag Trace';
```

Here is the output for this example:

```
/ora01/app/oracle/diag/rdbms/o18c/o18c/trace
```

Next, create a directory object that points to the diagnostic trace directory:

```
SQL> create directory t_loc as '/ora01/app/oracle/diag/rdbms/o18c/o18c/trace';
```

Now, create an external table that maps to the database alert log OS file. In this example, the database name is o18c, and thus the alert log file name is `alert_o18c.log`:

```
SQL> create table alert_log_file(
  alert_text varchar2(4000))
organization external
( type                 oracle_loader
  default directory t_loc
  access parameters (
    records delimited by newline
    nobadfile
    nologfile
    nodiscardfile
    fields terminated by '#$~=ui$X'
    missing field values are null
    (alert_text)
  )
  location ('alert_o18c.log')
)
reject limit unlimited;
```

You can query the table via SQL queries; for example,

```
SQL> select * from alert_log_file where alert_text like 'ORA-%';
```

This allows you to use SQL to view and report on the contents of the alert log. You may find this a convenient way to provide SQL access to otherwise inaccessible OS files.

The `ACCESS PARAMETERS` clause of an external table's `ORACLE_LOADER` access driver may look familiar if you have previously worked with SQL*Loader. Table 14-1 describes some of the more commonly used access parameters. See the Oracle Database Utilities Guide, which can be freely downloaded from the Technology Network area of the Oracle web site (`http://otn.oracle.com`), for a full list of access parameters.

Table 14-1. *Selected Access Parameters for the ORACLE_LOADER Driver*

Access Parameter	Description
DELIMITED BY	Indicates which character delimits the fields
TERMINATED BY	Indicates how a field is terminated
FIXED	Specifies the size of records having a fixed length
BADFILE	Name of the file that stores records that can't be loaded because of an error
NOBADFILE	Specifies that a file shouldn't be created to hold records that can't be loaded because of errors
LOGFILE	Name of the file in which general messages are recorded when creating an external table
NOLOGFILE	Specifies that no log file should be created
DISCARDFILE	Names the file to which records are written that fail the LOAD WHEN clause
NODISCARDFILE	Specifies that no discard file should be created
SKIP	Skips the specified number of records in the file before loading
PREPROCESSOR	Specifies the user-named program that runs and modifies the contents of the file before Oracle loads the data
MISSING FIELD VALUES ARE NULL	Loads fields that have no data as NULL values

Unloading and Loading Data Using an External Table

External tables may also be used to select data from a regular database table and create a binary dump file. This is known as unloading data. The advantage of this technique is that the dump file is platform independent and can be used to move large amounts of data between servers of different platforms.

You can also encrypt or compress data, or both, when creating the dump file. Doing so provides you with an efficient and secure way of transporting databases between database servers.

Figure 14-2 illustrates the components in using an external table to unload and load data. On the source database (database A), you create a dump file, using an external table that selects data from a table named INV. After it is created, you copy the dump file to a destination server (database B) and subsequently load the file into the database, using an external table. using an external table.

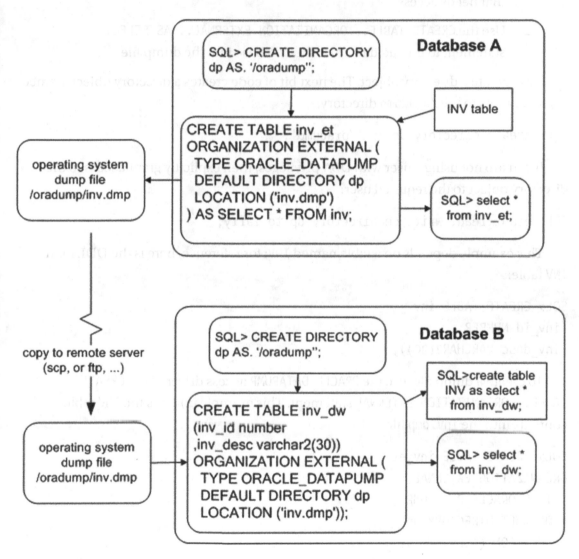

Figure 14-2. *Using external tables to unload and load data*

A small example illustrates the technique of using an external table to unload data. Here are the steps required:

1. Create a directory object that specifies where you want the dump file placed on disk. If you are not using a DBA account, then grant read and write access to the directory object to the database user that needs access.

2. Use the `CREATE TABLE...ORGANIZATION EXTERNAL...AS SELECT` statement to unload data from the database into the dump file.

First, create a directory object. The next bit of code creates a directory object, named DP, that points to the /oradump directory:

```
SQL> create directory dp as '/oradump';
```

If you are not using a user with DBA privileges, then explicitly grant access to the directory object to the required user:

```
SQL> grant read, write on directory dp to larry;
```

This example depends on a table named INV; for reference, here is the DDL for the INV table:

```
SQL> CREATE TABLE inv
(inv_id NUMBER,
 inv_desc VARCHAR2(30));
```

To create a dump file, use the `ORACLE_DATAPUMP` access driver of the `CREATE TABLE...ORGANIZATION EXTERNAL` statement. This example unloads the INV table's contents into the `inv.dmp` file:

```
SQL> CREATE TABLE inv_et
ORGANIZATION EXTERNAL (
  TYPE ORACLE_DATAPUMP
  DEFAULT DIRECTORY dp
  LOCATION ('inv.dmp')
)
AS SELECT * FROM inv;
```

The previous command creates two things:

- An external table named INV_ET, based on the structure and data within the INV table

- A platform-independent dump file named inv.dmp

Now, you can copy the inv.dmp file to a separate database server and base an external table on this dump file. The remote server (to which you copy the dump file) can be a platform different from the server on which you created the file. For example, you can create a dump file on a Windows box, copy to a Unix/Linus server, and select from the dump file via an external table. In this example the external table is named INV_DW:

```
SQL> CREATE TABLE inv_dw
(inv_id number
,inv_desc varchar2(30))
ORGANIZATION EXTERNAL (
  TYPE ORACLE_DATAPUMP
  DEFAULT DIRECTORY dp
  LOCATION ('inv.dmp')
);
```

After it's created, you can access the external table data from SQL*Plus:

```
SQL> select * from inv_dw;
```

You can also create and load data into regular tables, using the dump file:

```
SQL> create table inv as select * from inv_dw;
```

This provides a simple and efficient mechanism for transporting data from one platform to another.

Enabling Parallelism to Reduce Elapsed Time

To maximize the unload performance when you create a dump file via an external table, use the PARALLEL clause. This example creates two dump files, in parallel:

```
SQL> CREATE TABLE inv_et
ORGANIZATION EXTERNAL (
  TYPE ORACLE_DATAPUMP
```

```
  DEFAULT DIRECTORY dp
  LOCATION ('inv1.dmp','inv2.dmp')
)
PARALLEL 2
AS SELECT * FROM inv;
```

To access the data in the dump files, create a different external table that references the two dump files:

```
SQL> CREATE TABLE inv_dw
(inv_id number
,inv_desc varchar2(30))
ORGANIZATION EXTERNAL (
  TYPE ORACLE_DATAPUMP
  DEFAULT DIRECTORY dp
  LOCATION ('inv1.dmp','inv2.dmp')
);
```

You can now use this external table to select data from the dump files:

```
SQL> select * from inv_dw;
```

Compressing a Dump File

You can create a compressed dump file via an external table. For example, use the COMPRESS option of the ACCESS PARAMETERS clause:

```
SQL> CREATE TABLE inv_et
ORGANIZATION EXTERNAL (
  TYPE ORACLE_DATAPUMP
  DEFAULT DIRECTORY dp
  ACCESS PARAMETERS (COMPRESSION ENABLED BASIC)
  LOCATION ('inv1.dmp')
)
AS SELECT * FROM inv;
```

You should see quite good compression ratios when using this option. In my testing, the output dump file was 10 to 20 times smaller when compressed. Your mileage may vary, depending on the type data being compressed.

Starting with Oracle Database 12c, there are four levels of compression: BASIC, LOW, MEDIUM, and HIGH. Before using compression, ensure that the COMPATIBLE initialization parameter is set to 12.0.0 or higher.

Note   Using compression requires the Oracle Enterprise Edition, along with the Advanced Compression option.

Encrypting a Dump File

You can also create an encrypted dump file, using an external table. This example uses the ENCRYPTION option of the ACCESS PARAMETERS clause:

```
SQL> CREATE TABLE inv_et
ORGANIZATION EXTERNAL (
  TYPE ORACLE_DATAPUMP
  DEFAULT DIRECTORY dp
  ACCESS PARAMETERS
    (ENCRYPTION ENABLED)
  LOCATION ('inv1.dmp')
)
AS SELECT * FROM inv;
```

For this example to work, you need to have a security wallet in place and open for your database.

Note   Using encryption requires the Oracle Enterprise Edition along with the Advanced Security option.

ENABLING AN ORACLE WALLET

An Oracle Wallet is the mechanism Oracle uses to enable encryption. The wallet is an OS file that contains encryption keys. The wallet is enabled via the following steps:

1. Modify the SQLNET.ORA file to contain the location of the wallet:

```
ENCRYPTION_WALLET_LOCATION=
 (SOURCE=(METHOD=FILE) (METHOD_DATA=
   (DIRECTORY=/ora01/app/oracle/product/12.1.0.1/db_1/network/admin)))
```

2. Create the wallet file (ewallet.p12) with the ALTER SYSTEM command:

```
SQL> alter system set encryption key identified by foo;
```

3. Enable encryption:

```
SQL> alter system set encryption wallet open identified by foo;
```

See the Oracle Advanced Security Administrator's Guide, which can be freely downloaded from the Technology Network area of the Oracle web site (http://otn.oracle.com), for full details on implementing encryption.

You enable compression and encryption via the ACCESS PARAMETERS clause. Table 14-2 contains a listing of all access parameters available with the ORACLE_DATAPUMP access driver.

Table 14-2. *Parameters of the ORACLE_DATAPUMP Access Driver*

Access Parameter	Description
COMPRESSION	Compresses the dump file; DISABLED is the default value.
ENCRYPTION	Encrypts the dump file; DISABLED is the default value.
NOLOGFILE	Suppresses the generation of a log file
LOGFILE=[directory_object:] logfile_name	Allows you to name a log file
VERSION	Specifies the minimum version of Oracle that can read the dump file

Inline SQL from External Table

With Oracle 18c, it is possible to select directly from the file with the use of EXTERNAL without actually creating an external table in the data dictionary. This allows for external data to be part of a subquery, virtual view, or another transformation type of process.

Here is an example of how this works.

SELECT columns FROM EXTERNAL ((column definitions) TYPE [access_driver_type] external_table_properties [REJECT LIMIT clause])

```
SQL> SELECT first_name, last_name, hiredate, department_name from EXTERNAL(
(first_name varchare2(50),
last_name    varchar2(50),
hiredate           date,
department_name    varchar2(50))
TYPE ORACLE_LOADER
DEFAULT DIRECTORY EXT_DATA
ACCESS PARAMETERS (
RECORDS DELIMITED BY NEWLINE nobadfile, nologfile
fields date_format date mask "mm/dd/yy")
LOCATION ('empbydep.csv') REJECT LIMIT UNLIMITED) empbydep_external
where department='HR';
```

The empbydep_external table is not actually created as an external table, and this data is available to query and specify any of the columns or filter by a different selection in the WHERE CLAUSE. This is also possible with json and useful when accessing data APIs that are provided in the json format. This does not load the data into the table but can be queried and used in several different methods for views, reference data that is available by API to complete data sets in data integrations. Here is the example of the json file:

```
SQL> select * from external ((json_document CLOB)
TYPE ORACLE_LOADER
DEFAULT DIRECTORY EXT_DATA
ACCESS PARAMETERS (
RECORDS DELIMITED BY 0x'0A' FIELDS (json_document CHAR(5000)) )
location ('empbydep.json') REJECT LIMIT UNLIMITED) json_tab;
```

Summary

SQL*Loader is a useful utility for all types of data-loading tasks, and external tables are useful for data transformations in the process of loading or querying the data. Almost anything you can do with SQL*Loader, you can also do with an external table. The external table approach is advantageous because there are fewer moving parts and because the interface is SQL*Plus. Most DBAs and developers find SQL*Plus easier to use than a SQL*Loader control file.

You can easily use an external table to enable SQL*Plus access to OS flat files. You simply have to define the structure of the flat file in your `CREATE TABLE...ORGANIZATION EXTERNAL` statement. After the external table is created, you can select directly from the flat file, as if it were a database table. You can select from an external table, but you cannot insert, update, or delete.

When you create an external table, if required, you can then create regular database tables by using `CREATE TABLE AS SELECT` from the external table or use a view based on the external table for use in other queries. Doing so provides a fast and effective way to load data stored in external OS files.

The external table feature also allows you to select data from a table and write them to a binary dump file. The external table `CREATE TABLE...ORGANIZATION EXTERNAL` statement defines which tables and columns are used to unload the data. A dump file created in this manner is platform independent, meaning you can copy it to a server using a different OS and seamlessly load the data. Additionally, the dump file can be encrypted and compressed for secure and efficient transportation. You can also use parallel features to reduce the amount of time it takes to create the dump file.

External table design allows you to also query data directly from the file. This is also very useful for the json format, which is the format of which many data APIs might be available. Filtering of the data or a simplified way to load data into other tables is extremely useful for data integrations and ETL processes.

The next chapter deals with materialized views. These database objects provide you with a flexible, maintainable, and scalable mechanism for aggregating and replicating data.

CHAPTER 15

Materialized Views

Materialized view (MV) technology was introduced in Oracle Database version 7. This feature was originally called snapshots, and you can still see this nomenclature reflected in some data dictionary structures. An MV allows you to execute an SQL query at a point in time and store the result set in a table (either locally or in a remote database). After the MV is initially populated, you can later rerun the MV query and store the fresh results in the underlying table. There are three main uses for MVs:

- Replicating of data to offload query workloads to separate reporting databases

- Improving performance of queries by periodically computing and storing the results of complex aggregations of data, which lets users query point-in-time results (of the complex aggregations)

- Stopping the query from executing if the query rewrite does not happen.

The MV can be a query based on tables, views, and other MVs. The base tables are often referred to as master tables. When you create an MV, Oracle internally creates a table (with the same name as the MV) as well as an MV object (visible in DBA/ALL/USER_ OBJECTS).

Understanding MVs

Note The SALES table will be used as the basis for the majority of the examples in this chapter.

© Michelle Malcher and Darl Kuhn 2019
M. Malcher and D. Kuhn, *Pro Oracle Database 18c Administration*,
https://doi.org/10.1007/978-1-4842-4424-1_15

A good way of introducing MVs is to walk through how you would manually perform a task if the MV feature were not available. Suppose you have a table that stores sales data:

```
SQL> create table sales(
 sales_id  number
,sales_amt number
,region_id number
,sales_dtt date
,constraint sales_pk primary key(sales_id));
--
SQL> insert into sales values(1,101,10,sysdate-10);
SQL> insert into sales values(2,511,20,sysdate-20);
SQL> insert into sales values(3,11,30,sysdate-30);
SQL> commit;
```

And, you have a query that reports on historical daily sales:

```
SQL> select
sum(sales_amt) sales_amt
,sales_dtt
from sales
group by sales_dtt;
```

You observe from a database performance report that this query is executed thousands of times a day and is consuming a large amount of database resources. The business users use the report to display historical sales information and therefore do not need the query to be re-executed each time they run a report. To reduce the amount of resources the query is consuming, you decide to create a table and populate it as follows:

```
SQL> create table sales_daily as
select
 sum(sales_amt) sales_amt
,sales_dtt
from sales
group by sales_dtt;
```

After the table is created, you put in a daily process to delete from it and completely refresh it:

```
-- Step 1 delete from daily aggregated sales data:
SQL> delete from sales_daily;
--
-- Step 2 repopulate table with a snapshot of aggregated sales table:
SQL> insert into sales_daily
select
 sum(sales_amt) sales_amt
,sales_dtt
from sales
group by sales_dtt;
```

You inform the users that they can have subsecond query results by selecting from SALES_DAILY (instead of running the query that directly selects and aggregates from the master SALES table):

```
SQL> select * from sales_daily;
```

The prior procedure roughly describes an MV complete refresh process. Oracle's MV technology automates and greatly enhances this process. This chapter covers the procedures for implementing both basic and complex MV features. After reading this chapter and working through the examples, you should be able to create MVs to replicate and aggregate data in a wide variety of situations.

Before delving into the details of creating MVs, it is useful to cover basic terminology and helpful data dictionary views related to MVs. The next two sections briefly describe the various MV features and the many data dictionary views that contain MV metadata.

Note This chapter does not cover topics such as multimaster replication and updatable MVs. See the Oracle Advanced Replication Guide, which is available for download from the Technology Network area of the Oracle web site (http:// otn.oracle.com), for more details on those topics.

MV Terminology

A great many terms relate to refreshing MVs. You should be familiar with these terms before delving into how to implement the features. Table 15-1 defines the various terms relevant to MVs.

Table 15-1. *MV Terminology*

Term	Meaning
Materialized view (MV)	Database object used for replicating data and improving query performance
MV SQL statement	SQL query that defines what data are stored in the underlying MV base table
MV underlying table	Database table that has the same name as the MV and that stores the result of the MV SQL query
Master (base) table	Table that an MV references in its FROM clause of the MV SQL statement
Complete refresh	Process in which an MV is deleted from and completely refreshed with an MV SQL statement
Fast refresh	Process during which only DML changes (against base table) that have occurred since the last refresh are applied to an MV
MV log	Database object that tracks DML changes to the MV base table. An MV log is required for fast refreshes. It can be based on the primary key, ROWID, or object ID.
Simple MV	MV based on a simple query that can be fast refreshed
Complex MV	MV based on a complex query that isn't eligible for fast refresh
Build mode	Mode that specifies whether the MV should be immediately populated or deferred
Refresh mode	Mode that specifies whether the MV should be refreshed on demand, on commit, or never
Refresh method	Option that specifies whether the MV refresh should be complete or fast

(continued)

Table 15-1. (*continued*)

Term	Meaning
Query rewrite	Feature that allows the optimizer to choose to use MVs (instead of base tables) to fulfill the requirements of a query (even though the query doesn't directly reference the MVs)
Local MV	MV that resides in the same database as the base table(s)
Remote MV	MV that resides in a database separate from that of the base table(s)
Refresh group	Set of MVs refreshed at the same consistent transactional point

Refer back to Table 15-1 as you read the rest of this chapter. These terms and concepts are explained and expounded on in subsequent sections.

Referencing Useful Views

When you are working with MVs, sometimes it is hard to remember which data dictionary view to query under a particular circumstance. A wide variety of data dictionary views are available. Table 15-2 contains a description of the MV-related data dictionary views. Examples of using these views are shown throughout this chapter where appropriate. These views are invaluable for troubleshooting, diagnosing issues, and understanding your MV environment.

Table 15-2. *MV Data Dictionary View Definitions*

Data Dictionary View	Meaning
DBA/ALL/USER_MVIEWS	Information about MVs, such as owner, base query, last refresh time, and so on
DBA/ALL/USER_MVIEW_REFRESH_TIMES	MV last refresh times, MV names, master table, and master owner
DBA/ALL/USER_REGISTERED_MVIEWS	All registered MVs; helps identify which MVs are using which MV logs
DBA/ALL/USER_MVIEW_LOGS	MV log information

(*continued*)

Table 15-2. (*continued*)

Data Dictionary View	Meaning
DBA/ALL/USER_BASE_TABLE_MVIEWS	Base table names and last refresh dates for tables that have MV logs
DBA/ALL/USER_MVIEW_AGGREGATES	Aggregate functions that appear in SELECT clauses for MVs
DBA/ALL/USER_MVIEW_ANALYSIS	Information about MVs. Oracle recommends that you use DBA/ALL/USER_MVIEWS instead of these views.
DBA/ALL/USER_MVIEW_COMMENTS	Any comments associated with MVs
DBA/ALL/USER_MVIEW_DETAIL_PARTITION	Partition and freshness information
DBA/ALL/USER_MVIEW_DETAIL_SUBPARTITION	Subpartition and freshness information
DBA/ALL/USER_MVIEW_DETAIL_RELATIONS	Local tables and MVs that an MV is dependent on
DBA/ALL/USER_MVIEW_JOINS	Joins between two columns in the WHERE clause of an MV definition
DBA/ALL/USER_MVIEW_KEYS	Columns or expressions in the SELECT clause of an MV definition
DBA/ALL/USER_TUNE_MVIEW	Result of executing the DBMS_ADVISOR. TUNE_MVIEW procedure
V$MVREFRESH	Information about MVs currently being refreshed
DBA/ALL/USER_REFRESH	Details about MV refresh groups
DBA_RGROUP	Information about MV refresh groups
DBA_RCHILD	Children in an MV refresh group

Creating Basic Materialized Views

This section covers how to create an MV. The two most common configurations used are as follows:

- Creating complete refresh MVs that are refreshed on demand

- Creating fast refresh MVs that are refreshed on demand

It is important to understand these basic configurations. They lay the foundation for everything else you do with the MV feature. Therefore, this section starts with these basic configurations. Later, the section covers more advanced configurations.

Creating a Complete Refreshable MV

This section explains how to set up an MV that is periodically completely refreshed, which is about the simplest example possible. Complete refreshes are appropriate for MVs that have base tables in which significant portions of the rows change from one refresh interval to the next. Complete refreshes are also required in situations in which a fast refresh is not possible because of restrictions imposed by Oracle (more on this later in this section; see also the section "Manually Refreshing MVs from SQL *Plus" later in this chapter).

Note   To create an MV, you need both the CREATE MATERIALIZED VIEW system privilege and the CREATE TABLE system privilege. If a user creating MVs doesn't own the base table, then SELECT access on the base table is also required to perform a refresh-on-commit ON COMMIT REFRESH.

The MV example in this section is based on the previously created SALES table. Suppose you wanted to create an MV that reports on daily sales. Use the CREATE MATERIALIZED VIEW...AS SELECT statement to do this. The following statement names the MV, specifies its attributes, and defines the SQL query on which the MV is based:

```
SQL> create materialized view sales_daily_mv
segment creation immediate
refresh
complete
on demand
as
select
 sum(sales_amt) sales_amt
,trunc(sales_dtt) sales_dtt
from sales
group by trunc(sales_dtt);
```

The SEGMENT CREATION IMMEDIATE clause is available with Oracle 11g Release 2 and higher. This clause instructs Oracle to create the segment and allocate an extent when you create the MV. This was the behavior in previous versions of Oracle. If you do not want immediate segment creation, use the SEGMENT CREATION DEFERRED clause. If the newly created MV contains any rows, then segments are created, and extents are allocated, regardless of whether you use SEGMENT CREATION DEFERRED.

Let's look at the USER_MVIEWS data dictionary to verify that the MV was created as expected. Run this query:

```
SQL> select mview_name, refresh_method, refresh_mode
,build_mode, fast_refreshable
from user_mviews
where mview_name = 'SALES_DAILY_MV';
```

Here is the output for this MV:

```
MVIEW_NAME       REFRESH_ REFRES BUILD_MOD FAST_REFRESHABLE
---------------- -------- ------ --------- ------------------
SALES_DAILY_MV   COMPLETE DEMAND IMMEDIATE DIRLOAD_LIMITEDDML
```

It is also informative to inspect the USER_OBJECTS and USER_SEGMENTS views to see what has been created. When you query USER_OBJECTS, note that an MV and table object have been created:

```
SQL> select object_name, object_type
from user_objects
where object_name like 'SALES_DAILY_MV'
order by object_name;
```

Here is the corresponding output:

```
OBJECT_NAME           OBJECT_TYPE
--------------------  -----------------------
SALES_DAILY_MV        MATERIALIZED VIEW
SALES_DAILY_MV        TABLE
```

The MV is a logical container that stores data in a regular database table. Querying the USER_SEGMENTS view shows the base table, its primary key index, and the table that stores data returned by the MV query:

```
SQL> select segment_name, segment_type
from user_segments
where segment_name like '%SALES_DAILY%'
order by segment_name;
```

Here is the output for this example:

```
SEGMENT_NAME                  SEGMENT_TYPE
--------------------------    ------------------
I_SNAP$_SALES_DAILY_MV        INDEX
SALES_DAILY                   TABLE
SALES_DAILY_MV                TABLE
```

In the prior output the I_SNAP$_SALES_DAILY_MV is a unique index associated with the MV that Oracle automatically creates to help improve refresh performance. Recall that the MV feature was originally called snapshots, and so sometimes you will find objects with names derived from the early days of the feature.

Finally, let's look at how to refresh the MV. Here are data contained in the MV:

```
SQL> select sales_amt, to_char(sales_dtt,'dd-mon-yyyy') from sales_daily_mv;
```

Here is the output:

```
SALES_AMT TO_CHAR(SALES_DTT,'D
---------- --------------------/
       101 20-jan-2013
       511 10-jan-2013
        11 31-dec-2012
```

Next, insert some additional data into the base SALES table:

```
SQL> insert into sales values(4,99,200,sysdate);
SQL> insert into sales values(5,127,300,sysdate);
SQL> commit;
```

Now, you attempt to initiate a fast refresh of the MV, using the REFRESH procedure of the DBMS_MVIEW package. This example passes two parameters to the REFRESH procedure: the name and the refresh method. The name is SALES_DAILY_MV, and the parameter is F (for fast):

```
SQL> exec dbms_mview.refresh('SALES_DAILY_MV','F');
```

Because this MV was not created in conjunction with an MV log, a fast refresh is not possible. The following error is thrown:

```
ORA-23413: table "MV_MAINT"."SALES" does not have a materialized view log
```

Instead, a complete refresh is initiated. The parameter passed in is C (for complete):

```
SQL> exec dbms_mview.refresh('SALES_DAILY_MV','C');
```

The output indicates success:

```
PL/SQL procedure successfully completed.
```

Now, when you select from the MV, it returns data showing that more information has been added:

```
SQL> select sales_amt, to_char(sales_dtt,'dd-mon-yyyy') from sales_daily_mv;
```

Here is the output:

```
 SALES_AMT TO_CHAR(SALES_DTT,'D
---------- --------------------
       101 20-jan-2013
       226 30-jan-2013
       511 10-jan-2013
        11 31-dec-2012
```

Figure 15-1 illustrates the architectural components that are new to MVs; pause for a few minutes here, and make sure you understand all the components.

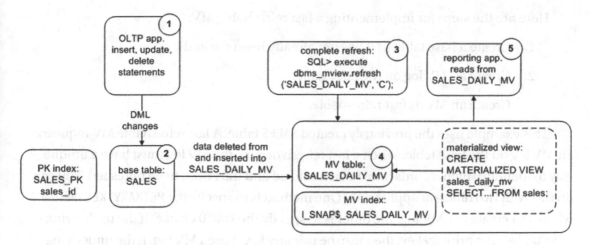

Figure 15-1. *Architectural components of a complete refresh MV*

This diagram illustrates that a complete refresh is not difficult to understand. The numbers show the flow of data in the complete refresh process:

1. Users/applications create transactions.

2. Data are committed in the base table.

3. A complete refresh is manually initiated with the DBMS_MVIEW package.

4. Data in the underlying MV are deleted and completely refreshed with the contents of the base table.

5. Users can query data from the MV, which contains a point-in-time snapshot of the base table's data.

In the next section, a more complicated example shows you how to set up a fast refreshable MV.

Creating a Fast Refreshable MV

When you create a fast refreshable MV, it first populates the MV table with the entire result set of the MV query. After the initial result set is in place, only data modified (in the base table) since the last refresh need to be applied to the MV. In other words, any updates, inserts, or deletes from the master table that have occurred since the last refresh are copied over. This feature is appropriate when you have a small number of changes to a base table over a period of time compared with the total number of rows in the table.

591

Here are the steps for implementing a fast refreshable MV:

1. Create a base table (if it has not already been created).

2. Create an MV log on the base table.

3. Create an MV as fast refreshable.

This example uses the previously created SALES table. A fast refreshable MV requires an MV log on the base table. When a fast refresh occurs, the MV log must have a unique way to identify which records have been modified and thus need to be refreshed. You can do this with two different approaches. One method is to specify the PRIMARY KEY clause when you create the MV log; the other is to specify the ROWID clause. If the underlying base table has a primary key, then use the primary key–based MV log. If the underlying base table has no primary key, then you have to create the MV log, using ROWID. In most cases, you will probably have a primary key defined for every base table. However, the reality is that some systems are poorly designed or have some rare reason for a table not to have a primary key.

In this example, a primary key is defined on the base table, so you create the MV log with the PRIMARY KEY clause:

```
SQL> create materialized view log on sales with primary key;
```

If there was no primary key defined on the base table, this error is thrown when attempting to create the MV log:

```
ORA-12014: table does not contain a primary key constraint
```

If the base table has no primary key, and you do not have the option of adding one, you must specify ROWID when you create the MV log:

```
SQL> create materialized view log on sales with rowid;
```

When you use a primary key-based fast refreshable MV, the primary key column(s) of the base table must be part of the fast refreshable MV SELECT statement;see the section "Creating a Fast Refreshable MV Based on a Complex Query" later in the chapter). For this example, there will be no aggregated columns in the MV. This type of MV would typically be used to replicate data from one environment to another: there will be no aggregated columns in the MV. This type of MV would typically be used to replicate data from one environment to another:

```
SQL> create materialized view sales_rep_mv
segment creation immediate
refresh
  with primary key
  fast
  on demand
as
select
 sales_id
,sales_amt
,trunc(sales_dtt) sales_dtt
from sales;
```

At this point, it is useful to inspect the objects that are associated with the MV. The following query selects from USER_OBJECTS:

```
SQL> select object_name, object_type
from user_objects
where object_name like '%SALES%'
order by object_name;
```

Here are the objects that have been created:

OBJECT_NAME	OBJECT_TYPE
MLOG$_SALES	TABLE
RUPD$_SALES	TABLE
SALES	TABLE
SALES_PK	INDEX
SALES_PK1	INDEX
SALES_REP_MV	TABLE
SALES_REP_MV	MATERIALIZED VIEW

A few objects in the previous output require some explanation:

- `MLOG$_SALES`

- `RUPD$_SALES`

- `SALES_PK1`

First, when an MV log is created, a corresponding table is also created that stores the rows in the base table that changed and how they changed (insert, update, or delete). The MV log table name follows the format `MLOG$_<base table name>`.

A table is also created with the format `RUPD$_<base table name>`Oracle automatically creates this `RUPD$` table when you create a fast refreshable MV, using a primary key. The table is there to support the updatable MV feature. You do not have to worry about this table unless you are dealing with updatable MVs (see the Oracle Advanced Replication Guide for more details on updatable MVs). If you're not using the updatable MV feature, then you can ignore the `RUPD$` table. table.

Furthermore, Oracle creates an index with the format `<base table name>_PK1`. This index is automatically created for primary key-based MVs and is based on the primary key column(s) of the base table. If this is a `ROWID` instead of a primary key, then the index name has the format `I_SNAP$_<table_name>` and is based on the `ROWID`. If you do not explicitly name the primary key index on the base table, then Oracle gives the MV table primary key index a system-generated name, such as `SYS_C008780`.

Now that you understand the underlying architectural components, let's look at the data in the MV:

```
SQL> select sales_amt, to_char(sales_dtt,'dd-mon-yyyy')
from sales_rep_mv
order by 2;
```

Here is the output:

```
SALES_AMT TO_CHAR(SALES_DTT,'D
---------- --------------------
       511 10-jan-2013
       101 20-jan-2013
       127 30-jan-2013
        99 30-jan-2013
        11 31-dec-2012
```

Let's add two records to the base SALES table:

```
SQL> insert into sales values(6,99,20,sysdate-6);
SQL> insert into sales values(7,127,30,sysdate-7);
SQL> commit;
```

At this point, it is instructional to inspect the M$LOG table. You should see two records that identify how the data in the SALES table have changed:

```
SQL> select count(*) from mlog$_sales;
```

There are two records:

```
  COUNT(*)
----------
         2
```

Next, let's refresh the MV. This MV is fast refreshable, so you call the REFRESH procedure of the DBMS_MVIEW package with the F (for fast) parameter:

```
SQL> exec dbms_mview.refresh('SALES_REP_MV','F');
```

A quick inspection of the MV shows two new records:

```
SQL> select sales_amt, to_char(sales_dtt,'dd-mon-yyyy')
from sales_rep_mv
order by 2;
```

Here is some sample output:

```
SALES_AMT TO_CHAR(SALES_DTT,'D
---------- --------------------
       511 10-jan-2013
       101 20-jan-2013
       127 23-jan-2013
        99 24-jan-2013
       127 30-jan-2013
        99 30-jan-2013
        11 31-dec-2012
```

Additionally, the count of the MLOG$ has dropped to zero. After the MV refresh is complete, those records are no longer required:

```
SQL> select count(*) from mlog$_sales;
```

Here is the output:

```
  COUNT(*)
----------
         0
```

You can verify the last method whereby an MV was refreshed by querying the USER_ MVIEWS view:

```
SQL> select mview_name, last_refresh_type, last_refresh_date
from user_mviews
order by 1,3;
```

Here is some sample output:

```
MVIEW_NAME                         LAST_REF LAST_REFR
-------------------------- -------- ---------
SALES_REP_MV                       FAST      30-JAN-13
```

Figure 15-2 illustrates the architectural components that are new to MVs; once again, understanding of these components is important, so pause for a few minutes here.

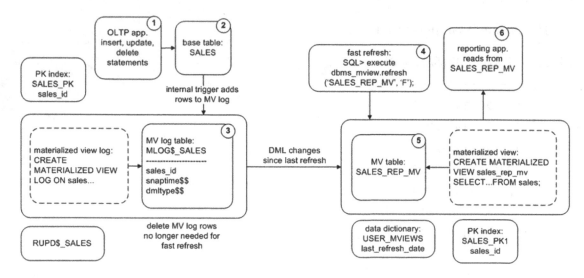

Figure 15-2. *Architectural components of a fast refreshable MV*

The numbers in the diagram describe the flow of data for a fast refreshable MV:

1. Users create transactions.

2. Data are committed in the base table.

3. An internal trigger on the base table populates the MV log table.

4. A fast refresh is initiated via the DBMS_MVIEW package.

5. DML changes that have been created since the last refresh are applied to the MV. Rows no longer needed by the MV are deleted from the MV log.

6. Users can query data from the MV, which contains a point-in-time snapshot of the base table's data.

When you have a good understanding of the architecture of a fast refresh, you will not have difficulty learning advanced MV concepts. If this is the first time looking atMVs, it is important to realize that an MV's data are stored in a regular database table. This will help you understand architecturally what is and is not possible. For the most part, because the MV and MV log are based on tables, most features available with a regular database table can also be applied to the MV table and MV log table. For instance, the following Oracle features are readily applied to MVs:

- Storage and tablespace placement

- Indexing

- Partitioning

- Compression

- Encryption

- Logging

- Parallelism

The next section shows examples of how to create MVs with various features.

Going Beyond the Basics

Numerous MV features are available. Many are related to attributes that you can apply to any table, such as storage, indexing, compression, and encryption. Other features are related to the type of MV created and how it is refreshed. These features are described in the next several sections.

Creating MVs and Specifying Tablespace for MVs and Indexes

Every MV has an underlying table associated with it. Additionally, depending on the type of MV, an index may be automatically created. When you create an MV, you can specify the tablespace and storage characteristics for both the underlying table and index. The next example shows how to specify the tablespace to be used for the MV table and the index:

```
SQL> create materialized view sales_mv
tablespace users
using index tablespace users
refresh with primary key
  fast on demand
as
select sales_id ,sales_amt, sales_dtt
from sales;
```

Creating Indexes on MVs

An MV stores its data in a regular database table. Therefore, you can create indexes on the underlying table (just as you can for any other table). In general, follow the same guidelines for creating an index on an MV table as you would a regular table (see Chapter 8 for more details on creating indexes). Keep in mind that although indexes can significantly improve query performance, overhead is associated with maintaining the index for any inserts, updates, and deletes. Indexes also consume disk space.

Listed next is an example of creating an index based on a column in an MV. The syntax is the same as for creating an index on a regular table:

```
SQL> create index sales_mv_idx1 on sales_mv(sales_dtt) tablespace users;
```

You can display the indexes created for an MV by querying the USER_INDEXES view:

```
SQL> select a.table_name, a.index_name
from user_indexes a
    ,user_mviews  b
where a.table_name = b.mview_name;
```

Note   If you create, using the WITH PRIMARY KEY clause, a simple MV that selects from a base table that has a primary key, Oracle automatically creates an index on the corresponding primary key columns in the MV. If you create, using the WITH ROWID clause, a simple MV that selects from a base table that has a primary key, Oracle automatically creates an index named I_SNAP$_<table_name> on a hidden column named M_ROW$$.

Partitioning MVs

You can partition an MV table like any other table in the database. If you work with large MVs, you may want to consider partitioning to better manage and maintain a large table. Use the PARTITION clause when you create the MV. This example builds an MV that is partitioned by hash on SALES_ID:

```
SQL> create materialized view sales_mv
partition by hash (sales_id)
partitions 4
refresh on demand complete with rowid
as
select sales_id, sales_amt, region_id, sales_dtt
from sales;
```

The result set from the query is stored in a partitioned table. You can view the partition details for this table in USER_TAB_PARTITIONS and USER_PART_TABLES (just like any other partitioned table in your database). See Chapter 12 for more details on partitioning strategies and maintenance.

Compressing an MV

As mentioned earlier, when you create an MV, an underlying table is created to store the data. Because this table is a regular database table, you can implement features such as compression; for example,

```
SQL> create materialized view sales_mv
compress
as
select sales_id, sales_amt
from sales;
```

You can confirm the compression details with the following query:

```
SQL> select table_name, compression, compress_for
from user_tables
where table_name='SALES_MV';
```

Here is the output:

```
TABLE_NAME                           COMPRESS  COMPRESS_FOR
------------------------------------ --------  ------------
SALES_MV                             ENABLED   BASIC
```

> **Note**   Basic table compression does not require an extra license from Oracle, whereas ROW STORE COMPRESS ADVANCED compression (prior to 12c; this was enabled via COMPRESS FOR OLTP) calls for the Advanced Compression option, which does require an extra license from Oracle. See Oracle Database Licensing Information, available from the Technology Network area of the Oracle Web site (http://otn.oracle.com), for details.

Encrypting MV Columns

As mentioned earlier, when you create an MV, an underlying table is created to store the data. Because this table is a regular database table, you can implement features such as encryption of columns; for example,

```
SQL> create materialized view sales_mv
(sales_id    encrypt no salt
,sales_amt   encrypt)
as
select
 sales_id
,sales_amt
from sales;
```

For the previous statement to work, you must create and open a security wallet for your database. This feature requires the Advanced Security option from Oracle. Since the MV is stored in a tablespace, the encryption can also be done at the tablespace level instead of just a column.

You can verify that encryption is in place by describing the MV:

```
SQL> desc sales_mv
Name                              Null?    Type
--------------------------------- -------- ---------------------------
SALES_ID                          NOT NULL NUMBER ENCRYPT
SALES_AMT                                  NUMBER ENCRYPT
```

ENABLING AN ORACLE WALLET

An Oracle Wallet is the mechanism Oracle uses to enable encryption. The wallet is an OS file that contains encryption keys. The wallet is enabled via the following steps:

1. Modify the SQLNET.ORA file to contain the location of the wallet:

```
ENCRYPTION_WALLET_LOCATION=
 (SOURCE=(METHOD=FILE) (METHOD_DATA=
   (DIRECTORY=/ora01/app/oracle/product/18.1.0.1/db_1/network/admin)))
```

2. Create the wallet file (ewallet.p18) with the ALTER SYSTEM command:

```
SQL> alter system set encryption key identified by foo;
```

---

3.   Enable encryption:

```
SQL> alter system set encryption wallet open identified by foo;
```

See the Oracle Advanced Security Administrator's Guide, which can be freely downloaded from the Technology Network area of the Oracle web site (http://otn.oracle.com), for full details on implementing encryption.

Building an MV on a Prebuilt Table

In data warehouse environments, sometimes you need to create a table, populate it with large quantities of data, and then transform it into an MV. Or, you may be replicating a large table and find that it is more efficient to initially populate the remote MV by prebuilding the table with data, using Data Pump. Listed next are the steps for building an MV on a prebuilt table:

1.   Create a table.

2.   Populate it with data.

3.   Create an MV on the table created in step 1.

Here is a simple example to illustrate the process. First, you create a table:

```
SQL> create table sales_mv
(sales_id    number
,sales_amt number);
```

Now, populate the table with data. For instance, in a data warehouse environment, a table can be loaded using Data Pump, SQL*Loader, or external tables.

Finally, run the CREATE MATERIALIZED VIEW...ON PREBUILT TABLE statement to turn the table into an MV. The MV name and the table name must be identical. Additionally, each column in the query must correspond to a column in the table; for example,

```
SQL> create materialized view sales_mv
on prebuilt table
using index tablespace users
as
select sales_id, sales_amt
from sales;
```

Now, the SALES_MV object is an MV. If you attempt to drop the SALES_MV table, the following error is thrown, indicating that SALES_MV is now an MV:

```
SQL> drop table sales_mv;
ORA-12083: must use DROP MATERIALIZED VIEW to drop "MV_MAINT"."SALES_MV"
```

The prebuilt-table feature is useful in data warehouse environments, in which typically there are long periods when a base table is not being actively updated. This gives you time to load a prebuilt table and ensure that its contents are identical to those of the base table. After you create the MV on the prebuilt table, you can fast refresh the MV and keep it in sync with the base table.

If your base table (specified in the SELECT clause of the MV) is continuously being updated, then creating an MV on a prebuilt table may not be a viable option. This is because there is no way to ensure that the prebuilt table will stay in sync with the base table.

Note   For MVs created on prebuilt tables, if you subsequently issue a DROP MATERIALIZED VIEW statement, the underlying table isn't dropped. This has some interesting implications when you need to modify a base table (such as adding a column). See the section "Modifying Base Table DDL and Propagating to MVs," later in this chapter, for details.

Creating an Unpopulated MV

When you create an MV, you have the option of instructing Oracle whether or not to initially populate the MV with data. For example, if it takes several hours to initially build an MV, you may want to first define the MV and then populate it as a separate job.

This example uses the BUILD DEFERRED clause to instruct Oracle not to initially populate the MV with the results of the query:

```
SQL> create materialized view sales_mv
tablespace users
build deferred
refresh complete on demand
as
select sales_id, sales_amt
from sales;
```

At this point, querying the MV results in zero rows returned. At some later point, you can initiate a complete refresh to populate the MV with data.

Creating an MV Refreshed on Commit

You may be required, when data are modified in the master table, to have them immediately copied to an MV. In this scenario, use the ON COMMIT clause when you create the MV. The master table must have an MV log created on it for this technique to work:

```
SQL> create materialized view log on sales with primary key;
```

Next, an MV is created that refreshes on commit:

```
SQL> create materialized view sales_mv
refresh
on commit
as
select sales_id, sales_amt from sales;
```

As data are inserted and committed in the master table, any changes are also available in the MV that would be selected by the MV query.

The ON COMMIT refreshable MV has a few restrictions you need to be aware of:

- The master table and MV must be in the same database.

- You cannot execute a distributed transaction on the base table.

- This approach is not supported with MVs that contain object types or Oracle-supplied types.

Also consider the overhead associated with committing data simultaneously in two places; this can affect the performance of a high-transaction OLTP system. Additionally, if there is any problem with updating the MV, then the base table cannot commit a transaction. For example, if the tablespace in which the MV is created becomes full (and cannot allocate another extent), you see an error such as this when trying to insert into the base table:

```
ORA-12008: error in materialized view refresh path
ORA-01653: unable to extend table MV_MAINT.SALES_MV by 16 in tablespace...
```

For these reasons, you should use this feature only when you are sure it would not affect performance or availability.

Note   You cannot specify that an MV be refreshed with both ON COMMIT and ON DEMAND. In addition, ON COMMIT is not compatible with the START WITH and NEXT clauses of the CREATE MATERIALIZED VIEW statement.

Creating a Never Refreshable MV

You may never want an MV to be refreshed. For example, you may want to guarantee that you have a snapshot of a table at a point in time for auditing purposes. Specify the NEVER REFRESH clause when you create the MV to achieve this:

```
SQL> create materialized view sales_mv
never refresh
as
select sales_id, sales_amt
from sales;
```

If you attempt to refresh a nonrefreshable MV, you receive this error:

```
ORA-23538: cannot explicitly refresh a NEVER REFRESH materialized view
```

You can alter a never refreshable view to be refreshable. Use the ALTER MATERIALIZED VIEW statement to do this:

```
SQL> alter materialized view sales_mv refresh on demand complete;
```

You can verify the refresh mode and method with the following query:

```
SQL> select mview_name, refresh_mode, refresh_method from user_mviews;
```

Creating MVs for Query Rewrite

Query rewrite allows the optimizer to recognize that an MV can be used to fulfill the requirements of a query instead of using the underlying master (base) tables. If you have an environment in which users frequently write their own queries and are unaware of the available MVs, this feature can greatly help with performance. There are three prerequisites for enabling query rewrite:

- Oracle Enterprise Edition

- Setting database initialization parameter QUERY_REWRITE_ENABLED to TRUE

- MV either created or altered with the ENABLE QUERY REWRITE clause

This example creates an MV with query rewrite enabled:

```
SQL> create materialized view sales_daily_mv
segment creation immediate
refresh
complete
on demand
enable query rewrite
as
select
 sum(sales_amt) sales_amt
,trunc(sales_dtt) sales_dtt
from sales
group by trunc(sales_dtt);
```

You can verify that query rewrite is in use by examining a query's explain plan via the autotrace utility:

```
SQL> set autotrace trace explain
```

Now, suppose a user runs the following query, unaware that an MV exists that already aggregates the required data:

```
SQL> select
 sum(sales_amt) sales_amt
,trunc(sales_dtt) sales_dtt
from sales
group by trunc(sales_dtt);
```

Here is a partial listing of autotrace output that verifies that query rewrite is in use:

```
---------------------------------------------------------------------------
| Id  | Operation                  | Name           | Cost (%CPU)| Time     |
---------------------------------------------------------------------------
|   0 | SELECT STATEMENT           |                |     3   (0)| 00:00:01 |
|   1 |   MAT_VIEW REWRITE ACCESS FULL| SALES_DAILY_MV |     3   (0)| 00:00:01 |
---------------------------------------------------------------------------
```

As you can see from the prior output, even though the user selected directly from the SALES table, the optimizer determined that it could more efficiently satisfy the results of the query by accessing the MV.

You can tell if query rewrite is enabled for an MV by selecting the REWRITE_ENABLED column from USER_MVIEWS:

```
SQL> select mview_name, rewrite_enabled, rewrite_capability
from user_mviews
where mview_name = 'SALES_DAILY_MV';
```

If for any reason a query is not using the query rewrite functionality, and you think it should be, use the EXPLAIN_REWRITE procedure of the DBMS_MVIEW package to diagnose issues.

Creating a Fast Refreshable MV Based on a Complex Query

In many situations, when you base an MV on a query that joins multiple tables, it is deemed complex and therefore is available only for a complete refresh. However, in some scenarios, you can create a fast refreshable MV when you reference two tables that are joined together in the MV query.

This section describes how to use the EXPLAIN_MVIEW procedureDBMS_MVIEW to determine whether it is possible to fast refresh a complex query. To help you completely understand the example, this section shows the SQL used to create the base tables. Say you have two base tables, defined as follows:

```
SQL> create table region(
 region_id number
,reg_desc varchar2(30)
```

```
,constraint region_pk primary key(region_id));
--
SQL> create table sales(
 sales_id  number
,sales_amt number
,region_id number
,sales_dtt date
,constraint sales_pk primary key(sales_id)
,constraint sales_fk1 foreign key (region_id) references region(region_
id));
```

Additionally, REGION and SALES have MV logs created on them, as shown:

```
SQL> create materialized view log on region with primary key;
SQL> create materialized view log on sales with primary key;
```

Also, for this example, the base tables have these data inserted into them:

```
SQL> insert into region values(10,'East');
SQL> insert into region values(20,'West');
SQL> insert into region values(30,'South');
SQL> insert into region values(40,'North');
--
SQL> insert into sales values(1,100,10,sysdate);
SQL> insert into sales values(2,200,20,sysdate-20);
SQL> insert into sales values(3,300,30,sysdate-30);
```

Suppose you want to create an MV that joins the REGION and SALES base tables as follows:

```
SQL> create materialized view sales_mv
as
select
 a.sales_id
,b.reg_desc
from sales  a
    ,region b
where a.region_id = b.region_id;
```

Next, let's attempt to fast refresh the MV:

```
SQL> exec dbms_mview.refresh('SALES_MV','F');
```

This error is thrown:

```
ORA-12032: cannot use rowid column from materialized view log...
```

The error indicates that the MV has issues and cannot be fast refreshed. To determine whether this MV can become fast refreshable, use the output of the EXPLAIN_ MVIEW procedure of the DBMS_MVIEW package. This procedure requires that you first create an MV_CAPABILITIES_TABLE. Oracle provides a script to do this. Run this script as the owner of the MV:

```
SQL> @?/rdbms/admin/utlxmv.sql
```

After you create the table, run the EXPLAIN_MVIEW procedure to populate it:

```
SQL> exec dbms_mview.explain_mview(mv=>'SALES_MV',stmt_id=>'100');
```

Now, query MV_CAPABILITIES_TABLE to see what potential issues this MV may have:

```
SQL> select capability_name, possible, msgtxt, related_text
from mv_capabilities_table
where capability_name like 'REFRESH_FAST_AFTER%'
and statement_id = '100'
order by 1;
```

Next is a partial listing of the output. The P (for possible) column contains an N (for no) for every fast refresh possibility:

CAPABILITY_NAME	P	MSGTXT	RELATED_TEXT
REFRESH_FAST_AFTER_INSERT	N	the SELECT list does not have the rowids of all the detail tables	B
REFRESH_FAST_AFTER_INSERT	N	mv log must have ROWID	MV_MAINT.REGION
REFRESH_FAST_AFTER_INSERT	N	mv log must have ROWID	MV_MAINT.SALES

MSGTXT indicates the issues: The MV logs need to be ROWID based, and the ROWID of the tables must appear in the SELECT clause. So, first drop and re-create the MV logs with ROWID (instead of a primary key):

```
SQL> drop materialized view log on region;
SQL> drop materialized view log on sales;
--
SQL> create materialized view log on region with rowid;
SQL> create materialized view log on sales with rowid;
--
SQL> drop materialized view sales_mv;
--
SQL> create materialized view sales_mv
as
select
 a.rowid sales_rowid
,b.rowid region_rowid
,a.sales_id
,b.reg_desc
from sales  a
    ,region b
where a.region_id = b.region_id;
```

Next, reset the MV_CAPABILITIES_TABLE, and repopulate it via the EXPLAIN_MVIEW procedure:

```
SQL> delete from mv_capabilities_table where statement_id=100;
SQL> exec dbms_mview.explain_mview(mv=>'SALES_MV',stmt_id=>'100');
```

The output shows that it is now possible to fast refresh the MV:

```
CAPABILITY_NAME                  P MSGTXT                    RELATED_TEXT
-------------------------------- - -------------------------- ------------
REFRESH_FAST_AFTER_ANY_DML       Y
REFRESH_FAST_AFTER_INSERT        Y
REFRESH_FAST_AFTER_ONETAB_DML    Y
```

Execute the following statement to see if the fast refresh works:

```
SQL> exec dbms_mview.refresh('SALES_MV','F');
PL/SQL procedure successfully completed.
```

The EXPLAIN_MVIEW procedure is a powerful tool that allows you to determine whether a refresh capability is possible and, if it is not possible, why it is not and how to potentially resolve the issue.

Viewing MV DDL

To quickly view the SQL query on which an MV is based, select from the QUERY column of DBA/ALL/USER_MVIEWS. If you are using SQL*Plus, first set the LONG variable to a value large enough to display the entire contents of a LONG column:

```
SQL> set long 5000
SQL> select query from dba_mviews where mview_name=UPPER('&&mview_name');
```

To view the entire DDL required to re-create an MV, use the DBMS_METADATA package (you also need to set the LONG variable to a large value if using SQL*Plus):

```
SQL> select dbms_metadata.get_ddl('MATERIALIZED_VIEW','SALES_MV') from dual;
```

Here is a partial listing of the output for this example:

```
DBMS_METADATA.GET_DDL('MATERIALIZED_VIEW','SALES_MV')
-----------------------------------------------------------------------------

  CREATE MATERIALIZED VIEW "MV_MAINT"."SALES_MV" ("SALES_ROWID", "REGION_ROWID",
 "SALES_ID", "REG_DESC")
  ORGANIZATION HEAP PCTFREE 10 PCTUSED 40 INITRANS 1 MAXTRANS 255
```

This output shows the DDL that Oracle thinks is required to re-create the MV. This is usually the most reliable way to generate the DDL associated with an MV.

Dropping an MV

You may occasionally need to drop an MV. Perhaps a view is no longer being used, or you may need to drop and re- create an MV to change the underlying query on which the MV is based (such as adding a column). Use the DROP MATERIALIZED VIEW command to drop an MV; for example,

```
SQL> drop materialized view sales_mv;
```

When you drop an MV, the MV object, the table object, and any corresponding indexes are also dropped. Dropping an MV doesn't affect any MV logs—an MV log is dependent only on the master table.

You can also specify that the underlying table be preserved. You may want to do this if you are troubleshooting and need to drop the MV definition but keep the MV table and data; for example,

```
SQL> drop materialized view sales_mv preserve table;
```

In this scenario, you can also use the underlying table later as the basis for an MV by building the MV, using the ON PREBUILT TABLE clause.

If the MV was originally built using the ON PREBUILT TABLE clause, then when you drop the MV, the underlying table is not dropped. If you want the underlying table dropped, you must use a DROP TABLE statement:

```
SQL> drop materialized view sales_mv;
SQL> drop table sales_mv;
```

Modifying MVs

The following sections describe common maintenance tasks associated with MVs. Topics covered include how to modify an MV to reflect column changes that have been applied to the base table sometime after the MV was initially created and modifying attributes such as logging and parallelism.

Modifying Base Table DDL and Propagating to MVs

A common task involves adding a column to or dropping a column from a base table (because business requirements have changed). After the column is added to or dropped from the base table, you want those DDL changes to be reflected in any dependent MVs. You have a few options for propagating base table column changes to dependent MVs:

- Drop and re-create the MV with the new column definitions.

- Drop the MV, but preserve the underlying table, modify the MV table, and then re-create the MV (with the new column changes), using the ON PREBUILT TABLE clause.

- If the MV was originally created using the ON PREBUILT TABLE clause, drop the MV object, modify the MV table, and then re-create the MV (with the new column changes), using the ON PREBUILT TABLE clause.

With any of the prior options, you have to drop and recreate the MV so that it incorporates the new column changes in the base table. These approaches are described next.

Re-creating an MV to Reflect Base Table Modifications

Using the previously created SALES table, suppose you have an MV log and an MV, created as shown:

```
SQL> create materialized view log on sales with primary key;
--
SQL> create materialized view sales_mv
refresh with primary key
  fast on demand as
select sales_id ,sales_amt, sales_dtt
from sales;
```

Then, sometime later, a column is added to the base table:

```
SQL> alter table sales add(sales_loc varchar2(30));
```

You want the base table modification to be reflected in the MV. How do you accomplish this task? You know the MV contains an underlying table that stores the results. You decide to modify the underlying MV table directly:

```
SQL> alter table sales_mv add(sales_loc varchar2(30));
```

The alteration is successful. You next refresh the MV but realize that the additional column is not being refreshed. To understand why, recall that an MV is an SQL query that stores its results in an underlying table. Therefore, to modify an MV, you have to change the SQL query that the MV is based on. Because there is no ALTER MATERIALIZED

VIEW ADD/DROP/MODIFY <column> statement, you must do the following to add/delete columns in an MV:

1. Alter the base table.

2. Drop and re-create the MV to reflect the changes in the base table.

```
SQL> drop materialized view sales_mv;
--
SQL> create materialized view sales_mv
refresh with primary key
  complete on demand as
select sales_id, sales_amt, sales_dtt, sales_loc
from sales;
```

This approach may take a long time if large quantities of data are involved. You have downtime for any application that accesses the MV while it is being rebuilt. If you work in a data warehouse environment, then because of the amount of time it takes to refresh the MV completely, you may want to consider not dropping the underlying table. This option is discussed in the next section.

Altering an MV but Preserving the Underlying Table

When you drop an MV, you have the option of preserving the underlying table and its data. You may find this approach advantageous when you are working with large MVs in data warehouse environments. Here are the steps:

1. Alter the base table.

2. Drop the MV, but preserve the underlying table.

3. Modify the underlying table.

4. Re-create the MV, using the ON PREBUILT TABLE clause.

Here is a simple example to illustrate this procedure:

```
SQL> alter table sales add(sales_loc varchar2(30));
```

Drop the MV, but specify that you want to preserve the underlying table:

```
SQL> drop materialized view sales_mv preserve table;
```

Now, modify the underlying table:

```
SQL> alter table sales_mv add(sales_loc varchar2(30));
```

Next, create the MV, using the ON PREBUILT TABLE clause:

```
SQL> create materialized view sales_mv
on prebuilt table
refresh with primary key
  complete on demand as
select sales_id, sales_amt, sales_dtt, sales_loc
from sales;
```

This allows you to redefine the MV without dropping and completely refreshing the data. Be aware that if there is any DML activity against the base table during the MV rebuild operation, those transactions are not reflected in the MV when you attempt to refresh it. In data warehouse environments, you typically have a known schedule for loading base tables and therefore should be able to perform the MV alteration during a maintenance window in which no transactions are occurring in the base table.

Altering an MV Created on a Prebuilt Table

If you originally created an MV using the ON PREBUILT TABLE clause, then you can perform a procedure similar to the one shown in the previous section when preserving the underlying table. Here are the steps for modifying an MV that was created using the ON PREBUILT TABLE clause:

1. Alter the base table.

2. Drop the MV. For MVs built on prebuilt tables, this doesn't drop the underlying table.

3. Alter the prebuilt table.

4. Re-create the MV on the prebuilt table.

Here is a simple example to illustrate this process. First, the base table is altered:

```
SQL> alter table sales add(sales_loc varchar2(30));
```

Then, drop the MV:

```
SQL> drop materialized view sales_mv;
```

For MVs created on prebuilt tables, this does not drop the underlying table—only the MV object. Next, add a column to the prebuilt table:

```
SQL> alter table sales_mv add(sales_loc varchar2(30));
```

Now, you can rebuild the MV, using the prebuilt table with the new column added:

```
SQL> create materialized view sales_mv
on prebuilt table
refresh with primary key
  complete on demand as
select sales_id, sales_amt, sales_dtt, sales_loc
from sales;
```

This process has the advantage of allowing you to modify an MV definition without dropping the underlying table. You have to drop the MV, alter the underlying table, and then re-create the MV with the new definition. If the underlying table contains a large amount of data, this method can prevent unwanted downtime.

As mentioned in the previous section, you need to be aware that if there is any DML activity against the base table during the MV rebuild operation, those transactions aren't reflected in the MV when you attempt to refresh it.

Toggling Redo Logging on an MV

Recall that an MV has an underlying database table. When you refresh an MV, this initiates transactions in the underlying table that result in the generation of redo (just as with a regular database table). In the event of a database failure, you can restore and recover all the transactions associated with an MV.

By default, redo logging is enabled when you create an MV. You have the option of specifying that redo not be logged when an MV is refreshed. To enable nologging, create the MV with the NOLOGGING option:

```
SQL> create materialized view sales_mv
nologging
refresh with primary key
  fast on demand as
select sales_id ,sales_amt, sales_dtt
from sales;
```

You can also alter an existing MV into nologging mode:

```
SQL> alter materialized view sales_mv nologging;
```

If you want to reenable logging, then do as follows:

```
SQL> alter materialized view sales_mv logging;
```

To verify that the MV has been switched to NOLOGGING, query the USER_TABLES view:

```
SQL> select a.table_name, a.logging
from user_tables a
    ,user_mviews b
where a.table_name = b.mview_name;
```

The advantage of enabling nologging is that refreshes take place more quickly. The refresh mechanism uses a direct path insert, which, when combined with NOLOGGING, eliminates most of the redo generation. The big downside is that if a media failure occurs soon after an MV has been refreshed, you cannot recover the data in the MV. In this scenario the first time you attempt to access the MV, you receive an error such as

```
ORA-01578: ORACLE data block corrupted (file # 5, block # 899)
ORA-01110: data file 5: '/u01/dbfile/o12c/users02.dbf'
ORA-26040: Data block was loaded using the NOLOGGING option
```

If you get the previous error, then you will most likely have to rebuild the MV to make the data accessible again. In many environments this may be acceptable. You save on database resources by not generating redo for the MV, but the downside is a longer restore process (in the event of a failure) that requires you to rebuild the MV.

Note   If your database is in force logging mode, then the NOLOGGING clause has no effect. The force logging mode is required in environments using Data Guard.

Altering Parallelism

Sometimes, an MV is created with a high degree of parallelism to improve the performance of the creation process:

```
SQL> create materialized view sales_mv
parallel 4
refresh with primary key
  fast on demand as
select sales_id ,sales_amt, sales_dtt
from sales;
```

After you create the MV, you may not need the same degree of parallelism associated with the underlying table. This is important because queries against the MV will start parallel threads of execution. In other words, you may require parallelism for building the MV quickly but do not want parallelism used when subsequently querying the MV. You can alter an MV's parallelism as follows:

```
SQL> alter materialized view sales_mv parallel 1;
```

You can check on the degree of parallelism by querying USER_TABLES:

```
SQL> select table_name, degree from user_tables where table_name=
upper('&mv_name');
```

Moving an MV

As the operating environment's conditions change, you may need to move an MV from one tablespace to another. In these scenarios, use the ALTER MATERIALIZED VIEW... MOVE TABLESPACE statement. This example moves the table associated with an MV to a different tablespace:

```
SQL> alter materialized view sales_mv move tablespace users;
```

If any indexes are associated with the MV table, the move operation renders them unusable. You can check the status of the indexes as follows:

```
SQL> select a.table_name, a.index_name, a.status
from user_indexes a
    ,user_mviews  b
where a.table_name = b.mview_name;
```

You must rebuild any associated indexes after moving the table; for example,

```
SQL> alter index sales_pk2 rebuild;
```

Managing MV Logs

MV logs are required for fast refreshable MVs. The MV log is a table that stores DML information for a master (base) table. The MV log is created in the same database as the master table with the same user that owns the master table. You need the CREATE TABLE privilege to create an MV log.

The MV log is populated by an Oracle internal trigger (that you have no control over). This internal trigger inserts a row into the MV log after an INSERT, UPDATE, or DELETE on the master table. You can view the internal triggers in use by querying DBA/ALL/USER_INTERNAL_TRIGGERS.

An MV log is associated with only one table, and each master table can have only one MV log defined for it. You can create an MV log on a table or on another MV. Multiple fast refreshable MVs can use one MV log.

After an MV performs a fast refresh, any records in the MV log that are no longer needed are deleted. In the event that multiple MVs are using one MV log, then records are purged from the MV log only once they are not required by any of the fast refreshable MVs.

Table 15-3 defines the terms used with MV logs. These terms are referred to in the following sections in this chapter that relate to MV logs.

Table 15-3. *MV Log Terminology and Features*

Term	Meaning
Materialized view (MV) log	Database object that tracks DML changes to MV base table; required for fast refreshes
Primary key MV log	MV log that uses the base table primary key to track DML changes
ROWID MV log	MV log that uses the base table ROWID to track DML changes
Commit SCN MV log	MV log based on the commit SCN instead of a timestamp
Object ID	Object identifier used to track DML changes
Filter column	Nonprimary key column referenced by an MV subquery; required for some fast refresh scenarios
Join column	Nonprimary key column that defines a join in the subquery WHERE clause; required for some fast refresh scenarios
Sequence	Sequence value required for some fast refresh scenarios
New values	Specifies that old and new values be recorded in the MV log; required for single-table aggregate views to be eligible for fast refresh

Creating an MV Log

Fast refreshable views require an MV log to be created on the master (base) table. Use the CREATE MATERIALIZED VIEW LOG command to create an MV log. This example creates an MV log on the SALES table, specifying that the primary key should be used to identify rows in the MV log:

```
SQL> create materialized view log on sales with primary key;
```

You can also specify storage information, such as the tablespace name:

```
SQL> create materialized view log on sales
pctfree 5
tablespace users
with primary key;
```

When you create an MV log on a table, Oracle creates a table to store the changes since the last refresh to a base table. The name of the MV log table follows this format: MLOG$_<master_table_name>. You can use the SQL*Plus DESCRIBE statement to view the columns of the MV log:

```
SQL> desc mlog$_sales;
Name                                  Null?    Type
----------------------------------    -------- ----------------------------
 SALES_ID                                      NUMBER
 SNAPTIME$$                                     DATE
 DMLTYPE$$                                      VARCHAR2(1)
 OLD_NEW$$                                      VARCHAR2(1)
 CHANGE_VECTOR$$                                RAW(255)
 XID$$                                          NUMBER
```

You can query this underlying MLOG$ table to determine the number of transactions since the last refresh. After each refresh the MV log table is purged. If multiple MVs use the MV log, the log table is not purged until all dependent MVs are refreshed.

If you create the MV log on a table with a primary key, then a RUPD$_<master_table_name> table is also created. This table is used for updatable MVs. If you are not using the updatable MV feature, then this table is never used, and you can ignore it.

When you create an MV log, you can specify that it uses one of the following clauses to uniquely identify rows in the MV log table:

- WITH PRIMARY KEY

- WITH ROWID

- WITH OBJECT ID

If the master table has a primary key, use WITH PRIMARY KEY when you create the MV log. If the master table does not have a primary key, you have to use WITH ROWID to specify that a ROWID value be used to uniquely identify MV log records. You can use WITH OBJECT ID when you create an MV log on an object table.

Oracle uses the SNAPTIME$$ column to determine which records need to be refreshed or purged, or both. You have the option of creating a COMMIT SCN–based MV log (not based on a timestamp). This type of MV log uses the SCN of a transaction to determine which records need to be applied to any dependent MVs. COMMIT SCN–based MV logs are more efficient than timestamp-based MV logs. Use the WITH COMMIT SCN clause to do this:

```
SQL> create materialized view log on sales with commit scn;
```

You can view whether an MV log is SCN based by querying USER_MVIEW_LOGS:

```
SQL> select log_table, commit_scn_based from user_mview_logs;
```

Note   MV logs created with COMMIT SCN do not have a SNAPTIME$$ column.

Indexing MV Log Columns

Sometimes, you may need better performance from your fast refreshing MVs. One way to do this is through indexes on columns of the MV log table. In particular, Oracle uses the SNAPTIME$$ column or the primary key column, or both, when refreshing or purging. Therefore, indexes on these columns can improve performance:

```
SQL> create index mlog$_sales_idx1 on mlog$_sales(snaptime$$);
SQL> create index mlog$_sales_idx2 on mlog$_sales(sales_id);
```

You should not add indexes just because you think it may be a good idea. Only add indexes on the MV log tables when you have known performance issues with fast refreshes. Keep in mind that adding indexes consumes resources in the database. Oracle has to maintain the index for DML operations on the table, and an index uses disk space.

Viewing Space Used by an MV Log

You should consider periodically checking the space consumed by an MV log. If the space consumed is growing (and never shrinking), you may have an issue with an MV not successfully refreshing and hence causing the MV log never to be purged. Here is a query to check the space of MV logs:

```
SQL> select segment_name, tablespace_name
,bytes/1024/1024 meg_bytes, extents
from dba_segments
where segment_name like 'MLOG$%'
order by meg_bytes;
```

Here is some sample output:

```
SEGMENT_NAME          TABLESPACE_NAME                   MEG_BYTES    EXTENTS
--------------------  --------------------------------  ----------  ----------
MLOG$_USERS           MV_DATA                                 1609        3218
MLOG$_ASSET_ATTRS     MV_DATA                               3675.5        7351
```

This output indicates that a couple of MV logs most likely have purging issues. In this situation, there are probably multiple MVs that are using the MV log, and one of them is not refreshing on a daily basis, thus preventing the log from being purged.

You may run into a situation in which an MV log has not been purged for quite some time. This can happen because you have multiple MVs using the same MV log, and one of those MVs is not successfully refreshing anymore. This can happen when a DBA builds a development environment and connects development MVs to the production environment (it should not happen, but it does). At some later point in time, the DBA drops the development database. The production environment still has information regarding the remote development MV and would not purge MV log records because it would need the log data for a fast refreshable MV, which is not the case.

In these scenarios, you should determine which MVs are using the log (see the section "Determining How Many MVs Reference a Central MV Log" later in this chapter), and resolve any issues. After the problem is solved, check the space being used by the log, and see if it can be shrunk (see the next section, "Shrinking the Space in an MV Log"). Monitoring the space of the MVs and MVs logs is important in this case and can provide insight into these issues.

Shrinking the Space in an MV Log

If an MV log does not successfully delete records, it grows large. After you resolve the issue, and the records are deleted from the MV log, you can set the high-water mark for the MV log table to a high value. But, doing so may cause performance issues and also unnecessarily consumes disk space. In this situation, consider shrinking the space used by the MV log.

In this example, MLOG$_SALES had a problem with purging records because of an associated MV not successfully refreshing. This MV log subsequently grew large. The issue was identified and resolved, and now the log's space needs to be reduced. To shrink the space in an MV log, first enable row movement on the appropriate MV log MLOG$ table:

```
SQL> alter table mlog$_sales enable row movement;
```

Next, issue the ALTER MATERIALIZED VIEW LOG ON...SHRINK statement. Note that the table name (after the keyword ON) is that of the master table:

```
SQL> alter materialized view log on sales shrink space;
```

This statement may take a long time, depending on the amount of space it shrinks. After the statement finishes, you can disable row movement:

```
SQL> alter table mlog$_sales disable row movement;
```

You can verify that the space has been reduced by running the query from the prior section, which selects from DBA_SEGMENTS.

Checking the Row Count of an MV Log

As mentioned earlier, sometimes there are problems with an MV's refreshing, and this results in the building up of a large number of rows in the corresponding MV log table. This can happen when multiple MVs are using one MV log, and one of the MVs can't perform a fast refresh. In this situation the MV log continues to grow until the issue is resolved.

One way of detecting whether an MV log isn't being purged is to check the row counts of the MV log tables periodically. The following query uses SQL to generate an SQL that creates a script that checks row counts for MV log tables owned by the currently connected user:

```
SQL> set head off pages 0 lines 132 trimspool on
SQL> spo mvcount_dyn.sql
SQL> select 'select count(*) || ' || "" || ': ' || table_name || ""
|| ' from ' || table_name || ';'
from user_tables
where table_name like 'MLOG%';
SQL> spo off;
```

This script generates a script named mvcount_dyn.sql, containing the SQL statements to select row counts from the MLOG$ tables. When you are inspecting row counts, you must be somewhat familiar with your application and have an idea of what a normal row count is. Here is some sample code generated by the previous script:

```
SQL> select count(*) || ': MLOG$_SALES' from MLOG$_SALES;
SQL> select count(*) || ': MLOG$_REGION' from MLOG$_REGION;
```

Moving an MV Log

You may need to move an MV log because the initial creation script did not specify the correct tablespace. A common scenario is that the tablespace is not specified, and the MV log is placed by default in a tablespace such as USERS. You can verify the tablespace information with this query:

```
SQL> select table_name, tablespace_name
from user_tables
where table_name like 'MLOG%';
```

If any MV log tables need to be relocated, use the ALTER MATERIALIZED VIEW LOG ON <table_name> MOVE statement. Note that you specify the name of the master table (and not the underlying MLOG$ table) on which the MV is created:

```
SQL> alter materialized view log on sales move tablespace users;
```

Also keep in mind that when you move a table, any associated indexes are rendered unusable (because the ROWID of every record in the table has just changed). You can check the status of the indexes as shown:

```
SQL> select a.table_name, a.index_name, a.status
from user_indexes a
   ,user_mview_logs b
where a.table_name = b.log_table;
```

Any unusable indexes must be rebuilt. Here is an example of rebuilding an index:

```
SQL> alter index mlog$_sales_idx2 rebuild;
```

Dropping an MV Log

There are a couple of reasons why you may want to drop an MV log:

- You initially created an MV log, but requirements have changed and you no longer need it.

- The MV log has grown large and is causing performance issues, and you want to drop it to reset the size.

Before you drop an MV log, you can verify the owner, master table, and MV log table with the following query:

```
SQL> select
 log_owner
,master      -- master table
,log_table
from user_mview_logs;
```

Use the DROP MATERIALIZED VIEW LOG ON statement to drop an MV log. You do not need to know the name of the MV log, but you do need to know the name of the master table on which the log was created. This example drops the MV log on the SALES table:

```
SQL> drop materialized view log on sales;
```

You should see the following message if successful:

```
Materialized view log dropped.
```

If you have permissions, and you do not own the table on which the MV log is created, you can specify the schema name when dropping the MV log:

```
SQL> drop materialized view log on <schema>.<table>;
```

If you are cleaning up an environment and want to drop all MV logs associated with a user, then use SQL to generate SQL to accomplish this. The following script creates the SQL required to drop all MV logs owned by the currently connected user:

```
SQL> set lines 132 pages 0 head off trimspool on
SQL> spo drop_dyn.sql
SQL> select 'drop materialized view log on ' || master || ';'
from user_mview_logs;
SQL> spo off;
```

The previous SQL*Plus code creates a script named drop_dyn.sql, containing the SQL statements that can be used to drop all MV logs for a user.

Refreshing MVs

Typically, you refresh MVs at periodic intervals. You can either refresh the MVs manually or automate this task. The following sections cover these related topics:

- Manually refreshing MVs from SQL*Plus

- Automating refreshes, using a shell script and scheduling utility

- Automating refreshes, using the built-in Oracle job scheduler

---

Note If you require that a group of MV be refreshed as a set, see the section "Managing MVs in Groups" later in this chapter.

Manually Refreshing MVs from SQL*Plus

You will need to refresh an MV periodically so as to synchronize it with the base table. To do this, use SQL*Plus to call the REFRESH procedure of the DBMS_MVIEW package. The procedure takes two parameters: the MV name and the refresh method. This example uses the EXEC[UTE] statement to call the procedure. The MV being refreshed is SALES_MV, and the refresh method is F (for fast):

```
SQL> exec dbms_mview.refresh('SALES_MV','F');
```

You can also manually run a refresh from SQL*Plus, using an anonymous block of PL/SQL. This example performs a fast refresh:

```
SQL> begin
    dbms_mview.refresh('SALES_MV','F');
    end;
    /
```

Additionally, you can use a question mark (?) to invoke the force refresh method. This instructs Oracle to perform a fast refresh if possible. If a fast refresh is not possible, then Oracle performs a complete refresh:

```
SQL> exec dbms_mview.refresh('SALES_MV','?');
```

You can also use a C (for complete) to specifically execute the complete refresh method:

```
SQL> exec dbms_mview.refresh('SALES_MV','C');
```

MVS VS. RESULT CACHE

Oracle has a result cache feature that stores the result of a query in memory and makes that result set available to any subsequent identical queries that are issued. If a subsequent identical query is issued, and none of the underlying table data have changed since the original query was issued, Oracle makes the result available to the subsequent query. For databases with relatively static data and many identical queries being issued, using the result cache can significantly improve performance.

How do MVs compare with the result cache? Recall that an MV stores the result of a query in a table and makes that result available to reporting applications. The two features sound similar but differ in a couple of significant ways:

1. The result cache stores results in memory. An MV stores results in a table.

2. The result cache needs to be refreshed any time the underlying data in the tables change. MVs are refreshed on commit or at a periodic interval (such as on a daily basis). Because of this MVs can have stale data if not refreshed.

The result cache can significantly improve performance if you have long-running queries that operate on relatively static data. MVs are better suited for replicating data and storing the results of complex queries that only require new results on a periodic basis (such as daily, weekly, or monthly).

Creating an MV with a Refresh Interval

When you initially create an MV, you have the option of specifying START WITH and NEXT clauses, that instruct Oracle to set up an internal database job (via the DBMS_SCHEDULER package) to initiate the refresh of an MV on a periodic basis. The START WITH parameter specifies the date you want the first refresh of an MV to occur. The NEXT parameter specifies a date expression that Oracle uses to calculate the interval between refreshes. For instance, this MV initially refreshes 1 minute in the future (sysdate+1/1440) and subsequently refreshes on a daily basis (sysdate+1):

```
SQL> create materialized view sales_mv
refresh
with primary key
fast on demand
start with sysdate+1/1440
next sysdate+1
as
select sales_id, sales_amt, sales_dtt
from sales;
```

You can view details of the scheduled job by querying USER_JOBS:

```
SQL> select job, schema_user
,to_char(last_date,'dd-mon-yyyy hh24:mi:ss') last_date
,to_char(next_date,'dd-mon-yyyy hh24:mi:ss') next_date
,interval, broken
from user_jobs;
```

Here is some sample output:

```
JOB  SCHEMA_USE  LAST_DATE            NEXT_DATE            INTERVAL      B
---- ----------  -------------------- -------------------- ------------ -
   1 MV_MAINT    28-jan-2013 14:55:33 29-jan-2013 14:55:33 sysdate+1     N
```

You can also view job information in the USER_REFRESH view:

```
SQL> select rowner, rname, job
,to_char(next_date,'dd-mon-yyyy hh24:mi:ss')
,interval, broken
from user_refresh;
```

Here is some sample output:

```
ROWNER      RNAME        JOB TO_CHAR(NEXT_DATE,'DD-MON-YYY INTERVAL      B
----------  ----------   ---- ------------------------------ ------------ -
MV_MAINT    SALES_MV        1 29-jan-2013 14:55:33                sysdate+1     N
```

When you drop an MV, the associated job is also removed. If you want to remove a job manually, use the REMOVE procedure DBMS_JOB. This example removes job number 1, which was identified from the previous queries:

```
SQL> exec dbms_job.remove(1);
```

Note   You cannot use START WITH or NEXT in conjunction with an MV that refreshes ON COMMIT.

Efficiently Performing a Complete Refresh

When an MV does a complete refresh, the default behavior is to use a DELETE statement to remove all records from the MV table. After the delete is finished, records are selected from the master table and inserted into the MV table. The delete and insert are done as one transaction; this means that anybody selecting from the MV during the complete refresh process sees the data as they existed before the DELETE statement. Anybody accessing the MV immediately after the INSERT commits sees a fresh view of the data.

In some scenarios, you may want to modify this behavior. If a large amount of data are being refreshed, the DELETE statement can take a long time. You have the option of instructing Oracle to perform the removal of data as efficiently as possible via the ATOMIC_REFRESH parameter. When this parameter is set to FALSE, it allows Oracle to use a TRUNCATE statement instead of a DELETE when performing a complete refresh:

```
SQL> exec dbms_mview.refresh('SALES_MV',method=>'C',atomic_refresh=>false);
```

TRUNCATE works faster than DELETE for large data sets because TRUNCATE does not have the overhead of generating redo. The disadvantage of using the TRUNCATE statement is that a user selecting from the MV may see zero rows while the refresh is taking place.

Handling the ORA-12034 Error

When you attempt to perform a fast refresh of an MV, you may sometimes get the ORA-12034 error; for example,

```
SQL> exec dbms_mview.refresh('SALES_MV','F');
```

The statement subsequently throws this error message:

```
ORA-12034: materialized view log on "MV_MAINT"."SALES" younger than last
refresh
```

To resolve this error, try to refresh the MV completely:

```
SQL> exec dbms_mview.refresh('SALES_MV','C');
```

After the complete refresh has finished, you should be able to perform a fast refresh without receiving an error:

```
SQL> exec dbms_mview.refresh('SALES_MV','F');
```

The ORA-12034 error is thrown when Oracle determines that the MV log was created after the last refresh took place in the associated MV. In other words, the MV log is younger than the last refresh of MV. There are several possible causes:

- The MV log was dropped and re-created.

- The MV log was purged.

- The master table was reorganized.

- The master table was truncated.

- The previous refresh failed.

In this situation, the transactions may have been created between the last refresh time of the MV and when the MV log was created. In this scenario, you have to first perform a complete refresh before you can start using the fast refresh mechanism.

Monitoring MV Refreshes

The following sections contain some very handy examples of how to monitor MV refresh jobs. Examples include how to view the last refresh time, determine whether a job is currently executing, establish the progress of a refresh job, and check to see whether MVs have not refreshed within the last day. Scripts such as these are invaluable for troubleshooting and diagnosing refresh problems.

Viewing MVs' Last Refresh Times

When you are troubleshooting issues with MVs, usually the first item to check is the LAST_REFRESH_DATE in DBA/ALL/USER_MVIEWS. Viewing this information allows you to see whether the MVs are refreshing on schedule. Run this query as the owner of the MV to display the last refresh date:

```
SQL> select mview_name
,to_char(last_refresh_date,'dd-mon-yy hh24:mi:ss')
,refresh_mode, refresh_method
from user_mviews;
```

The LAST_REFRESH_DATE column of DBA/ALL/USER_MVIEWS shows the last date and time that an MV successfully finished refreshing. The LAST_REFRESH_DATE is NULL if the MV has never successfully refreshed.

Determining Whether a Refresh Is in Progress

If you need to know what MVs are running, use this query:

```
SQL> select sid, serial#, currmvowner, currmvname from v$mvrefresh;
```

Here is some sample output:

```
    SID    SERIAL# CURRMVOWNER             CURRMVNAME
---------- --------- ----------------------- --------------------
    108       3037 MV_MAINT                SALES_MV
```

Monitoring Real-Time Refresh Progress

If you deal with large MVs, the next query shows you the real-time progress of the refresh operation. When you are troubleshooting issues, this query can be very useful. Run the following script as the user, with privileges on the internal SYS tables:

```
SQL> column "MVIEW BEING REFRESHED" format a25
SQL> column inserts format 9999999
SQL> column updates format 9999999
SQL> column deletes format 9999999
--
SQL> select
  currmvowner_knstmvr || '.' || currmvname_knstmvr "MVIEW BEING REFRESHED",
  decode(reftype_knstmvr, 1, 'FAST', 2, 'COMPLETE', 'UNKNOWN') reftype,
  decode(groupstate_knstmvr, 1, 'SETUP', 2, 'INSTANTIATE',
     3, 'WRAPUP', 'UNKNOWN') STATE,
  total_inserts_knstmvr inserts,
  total_updates_knstmvr updates,
  total_deletes_knstmvr deletes
from x$knstmvr x
where type_knst = 6
and exists (select 1
            from v$session s
            where s.sid=x.sid_knst
            and s.serial#=x.serial_knst);
```

When an MV first starts refreshing, you see this output:

MVIEW BEING REFRESHED	REFTYPE	STATE	INSERTS	UPDATES	DELETES
MV_MAINT.SALES_MV	UNKNOWN	SETUP	0	0	0

After a few seconds the MV reaches the INSTANTIATE state:

| MV_MAINT.SALES_MV | FAST | INSTANTIATE | 0 | 0 | 0 |

As the MV refreshes, the INSERTS, UPDATES, and DELETES columns are updated appropriately:

| MV_MAINT.SALES_MV | FAST | INSTANTIATE | 860 | 274 | 0 |

When the MV is almost finished refreshing, it reaches the WRAPUP state:

```
MV_MAINT.SALES_MV                FAST      WRAPUP              5284        1518           0
```

After the MV has completed refreshing, the query returns no rows:

```
no rows selected
```

As you can imagine, this query can be quite useful for troubleshooting and diagnosing MV refresh issues.

Checking Whether MVs Are Refreshing Within a Time Period

When you are dealing with MVs, it is nice to have an automated way of determining whether refreshes are occurring. Use the following shell script to detect which MVs have not refreshed within the last day and then send an e-mail if any are detected:

```
#!/bin/bash
# Source oracle OS variables, see Chapter 2 for details
. /etc/oraset $1
#
crit_var=$(sqlplus -s <<EOF
mv_maint/foo
SET HEAD OFF FEED OFF
SELECT count(*) FROM user_mviews
WHERE sysdate-last_refresh_date > 1;
EOF)
#
if [ $crit_var -ne 0 ]; then
  echo $crit_var
  echo "mv_ref refresh problem with $1" | mailx -s "mv_ref problem" \
dkuhn@gmail.com
else
  echo $crit_var
  echo "MVs ok"
fi
#
exit 0
```

This script takes the output of the SQL*Plus statement and returns it to the shell crit_var variable. If any MVs for the REP_MV user haven't refreshed within the last day, then the crit_var variable has a nonzero value. If crit_var isn't equal to zero, then an e-mail is sent, indicating that there is an issue.

Creating Remote MV Refreshes

You can create MVs that select from remote tables, MVs, or views, or a combination of these. Doing so allows you to quickly and efficiently replicate data. The setup for basing MVs on remote objects is as follows:

1. Ensure that Oracle Net connectivity exists from the replicated database environment to the database with the master tables. If you do not have this connectivity, you can't replicate using MVs.

2. Obtain access to a user account in the remote database that has access to the remote tables, MVs, or views that you want to replicate.

3. For fast refreshes, create an MV log on the master (base) table. You only need to do this if you intend to perform fast refreshes.

4. Create a database link in the replicated database environment that points to the master database.

5. Create MVs in the replicated database environment that access remote master objects via the database link created in step 4.

Here is a simple example. First, ensure that you can establish Oracle Net connectivity from the replicated environment to the master database. You can verify connectivity and ensure that you can log in to the master database by connecting via SQL*Plus from the replicated database environment to the remote master. From the command prompt on the database that will contain the MVs, attempt to connect to the user REP_MV in the master database named ENGDEV on the XENGDB server:

```
$ sqlplus rep_mv/foo@'xengdb:1522/engdev'
```

When you are connected to the remote master database, you have access to the tables that you base the MV on. In this example the name of the remote master table is SALES:

```
SQL> select count(*) from sales;
```

CHAPTER 15   MATERIALIZED VIEWS

Next, create a database link in the database that will contain the MVs. The database link points to the user in the remote master database:

```
SQL> create database link engdev
connect to rep_mv identified by foo
using 'xengdb:1522/engdev';
```

Now, create an MV that accesses the master SALES table:

```
SQL> create materialized view sales_mv
refresh complete on demand
as
select
 sales_id
,sales_amt
from sales@engdev;
```

You access the remote database by appending the @<database_link_name> to the table name. This instructs Oracle to select from the remote table. The remote table's location is defined in the CREATE DATABASE LINK statement.

Understanding Remote-Refresh Architectures

You can use numerous configurations with remotely refreshed MVs. This section details three common scenarios; you can build on them to meet most remote-replication needs.

Figure 15-3 shows a common configuration using MV logs on the master OLTP database. The remote database uses MV logs to enable fast refreshes. This configuration is typically used when you cannot report directly from an OLTP database because of concern that the reporting activity will greatly hamper production performance. This architecture is also useful when you have users on the other side of the planet, and you want to replicate data to a database that is physically closer to them so that they have acceptable reporting performance.

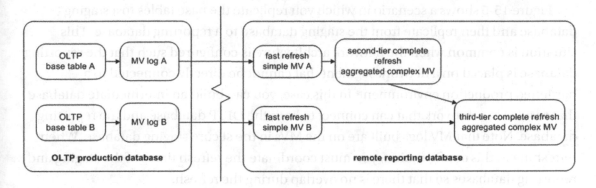

Figure 15-3. *Remote refresh, using MV logs at a master site*

Figure 15-4 illustrates a scenario in which you are not allowed to create MV logs on the master base tables. This may happen because another team or organization owns the master (base) database, and the owners are unwilling to let you create MV logs in the master environment. In this case, you have to use complete MV refreshes to the remote reporting database. This architecture is also appropriate when a large percentage of the base table records are modified each day. In this situation, a complete refresh may be more efficient than a fast refresh (because you are replicating most of the data, not just a small subset).

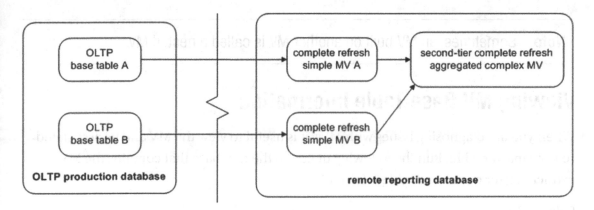

Figure 15-4. *Remote refresh, using complete MV refreshes*

Figure 15-5 shows a scenario in which you replicate the base tables to a staging database and then replicate from the staging database to a reporting database. This situation is common when the network architecture is configured such that the reporting database is placed on a network segment that cannot be directly connected to a hardened production environment. In this case, you can build an intermediate database that resides in a network that can connect to both the OLTP database and the reporting database. Note that MV logs built are on the MVs in the secure staging database. When refreshing in this configuration, you must coordinate the refresh times of the staging and reporting databases so that there is no overlap during the refresh.

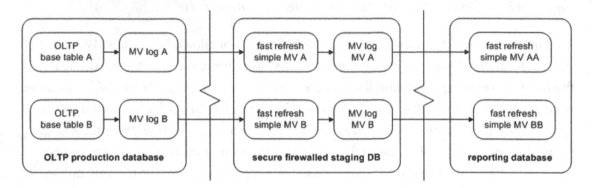

Figure 15-5.   *Two-hop remote fast MV refresh*

Note   Sometimes, an MV built on another MV is called a nested MV.

Viewing MV Base Table Information

When you are diagnosing issues with MVs, it is useful to view the MV and its associated remote master table. Run the following query on the database that contains the MV to extract master owner and table information:

```
SQL> select
 owner         mv_owner
,name          mv_name
,master_owner  mast_owner
,master        mast_table
from dba_mview_refresh_times
order by 1,2;
```

The previous query reports on each MV and the master table it is based on. The base table can be local or remote.

Determining How Many MVs Reference a Central MV Log

Say you have one master table with an MV log. Additionally, more than one remote MV uses the central master MV log. Figure 15-6 illustrates this configuration.

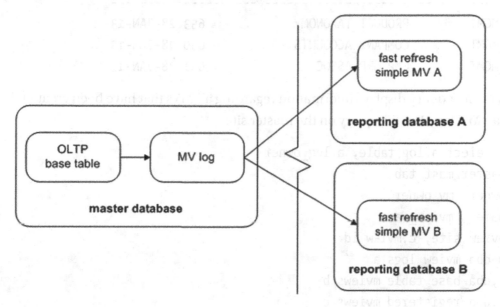

Figure 15-6. *Multiple remote MVs using the same centralized MV log*

In this situation, Oracle keeps records in the MV log until all MVs have refreshed. For example, suppose MV A has a LAST_REFRESH_DATE of July 1, 2013, and MV B has a LAST_REFRESH_DATE of September 1, 2013. Then, MV A refreshes on October 1, 2013. The master log only purges records older than September 1, 2013 (because the more recent log records are still needed by MV B).

If an MV was dropped and unable to unregister itself from a master MV log table, then records grow indefinitely in the master MV log table. To resolve this issue, you need information regarding which MVs are tied to which MV logs. This query displays the master table owner information and the SNAPID (MV ID) of all dependent MVs:

```
SQL> select mowner
,master base_table
,snapid, snaptime
from sys.slog$;
```

Here is some sample output that shows two MVs connected to one MV log:

```
MOWNER              BASE_TABLE              SNAPID SNAPTIME
---------------     --------------------    ---------- ---------
INV_MGMT            PRODUCT_TAXONOMY           653 28-JAN-13
INV_MGMT            COMPANY_ACCOUNTS           650 28-JAN-13
INV_MGMT            CMP_GRP_ASSOC              651 28-JAN-13
```

The next query displays information regarding all MVs that have been created that tie into an MV log. Run this query on the master site:

```
SQL> select a.log_table, a.log_owner
,b.master mast_tab
,c.owner  mv_owner
,c.name   mview_name
,c.mview_site, c.mview_id
from dba_mview_logs a
    ,dba_base_table_mviews b
    ,dba_registered_mviews c
where b.mview_id = c.mview_id
and    b.owner   = a.log_owner
and    b.master  = a.master
order by a.log_table;
```

Here is some sample output:

```
LOG_TABLE               LOG_OWNE   MAST_TAB        MV_OWN   MVIEW_NAME
-------------------     --------   -------------   ------   ----------------
MVIEW_S     MVIEW_ID
-------     -------
MLOG$_CMP_GRP_ASSOC     INV_MGMT   CMP_GRP_ASSOC   REP_MV   CMP_GRP_ASSOC_MV
DWREP       651
MLOG$_CMP_GRP_ASSOC     INV_MGMT   CMP_GRP_ASSOC   TSTDEV   CMP_GRP_ASSOC_MV
ENGDEV      541
```

When you drop a remote MV, it should unregister from the master database. However, this does not always happen. A remote database may get wiped out (e.g., a short-term development database), and the MV does not get a chance to unregister itself (via the DROP MATERIALIZED VIEW statement). In this situation the MV log is unaware that a dependent MV is no longer available and therefore keeps records indefinitely.

To purge unwanted MV information from the database that contains the MV log, execute the PURGE_MVIEW_FROM_LOG procedure of DBMS_MVIEW. This example passes in the ID of the MV to be purged:

```
SQL> exec dbms_mview.purge_mview_from_log(541);
```

This statement should update the data dictionary and remove information from the internal table SLOG$ and DBA_REGISTERED_MVIEWS. If the MV being purged is the oldest MV associated with the MV log table, the associated old records are also deleted from the MV log.

If a remote MV is no longer available but is still registered with the MV log table, you can manually unregister it at the master site. Use the UNREGISTER_MVIEW procedure of the DBMS_MVIEW package to unregister a remote MV. To do this, you need to know the remote MV owner, MV name, and MV site (available from the output of the previous query in this section):

```
SQL> exec dbms_mview.unregister_mview('TSTDEV','CMP_GRP_ASSOC_MV','ENGDEV');
```

If successful, the prior operation removes a record from DBA_REGISTERED_MVIEWS.

Managing MVs in Groups

An MV group is a useful feature that enables you to refresh a set of MVs at a consistent transactional point in time. If you refresh MVs based on master tables that have parent–child relationships, then you should most likely use a refresh group. This method guarantees that you would not have any orphaned child records in your set of refreshed MVs. The following sections describe how to create and maintain MV refresh groups.

Note   You use the DBMS_REFRESH package to accomplish most of the tasks involved in managing MV refresh groups. This package is fully documented in the Oracle Advanced Replication Management API Reference Guide, which is available for download from the Technology Network area of the Oracle Web site (http:// otn.oracle.com).

Creating an MV Group

You use the MAKE procedure of the DBMS_REFRESH package to create an MV group. When you create an MV group, you must specify a name, a comma-separated list of MVs in the group, the next date to refresh, and the interval used to calculate the next refresh time. Here is an example of a group that consists of two MVs:

```
SQL> begin
  dbms_refresh.make(
    name       => 'SALES_GROUP'
    ,list      => 'SALES_MV, SALES_DAILY_MV'
    ,next_date => sysdate-100
    ,interval  => 'sysdate+1'
);
end;
/
```

When you create an MV group, Oracle automatically creates a database job to manage the refresh of the group. You can view the details of an MV group by querying from DBA/ALL/USER_REFRESH:

```
SQL> select rname, job, next_date, interval from user_refresh;
```

Here is some sample output:

```
RNAME             JOB   NEXT_DATE            INTERVAL
---------------   ----  -------------------  --------------
SALES_GROUP        3    20-OCT-12            sysdate+1
```

Altering an MV Refresh Group

You can alter characteristics of a refresh group, such as the refresh date or interval. If you rely on a database job for your refresh mechanism, then you may occasionally need to tweak your refresh characteristics. Use the CHANGE function of the DBMS_REFRESH package to achieve this. The following example changes the INTERVAL calculation:

```
SQL> exec dbms_refresh.change(name=>'SALES_GROUP',interval=>'SYSDATE+2');
```

Again, you need to change refresh intervals only if you are using the internal database job to initiate the materialized group refresh. You can verify the details of a refresh group's interval and job information with this query:

```
SQL> select a.job, a.broken, b.rowner, b.rname, b.interval
from dba_jobs    a
   ,dba_refresh b
where a.job = b.job
order by a.job;
```

Here is the output for this example:

```
JOB  B ROWNER     RNAME            INTERVAL
---- - ---------- ---------------- ----------------
   3 N MV_MAINT   SALES_GROUP      SYSDATE+2
```

Refreshing an MV Group

After you have created a group, you can manually refresh it, using the REFRESH function of the DBMS_REFRESH package. This example refreshes the group that you previously created:

```
SQL> exec dbms_refresh.refresh('SALES_GROUP');
```

If you inspect the LAST_REFRESH_DATE column of USER_MVIEWS, you will note that all MVs in the group have the same refresh time. This is the expected behavior because the MVs in the group are all refreshed at a consistent transactional point in time.

DBMS_MVIEW vs. DBMS_REFRESH

You may have noted that you can use the DBMS_MVIEW package to refresh a group of MVs. For instance, you can refresh a set of MVs in a list as follows, using DBMS_MVIEW:

```
SQL> exec dbms_mview.refresh(list=>'SALES_MV,SALES_DAILY_MV');
```

This method refreshes each MV in the list in a single transaction. It is the equivalent of using an MV group. However, when you use DBMS_MVIEW, you have the option of setting the ATOMIC_REFRESH parameter to TRUE (default) or FALSE. For example, here the ATOMIC_REFRESH parameter is set to FALSE:

```
SQL> exec dbms_mview.refresh(list=>'SALES_MV,SALES_DAILY_MV',atomic_
refresh=>false);
```

This setting instructs DBMS_MVIEW to refresh each MV in the list as a separate transaction. The previous line of code is equivalent to the following two lines:

```
SQL> exec dbms_mview.refresh(list=>'SALES_MV', atomic_refresh=>false);
SQL> exec dbms_mview.refresh(list=>'SALES_DAILY_MV', atomic_
refresh=>false);
```

Compare that with the behavior of DBMS_REFRESH, which is the package you should use to set up and maintain an MV group. The DBMS_REFRESH package always refreshes a group of MVs as a consistent transaction.

If you always need a set of MVs to be refreshed as a transactionally consistent group, use DBMS_REFRESH. If you need some flexibility as to whether a list of MVs is refreshed as a consistent transaction (or not), use DBMS_MVIEW.

Determining MVs in a Group

When you are investigating issues with an MV refresh group, a good starting point is to display which MVs the group contains. Query the data dictionary views DBA_RGROUP and DBA_RCHILD, and see the MVs in a refresh group:

```
SQL> select a.owner
 ,a.name mv_group
 ,b.name mv_name
from dba_rgroup a
    ,dba_rchild b
where a.refgroup = b.refgroup
and    a.owner    = b.owner
order by a.owner, a.name, b.name;
```

Here is a snippet of the output:

```
OWNER       MV_GROUP             MV_NAME
----------  -------------------- --------------------
MV_MAINT    SALES_GROUP          SALES_DAILY_MV
MV_MAINT    SALES_GROUP          SALES_MV
```

In the DBA_RGROUP view, the NAME column represents the name of the refresh group. The DBA_RCHILD view contains the name of each MV in the refresh group.

Adding an MV to a Refresh Group

As your business requirements change, you occasionally need to add an MV to a group. Use the ADD procedure of the DBMS_REFRESH package to accomplish this task:

```
SQL> exec dbms_refresh.add(name=>'SALES_GROUP',list=>'PRODUCTS_MV,USERS_MV');
```

You must specify a name and provide a comma-separated list of the MV names to add. The newly added MVs are refreshed the next time the group is refreshed.

The other way to add an MV to a group is to drop the group and re-create it with the new MV. However, it is usually preferable to add an MV.

Removing MVs from a Refresh Group

Sometimes, you need to remove an MV from a group. To do this, use the SUBTRACT function of the DBMS_REFRESH package. This example removes one MV from a group:

```
SQL> exec dbms_refresh.subtract(name=>'SALES_GROUP',list=>'SALES_MV');
```

You have to specify the name of the MV group and provide a comma-separated list containing the names of the MVs you want to remove.

The other way to remove an MV from a group is to drop the group and re-create it without the unwanted MV(s). However, it is usually preferable to remove an MV.

Dropping an MV Refresh Group

If you need to drop an MV refresh group, use the DESTROY procedure of the DBMS_REFRESH package. This example drops the MV group named SALES_GROUP:

```
SQL> exec dbms_refresh.destroy('SALES_GROUP');
```

This method only drops the MV refresh-group object—it does not drop any of the actual MVs. If you need to also drop the MVs, use the DROP MATERIALIZED VIEW statement.

Summary

Sometimes, the term *materialized view* confuses people who are new to the technology. Perhaps Oracle should have named this feature "periodically purge and repopulate a table that contains the results of a query," but that is probably too long a phrase. Regardless, when you understand the power of this tool, you can use it to replicate and aggregate large amounts of data. You can greatly improve the performance of queries by periodically computing and storing the results of complex aggregations of data.

MVs can be fast refreshable, which means that they copy over only changes from the master table that have occurred since the last refresh. To use this type of MV, you must create an MV log on the master table. It is not always possible to create an MV log; in these scenarios, the MV must be completely refreshed.

If need be, you can also compress and encrypt the data with an MV. This allows for better space management and security. Additionally, you can partition the underlying table used by an MV, to allow for greater scalability, performance, and availability.

There are plenty of options for MVs to be able to use this data for reporting, another database, integrations and data APIs. It is important to discuss the use of the data in order to provide the right refresh plan and understand the data that is being provided in the MVs.

The last several chapters have focused on specialized database features that DBAs often use. These include large objects, partitioning, Data Pump, external tables, and MVs. The book now shifts focus to one of the most important topics a DBA must be familiar with: backup and recovery. User-managed backups and RMAN are covered in the next several chapters.

CHAPTER 16

User-Managed Backup and Recovery

All DBAs should know how to back up a database. Even more critical, a DBA must be able to restore and recover a database. When media failures occur, everybody looks to the DBA to get the database up and running. There are two common, yet very different, Oracle approaches for backup and recovery:

- User-managed approach
- RMAN approach

User-managed backups are aptly named because you manually perform all steps associated with the backup or recovery, or both. There are two types of user-managed backups: cold backups and hot backups. Cold backups are sometimes called offline backups because the database is shut down during the backup process. Hot backups are also referred to as online backups because the database is available during the backup procedure.

RMAN is Oracle's backup and recovery tool. It simplifies and manages most aspects of backup and recovery. For Oracle backup and recovery, you should use RMAN. RMAN automatically determines which data files need to be backed up, locations, and how to restore and recover. So, why have a chapter about user-managed backups when this approach has been gathering dust for more than a decade? Consider the following reasons for understanding user-managed backup and recovery:

- You still find shops using user-managed backup and recovery techniques. Therefore, you are required to be knowledgeable about this technology.

- It is possible that during a recovery or backup failure, using this approach will help troubleshoot an issue or resolve a backup issue.

© Michelle Malcher and Darl Kuhn 2019
M. Malcher and D. Kuhn, *Pro Oracle Database 18c Administration*,
https://doi.org/10.1007/978-1-4842-4424-1_16

- Solidify your understanding of the Oracle backup and recovery architecture. This helps immensely when you are troubleshooting issues with any backup and recovery tool and lays the foundation of core knowledge for key Oracle tools, such as RMAN and Data Guard.

- You will more fully appreciate RMAN and the value of its features.

- Nightmarish database recovery stories recounted by the old DBAs will now make sense.

For these reasons, you should be familiar with user-managed backup and recovery techniques. Manually working through the scenarios in this chapter will greatly increase your understanding of which files are backed up and how they are used in a recovery. You will be much better prepared to use RMAN. RMAN makes much of backup and recovery automated and push-button. However, knowledge of how to back up and recover a database manually helps you think through and troubleshoot issues with any type of backup technology.

This chapter begins with cold backups. These types of backups are viewed as the simplest form of user-managed backup because even a system administrator can implement them. Next, the chapter discusses hot backups. You also investigate several common restore-and-recovery scenarios. These examples build your base knowledge of Oracle backup and recovery internals.

Tip   In Oracle Database 12c, you can perform user-managed hot backups and cold backups on pluggable databases; the user-managed backup and recovery technology works fine. Just as with other Oracle databases, it is strongly recommended that you use RMAN to manage backup and recovery in a pluggable environment. User-managed backup tasks quickly become unwieldy, in which the DBA must manage this information for the root container and, potentially, numerous pluggable databases.

Implementing a Cold-Backup Strategy

You perform a user-managed cold backup by copying files after the database has been shut down. This type of backup is also known as an offline backup. Your database can be in either noarchivelog mode or archivelog mode when you make a cold backup.

DBAs tend to think of a cold backup as being synonymous with a backup of a database in noarchivelog mode. That is not correct. You can make a cold backup of a database in archivelog mode, which might be used before a data center move or a large migration requiring an outage. A cold backup is a backup of the database while it is shut down, which means there is not a difference if the database is in archivelog or noarchivelog mode. It is a backup at a point in time and, if used to restore, can only be restored to that point.

Making a Cold Backup of a Database

One main reason for making a cold backup of a database in noarchivelog mode is to give you a way to restore a database back to a point in time in the past. You should use this type of backup only if you do not need to recover transactions that occurred after the backup. It is not possible to take hot backups, or while the database is started and running, of a database in noarchivelog mode because the changes cannot be captured as part of the backup. This type of backup and recovery strategy is acceptable only if your business requirements allow for the loss of data and downtime. Rarely would you ever implement this type of backup and recovery solution for a production business database since it is normal for the production database to be in archivelog mode.

Having said that, there are some good reasons to implement this type of backup. One common use is to make a cold backup of a development/test/training database and periodically reset the database back to the baseline. This gives you a way to restart a performance test or a training session with the same point-in-time snapshot of the database.

Tip   Consider using the Flashback Database feature to set your database back to a point in time in the past (see Chapter 19 for more details).

The example in this section shows you how to make a backup of every critical file in your database: all control files, data files, and online redo log files. With this type of backup, you can easily restore your database back to the point in time when the backup was made. The main advantages of this approach are that it is conceptually simple and easy to implement. Here are the steps required for a cold backup of a database:

1. Determine where to copy the backup files and how much space is required.

2. Identify the locations and names of the database files to copy.

3. Shut down the database with the IMMEDIATE, TRANSACTIONAL, or NORMAL clause.

4. Copy the files (identified in step 2) to the backup location (determined in step 1).

5. Restart your database.

The following sections elaborate on these steps.

Step 1. Determine Where to Copy the Backup Files and How Much Space Is Required

Ideally, the backup location should be on a set of disks separate from your live data files location. However, in many shops, you may not have a choice and may be told which mount points are to be used by the database. For this example, the backup location is the directory /u01/cbackup/o18c. To get a rough idea of how much space you need to store one copy of the backups, you can run this query:

```
SQL> select sum(sum_bytes)/1024/1024 m_bytes
from(
select sum(bytes) sum_bytes from v$datafile
union
select (sum(bytes) * members) sum_bytes from v$log
group by members);
```

You can verify how much operating disk space is available with the Linux/Unix df (disk free) command. Make sure that the amount of disk space available at the OS is greater than the sum returned from the prior query:

```
$ df -h
```

Tip   Temporary files are only needed to be backed up if the database is before release 10g.

Step 2. Identify the Locations and Names of the Database Files to Copy

Run this query to list the names (and paths) of the files that are included in a cold backup of a noarchivelog mode database:

```
SQL> select name from v$datafile
union
select name from v$controlfile
union
select member from v$logfile;
```

BACKING UP ONLINE REDO LOGS (OR NOT)

Do you need to back up the online redo logs? No; you never need to back up the online redo logs as part of any type of backup. Then, why do DBAs back up the online redo logs as part of a cold backup? One reason is that it makes the restore process for the noarchivelog mode scenario slightly easier. The online redo logs are required to open the database in a normal manner.

If you back up all files (including the online redo logs), then to get your database back to the state it was in at the time of the backup, you restore all files (including the online redo logs) and start up your database.

Step 3. Shut Down the Database

Connect to your database as the SYS (or as a SYSDBA-privileged user), and shut down your database, using IMMEDIATE, TRANSACTIONAL, or NORMAL. In almost every situation, using IMMEDIATE is the preferred method. This mode disconnects users, rolls back incomplete transactions, and shuts down the database:

```
$ sqlplus / as sysdba
SQL> shutdown immediate;
```

Step 4. Create Backup Copies of the Files

For every file identified in step 2, use an OS utility to copy the files to a backup directory (identified in step 1). In this simple example, all the data files, control files, temporary database files, and online redo logs are in the same directory. In production environments, you will most likely have files spread out in several different directories. This example uses the Linux/Unix cp command to copy the database files from /u01/dbfile/o18c to the /u01/cbackup/o18c directory:

```
$ cp /u01/dbfile/o18c/*.*  /u01/cbackup/o18c
```

Step 5. Restart Your Database

After all the files are copied, you can start up your database:

```
$ sqlplus / as sysdba
SQL> startup;
```

Restoring a Cold Backup in Noarchivelog Mode with Online Redo Logs

The next example explains how to restore from a cold backup of a database in noarchivelog mode. If you included the online redo logs as part of the cold backup, you can include them when you restore the files. Here are the steps involved in this procedure:

1. Shut down the instance.

2. Copy the data files, online redo logs, and control files back from the backup to the live database data file locations.

3. Start up your database.

These steps are detailed in the following sections.

Step 1. Shut Down the Instance

Shut down the instance, if it is running. In this scenario, it does not matter how you shut down the database, because you are restoring back to a point in time (with no recovery of transactions). Any files in the live database directory locations are overwritten when the backup files are copied back. If your instance is running, you can abruptly abort it. As a SYSDBA-privileged user, do the following:

```
$ sqlplus / as sysdba
SQL> shutdown abort;
```

Step 2. Copy the Files Back from the Backup

This step does the reverse of the backup: you are copying files from the backup location to the live database file locations. In this example, all the backup files are located in the /u01/cbackup/o18c directory, and all files are being copied to the /u01/dbfile/o18c directory:

```
$ cp /u01/cbackup/o18c/*.*  /u01/dbfile/o18c
```

Step 3. Start Up the Database

Connect to your database as SYS (or a user that has SYSDBA privileges), and start up your database:

```
$ sqlplus / as sysdba
SQL> startup;
```

After you finish these steps, you should have an exact copy of your database as it was when you made the cold backup. It is as if you set your database back to the point in time when you made the backup.

Restoring a Cold Backup in Noarchivelog Mode Without Online Redo Logs

As mentioned earlier, you do not ever need the online redo logs when restoring from a cold backup. If you made a cold backup of your database in noarchivelog mode and did not include the online redo logs as part of the backup, the steps to restore are nearly identical to the steps in the previous section. The main difference is that the last step requires you to open your database, using the OPEN RESETLOGS clause. Here are the steps:

1. Shut down the instance.

2. Copy the control files and data files back from the backup.

3. Start up the database in mount mode.

4. Open the database with the OPEN RESETLOGS clause.

Step 1. Shut Down the Instance

Shut down the instance, if it is running. In this scenario, it does not matter how you shut down the database, because you are restoring back to a point in time. As a SYSDBA-privileged user, do the following:

```
$ sqlplus / as sysdba
SQL> shutdown abort;
```

Step 2. Copy the Files Back from the Backup

Copy the control files and data files from the backup location to the live data file locations:

```
$ cp <backup directory>/*.*   <live database file directory>
```

Step 3. Start Up the Database in Mount Mode

Connect to your database as SYS or a user with SYSDBA privileges, and start the database in mount mode:

```
$ sqlplus / as sysdba
SQL> startup mount
```

Step 4. Open the Database with the OPEN RESETLOGS Clause

Open your database for use with the OPEN RESETLOGS clause:

```
SQL> alter database open resetlogs;
```

If you see the `Database altered` message, the command was successful. However, you may see this error:

```
ORA-01139: RESETLOGS option only valid after an incomplete database
recovery
```

In this case, issue the following command:

```
SQL> recover database until cancel;
```

You should see this message:

```
Media recovery complete.
```

Now, attempt to open your database with the `OPEN RESETLOGS` clause:

```
SQL> alter database open resetlogs;
```

This statement instructs Oracle to re-create the online redo logs. Oracle uses information in the control file for the placement, name, and size of the redo logs. If there are old online redo log files in those locations, they are overwritten.

If you are monitoring your `alert.log` throughout this process, you may see ORA-00312 and ORA-00313. This means that Oracle cannot find the online redo log files; this is okay, because these files are not physically available until they are re-created by the `OPEN RESETLOGS` command.

Scripting a Cold Backup and Restore

It is instructional to view how to script a cold backup. The basic idea is to dynamically query the data dictionary to determine the locations and names of the files to be backed up. This is preferable to hard-coding the directory locations and file names in a script. The dynamic generation of a script is less prone to errors and surprises (e.g., the addition of new data files to a database but not to an old, hard-coded backup script).

Note   The scripts in this section are not meant to be production-strength backup and recovery scripts. Rather, they illustrate the basic concepts of scripting a cold backup and subsequent restore.

The first script in this section makes a cold backup of a database. Before you use the cold backup script, you need to modify these variables in the script to match your database environment:

- ORACLE_SID

- ORACLE_HOME

- cbdir

The cbdir variable specifies the name of the backup-directory location. The script creates a file named coldback.sql, which is executed from SQL*Plus to initiate a cold backup of the database:

```
#!/bin/bash
ORACLE_SID=o18c
ORACLE_HOME=/u01/app/oracle/product/18.1.0.1/db_1
PATH=$PATH:$ORACLE_HOME/bin
#
sqlplus -s <<EOF
/ as sysdba
set head off pages0 lines 132 verify off feed off trimsp on
define cbdir=/u01/cbackup/o18c
spool coldback.sql
select 'shutdown immediate;' from dual;
select '!cp ' || name || ' ' || '&&cbdir'   from v\$datafile;
select '!cp ' || member || ' ' || '&&cbdir' from v\$logfile;
select '!cp ' || name || ' ' || '&&cbdir'   from v\$controlfile;
select 'startup;' from dual;
spool off;
@@coldback.sql
EOF
exit 0
```

This file generates commands that are to be executed from an SQL*Plus script to make a cold backup of a database. You place an exclamation mark (!) in front of the Unix cp command to instruct SQL*Plus to host out to the OS to run the cp command. You also place a backward slash (\) in front of each dollar sign ($) when referencing v$ data dictionary views; this is required in a Linux/Unix shell script. The \ escapes the $ and tells the shell script not to treat the $ as a special character (the $ normally signifies a shell variable).

After you run this script, here is a sample of the copy commands written to the coldback.sql script:

```
shutdown immediate;
!cp /u01/dbfile/o18c/system01.dbf /u01/cbackup/o18c
!cp /u01/dbfile/o18c/sysaux01.dbf /u01/cbackup/o18c
!cp /u01/dbfile/o18c/undotbs01.dbf /u01/cbackup/o18c
!cp /u01/dbfile/o18c/users01.dbf /u01/cbackup/o18c
!cp /u01/dbfile/o18c/tools01.dbf /u01/cbackup/o18c
!cp /u01/oraredo/o18c/redo02a.rdo /u01/cbackup/o18c
!cp /u02/oraredo/o18c/redo02b.rdo /u01/cbackup/o18c
!cp /u01/oraredo/o18c/redo01a.rdo /u01/cbackup/o18c
!cp /u02/oraredo/o18c/redo01b.rdo /u01/cbackup/o18c
!cp /u01/oraredo/o18c/redo03a.rdo /u01/cbackup/o18c
!cp /u02/oraredo/o18c/redo03b.rdo /u01/cbackup/o18c
!cp /u01/dbfile/o18c/control01.ctl /u01/cbackup/o18c
!cp /u01/dbfile/o18c/control02.ctl /u01/cbackup/o18c
startup;
```

While you make a cold backup, you should also generate a script that provides the commands to copy data files, log files, and control files back to their original locations. You can use this script to restore from the cold backup. The next script in this section dynamically creates a coldrest.sql script that copies files from the backup location to the original data file locations. You need to modify this script in the same manner that you modified the cold backup script (i.e., change the ORACLE_SID, ORACLE_HOME, and cbdir variables to match your environment):

```
#!/bin/bash
ORACLE_SID=o18c
ORACLE_HOME=/u01/app/oracle/product/18.1.0.1/db_1
PATH=$PATH:$ORACLE_HOME/bin
#
sqlplus -s <<EOF
/ as sysdba
```

```
set head off pages0 lines 132 verify off feed off trimsp on
define cbdir=/u01/cbackup/o18c
define dbname=$ORACLE_SID
spo coldrest.sql
select 'shutdown abort;' from dual;
select '!cp ' || '&&cbdir/' || substr(name, instr(name,'/',-1,1)+1) ||
       ' ' || name   from v\$datafile;
select '!cp ' || '&&cbdir/' || substr(member, instr(member,'/',-1,1)+1) ||
       ' ' || member from v\$logfile;
select '!cp ' || '&&cbdir/' || substr(name, instr(name,'/',-1,1)+1) ||
       ' ' || name   from v\$controlfile;
select 'startup;' from dual;
spo off;
EOF
exit 0
```

This script creates a script, named `coldrest.sql`, that generates the copy commands to restore your data files, log files, and control files back to their original locations. After you run this shell script, here is a snippet of the code in the `coldrest.sql` file:

```
shutdown abort;
!cp /u01/cbackup/o18c/system01.dbf /u01/dbfile/o18c/system01.dbf
!cp /u01/cbackup/o18c/sysaux01.dbf /u01/dbfile/o18c/sysaux01.dbf
!cp /u01/cbackup/o18c/undotbs01.dbf /u01/dbfile/o18c/undotbs01.dbf
!cp /u01/cbackup/o18c/users01.dbf /u01/dbfile/o18c/users01.dbf
!cp /u01/cbackup/o18c/tools01.dbf /u01/dbfile/o18c/tools01.dbf

...
!cp /u01/cbackup/o18c/redo03b.rdo /u02/oraredo/o18c/redo03b.rdo
!cp /u01/cbackup/o18c/control01.ctl /u01/dbfile/o18c/control01.ctl
!cp /u01/cbackup/o18c/control02.ctl /u01/dbfile/o18c/control02.ctl
startup;
```

If you need to restore from a cold backup using this script, log in to SQL*Plus as SYS, and execute the script:

```
$ sqlplus / as sysdba
SQL> @coldrest.sql
```

1. For the restore of a database in archivelog mode, it is the same if from a cold or hot backup. These restore examples are covered in sections "Performing a Complete Recovery of an Archivelog Mode Database" and "Performing an Incomplete Recovery of an Archivelog Mode Database" later in this chapter.

UNDERSTANDING THE MECHANICS DOES MATTER

Knowing how a hot backup works also helps in untangling and surviving difficult RMAN scenarios. RMAN is a sophisticated tool and yet provides simplified management of backup and recovery. With just a few commands, you can back up, restore, and recover your database. However, if there is a failure with any RMAN command or step, an understanding of Oracle's underlying internal restore-and-recovery architecture pays huge dividends. A detailed knowledge of how to restore and recover from a hot backup helps you logically think your way through any RMAN scenario.

Knowing that RMAN is restoring a file from a backup and can perform the recovery, relates back to how to restore a data file through the copy commands without RMAN. The few things that can go wrong with RMAN in a restore should be listed as part of the testing documentation in order to work through the issues with RMAN in order to continue with the recovery, if not, document the commands through the command line to copy files, and recover the data file.

Similarly, effort you put into understanding how backup and recovery is implemented pays off in the long run. You actually have less to remember—because your understanding of the underlying operation enables you to think through problems and solve them in ways that checklists do not.

Implementing a Hot Backup Strategy

As discussed previously, RMAN should be your tool of choice for any type of Oracle database backup (either online or offline). RMAN is more efficient than user-managed backups and improves the process as well as offers a framework to schedule and maintain backup and recovery internals is to make a hot backup and then use that backup to restore and recover your database. Manually issuing the commands involved in a hot backup, followed by a restore and recovery, helps you understand the role of each type of file (control files, data files, archive redo logs, online redo logs) in a restore-and-recovery scenario.

The following sections begin by showing you how to implement a hot backup. They also provide basic scripts that you can use to automate the hot backup process. Later sections explain some of the internal mechanics of a hot backup and clarify why you must put tablespaces in backup mode before the hot backup takes place.

Making a Hot Backup

Here are the steps required for a hot backup:

1. Ensure that the database is in archivelog mode.

2. Determine where to copy the backup files.

3. Identify which files need to be backed up.

4. Note the maximum sequence number of the online redo logs.

5. Alter the database/tablespace into backup mode.

6. Copy the data files with an OS utility to the location determined in step 2.

7. Alter the database/tablespace out of backup mode.

8. Archive the current online redo log, and note the maximum sequence number of the online redo logs.

9. Back up the control file.

10. Back up any archive redo logs generated during the backup.

These steps are covered in detail in the following sections.

Step 1. Ensure That the Database Is in Archivelog Mode

Run the following command to check the archivelog mode status of your database:

```
SQL> archive log list;
```

The output shows that this database is in archivelog mode:

```
Database log mode              Archive Mode
Automatic archival             Enabled
Archive destination            /u01/oraarch/o18c
```

If you are not sure how to enable archiving, see Chapter 5 for details.

Step 2. Determine Where to Copy the Backup Files

Now, determine the backup location. For this example, the backup location is the directory /u01/hbackup/o18c. To get a rough idea of how much space you need, you can run this query:

```
SQL> select sum(bytes) from dba_data_files;
```

Ideally, the backup location should be on a set of disks separate from your live data files. But, in practice, many times you are given a slice of space on a SAN and have no idea about the underlying disk layout. In these situations, you rely on redundancies being built into the SAN hardware (RAID disks, multiple controllers, and so on) to ensure high availability and recoverability.

Step 3. Identify Which Files Need to Be Backed Up

For this step, you only need to know the locations of the data files:

```
SQL> select name from v$datafile;
```

When you get to step 5, you may want to consider altering tablespaces one at a time into backup mode. If you take that approach, you need to know which data files are associated with which tablespace:

```
SQL> select tablespace_name, file_name
from dba_data_files
order by 1,2;
```

Step 4. Note the Maximum Sequence Number of the Online Redo Logs

To successfully recover using a hot backup, you require, at minimum, all the archive redo logs that were generated during the backup. For this reason, you need to note the archivelog sequence before starting the hot backup:

```
SQL> select thread#, max(sequence#)
from v$log
group by thread#
order by thread#;
```

Step 5. Alter the Database/Tablespaces into Backup Mode

You can put all your tablespaces into backup mode at the same time, using the ALTER DATABASE BEGIN BACKUP statement:

```
SQL> alter database begin backup;
```

If it is an active OLTP database, doing this can greatly degrade performance. This is because when a tablespace is in backup mode, Oracle copies a full image of any block (when it is first modified) to the redo stream (see the section "Understanding the Split-Block Issue," later in this chapter, for more details).

The alternative is to alter only one tablespace at a time into backup mode. After the tablespace has been altered into backup mode, you can copy the associated data files (step 6) and then alter the tablespace out of backup mode (step 7). You have to do this for each tablespace:

```
SQL> alter tablespace <tablespace_name> begin backup;
```

Step 6. Copy the Data Files with an OS Utility

Use an OS utility (Linux/Unix cp command) to copy the data files to the backup location. In this example, all the data files are in one directory, and they are all copied to the same backup directory:

```
$ cp /u01/dbfile/o18c/*.dbf  /u01/hbackup/o18c
```

Step 7. Alter the Database/Tablespaces out of Backup Mode

After you are finished copying all your data files to the backup directory, you need to alter the tablespaces out of backup mode. This example alters all tablespaces out of backup mode at the same time:

```
SQL> alter database end backup;
```

If you are altering your tablespaces into backup mode one at a time, you need to alter each tablespace out of backup mode after its data files have been copied:

```
SQL> alter tablespace <tablespace_name> end backup;
```

If you do not take the tablespaces out of backup mode, you can seriously degrade performance and compromise the ability to recover your database. I have also seen RMAN failure leave a tablespace or datafile in backup mode and cause future backups also to fail, and this same check will show if there is something still in backup mode. You can verify that no data files have an ACTIVE status with the following query:

```
SQL> alter session set nls_date_format = 'DD-MON-RRRR HH24:MI:SS';
SQL> select * from v$backup where status='ACTIVE';
```

Note Setting the NLS_DATE_FORMAT parameter appropriately will allow you to see the exact date/time when the data file was placed into backup mode. This is useful for determining the starting sequence number of the archivelog needed, in the event that the data file needs to be recovered.

Step 8. Archive the Current Online Redo Log, and Note the Maximum Sequence Number of the Online Redo Logs

The following statement instructs Oracle to archive any unarchived online redo logs and to initiate a log switch. This ensures that an end-of-backup marker is written to the archive redo logs:

```
SQL> alter system archive log current;
```

Also, note the maximum online redo log sequence number. If a failure occurs immediately after the hot backup, you need any archive redo logs generated during the hot backup to fully recover your database:

```
SQL> select thread#, max(sequence#)
from v$log
group by thread#
order by thread#;
```

Step 9. Back Up the Control File

For a hot backup, you cannot use an OS copy command to make a backup of the control file. Oracle's hot backup procedure specifies that you must use the ALTER DATABASE BACKUP CONTROLFILE statement. This example makes a backup of the control file and places it in the same location as the database backup files:

```
SQL> alter database backup controlfile
     to '/u01/hbackup/o18c/controlbk.ctl' reuse;
```

The REUSE clause instructs Oracle to overwrite the file if it already exists in the backup location.

Step 10. Back Up Any Archive Redo Logs Generated During the Backup

Back up the archive redo logs that were generated during the hot backup. You can do this with an OS copy command:

```
$ cp <archive redo logs generated during backup>  <backup directory>
```

This procedure guarantees that you have the logs, even if a failure should occur soon after the hot backup finishes. Be sure you do not back up an archive redo log that is currently being written to by the archiver process—doing so results in an incomplete copy of that file. Sometimes, DBAs script this process by checking the maximum SEQUENCE# with the maximum RESETLOGS_ID in the V$ARCHIVED_LOG view. Oracle updates that view when it is finished copying the archive redo log to disk. Therefore, any archive redo log file that appears in the V$ARCHIVED_LOG view should be safe to copy.

Scripting Hot Backups

The script in this section covers the minimal tasks associated with a hot backup. For a production environment, a hot backup script can be quite complex. The script given here provides you with a baseline of what you should include in a hot backup script. You need to modify these variables in the script for it to work in your environment:

- ORACLE_SID

- ORACLE_HOME

- hbdir

The ORACLE_SID OS variable defines your database name. The ORACLE_HOME OS variable defines where you installed the Oracle software. The SQL*Plus hbdir variable points to the directory for the hot backups.

```
#!/bin/bash
ORACLE_SID=o18c
ORACLE_HOME=/u01/app/oracle/product/18.1.0.1/db_1
PATH=$PATH:$ORACLE_HOME/bin
#
sqlplus -s <<EOF
/ as sysdba
set head off pages0 lines 132 verify off feed off trimsp on
define hbdir=/u01/hbackup/o18c
spo hotback.sql
select 'spo &&hbdir/hotlog.txt' from dual;
select 'select max(sequence#) from v\$log;' from dual;
select 'alter database begin backup;' from dual;
select '!cp ' || name || ' ' || '&&hbdir' from v\$datafile;
select 'alter database end backup;' from dual;
select 'alter database backup controlfile to ' || "" || '&&hbdir'
    || '/controlbk.ctl'  || "" || ' reuse;' from dual;
select 'alter system archive log current;' from dual;
select 'select max(sequence#) from v\$log;' from dual;
select 'select member from v\$logfile;' from dual;
```

```
select 'spo off;' from dual;
spo off;
@@hotback.sql
EOF
```

The script generates a hotback.sql script. This script contains the commands for performing the hot backup. Here is a listing of the hotback.sql script for a test database:

```
spo /u01/hbackup/o18c/hotlog.txt
select max(sequence#) from v$log;
alter database begin backup;
!cp /u01/dbfile/o18c/system01.dbf /u01/hbackup/o18c
!cp /u01/dbfile/o18c/sysaux01.dbf /u01/hbackup/o18c
!cp /u01/dbfile/o18c/undotbs01.dbf /u01/hbackup/o18c
!cp /u01/dbfile/o18c/users01.dbf /u01/hbackup/o18c
!cp /u01/dbfile/o18c/tools01.dbf /u01/hbackup/o18c
alter database end backup;
alter database backup controlfile to '/u01/hbackup/o18c/controlbk.ctl' reuse;
alter system archive log current;
select max(sequence#) from v$log;
select member from v$logfile;
spo off;
```

You can run this script manually from SQL*Plus, like this:

```
SQL> @hotback.sql
```

Caution   If the previous script fails on a statement before ALTER DATABASE END BACKUP is executed, you must take your database (tablespaces) out of backup mode by manually running ALTER DATABASE END BACKUP from SQL*Plus (as the SYS user).

While you generate the hot backup script, it is prudent to generate a script that you can use to copy the data files from a backup directory. You have to modify the `hbdir` variable in this script to match the location of the hot backups for your environment. Here is a script that generates the copy commands:

```
#!/bin/bash
ORACLE_SID=o18c
ORACLE_HOME=/u01/app/oracle/product/18.1.0.1/db_1
PATH=$PATH:$ORACLE_HOME/bin
#
sqlplus -s <<EOF
/ as sysdba
set head off pages0 lines 132 verify off feed off trimsp on
define hbdir=/u01/hbackup/o18c/
define dbname=$ORACLE_SID
spo hotrest.sql
select '!cp ' || '&&hbdir' || substr(name,instr(name,'/',-1,1)+1)
       || ' ' || name from v\$datafile;
spo off;
EOF
#
exit 0
```

For my environment, here is the code generated that can be executed from SQL*Plus to copy the data files back from the backup directory, if a failure should occur:

```
!cp /u01/hbackup/o18c/system01.dbf /u01/dbfile/o18c/system01.dbf
!cp /u01/hbackup/o18c/sysaux01.dbf /u01/dbfile/o18c/sysaux01.dbf
!cp /u01/hbackup/o18c/undotbs01.dbf /u01/dbfile/o18c/undotbs01.dbf
!cp /u01/hbackup/o18c/users01.dbf /u01/dbfile/o18c/users01.dbf
!cp /u01/hbackup/o18c/tools01.dbf /u01/dbfile/o18c/tools01.dbf
```

In this output, you can remove the exclamation point (!)from each line if you prefer to run the commands from the OS prompt. The main idea is that these commands are available in the event of a failure, so you know which files have been backed up to which location and how to copy them back.

Tip   Do not use user-managed hot backup technology for online backups; use RMAN. RMAN does not need to place tablespaces in backup mode and automates nearly everything related to backup and recovery.

Understanding the Split-Block Issue

To perform a hot backup, one critical step is to alter a tablespace into backup mode before you copy any of the data files associated with the tablespace, using an OS utility. To understand why you have to alter a tablespace into backup mode, you must be familiar with what is sometimes called the split- (or fractured-) block issue.

Recall that the size of a database block is often different from that of an OS block. For instance, a database block may be sized at 8KB, whereas the OS block size is 4KB. As part of the hot backup, you use an OS utility to copy the live data files. While the OS utility is copying the data files, the possibility exists that database writers are writing to a block simultaneously. Because the Oracle block and the OS block are different sizes, the following may happen:

1.   The OS utility copies part of the Oracle block.

2.   A moment later, a database writer updates the entire block.

3.   A split second later, the OS utility copies the latter half of the Oracle block.

This can result in the OS copy of the block's being inconsistent with what Oracle wrote to the OS. Figure 16-1 illustrates this concept.

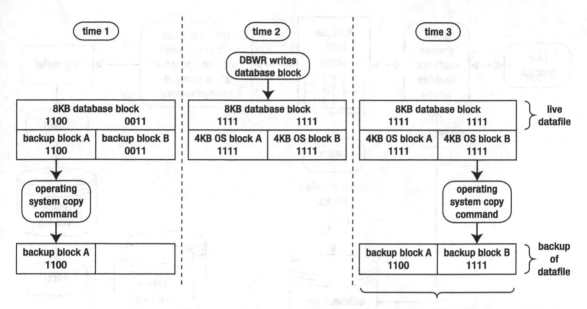

Figure 16-1. *Hot backup split- (or fractured-) block issue*

Looking at Figure 16-1, the block copied to disk at time 3 is corrupt, as far as Oracle is concerned. The first half of the block is from time 1, and the latter half is copied at time 3. When you make a hot backup, you are guaranteeing block-level corruption in the backups of the data files.

To understand how Oracle resolves the split-block issue, first consider a database operating in its normal mode (not in backup mode). The redo information that is written to the online redo logs is only what Oracle needs, to reapply transactions. The redo stream contains entire blocks of data. Oracle only records a change vector in the redo stream that specifies which block changed and how it was changed. Figure 16-2 shows Oracle operating under normal conditions.

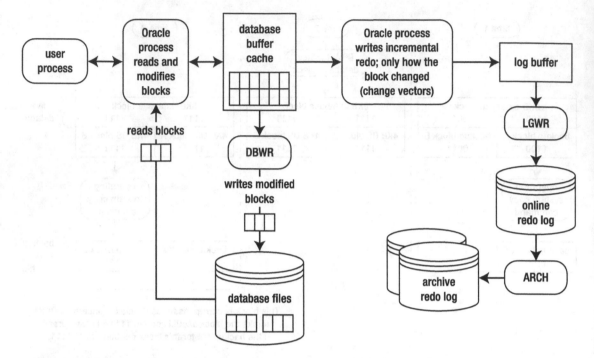

Figure 16-2. *Oracle normally only writes change vectors to the redo stream*

Now, consider what happens during a hot backup. For a hot backup, before you copy the data files associated with a tablespace, you must first alter the tablespace into backup mode. While in this mode, before Oracle modifies a block, the entire block is copied to the redo stream. Any subsequent changes to the block only require that the normal redo-change vectors be written to the redo stream. This is illustrated in Figure 16-3.

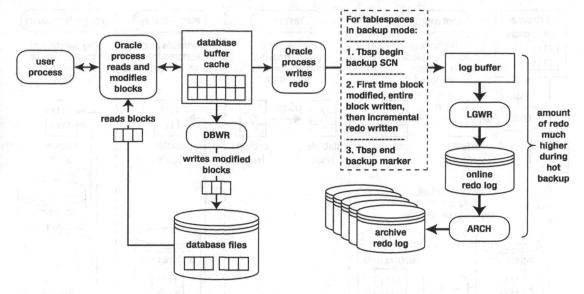

Figure 16-3. *Entire blocks are written to the redo stream*

To understand why Oracle logs the entire block to the redo stream, consider what happens during a restore and recovery. First, the backup files from the hot backup are restored. As explained earlier, these backup files contain corrupt blocks, owing to the split-block issue. But it does not matter, because once Oracle recovers the data files, for any block that was modified during the hot backup, Oracle has an image copy of the block as it was before it was modified. Oracle uses the copy of the block it has in the redo stream as a starting point for the recovery (of that block). This process is illustrated in Figure 16-4.

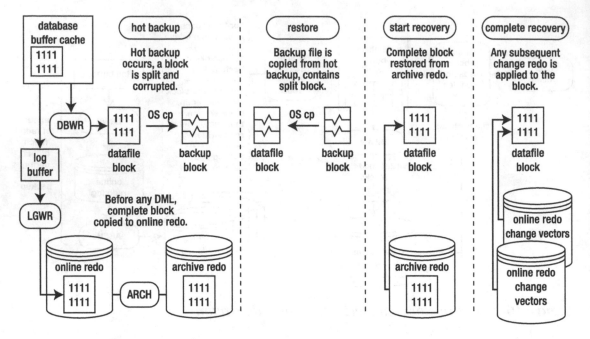

Figure 16-4. *Restore and recovery of a split block*

In this way, it does not matter if there are corrupt blocks in the hot backup files. Oracle always starts the recovery process for a block from a copy of the block (as it was before it was modified) in the redo stream.

Understanding the Need for Redo Generated During Backup

What happens if you experience a failure soon after you make a hot backup? Oracle knows when a tablespace was put in backup mode (begin backup system SCN written to the redo stream), and Oracle knows when the tablespace was taken out of backup mode (end-of-backup marker written to the redo stream). Oracle requires every archive redo log generated during that time frame to successfully recover the data files.

Figure 16-5 shows that, at minimum, the archive redo logs from sequence numbers 100 to 102 are required to recover the tablespace. These archive redo logs were generated during the hot backup.

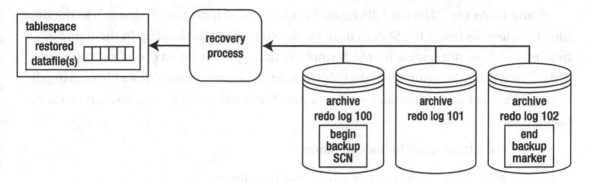

Figure 16-5. *Recovery applied*

If you attempt to stop the recovery process before all redo between the begin and end markers has been applied to the data file, Oracle throws this error:

```
ORA-01195: online backup of file 1 needs more recovery to be consistent
```

All redo generated during the hot backup of a tablespace must be applied to the data files before they can be opened. Oracle, at a minimum, needs to apply everything between the begin-backup SCN marker and the end-backup marker, to account for every block modified while the tablespace was in backup mode. This redo is in the archive redo log files; or, if the failure happened right after the backup ended, some of the redo may not have been archived and may be in the online redo logs. Therefore, you have to instruct Oracle to apply what's in the online redo logs.

Understanding That Data Files Are Updated

Note that, in Figures 16-2 and 16-3, the behavior of the database writer is, for the most part, unchanged throughout the backup procedure. The database writer continues to write blocks to data files, regardless of the backup mode of the database. The database writer does not care if a hot backup is taking place; its job is to write blocks from the buffer cache to the data files.

Every once in a while, you run into a DBA who states that the database writer does not write to data files during user-managed hot backups. This is a widespread misconception. Use some common sense: If the database writer is not writing to the data files during a hot backup, then where are the changes being written? If the transactions are being written to somewhere other than the data files, how would those data files be resynchronized after the backup? It does not make any sense.

Some DBAs say, "The data file header is frozen, which means no changes to the data file." Oracle does freeze the SCN to indicate the start of the hot backup in the data file header and does not update that SCN until the tablespace is taken out of backup mode. This "frozen SCN"does not mean that blocks are not being written to data files during the backup. You can easily demonstrate that a data file is written to during backup mode by doing this:

1. Put a tablespace in backup mode:

    ```
    SQL> alter tablespace users begin backup;
    ```

2. Create a table that has a character field:

    ```
    SQL> create table cc(cc varchar2(20)) tablespace users;
    ```

3. Insert a string into that table:

    ```
    SQL> insert into cc values('DBWR does write');
    ```

4. Force a checkpoint (which ensures that all modified buffers are written to disk):

    ```
    SQL> alter system checkpoint;
    ```

5. From the OS, use the `strings` and `grep` commands to search for the string in the data file:

    ```
    $ strings /u01/dbfile/o18c/users01.dbf | grep "DBWR does write"
    ```

6. Here is the output, proving that the database writer did write the data to disk:

    ```
    DBWR does write
    ```

7. Do not forget to take the tablespace out of backup mode:

    ```
    SQL> alter tablespace users end backup;
    ```

Performing a Complete Recovery of an Archivelog Mode Database

The term *complete recovery* means that you can recover all transactions that were committed before a failure occurred. *Complete recovery* does not mean you that completely restore and recover the entire database. For instance, if only one data file has experienced media failure, you need to restore and recover only the damaged data file to perform a complete recovery.

Tip   If you have access to a test or development database, take the time to walk through every step in each of the examples that follow. Going through these steps can teach you more about backup and recovery than any documentation.

The steps outlined here apply to any database backed up while in archivelog mode. It does not matter if you made a cold backup or hot backup. The steps to restore and recover data files are the same, as long as the database was in archivelog mode during the backup. For a complete recovery, you need the following:

- To be able to restore the data files that have experienced media failure

- Access to all archive redo logs generated since the last backup was started

- Intact online redo logs

Here is the basic procedure for a complete recovery:

1. Place the database in mount mode; this prevents normal user transaction processing from reading/writing to data files being restored. (If you are not restoring the SYSTEM or UNDO tablespace, you have the option of opening the database and manually taking the data files offline before restoring them. If you do this, make sure you place the data files online after the recovery is complete.)

2. Restore the damaged data files with an OS copy utility.

3. Issue the appropriate SQL*Plus RECOVER command to apply any information required in the archive redo logs and online redo logs.

4. Alter the database open.

The next several sections demonstrate some common complete restore-and-recovery scenarios. You should be able to apply these basic scenarios to diagnose and recover from any complex situation you find yourself in.

Restoring and Recovering with the Database Offline

This section details a simple restore-and-recovery scenario. Described next are the steps to simulate a failure and then perform a complete restore and recovery. Try this scenario in a development database. Ensure that you have a good backup and that you are not trying this experiment in a database that contains critical business data.

Before you start this example, create a table, and insert some data. This table and data are selected from the end of the complete recovery process to demonstrate a successful recovery:

```
SQL> create table foo(foo number) tablespace users;
SQL> insert into foo values(1);
SQL> commit;
```

Now, switch the online logs several times. Doing so ensures that you have to apply archive redo logs as part of the recovery:

```
SQL> alter system switch logfile;
```

The forward slash (/) reruns the most recently executed SQL statement:

```
SQL> /
SQL> /
SQL> /
```

Next, simulate a media failure by renaming the data file associated with the USERS tablespace. You can identify the name of this file with this query:

```
SQL> select file_name from dba_data_files where tablespace_name='USERS';

FILE_NAME
----------------------------------
/u01/dbfile/o18c/users01.dbf
```

From the OS, rename the file:

```
$ mv /u01/dbfile/o18c/users01.dbf /u01/dbfile/o18c/users01.dbf.old
```

And, attempt to stop your database:

```
$ sqlplus / as sysdba
SQL> shutdown immediate;
```

You should see an error such as this:

```
ORA-01116: error in opening database file ...
```

If this were a real disaster, it would be prudent to navigate to the data file directory, list the files, and see if the file in question was in its correct location. You should also inspect the alert.log file to see if any relevant information is logged there by Oracle.

Now that you have simulated a media failure, the next several steps walk you through a restore and complete recovery.

Step 1. Place Your Database in Mount Mode

Before you place your database in mount mode, you may need to first shut it down, using ABORT:

```
$ sqlplus / as sysdba
SQL> shutdown abort;
SQL> startup mount;
```

Step 2. Restore the Data File from the Backup

The next step is to copy from the backup the data file that corresponds to the one that has had a failure:

```
$ cp /u01/hbackup/o18c/users01.dbf /u01/dbfile/o18c/users01.dbf
```

At this point, it is instructional to ponder what Oracle would do if you attempted to start your database. When you issue the ALTER DATABASE OPEN statement, Oracle inspects the SCN in the control file for each data file. You can examine this SCN by querying V$DATAFILE:

```
SQL> select checkpoint_change# from v$datafile where file#=4;


CHECKPOINT_CHANGE#
------------------
          3543963
```

Oracle compares the SCN in the control file with the SCN in the data file header. You can check the SCN in the data file header by querying V$DATAFILE_HEADER; for example,

```
SQL> select file#, fuzzy, checkpoint_change#
from v$datafile_header
where file#=4;

     FILE# FUZ CHECKPOINT_CHANGE#
---------- --- ------------------
         4 YES            3502285
```

Note that the SCN recorded in V$DATAFILE_HEADER is less than the SCN in V$DATAFILE for the same data file. If you attempt to open your database, Oracle throws an error stating that media recovery is required (meaning that you need to apply redo) to synchronize the SCN in the data file with the SCN in the control file. The FUZZY column is set to YES. This indicates that redo must be applied to the data file before it can be opened for use. Here is what happens when you try to open the database at this point:

```
SQL> alter database open;

alter database open;
alter database open
*
ERROR at line 1:
ORA-01113: file 4 needs media recovery...
```

Oracle does not let you open the database until the SCN in all data file headers matches the corresponding SCN in the control file.

Step 3. Issue the Appropriate RECOVER Statement

The archive redo logs and online redo logs have the information required to catch up the data file SCN to the control file SCN. You can apply redo to the data file that needs media recovery by issuing one of the following SQL*Plus statements:

- RECOVER DATAFILE

- RECOVER TABLESPACE

- RECOVER DATABASE

Because only one data file in this example needs to be recovered, the RECOVER DATAFILE statement is appropriate. However, keep in mind that you can run any of the previously listed RECOVER statements, and Oracle will figure out what needs to be recovered. In this particular scenario, you may find it easier to remember the name of the tablespace that contains the restored data file(s) than to remember the data file name(s). Next, any data files that need recovery in the USERS tablespace are recovered:

```
SQL> recover tablespace users;
```

At this point, Oracle uses the SCN in the data file header to determine which archive redo log or online redo log to use to begin applying redo. You can view the starting log sequence number that RMAN will use to begin the recovery process via the following query:

```
SQL> select
 HXFNM file_name
,HXFIL file_num
,FHTNM tablespace_name
,FHTHR thread
,FHRBA_SEQ sequence
from X$KCVFH
where FHTNM = 'USERS';
```

If all the redo required is in the online redo logs, Oracle applies that redo and displays this message:

```
Media recovery complete.
```

If Oracle needs to apply redo that is only contained in archived redo logs (meaning that the online redo log that contained the appropriate redo has already been overwritten), you are prompted with a recommendation from Oracle as to which archive redo log to apply first:

```
ORA-00279: change 3502285 generated at 11/02/2018 10:49:39 needed for
thread 1
ORA-00289: suggestion : /u01/oraarch/o18c/1_1_798283209.dbf
ORA-00280: change 3502285 for thread 1 is in sequence #1

Specify log: {<RET>=suggested | filename | AUTO | CANCEL}
```

You can press Enter or Return (<RET>) to have Oracle apply the suggested archive redo log file, specify a file name, specify AUTO to instruct Oracle to apply any suggested files automatically, or type CANCEL to cancel out of the recovery operation.

In this example, specify AUTO. Oracle applies all redo in all archive redo log files and online redo log files to perform a complete recovery:

```
AUTO
```

The last message displayed after all required archive redo and online redo have been applied is this:

```
Log applied.
Media recovery complete.
```

Step 4. Alter Your Database Open

After the media recovery is complete, you can open your database:

```
SQL> alter database open;
```

You can now verify that the transaction you committed just prior to the media failure was restored and recovered:

```
SQL> select * from foo;

       FOO
----------
        1
```

Restoring and Recovering with a Database Online

If you lose a data file associated with a tablespace other than SYSTEM and UNDO, you can restore and recover the damaged data file while leaving the database online. For this to work, any data files being restored and recovered must be taken offline first. You may be alerted to an issue with a data file in which a user is attempting to update a table and sees an error such as this:

```
SQL> insert into foo values(2);

ORA-01116: error in opening database file ...
```

You navigate to the OS directory that contains the data file and determine that it has been erroneously removed by a system administrator.

In this example, the data file associated with the USERS tablespace is taken offline and subsequently restored and recovered while the rest of the database remains online. First, place take the data file offline:

```
SQL> alter database datafile '/u01/dbfile/o18c/users01.dbf' offline;
```

Now, restore the appropriate data file from the backup location:

```
$ cp /u01/hbackup/o18c/users01.dbf /u01/dbfile/o18c/users01.dbf
```

In this situation, you cannot use RECOVER DATABASE. The RECOVER DATABASE statement attempts to recover all data files in the database, of which the SYSTEM tablespace is part. The SYSTEM tablespace cannot be recovered while the database is online. If you use the RECOVER TABLESPACE, all data files associated with the tablespace must be offline. In this case, it is more appropriate to recover at the data file level of granularity:

```
SQL> recover datafile '/u01/dbfile/o18c/users01.dbf';
```

Oracle inspects the SCN in the data file header and determines which archive redo log or online redo log to use to start applying redo. If all redo required is in the online redo logs, you see this message:

```
Media recovery complete.
```

If the starting point for redo is contained only in an archive redo log file, Oracle suggests which file to start with:

```
ORA-00279: change 3502285 generated at 11/02/2018 10:49:39 needed for
thread 1
ORA-00289: suggestion : /u01/oraarch/o18c/1_1_798283209.dbf
ORA-00280: change 3502285 for thread 1 is in sequence #1

Specify log: {<RET>=suggested | filename | AUTO | CANCEL}
```

You can type AUTO to have Oracle apply all required redo in archive redo log files and online redo log files:

```
AUTO
```

If successful, you should see this message:

```
Log applied.
Media recovery complete.
```

You can now bring the data file back online:

```
SQL> alter database datafile '/u01/dbfile/o18c/users01.dbf' online;
```

If successful, you should see this:

```
Database altered.
```

Restoring Control Files

When you are dealing with user-managed backups, you usually restore the control file in one of these situations:

- A control file is damaged, and the file is multiplexed.

- All control files are damaged.

These two situations are covered in the following sections.

Restoring a Damaged Control File When Multiplexed

If you configure your database with more than one control file, you can shut down the database and use an OS command to copy an existing control file to the location of the missing control file. For example, from the initialization file, you know that two control files are used for this database:

```
SQL> show parameter control_files
```

NAME	TYPE	VALUE
control_files	string	/u01/dbfile/o18c/control01.ctl
		,/u02/dbfile/o18c/control02.ctl

Suppose the control02.ctl file has become damaged. Oracle throws this error when querying the data dictionary:

```
ORA-00210: cannot open the specified control file...
```

When a good control file is available, you can shut down the database, move the old/bad control file (this preserves it, in the event that it is later needed for root cause analysis), and copy the existing good control file to the name and location of the bad control file:

```
SQL> shutdown abort;
```

```
$ mv /u02/dbfile/o18c/control02.ctl /u02/dbfile/o18c/control02.ctl.old
$ cp /u01/dbfile/o18c/control01.ctl /u02/dbfile/o18c/control02.ctl
```

Now, restart the database:

```
SQL> startup;
```

In this manner, you can restore a control file from an existing control file.

Restoring When All Control Files Are Damaged

If you lose all of your control files, you can restore one from a backup, or you can re-create the control file. As long as you have all your data files and any required redo (archive redo and online redo), you should be able to recover your database completely. The steps for this scenario are as follows:

1. Shut down the database.

2. Restore a control file from the backup.

3. Start the database in mount mode, and initiate database recovery, using the RECOVER DATABASE USING BACKUP CONTROLFILE clause.

4. For a complete recovery, manually apply the redo contained in the online redo logs.

5. Open the database with the OPEN RESETLOGS clause.

In this example, all control files for the database were accidentally deleted, and Oracle subsequently reports this error:

```
ORA-00210: cannot open the specified control file...
```

Step 1. Shut Down the Database

First, shut down the database:

```
SQL> shutdown abort;
```

Step 2. Restore the Control File from the Backup

This database was configured with just one control file, which you copy back from the backup location, as shown:

```
$ cp /u01/hbackup/o18c/controlbk.ctl /u01/dbfile/o18c/control01.ctl
```

If more than one control file is being used, you have to copy the backup control file to each control file and location name listed in the CONTROL_FILES initialization parameter.

Step 3. Start the Database in Mount Mode, and Initiate Database Recovery

Next, start the database in mount mode:

```
SQL> startup mount;
```

After the control file(s) and data files have been copied back, you can perform a recovery. Oracle knows that the control file was from a backup (because it was created with the ALTER DATABASE BACKUP CONTROLFILE statement), so the recovery must be performed with the USING BACKUP CONTROLFILE clause:

```
SQL> recover database using backup controlfile;
```

At this point, you are prompted for the application of archive redo log files:

```
ORA-00279: change 3584431 generated at 11/02/2018 11:48:46 needed for
thread 1
ORA-00289: suggestion : /u01/oraarch/o18c/1_8_798283209.dbf
ORA-00280: change 3584431 for thread 1 is in sequence #8

Specify log: {<RET>=suggested | filename | AUTO | CANCEL}
```

Type AUTO to instruct the recovery process to apply all archive redo logs automatically:

```
AUTO
```

The recovery process applies all available archive redo logs. The recovery process has no one way of determining where the archive redo stream ends and therefore tries to apply an archive redo log that does not exist, resulting in a message such as this:

```
ORA-00308: cannot open archived log '/u01/oraarch/o18c/1_10_798283209.dbf'
ORA-27037: unable to obtain file status
```

The prior message is to be expected. Now, attempt to open the database:

```
SQL> alter database open resetlogs;
```

Oracle throws the following error in this situation:

```
ORA-01113: file 1 needs media recovery
ORA-01110: data file 1: '/u01/dbfile/o18c/system01.dbf'
```

685

Step 4. Apply Redo Contained in the Online Redo Logs

Oracle needs to apply more redo to synchronize the SCN in the control file with the SCN in the data file header. In this scenario, the online redo logs are still intact and contain the required redo. To apply redo contained in the online redo logs, first identify the locations and names of the online redo log files:

```
SQL> select a.sequence#, a.status, a.first_change#, b.member
from v$log a, v$logfile b
where a.group# = b.group#
order by a.sequence#;
```

Here is the partial output for this example:

```
SEQUENCE#  STATUS           FIRST_CHANGE#    MEMBER
---------- ---------------  ---------------  ----------------------
        6  INACTIVE         3543960          /u01/oraredo/o12c/redo03a.rdo
        6  INACTIVE         3543960          /u02/oraredo/o12c/redo03b.rdo
        7  INACTIVE         3543963          /u02/oraredo/o12c/redo01b.rdo
        7  INACTIVE         3543963          /u01/oraredo/o12c/redo01a.rdo
        8  CURRENT          3583986          /u02/oraredo/o12c/redo02b.rdo
        8  CURRENT          3583986          /u01/oraredo/o12c/redo02a.rdo
```

Now, reinitiate the recovery process:

```
SQL> recover database using backup controlfile;
```

The recovery process prompts for an archive redo log that does not exist:

```
ORA-00279: change 3584513 generated at 11/02/2018 11:50:50 needed for
thread 1
ORA-00289: suggestion : /u01/oraarch/o18c/1_10_798283209.dbf
ORA-00280: change 3584513 for thread 1 is in sequence #10

Specify log: {<RET>=suggested | filename | AUTO | CANCEL}
```

Instead of supplying the recovery process with an archive redo log file, type in the name of a current online redo log file (you may have to attempt each online redo log until you find the one that Oracle needs). This instructs the recovery process to apply any redo in the online redo log:

```
/u01/oraredo/o18c/redo01a.rdo
```

You should see this message when the correct online redo log is applied:

```
Log applied.
Media recovery complete.
```

Step 5. Open the Database with RESETLOGS

The database is completely recovered at this point. It is important after this type of recovery that a new backup performed against the database. However, because a backup control file was used for the recovery process, the database must be opened with the RESETLOGS clause:

```
SQL> alter database open resetlogs;
```

Upon success, you should see this:

```
Database altered.
```

Performing an Incomplete Recovery of an Archivelog Mode Database

Incomplete recovery means that you do not restore all transactions that were committed before the failure. With this type of recovery, you are recovering to a point in time in the past, and transactions are lost. This is why incomplete recovery is also known as database point-in-time recovery (DBPITR).

Incomplete recovery does not mean that you are restoring and recovering only a subset of data files. In fact, with most incomplete scenarios, you have to restore all data files from the backup as part of the procedure. If you do not want to recover all data files, you first need to take offline any data files you do not intend to participate in the incomplete recovery process. When you initiate the recovery, Oracle will only recover data files that have an ONLINE value in the STATUS column of V$DATAFILE_HEADER.

You may want to perform an incomplete recovery for many different reasons:

- You attempt to perform a complete recovery but are missing the required archive redo logs or unarchived online redo log information.

- You want to restore the database back to a point in time in the past just prior to an erroneous user error (deleted data, dropped table, and so on).

- You have a testing environment. (Flashback database might be an option here.)

You can perform user-managed incomplete recovery three ways:

- Cancel based

- SCN based

- Time based

Cancel based allows you to apply archive redo and halt the process at the boundary, based on an archive redo log file. For instance, say you are attempting to restore and recover your database, and you realize that you are missing an archive redo log. You have to stop the recover process at the point of your last good archive redo log. You initiate cancel-based incomplete recovery with the CANCEL clause of the RECOVER DATABASE statement:

```
SQL> recover database until cancel;
```

If you want to recover up to and including a certain SCN number, use SCN-based incomplete recovery. You may know from the alert log or from the output of LogMiner the point to which you want to restore to a certain SCN. Use the UNTIL CHANGE clause to perform this type of incomplete recovery:

```
SQL> recover database until change 12345;
```

If you know the time at which you want to stop the recovery process, use time-based incomplete recovery. For example, you may know that a table was dropped at a certain time and want to restore and recover the database up to the specified time. The format for a time-based recovery is always as follows: YYYY-MM-DD:HH24:MI:SS. Here is an example:

```
SQL> recover database until time '2018-10-21:02:00:00';
```

When you perform an incomplete recovery, you have to restore all data files that you plan to have online when the incomplete restoration is finished. Here are the steps for an incomplete recovery:

1. Shut down the database.

2. Restore all the data files from the backup.

3. Start the database in mount mode.

4. Apply redo (roll forward) to the desired point, and halt the recovery process (use cancel-, SCN-, or time-based recovery).

5. Open the database with the OPEN RESETLOGS clause.

The following example performs a cancel-based incomplete recovery. If the database is open, shut it down:

```
$ sqlplus / as sysdba
SQL> shutdown abort;
```

Next, copy all data files from the backup (either a cold or hot backup). This example restores all data files from a hot backup. For this example, the current control file is intact and does not need to be restored. Here is a snippet of the OS copy commands for the database being restored:

```
cp /u01/hbackup/o18c/system01.dbf /u01/dbfile/o18c/system01.dbf
cp /u01/hbackup/o18c/sysaux01.dbf /u01/dbfile/o18c/sysaux01.dbf
cp /u01/hbackup/o18c/undotbs01.dbf /u01/dbfile/o18c/undotbs01.dbf
cp /u01/hbackup/o18c/users01.dbf /u01/dbfile/o18c/users01.dbf
cp /u01/hbackup/o18c/tools01.dbf /u01/dbfile/o18c/tools01.dbf
```

After the data files have been copied back, you can initiate the recovery process. This example performs a cancel-based incomplete recovery:

```
$ sqlplus / as sysdba
SQL> startup mount;
SQL> recover database until cancel;
```

At this point, the Oracle recovery process suggests an archive redo log to apply:

```
ORA-00279: change 3584872 generated at 11/02/2018 12:02:32 needed for
thread 1
ORA-00289: suggestion : /u01/oraarch/o18c/1_1_798292887.dbf
ORA-00280: change 3584872 for thread 1 is in sequence #1

Specify log: {<RET>=suggested | filename | AUTO | CANCEL}
```

Apply the logs up to the point you where want to stop, and then type CANCEL:

```
CANCEL
```

This stops the recovery process. Now, you can open the database with the RESETLOGS clause:

```
SQL> alter database open resetlogs;
```

The database has been opened to a point in time in the past. The recovery is deemed incomplete because not all redo was applied.

Tip   Now would be a good time to get a good backup of your database. This will give you a clean point from which to initiate a restore and recovery should a failure happen soon after you have opened your database.

PURPOSE OF OPEN RESETLOGS

Sometimes, you are required to open your database with the OPEN RESETLOGS clause. You may do this when recreating a control file, performing a restore and recovery with a backup control file, or performing an incomplete recovery. When you open your database with the OPEN RESETLOGS clause, it either wipes out any existing online redo log files or, if the files do not exist, re-creates them. You can query the MEMBER column of V$LOGFILE to see which files are involved in an OPEN RESETLOGS operation.

Why would you want to wipe out what's in the online redo logs? Take the example of an incomplete recovery, in which the database is deliberately opened to a point in time in the past. In this situation, the SCN information in the online redo logs contains transaction data that will never be recovered. Oracle forces you to open the database with OPEN RESETLOGS to purposely wipe out that information.

When you open your database with OPEN RESETLOGS, you create a new incarnation of your database and reset the log sequence number back to 1. Oracle requires a new incarnation so as to avoid accidentally using any old archive redo logs (associated with a separate incarnation of the database), in the event that another restore and recovery is required.

Summary

Some studies have indicated that airplane pilots who are over dependent on autopilot technology are less able to cope with catastrophic in-flight problems than the pilots who have spent considerable time flying without autopilot assistance. The over-autodependent pilots tend to forget key procedures when serious problems arise, whereas pilots who are not as dependent on autopilot are more adept at diagnosing and resolving stressful in-flight failures.

Similarly, DBAs who understand how to backup, restore, and recover a database manually, using user-managed techniques, are more proficient at troubleshooting and resolving serious backup and recovery problems than DBAs who only navigate backup and recovery technology via screens. This is why this chapter is included in the book. Understanding what happens at each step and why the step is required is vital for complete knowledge of the Oracle backup and recovery architecture. Having additional knowledge and tools in a stressful recovery scenario is extremely valuable. This awareness translates into key troubleshooting skills when you are using Oracle tools such as RMAN (backup and recovery), Enterprise Manager, and Data Guard (disaster recovery, high availability, and replication).

The user-managed backup and recovery techniques covered in this chapter are not taught or used much anymore. Most DBAs are (and should be) using RMAN for their Oracle backup and recovery requirements. However, it is critical for you to understand how cold backups and hot backups work. You may find yourself employed in a shop in which old technology has been implemented and needing to restore and recover the database, troubleshoot, or assist in migrating to RMAN. In these scenarios, you must fully understand the old backup technologies.

Now that you have an in-depth understanding of Oracle backup and recovery mechanics, you are ready to investigate RMAN. The next several chapters examine how to configure and use RMAN for production-strength backup and recovery.

CHAPTER 17

Configuring RMAN

Oracle Recovery Manager (RMAN) is provided by default when you install the Oracle software (for both the Standard Edition and Enterprise Edition). RMAN offers a robust and flexible set of backup and restore features. The following list highlights some of the most salient qualities:

- Easy-to-use commands for backup, restore, and recovery.

- Ability to track which files have been backed up and where to.

- Manages the deletion of obsolete backups and archivelogs.

- Parallelization: can use multiple processes for backup, restore, and recovery.

- Incremental backups that only back up changes since the previous backup.

- Ability to apply incremental backups to an image copy.

- Recovery at the database, tablespace, data file, table, or block level.

- Advanced compression and encryption features.

- Integration with media managers for tape backups.

- Backup validation and testing. Restore validation and testing.

- Cross-platform data conversion.

- Data Recovery Advisor, which assists with diagnosing failures and proposing solutions.

- Ability to detect corrupt blocks in data files.

- Advanced reporting capabilities from the RMAN command line.

© Michelle Malcher and Darl Kuhn 2019
M. Malcher and D. Kuhn, *Pro Oracle Database 18c Administration*,
https://doi.org/10.1007/978-1-4842-4424-1_17

The goal of this chapter is to present enough information about RMAN that you can make reasonable decisions about how to implement a solid backup strategy. The basic RMAN components are described first, after which you walk through many of the decision points involved in implementing RMAN.

Note   The RMAN-related chapters in this book are not intended to be a complete reference on all aspects of backup and restore. That would take an entire book. These chapters contain the basic information you need to successfully use RMAN. If you require advanced RMAN information regarding backup, restore, and recovery, see *RMAN Recipes for Oracle Database 12c*, second edition, by Darl Kuhn, Sam Alapati, and Arup Nanda (Apress, 2013).

Understanding RMAN

RMAN ecosystem consists of many different components. Figure 17-1 shows the interactions of the main RMAN pieces. Refer back to this diagram when reading through this section.

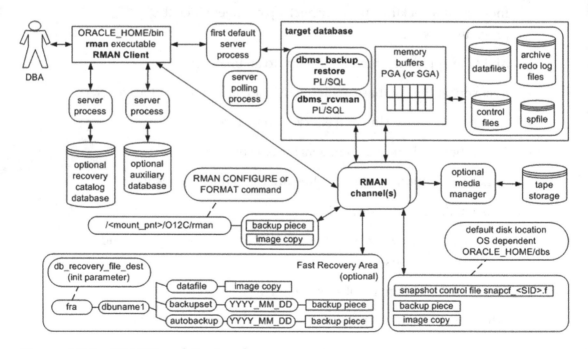

Figure 17-1. *RMAN architectural components*

The following list describes the RMAN architectural components:

DBA: Human interaction to ensure successful backups and restores.

Target database: The database being backed up by RMAN. You connect to the target database with the RMAN command-line TARGET parameter (see the next section for more details).

RMAN client: The rman utility from which you issue BACKUP, RESTORE, and RECOVER commands. On most database servers, the rman utility is located in the ORACLE_HOME/bin directory (along with all the other Oracle utilities, such as sqlplus and expdp).

Oracle server processes: When you execute the rman client and connect to the target database, two Oracle server background processes are started. The first default server process interacts with the PL/SQL packages to coordinate the backup activities. The secondary polling process occasionally updates Oracle data dictionary structures.

Channel (s): The Oracle server processes for handling I/O between files being backed up (or restored) and the backup device (disk or tape).

PL/SQL packages: RMAN uses two internal PL/SQL packages (owned by SYS) to perform backup and restore tasks: DBMS_RCVMAN and DBMS_BACKUP_RESTORE. DBMS_RCVMAN accesses information in the control file and passes that to the RMAN server processes. The DBMS_BACKUP_RESTORE package performs most of RMAN's work. For example, this package creates the system calls that direct the channel processes to perform B&R operations.

Memory buffers (PGA or SGA): RMAN uses a memory area in the PGA (and sometimes in the SGA) as a buffer when reading from data files and copying subsequent blocks to back up files.

Auxiliary database: A database to which RMAN restores target database data files for the purpose of duplicating a database, creating a Data Guard standby database, or performing a database point in time recovery (DBPITR).

Backup/Back up: Can be either a noun or a verb. The physical files (backup) that store the backed-up files; or, the act of copying and archiving (backing up) files. Backups can consist of backup sets and backup pieces or image copies.

Backup set: When you run an RMAN BACKUP command, by default, it creates one or more backup sets. A backup set is a logical RMAN construct that groups backup piece files. You can think of the relationship of a backup set to a backup piece as similar to the relationship between a tablespace and a data file: one is a logical construct, the other is a physical file.

Backup piece file: RMAN binary backup files. Each logical backup set consists of one or more backup piece files. These are the physical files that RMAN creates on disk or tape. They are binary, proprietary format files that only RMAN can read or write to. A backup piece can contain blocks from many different data files. Backup piece files are typically smaller than data files, because backup pieces only contain blocks that have been used in the data files.

Image copy: Initiated with the BACKUP AS COPY command. A type of backup in which RMAN creates identical copies of a data file, archivelog file, or control file. Image copies can be operated on by OS utilities such as the Linux cp and mv commands. Image copies are used as part of incrementally updated image backups. Sometimes, it is preferable to use image copies rather than backup sets if you need to be able to restore quickly.

Recovery catalog: An optional database schema that contains tables used to store metadata information regarding RMAN backup operations. Oracle strongly recommends using a recovery catalog, because it provides more options for backup and restore. The catalog is normally remote and does not have to be in each of the databases.

Media manager: Third-party software that allows RMAN to back up files directly to tape. Backing up to tape is desirable when you do not have enough room to back up directly to disk or when disaster recovery requirements necessitate a backup to storage that can be easily moved offsite.

Fast Recovery Area (FRA): A disk area that RMAN can use for backups. You can also use the FRA to multiplex control files and online redo logs. You instantiate a fast recovery with the database initialization parameters DB_RECOVERY_FILE_DEST_SIZE and DB_RECOVERY_FILE_DEST.

Snapshot control file: RMAN requires a read-consistent view of the control file when either backing up the control file or synchronizing with the recovery catalog (if it is being used). In these situations, RMAN first creates a temporary copy (snapshot) of the control file. This allows RMAN to use a version of the control file that is guaranteed not to change while backing up the control file or synchronizing with the recovery catalog being used). In these situations, RMAN first creates a temporary copy (snapshot) of the control file. This allows RMAN to use a version of the control file that is guaranteed not to change while backing up the control file or synchronizing with the recovery catalog.

You can make several types of backups with RMAN:

Full backup: All modified blocks associated with the data file are backed up. A full backup is not a backup of the entire database. For example, you can make a full backup of one data file.

Incremental level 0 backup: Backs up the same blocks as a full backup. The only difference between a level 0 backup and a full backup is that you can use a level 0 backup with other incremental backups, but not a full backup.

Incremental level 1 backup: Backs up only blocks that have been modified since the previous backup. Level 1 incremental backups can be either differential or cumulative. A differential level 1 backup is the default and backs up all blocks that have been modified since the last level 0 or level 1 backup. A cumulative level 1 backup backs up all blocks that have changed since the last level 0 backup.

Incrementally updated backup: First creates an image copy of the data files, after which subsequent backups are incremental backups that are merged with the image copy. This is an efficient way to use image copies for backups. Media recoveries using incrementally updated backups are fast because the image copy of the data file is used during the restore.

Block change tracking: Database feature that keeps track of blocks that have changed in the database. A record of the changed blocks is kept in a binary file. RMAN can use the contents of the binary file to improve the performance of incremental backups: instead of having to scan all modified blocks in a data file, RMAN can determine which blocks have changed from the binary block change tracking.

Archivelog backups: This performs the backup of the archivelogs and allows for freeing up space in the archivelog directory. Archivelog backups are normally included as part of the data files but can also be run separately to manage the disk space for the archivelogs.

Now that you understand the RMAN architectural components and the types of backups you can make, you are ready to start up RMAN and configure it for your environment.

Starting RMAN

To connect to RMAN, you need to establish:

- OS environment variables

- Access to a privileged OS account or a database user with SYSBACKUP privileges

The easiest way to connect to RMAN is to log in to the server on which the target database resides as the owner of the Oracle software (usually named `oracle`, on Linux/Unix boxes). When you log in as `oracle`, you need to establish several OS variables before you can use utilities such as `rman` and `sqlplus`. Setting these required OS variables is covered in detail in Chapter 2. RMAN can be run from another server with the Oracle software installed. The service or SID name is what is needed to connect to the target database in order to perform the backup.

At minimum, you need to set `ORACLE_HOME` and `ORACLE_SID`. Additionally, it is convenient if the `PATH` variable includes the directory `ORACLE_HOME/bin`. This is the directory that contains the Oracle utilities.

After you have established your OS variables, you can invoke RMAN from the OS, as shown:

```
$ rman target /
Or
$ rman target backupuser@ora18c
```

When connecting to RMAN, you do not have to specify the `AS SYSDBA` clause (as you do when connecting to a database as a privileged user in SQL*Plus). This is because RMAN always requires that you connect as a database user with SYSDBA privileges. Any user will need to have the SYSBACKUP role granted to it in order to perform the backups.

Tip   New in Oracle Database 12c, the SYSBACKUP privilege allows you to assign privileges to a user that include only the permissions needed to perform backup and restore operations. The SYSBACKUP privilege contains the subset of SYSDBA privileges required for carrying out such operations.

The previous example of logging in to RMAN uses OS authentication. This type of authentication means that if you can log in to an authorized OS account (such as the owner of the Oracle software, usually `oracle`), then you are allowed to connect to the database without having to provide a username and password. You administer OS authentication by assigning special groups to OS accounts. When you install the Oracle binaries in a Linux/Unix environment, you are required to specify at the time of installation the names of the OS groups that are assigned the database privileges of SYSDBA, SYSOPER, SYSBACKUP—typically, the `dba`, `oper`, and `backupdba` groups, respectively (see Chapter 1 for details). As part of an enterprise backup solution, it would be recommended to create a separate user for backups in order to perform the backups to disk or tape and schedule to run automatically.

(NOT) CALLING RMAN FROM SQL*PLUS

It is very typical to be in a SQLPLUS session and accidentally attempt an RMAN command or just try running RMAN from SQLPLUS. Well, it does not work:

```
SQL> rman
SP2-0042: unknown command "rman" - rest of line ignored.
```

The answer is short: the rman client is an OS utility, not an SQL*Plus function. You must invoke the rman client from the OS prompt.

RMAN Architectural Decisions

If archiving is enabled for your database (see Chapter 5 for details on archiving), you can use RMAN out of the box to run commands such as this to back up your entire target database:

```
$ rman target /
RMAN> backup database;
```

If you experience a media failure, you can restore all data files, as follows:

```
RMAN> shutdown immediate;
RMAN> startup mount;
RMAN> restore database;
```

After your database is restored, you can fully recover it:

```
RMAN> recover database;
RMAN> alter database open;
```

You are good to go, right? No, not quite. RMAN's default attributes are reasonably set for simple backup requirements. The RMAN out-of-the-box settings may be appropriate for small development or test databases. But, for any type of business-critical database, you need to consider carefully where the backups are stored, how long to store backups on disk or tape, which RMAN features are appropriate for the database, and so on. The following sections in this chapter walk you through many of the backup and recovery architectural decisions necessary for implementing RMAN in a production environment. RMAN has a vast and robust variety of options for customizing backups, managing backup files, and performing restores; and, typically, you do not need to implement many of RMAN's features. However, each time you implement RMAN to back up a production database, you should think through each decision point and decide whether you require an attribute.

Table 17-1 summarizes the RMAN implementation on in subsequent sections. Many DBAs will have differing opinions concerning some of these recommendations; that is fine. The point is that you need to consider each architectural aspect and determine what makes sense for your business requirements fine.

Table 17-1. *Overview of Architectural Decisions and Recommendations*

Decision Point	Recommendation
1. Running the RMAN client remotely or locally	Run the client locally on the target database server.
2. Specifying the backup user	Create a user for performing backups.
3. Using online or offline backups	Depends on your business requirements. Most production databases require online backups, which means that you must enable archiving.
4. Setting the archivelog destination and file format	If you are using an FRA, archive logs are written there with a default format. To use the LOG_ARCHIVE_DEST_N initialization parameter to specifically set the location outside the FRA.

(*continued*)

Table 17-1. (*continued*)

Decision Point	Recommendation
5. Configuring the RMAN backup location and file format	Depends on your business requirements. Some shops require tape backups. If you are using disk, place the backups in the FRA, or specify a location via channel settings. Using FRA will allow for increasing the storage sizing dynamically. Backups to tape can be run after creating the backup set and is normally more efficient.
6. Setting the autobackup of the control file	Always enable autobackup of the control file.
7. Specifying the location of the autobackup of the control file	Either place it in the FRA, or configure a location. It makes sense to write the autobackup of the control file to the same location as that of the database backups.
8. Backing up archivelogs	Depends on your business requirements. For many environments, backing up the archivelogs can be done just on a daily basis, with the same command use to back up the database or triggered when space requires it.
9. Determining the location for the snapshot control file	Use the default location.
10. Using a recovery catalog	Depends on your business requirements. Oracle recommends that you do use a recovery catalog. If the RMAN retention policy is greater than CONTROL_FILE_RECORD_KEEP_TIME, then I recommend that you use a recovery catalog.
11. Using a media manager	This is required for backing up directly to tape.
12. Setting the CONTROL_FILE_RECORD_KEEP_TIME initialization parameter	Usually, the default of 7 days is sufficient.
13. Configuring RMAN's backup retention policy	Depends on your database and business requirements. For many environments, I use a backup retention redundancy of 1 or 2.

(*continued*)

Table 17-1. *(continued)*

Decision Point	Recommendation
14. Configuring the archivelogs' deletion policy	Depends on your database and business requirements. In many scenarios, applying the backup retention policy to the archivelogs is sufficient (this is the default behavior).
15. Setting the degree of parallelism	Depends on the available hardware resources and business requirements. For most production servers, on which there are multiple CPUs, configure a degree of parallelism of 2 or more based on CPUs available.
16. Using backup sets or image copies	Backup sets are generally smaller than image copies and easier to manage.
17. Using incremental backups	Use incremental backups for large databases when a small percentage of the database changes between backups and when you want to conserve on disk space. Use incremental backups in a large database and data warehouse-type databases.
18. Using incrementally updated backups	Use this approach if you require image copies of data files.
19. Using block change tracking	Use this to improve the performance of incremental backups. For large, data warehouse-type databases, block change tracking can result in significant time savings for backups because it keeps track of the blocks changed so the backup does not have to read the headers to determine if the block has changed.
20. Configuring binary compression	Depends on your business requirements. Compressed backups consume less space but require more CPU resources (and time) for backup and restore operations.
21. Configuring encryption	Depends on your business requirements.
22. Configuring miscellaneous settings	You can set many channel-related properties, such as the backup set size and backup piece size. Configure as needed.
23. Configuring informational output	Configure the OS variable NLS_DATE_FORMAT to display date and time. Use SET ECHO ON and SHOW ALL to display RMAN commands and settings.

1. Running the RMAN Client Remotely or Locally

It is possible to run the rman utility from a remote server and connect to a target database via Oracle Net:

```
$ rman target sys/foo@remote_db
```

This allows you to run RMAN backups on disparate remote servers from one central location. When you run RMAN remotely, the backup files are always created on the target database server.

When running locally and after the database environment variables are configured, RMAN can be run like this:

```
$ rman target /
```

If you run RMAN remotely, you need to be sure the remote rman executable is compatible with the target database. For example, you may establish that the remote rman executable you are running is an Oracle Database 12c version of the RMAN client, and it is compatible with several earlier versions of Oracle database. If you run the rman client locally on the target server, there is never a compatibility issue because the rman client is always the same version as the target database.

2. Specifying the Backup User

As discussed previously, RMAN requires that you use a database user with SYSDBA privileges. Whether I'm running RMAN from the command line or invoking RMAN in a script, in most scenarios, using a backup user is appropriate. For example, here is how to connect to RMAN from the command line:

```
$ rman target BACKUPUSER/$password
```

Some DBAs do not use this approach; they opt to set up a user separate from SYS and cite security concerns as a rationale for doing this. The password variable can either read in the password from a secured encrypted file or use another method for getting the password. Other examples in this chapter will probably be showing the use for the SYS users:

```
$ rman target
```

3. Using Online or Offline Backups

Most production databases have 24-7 availability requirements. Therefore, your only option is online RMAN backups. Your database must be in archivelog mode for online backups. You need to consider carefully how to place archivelogs, how to format them, how often to back them up, and how long to retain them before deletion. These topics are discussed in subsequent sections.

Note   If you make offline backups, you must shut down your database with IMMEDIATE, NORMAL, or TRANSACTIONAL and then place it in mount mode. RMAN needs the database in mount mode so that it can read from and write to the control file.

---

4. Setting the Archivelog Destination and File Format

Enabling archive redo log mode is a prerequisite for making online backups (see Chapter 5 for a full discussion of architectural decisions regarding the archivelog destination and format and how to enable/disable archivelog mode).

When archivelog mode is enabled, Oracle writes the archivelogs to one or more of the following locations (you can configure archivelogs to be written to the FRA as well as to several other locations that you manually set via initialization parameters):

- Default location

- FRA (Fast Recovery Area)

- Location specified via the LOG_ARCHIVE_DEST_N initialization parameter(s)

If you do not use an FRA, and if you do not explicitly set the archivelog destination via a LOG_ARCHIVE_DEST_N initialization parameter, then by default the archivelogs are written to an OS-dependent location. On many Linux/Unix boxes the default location is the ORACLE_HOME/dbs directory. The default file name format for archivelogs is %t_%s_%r.dbf. The format is a shorthand to reference date, backup set number, etc. The %t is timestamp, %s is log sequence number and %r is reset logs ID.

If you enable an FRA (and do not set LOG_ARCHIVE_DEST_N), then, by default, the archivelogs are written to a directory in the FRA. The default file name format of the of archivelog files created in the FRA is an Oracle Managed File (OMF) format. The files are stored in a subdirectory given the same name as the database's unique name; for example,

```
/<fra>/<dbuname>/archivelog/<YYYY_MM_DD>/o1_mf_1_1078_68dx5dyj_.arc
```

It is recommended to use an FRA. To use the LOG_ARCHIVE_DEST_N parameter to set the location of the archivelog files, follow this example:

```
log_archive_dest_1='LOCATION=/oraarch1/CHNPRD'
```

Here is also a preferred format for the default archivelog file name:

```
log_archive_format='%t_%s_%r.arc'
```

Sometimes, DBAs use .dbf as an extension for both data files and archivelog files. I prefer to use .arc for the archivelog files. The .arc extension avoids the potentially confusing task of identifying a file as an archivelog file or a live database data file.

5. Configuring the RMAN Backup Location and File Format

When you run a BACKUP command for disk-based backups, RMAN creates backup pieces in one of the following locations:

- Default location
- FRA
- Location specified via the BACKUP...FORMAT command
- Location specified via the CONFIGURE CHANNEL...FORMAT command

Default Location

If you do not configure any RMAN variables and do not set up an FRA, by default RMAN allocates one disk-based channel and writes the backup files to a default location. For example, you can run the following command without configuring any RMAN parameters:

```
RMAN> backup database;
```

The default location varies by OS. In many Linux/Unix environments, the default location is ORACLE_HOME/dbs. The default format of the name of the backup files created is an OMF format; for example,

```
<ORACLE_HOME>/dbs/01ln9g7e_1_1
```

Tip   The default location is okay for small development databases. However, for most other environments (especially production), you will need to plan ahead for how much disk space you will need for backups and explicitly set the location for the backups via one of the other methods (such as implementing an FRA or CONFIGURE CHANNEL).

FRA

When backing up to disk, if you do not explicitly instruct RMAN to write the backups to a specific location (via the FORMAT or CONFIGURE command), you are using an FRA, RMAN automatically writes the backup files to directories in the FRA. When you are using an FRA, RMAN automatically creates separate directories when backing up a database for the first time on a given date. The files are stored in a subdirectory with the same name as the database's unique name. Also, the default format of the name of the backup files created in the FRA is an OMF format; for example,

```
/<fra>/<dbuname>/backupset/<YYYY_MM_DD>/o1_mf_nnndf_TAG20100907T025402_
68czfbdf_.bkp
```

Dynamically being able to set the size or location of the FRA is available with SYSTEM parameters. This is useful if the backsets are still being purged or archivelogs are filling up the space; instead of hoping a backup or move of files completes, the FRA size can be adjusted, and then you can shrink it back down to the original size.

BACKUP...FORMAT

If you have configured an FRA and do not want to place RMAN backup files in the FRA automatically, you can directly specify where you want backups to be placed when you issue the B command; for example,

```
RMAN> backup database format '/u01/O18C/rman/rman_%U.bkp';
```

Here is a corresponding file generated by RMAN:

```
/u01/O18C/rman/rman_0jnv0557_1_1.bkp
```

The %U instructs RMAN to dynamically construct a unique string for the backup file name. A unique name is required in most situations, because RMAN won't write over the top of a file that already exists. This is important, because if you instruct RMAN to write in parallel, it needs to create unique file names for each channel; for example,

```
RMAN> configure device type disk parallelism 2;
```

Now, when you run the BACKUP command, you see this message:

```
RMAN> backup database format '/u01/O18C/rman/rman_%U.bkp';
```

RMAN allocates multiple channels and writes in parallel to two different backup files. The U% in the format string guarantees that unique file names are created.

CONFIGURE CHANNEL...FORMAT

When writing to multiple disk locations, it is easier to specify the directories using CONFIGURE CHANNEL...FORMAT. Here is a typical configuration specifying the following:

```
RMAN> configure device type disk parallelism 3;
RMAN> configure channel 1 device type disk format '/u01/O18C/rman/rman1_%U.bk';
RMAN> configure channel 2 device type disk format '/u02/O18C/rman/rman2_%U.bk';
RMAN> configure channel 3 device type disk format '/u03/O18C/rman/rman3_%U.bk';
```

In these lines of code, you should configure the device-type parallelism degree to match the number of channels that you allocated. RMAN only allocates the number of channels as specified by the degree of parallelism; other configured channels are ignored. For instance, if you specify a degree of parallelism of 2, RMAN allocates only two channels, regardless of the number of channels you configured via the CONFIGURE CHANNEL command.

In this example of configuring three channels, suppose the BACKUP command is issued, like this:

```
RMAN> backup database;
```

RMAN allocates three channels, all on separate mount points (/u01, /u02, /u03), and writes in parallel to the specified locations. RMAN creates as many backup pieces in the three locations as it deems necessary to create a backup of the database.

If you need to unconfigure a channel, do so as follows:

```
RMAN> configure channel 3 device type disk clear;
```

Note   Also consider what happens if you configure a degree of parallelism higher than the number of preconfigured channels. RMAN will open a channel for each degree of parallelism, and if the number of channels opened is greater than the number of preconfigured channels, for the unconfigured channels, RMAN will write backup files to the FRA (if configured) or the default location.

6. Setting the Autobackup of the Control File

You should always configure RMAN to back up the control file automatically after running any RMAN BACKUP or COPY command or after you make physical changes to the database that result in updates to the control file (such as adding/removing a data file). Use the SHOW command to display the current setting of the control file autobackup:

```
RMAN> show controlfile autobackup;
```

Here is some sample output:

```
RMAN configuration parameters for database with db_unique_name O18C are:
CONFIGURE CONTROLFILE AUTOBACKUP ON;
```

The following line of code shows how to enable automatic backup of the control file feature:

```
RMAN> configure controlfile autobackup on;
```

The automatic control file backup always goes into its own backup set. When autobackup of the control file is enabled, if you are using an spfile, it is automatically backed up along with the control file.

If, for any reason, you want to disable automatic backup of the control file, you can do so as follows:

```
RMAN> configure controlfile autobackup off;
```

Note   If autobackup of the control file is off, then any time you back up data file 1 (SYSTEM tablespace data file), RMAN automatically backs up the control file.

---

7. Specifying the Location of the Autobackup of the Control File

When you enable autobackup of the control file, RMAN creates the backup of the control file in one of the following locations:

- Default location

- FRA

- Location specified via the `CONFIGURE CONTROLFILE AUTOBACKUP FORMAT` command

If you are not using an FRA, or if you have not specified a location for the control file autobackups, the control file autobackup is written to an OS-dependent default location. In Linux/Unix environments, the default location is `ORACLE_HOME/dbs`; for example,

```
/u01/app/oracle/product/18.1.0.1/db_1/dbs/c-3423216220-20130109-01
```

If you have enabled an FRA, then RMAN automatically writes the control file autobackup files to directories in the FRA, using an OMF format for the name; for example,

```
/<fra>/<dbuname>/autobackup/<YYYY_MM_DD>/o1_mf_s_729103049_68fho9z2_.bkp
```

Control file backups can be placed in the same directory that the database backups are in. Here is an example:

```
RMAN> configure controlfile autobackup format for device type disk to
'/u01/O18C/rman/rman_ctl_%F.bk';
```

If you want to set the autobackup format back to the default, do so as follows:

```
RMAN> configure controlfile autobackup format for device type disk clear;
```

8. Backing Up Archivelogs

You should back up your archivelogs on a regular basis. The archivelog files should not be removed from disk until you have backed them up at least once. I usually like to keep on disk any archivelogs that have been generated since the last good RMAN backup.

Generally, I instruct RMAN to back up the archivelogs while the data files are being backed up. This is a sufficient strategy in most situations. Here is the command to back up the archivelogs along with the data files:

```
RMAN> backup database plus archivelog;
```

Sometimes, if your database generates a great deal of redo, you may need to back up your archivelogs at a frequency different from that of the data files. DBAs may back up the archivelogs two or three times a day; after the logs are backed up, the DBAs delete them to make room for more current archivelog files.

In most situations, you do not need any archivelogs that were generated before your last good backup. For example, if a data file has experienced media failure, you need to restore the data file from a backup and then apply any archivelogs that were generated during and after the backup of the data file.

On some occasions, you may need archivelogs that were generated before the last backup. For instance, you may experience a media failure, attempt to restore your database from the last good backup, find corruption in that backup, and therefore need to restore from an older backup. At that point, you need a copy of all archivelogs that have been generated since that older backup was made.

9. Determining the Location for the Snapshot Control File

RMAN requires a read-consistent view of the control file for the following tasks:

- Synchronizing with the recovery catalog

- Backing up the current control file

RMAN creates a snapshot copy of the current control file that it uses as a read-consistent copy while it is performing these tasks. This ensures that RMAN is working from a copy of the control file that is not being modified.

The default location of the snapshot control file is OS specific. On Linux platforms, the default location/format is `ORACLE_HOME/dbs/snapcf_@.f`. Note that the default location is not in the FRA.

You can display the current snapshot control file details, using the `SHOW` command:

```
RMAN> show snapshot controlfile name;
```

Here is some sample output:

```
CONFIGURE SNAPSHOT CONTROLFILE NAME TO
 '/ora01/app/oracle/product/18.1.0.1/db_1/dbs/snapcf_o18c.f'; # default
```

For most situations, the default location and format of the snapshot control file are sufficient. This file does not use much space or have any intensive I/O requirements. I recommend that you use the default setting.

If you have a good reason to configure the snapshot control file to a nondefault location, you can do so as follows:

```
RMAN> configure snapshot controlfile name to '/u01/O18C/rman/snapcf.ctl';
```

If you accidentally configure the snapshot control file location to a nonexistent directory, then when running a `BACKUP` or `COPY` command, the autobackup of the control file will fail, with this error:

```
ORA-01580: error creating control backup file ...
```

You can set the snapshot control file back to the default, like this:

```
RMAN> configure snapshot controlfile name clear;
```

10. Using a Recovery Catalog

RMAN always stores its latest backup operations in the target database control file. You can set up an optional recovery catalog to store metadata regarding RMAN backups. The recovery catalog is a separate schema (usually in a database different from that of the target database) that contains database objects (tables, indexes, and so on) that store the RMAN backup information. The recovery catalog does not store RMAN backup pieces—only backup metadata.

The main advantages of using a recovery catalog are as follows:

- Provides a secondary repository for RMAN metadata. If you lose all your control files and backups of your control files, you can still retrieve RMAN metadata from the recovery catalog.

- Stores RMAN metadata for a much longer period than is possible when you just use a control file for the repository.

- Offers access to all RMAN features. Some restore and recovery features are simpler when using a recovery catalog.

The disadvantage of using a recovery catalog is that this is another database you have to set up, maintain, and back up. Additionally, when you start a backup and attempt to connect to the recovery catalog, if the recovery catalog is not available for any reason (server down, network issues, and so on), you can continue with the backup without a recovery catalog.

You must also be aware of versioning aspects when using a recovery catalog. You need to make sure the version of the database you use to store the recovery catalog is compatible with the version of the target database. When you upgrade a target database, be sure the recovery catalog is upgraded (if necessary).

Note   See Chapter 18 for details on how to implement a recovery catalog.

---

11. Using a Media Manager

A media manager is required for RMAN to back up directly to tape. Several vendors provide this feature (for a cost). Media managers are used in large database environments, such as data warehouses, in which you may not have enough room to back up a database to disk. You may also have a disaster recovery requirement to back up directly to tape.

If you have such requirements, then you should purchase a media management package and implement it. If you do not need to back up directly to tape, there's no need to implement a media manager. RMAN works fine backing up directly to disk. The backup files can be copied off to tape for offsite storage and because of retention policies. If copying to tape, you can have a job run the RMAN backup and then initiate the copy to tape. The backup files need to be complete and not in the middle of a backup; otherwise there is the risk of only getting partial files copied to tape.

Tip   See Chapter 20 for details on how to implement Oracle Secure Backup as a media management layer.

---

12. Setting the CONTROL_FILE_RECORD_KEEP_TIME Initialization Parameter

The CONTROL_FILE_RECORD_KEEP_TIME initialization parameter specifies the minimum number of days a reusable record in the control file is retained before the record can be overwritten. The RMAN metadata are stored in the reusable section of the control file and therefore are eventually overwritten.

If you are using a recovery catalog, then you do not need to worry about this parameter because RMAN metadata are stored in the recovery catalog indefinitely. Therefore, when you use a recovery catalog, you can access any historical RMAN metadata.

If you are using only the control file as the RMAN metadata repository, then the information stored there will eventually be overwritten. The default value for CONTROL_FILE_RECORD_KEEP_TIME is 7 days:

```
SQL> show parameter control_file_record_keep_time

NAME                                 TYPE        VALUE
------------------------------------ ----------- --------------------------
control_file_record_keep_time        integer     7
```

You can set the value to anything from 0 to 365 days. Setting the value to 0 means that the RMAN metadata information can be overwritten at any time.

The CONTROL_FILE_RECORD_KEEP_TIME parameter was more critical in older versions of Oracle, in which it was not easy to repopulate the control file with RMAN information, in the event that metadata were overwritten. The C command can be used to quickly make the control file aware of RMAN backup files.

If you run daily backups, then I recommend that you leave this parameter at 7 days. However, if you only back up your database once a month, or if, for some reason, you have a retention policy greater than 7 days, and you are not using a recovery catalog, then you may want to consider increasing the value. The downside to increasing this parameter is that if you have a significant amount of RMAN backup activity, this can increase the size of your control file.

13. Configuring RMAN's Backup Retention Policy

RMAN retention policies allow you to specify how long you want to retain backups. RMAN has two mutually exclusive methods of specifying a retention policy:

- Recovery window

- Number of backups (redundancy)

Recovery Window

With a recovery window, you specify a number of days in the past for which you want to be able recover to any point in that window. For example, if you specify a retention policy window of 5 days, then RMAN does not mark as obsolete backups of data files and archivelogs that are required to be able to restore to any point in that 5-day window:

```
RMAN> configure retention  policy to recovery window of 5 days;
```

For the specified recovery, RMAN may need backups older than the 5-day window because it may need an older backup to start with to be able to recover to the recovery point specified. For cxample, suppose your last good backup was made 6 days ago, and now you want to recover to 4 days in the past. For this recovery window, RMAN needs the backup from 6 days ago to restore and recover to the point specified.

Redundancy

You can also specify that RMAN keep a minimum number of backups. For instance, if redundancy is set to 2, then RMAN does not mark as obsolete the latest two backups of data files and archivelog files:

```
RMAN> configure retention policy to redundancy 2;
```

I find that a retention policy based on redundancy is easier to work with and more predictable with regard to how long backups are retained. If I set redundancy to 2, I know that RMAN will not mark as obsolete the latest two backups. In contrast, the recovery window retention policy depends on the frequency of the backups and the window length to determine whether a backup is obsolete.

Deleting Backups, Based on Retention Policy

You can report on backups that RMAN has determined to be obsolete per the retention policy, as follows:

RMAN> report obsolete;

To delete obsolete backups, run the DELETE OBSOLETE command:

RMAN> delete obsolete;

You are prompted with this:

Do you really want to delete the above objects (enter YES or NO)?

If you are scripting the procedure, you can specify the delete not to prompt for input:

RMAN> delete noprompt obsolete;

I usually have the DELETE NOPROMPT OBSOLETE command coded into the shell script that backs up the database. This instructs RMAN to delete any obsolete backups and obsolete archivelogs, as specified by the retention policy (see the section "Segueing from Decisions to Action," later in this chapter, for an example of how to automate the deleting of obsolete backups with a shell script).

Clearing the Retention Policy

The default retention policy is redundancy of 1. You can completely disable the RMAN retention policy via the TO NONE command.

RMAN> configure retention policy to none;

When the policy is set to NONE, no backups are ever considered obsolete and therefore cannot be removed via the DELETE OBSOLETE command. This normally is not the behavior you want. You want to let RMAN delete backups per a retention policy based on a window or number of backups.

To set the retention policy back to the default, use the CLEAR command:

RMAN> configure retention policy clear;

14. Configuring the Archivelogs' Deletion Policy

In most scenarios, I have RMAN delete the archivelogs based on the retention policy of the database backups. This is the default behavior. You can view the database retention policy, using the SHOW command:

```
RMAN> show retention policy;
CONFIGURE RETENTION POLICY TO REDUNDANCY 1; # default
```

To remove archivelogs (and backup pieces) based on the database retention policy, run the following:

```
RMAN> delete obsolete;
```

As of Oracle Database 11g, you can specify an archivelog deletion policy that is separate from that of the database backups. This deletion policy applies to archivelogs both outside and in the FRA.

Note   Prior to Oracle Database 11g, the archive deletion policy only applied to archivelogs associated with a standby database.

To configure an archivelog deletion policy, use the CONFIGURE ARCHIVELOG DELETION command. The following command configures the archive redo deletion policy so that archivelogs aren't deleted until they have been backed up twice to disk:

```
RMAN> configure archivelog deletion policy to backed up 2 times to device
type disk;
```

To have RMAN delete obsolete archivelogs, as defined by the archivelog deletion policy, issue the following command:

```
RMAN> delete archivelog all;
```

Tip   Run the CROSSCHECK command before running the DELETE command. Doing so ensures that RMAN is aware of whether a file is on disk.

To see whether a retention policy has been set specifically for the archivelog files, use this command:

```
RMAN> show archivelog deletion policy;
```

To clear the archive deletion policy, do this:

```
RMAN> configure archivelog deletion policy clear;
```

15. Setting the Degree of Parallelism

You can significantly increase the performance of RMAN backup and restore operations if your database server is equipped with the hardware to support multiple channels. If your server has multiple CPUs and multiple storage devices (disks or tape devices), then you can improve performance by enabling multiple backup channels.

If you require better performance from backup and restore operations and have hardware that facilitates parallel operations, you should enable parallelism and perform tests to determine the optimal degree. If your hardware can take advantage of parallel RMAN channels, there is little downside to enabling parallelism.

If you have multiple CPUs, but just one storage device location, you can enable multiple channels to write to and read from one location. For example, if you are backing up to an FRA, you can still take advantage of multiple channels by enabling parallelism. Suppose you have four CPUs on a server and want to enable a corresponding degree of parallelism:

```
RMAN> configure device type disk parallelism 4;
```

You can also write to separate locations in parallel by configuring multiple channels associated with different mount points; for example,

```
RMAN> configure device type disk parallelism 4;
RMAN> configure channel 1 device type disk format '/u01/O18C/rman/rman1_%U.bk';
RMAN> configure channel 2 device type disk format '/u02/O18C/rman/rman2_%U.bk';
RMAN> configure channel 3 device type disk format '/u03/O18C/rman/rman3_%U.bk';
RMAN> configure channel 4 device type disk format '/u04/O18C/rman/rman4_%U.bk';
```

This code configures four channels that write to separate locations on disk. When you configure separate channels for different locations, make sure you enable the degree of parallelism to match the number of configured device channels. If you allocate more channels than the specified degree of parallelism, RMAN only writes to the number of channels specified by the degree of parallelism and ignores the other channels.

If you need to clear the degree of parallelism, you can do so as follows:

```
RMAN> configure device type disk clear;
```

Similarly, to clear the channel device types, use the CLEAR command. This example clears channel 4:

```
RMAN> configure channel 4 device type disk clear;
```

16. Using Backup Sets or Image Copies

When you issue an RMAN BACKUP command, you can specify that the backup be one of the following:

- Backup set

- Image copy

A backup set is the default type of RMAN backup. A backup set contains backup pieces, which are binary files that only RMAN can write to or read from. Backup sets are desirable because they are generally smaller than the data files being backed up. RMAN automatically attempts to create backup pieces with unused block compression. In this mode, RMAN reads a bitmap to determine which blocks are allocated and only reads from those blocks in the data files. This feature is supported only for disk-based backup sets and Oracle Secure Backup tape backups.

Note   RMAN can also create backup sets using true binary compression. This is the type of compression you get from an OS compression utility (such as `zip`). Oracle supports several levels of binary compression. The BASIC compression algorithm is available without an additional license. Oracle provides further compression features with the Oracle Advanced Compression option (see the section "Configuring Binary Compression," later in this chapter, for details on how to enable binary compression).

When you create a backup as a backup set, the binary backup piece files can only be manipulated by RMAN processes. Some DBAs view this as a disadvantage because they must use RMAN to back up and restore these files (you have no direct access to or control over the backup pieces). But these perceptions are not warranted. Unless you hit a rare bug, RMAN is dependable and works reliably in all backup and restore situations.

Contrast the backup set with an image copy. An image copy creates a byte-for-byte identical copy of each data file. The advantage of creating an image copy is that (if necessary) you can manipulate the image copy without using RMAN (as with an OS copy utility). Additionally, in the event of a media failure, an image copy is a fast method of restoring data files, because RMAN only has to copy the file back from the backup location (there is no reconstructing of the data file, because it is an exact copy).

The size of the backup to disk is almost always a concern. Backup sets are more efficient regarding disk space consumption. Because backup sets can take advantage of RMAN compression, there is also less I/O involved, compared with an image copy. In many environments, reducing the I/O so as not to impact other applications is a concern.

However, if you feel that you need direct control over the backup files that RMAN creates, or you are in an environment in which the speed of the restore process is paramount, consider using image copies.

17. Using Incremental Backups

Incremental backup strategies are appropriate for large databases in which only a small portion of the database blocks change from one backup to the next. If you are in a data warehouse environment, you may want to consider an incremental backup strategy, because it can greatly reduce the size of your backups. For example, you may want to run a weekly level 0 backup and then run a daily level 1 incremental backup.

The term *RMAN level 0 incremental backup* doesn't exactly describe itself very well, either. A level 0 incremental backup is backing up the same blocks as a full backup. In other words, the following two commands back up the same blocks in a database:

```
RMAN> backup as backupset full database;
RMAN> backup as backupset incremental level=0 database;
```

The only difference between the prior two commands is that an incremental level 0 backup can be used in conjunction with other incremental backups, whereas a full backup cannot participate in an incremental backup strategy. Therefore, I almost always prefer to use the INCREMENTAL LEVEL=0 syntax (as opposed to a full backup); it gives me the flexibility to use the level 0 incremental backup along with subsequent incremental level 1 backups.

18. Using Incrementally Updated Backups

Incrementally updated backups are an efficient way to implement an image copy backup strategy. This technique instructs RMAN to first create image copies of data files; then, the next time the backup runs, instead of creating a fresh set of image copies, RMAN makes an incremental backup (changes to blocks since the image copy was created) and applies that incremental backup to the image copies.

If you have the disk space available for full image copies of your database and you want the flexibility to use the image copies directly, in the event of a media failure, consider this backup strategy.

One potential disadvantage of this approach is that if you are required to restore and recover to some point in the past, you can only restore and recover to the point at which the image copies were last updated with the incremental backup.

19. Using Block Change Tracking

This feature keeps track of when a database block changes. The idea is that if you are using an incremental backup strategy, you can enhance performance, because by implementing this feature, RMAN does not have to scan each block (under the high-water mark) in the data files to determine whether it needs to be backed up. Rather, RMAN only has to access the block change tracking file to find which blocks have changed since the last backup and directly access those blocks. If you work in a large, data warehouse environment and are using an incremental backup strategy, consider enabling block change tracking to enhance performance.

Note   See Chapter 18 for more details on implementing incremental and block change backup and restores.

---

20. Configuring Binary Compression

You can configure RMAN to use true binary compression when generating backup sets. You can enable compression in one of two ways:

- Specify AS COMPRESSED BACKUPSET with the BACKUP command.

- Use a one-time CONFIGURE command.

Here is an example of backing up with compression when issuing the BACKUP command:

```
RMAN> backup as compressed backupset database;
```

In this example, compression is configured for the disk device:

```
RMAN> configure device type disk backup type to compressed backupset;
```

If you need to clear the device-type compression, issue this command:

```
RMAN> configure device type disk clear;
```

The default compression algorithm proves to be quite efficient. For a typical database, the backups are usually approximately four to five times smaller than the regular backups. Of course, your compression results may vary, depending on your data.

Why not compress all backups? Compressed backups consume more CPU resources and take longer to create and restore from, but they result in less I/O, spread out over a longer period. If you have multiple CPUs, and the speed of making a backup isn't an issue, then you should consider compressing your backups.

You can view the type of compression enabled, using the SHOW command:

```
RMAN> show compression algorithm;
```

Here is some sample output:

```
CONFIGURE COMPRESSION ALGORITHM 'BASIC' AS OF RELEASE 'DEFAULT'
OPTIMIZE FOR LOAD TRUE ; # default
```

The basic compression algorithm does not require an extra license from Oracle. If you have a license for the Advanced Compression option, then you have available three additional configurable levels of binary compression; for example,

```
RMAN> configure compression algorithm 'HIGH';
RMAN> configure compression algorithm 'MEDIUM';
RMAN> configure compression algorithm 'LOW';
```

In my experience the prior compression algorithms are very efficient, both in compression ratios and time taken to create backups.

You can query V$RMAN_COMPRESSION_ALGORITHM to view details regarding the compression algorithms available for your release of the database. To reset the current compression algorithm to the default of BASIC, use the CLEAR command:

```
RMAN> configure compression algorithm clear;
```

21. Configuring Encryption

You may be required to encrypt backups. Some shops especially require this for backups that contain sensitive data and that are stored offsite. To use encryption when backing up, you must use the Oracle Enterprise Edition and possess a license for the Advanced Security option.

If you have configured a security wallet (see the Oracle Advanced Security Administrator's Guide, which can be freely downloaded from the Technology Network area of the Oracle web site (http://otn.oracle.com, for details), you can configure transparent encryption for backups, as shown:

```
RMAN> configure encryption for database on;
```

Any backups that you make now will be encrypted. If you need to restore from a backup, it is automatically unencrypted (assuming the same security wallet is in place as when you encrypted the backup). To disable encryption, use the C command:

```
RMAN> configure encryption for database off;
```

Encrypted tablespaces will remain encrypted in the backup sets. The configuration for backup encryption does not need to be on for this, but only the tablespaces that are encrypted will remain encrypted.

You can also clear the encryption setting with CLEAR:

```
RMAN> configure encryption for database clear;
```

You can query V$RMAN_ENCRYPTION_ALGORITHMS to view details regarding the encryption algorithms available for your release of the database.

RUNNING SQL FROM WITHIN RMAN

Starting with Oracle Database 12c, you can run SQL statements (and see the results) directly from within RMAN:

```
RMAN> select * from v$rman_encryption_algorithms;
```

Prior to 12c, you could run the prior SQL statement with the RMAN `sql` command, but no results would be displayed:

```
RMAN> sql 'select * from v$rman_encryption_algorithms';
```

The RMAN `sql` command was meant more for running commands such as ALTER SYTEM:

```
RMAN> sql 'alter system switch logfile';
```

Now, in 12c, you can run the SQL directly:

```
RMAN> alter system switch logfile;
```

This ability to run SQL from within RMAN is a really nice enhancement; it allows you to see the results of SQL queries and eliminates the need for specifying the `sql` keyword as well as for placing quotation marks around the SQL command itself.

---

22. Configuring Miscellaneous Settings

RMAN provides a flexible number of channel configuration commands. You will occasionally need to use them, depending on special circumstances and the requirements for your database. Here are some of the options:

- Maximum backup set size
- Maximum backup piece size
- Maximum rate
- Maximum open files

By default, the maximum backup set size is unlimited. You can use the MAXSETSIZE parameter with the CONFIGURE or BACKUP command to specify the overall maximum backup set size. Make sure the value of this parameter is at least as great as the largest data file being backed up by RMAN. Here is an example:

```
RMAN> configure maxsetsize to 2g;
```

Sometimes, you may want to limit the overall size of a backup piece because of physical limitations of storage devices. Use the MAXPIECESIZE parameter of the CONFIGURE CHANNEL or ALLOCATE CHANNEL command do this; for example,

```
RMAN> configure channel device type disk maxpiecesize = 2g;
```

If you need to set the maximum number of bytes that RMAN reads each second on a channel, you can do so, using the RATE parameter. This configures the maximum read rate for channel 1 to 200MB per second:

```
configure channel 1 device type disk rate 200M;
```

If you have a limit on the number of files you can have open simultaneously, you can specify a maximum open files number via the MAXOPENFILES parameter:

```
RMAN> configure channel 1 device type disk maxopenfiles 32;
```

You may need to configure any of these settings when you need to make RMAN aware of some OS or hardware limitation. You will rarely need to use these parameters but should know of them.

23. Configuring Informational Output

A good practice is to always set the OS NLS_DATE_FORMAT variable (before running RMAN) so that both the date and time information are displayed in the RMAN log instead of just the date, which is the default:

```
export NLS_DATE_FORMAT='dd-mon-yyyy hh24:mi:ss'
```

This is useful during troubleshooting, especially when RMAN fails, because we can use the exact date/time information for when the RMAN error occurred and compare it with the alert.log and OS/MML logs to verify what other events occurred in the database/server.

Also consider executing SET ECHO ON to ensure that RMAN commands are displayed within the log before the command is executed. Execute SHOW ALL as well to display the current settings of RMAN variables. These settings are useful when troubleshooting and tuning.

CLEARING ALL RMAN CONFIGURATIONS

There is no CLEAR ALL command for resetting all RMAN configurations back to the default values. However, you can easily simulate this by running a script that contains CONFIGURE... CLEAR commands:

```
CONFIGURE RETENTION POLICY clear;
CONFIGURE BACKUP OPTIMIZATION clear;
CONFIGURE DEFAULT DEVICE TYPE clear;
CONFIGURE CONTROLFILE AUTOBACKUP clear;
CONFIGURE CONTROLFILE AUTOBACKUP FORMAT FOR DEVICE TYPE DISK clear;
CONFIGURE DEVICE TYPE DISK clear;
CONFIGURE DATAFILE BACKUP COPIES FOR DEVICE TYPE DISK clear;
CONFIGURE CHANNEL 1 DEVICE TYPE DISK clear;
CONFIGURE CHANNEL 2 DEVICE TYPE DISK clear;
CONFIGURE CHANNEL 3 DEVICE TYPE DISK clear;
CONFIGURE ARCHIVELOG BACKUP COPIES FOR DEVICE TYPE DISK clear;
CONFIGURE MAXSETSIZE clear;
CONFIGURE ENCRYPTION FOR DATABASE clear;
CONFIGURE ENCRYPTION ALGORITHM clear;
CONFIGURE COMPRESSION ALGORITHM clear;
CONFIGURE RMAN OUTPUT clear; # 12c
CONFIGURE ARCHIVELOG DELETION POLICY clear;
CONFIGURE SNAPSHOT CONTROLFILE NAME clear;
```

Depending on what you have set (and the version of your database), you may need to set additional configurations.

Segueing from Decision to Action

Now that you have a good understanding of what types of decisions you should make before implementing RMAN, it is instructional to view a script that implements some of these components. Scripts can be used to automate the RMAN backups. These shell scripts are automated through a scheduling utility such as cron. RMAN can also be run from Oracle Enterprise Manager. Additionally, if there are tools that are used to copy files to tape or other schedulers, RMAN scripts can be included in these jobs; however, there is less flexibility if the RMAN script does not remain on the database side.

This section contains a typical shell script for RMAN backups. The shell script has line numbers in the output for reference in the discussion of the architectural decisions there were made when writing the script. (If you copy the script, take out the line numbers before running it.)

Following is the script. Table 17-2 details every RMAN architectural decision point covered in this chapter, how it is implemented (or not) in the shell script, and the corresponding line number in the shell script. The script does not cover every aspect of how to use RMAN. If you use the script, be sure to modify it to meet the requirements and RMAN standards for your own environment:

```
1 #!/bin/bash
2 HOLDSID=${1}  # SID name
3 PRG=`basename $0`
4 USAGE="Usage: ${PRG} <database name> "
5 if [ -z "${HOLDSID}" ]; then
6    echo "${USAGE}"
7    exit 1
8 fl
9 #-----------------------------------------------
10 # source environment variables (see Chapter 2 for details on oraset)
11 . /etc/oraset $HOLDSID
12 BOX=`uname -a | awk '{print$2}'`
13 MAILX='/bin/mailx'
14 MAIL_LIST='dkuhn@gmail.com'
15 export NLS_DATE_FORMAT='dd-mon-yyyy hh24:mi:ss'
16 date
17 #-----------------------------------------------
```

```
18 LOCKFILE=/tmp/$PRG.lock
19 if [ -f $LOCKFILE ]; then
20   echo "lock file exists, exiting..."
21   exit 1
22 else
23   echo "DO NOT REMOVE, $LOCKFILE" > $LOCKFILE
24 fi
25 #------------------------------------------------
26 rman nocatalog <<EOF
27 connect target /
28 set echo on;
29 show all;
30 crosscheck backup;
31 crosscheck copy;
32 configure controlfile autobackup on;
33 configure controlfile autobackup format for device type disk to
   '/u01/O18C/rman/o18c_ctl_%F.bk';
34 configure retention policy to redundancy 1;
35 configure          device type disk parallelism 2;
36 configure channel 1 device type disk format '/u01/O18C/rman/o18c_%U.bk';
37 configure channel 2 device type disk format '/u02/O18C/rman/o18c_%U.bk';
38 backup as compressed backupset incremental level=0 database plus archivelog;
39 delete noprompt obsolete;
40 EOF
41 #------------------------------------------------
42 if [ $? -ne 0 ]; then
43   echo "RMAN problem..."
44   echo "Check RMAN backups" | $MAILX -s "RMAN issue: $ORACLE_SID on
   $BOX" $MAIL_LIST
45 else
46   echo "RMAN ran okay..."
47 fi
48 #------------------------------------------------
49 if [ -f $LOCKFILE ]; then
50   rm $LOCKFILE
```

```
51 fi
52 #------------------------------------------------
53 date
54 exit 0
```

Table 17-2. *Implementation of Architectural Decisions*

Decision Point	Implementation in Script	Line Number in Script
1. Running the RMAN client remotely or locally	Running script locally on the database server	Line 26, connecting locally (not a network connection)
2. Specifying the backup user	Using SYS to connect	Line 27, starting rman connecting with forward slash (/)
3. Using online or offline backups	Online backup	N/A. Database is assumed to be up during the backup
4. Setting the archivelog destination and file format	LOG_ARCHIVE_DEST_N and LOG_ARCHIVE_FORMAT initialization parameters set outside the script in a database parameter file	N/A; set outside the script
5. Configuring the RMAN backup location and file format	Using the CONFIGURE command directly in the script	Lines 33–37
6. Setting the autobackup of the control file	Enabled in the script	Line 32
7. Specifying the location of the autobackup of the control file	Placed in the same directory as the backups	Line 33
8. Backing up archivelogs	Backing up with the rest of the database; specifically, using the PLUS ARCHIVELOG clause	Line 38

(*continued*)

Table 17-2. (*continued*)

Decision Point	Implementation in Script	Line Number in Script
9. Determining the location for the snapshot control file	Using the default location	N/A
10. Using a recovery catalog	Not using	Line 26, connecting as `nocatalog`
11. Using a media manager	Not using	Lines 35–37, `device type disk`
12. Setting the `CONTROL_FILE_RECORD_KEEP_TIME` initialization parameter	Using the default	N/A
13. Configuring RMAN's backup retention policy	Configuring to a redundancy of 1, cross-checking, and deleting obsolete backups and archivelog files	Line 34, configuring; lines 30 and 31 crosscheck; line 39, using RMAN to delete old files
14. Configuring the archivelogs' deletion policy	Using the same retention policy applied to the backups	N/A
15. Setting the degree of parallelism	Setting a degree of 2	Lines 35–37
16. Using backup sets or image copies	Using backup sets	Line 38
17. Using incremental backups	Incremental level 0, the same as a full backup	Line 38
18. Using incrementally updated backups	Not using	N/A
19. Using block change tracking	Not using	N/A
20. Configuring binary compression	Using basic compression	Line 38
21. Configuring encryption	Not using	N/A
22. Configuring miscellaneous settings	Not using	N/A
23. Configuring informational output	Setting	Lines 15, 28, and 29

A few aspects of this script need further discussion. Line 11 sets the required OS variables by running a script named oraset (see Chapter 2 for details on running oraset and sourcing OS variables). Many DBAs choose to hard-code OS variables, such as ORACLE_HOME and ORACLE_SID, into the script. However, you should avoid hard-coding variables and instead use a script to source the required variables. Running a script is much more flexible, especially when you have many databases on a box with different versions of Oracle installed.

Line 15 sets the NLS_DATE_FORMAT OS variableyou are debugging and diagnoses issues. By default, RMAN displays only the date component. Knowing just the date when a command ran is rarely enough information to determine the timing of the commands as they were executed. At minimum, you need to see hours and minutes (along with the date).

Lines 18–24 check for the existence of a lock file. You do not want to run this script if it is already running. The script checks for the lock file, and, if it exists, the script exits. After the backup has finished, the lock file is removed (lines 49–51).

Line 28 sets the ECHO parameter to on. This instructs RMAN to display in the output the command before running it. This can be invaluable for debugging issues. Line 29 displays all the configurable variables. This also comes in handy for troubleshooting issues because you can see what the RMAN variables were set to before any commands are executed.

Lines 32–37 use the CONFIGURE command. These commands run each time the script is executed. Why do that? You only need to run a CONFIGURE command once, and it is stored in the control file—you do not have to run it again, right? That is correct. However, I've occasionally been burned when a DBA with poor habits configured a setting for a database and didn't tell anybody, and I didn't discover the misconfiguration until I attempted to make another backup. I strongly prefer to place the CONFIGURE commands in the script so that the behavior is the same, regardless of what another DBA may have done outside the script. The CONFIGURE settings in the script also act as a form of documentation: I can readily look at the script and determine how settings have been configured.

Lines 30 and 31 run CROSSCHECK commands. Why do that? Sometimes, files go missing, or a rogue DBA may remove archivelog files from disk with an OS command outside RMAN. When RMAN runs, if it can't find files that it thinks should be in place, it throws an error and stops the backup. I prefer to run the CROSSCHECK command and let RMAN reconcile which files it thinks should be on disk with those that are actually on disk. This keeps RMAN running smoothly.

You run `DELETE NOPROMPT OBSOLETE` on line 39. This removes all backup files and archivelog files that have been marked as `OBSOLETE` by RMAN, as defined by the retention policy. This lets RMAN manage which files should be kept on disk. I prefer to run the `DELETE` command after the backup has finished (as opposed to running it before the backup). The retention policy is defined as 1, so if you run `DELETE` after the backup, RMAN leaves one backup copy on disk. If you run `DELETE` before the backup, RMAN leaves one copy of the backup on disk. After the backup runs, there are be two copies of the backup on disk, which I do not have room for on this server.

You can execute the shell script from the Linux/Unix scheduling utility `cron`, as follows:

```
0 16 * * * $HOME/bin/rmanback.bsh INVPRD >$HOME/bin/log/INVPRDRMAN.log 2>&1
```

The script runs daily at 1600 hours military time on the database server. A log file is created (`INVPRDRMAN.log`) to capture any output and errors associated with the RMAN job. See Chapter 21 for details on automating jobs through `cron`.

Again, the script in this section is basic; you will no doubt want to enhance and modify it to meet your requirements. This script gives you a starting point, with concrete RMAN recommendations and how to implement them.

Summary

RMAN is not only the backup tool for Oracle database but the restore and recovery manager. If you are still using the older, user-managed backup technologies, then I strongly recommend that you switch to RMAN. RMAN contains a powerful set of features that are unmatched by any other backup tool available. RMAN is easy to use and configure. It will save you time and effort and give you peace of mind when you are implementing a rock-solid restore and backup strategy.

If you are new to RMAN, it may not be obvious which features should always be enabled and implemented and, likewise, which aspects you will rarely need. This chapter contains a checklist that walks you through each architectural decision point. Many of the strategies need to be discussed to make sure that the business requirements are going to be met. The point is that you should carefully consider each component and how to implement the features that make sense.

The chapter ended with a real-world example of a script used to implement RMAN in a production environment. Now that you have a good idea of RMAN's features and how to use them, you are ready to start making backups. The next chapter deals with RMAN backup scenarios.

CHAPTER 18

RMAN Backups and Reporting

Chapter 17 provided the details on configuring RMAN and using specialized features to control the behavior of RMAN. After you consider which features you require, you are ready to create backups. RMAN can back up the following types of files:

- Data files
- Control files
- Archived redo log files
- spfiles
- Backup pieces

For most scenarios, you will use RMAN to back up data files, control files, and archivelog files. If you have the autobackup of the control file feature enabled, then RMAN will automatically back up the control file and the spfile when a BACKUP or COPY command is issued. You can also back up the backup piece files that RMAN has created.

RMAN does not back up Oracle Net files, password files, block change tracking files, flashback logs, or the Oracle binary files (files created when you installed Oracle). If required, you should put in place OS backups that include those files.

Also note that RMAN does not back up online redo log files. If you were to back up the online redo log files, it would be pointless to restore them. The online redo log files contain the latest redo generated by the database. You would not want to overwrite them from a backup with old redo information. When your database is in archivelog mode, the online redo log files contain the most recently generated transactions required to perform complete recovery.

© Michelle Malcher and Darl Kuhn 2019
M. Malcher and D. Kuhn, *Pro Oracle Database 18c Administration*,
https://doi.org/10.1007/978-1-4842-4424-1_18

This chapter details many of the features related to running the RMAN BACKUP command. Also covered are creating a recovery catalog and techniques for logging output and reporting on RMAN backup operations. This chapter begins by discussing a few common practices used to enhance what is displayed in the RMAN output when running commands.

Preparing to Run RMAN Backup Commands

Before running RMAN backups, it usually makes sense to set a few things so as to enhance what is shown in the output. You do not need to set these variables every time you log in and run an RMAN command. However, when troubleshooting or debugging issues, it is almost always a good idea to perform the following tasks:

- Set NLS_DATE_FORMAT OS variable

- Set ECHO

- Show RMAN variables

The bulleted items are discussed in the following sections.

Setting NLS_DATE_FORMAT

Before running any RMAN job, set the OS variable NLS_DATE_FORMAT to include a time (hours, minutes, seconds) component; for example,

```
$ export NLS_DATE_FORMAT='dd-mon-yyyy hh24:mi:ss'
```

Additionally, if a shell script calls RMAN, put the prior line directly in the shell script (see the shell script at the end of Chapter 17 for an example):

```
NLS_DATE_FORMAT='dd-mon-yyyy hh24:mi:ss'
```

This ensures that when RMAN displays a date, it always includes the hours, minutes, and seconds as part of the output. By default, RMAN only includes the date component (DD-MON-YY) in the output. For instance, without setting NLS_DATE_FORMAT, when starting a backup, here is what RMAN displays:

```
Starting backup at 11-JAN-13
```

When you set the NLS_DATE_FORMAT OS variable to include a time component, the output will look like this instead:

```
Starting backup at 11-jan-2013 16:43:04
```

When troubleshooting, it is essential to have a time component so that you can determine how long a command took to run or how long a command was running before a failure occurred. Oracle Support will almost always ask you to set this variable to include the time component before capturing output and sending it to them.

The only downside to setting the NLS_DATE_FORMAT is that if you set it to a value unknown to RMAN, connectivity issues can occur. For example, here the NLS_DATE_FORMAT is set to an invalid value:

```
$ export NLS_DATE_FORMAT='dd-mon-yyyy hh24:mi:sd'
$ rman target /
```

When set to an invalid value, you get this error when logging in to RMAN:

```
RMAN-03999: Oracle error occurred while converting a date: ORA-01821:
```

To unset the NLS_DATE_FORMAT variable, set it to a blank value, like so:

```
$ export NLS_DATE_FORMAT="
```

Setting ECHO

Another value that should be set in RMAN scripts is the ECHO command, seen here:

```
RMAN> set echo on;
```

This instructs RMAN to display the command that it is running in the output, so you can see what RMAN command is running, along with any relevant error or output messages associated with the command. This is especially important when you are running RMAN commands within scripts, because you are not directly typing in a command (and may not know what command was issued within the shell script). For example, without SET ECHO ON, here is what is displayed in the output for a command:

```
Starting backup at...
```

With SET ECHO ON, this output shows the actual command that was run:

```
backup datafile 4;
Starting backup at...
```

From the prior output, you can see which command is running, when it started, and so on.

Showing Variables

Another good practice is to run the SHOW ALL command within any script, as follows:

```
RMAN> show all;
```

This displays all the RMAN configurable variables. When troubleshooting, you may not be aware of something that another DBA has configured. This gives you a snapshot of the settings as they were when the RMAN session executed.

Running Backups

Before you run an RMAN backup, make sure you read Chapter 17 for details on how to configure RMAN with settings for a production environment. For production databases, run RMAN from Oracle Cloud Control or a shell script similar to the one shown at the end of Chapter 17. Within the shell script, it is useful to configure every aspect of RMAN to use for a particular database. If you run RMAN out of the box, with its default settings, you will be able to back up your database. However, these settings will not be adequate for most production database applications.

Backing Up the Entire Database

If you are not sure where RMAN will be backing up your database files, you need to read Chapter 17, because it describes how to configure RMAN to create the backup files in the location of your choice. To configure RMAN to write to specific locations on disk (note that the CONFIGURE command must be executed before you run the BACKUP command):

```
RMAN> configure channel 1 device type disk format '/u01/O18C/rman/rman1_%U.bk';
```

After a backup location is configured, use a command similar to the one shown next to back up the entire database:

```
RMAN> backup incremental level=0 database plus archivelog;
```

This command ensures that RMAN will back up all data files in the database, all available archivelogs generated prior to the backup, and all archivelogs generated during the backup. This command also ensures that you have all the data files and archivelogs that would be required to restore and recover your database.

If you have the autobackup of the control file feature enabled, run this command next:

```
RMAN> configure controlfile autobackup on;
```

The last task RMAN does as part of the backup is to generate a backup set that contains a backup of the control file. This control file will contain all information regarding the backup that took place and any archivelogs that were generated during the backup.

Tip   Always enable the autobackup of the control file feature.

There are many nuances to the RMAN BACKUP command. For production databases, it is usually recommended to back up the database with the BACKUP INCREMENTAL LEVEL=0 DATABASE PLUS ARCHIVELOG command. That is generally sufficient. However, you will encounter many situations in which you need to run a backup that uses a specific RMAN feature, or you might troubleshoot an issue requiring that you be aware of the other ways to invoke an RMAN backup. These aspects are discussed in the next several sections.

Full Backup vs. Incremental Level=0

The term *RMAN full backup* sometimes causes confusion. A more apt way of phrasing this task would be *RMAN backing up all modified blocks within one or more data files*. The term *full* does not mean that all blocks are backed up or that all data files are backed up. It simply means that all blocks that would be required to rebuild a data file (in the event of a failure) are being backed up. You can take a full backup of a single data file, and the contents of that backup piece may be quite a bit smaller than the data file itself.

Backup Sets vs. Image Copies

The default backup mode of RMAN instructs it to back up only blocks that have been used in a data file; these are known as backup sets. RMAN can also make byte-for-byte copies of the data files; these are known as image copies. Creating a backup set is the default type of backup that RMAN creates. The next command creates a backup set backup of the database:

```
RMAN> backup database;
```

If you prefer, you can explicitly place the AS BACKUPSET command when creating backups:

```
RMAN> backup as backupset database;
```

You can instruct RMAN to create image copies by using the AS COPY command. This command creates image copies of every data file in the database:

```
RMAN> backup as copy database;
```

Because image copies are identical copies of the data files, they can be directly accessed by the DBA with OS commands. For example, say you had a media failure, and you did not want to use RMAN to restore an image copy. You could use an OS command to copy the image copy of a data file to a location where it could be used by the database. In contrast, a backup set consists of binary files that only the RMAN utility can write to or read from.

It is preferred to use backup sets when working with RMAN. The backup sets tend to be smaller than the data files and can have true binary compression applied to them. Also, it is not inconvenient to use RMAN as the mechanism for creating backup files that only RMAN can restore. Using RMAN with backup sets is efficient and very reliable and extremely useful in the time of restore.

Backing Up Tablespaces

RMAN has the ability to back up at the database level (as shown in the prior section), the tablespace level, or, even more granularly, at the data file level. When you back up a tablespace, RMAN backs up any data files associated with the tablespaces(s) that you specify.

For instance, the following command will back up all the data files associated with the SYSTEM and SYSAUX tablespaces:

```
RMAN> backup tablespace system, sysaux;
```

One scenario to use the tablespace level is if a new tablespace has been recently added and you want to take a backup of just the data files associated with the newly added tablespace. Note that when restore and backup issues, it is often more efficient to work with one tablespace and especially a data block (because it is generally much faster to back up one tablespace than the entire database).

Backing Up Data Files

You may occasionally need to back up individual data files. For example, when troubleshooting issues with backups, it is often helpful to attempt to successfully back up one data file. You can specify data files by file name or by file number, as follows:

```
RMAN> backup datafile '/u01/dbfile/o18c/system01.dbf';
```

In this example, file numbers are specified:

```
RMAN> backup datafile 1,4;
```

Here are some other examples of backing up data files, using various features:

```
RMAN> backup as copy datafile 4;
RMAN> backup incremental level 1 datafile 4;
```

Tip   Use the RMAN REPORT SCHEMA command to list tablespace, data file name, and data file number information.

Backing Up the Control File

The most reliable way to back up the control file is to configure the autobackup feature:

```
RMAN> configure controlfile autobackup on;
```

This command ensures that the control file is automatically backed up when a BACKUP or COPY command is issued. Enable the autobackup of the control file feature, and then you never have to worry about explicitly issuing a separate command to back up the control file. When in this mode, the control file is always created in its own backup set and backup piece after the data file backup pieces have been created.

If you need to back up the control file manually, you can do so like this:

```
RMAN> backup current controlfile;
```

The location of the backup is either a default OS location, the FRA, or a manually configured location:

```
RMAN> configure controlfile autobackup format for device type disk to
'/u01/O18C/rman/rman_ctl_%F.bk';
```

Backing Up the spfile

If you have enabled the autobackup of the control file feature, the spfile will be backed up automatically (along with the control file) anytime a BACKUP or COPY command is issued. If you need to back up the spfile manually, use the following command:

```
RMAN> backup spfile;
```

The location of the file that contains the backup of the spfile is dependent on what you have configured for the autobackup of the control file (see the previous section for an example). By default, if you do not use an FRA, and have not explicitly configured a location via a channel, then for Linux/Unix servers, the backup goes to the ORACLE_HOME/dbs directory.

Note   RMAN can only back up the spfile if the instance was started using a spfile.

Backing Up Archivelogs

Archivelogs can run in backups separately from the database backups and with backups. Because of the space of the FRA and amount of archivelogs being generated, an archivelog backup can run several times a day. Even if this runs separately, it should also run along with the backup of the database using the following command:

```
RMAN> backup incremental level=0 database plus archivelog;
```

However, you will occasionally find yourself in a situation in which you need to take a special, one-off backup of the archivelogs. You can issue the following command to back up the archivelogs files:

```
RMAN> backup archivelog all;
```

If you have a mount point that is nearly full, and you determine that you want to back up the archivelogs (so that they exist in a backup file), but then you want to immediately delete the files (that were just backed up) from disk, you can use the following syntax to back up the archivelogs and then have RMAN delete them from the storage media:

```
RMAN> backup archivelog all delete input;
```

Listed next are some other ways in which you can back up the archivelog files:

```
RMAN> backup archivelog sequence 300;
RMAN> backup archivelog sequence between 300 and 400 thread 1;
RMAN> backup archivelog from time "sysdate-7" until time "sysdate-1";
```

If an archivelog has been removed from disk manually via an OS delete command, RMAN will throw the following error when attempting to back up the nonexistent archivelog file:

```
RMAN-06059: expected archived log not found, loss of archived log
compromises recoverability
```

In this situation, first run a CROSSCHECK command to let RMAN know which files are physically available on disk:

```
RMAN> crosscheck archivelog all;
```

Backing Up FRA

If you use an FRA, one nice RMAN feature is that you can back up all the files in that location with one command. If you are using a media manager and have a tape backup channel enabled, you can back up everything in the FRA to tape, like this:

```
RMAN> backup device type sbt_tape recovery area;
```

You can also back up the FRA to a location on disk. Use the TO DESTINATION command to accomplish this:

```
RMAN> backup recovery area to destination '/u01/O18C/fra_back';
```

RMAN will automatically create directories as required beneath the directory specified by the TO DESTINATION command.

Note   The format of the subdirectory under the directory TO_DESTINATION> is db_uniuqe_name/backupset/YYYY_MM_DD.

RMAN will back up full backups, incremental backups, control file autobackups, and archivelog files. Keep in mind that flashback logs, online redo log files, and the current control file are not backed up.

Excluding Tablespaces from Backups

Suppose you have a tablespace that contains noncritical data, and you do not ever want to back it up. RMAN can be configured to exclude such tablespaces from the backup. To determine if RMAN is currently configured to exclude any tablespaces, run this command:

```
RMAN> show exclude;
RMAN configuration parameters for database with db_unique_name O18C are:
RMAN configuration has no stored or default parameters
```

Use the EXCLUDE command to instruct RMAN as to which tablespaces not to back up:

```
RMAN> configure exclude for tablespace users;
```

Now, for any database-level backups, RMAN will exclude the data files associated with the USERS tablespace. You can instruct RMAN to back up all data files and any excluded tablespaces with this command:

```
RMAN> backup database noexclude;
```

You can clear the exclude setting via the following command:

```
RMAN> configure exclude for tablespace users clear;
```

Backing Up Data Files Not Backed Up

Suppose you have just added several data files to your database, and you want to ensure that you have a backup of them. You can issue the following command to instruct Oracle to back up data files that have not yet been backed up:

```
RMAN> backup database not backed up;
```

You can also specify a time range for such files that have not yet been backed up. Say you discover that your backups have not been running for the last several days, and you want to back up everything that has not been backed up within the last 24 hours. The following command backs up all data files that have not been backed up within the last day:

```
RMAN> backup database not backed up since time='sysdate-1';
```

The prior command is also useful if, for any reason (a power failure in the data center, your backup directory's becoming full during backups, and so on), your backups aborted. After you have resolved the issue that caused your backup job to fail, you can issue the previous command, and RMAN will back up only the data files that have not been backed up in the specified time period.

Skipping Read-Only Tablespaces

Because data in read-only tablespaces cannot change, you may only want to back up read-only tablespaces once and then skip them in subsequent backups. Use the SKIP READONLY command to achieve this:

```
RMAN> backup database skip readonly;
```

Keep in mind that when you skip read-only tablespaces, you will need to keep available a backup that contains these tablespaces. As long as you only issue the RMAN command DELETE OBSOLETE, the RMAN backup set containing the read-only tablespaces will be retained and not deleted, even if that RMAN backup set contains other read-write tablespaces.

Skipping Offline or Inaccessible Files

Suppose you have one data file that is missing or corrupt, and you do not have a backup of it, so you cannot restore and recover it. You cannot start your database in this situation:

```
SQL> startup;
ORA-01157: cannot identify/lock data file 6 - see DBWR trace file
ORA-01110: data file 6: '/u01/dbfile/o18c/reg_data01.dbf'
```

In this scenario, you will have to take the data file offline before you can start your database:

```
SQL> alter database datafile '/u01/dbfile/o18c/reg_data01.dbf' offline for drop;
```

Now, you can open your database:

```
SQL> alter database open;
```

Suppose you then attempt to run an RMAN backup:

```
RMAN> backup database;
```

The following error is thrown when RMAN encounters a data file that it cannot back up:

```
RMAN-03002: failure of backup command at ...
RMAN-06056: could not access datafile 6
```

In this situation, you will have to instruct RMAN to exclude the offline data file from the backup. The SKIP OFFLINE command instructs RMAN to ignore data files with an offline status:

```
RMAN> backup database skip offline;
```

If a file has gone completely missing, use SKIP INACCESSIBLE to instruct RMAN to ignore files that are not available on disk. This might happen if the data file was deleted using an OS command. Here is an example of excluding inaccessible data files from the RMAN backup:

```
RMAN> backup database skip inaccessible;
```

You can skip read-only, offline, and inaccessible data files with one command:

```
RMAN> backup database skip readonly skip offline skip inaccessible;
```

When dealing with offline and inaccessible files, you should figure out why the files are offline or inaccessible and try to resolve any issues.

Backing Up Large Files in Parallel

Normally, RMAN will only use one channel to back up a single data file. When you enable parallelism, it allows RMAN to spawn multiple processes to back up multiple files. However, even when parallelism is enabled, RMAN will not use parallel channels simultaneously to back up one data file.

You can instruct RMAN to use multiple channels to back up one data file in parallel. This is known as a multisection backup. This feature can speed up the backups of very large data files. Use the SECTION SIZE parameter to make a multisection backup. The following example configures two parallel channels to back up one file:

```
RMAN> configure device type disk parallelism 2;
RMAN> configure channel 1 device type disk format '/u01/O18C/rman/r1%U.bk';
RMAN> configure channel 2 device type disk format '/u02/O18C/rman/r2%U.bk';
RMAN> backup section size 2500M datafile 10;
```

When this code runs, RMAN will allocate two channels to back up the specified data file in parallel.

Note   If you specify a section size greater than the size of the data file, RMAN will not back up the file in parallel.

Adding RMAN Backup Information to the Repository

Suppose you have had to re-create your control file. The process of re-creating the control file wipes out any information regarding RMAN backups. However, you want to make the newly created control file aware of RMAN backups sitting on disk. In this situation, use the CATALOG command to populate the control file with RMAN metadata.

For example, if all the RMAN backup files are kept in the /u01/O18C/rman directory, you can make the control file aware of these backups files in the directory, as follows:

```
RMAN> catalog start with '/u01/O18C/rman';
```

This instructs RMAN to look for any backup pieces, image copies, control file copies, and archivelogs in the specified directory, and, if found, to populate the control file with the appropriate metadata. For this example, two backup piece files are found in the given directory:

```
searching for all files that match the pattern /u01/O18C/rman

List of Files Unknown to the Database
=======================================
File Name: /u01/O18C/rman/r1otlns9oo_1_1.bk
File Name: /u01/O18C/rman/r1xyklnrveg_1_1.bk

Do you really want to catalog the above files (enter YES or NO)?
```

If you enter YES, then metadata regarding the backup files will be added to the control file. In this way, the CATALOG command allows you to make the RMAN repository (control file and recovery catalog) aware of files that RMAN can work with for backup and recovery.

You can also instruct RMAN to catalog any files in the FRA that the control file is not currently aware of, like this:

```
RMAN> catalog recovery area;
```

Additionally, you can catalog specific files. This example instructs RMAN to add metadata to the control file for a specific backup piece file:

```
RMAN> catalog backuppiece '/u01/O18C/rman/r159nv562v_1_1.bk';
```

Taking Backups of Pluggable Databases

Starting with Oracle Database 12c, you can create pluggable databases within a root container database (see Chapter 22 for more details). If you are using this option, there are a few features to be aware of in regard to backups:

- While connected to the root container, you can back up all the data files within the database or just the root database data files; a specific pluggable database; or specific tablespaces or data files, or a combination of these.

- While connected to a pluggable database, you can only back up data files associated with that pluggable database.

The bulleted items are detailed in the following two sections.

While Connected to the Root Container

Suppose you are connected to the root container as SYS and want to back up all data files (including any data files with associated pluggable databases). First, verify that you are indeed connected to the root container as SYS:

```
RMAN> SELECT SYS_CONTEXT('USERENV', 'CON_ID')    AS con_id,
      SYS_CONTEXT('USERENV', 'CON_NAME')          AS cur_container,
      SYS_CONTEXT('USERENV', 'CURRENT_SCHEMA') AS cur_user
      FROM DUAL;
```

Here is some sample output:

```
CON_ID              CUR_CONTAINER        CUR_USER
------------------- -------------------- --------------------
1                   CDB$ROOT             SYS
```

Now, to back up all data files, both in the root container and in any associated pluggable databases, do so as follows:

```
RMAN> backup database;
```

If you want to back up only the data files associated with the root container, then specify ROOT:

```
RMAN> backup database root;
```

You can also back up a specific pluggable database:

```
RMAN> backup pluggable database salespdb;
```

Additionally, you can back up specific tablespaces within a pluggable database:

```
RMAN> backup tablespace SALESPDB:SALES;
```

Also, you can specify the file name to back up any data file within the root container or associated pluggable databases:

```
RMAN> backup datafile '/ora01/app/oracle/oradata/CDB/salespdb/sales01.dbf';
```

While Connected to a Pluggable Database

First, start RMAN, and connect to the pluggable database you want to back up. You must connect as a user with SYSDBA or SYSBACKUP privileges. Also, there must be a listener running for the PDB service. This example connects to the SALESPDB pluggable database:

```
$ rman target sys/foo@salespdb
```

Once connected to a pluggable database, you can only back up data files specific to that database. Therefore, for this example, the following command takes a backup of just data files associated with the SALESPDB pluggable database:

```
RMAN> backup database;
```

This example backs up the data files associated with the pluggable database SYSTEM tablespace:

```
RMAN> backup tablespace system;
```

I should emphasize again that when you are connected directly to a pluggable database, you can only back up data files associated with that database. You cannot back up data files associated with the root container or with any other pluggable databases within the container. Figure 18-1 illustrates this concept. A connection as SYSDBA to the SALESPDB pluggable database can only back up and view data files related to that database. The SYSDBA connection cannot see outside its pluggable box in regard to data files and RMAN backups of data files. In contrast, the SYSDBA connection to the root container can back up all data files (root, seed, and all pluggable databases) as well as access RMAN backups that were initiated from a connection to a pluggable database.

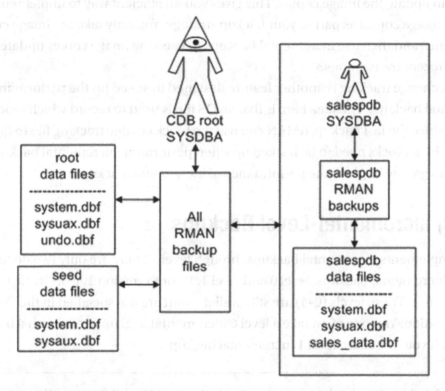

Figure 18-1. *Purview of a SYSDBA connection to root container vs. a SYSDBA connection to a pluggable database*

Creating Incremental Backups

RMAN has three separate and distinct incremental backup features:

- Incremental-level backups

- Incrementally updating backups

- Block change tracking

With incremental-level backups, RMAN only backs up the blocks that have been modified since a previous backup. Incremental backups can be applied to the entire database, tablespaces, or data files. Incremental-level backups are the most commonly used incremental feature with RMAN.

Incrementally updating backups is a separate feature from incremental-level backups. These backups take image copies of the data files and then use incremental backups to update the image copies. This gives you an efficient way to implement and maintain image copies as part of your backup strategy. You only take the image copy backup once and then use incremental backups to keep the image copies updated with the most recent transactions.

Block change tracking is another feature designed to speed up the performance of incremental backups. The idea here is that an OS file is used to record which blocks have changed since the last backup. RMAN can use the block change tracking file to quickly identify which blocks need to be backed up when performing incremental backups. This feature can greatly improve the performance of incremental backups.

Taking Incremental-Level Backups

RMAN implements incremental backups through levels. There are only two documented levels of incremental backups: level 0 and level 1. Prior to version 10g of Oracle offer five levels, 0–4. These levels (0–4) are still available but are not specified in the Oracle documentation. You must first take a level 0 incremental backup to establish a baseline, after which you can take a level 1 incremental backup.

Note   A full backup backs up the same blocks as a level 0 backup. However, you cannot use a full backup with incremental backups. Furthermore, you have to start an incremental backup strategy with a level 0 backup. If you attempt to take a level 1 backup, and no level 0 exists, RMAN will automatically take a level 0 backup.

Here is an example of taking an incremental level 0 backup:

```
RMAN> backup incremental level=0 database;
```

Suppose for the next several backups you want to back up only the blocks that have changed since the last incremental backup. This line of code takes a level 1 backup:

```
RMAN> backup incremental level=1 database;
```

There are two different types of incremental backups: differential and cumulative. Which type you use depends on your requirements. Differential backups (the default) are smaller but take more time to recover from. Cumulative backups are larger than differential backups but require less recovery time.

A differential incremental level 1 backup instructs RMAN to back up blocks that have changed since the last level 1 or level 0 backup, whereas a cumulative incremental level 1 backup instructs RMAN to back up blocks that have changed since the last level 0 backup. Cumulative incremental backups, in effect, ignore any level 1 incremental backups.

Note   The RMAN incremental level 0 backups are used to restore the data files, whereas the RMAN incremental level 1 backups are used to recover the data files.

When using incremental backups, the default is differential. If you require cumulative backups, you must specify the key word CUMULATIVE. Here is an example of taking a cumulative level 1 backup:

```
RMAN> backup incremental level=1 cumulative database;
```

Here are some examples of taking incremental backups at a more granular level than the database:

```
RMAN> backup incremental level=0 tablespace sysaux;
RMAN> backup incremental level=1 tablespace sysaux plus archivelog;
RMAN> backup incremental from scn 4343352 datafile 3;
```

Making Incrementally Updating Backups

The basic idea behind an incrementally updating backup is to create image copies of data files and then use incremental backups to update the image copies. In this manner, you have image copies of your database that are kept somewhat current. This can be an efficient way to combine image copy backups with incremental backups.

To understand how this backup technique works, you will need to inspect the commands that perform an incrementally updating backup. The following lines of RMAN code are required to enable this feature:

```
run{recover copy of database with tag 'incupdate';
backup incremental level 1 for recover of copy with tag 'incupdate'
database;}
```

In the first line a tag is specified (this example uses incupdate). You can use whatever you want for the tag name; the tag name lets RMAN associate the backup files being used each time the commands are run. This code will perform as follows the first time you run the script:

- RECOVER COPY generates a message saying there is nothing for it to do.

- If no image copies exist, the BACKUP INCREMENTAL creates an image copy of the database data files.

You should see messages such as this in the output when the RECOVER COPY and BACKUP INCREMENTAL commands run the first time:

```
no copy of datafile 1 found to recover
...
no parent backup or copy of datafile 1 found
...
```

The second time you run the incrementally updating backup, it does as follows:

- RECOVER COPY again generates a message saying it has nothing to do.

- BACKUP INCREMENTAL makes an incremental level 1 backup and assigns it the tag name specified; this backup will subsequently be used by the RECOVER COPY command.

The third time you run the incrementally updating backup, it does this:

- Now that an incremental backup has been created, the RECOVER COPY applies the incremental backup to the image copies.

- BACKUP INCREMENTAL makes an incremental level 1 backup and assigns it the tag name specified; this backup will subsequently be used by the RECOVER COPY command.

Going forward, each time you run the two lines of code, you will have a regularly repeating backup pattern. If you use image copies for backups, you might consider using an incrementally updating backup strategy, because with it, you avoid creating entire image copies whenever the backup runs. The image copies are updated each time the backup runs with the incremental changes from the previous backup.

Using Block Change Tracking

Block change tracking is the process in which a binary file is used to record changes to database data file blocks. The idea is that incremental backup performance can be improved because RMAN can use the block change tracking file to pinpoint which blocks have changed since the last backup. This saves a great deal of time because otherwise RMAN would have to scan all the blocks that had been backed up to determine if they had changed since the last backup.

Listed next are the steps for enabling block change tracking:

1. If not already enabled, set the DB_CREATE_FILE_DEST parameter to a location (that already exists on disk); for example,

```
SQL> alter system set db_create_file_dest='/u01/O18C/bct' scope=both;
```

2. Enable block change tracking via the ALTER DATABASE command:

```
SQL> alter database enable block change tracking;
```

This example creates a file with an OMF name in the directory specified by DB_CREATE_FILE_DEST. In this example the file created is given this name:

```
/u01/O18C/bct/O18C/changetracking/o1_mf_8h0wmng1_.chg
```

You can also enable block change tracking by directly specifying a file name, which does not require that DB_CREATE_FILE_DEST be set; for example,

```
SQL> alter database enable block change tracking using file
'/u01/O18C/bct/btc.bt';
```

You can verify the details of block change tracking by running the following query:

```
SQL> select * from v$block_change_tracking;
```

For space-planning purposes, the size of the block change tracking file is approximately 1/30,000 the size of the total size of the blocks being tracked in the database. Therefore, the size of the block change tracking file is proportional to the size of the database and not to the amount of redo generated.

To disable block change tracking, run this command:

```
SQL> alter database disable block change tracking;
```

Note When you disable block change tracking, Oracle will automatically delete the block change tracking file.

Checking for Corruption in Data Files and Backups

You can use RMAN to check for corruption in data files, archivelogs, and control files. You can also verify whether a backup set is restorable. The RMAN VALIDATE command is used to perform these types of integrity checks. There are three ways you can run the VALIDATE command:

- VALIDATE
- BACKUP...VALIDATE
- RESTORE...VALIDATE

Note The stand-alone VALIDATE command is available in Oracle Database 11g and higher. The BACKUP...VALIDATE and RESTORE...VALIDATE commands are available in Oracle Database 10g and higher.

Using VALIDATE

The VALIDATE command can be used as a stand-alone to check for missing files or physical corruption in database data files, archivelog files, control files, spfiles, and backup set pieces. For example, this command will validate all data files and the control files:

```
RMAN> validate database;
```

You can also validate just the control file, as follows:

```
RMAN> validate current controlfile;
```

You can validate the archivelog files, like so:

```
RMAN> validate archivelog all;
```

You may want to combine all the prior integrity checks into one command, as shown:

```
RMAN> validate database include current controlfile plus archivelog;
```

Under normal conditions, the VALIDATE command only checks for physical corruption. You can specify that you also want to check for logical corruption by using the CHECK LOGICAL clause:

```
RMAN> validate check logical database include current controlfile plus archivelog;
```

VALIDATE has a variety of uses. Here are a few more examples:

```
RMAN> validate database skip offline;
RMAN> validate copy of database;
RMAN> validate tablespace system;
RMAN> validate datafile 3 block 20 to 30;
RMAN> validate spfile;
RMAN> validate backupset <primary_key_value>;
RMAN> validate recovery area;
```

If you are using the Oracle Database 12c pluggable database feature, you can validate specific databases within the container. While connected as SYS to the root container, validate any associated pluggable databases:

```
RMAN> validate pluggable database salespdb;
```

If RMAN detects any corrupt blocks, the V$DATABASE_BLOCK_CORRUPTION is populated. This view contains information on the file number, block number, and number of blocks affected. You can use this information to perform a block-level recovery (see Chapter 19 for more details).

> **Note**   Physical corruption is a change to a block, such that its contents do not match the physical format that Oracle expects. By default, RMAN checks for physical corruption when backing up, restoring, and validating data files. With logical corruption, a block is in the correct format, but the contents are not consistent with what Oracle expects, such as in a row piece or an index entry.

Using BACKUP...VALIDATE

The BACKUP...VALIDATE command is very similar to the VALIDATE command, in that it can check to see if data files are available and if the data files contain any corrupt blocks; for example,

```
RMAN> backup validate database;
```

This command does not actually create any backup files; it only reads the data files and checks for corruption. Like the VALIDATE command, BACKUP VALIDATE, by default, only checks for physical corruption. You can instruct it to check as well for logical corruption, as shown:

```
RMAN> backup validate check logical database;
```

Here are some variations of the BACKUP...VALIDATE command:

```
RMAN> backup validate database current controlfile;
RMAN> backup validate check logical database current controlfile plus
archivelog;
```

Also like the VALIDATE command, BACKUP...VALIDATE will populate V$DATABASE_BLOCK_CORRUPTION if it detects any corrupt blocks. The information in this view can be used to determine which blocks can potentially be restored by block-level recovery (see Chapter 19 for more details.

Using RESTORE...VALIDATE

The RESTORE...VALIDATE command is used to verify backup files that would be used in a restore operation. This command validates backup sets, data file copies, and archivelog files:

```
RMAN> restore validate database;
```

No actual files are restored when using RESTORE...VALIDATE. This means that you can run the command while the database is online and available.

Using a Recovery Catalog

When you use a recovery catalog, it is possible to create the recovery catalog user in the same database, on the same server, as your target database. However, that approach is not recommended because you do not want the availability of your target database or of the server on which the target database resides to affect the recovery catalog. Therefore, you should create the recovery catalog database on a server different from that of your target databases. The recovery catalog can be used for the whole database environment depending on sizing, but remember it normally is going to store the information stored in control files.

Creating a Recovery Catalog

When I use a recovery catalog, I prefer to have a dedicated database that is used only for the recovery catalog. This ensures that the recovery catalog is not affected by any maintenance or downtime required by another application (and vice versa).

Listed next are the steps for creating a recovery catalog:

1. Create a database on a server different from that of your target database, to be used for the recovery catalog. Make sure the database is adequately sized. I have found that Oracle's recommended sizes are usually much too small. Here are some adequate recommendations for initial sizing:

   SYSTEM tablespace: 500MB

   SYSAUX tablespace: 500MB

   TEMP tablespace: 500MB

   UNDO tablespace: 500MB

   Online redo logs: 25MB each; three groups, multiplexed with two members per group

   RECCAT tablespace: 500MB

2. Create a tablespace to be used by the recovery catalog user. I recommend giving the tablespace a name such as RECCAT so that it is readily identifiable as the tablespace that contains the recovery catalog metadata:

```
SQL> CREATE TABLESPACE reccat
  DATAFILE '/u01/dbfile/O12C/reccat01.dbf' SIZE 500M
  EXTENT MANAGEMENT LOCAL UNIFORM SIZE 128k
  SEGMENT SPACE MANAGEMENT AUTO;
```

3. Create a user that will own the tables and other objects used to store the target database metadata. I recommend giving the recovery catalog user a name such as RCAT so that it is readily identifiable as the user that owns the recovery catalog objects. Also, grant the RECOVERY_CATALOG_OWNER role to the RCAT user as well as CREATE SESSION:

```
SQL> CREATE USER rcat IDENTIFIED BY foo
TEMPORARY TABLESPACE temp
DEFAULT TABLESPACE reccat
QUOTA UNLIMITED ON reccat;
--
GRANT RECOVERY_CATALOG_OWNER TO rcat;
GRANT CREATE SESSION TO rcat;
```

4. Connect through RMAN as RCAT, and create the recovery catalog objects:

```
$ rman catalog rcat/foo
```

5. Now, run the CREATE CATALOG command:

```
RMAN> create catalog;
RMAN> exit;
```

6. This command may take a few minutes to run. When it is finished, you can verify that the tables were created with the following query:

```
$ sqlplus rcat/foo
SQL> select table_name from user_tables;
```

7. Here is a small sample of the output:

```
TABLE_NAME
------------------------------
DB
NODE
CONF
DBINC
```

Registering a Target Database

Now, you can register a target database with the recovery catalog. Log in to the target database server. Ensure that you can establish Oracle Net connectivity to the recovery catalog database. For instance, one approach is to populate the TNS_ADMIN/tnsnames.ora file with an entry that points to the remote database. On the target database server, register the recovery catalog, as follows:

```
$ rman target / catalog rcat/foo@rcat
```

When you connect, you should see verification that you are connecting to both the target and the recovery catalog:

```
connected to target database: O18C (DBID=3423216220)
connected to recovery catalog database
```

Next, run the REGISTER DATABASE command:

```
RMAN> register database;
```

Now, you can run backup operations and have the metadata about the backup tasks written to both the control file and the recovery catalog. Make sure you connect to the recovery catalog, along with the target database, each time you run RMAN commands:

```
$ rman target / catalog rcat/foo@rcat
RMAN> backup database;
```

Backing Up the Recovery Catalog

Make certain you include a strategy for backing up and recovering the recovery catalog database. For the most protection, be sure the recovery catalog database is in archivelog mode, and use RMAN to back up the database.

You can also use a tool such as Data Pump to take a snapshot of the database. The downside to using Data Pump is that you can potentially lose some information in the recovery catalog that was created after the Data Pump export.

Keep in mind that if you experience a complete failure on your recovery catalog database server, you can still use RMAN to back up your target databases; you just cannot connect to the recovery catalog. Therefore, any scripts that instruct RMAN to connect to the target and the recovery catalog must be modified.

Also, if you completely lose a recovery catalog and do not have a backup, one option is to re-create it from scratch. As soon as you re-create it, you reregister the target databases with the recovery catalog. You lose any long-term historical recovery catalog metadata.

Synchronizing the Recovery Catalog

You may have an issue with the network that renders the recovery catalog inaccessible. In the meantime, you connect to your target database and perform backup operations. Sometime later, the network issues are resolved, and you can again connect to the recovery catalog.

In this situation, you need to resynchronize the recovery catalog with the target database so that the recovery catalog is aware of any backup operations that are not stored in it. Run the following command to ensure that the recovery catalog has the most recent backup information:

```
$ rman target / catalog rcat/foo@rcat
RMAN> resync catalog;
```

Keep in mind that you have to resynchronize the catalog only if, for some reason, you are performing backup operations without connecting to the catalog. Under normal conditions, you do not have to run the RESYNC command.

Recovery Catalog Versions

I recommend that you create a recovery catalog for each version of the target databases that you are backing up. Doing so will save you some headaches with compatibility issues and upgrades. I have found it easier to use a recovery catalog when the database version of the rman client is the same version used when creating the catalog.

Yes, having multiple versions of the recovery catalog can cause some confusion. However, if you are in an environment in which you have several different versions of the Oracle database, then multiple recovery catalogs may be more convenient.

Dropping a Recovery Catalog

If you determine that you are not using a recovery catalog and that you no longer need the data, you can drop it. To do so, connect to the recovery catalog database as the catalog owner, and issue the DROP CATALOG command:

```
$ rman catalog rcat/foo
RMAN> drop catalog;
```

You are prompted as follows:

```
recovery catalog owner is RCAT
enter DROP CATALOG command again to confirm catalog removal
```

If you enter the DROP CATALOG command again, all the objects in the recovery catalog are removed from the recovery catalog database. It would be recommended to take a back of the catalog before performing any drop commands or after registering databases.

The other way to drop a catalog is to drop the owner. To do so, connect to the recovery catalog as a user with DBA privileges, and issue the DROP USER statement:

```
$ sqlplus system/manager
SQL> drop user rcat cascade;
```

SQL*Plus does not prompt you twice; it does as you instructed and drops the user and its objects. Again, the only reason to do this is when you are certain you do not need the recovery catalog or its data any longer. Use caution when dropping a user or the recovery catalog: another good practice is that you take a Data Pump export of the recovery catalog owner before dropping it.

Logging RMAN Output

When troubleshooting RMAN output or checking the status of a backup job, it is essential to have a record of what RMAN ran and the status of each command. There are several methods for logging RMAN output. Some are built-in aspects of the Linux/Unix OS. Others are RMAN-specific features:

- Linux/Unix redirect output to file
- Linux/Unix logging commands
- RMAN SPOOL LOG command
- V$RMAN_OUTPUT view

These logging features are discussed in the next sections.

Redirecting Output to a File

The shell scripts are usually run automatically from a scheduling tool such as cron. When running RMAN commands in this fashion, capture the output by instructing the shell command to redirect standard output messaging and standard error messaging to a log file. This is done with the redirection (>) character. This example runs a shell script (rmanback.bsh) and redirects both standard output and standard error output to a log file named rmanback.log:

```
$ rmanback.bsh 1>/home/oracle/bin/log/rmanback.log 2>&1
```

Here, 1> instructs standard output to be redirected to the specified file. The 2>&1 instructs the shell script to send standard error output to the same location as standard output.

Tip   For further details on how DBAs use shell scripts and Linux features, see *Linux Recipes for Oracle DBAs* by Darl Kuhn (Apress, 2008).

762

Capturing Output with Linux/Unix Logging Commands

You can instruct Linux/Unix to create a log file to capture any output that is also being displayed on your screen. This can be done in one of two ways:

- tee
- script

Capturing Output with tee

When you start RMAN, you can send the output you see on your screen to an OS text file, using the tee command:

```
$ rman | tee /tmp/rman.log
```

Now, you can connect to the target database and run commands. All the output seen on your screen will be logged to the /tmp/rman.log file:

```
RMAN> connect target /
RMAN> backup database;
RMAN> exit;
```

The tee party session stops writing to the log file when you exit RMAN.

Capturing Output with script

The script command is useful because it instructs the OS to log any output that appears at the terminal to a log file. To capture all output, run the script command before connecting to RMAN:

```
$ script /tmp/rman.log
Script started, file is /tmp/rman.log
$ rman target /
RMAN> backup database;
RMAN> exit;
```

To end a script session, press Ctrl+D, or type exit. The tmp/rman.log file will contain all output that was displayed on your screen. The script command is useful when you need to capture all the output from a particular time range. For example, you may be running RMAN commands, exiting from RMAN, running SQL*Plus commands, and so on. The script session lasts from the point at which you start `script` to the point at which you press Ctrl+D.

Logging Output to a File

An easy way to capture RMAN output is to use the SPOOL LOG command to send the output to a file. This example spools a log file from within RMAN:

```
RMAN> spool log to '/tmp/rmanout.log'
RMAN> set echo on;
RMAN> <run RMAN commands>
RMAN> spool log off;
```

By default, the SPOOL LOG command will overwrite an existing file. If you want to append to the log file, use the keyword APPEND:

```
RMAN> spool log to '/tmp/rmanout.log' append
```

You can also direct output to a log file when starting RMAN on the command line, which will overwrite an existing file:

```
$ rman target / log /tmp/rmanout.log
```

You can also append to the log file, as follows:

```
$ rman target / log /tmp/rmanout.log append
```

When you use SPOOL LOG as shown in the previous examples, the output goes to a file and not to your terminal. Therefore, I hardly ever use SPOOL LOG when running RMAN interactively. The command is mainly a tool for capturing output when running RMAN from scripts.

Querying for Output in the Data Dictionary

If you do not capture any RMAN output, you can still view the most recent RMAN output by querying the data dictionary. The V$RMAN_OUTPUT view contains messages recently reported by RMAN:

```
SQL> select sid, recid, output
from v$rman_output
order by recid;
```

The V$RMAN_OUTPUT view is an in-memory object that holds up to 32,768 rows. Information in this view is cleared out when you stop and restart your database. The view is handy when you are using the RMAN SPOOL LOG command to spool output to a file and cannot view what is happening at your terminal.

RMAN Reporting

There are several different methods for reporting on the RMAN environment:

- LIST command

- REPORT command

- Query metadata via data dictionary views

When first learning RMAN, the difference between the LIST and REPORT commands may seem confusing because the distinction between the two is not clear-cut. In general, I use the LIST command to view information about existing backups and the REPORT command to determine which files need to be backed or to display information on obsolete or expired backups.

SQL queries can provide details for specialized reports (not available via LIST or REPORT) or for automating reports: for example, generally implementing an automated check via a shell script and SQL that reports whether the RMAN backups have run within the last day.

Using LIST

When investigating issues with RMAN backups, usually one of the first tasks I undertake is connecting to the target database and running the LIST BACKUP command. This command allows you to view backup sets, backup pieces, and the files included in the backup:

```
RMAN> list backup;
```

The command shows all RMAN backups recorded in the repository. You may want to spool the backups to an output file so that you can save the output and then use an OS editor to search through and look for specific strings in the output.

To get a summarized view of backup information, use the LIST BACKUP SUMARY command:

```
RMAN> list backup summary;
```

You can also use the LIST command to report just image copy information:

RMAN> list copy;

To list all files that have been backed up, and the associated backup set, issue the following command:

RMAN> list backup by file;

These commands display archivelogs on disk:

RMAN> list archivelog all;
RMAN> list copy of archivelog all;

Also, this command lists the backups of the archivelogs (and which archivelogs are contained in which backup pieces):

RMAN> list backup of archivelog all;

There are a great many ways in which you can run the LIST command (and, likewise, the REPORT command, covered in the next section). The prior methods are the ones you will run most of the time. See the Oracle Database Backup and Recovery Reference Guide, available from the Technology Network area of the Oracle web site (http://otn. oracle.com), for a complete list of options.

Using REPORT

The RMAN REPORT command is useful for reporting on a variety of details. You can quickly view all the data files associated with a database, as follows:

RMAN> report schema;

The REPORT command provides detailed information about backups marked obsolete via the RMAN retention policy; for example,

RMAN> report obsolete;

You can report on data files that need to be backed up, as defined by the retention policy, like this:

RMAN> report need backup;

There are several ways to report on data files that need to be backed up. Here are some other examples:

```
RMAN> report need backup redundancy 2;
RMAN> report need backup redundancy 2 datafile 2;
```

The REPORT command may also be used for data files that have never been backed up or that may contain data created from a NOLOGGING operation. For example, say you have direct-path loaded data into a table, and the data file in which the table resides has not been backed up. The following command will detect these conditions:

```
RMAN> report unrecoverable;
```

Using SQL

There are a number of data dictionary views available for querying about backup information. Table 18-1 describes RMAN-related data dictionary views. These views are available regardless of your use of a recovery catalog (the information in these views is derived from the control file).

Table 18-1. *Description of RMAN Backup Data Dictionary Views*

View Name	Information Provided
V$RMAN_BACKUP_JOB_DETAILS	RMAN backup jobs
V$BACKUP	Backup status of online data files placed in backup mode (for hot backups)
V$BACKUP_ARCHIVELOG_DETAILS	Archive logs backed up
V$BACKUP_CONTROLFILE_DETAILS	Control files backed up
V$BACKUP_COPY_DETAILS	Control file and data file copies
V$BACKUP_DATAFILE	Control files and data files backed up
V$BACKUP_DATAFILE_DETAILS	Data files backed up in backup sets, image copies, and proxy copies
V$BACKUP_FILES	Data files, control files, spfiles, and archivelogs backed up

(continued)

Table 18-1. (*continued*)

View Name	Information Provided
V$BACKUP_PIECE	Backup piece files
V$BACKUP_PIECE_DETAILS	Backup piece details
V$BACKUP_SET	Backup sets
V$BACKUP_SET_DETAILS	Backup set details

Sometimes, DBAs new to RMAN have a hard time grasping the concept of backups, backup sets, backup pieces, and data files and how they relate. I find the following query useful when discussing RMAN backup components. This query will display backup sets, the backup pieces with the set, and the data files that are backed up within the backup pieces:

```
SQL> SET LINES 132 PAGESIZE 100
SQL> BREAK ON REPORT ON bs_key ON completion_time ON bp_name ON file_name
SQL> COL bs_key    FORM 99999 HEAD "BS Key"
SQL> COL bp_name   FORM a40   HEAD "BP Name"
SQL> COL file_name FORM a40   HEAD "Datafile"
SQL> --
SQL> SELECT
 s.recid                 bs_key
,TRUNC(s.completion_time) completion_time
,p.handle                bp_name
,f.name                  file_name
FROM v$backup_set        s
    ,v$backup_piece      p
    ,v$backup_datafile   d
    ,v$datafile          f
WHERE p.set_stamp = s.set_stamp
AND   p.set_count = s.set_count
AND   d.set_stamp = s.set_stamp
AND   d.set_count = s.set_count
AND   d.file#     = f.file#
```

```
ORDER BY
 s.recid
,p.handle
,f.name;
```

The output here has been shortened to fit on the page:

```
BS Key COMPLETIO BP Name                              Datafile
------ --------- ------------------------------------ --------------------------------
   159 11-JAN-18 /u01/O18C/rman/r16qnv59jj_1_1.bk     /u01/dbfile/o18c/inv_data2.dbf
                                                      /u01/dbfile/o18c/lob_data01.dbf
                                                      /u01/dbfile/o18c/p14_tbsp.dbf
                                                      /u01/dbfile/o18c/p15_tbsp.dbf
                                                      /u01/dbfile/o18c/p16_tbsp.dbf
```

Sometimes, it is useful to report on the performance of RMAN backups. The following query reports on the time taken for an RMAN backup per session.

```
SQL> COL hours              FORM 9999.99
SQL> COL time_taken_display FORM a20
SQL> SET LINESIZE 132
SQL> --
SQL> SELECT
 session_recid
,compression_ratio
,time_taken_display
,(end_time - start_time) * 24 as hours
,TO_CHAR(end_time,'dd-mon-yy hh24:mi') as end_time
FROM v$rman_backup_job_details
ORDER BY end_time;
```

Here is some sample output:

```
SESSION_RECID COMPRESSION_RATIO TIME_TAKEN_DISPLAY     HOURS END_TIME
------------- ----------------- -------------------- -------- ----------------
           15                 1 00:05:08                  .09 11-jan-18 13:41
           27        3.79407176 00:00:09                  .00 11-jan-18 13:52
           33        1.19992137 00:05:01                  .08 11-jan-18 14:07
```

The contents of V$RMAN_BACKUP_JOB_DETAILS are summarized by a session connection to RMAN. Therefore, the report output is more accurate if you connect to RMAN (establishing a session) and then exit out of RMAN after the backup job is complete. If you remain connected to RMAN while running multiple backup jobs, the query output reports on all backup activity while connected (for that session).

You should have an automated method of detecting whether or not RMAN backups are running and if data files are being backed up. One reliable method of automating such a task is to embed SQL into a shell script and then run the script on a periodic basis from a scheduling utility such as cron.

I typically run two basic types of checks regarding the RMAN backups:

- Have the RMAN backups run recently?

- Are there any data files that have not been backed up recently?

The following shell script checks for these conditions. You will need to modify the script and provide it with a username and password for a user that can query the data dictionary objects referenced in the script and also change the e-mail address of where messages are sent. When running the script, you will need to pass in two variables: the Oracle SID and the threshold number of past days that you want to check for the last time the backups ran or for when a data file was backed up.

```
#!/bin/bash
#
if [ $# -ne 2 ]; then
  echo "Usage: $0 SID threshold"
  exit 1
fi
# source oracle OS variables
. /var/opt/oracle/oraset $1
crit_var=$(sqlplus -s <<EOF
/ as sysdba
SET HEAD OFF FEEDBACK OFF
SELECT COUNT(*) FROM
(SELECT (sysdate - MAX(end_time)) delta
 FROM v\$rman_backup_job_details) a
WHERE a.delta > $2;
EOF)
```

```
#
if [ $crit_var -ne 0 ]; then
  echo "rman backups not running on $1" | mailx -s "rman problem" dkuhn@
  gmail.com
else
  echo "rman backups ran ok"
fi
#-----------------------------------------------
crit_var2=$(sqlplus -s <<EOF
/ as sysdba
SET HEAD OFF FEEDBACK OFF
SELECT COUNT(*)
FROM
(
SELECT name
FROM v\$datafile
MINUS
SELECT DISTINCT
 f.name
FROM v\$backup_datafile d
    ,v\$datafile       f
WHERE d.file#    = f.file#
AND   d.completion_time > sysdate - $2);
EOF)
#
if [ $crit_var2 -ne 0 ]; then
  echo "datafile not backed up on $1" | mailx -s "backup problem" dkuhn@
  gmail.com
else
  echo "datafiles are backed up..."
fi
#
exit 0
```

For example, to check if backups have been running successfully within the past 2 days, run the script (named `rman_chk.bsh`):

```
$ rman_chk.bsh INVPRD 2
```

The prior script is basic but effective. You can enhance it as required for your RMAN environment.

Summary

RMAN offers many flexible and feature-rich options for backups. By default, RMAN backs up only blocks that have been modified in the database. The incremental features allow you to back up only blocks that have been modified since the last backup. These incremental features are particularly useful in reducing the size of backups in large database environments, in which only a small percentage of data in the database changes from one backup to the next.

You can instruct RMAN to back up every block in each data file via an image copy. An image copy is a block-for-block identical copy of the data file. Image copies have the advantage of being able to restore the backup files directly from the backup (without using RMAN). You can use the incrementally updated backup feature to implement an efficient hybrid of image copy backups and incremental backups.

There are configurations that will help match recovery strategies and requirements from image copies with incremental backups to backup sets and archivelogs. The CDB and PDB databases can all be backed up in the CDB, but when connecting to a PDB as target, only the PDB can be backed up. Database data block changes can be backed up along with tablespaces, data files, and databases.

RMAN contains built-in commands for reporting on many aspects of backups. The LIST command reports on backup activity. The REPORT command is useful for determining which files need to be backed up, as dictated by the retention policy.

After you have successfully configured RMAN and created backups, you are in a position to be able to restore and recover your database in the event of a media failure. Backups are only as good as the ability to restore the database. Restore and recovery topics are detailed in the next chapter.

CHAPTER 19

RMAN Restore and Recovery

There are quite a few stories I can tell you about needing to recover and even the monthly drills that were practiced to perform restores. A backup is only good if you can restore; hopefully it is not needed, but a restore process needs to be documented, tested, and practiced. Practicing allows for errors to occur and document strange things that can happen, so in the moment of panic and needing to complete the restore under pressure, the years of practice will help. It will also help verify that there are good backups available, as described by the co-author in a tale from a DBA:

A couple of years ago, I was out on a long Saturday morning bike ride. About halfway through the ride, my cell phone rang. It was one of the data center operational support technicians. He told me that a mission critical database server was acting strange and that I should log in as soon as possible and make sure things were okay. I told him that I was about 15 minutes from being able to log in. So, I scurried home as fast as I could to check out the production box. When I got home and logged in to the database server, I tried to start SQL*Plus and immediately got an error indicating that the SQL*Plus binary file had corruption. Great. I couldn't even log in to SQL*Plus. This was not good.

I had the SA restore the Oracle binaries from an OS backup. I started SQL*Plus. The database had crashed, so I attempted to start it. The output indicated that there was a media failure with all the data files. After some analysis, it was discovered that there had been some filesystem issues and that all these files on disk were corrupt:

- Data files
- Control files
- Archive redo logs

© Michelle Malcher and Darl Kuhn 2019
M. Malcher and D. Kuhn, *Pro Oracle Database 18c Administration*,
https://doi.org/10.1007/978-1-4842-4424-1_19

- Online redo log files

- RMAN backup pieces

This was almost a total disaster. My director asked about our options. I responded, "All we have to do is restore the database from our last tape backup, and we'll lose whatever data are in archive redo logs that haven't been backed up to tape yet."

The storage administrators were called in and instructed to restore the last set of RMAN backups that had been written to tape. About 15 minutes later, we could hear the tape guys talking to each other in hushed voices. One of them said, "We are sooooo hosed. We do not have any tape backups of RMAN for any databases on this box."

That was a dark moment. The worst-case scenario was to rebuild the database from DDL scripts and lose 3 years of production data. Not a very palatable option.

After looking around the production box, I discovered that the prior production support DBAwho, ironically, had just been let go a few days before, owing to budget cuts) had implemented a job to copy the RMAN backups to another server in the production environment. The RMAN backups on this other server were intact. I was able to restore and recover the production database from these backups. We lost about a day's worth of data (between corrupt archive logs and downtime, in which no incoming transactions were allowed), but we were able to get the database restored and recovered approximately 20 hours after the initial phone call. That was a long day.

Most situations in which you need to restore and recover will not be as bad as the one just described. Even in places where there are safeguards and little natural disasters, there always seems to be something that occurs to make you want to test the recovery and validate the backups. However, the previous scenario does highlight the need for the following:

- A backup strategy

- A DBA with backup and recovery skills

- A restore-and-recovery strategy, including a requirement to test the restore and recovery periodically

This chapter walks you through restore and recovery, using RMAN. The chapter covers many of the common tasks you will have to perform when dealing with media failures.

Determining if Media Recovery Is Required

The term *media recovery* means the restoration of files that have been lost or damaged, owing to the failure of the underlying storage media (usually a disk of some sort) or accidental removal of files. Usually, you know that media recovery is required through an error such as the following:

```
ORA-01157: cannot identify/lock data file 1 - see DBWR trace file
ORA-01110: data file 1: '/u01/dbfile/o12c/system01.dbf'
```

The error may be displayed on your screen when performing DBA tasks, such as stopping and starting the database. Or, you might see such an error in a trace file or the alert.log file. It is also possible that since the file has not been written to or because of the OS, the error might be delayed in appearing. If you do not notice the issue right away, with a severe media failure, the database will stop processing transactions, and users will start calling you.

To understand how Oracle determines that media recovery is required, you must first understand how Oracle determines that everything is okay. When Oracle shuts down normally (IMMEDIATE, TRANSACTIONAL, NORMAL), part of the shutdown process is to flush all modified blocks (in memory) to disk, mark the header of each data file with the current SCN, and update the control file with the current SCN information.

Upon startup, Oracle checks to see if the SCN in the control file matches the SCN in the header of the data files. If there is a match, then Oracle attempts to open the data files and online redo log files. If all files are available and can be opened, Oracle starts normally. The following query compares the SCN in the control file (for each data file) with the SCN in the data file header:

```
SQL> SET LINES 132
SQL> COL name            FORM a40
SQL> COL status          FORM A8
SQL> COL file#           FORM 9999
SQL> COL control_file_SCN FORM 999999999999999
SQL> COL datafile_SCN    FORM 999999999999999
--
SQL> SELECT
 a.name
,a.status
```

```
,a.file#
,a.checkpoint_change# control_file_SCN
,b.checkpoint_change# datafile_SCN
,CASE
   WHEN ((a.checkpoint_change# - b.checkpoint_change#) = 0) THEN 'Startup
   Normal'
   WHEN ((b.checkpoint_change#) = 0)                        THEN 'File Missing?'
   WHEN ((a.checkpoint_change# - b.checkpoint_change#) > 0) THEN 'Media
   Rec. Req.'
   WHEN ((a.checkpoint_change# - b.checkpoint_change#) < 0) THEN 'Old
   Control File'
   ELSE 'what the ?'
 END datafile_status
FROM v$datafile        a -- control file SCN for datafile
    ,v$datafile_header b -- datafile header SCN
WHERE a.file# = b.file#
ORDER BY a.file#;
```

If the control file SCN values are greater than the data file SCN values, then media recovery is most likely required. This would be the case if you restored a data file from a backup, and the SCN in the restored data file had an SCN less than the data file in the current control file.

Tip   The V$DATAFILE_HEADER view uses the physical data file on disk as its source. The V$DATAFILE view uses the control file as its source.

You can also directly query the V$DATAFILE_HEADER for more information. The ERROR and RECOVER columns report any potential problems. For example, a YES or null value in the RECOVER column indicates that there is a problem:

```
SQL> select file#, status, error, recover from v$datafile_header;
```

Here is some sample output:

```
FILE# STATUS  ERROR                 REC
----------- -------  --------------------- ---
        1 ONLINE  FILE NOT FOUND
        2 ONLINE                        NO
        3 ONLINE                        NO
```

Determining What to Restore

Media recovery requires that you perform manual tasks to get your database back in one piece. These tasks usually involve a combination of RESTORE and RECOVER commands. You will have to issue an RMAN RESTORE command if, for some reason (accidental deleting of files, disk failure, and so on), your data files have experienced media failure.

How the Process Works

When you issue the RESTORE command, RMAN automatically decides how to extract the data files from any of the following available backups:

- Full database backup

- Incremental level-0 backup

- Image copy backup generated by BACKUP AS COPY command

After the files are restored from a backup, you are required to apply redo to them via the RECOVER command. When you issue the RECOVER command, Oracle examines the SCNs in the affected data files and determines whether any of them need to be recovered. If the SCN in the data file is less than the corresponding SCN in the control file, then media recovery will be required.

Oracle retrieves the data file SCN and then looks for the corresponding SCN in the redo stream to establish where to start the recovery process. If the starting recovery SCN is in the online redo log files, the archivelog files are not required for recovery.

During a recovery, RMAN automatically determines how to apply redo. First, RMAN applies any incremental backups available that are greater than level 0, such as the incremental level 1. Next, any archivelog files on disk are applied. If the archivelog files do not exist on disk, RMAN attempts to retrieve them from a backup set.

To be able to perform a complete recovery, all the following conditions need to be true:

- Your database is in archivelog mode.

- You have a good baseline backup of your database.

- You have any required redo that has been generated since the backup (archivelog files, online redo log files, or incremental backups that RMAN can use for recovery instead of applying redo).

There are a wide variety of restore-and-recovery scenarios. How you restore and recover depends directly on your backup strategy and which files have been damaged. Listed next are the general steps to follow when facing a media failure:

1. Determine which files need to be restored.

2. Depending on the damage, set your database mode to nomount, mount, or open.

3. Use the RESTORE command to retrieve files from RMAN backups.

4. Use the RECOVER command for data files requiring recovery.

5. Open your database.

Your particular restore-and-recovery scenario may not require that all the previous steps be performed. For instance, you may just want to restore your spfile, which does not require a recovery step.

The first step in the restore-and-recovery process is to determine which files have experienced media failure. You can usually determine which files need to be restored from the following sources:

- Error messages displayed on your screen, either from RMAN or SQL*Plus

- Alert.log file and corresponding trace files

- Data dictionary views

Additionally, to the previously listed methods, you should consider the Data Recovery Advisor for obtaining information about the extent of a failure and corresponding corrective action.

Using Data Recovery Advisor

The Data Recovery Advisor tool was introduced in Oracle Database 11g. In the event of a media failure, this tool will display the details of the failure, recommend corrective actions, and perform the recommended actions if you specify that it do so. It is like having another set of eyes to provide feedback when in a restore-and-recovery situation. There are four modes to Data Recovery Advisor:

- Listing failures
- Suggesting corrective action
- Running commands to repair failures
- Changing the status of a failure

The Data Recovery Advisor is invoked from RMAN. You can think of the Data Recovery Advisor as a set of RMAN commands that can assist you when dealing with media failure.

Listing Failures

When using the Data Recovery Advisor, the LIST FAILURE command is used to display any issues with the data files, control files, or online redo logs:

```
RMAN> list failure;
```

If there are no detected failures, you will see a message indicating that there are no failures. Here is some sample output indicating that there may be an issue with a data file:

```
List of Database Failures
=========================

Failure ID Priority Status    Time Detected Summary
---------- -------- --------- ------------- -------
6222       CRITICAL OPEN      12-JAN-18     System datafile 1:
 '/u01/dbfile/o18c/system01.dbf' is missing
```

To display more information about the failure, use the DETAIL clause:

```
RMAN> list failure 6222 detail;
```

Here is the additional output for this example:

```
Impact: Database cannot be opened
```

With this type of failure, the prior output indicates that the database cannot be opened.

Tip   If you suspect there is a media failure, yet the Data Recovery Advisor is not reporting any issues, run the VALIDATE DATABASE command to verify that the database is intact.

Suggesting Corrective Action

The ADVISE FAILURE command gives advice about how to recover from potential problems detected by the Data Recovery Advisor. If you have multiple failures with your database, you can directly specify the failure ID to get advice on a given failure, like so:

```
RMAN> advise failure 6222;
```

Here is a snippet of the output for this particular issue:

```
Optional Manual Actions
=======================
1. If file /u01/dbfile/o18c/system01.dbf was unintentionally renamed or moved,
restore it

Automated Repair Options
========================
Option Repair Description
------ ------------------
1      Restore and recover datafile 1
  Strategy: The repair includes complete media recovery with no data loss
  Repair script: /ora01/app/oracle/diag/rdbms/o18c/o18c/hm/reco_4116328280.hm
```

In this case, the Data Recovery Advisor created a script that can be used to potentially fix the problem. The contents of the repair script can be viewed with an OS utility; for example,

```
$ cat /ora01/app/oracle/diag/rdbms/o18c/o18c/hm/reco_4116328280.hm
```

Here are the contents of the script for this example:

```
# restore and recover datafile
restore ( datafile 1 );
recover datafile 1;
sql 'alter database datafile 1 online';
```

After reviewing the script, you can decide to run the suggested commands manually, or you can have the Data Recovery Advisor run the script via the REPAIR command (see the next section for details).

Repairing Failures

If you have identified a failure and viewed the recommended advice, you can proceed to the repair work. If you want to inspect what the REPAIR FAILURE command will do without actually running the commands, use the PREVIEW clause:

```
RMAN> repair failure preview;
```

Before you run the REPAIR FAILURE command, ensure that you first run the LIST FAILURE and ADVISE FAILURE commands from the same connected session. In other words, the RMAN session that you are in must run the LIST and ADVISE commands within the same session before running the REPAIR command.

If you are satisfied with the repair suggestions, then run the REPAIR FAILURE command:

```
RMAN> repair failure;
```

You will be prompted at this point for confirmation:

```
Do you really want to execute the above repair (enter YES or NO)?
```

Type YES to proceed:

```
YES
```

If all goes well, you should see a final message such as this in the output:

```
repair failure complete
```

Note   You can run the Data Recovery Advisor commands from the RMAN command prompt or from Enterprise Manager.

In this way, you can use the RMAN commands LIST FAILURE, ADVISE FAILURE, and REPAIR FAILURE to resolve media failures.

Changing the Status of a Failure

One last note on the Data Recovery Advisor: if you know that you have had a failure and that it is not critical (e.g., a data file missing from a tablespace that is no longer used), then use the CHANGE FAILURE command to alter the priority of a failure. In this example, there is a missing data file that belongs to a noncritical tablespace. First, obtain the failure priority via the LIST FAILURE command:

```
RMAN> list failure;
```

Here is some sample output:

```
Failure ID Priority Status    Time Detected Summary
---------- -------- --------- ------------- -------
5          HIGH     OPEN      12-JAN-18     One or more non-system datafiles
                                            are missing
```

Next, change the priority from HIGH to LOW with the CHANGE FAILURE command:

```
RMAN> change failure 5 priority low;
```

You will be prompted to confirm that you really do want to change the priority:

```
Do you really want to change the above failures (enter YES or NO)?
```

If you do want to change the priority, then type YES, and press the Enter key. If you run the LIST FAILURE command again, you will see that the priority has now been changed to LOW:

```
RMAN> list failure low;
```

Using RMAN to Stop/Start Oracle

You can use RMAN to stop and start your database with methods that are almost identical to those available through SQL*Plus. When performing restore-and-recovery operations, it is often more convenient to stop and start your database from within RMAN. The following RMAN commands can be used to stop and start your database:

- SHUTDOWN

- STARTUP

- ALTER DATABASE

Shutting Down

The SHUTDOWN command works the same from RMAN as it does from SQL*Plus. There are four types of shutdown: ABORT, IMMEDIATE, NORMAL, and TRANSACTIONAL. I usually first attempt to stop a database using SHUTDOWN IMMEDIATE. Here are some examples:

```
RMAN> shutdown immediate;
RMAN> shutdown abort;
```

If you do not specify a shutdown option, NORMAL is the default. Shutting down a database with NORMAL is rarely viable, as this mode waits for currently connected users to disconnect at their leisure.

Starting Up

As with SQL*Plus, you can use a combination of STARTUP and ALTER DATABASE commands with RMAN to step the database through startup phases, like this:

```
RMAN> startup nomount;
RMAN> alter database mount;
RMAN> alter database open;
```

Here is another example:

```
RMAN> startup mount;
RMAN> alter database open;
```

If you want to start the database with restricted access, use the DBA option:

```
RMAN> startup dba;
```

Tip   Starting with Oracle Database 12c, you can run all SQL statements directly from within RMAN without having to specify the RMAN `sql` command.

Complete Recovery

As discussed in Chapter 16, the term *complete recovery* means that you can restore all transactions that were committed before a failure occurred. *Complete recovery* does not mean that you are restoring and recovering all data files in your database. For instance, you are performing a complete recovery if you have a media failure with one data file, and you restore and recover the one data file. For complete recovery, the following conditions must be true:

- Your database is in archivelog mode.

- You have a good baseline backup of the data files that have experienced media failure.

- You have any required redo that has been generated since the last backup.

- All archive redo logs start from the point at which the last backup began.

- Any incremental backups that RMAN can use for recovery are available (if using).

- Online redo logs that contain transactions that have not yet been archived are available.

If you have experienced a media failure, and you have the required files to perform a complete recovery, then you can restore and recover your database.

Testing Restore and Recovery

You can determine which files RMAN will use for restore and recovery before you
actually perform the restore and recovery. You can also instruct RMAN to verify the
integrity of the backup files that will be used for the restore and recovery.

Previewing Backups Used for Recovery

Use the RESTORE...PREVIEW command to list the backups and archive redo log files
that RMAN will use to restore and recover database data files. The RESTORE...PREVIEW
command does not actually restore any files. Rather, it lists the backup files that will be
used for a restore operation. This example previews in detail the backups required for
restore and recovery for the entire database:

```
RMAN> restore database preview;
```

You can also preview require backup files at a summarized level of detail:

```
RMAN> restore database preview summary;
```

Here is a snippet of the output:

```
List of Backup Sets
===================
BS Key  Type LV Size       Device Type Elapsed Time Completion Time
------- ---- -- ---------- ----------- ------------ ---------------
224     Full    775.37M    DISK        00:02:22     12-JAN-18
        BP Key: 229  Status: AVAILABLE  Compressed: NO  Tag: TAG20130112T120713
        Piece Name: /u02/O18C/rman/r29gnv7q7i_1_1.bk
  List of Datafiles in backup set 224
  File LV Type Ckp SCN    Ckp Time  Name
  ---- -- ---- ---------- --------- ----
  1       Full 4586940    12-JAN-18 /u01/dbfile/o18c/system01.dbf
  3       Full 4586940    12-JAN-18 /u01/dbfile/o18c/undotbs01.dbf
  4       Full 4586940    12-JAN-18 /u01/dbfile/o18c/users01.dbf
```

Here are some more examples of how to preview backups required for restore and recovery:

```
RMAN> restore tablespace system preview;
RMAN> restore archivelog from time 'sysdate -1' preview;
RMAN> restore datafile 1, 2, 3 preview;
```

Validating Backup Files Before Restoring

There are several levels of verification that you can perform on backup files without actually restoring anything. If you just want RMAN to verify that the files exist and check the file headers, then use the RESTORE...VALIDATE HEADER command, as shown:

```
RMAN> restore database validate header;
```

This command only validates the existence of backup files and checks the file headers. You can further instruct RMAN to verify the integrity of blocks within backup files required to restore the database data files via the RESTORE...VALIDATE command (sans the HEADER clause). Again, RMAN will not restore any data files in this mode:

```
RMAN> restore database validate;
```

This command only checks for physical corruption within the backup files. You can also check for logical corruption (along with physical corruption), as follows:

```
RMAN> restore database validate check logical;
```

Here are some other examples of using RESTORE...VALIDATE:

```
RMAN> restore datafile 1,2,3 validate;
RMAN> restore archivelog all validate;
RMAN> restore controlfile validate;
RMAN> restore tablespace system validate;
```

Testing Media Recovery

The prior sections covered reporting and verifying the restore operations. You can also instruct RMAN to verify the recovery process via the RECOVER...TEST command. Before performing a test recovery, you need to ensure that the data files being recovered are offline. Oracle will throw an error for any online data files being recovered in test mode.

In this example, the tablespace USERS is restored first, and then a trial recovery is performed:

```
RMAN> connect target /
RMAN> startup mount;
RMAN> restore tablespace users;
RMAN> recover tablespace users test;
```

If there are any missing archive redo logs that are required for recovery, the following error is thrown:

```
RMAN-06053: unable to perform media recovery because of missing log
RMAN-06025: no backup of archived log for thread 1 with sequence 6 ...
```

If the testing of the recovery succeeded, you will see messages such as the following, indicating that the application of redo was tested but not applied:

```
ORA-10574: Test recovery did not corrupt any data block
ORA-10573: Test recovery tested redo from change 4586939 to 4588462
ORA-10572: Test recovery canceled due to errors
ORA-10585: Test recovery can not apply redo that may modify control file
```

Here are some other examples of testing the recovery process:

```
RMAN> recover database test;
RMAN> recover tablespace users, tools test;
RMAN> recover datafile 1,2,3 test;
```

Restoring and Recovering the Entire Database

The RESTORE DATABASE command will restore every data file in your database. The exception to this is when RMAN detects that data files have already been restored; in that case, it will not restore them again. If you want to override that behavior, use the FORCE command.

When you issue the RECOVER DATABASE command, RMAN will automatically apply redo to any data files that need recovery. The recovery process includes applying changes found in the following files:

- Incremental backup pieces (applicable only if using incremental backups)

- Archivelog files (generated since the last backup or incremental backup applied)

- Online redo log files (current and unarchived)

You can open your database after the restore-and-recovery process is complete. Complete database recovery works only if you have good backups of your database and access to all redo generated after the backup was taken. You need all the redo required to recover the database data files. If you do not have all the required redo, then you will most likely have to perform an incomplete recovery (see the section "Incomplete Recovery" later in this chapter).

Note Your database has to be at least mounted to restore data files, using RMAN. This is because RMAN reads information from the control file during the restore-and-recovery process.

You can perform a complete database-level recovery with either the current control file or a backup control file.

Using the Current Control File

You must first put your database in mount mode to perform a database-wide restore and recovery. This is because Oracle will not allow you to operate your database in open mode while data files associated with the SYSTEM tablespace are being restored and recovered. In this situation, start up the database in mount mode, issue the RESTORE and RECOVER commands, and then open the database, like so:

```
$ rman target /
RMAN> startup mount;
RMAN> restore database;
RMAN> recover database;
RMAN> alter database open;
```

If everything goes as expected, the last message you should see is this:

```
Statement processed
```

Using the Backup Control File

This technique uses an autobackup of the control file retrieved from the FRA. (see the section "Restoring a Control File," later in this chapter, for more examples of how to restore your control file). In this scenario, the control file is first retrieved from a backup before restoring and recovering the database:

```
$ rman target /
RMAN> startup nomount;
RMAN> restore controlfile from autobackup;
RMAN> alter database mount;
RMAN> restore database;
RMAN> recover database;
RMAN> alter database open resetlogs;
```

If successful, the last message you should see is this:

```
Statement processed
```

Restoring and Recovering Tablespaces

Sometimes you will have a media failure that is localized to a particular tablespace or set of tablespaces. In this situation, it is appropriate to restore and recover at the tablespace level of granularity. The RMAN RESTORE TABLESPACE and RECOVER TABLESPACE commands will restore and recover all data files associated with the specified tablespace(s).

Restoring Tablespaces While the Database Is Open

If your database is open, then you must take offline the tablespace you want to restore and recover. You can do this for any tablespace except SYSTEM and UNDO. This example restores and recovers the USERS tablespace while the database is open:

```
$ rman target /
RMAN> alter tablespace users offline immediate;
RMAN> restore tablespace users;
```

```
RMAN> recover tablespace users;
RMAN> alter tablespace users online;
```

After the tablespace is brought online, you should see a message such as this:

```
sql statement: alter tablespace users online
```

Restoring Tablespaces While the Database Is in Mount Mode

Usually when performing a restore and recovery, DBAs will shut down the database and restart it in mount mode in preparation for performing the recovery. Placing a database in mount mode ensures that no users are connecting to the database and that no transactions are transpiring.

Also, if you are restoring and recovering the SYSTEM tablespace, then you must start the database in mount mode. Oracle does not allow for restoring and recovering the SYSTEM tablespace data files while the database is open. This next example restores the SYSTEM tablespace while the database is in mount mode:

```
$ rman target /
RMAN> shutdown immediate;
RMAN> startup mount;
RMAN> restore tablespace system;
RMAN> recover tablespace system;
RMAN> alter database open;
```

If successful, the last message you should see is this:

```
Statement processed
```

Restoring Read-Only Tablespaces

RMAN will restore read-only tablespaces along with the rest of the database when you issue a RESTORE DATDABASE command. For example, the following command will restore all data files (including those in read-only mode):

```
RMAN> restore database;
```

Note   If you are using a backup that was created after the read-only tablespace was placed in read-only mode, then no recovery is necessary for the read-only data files. In this situation, no redo has been generated for the read-only tablespace since it was backed up.

Restoring Temporary Tablespaces

You do not have to restore or re-create missing locally managed temporary tablespace temp files. When you open your database for use, Oracle automatically detects and re-creates locally managed temporary tablespace temp files.

When Oracle automatically re-creates a temporary tablespace, it will log a message to your target database alert.log such as this:

```
Re-creating tempfile <your temporary tablespace filename>
```

If, for any reason, your temporary tablespace becomes unavailable, you can also re-create it yourself. Because there are never any permanent objects in temporary tablespaces, you can simply re-create them as needed. Here is an example of how to create a locally managed temporary tablespace:

```
SQL> CREATE TEMPORARY TABLESPACE temp TEMPFILE
'/u01/dbfile/o18c/temp01.dbf' SIZE 1000M
EXTENT MANAGEMENT
LOCAL UNIFORM SIZE 512K;
```

If your temporary tablespace exists, but the temporary data files are missing, you can just add them, as shown:

```
SQL> alter tablespace temp
add tempfile '/u01/dbfile/o18c/temp02.dbf' SIZE 5000M REUSE;
```

Restoring and Recovering Data Files

A data file-level restore and recovery works well when a media failure is confined to a small set of data files. With data file-level recoveries, you can instruct RMAN to restore and recover either with a data file name or data file number. For data files not associated with the SYSTEM or UNDO tablespaces, you have the option of restoring and recovering while the database remains open. While the database is open, however, you must first take offline any data files being restored and recovered.

Restoring and Recovering Data Files While the Database Is Open

Use the RESTORE DATAFILE and RECOVER DATAFILE commands to restore and recover at the data file level. When your database is open, you are required to take offline any data files that you are attempting to restore and recover. This example restores and recovers data files while the database is open:

```
RMAN> alter database datafile 4, 5 offline;
RMAN> restore datafile 4, 5;
RMAN> recover datafile 4, 5;
RMAN> alter database datafile 4, 5 online;
```

Tip   Use the RMAN REPORT SCHEMA command to list data file names and file numbers. You can also query the NAME and FILE# columns of V$DATAFILE to take names and numbers.

You can also specify the name of the data file that you want to restore and recover; for example,

```
RMAN> alter database datafile '/u01/dbfile/o18c/users01.dbf' offline;
RMAN> restore datafile '/u01/dbfile/o18c/users01.dbf';
RMAN> recover datafile '/u01/dbfile/o18c/users01.dbf';
RMAN> alter database datafile '/u01/dbfile/o18c/users01.dbf' online;
```

Restoring and Recovering Data Files While the Database Is Not Open

In this scenario, the database is first shut down and then started in mount mode. You can restore and recover any data file in your database while the database is not open. This example shows the restoring of data file 1, which is associated with the SYSTEM tablespace:

```
$ rman target /
RMAN> shutdown abort;
RMAN> startup mount;
```

```
RMAN> restore datafile 1;
RMAN> recover datafile 1;
RMAN> alter database open;
```

You can also specify the file name when performing a data file recovery:

```
$ rman target /
RMAN> shutdown abort;
RMAN> startup mount;
RMAN> restore datafile '/u01/dbfile/o18c/system01.dbf';
RMAN> recover datafile '/u01/dbfile/o18c/system01.dbf';
RMAN> alter database open;
```

Restoring Data Files to Nondefault Locations

Sometimes a failure will occur that renders the disks associated with a mount point inoperable. In these situations, you will need to restore and recover the data files to a location different from the one where they originally resided. Another typical need for restoring data files to nondefault locationsis for filcs that you are restoring to a different database server, on which the mount points are completely different from those of the server on which the backup originated.

Use the SET NEWNAME and SWITCH commands to restore data files to nondefault locations. Both of these commands must be run from within an RMAN run{} block. You can think of using SET NEWNAME and SWITCH as a way to rename data files (similar to the SQL*Plus ALTER DATABASE RENAME FILE statement).

This example changes the location of data files when doing a restore and recover. First, place the database in mount mode:

```
$ rman target /
RMAN> startup mount;
```

Then, run the following block of RMAN code:

```
run{
set newname for datafile 4 to '/u02/dbfile/o18c/users01.dbf';
set newname for datafile 5 to '/u02/dbfile/o18c/users02.dbf';
restore datafile 4, 5;
switch datafile all; # Updates repository with new datafile location.
```

```
recover datafile 4, 5;
alter database open;
}
```

This is a partial listing of the output:

```
datafile 4 switched to datafile copy
input datafile copy RECID=79 STAMP=804533148 file
name=/u02/dbfile/o18c/users01.dbf
datafile 5 switched to datafile copy
input datafile copy RECID=80 STAMP=804533148 file
name=/u02/dbfile/o18c/users02.dbf
```

If the database is open, you can place the data files offline and then set their new names for restore and recovery, as follows:

```
run{
alter database datafile 4, 5 offline;
set newname for datafile 4 to '/u02/dbfile/o18c/users01.dbf';
set newname for datafile 5 to '/u02/dbfile/o18c/users02.dbf';
restore datafile 4, 5;
switch datafile all; # Updates repository with new datafile location.
recover datafile 4, 5;
alter database datafile 4, 5 online;
}
```

Performing Block-Level Recovery

Block-level corruption is rare and is usually caused by some sort of I/O error. It can rescue you from having to do a complete restore of a datafile with recovery. I have actually run into this issue once before, and now with block checking and auto repair with ASM, this might even become rarer. However, if you do have an isolated corrupt block within a large data file, it is nice to have the option of performing a block-level recovery. Block-level recovery is useful when a small number of blocks are corrupt within a data file. Block recovery is not appropriate if the entire data file needs media recovery.

RMAN will automatically detect corrupt blocks whenever a BACKUP, VALIDATE, or BACKUP VALIDATE command is run. Details on corrupt blocks can be viewed in the V$DATABASE_BLOCK_CORRUPTION view. In the following example the regular backup job has reported a corrupt block in the output:

```
ORA-19566: exceeded limit of 0 corrupt blocks for file...
```

Querying the V$DATABASE_BLOCK_CORRUPTION view indicates which file contains corruption:

```
SQL> select * from v$database_block_corruption;

     FILE#     BLOCK#     BLOCKS CORRUPTION_CHANGE# CORRUPTIO     CON_ID
---------- ---------- ---------- ------------------ --------- ----------
         4         20          1                  0 ALL ZERO           0
```

Your database can be either mounted or open when performing block-level recovery. You do not have to take offline the data file being recovered. You can instruct RMAN to recover all blocks reported in V$DATABASE_BLOCK_CORRUPTION, as shown:

```
RMAN> recover corruption list;
```

If successful, the following message is displayed:

```
media recovery complete...
```

Another way to recover the block is to specify the data file and block number, like so:

```
RMAN> recover datafile 4 block 20;
```

It is preferable to use the RECOVER CORRUPTION LIST syntax because it will clear out any blocks recovered from the V view.

Note   RMAN cannot perform block-level recovery on block 1 (data file header) of the data file.

Block-level media recovery allows you to keep your database available and also reduces the mean time to recovery, as only the corrupt blocks are offline during the recovery. Your database must be in archivelog mode for performing block-level recoveries. RMAN can restore the block from the flashback logs (if available). If the flashback logs are not available, then RMAN will attempt to restore the block from a full backup, a level-0 backup, or an image copy backup generated by the BACKUP AS COPY command. After the block has been restored, any required archivelogs must be available to recover the block. RMAN cannot perform block media recovery using incremental level-1 (or higher) backups.

Restoring a Container Database and Its Associated Pluggable Databases

Starting with Oracle Database 12c, you can create pluggable databases within one container database (see Chapter 22 for details). When dealing with container and associated pluggable databases, there are three basic scenarios:

- All data files have experienced media failure (container root data files as well as all associated pluggable database data files).

- Just the data files associated with the container root database have experienced media failure.

- Only data files associated with a pluggable database have experienced media failure.

The prior scenarios are covered in the following sections.

Restoring and Recovering All Data Files

To restore and recover all data files associated with a container database (this includes the root container, the seed container, and all associated pluggable databases), use RMAN to connect to the container database as a user with sysdba or sysbackup privileges. Because the data files associated with the root system tablespace are being restored, the database must be started in mount mode (and not open):

```
$ rman target /
RMAN> startup mount;
RMAN> restore database;
RMAN> recover database;
RMAN> alter database open;
```

Keep in mind that when you open a container database, this does not, by default, open the associated pluggable databases. You can do that from the root container, as follows:

```
RMAN> alter pluggable database all open;
```

Restoring and Recovering Root Container Data Files

If just data files associated with the root container have been damaged, then you can restore and recover at the root level. In this example, the root container's system data file is being restored, so the database must not be open. The following commands instruct RMAN to restore only the data files associated with the root container database, via the keyword root:

```
$ rman target /
RMAN> startup mount;
RMAN> restore database root;
RMAN> recover database root;
RMAN> alter database open;
```

In the prior code the `restore database root` command instructs RMAN to restore only data files associated with the root container database. After the container database is opened, you must open any associated pluggable databases. You can do so from the root container, as shown:

```
RMAN> alter pluggable database all open;
```

You can check the status of your pluggable databases via this query:

```
SQL> select name, open_mode from v$pdbs;
```

Restoring and Recovering a Pluggable Database

You have two options for restoring and recovering a pluggable database:

- Connect as the container root user, and specify the pluggable database to be restored and recovered.

- Connect directly to the pluggable database as a privileged pluggable-level user, and issue RESTORE and RECOVER commands.

This first example connects to the root container and restores and recovers the data files associated with the salespdb pluggable database. For this to work, the pluggable database must not be open (because the pluggable database's system data files are also being restored and recovered):

```
$ rman target /
RMAN> alter pluggable database salespdb close;
RMAN> restore pluggable database salespdb;
RMAN> recover pluggable database salespdb;
RMAN> alter pluggable database salespdb open;
```

You can also connect directly to a pluggable database and perform restore and recovery operations. When connected directly to the pluggable database, the user only has access to the data files associated with the pluggable database:

```
$ rman target sys/foo@salespdb
RMAN> shutdown immediate;
RMAN> restore database;
RMAN> recover database;
RMAN> alter database open;
```

Note   When you are connected directly to a pluggable database, you cannot specify the name of the pluggable database as part of the RESTORE and RECOVER commands. In this situation, you will get an RMAN-07536: command not allowed when connected to a Pluggable Database error.

The prior code only affects data files associated with the pluggable database to which you are connected. The pluggable database needs to be closed for this to work. However, the root container database can be open or mounted. Also, you must use a backup that was taken while connected to the pluggable database as a privileged user. The privileged pluggable database user cannot access backups of data files initiated by the root container database privileged user.

Restoring Archivelog Files

RMAN will automatically restore any archivelog files that it needs during a recovery process. You normally do not need to restore archivelog files manually. However, you may want to do so if any of the following situations apply:

- You need to restore archivelog files in anticipation of later performing a recovery; the idea is that if the archivelog files are already restored, it will speed the recovery operation.

- You are required to restore the archivelog files to a nondefault location, either because of media failure or because of storage space issues.

- You need to restore specific archivelog files in order to inspect them via LogMiner.

If you have enabled an FRA, then RMAN will, by default, restore archivelog files to the destination defined by the initialization parameter DB_RECOVERY_FILE_DEST. Otherwise, RMAN uses the LOG_ARCHIVE_DEST_N initialization parameter (where N is usually 1) to determine where to restore the archivelog files.

If you restore archivelog files to a nondefault location, RMAN knows the location they were restored to and automatically finds these files when you issue any subsequent RECOVER commands. RMAN will not restore archivelog files that it determines are already on disk. Even if you specify a nondefault location, RMAN will not restore an archivelog file to disk if the file already exists. In this situation, RMAN simply returns a message stating that the archivelog file has already been restored. Use the FORCE option to override this behavior.

If you are uncertain of the sequence numbers to use during a restore of log files, you can query the V$LOG_HISTORY view.

Tip   Keep in mind that you cannot restore an archivelog that you never backed up. Also, you cannot restore an archivelog if the backup file containing the archivelog is no longer available. Run the LIST ARCHIVELOG ALL command to view archivelogs currently on disk, and LIST BACKUP OF ARCHIVELOG ALL to verify which archivelog files are in available RMAN backups.

Restoring to the Default Location

The following command will restore all archivelog files that RMAN has backed up:

```
RMAN> restore archivelog all;
```

If you want to restore from a specified sequence, use the FROM SEQUENCE clause. You may want to run this query first to establish the most recent log files and sequence numbers that have been generated:

```
SQL> select sequence#, first_time from v$log_history order by 2;
```

This example restores all archivelog files from sequence 68:

```
RMAN> restore archivelog from sequence 68;
```

If you want to restore a range of archivelog files, use the FROM SEQUENCE and UNTIL SEQUENCE clauses or the SEQUENCE BETWEEN clause, as shown. The following commands restore archivelog files from sequence 68 through sequence 78, using thread 1:

```
RMAN> restore archivelog from sequence 68 until sequence 78 thread 1;
RMAN> restore archivelog sequence between 68 and 78 thread 1;
```

By default, RMAN will not restore an archivelog file if it is already on disk. You can override this behavior if you use the FORCE, like so:

```
RMAN> restore archivelog from sequence 1 force;
```

Restoring to a Nondefault Location

Use the SET ARCHIVELOG DESTINATION clause if you want to restore archivelog files to a location different from the default. The following example restores to the nondefault location /u01/archtemp. The option of the SET command must be executed from within an RMAN run{} block.

```
run{
set archivelog destination to '/u01/archtemp';
restore archivelog from sequence 8 force;
}
```

Space is the main reason for having to do this, but these types of restores are great test and practice cases to work through to experience this behavior and document for the "just in case" scenario.

Restoring a Control File

If you are missing one control file, and you have multiple copies, then you can shut down your database and simply restore the missing or damaged control file by copying a good control file to the correct location and name of the missing control file (see Chapter 5 for details). This works if only all except one file are corrupted and the multiple copies are truly on separate disks. If there is a disk or controller failure, it is possible that at least one of the control files is still available. Part of the RMAN strategy is to take the backup of the control file for these issues.

Listed next are three typical scenarios when restoring a control file:

- Using a recovery catalog

- Using an autobackup

- Specifying a backup file name

Using a Recovery Catalog

When you are connected to the recovery catalog, you can view backup information about your control files even while your target database is in nomount mode. To list backups of your control files, use the LIST command, as shown:

```
$ rman target / catalog rcat/foo@rcat
RMAN> startup nomount;
RMAN> list backup of controlfile;
```

If you are missing all your control files, and you are using a recovery catalog, then issue the STARTUP NOMOUNT and the RESTORE CONTROLFILE commands:

```
RMAN> startup nomount;
RMAN> restore controlfile;
```

RMAN restores the control files to the location defined by your CONTROL_FILES initialization parameter. You should see a message indicating that your control files have been successfully copied back from an RMAN backup piece. You can now alter your database into mount mode and perform any additional restore-and-recovery commands required for your database.

Note   When you restore a control file from a backup, you are required to perform media recovery on your entire database and open your database with the OPEN RESETLOGS command, even if you did not restore any data files. You can determine whether your control file is a backup by querying the CONTROLFILE_TYPE column of the V$DATABASE view.

Using an Autobackup

When you enable the autobackup of your control file and are using an FRA, restoring your control file is fairly simple. First, connect to your target database, then issue a STARTUP NOMOUNT command, followed by the RESTORE CONTROLFILE FROM AUTOBACKUP command, like this:

```
$ rman target /
RMAN> startup nomount;
RMAN> restore controlfile from autobackup;
```

RMAN restores the control files to the location defined by your CONTROL_FILES initialization parameter. You should see a message indicating that your control files have been successfully copied back from an RMAN backup piece. Here is a snippet of the output:

```
channel ORA_DISK_1: control file restore from AUTOBACKUP complete
```

You can now alter your database into mount mode and perform any additional restore-and-recovery commands required for your database. Practicing this example would be to move your control files off to another directory in a TEST environment and walk through the restore options. Copying off the files allow you to quickly get back up and running by moving them back, but it does give you practice with these restores.

Specifying a Backup File Name

When restoring a database to a different server, these are generally the first few steps in the process: take a backup of the target database, copy to the remote server, and then restore the control file from the RMAN backup. In these scenarios, the name of the backup piece is known that contains the control file. Here is an example in which you instruct RMAN to restore a control file from a specific backup piece file:

```
RMAN> startup nomount;
RMAN> restore controlfile from
'/u01/O18C/rman/rman_ctl_c-3423216220-20130113-01.bk';
```

The control file will be restored to the location defined by the `CONTROL_FILES` initialization parameter.

Restoring the spfile

You might want to restore a `spfile` for several different reasons:

- You accidentally set a value in the `spfile` that keeps your instance from starting.

- You accidentally deleted the `spfile`.

- You are required to see what the `spfile` looked like at some point in time in the past.

One scenario (this has happened to me more than once) is that you are using a `spfile`, and one of the DBAs on your team does something inexplicable, such as this:

```
SQL> alter system set processes=1000000 scope=spfile;
```

The parameter is changed in the `spfile` on disk, but not in memory. Sometime later, the database is stopped for some maintenance. When attempting to start the database, you cannot even get the instance to start in a nomount state. This is because a parameter has been set to a ridiculous value that will consume all the memory on the box. In this scenario, the instance may hang, or you may see one or more of the following messages:

```
ORA-01078: failure in processing system parameters
ORA-00838: Specified value of ... is too small
```

If you have an RMAN backup available that has a copy of the spfile as it was before it was modified, you can simply restore the spfile. If you are using a recovery catalog, here is the procedure for restoring the spfile:

```
$ rman target / catalog rcat/foo@rcat
RMAN> startup nomount;
RMAN> restore spfile;
```

- If you are not using a recovery catalog, there are a number of ways to restore your spfile. The approach you take depends on several variables, such as whether you are using an FRA.

- You have configured a channel backup location for the autobackup.

- You are using the default location for autobackups.

This is a general overview of these scenarios to show steps that need to be taken, but not every detail is listed here. Determine the location of the backup piece that contains the backup of the spfile and do the restore, like this:

```
RMAN> startup nomount force;
RMAN> restore spfile to '/tmp/spfile.ora'
      from '/u01/O18C/rman/rman_ctl_c-3423216220-20130113-00.bk';
```

You should see a message such as this:

```
channel ORA_DISK_1: SPFILE restore from AUTOBACKUP complete
```

In this example the spfile is restored to the /tmp directory. Once restored, you can copy the spfile to ORACLE_HOME/dbs, with the proper name. For my environment (database name: o18c) this would be as follows:

```
$ cp /tmp/spfile.ora $ORACLE_HOME/dbs/spfileo18c.ora
```

Note   For a complete description of all possible spfile and control file restore scenarios, see *RMAN Recipes for Oracle Database 12c, second edition*, by Darl Kuhn, Sam Alapati, and Arup Nanda (Apress, 2013).

Incomplete Recovery

The term *incomplete database recovery* means that you cannot recover all committed transactions. *Incomplete* means that you do not apply all redo to restore up to the point of the last committed transaction that occurred in your database. In other words, you are restoring and recovering to a point in time in the past. For this reason, incomplete database recovery is also called database point-in-time recovery (DBPITR). Typically, you perform incomplete database recovery for one of the following reasons:

- You do not have all the redo required to perform a complete recovery. You are missing either the archivelog files or the online redo log files that are required for complete recovery. This situation could arise because the required redo files are damaged or missing.

- You purposely want to roll back the database to a point in time in the past. For example, you would do this if somebody accidentally truncated a table, and you intentionally wanted to roll back the database to just before the truncate table command was issued.

Incomplete database recovery consists of two : restore and recovery. The restore step re-creates data files, and the recover step applies redo up to the specified point in time. The restore process can be initiated from RMAN in a couple of different ways:

- `RESTORE DATABASE UNTIL`
- `FLASHBACK DATABASE` (May not need the restore depending on the UNDO information)

For the majority of incomplete database recovery circumstances, you use the `RESTORE DATABASE UNTIL` command to instruct RMAN to retrieve data files from the RMAN backup files. This type of incomplete database recovery is the main focus of this section of the chapter. The Flashback Database feature is covered in the section "Flashing Back a Database" later in this chapter.

The `UNTIL` portion of the `RESTORE DATABASE` command instructs RMAN to retrieve data files from a point in time in the past, based on one of the following methods:

- Time
- SCN
- Log sequence number
- Restore point

The RMAN RESTORE DATABASE UNTIL command will retrieve all data files from the most recent backup set or image copy. RMAN will automatically determine from the UNTIL clause which backup set contains the required data files. If you omit the UNTIL clause of the R command, RMAN will retrieve data files from the latest available backup set or image copy. In some situations, this may be the behavior you desire. It is recommended that you use the UNTIL clause to ensure that RMAN restores from the correct backup set. When you issue the RESTORE DATABASE UNTIL command, RMAN will establish how to extract the data files from any of the following types of backups:

- Full database backup

- Incremental level-0 backup

- Image copy backup generated by the BACKUP AS COPY command

You cannot perform an incomplete database recovery on a subset of your database's online data files. When performing incomplete database recovery, all the checkpoint SCNs for all online data files must be synchronized before you can open your database with the ALTER DATABASE OPEN RESETLOGS command. You can view the data file header SCNs and the status of each data file via this SQL query:

```
SQL> select file#, status, fuzzy,
error, checkpoint_change#,
to_char(checkpoint_time,'dd-mon-rrrr hh24:mi:ss') as checkpoint_time
from v$datafile_header;
```

Note The FUZZY column V$DATAFILE_HEADER contains data files that have one or more blocks with an SCN value greater than or equal to the checkpoint SCN in the data file header. If a data file is restored and has a FUZZY value of YES, then media recovery is required.

The only exception to this rule of not performing an incomplete recovery on a subset of online database files is a tablespace point-in-time recovery (TSPITR), which uses the RECOVER TABLESPACE UNTIL command. TSPITR is used in rare situations; it restores and recovers only the tablespace(s) you specify.

The recovery portion of an incomplete database recovery is always initiated with the RECOVER DATABASE UNTIL command. RMAN will automatically recover your database up to the point specified with the UNTIL clause. Just like the RESTORE command, you can recover up to the time, change/SCN, log sequence number, or restore point. When RMAN reaches the specified point, it will automatically terminate the recovery process.

Note   Regardless of what you specify in the UNTIL clause, RMAN will convert that into a corresponding UNTIL SCN clause and assign the appropriate SCN. This is to avoid any timing issues, particularly those caused by Daylight Saving Time.

During a recovery, RMAN will automatically determine how to apply redo. First, RMAN will apply any incremental backups available. Next, any archivelog files on disk will be applied. If the archivelog files do not exist on disk, then RMAN will attempt to retrieve them from a backup set. If you want to apply redo as part of an incomplete database recovery, the following conditions must be true:

- Your database is in archivelog mode.

- You have a good backup of all data files.

- You have all redo required to restore up to the specified point.

When performing an incomplete database recovery with RMAN, you must have your database in mount mode. RMAN needs the database in mount mode to be able to read and write to the control file. Also, with an incomplete database recovery, any SYSTEM tablespace data files are always recovered. Oracle will not allow your database to be open while restoring the SYSTEM tablespace data file(s).

Note   After incomplete database recovery is performed, you are required to open your database with the ALTER DATABASE OPEN RESETLOGS command. Any time after issuing an ALTER DATABASE OPEN RESETLOGS, make sure a new backup is taken to be able to have available after this point as other backups may become invalid if trying to restore to after the resetlogs.

Depending on the scenario, you can use RMAN to perform a variety of incomplete recovery methods. The next section discusses how to determine what type of incomplete recovery to perform.

Determining the Type of Incomplete Recovery

Time-based restore and recovery is commonly used when you know the approximate date and time to which you want to recover your database. For instance, you may know approximately the time you want to stop the recovery process, but not a particular SCN.

Log sequence-based and cancel-based recovery work well in situations in which you have missing or damaged log files. In such scenarios, you can recover only up to your last good archivelog file.

SCN-based recovery works well if you can pinpoint the SCN at which you want to stop the recovery process. You can retrieve SCN information from views such as V$LOG and V$LOG_HISTORY. You can also use tools such as LogMiner to retrieve the SCN of a particular SQL statement.

Restore point recoveries work only if you have established restore points. In these situations, you restore and recover up to the SCN associated with the specified restore point.

TSPITR is used in situations in which you need to restore and recover just a few tablespaces. You can use RMAN to automate many of the tasks associated with this type of incomplete recovery.

Performing Time-Based Recovery

To restore and recover your database back to a point in time in the past, you can use either the UNTIL TIME clause of the RESTORE and RECOVER commands or the SET UNTIL TIME clause within a run{} block. It is very useful to have run{} blocks of code with the correct syntax available to replace a TIME to be able to perform the restores without having to search for the syntax. Using these examples in the book and running test and practice restores will give you the blocks of code needed to have ready to use. RMAN will restore and recover the database up to, but not including, the specified time. In other words, RMAN will restore any transactions committed prior to the time specified. RMAN automatically stops the recovery process when it reaches the time you specified.

The default date format that RMAN expects is YYYY-MM-DD:HH24:MI:SS. However, it is recommended to use the TO_DATE function and specifying a format mask. This eliminates ambiguities with different national date formats and having to set the OS

NLS_DATE_FORMAT variable. The following example specifies a time when issuing the restore and recover commands:

```
$ rman target /
RMAN> startup mount;
RMAN> restore database until time
      "to_date('15-jan-2018 12:20:00', 'dd-mon-rrrr hh24:mi:ss')";
RMAN> recover database until time
      "to_date('15-jan-2018 12:20:00', 'dd-mon-rrrr hh24:mi:ss')";
RMAN> alter database open resetlogs;
```

If everything goes well, you should see output such as this:

```
Statement processed
```

Performing Log Sequence-Based Recovery

Usually this type of incomplete database recovery is initiated because you have a missing or damaged archivelog file. If that is the case, you can recover only up to your last good archivelog file, because you cannot skip a missing archivelog.

How you determine which archivelog file to restore up to (but not including) will vary. For example, if you are physically missing an archivelog file, and RMAN cannot find it in a backup set, you will receive a message such as this when trying to apply the missing file:

```
RMAN-06053: unable to perform media recovery because of missing log
RMAN-06025: no backup of archived log for thread 1 with sequence 19...
```

Based on the previous error message, you would restore up to (but not including) log sequence 19.

```
$ rman target /
RMAN> startup mount;
RMAN> restore database until sequence 19;
RMAN> recover database until sequence 19;
RMAN> alter database open resetlogs;
```

If successful, you should see output such as this:

```
Statement processed
```

> **Note**   Log sequence-based recovery is similar to user-managed cancel-based recovery. See Chapter 16 for details on a user-managed cancel-based recovery.

Performing SCN-Based Recovery

SCN-based incomplete database recovery works in situations in which you know the SCN value at which you want to end the restore-and-recovery session. RMAN will recover up to, but not including, the specified SCN. RMAN automatically terminates the restore process when it reaches the specified SCN.

You can view your database SCN information in several ways:

- Using LogMiner to determine an SCN associated with a DDL or DML statement

- Looking in the alert.log file

- Looking in your trace files

- Querying the FIRST_CHANGE# column of VLOG, VLOG_HISTORY and V$ARCHIVED_LOG

After establishing the SCN to which you want to restore, use the UNTIL SCN clause to restore up to, but not including, the SCN specified. The following example restores all transactions that have an SCN that is less than 95019865425:

```
$ rman target /
RMAN> startup mount;
RMAN> restore database until scn 95019865425;
RMAN> recover database until scn 95019865425;
RMAN> alter database open resetlogs;
```

If everything goes well, you should see output such as this:

```
Statement processed
```

Restoring to a Restore Point

There are two types of restore points: normal and guaranteed. The main difference between a guaranteed restore point and a normal restore point is that a guaranteed restore point is not eventually aged out of the control file; a guaranteed restore point will persist until you drop it. Guaranteed restore points do require an FRA. However, for incomplete recovery using a guaranteed restore point, you do not have to have flashback database enabled.

You can create a normal restore point using SQL*Plus, as follows:

```
SQL> create restore point MY_RP;
```

This command creates a restore point, named MY_RP, which is associated with the SCN of the database at the time the command was issued. You can view the current SCN of your database, as shown:

```
SQL> select current_scn from v$database;
```

You can view restore point information in the V$RESTORE_POINT view, like so:

```
SQL> select name, scn from v$restore_point;
```

The restore point acts like a synonym for the particular SCN. The restore point allows you to restore and recover to an SCN without having to specify a number. RMAN will restore and recover up to, but not including, the SCN associated with the restore point.

This example restores and recovers to the MY_RP restore point:

```
$ rman target /
RMAN> startup mount;
RMAN> restore database until restore point MY_RP;
RMAN> recover database until restore point MY_RP;
RMAN> alter database open resetlogs;
```

Restoring Tables to a Previous Point

Starting with Oracle Database 12c, you can restore individual tables from RMAN backups via the RECOVER TABLE command. This gives you the ability to restore and recover a table back to a point in time in the past.

The table-level restore feature uses a temporary auxiliary instance and the Data Pump utility. Both the auxiliary instance and Data Pump create temporary files when restoring the table. Before initiating a table-level restore, first create two directories: one to hold files used by the auxiliary instance and one to store a Data Pump dump file:

```
$ mkdir /tmp/oracle
$ mkdir /tmp/recover
```

The prior two directories are referenced within the RECOVER TABLE command via the AUXILIARY DESTINATION and DATAPUMP DESTINATION clauses. In the following bit of code, the INV table, owned by MV_MAINT, is restored as it was at a prior SCN:

```
RMAN> recover table mv_maint.inv
until scn 4689805
auxiliary destination '/tmp/oracle'
datapump destination '/tmp/recover';
```

Providing that RMAN backups are available that contain the state of the table at the specified SCN, a table-level restore and recovery is performed.

Note   You can also restore a table to an SCN, a point in time, or a log sequence number.

When RMAN performs a table-level recovery, it automatically creates a temporary auxiliary database, uses Data Pump to export the table, and then imports the table back into the target database as it was at the specified restore point. After the restore is finished, the auxiliary database is dropped, and Data Pump dump file is removed.

Tip   Although the RECOVER TABLE command is a nice enhancement, I would recommend that, if you have an accidentally dropped table, you first explore using the recycle bin or Flashback Table to Before Drop feature to restore the table. Or, if the table was erroneously deleted from, then use the Flashback Table feature to restore the table back to a point in time in the past. It might even be possible to restore from a FLASBACK QUERY using CTAS (create table as). If neither of the prior options are viable, then consider using the RMAN Recover Table feature.

Flashing Back a Table

To simplify recovery of an accidentally dropped table, Oracle introduced the Flashback Table feature. Oracle offers two different types of Flashback Table operations:

- FLASHBACK TABLE TO BEFORE DROP quickly undrops a previously dropped table. This feature uses a logical container named the recycle bin.

- FLASHBACK TABLE flashes back to a recent point in time to undo the effects of undesired DML statements. You can flash back to an SCN, a timestamp, or a restore point.

Oracle introduced FLASHBACK TABLE TO BEFORE DROP to allow you to quickly recover a dropped table. When you drop a table, if you do not specify the PURGE clause, Oracle does not drop the table—instead, the table is renamed. Any tables you drop (that Oracle renames) are placed in the recycle bin. The recycle bin provides you with an efficient way to view and manage dropped objects.

Note To use the Flashback Table feature, you do not need to implement an FRA, nor do you need Flashback Database to be enabled.

The FLASHBACK TABLE TO BEFORE DROP operation only works if your database has the recycle bin feature enabled (which it is by default). You can check the status of the recycle bin, as follows:

```
SQL> show parameter recyclebin
```

NAME	TYPE	VALUE
recyclebin	string	on

FLASHBACK TABLE TO BEFORE DROP

Here is an example. Suppose the INV table is accidentally dropped:

```
SQL> drop table inv;
```

Verify that the table has been renamed by viewing the contents of the recycle bin:

```
SQL> show recyclebin;
ORIGINAL NAME   RECYCLEBIN NAME                 OBJECT TYPE  DROP TIME
--------------- ------------------------------ ------------ ---------------
INV             BIN$ozIqhEFlcprgQ4TQTwq2uA==$0 TABLE        2018-01-11:12:16:49
```

The SHOW RECYCLEBIN statement shows only tables that have been dropped. To get a more complete picture of renamed objects, query the RECYCLEBIN view:

```
select object_name, original_name, type
from recyclebin;
```

Here is the output:

```
OBJECT_NAME                          ORIGINAL_NAM TYPE
------------------------------------ ------------ ---------------------------
BIN$ozIqhEFjcprgQ4TQTwq2uA==$0       INV_PK       INDEX
BIN$ozIqhEFkcprgQ4TQTwq2uA==$0       INV_TRIG     TRIGGER
BIN$ozIqhEFlcprgQ4TQTwq2uA==$0       INV          TABLE
```

In this output, the table also has a primary key that was renamed when the object was dropped. To undrop the table, do this:

```
SQL> flashback table inv to before drop;
```

The prior command restores the table to its original name. This statement, however, does not restore the index to its original name:

```
SQL> select index_name from user_indexes where table_name='INV';

INDEX_NAME
---------------------------------------------------
BIN$ozIqhEFjcprgQ4TQTwq2uA==$0
```

In this scenario, you have to rename the index:

```
SQL> alter index "BIN$ozIqhEFjcprgQ4TQTwq2uA==$0" rename to inv_pk;
```

You also have to rename any trigger objects in the same manner. If referential constraints were in place before the table was dropped, you must manually re-create them.

If, for some reason, you need to flash back a table to a name different from the original name, you can do so as follows:

```
SQL> flashback table inv to before drop rename to inv_bef;
```

Flashing Back a Table to a Previous Point in Time

If a table was erroneously deleted from, you have the option of flashing back the table to a previous point in time. The Flashback Table feature uses information in the undo tablespace to restore the table. The point in time in the past depends on your undo tablespace retention period, which specifies the minimum time that undo information is kept.

If the required flashback information is not in the undo tablespace, you receive an error such as this:

```
ORA-01555: snapshot too old
```

In other words, to be able to flash back to a point in time in the past, the required information in the undo tablespace must not have been overwritten.

FLASHBACK TABLE TO SCN

Suppose you are testing an application feature, and you want to quickly restore a table back to a specific SCN. As part of the application testing, you record the SCN before testing begins:

```
SQL> select current_scn from v$database;


CURRENT_SCN
-----------
   4760099
```

You perform some testing and then want to flash back the table to the SCN previously recorded. First, ensure that row movement is enabled for the table:

```
SQL> alter table inv enable row movement;
SQL> flashback table inv to scn 4760089;
```

The table should now reflect transactions that were committed as of the historical SCN value specified in the FLASHBACK statement.

FLASHBACK TABLE TO TIMESTAMP

You can also flash back a table to a prior point in time. For example, to flash back a table to 15 minutes in the past, first enable row movement, and then use FLASHBACK TABLE:

```
SQL> alter table inv enable row movement;
SQL> flashback table inv to timestamp(sysdate-1/96) ;
```

The timestamp you provide must evaluate to a valid format for an Oracle timestamp. You can also explicitly specify a time, as follows:

```
SQL> flashback table inv to timestamp
    to_timestamp('14-jan-18 12:07:33','dd-mon-yy hh24:mi:ss');
```

FLASHBACK TABLE TO RESTORE POINT

A restore point is a name associated with a timestamp or an SCN in the database. You can create a restore point that contains the current SCN of the database, as shown:

```
SQL> create restore point point_a;
```

Later, if you decide to flash back a table to that restore point, first enable row movement:

```
SQL> alter table inv enable row movement;
SQL> flashback table inv to restore point point_a;
```

The table should now contain transactions as they were at the SCN associated with the specified restore point.

FLASHING BACK A DATABASE

The Flashback Database featurebacks to a point in time in the past. Flashback Database uses information stored in flashback logs; it does not rely on restoring database files (as do cold backup, hot backup, and RMAN).

Tip   Flashback Database is not a substitute for a backup of your database. If you experience a media failure with a data file, you cannot use Flashback Database to flash back to before the failure. If a data file is damaged, you have to restore and recover, using a physical backup (hot, cold, or RMAN).

The Flashback Database feature may be desirable in situations in which you want to consistently reset your database back to a point in time in the past. For instance, you may periodically want to set a test or training database back to a known baseline. Or, you may be upgrading an application and, before making large-scale changes to the application database objects, mark the starting point. After the upgrade, if things do not go well, you want the ability to quickly reset the database back to the point in time before the upgrade took place.

There are several prerequisites for Flashback Database:

- The database must be in archivelog mode.

- You must be using an FRA.

- The Flashback Database feature must be enabled.

See Chapter 5 for details on enabling archivelog mode and/or enabling an FRA. You can verify the status of these features using the following SQL*Plus statements:

```
SQL> archive log list;
SQL> show parameter db_recovery_file_dest;
```

To enable the Flashback Database feature, alter your database into flashback mode, as shown:

```
SQL> alter database flashback on;
```

You can verify the flashback status, as follows:

```
SQL> select flashback_on from v$database;
```

After you enable Flashback Database, you can view the flashback logs in your FRA with this query:

```
SQL> select name, log#, thread#, sequence#, bytes
from v$flashback_database_logfile;
```

The range of time in which you can flash back is determined by the `DB_FLASHBACK_RETENTION_TARGET` parameter. This specifies the upper limit, in minutes, of how far your database can be flashed back.

You can view the oldest SCN and time you can flash back your database to by running the following SQL:

```
SQL> select
 oldest_flashback_scn
,to_char(oldest_flashback_time,'dd-mon-yy hh24:mi:ss')
from v$flashback_database_log;
```

If, for any reason, you need to disable Flashback Database, you can turn it off, as follows:

```
SQL> alter database flashback off;
```

You can use either RMAN or SQL*Plus to flash back a database. You can specify a point in time in the past, using one of the following:

- SCN

- Timestamp

- Restore point

- Last `RESETLOGS` operation (works from RMAN only)

This example creates a restore point:

```
SQL> create restore point flash_1;
```

Next, the application performs some testing, after which the database is flashed back to the restore point so that a new round of testing can begin:

```
SQL> shutdown immediate;
SQL> startup mount;
SQL> flashback database to restore point flash_1;
SQL> alter database open resetlogs;
```

At this point, your database should be transactionally consistent with how it was at the SCN associated with the restore point.

Restoring and Recovering to a Different Server

When you think about architecting your backup strategy, as part of the process, you must also consider how you are going to restore and recover. Your backups are only as good as the last time you tested a restore and recovery. A backup strategy can be rendered worthless without a good restore-and-recovery strategy. The last thing you want to happen is to have a media failure, go to restore your database, and then find out you are missing critical pieces, you do not have enough space to restore, something is corrupt, and so on.

One of the best ways to test an RMAN backup is to restore and recover it to a different database server. This will exercise all your backup, restore, and recovery DBA skills. If you can restore and recover an RMAN backup on a different server, it will give you confidence when a real disaster hits. You can think of all the prior material in this book as the building blocksof how backup and recovery works.

Note   RMAN does have a `DUPLICATE DATABASE` command, which works well for copying a database from one server to another. If you are going to be performing this type of task often, I would recommend that you use RMAN's duplicate database functionality. However, you may still have to copy a backup of a database manually from one server to another, especially when the security is such that you cannot directly connect a production server to a development environment. You can use RMAN to duplicate a database based on backups you copy from the target to the auxiliary server. See MOS note 874352.1 for details on targetless duplication.

In this example, the originating server and destination server have different mount points. Listed next are the high-level steps required to take an RMAN backup and use it to re-create a database on a separate server:

1. Create an RMAN backup on the originating database.

2. Copy the RMAN backup to the destination server. All steps that follow are performed on the destination database server.

3. Ensure that Oracle is installed.

4. Source the required OS variables.

5. Create an `init.ora` file for the database to be restored.

6. Create any required directories for data files, control files, and dump/trace files.

7. Start up the database in nomount mode.

8. Restore the control file from the RMAN backup.

9. Start up the database in mount mode.

10. Make the control file aware of the location of the RMAN backups.

11. Rename and restore the data files to reflect new directory locations.

12. Recover the database.

13. Set the new location for the online redo logs.

14. Open the database.

15. Add the temp file.

16. Rename the database (optional).

Each of the prior steps is covered in detail in the next several sections. Steps 1 and 2 occur on the source database server. All remaining steps are performed on the destination server. For this example, the source database is named o18c, and the destination database will be named DEVDB.

Furthermore, the originating server and destination server have different mount point names. On the source database, the data files and control files are here:

`/u01/dbfile/o18c`

On the destination database, the data files and control files will be renamed and restored to this directory:

`/ora01/dbfile/DEVDB`

The destination database online redo logs will be placed in this directory:

`/ora01/oraredo/DEVDB`

The destination database archive redo log file location will be set as follows:

`/ora01/arc/DEVDB`

Keep in mind that these are the directories used on servers in my test environment. You will have to adjust these directory names to reflect the directory structures on your database servers.

Step 1. Create an RMAN Backup on the Originating Database

When backing up a database, make sure you have the autobackup control file feature turned on. Also, include the archive redo logs as part of the backup, like so:

```
RMAN> backup database plus archivelog;
```

You can verify the names and locations of the backup pieces via the LIST BACKUP command. For example, this is what the backup pieces look like for the source database:

```
rman1_bonvb2js_1_1.bk
rman1_bqnvb2k5_1_1.bk
rman1_bsnvb2p3_1_1.bk
rman_ctl_c-3423216220-20130113-06.bk
```

In the prior output, the file with the c-3423216220 string in the name is the backup piece that contains the control file. You will have to inspect the output of your LIST BACKUP command to determine which backup piece contains the control file. You will need to reference that backup piece in step 8.

Step 2. Copy the RMAN Backup to the Destination Server

For this step, use a utility such as rsync or scp to copy the backup pieces from one server to another. This example uses the scp command to copy the backup pieces:

```
$ scp rman*  oracle@DEVBOX:/ora01/rman/DEVDB
```

In this example, the /ora01/rman/DEVDB directory must be created on the destination server before copying the backup files. Depending on your environment, this step might require copying the RMAN backups twice: once from the production server to a secure server and once from the secure server to a test server.

Note   If the RMAN backups are on tape instead of on disk, then the same media manager software must be installed/configured on the destination server. Also, that server must have direct access to the RMAN backups on tape.

Step 3. Ensure That Oracle Is Installed

Make sure you have the same version of the Oracle binaries installed on the destination server as you do on the originating database.

Step 4. Source the Required OS Variables

You need to establish the OS variables, such as ORACLE_SID, ORACLE_HOME, and PATH. Typically, the ORACLE_SID variable is initially set to match what it was on the original database. The database name will be changed as part of the last step in this recipe (optional). Here are the settings for ORACLE_SID and ORACLE_HOME on the destination server:

```
$ echo $ORACLE_SID
o18c
```

```
$ echo $ORACLE_HOME
/ora01/app/oracle/product/18.1.0.1/db_1
```

At this point, also consider adding the Oracle SID to the oratab file. If you plan on using this database after you have replicated it, then you should have an automated method for setting the required OS variables. See Chapter 2 for details on sourcing OS variables in conjunction with the oratab file.

Step 5. Create an init.ora File for the Database to Be Restored

Copy the init.ora file from the original server to the destination server, and modify it so that it matches the destination box in terms of any directory paths. Ensure that you change the parameters, such as the CONTROL_FILES, to reflect the new path directories on the destination server (/ora01/dbfile/DEVDB, in this example).

Initially, the name of the init.ora file is ORACLE_HOME/dbs/inito18c.ora, and the name of the database is o18c. Both will be renamed in a later step. Here are the contents of the init.ora file:

```
control_files='/ora01/dbfile/DEVDB/control01.ctl',
               '/ora01/dbfile/DEVDB/control02.ctl'
db_block_size=8192
db_name='o18c'
log_archive_dest_1='location=/ora01/arc/DEVDB'
job_queue_processes=10
memory_max_target=300000000
memory_target=300000000
open_cursors=100
os_authent_prefix="
processes=100
remote_login_passwordfile='EXCLUSIVE'
resource_limit=true
shared_pool_size=80M
sql92_security=TRUE
undo_management='AUTO'
undo_tablespace='UNDOTBS1'
workarea_size_policy='AUTO'
```

Step 6. Create Any Required Directories for Data Files, Control Files, and Dump/Trace Files

For this example, the directories /ora01/dbfile/DEVDB and /ora01/oraredo/DEVDB are created:

```
$ mkdir -p /ora01/dbfile/DEVDB
$ mkdir -p /ora01/oraredo/DEVDB
$ mkdir -p /ora01/arc/DEVDB
```

Step 7. Start Up the Database in Nomount Mode

You should now be able to start up the database in nomount mode:

```
$ rman target /
RMAN> startup nomount;
```

Step 8. Restore the Control File from the RMAN Backup

Next, restore the control file from the backup that was previously copied; for example,

```
RMAN> restore controlfile from
'/ora01/rman/DEVDB/rman_ctl_c-3423216220-20130113-06.bk';
```

The control file will be restored to all locations specified by the CONTROL_FILES
initialization parameter. Here is some sample output:

```
channel ORA_DISK_1: restore complete, elapsed time: 00:00:03
output file name=/ora01/dbfile/DEVDB/control01.ctl
output file name=/ora01/dbfile/DEVDB/control02.ctl
```

Step 9. Start Up the Database in Mount Mode

You should now be able to start up your database in mount mode:

```
RMAN> alter database mount;
```

At this point, your control files exist and have been opened, but none of the data files
or online redo logs exist yet.

Step 10. Make the Control File Aware of the Location of the RMAN Backups

First, use the CROSSCHECK command to let the control file know that none of the backups
or archive redo logs are in the same location that they were in on the original server:

```
RMAN> crosscheck backup; # Crosscheck backups
RMAN> crosscheck copy;   # Crosscheck image copies and archive logs
```

Then, use the CATALOG command to make the control file aware of the location and names of the backup pieces that were copied to the destination server.

Note   Do not confuse the CATALOG command with the recovery catalog schema. The CATALOG command adds RMAN metadata to the control file, whereas the recovery catalog schema is a user, generally created in a separate database, which can be used to store RMAN metadata.

In this example, any RMAN files that are in the /ora01/rman/DEVDB directory will be cataloged in the control file:

```
RMAN> catalog start with '/ora01/rman/DEVDB';
```

Here is some sample output:

```
List of Files Unknown to the Database
=======================================
File Name: /ora01/rman/DEVDB/rman1_bqnvb2k5_1_1.bk
File Name: /ora01/rman/DEVDB/rman1_bonvb2js_1_1.bk
File Name: /ora01/rman/DEVDB/rman_ctl_c-3423216220-20130113-06.bk
File Name: /ora01/rman/DEVDB/rman1_bsnvb2p3_1_1.bk

Do you really want to catalog the above files (enter YES or NO)?
```

Now, type YES (if everything looks okay). You should then be able to use the RMAN LIST BACKUP command to view the newly cataloged backup pieces:

```
RMAN> list backup;
```

Step 11. Rename and Restore the Data Files to Reflect New Directory Locations

If your destination server has the exact same directory structure as the original server directories, you can issue the RESTORE command directly:

```
RMAN> restore database;
```

However, when restoring data files to locations that are different from the original directories, you will have to use the SET NEWNAME command. Create a file that uses an RMAN run{} block that contains the appropriate SET NEWNAME and RESTORE commands. Here is a sample SQL script to generate a starting point for the run{} block:

```
SQL> set head off feed off verify off echo off pages 0 trimspool on
SQL> set lines 132 pagesize 0
SQL> spo newname.sql
--
SQL> select 'run{' from dual;
--
SQL> select
'set newname for datafile ' || file# || ' to ' || "" || name || "" || ';'
from v$datafile;
--
SQL> select
'restore database;' || chr(10) ||
'switch datafile all;' || chr(10) ||
'}'
from dual;
--
SQL> spo off;
```

After running the script, these are the contents of the newname.sql script that was generated:

```
run{
set newname for datafile 1 to '/u01/dbfile/o18c/system01.dbf';
set newname for datafile 2 to '/u01/dbfile/o18c/sysaux01.dbf';
set newname for datafile 3 to '/u01/dbfile/o18c/undotbs01.dbf';
set newname for datafile 4 to '/u01/dbfile/o18c/users01.dbf';
restore database;
switch datafile all;
}
```

Then, modify the contents of the newname.sql script to reflect the directories on the destination database server. Here is what the final newname.sql script looks like for this example:

```
run{
set newname for datafile 1 to '/ora01/dbfile/DEVDB/system01.dbf';
set newname for datafile 2 to '/ora01/dbfile/DEVDB/sysaux01.dbf';
set newname for datafile 3 to '/ora01/dbfile/DEVDB/undotbs01.dbf';
set newname for datafile 4 to '/ora01/dbfile/DEVDB/users01.dbf';
restore database;
switch datafile all;
}
```

Now, connect to RMAN, and run the prior script to restore the data files to the new locations:

```
$ rman target /
RMAN> @newname.sql
```

Here is a snippet of the output:

```
datafile 1 switched to datafile copy
input datafile copy RECID=5 STAMP=790357985 file
name=/ora01/dbfile/DEVDB/system01.dbf
```

All the data files have been restored to the new database server. You can use the RMAN REPORT SCHEMA command to verify that the files have been restored and are in the correct locations:

```
RMAN> report schema;
```

Here is some sample output:

```
RMAN-06139: WARNING: control file is not current for REPORT SCHEMA
Report of database schema for database with db_unique_name O12C
List of Permanent Datafiles
===========================
```

```
File Size(MB) Tablespace              RB segs Datafile Name
---- -------- -------------------- ------- ------------------------
1    500      SYSTEM               ***        /ora01/dbfile/DEVDB/system01.dbf
2    500      SYSAUX               ***        /ora01/dbfile/DEVDB/sysaux01.dbf
3    800      UNDOTBS1             ***        /ora01/dbfile/DEVDB/undotbs01.dbf
4    50       USERS                ***        /ora01/dbfile/DEVDB/users01.dbf

List of Temporary Files
=======================
File Size(MB) Tablespace              Maxsize(MB) Tempfile Name
---- -------- -------------------- ----------- --------------------
1    500      TEMP                 500         /u01/dbfile/o12c/temp01.dbf
```

From the prior output, you can see that the database name and temporary tablespace data file still do not reflect the destination database (DEVDB). These will be modified in subsequent steps.

Step 12. Recover the Database

Next, you need to apply any archive redo files that were generated during the backup. These should be included in the backup because the ARCHIVELOG ALL clause was used to take the backup. Initiate the application of redo via the RECOVER DATABASE command:

```
RMAN> recover database;
```

RMAN will restore and apply as many archive redo logs as it has in the backup pieces and then may throw an error when it reaches an archive redo log that does not exist; for example,

```
RMAN-06054: media recovery requesting unknown archived log for...
```

That error message is fine. The recovery process will restore and recover archive redo logs contained in the backups, which should be sufficient to open the database. The recovery process does not know where to stop applying archive redo logs and therefore will continue to attempt to do so until it cannot find the next log. Having said that, now is a good time to verify that your data files are online and not in a fuzzy state:

```
SQL> select file#, status, fuzzy, error, checkpoint_change#,
to_char(checkpoint_time,'dd-mon-rrrr hh24:mi:ss') as checkpoint_time
from v$datafile_header;
```

Step 13. Set the New Location for the Online Redo Logs

If your source and destination servers have the exact same directory structures, then you do not need to set a new location for the online redo logs (so you can skip this step).

However, if the directory structures are different, then you will need to update the control file to reflect the new directory for the online redo logs. I sometimes use an SQL script that generates SQL to assist with this step:

```
SQL> set head off feed off verify off echo off pages 0 trimspool on
SQL> set lines 132 pagesize 0
SQL> spo renlog.sql
SQL> select
'alter database rename file ' || chr(10)
|| "" || member || "" || ' to ' || chr(10) || "" || member || "" ||';'
from v$logfile;
SQL> spo off;
```

For this example, here is a snippet of the renlog.sql file that was generated:

```
SQL> alter database rename file
'/u01/oraredo/o18c/redo01a.rdo' to
'/u01/oraredo/o18c/redo01a.rdo';
...
SQL> alter database rename file
'/u02/oraredo/o18c/redo03b.rdo' to
'/u02/oraredo/o18c/redo03b.rdo';
```

The contents of `renlog.sql` need to be modified to reflect the directory structure on the destination server. Here is what `renlog.sql` looks like after being edited:

```
SQL> alter database rename file
'/u01/oraredo/o18c/redo01a.rdo' to
'/ora01/oraredo/DEVDB/redo01a.rdo';
...
SQL> alter database rename file
'/u02/oraredo/o18c/redo03b.rdo' to
'/ora01/oraredo/DEVDB/redo03b.rdo';
```

Update the control file by running the `renlog.sql` script:

```
SQL> @renlog.sql
```

You can select from V$LOGFILE to verify that the online redo log names are correct:

```
SQL> select member from v$logfile;
```

Here is the output for this example:

```
/ora01/oraredo/DEVDB/redo01a.rdo
/ora01/oraredo/DEVDB/redo02a.rdo
/ora01/oraredo/DEVDB/redo03a.rdo
/ora01/oraredo/DEVDB/redo01b.rdo
/ora01/oraredo/DEVDB/redo02b.rdo
/ora01/oraredo/DEVDB/redo03b.rdo
```

Make sure the directories exist on the new server that will contain the online redo logs. For this example, here is the `mkdir` command:

```
$ mkdir -p /ora01/oraredo/DEVDB
```

Step 14. Open the Database

You must open the database with the OPEN RESETLOGS command (because there are no redo logs, and they must be re-created at this point):

```
SQL> alter database open resetlogs;
```

If successful, you should see this message:

```
Statement processed
```

Note   Keep in mind that all the passwords from the newly restored copy are as they were in the source database. You will want to change the passwords in a replicated database, especially if it was copied from production.

Step 15. Add the Temp File

When you start your database, Oracle will automatically try to add any missing temp files to the database. Oracle will not be able to do this if the directory structure on the destination server is different from that of the source server. In this scenario, you will have to add any missing temp files manually. To do this, first take offline the temporary tablespace temp file. The file definition from the originating database is taken offline like so:

```
SQL> alter database tempfile '/u01/dbfile/o18c/temp01.dbf' offline;
SQL> alter database tempfile '/u01/dbfile/o18c/temp01.dbf' drop;
```

Next, add a temporary tablespace file to the TEMP tablespace that matches the directory structure of the destination database server:

```
SQL> alter tablespace temp add tempfile '/ora01/dbfile/DEVDB/temp01.dbf'
    size 100m;
```

You can run the REPORT SCHEMA command to verify that all files are in the correct locations.

Step 16. Rename the Database

This step is optional. If you need to rename the database to reflect the name for a development or test database, create a trace file that contains the CREATE CONTROLFILE statement, and use it to rename your database.

Tip   If you do not rename the database, be careful about connect and resync operations to the same recovery catalog used by the original/source database. This causes confusion in the recovery catalog as to which is the real source database and may jeopardize your ability to recover and restore the real source database.

The steps for renaming your database are as follows:

1. Generate a trace file that contains the SQL command to re-create the control files:

```
SQL> alter database backup controlfile to trace as '/tmp/cf.sql' resetlogs;
```

2. Shut down the database:

```
SQL> shutdown immediate;
```

3. Modify the /tmp/cf.sql trace file; be sure to specify SET DATABASE "<NEW DATABASE NAME>" in the top line of the output:

```
CREATE CONTROLFILE REUSE SET DATABASE "DEVDB" RESETLOGS ARCHIVELOG
    MAXLOGFILES 16
    MAXLOGMEMBERS 4
    MAXDATAFILES 1024
    MAXINSTANCES 1
    MAXLOGHISTORY 876
LOGFILE
  GROUP 1 (
    '/ora01/oraredo/DEVDB/redo01a.rdo',
    '/ora01/oraredo/DEVDB/redo01b.rdo'
  ) SIZE 50M BLOCKSIZE 512,
  GROUP 2 (
    '/ora01/oraredo/DEVDB/redo02a.rdo',
    '/ora01/oraredo/DEVDB/redo02b.rdo'
  ) SIZE 50M BLOCKSIZE 512,
  GROUP 3 (
    '/ora01/oraredo/DEVDB/redo03a.rdo',
    '/ora01/oraredo/DEVDB/redo03b.rdo'
```

```
) SIZE 50M BLOCKSIZE 512
DATAFILE
  '/ora01/dbfile/DEVDB/system01.dbf',
  '/ora01/dbfile/DEVDB/sysaux01.dbf',
  '/ora01/dbfile/DEVDB/undotbs01.dbf',
  '/ora01/dbfile/DEVDB/users01.dbf'
CHARACTER SET AL32UTF8;
```

> If you do not specify SET DATABASE in the top line of the prior
> script, when you run the script (as shown later in this example),
> you will receive an error such as this:

```
ORA-01161: database name ... in file header does not match...
```

4. Create an init.ora file that matches the new database name:

```
$ cd $ORACLE_HOME/dbs
$ cp init<old_sid>.ora init<new_sid>.ora
$ cp inito18c.ora initDEVDB.ora
```

5. Modify the DB_NAME variable within the new init.ora file (in this
    example, it is set to DEVDB):

```
db_name='DEVDB'
```

6. Set the ORACLE_SID OS variable to reflect the new SID name (in
    this example, it is set to DEVDB):

```
$ echo $ORACLE_SID
DEVDB
```

7. Start up the instance in nomount mode:

```
SQL> startup nomount;
```

8. Run the trace file (from step 2) to re-create the control file:

```
SQL> @/tmp/cf.sql
```

> **Note**   In this example, the control files already exist in the location specified by the CONTROL_FILES initialization parameter; therefore, the REUSE parameter is used in the CREATE CONTROL FILE statement.

   9. Open the database with OPEN RESETLOGS:

```
SQL> alter database open resetlogs;
```

   If successful, you should have a database that is a copy of the original database. All the data files, control files, archive redo logs, and online redo logs are in the new locations, and the database has a new name.

   10. As a last step, ensure that your temporary tablespace exists:

```
ALTER TABLESPACE TEMP ADD TEMPFILE '/ora01/dbfile/DEVDB/temp01.dbf'
    SIZE 104857600  REUSE AUTOEXTEND OFF;
```

> **Tip**   You can also use the NID utility to change the database name and database identifier (DBID). See MOS note 863800.1 for more details.

Summary

RMAN is an acronym for Recovery Manager. It is worth noting that Oracle did not name this tool Backup Manager. The Oracle team recognized that although backups are important, the real value of a backup and recovery tool is its ability to restore and recover the database. Being able to manage the recovery process is the critical skill. When a database is damaged and needs to be restored, everybody looks to the DBA to perform a smooth and speedy recovery of the database. Oracle DBAs should use RMAN to protect, secure, and ensure the availability of the company's data assets.

   The restore-and-recovery process is analogous to the healing process involved when you break a bone. Restoring data files from a backup and placing them in their original directories can be likened to setting a bone back to its original position. Recovering a data file is similar to the healing of a broken bone—returning the bone back to the state it was in before it was broken. However, the database recovery will not take as long as a bone healing. When you recover data files, you apply transactions (obtained from archive redo and online redo) to transform the restored data files back to the state they were in before the media failure occurred.

RMAN can be used for any type of restore-and-recovery scenario. Depending on the situation, RMAN can be used to restore the entire database, specific data files, control files, server parameter files, archive redo logs, or just specific data blocks. You can instruct RMAN to perform a complete or an incomplete recovery. It is important to set up scenarios and practice each one. This not only tests the backups but validates a successful restore can take place using the backups. A regular scheduled exercise or even a restore using the backup files to a DEV environment that can be schedule will provide these important tests. You will gain much confidence and fully understand backup and recovery internals once you can successfully restore a database to a server that is different from the original.

Automating Jobs

In almost any type of database environment—from development, to testing, to production—DBAs rely heavily on SQL statements, blocks of code, and scripts to perform tasks. Typical jobs that DBAs automate include the following:

- Shutdown and startup of databases and listeners
- Backups
- Validating the integrity of backups
- Checking for errors
- Removing old trace or log files
- Checking for errant processes
- Checking for abnormal conditions

Automation comes into play when these scripts, blocks of code, become part of a process that does not require DBA intervention to run. The tasks are performed regularly by scheduled processes or workflows that execute the necessary scripts without direct interaction. Routine maintenance jobs are normally the easiest jobs to automate and produce a check that it completed successfully, or possibly failed, for verification. What sometimes get complicated are the jobs that require a change or understanding of a failure to correct an continue without the human interaction to the process. Allowing a database for self-healing, tuning and patching is what Oracle 18c database has become. Oracle 18c is providing in the Oracle Cloud an autonomous database. These tasks happen as expected so that the DBA can work in other areas and provide consulting in data integrations, development, and data strategies.

Automating routine tasks allows DBAs to be much more effective and productive. Automated environments are inherently smoother running and more efficient than manually administered systems. DBA jobs that run automatically from scripts

© Michelle Malcher and Darl Kuhn 2019
M. Malcher and D. Kuhn, *Pro Oracle Database 18c Administration*,
https://doi.org/10.1007/978-1-4842-4424-1_20

consistently execute the same set of commands each time and therefore are less prone to human error and mistakes. Using Oracle 18c on-premise also allows for many of the tasks to be automated as well as the handful of scripts that are needed for applications and other maintenance jobs. Two scheduling utilities are described in this chapter:

- Oracle Scheduler

- Linux/Unix `cron` utility

There is of course the option to use an enterprise solution that is provided instead of the cron utility on every server. This allows for centralized management of the jobs. Since there are so many different options here, this chapter is not going to cover using an enterprise tool, but the scripts and jobs that are scheduled in cron and Oracle utility can also utilize the enterprise tool. This chapter begins by detailing the basic aspects of the Oracle Scheduler utility. This scheduler is available if you have an Oracle database installed. Oracle Scheduler can be used to schedule jobs in a wide variety of configurations.

Also covered in this chapter is how to use the Linux/Unix `cron` scheduling tool. In Linux/Unix environments, DBAs often use the `cron` scheduling utility to run jobs automatically. The `cron` utility is ubiquitous and easy to implement and use. If you are an Oracle DBA, you must be familiar with `cron`, because sooner or later, you will find yourself in an environment that relies heavily on this tool to automate database jobs. Other environments may not allow access to cron scheduling, so strategies of the jobs to be automated are important here in this chapter and can be implemented in another tool based on policies (probably security policies).

The last several sections in this chapter show you how to implement many real-world DBA jobs, such as automatically starting/stopping the database, monitoring, and OS file maintenance. You should be able to extend these scripts to meet the automation requirements of your environment.

Note   Enterprise Manager Grid/Cloud Control can also be used to schedule and manage automated jobs. If you work in a shop that uses Enterprise Manager, then it is appropriate to use this tool for automating your environment.

Automating Jobs with Oracle Scheduler

Oracle Scheduler is a tool that provides a way of automating the scheduling of jobs. Oracle Scheduler is implemented via the DBMS_SCHEDULER internal PL/SQL package. Oracle Scheduler offers a sophisticated set of features for scheduling jobs. DBMS_JOB is the older package for running jobs on the database. They both schedule and execute jobs against the database, but the Schedule offers additional features such as logging, privileged-based models, more detailed scheduling, and storing of the schedules. With these features, it is favorable to use the DBMS_SCHEDULER over DBMS_JOBS. The following sections of this chapter cover the basics of using Oracle Scheduler to automate jobs with simple requirements.

Tip   There are currently more than 70 procedures and functions available within the DBMS_SCHEDULER package. For complete details, see the Oracle Database PL/SQL Packages and Types Reference Guide, which is available for download from the Technology Network area of the Oracle web site (http://otn.oracle.com).

Creating and Scheduling a Job

The example in this section shows how to use DBMS_SCHEDULER to run an OS shell script on a daily basis. First, a shell script is created that contains an RMAN backup command. For this example, the shell script is named rmanback.bsh and is located in the /orahome/oracle/bin directory. The shell script also assumes that there is an /orahome/oracle/bin/log directory available. Here is the shell script:

```
#!/bin/bash
# source oracle OS variables; see chapter 2 for an example of oraset script
. /etc/oraset o18c
rman target / <<EOF
spool log to '/orahome/oracle/bin/log/rmanback.log'
backup database;
spool log off;
EOF
exit 0
```

Next, the CREATE_JOB procedure of the DBMS_SCHEDULER package is used to create a daily job. Next, connect as SYS or as the SYSBACKUP user with CREATE and ALTER JOB permissions, and execute the following command:

```
SQL> BEGIN
DBMS_SCHEDULER.CREATE_JOB(
job_name => 'RMAN_BACKUP',
job_type => 'EXECUTABLE',
job_action => '/orahome/oracle/bin/rmanback.bsh',
repeat_interval => 'FREQ=DAILY;BYHOUR=9;BYMINUTE=35',
start_date => to_date('17-01-2018','dd-mm-yyyy'),
job_class => '"DEFAULT_JOB_CLASS"',
auto_drop => FALSE,
comments => 'RMAN backup job',
enabled => TRUE);
END;
/
```

In the prior code the JOB_TYPE parameter can be one of the following types: STORED_PROCEDURE, PLSQL_BLOCK, EXTERNAL_SCRIPT, SQL_SCRIPT, or EXECUTABLE. In this example, an external shell script is executed, so the job is of type EXTERNAL.

The REPEAT_INTERVAL parameter is set to FREQ=DAILY;BYHOUR=9;BYMINUTE=35. This instructs the job to run daily, at 9:35 AM. The REPEAT_INTERVAL parameter of the CREATE_JOB is capable of implementing sophisticated calendaring frequencies. For instance, it supports a variety of yearly, monthly, weekly, daily, hourly, by the minute, and by the second schedules. The Oracle Database PL/SQL Packages and Types Reference Guide contains several pages of syntax details for just the REPEAT_INTERVAL parameter.

The JOB_CLASS parameter specifies which job class to assign the job to. Typically, you would create a job class and assign a job to that class, whereby the job would inherit the attributes of that particular class. For example, you may want all jobs in a particular class to have the same logging level or to purge log files in the same manner. There is a default job class that can be used if you have not created any job classes. The previous example uses the default job class.

Tip   Set up credentials for local and remote external jobs. Oracle can use default users, but for security policies and capturing of the execution of the job, it is better to create a user for authenticating the external jobs. DBMS_CREDENTIAL stores the user details and can store a Windows domain user, such as a service account, to execute these jobs. Credentials are owned by SYS and can also be managed using DBMS_CREDENTIAL.

The AUTO_DROP parameter is set to FALSE in this example. This instructs the Oracle Scheduler not to drop the job automatically after it runs (the default is TRUE).

Viewing Job Details

To view details about how a job is configured, query the DBA_SCHEDULER_JOBS view. This query selects information for the RMAN_BACKUP job:

```
SQL> SELECT job_name
 ,last_start_date
 ,last_run_duration
 ,next_run_date
 ,repeat_interval
FROM dba_scheduler_jobs
WHERE job_name='RMAN_BACKUP';
```

Each time a job runs, a record of the job execution is logged in the data dictionary. To check the status of a job execution, query the DBA_SCHEDULER_JOB_LOG view. There should be one entry for every time a job has run:

```
SQL> SELECT job_name
,log_date
,operation
,status
FROM dba_scheduler_job_log
WHERE job_name='RMAN_BACKUP';
```

Modifying Job Logging History

By default, the Oracle Scheduler keeps 30 days' worth of log history. You can modify the default retention period via the SET_SCHEDULER_ATTRIBUTE procedure. For example, this command changes the default number of days to 15:

```
SQL> exec dbms_scheduler.set_scheduler_attribute('log_history',15);
```

To remove the contents of the log history completely, use the PURGE_LOG procedure:

```
SQL> exec dbms_scheduler.purge_log();
```

Modifying a Job

You can modify various attributes of a job via the SET_ATTRIBUTE procedure. This example modifies the RMAN_BACKUP job to run weekly, on Mondays:

```
SQL> BEGIN
  dbms_scheduler.set_attribute(
    name=>'RMAN_BACKUP'
    ,attribute=>'repeat_interval'
    ,value=>'freq=weekly; byday=mon');
END;
/
```

You can verify the change by selecting the REPEAT_INTERVAL column from the DBA_SCHEDULER_JOBS view. Here is what the REPEAT_INTERVAL column now shows for the RMAN_BACKUP job:

```
21-JAN-18 12.00.00.200000 AM -07:00 freq=weekly; byday=mon
```

From the prior output, you can see that the job will run on the next Monday, and because no BYHOUR and BYMINUTE options were specified (when modifying the job), the job is scheduled to run at the default time of 12:00 AM.

Stopping a Job

If you have a job that has been running for an abnormally long period of time, you may want to abort it. Use the STOP_JOB procedure to stop a currently running job. This example stops the RMAN_BACKUP job while it is running:

```
SQL> exec dbms_scheduler.stop_job(job_name=>'RMAN_BACKUP');
```

The STATUS column of DBA_SCHEDULER_JOB_LOG will show STOPPED for jobs stopped using the STOP_JOB procedure.

Disabling a Job

You may want to temporarily disable a job because it is not running correctly. You need to ensure that the job does not run while you are troubleshooting the issue. Use the DISABLE procedure to disable a job:

```
SQL> exec dbms_scheduler.disable('RMAN_BACKUP');
```

If the job is currently running, consider stopping the job first or using the FORCE option of the DISABLE procedure:

```
SQL> exec dbms_scheduler.disable(name=>'RMAN_BACKUP',force=>true);
```

Enabling a Job

You can enable a previously disabled job via the ENABLE procedure of the DBMS_SCHEDULER package. This example re-enables the RMAN_BACKUP job:

```
SQL> exec dbms_scheduler.enable(name=>'RMAN_BACKUP');
```

Tip   You can check to see if a job has been disabled or enabled by selecting the ENABLED column from the DBA_SCHEDULER_JOBS view.

843

Copying a Job

If you have a current job that you want to clone, you can use the COPY_JOB procedure to accomplish this. The procedure takes two arguments: the old job name and the new job name. Here is an example of copying a job, where RMAN_BACKUP is a previously created job, and RMAN_NEW_BACK is the new job that will be created:

```
begin
  dbms_scheduler.copy_job('RMAN_BACKUP','RMAN_NEW_BACK');
end;
/
```

The copied job will be created but not enabled. You must enable the job first (see the previous section for an example) before it will run.

Running a Job Manually

You can manually run a job outside its regular schedule. You might want to do this to test the job to ensure that it is working correctly. Use the RUN_JOB procedure to initiate a job manually. This example manually runs the previously created RMAN_BACKUP job:

```
SQL> BEGIN
  DBMS_SCHEDULER.RUN_JOB(
  JOB_NAME => 'RMAN_BACKUP',
  USE_CURRENT_SESSION => FALSE);
END;
/
```

The USE_CURRENT_SESSION parameter instructs Oracle Scheduler to run the job as the current user (or not). A value of FALSE instructs the scheduler to run the job as the user who originally created and scheduled the job.

Deleting a Job

If you no longer require a job, you should delete it from the scheduler. Use the DOP_JOB procedure to permanently remove a job. This example removes the RMAN_BACKUP job:

```
SQL> BEGIN
  dbms_scheduler.drop_job(job_name=>'RMAN_BACKUP');
END;
/
```

The code will drop the job and remove any information regarding the dropped job from the DBA_SCHEDULER_JOBS view.

Oracle Scheduler vs. cron

DBAs often debate whether they should use Oracle Scheduler or the Linux/Unix cron utility for scheduling and automating tasks. These are some of the benefits that Oracle Scheduler has over cron:

- Can make the execution of a job dependent on the completion of another job

- Robust resource balancing and flexible scheduling features

- Can run jobs based on a database event

- The job does not need to check if the database is up and running

- Program's DBMS_SCHEDULER PL/SQL package syntax works the same, regardless of the OS

- Can run status reports, using the data dictionary

- The job does not need to pass the password through the cron job

- If working in a clustered environment, no need to worry about synchronizing multiple con tables for each node in the cluster

- Can be maintained and monitored via Enterprise Manager

The Oracle Scheduler is implemented via the DBMS_SCHEDULER PL/SQL package. As discussed previously, it is fairly easy to create and maintain jobs using this utility. Yet, despite Oracle Scheduler's benefits, many DBAs prefer to use a scheduling utility such as cron. These are some of the advantages of cron:

- Easy to use; simple, tried and true; only takes seconds to create or modify jobs

- Almost universally available on all Linux/Unix boxes; for the most part, runs nearly identically, regardless of the Linux/Unix platform (yes, there are minor differences)

- Database agnostic; operates independently of the database and works the same, regardless of the database vendor or version

- Works whether or not the database is available

The prior lists are not comprehensive but should give you a flavor of the uses of each scheduling tool. It is preferred to have the jobs be the same on all servers but even better to have a centralized way of managing the jobs and executing, such as Cloud Control or an enterprise scheduling tool. The following sections in this chapter provide information on how to implement and schedule automated jobs ia cron.

Note   If you are in a Windows environment, use the Task Scheduler utility to run batch jobs automatically. You can access the Task Scheduler by going to the Control Panel and then to Administrative Tools.

Automating Jobs via cron

The cron program is a job-scheduling utility that is ubiquitous in Linux/Unix environments. This tool derives its name from *chrónos* (the Greek word for "time"). The cron (the geek word for "scheduler") tool allows you to schedule scripts or commands to run at a specified time and repeat at a designated frequency.

How cron Works

When your Linux server boots up, a `cron` background process is automatically started to manage all `cron` jobs in the system. The `cron` background process is also known as the `cron` daemon. This process is started upon system startup by the `etc/init.d/crond` script. You can check to see whether the `cron` daemon process is running with the `ps` command:

```
$ ps -ef | grep crond | grep -v grep
root        3081      1  0  2012 ?          00:00:18 crond
```

On Linux boxes, you can also check to see whether the `cron` daemon is running, using the `service` command:

```
$ /sbin/service crond status
crond (pid  3081) is running...
```

The `root` user uses several files and directories when executing system `cron` jobs. The `etc/crontab` file contains commands for running system `cron` jobs. Here is a typical listing of the contents of the `etc/crontab` file:

```
SHELL=/bin/bash
PATH=/sbin:/bin:/usr/sbin:/usr/bin
MAILTO=root
HOME=/
# run-parts
01 * * * * root run-parts /etc/cron.hourly
02 4 * * * root run-parts /etc/cron.daily
22 4 * * 0 root run-parts /etc/cron.weekly
42 4 1 * * root run-parts /etc/cron.monthly
```

This `etc/crontab` file uses the `run-parts` utility to run scripts located in the following directories: `etc/cron.hourly`, `etc/cron.daily`, `etc/cron.weekly`, and `etc/cron.monthly`. If there is a system utility that needs to run other than on an hourly, daily, weekly, or monthly basis, then it can be placed in the `/etc/cron.d` directory.

Each user can create a `crontab` (also known as a `cron` table) file. This file contains the list of programs that you want to run at a specific time and interval. This file is usually located in the `var/spool/cron` directory. For every user who creates a `cron` table, there will be a file in the /var/spool/cron directory named after the user. As root, you can list the files in that directory, as shown:

```
# ls /var/spool/cron
oracle root
```

The cron background process is mostly idle. It wakes up once every minute and checks etc/crontab, etc/cron.d, and the user cron table files and determines whether there are any jobs that need to be executed.

Table 20-1 summarizes the purpose of the various files and directories used by cron. Knowledge of these files and directories will help you troubleshoot any issues as well as get a better understanding of cron.

Table 20-1. *Descriptions of Files and Directories Used by the cron Utility*

File	Purpose
/etc/init.d/crond	Starts the cron daemon upon system boot
/var/log/cron	System messages related to the cron process; useful for troubleshooting problems
/var/spool/ cron/<username>	User crontab files are stored in the /var/spool/cron directory
/etc/cron.allow	Specifies users who can create a cron table
/etc/cron.deny	Specifies users who are not allowed to create a cron table
/etc/crontab	The system cron table that has commands to run scripts located in the following directories: /etc/cron.hourly, /etc/cron.daily, /etc/cron.weekly, and /etc/cron.monthly
/etc/cron.d	Directory that contains cron tables for jobs that need to run on a schedule other than hourly, daily, weekly, or monthly
/etc/cron.hourly	Directory that contains system scripts to run on an hourly basis
/etc/cron.daily	Directory that contains system scripts to run on a daily basis
/etc/cron.weekly	Directory that contains system scripts to run on a weekly basis
/etc/cron.monthly	Directory that contains system scripts to run on a monthly basis

Enabling Access to cron

Sometimes when SAs set up a new box, they do not (by default) enable the use of cron for all users on the system. To verify whether you have access to cron, invoke the utility as follows:

```
$ crontab -e
```

If you receive the following error message, then you do not have access:

```
You (oracle) are not allowed to use this program (crontab)
```

To enable cron access as the root user, add oracle to the etc/cron.allow file with the echo command:

```
# echo oracle >> /etc/cron.allow
```

Once the oracle entry is added to the etc/cron.allow file, you can use the crontab utility to schedule a job.

Note   You can also use an editing utility (such as vi) to add an entry to the cron.allow file.

The root user can always schedule jobs with the crontab utility. Other users must be listed in the etc/cron.allow file. If the /etc/cron.allow file does not exist, then the OS user must not appear in the etc/cron.deny file. If neither the /etc/cron.allow nor the /etc/cron.deny file exists, then only the root user can access the crontab utility. (These rules may vary slightly, depending on the version of Linux/Unix you are using.)

On some Unix OSs (such as Solaris), the cron.allow and cron.deny files are located in the etc/cron.d directory. These files usually can only be modified by the root user.

Tip   On some Linux/Unix platforms, newer and more flexible variants of cron are available, such as the anacron utility. Use the man anacron command to view details on the implementation of this utility on your system.

Understanding cron Table Entries

Your cron table is a list of numbers and commands that the cron background process (cron daemon) will run at a specified time and schedule. The crontab utility expects entries to follow a well-defined format. It is a good idea to add a comment line at the beginning of your crontab file that documents the required format, like so:

```
# min(0-59) hr(0-23) dayMonth(1-31) monthYear(1-12) dayWeek(0/7-6)
commandOrScript
```

In the previous example, the number sign (#) in the cron file represents the start of a comment. Any text entered after # is ignored by cron.

Each entry in the crontab is a single line composed of six fields. The first five fields specify the execution time and frequency. Entries in these fields can be separated by commas or hyphens. A comma indicates multiple values for an entry, whereas a hyphen indicates a range of values. An entry can also be an asterisk (*), which indicates that all possible values are in effect. Here is an example to help clarify. The following entry sends an e-mail saying, "Wake up," every half hour, from 8 am to 4:30 PM, Monday through Friday:

```
0,30 8-16 * * 1-5 echo "wake up" | mailx -s "wake up" dkuhn@gmail.com
```

On some Linux systems, you can skip a value within a range by following the entry with /<integer>. For instance, if you wanted to run a job every other minute, use 0-59/2 in the minute column. You can also use a slash (/) with an asterisk to skip values. For instance, to run a job every fourth minute, you would use */4 in the minute column.

The sixth field in the crontab can be one or more Linux commands or a shell script. Or, put another way, the sixth column can be any combination of commands or a script that you can run on one line from the Linux command line.

The cron utility has a few quirks that need further explanation. The fifth column is the day of the week. Sunday is designated by either a 0 or a 7; Monday, by a 1; Tuesday, by a 2; and so on, to Saturday, which is indicated with a 6.

The hour numbers in the second column are in military time format, ranging from 0 to 23. The fourth column (month of the year) and fifth column (day of the week) can be represented with numeric values or by three-letter abbreviations. For example, the following entry in the crontab uses three-letter abbreviations for months and days:

```
0,30 8-16 * Jan-Dec Mon-Fri echo "wake up" | mailx -s "get up" dkuhn@gmail.com
```

There also appear to be overlapping columns, such as the third column (day of the month) and the fifth column (day of the week). These columns allow you to create flexible schedules for jobs that need to run on schedules such as the 1st and 15th day of the month or every Tuesday. Put an asterisk in the column that you are not using. If you need to run a job on the 1st and 15th and every Tuesday, then fill in both columns.

If you are running a shell script from cron that contains a call to an Oracle utility such as sqlplus or rman, ensure that you instantiate within the script any required OS variables, such as ORACLE_SID and ORACLE_HOME. If you do not source these variables, you will see errors such as the following when your shell script runs from cron:

```
sqlplus: command not found
```

When cron runs a script (in a user's crontab), it does not run the user's startup or login files (such as .bashrc). Therefore, any script (being run from cron) needs to explicitly set any required variables. You can directly set the variables within the script or call another script that exports these variables (such as Oracle's oraenv script).

Tip Do not schedule the jobs that you enter in cron to run all at the same time. Rather, spread them out so as not to bog down cron or the system at any particular point in time.

Scheduling a Job to Run Automatically

To schedule a job, you must add a line in your cron table, specifying the time you want the job to execute. There are two methods for adding entries in your cron table:

- Editing the cron table file directly
- Loading the cron table from a file

These two techniques are described in the following sections.

Editing the cron Table Directly

You an edit your cron table directly with the -e (editor) option of the crontab command:

```
$ crontab -e
```

When issuing the previous command, you will be presented with a file to edit. This file is known as your cron table (crontab). To schedule a script named backup.bsh to run daily, at 11:05 PM, enter the following line into your cron table:

```
5 23 * * * /home/oracle/bin/backup.bsh
```

Here, the 5 specifies that the job will run at 5 minutes after the top of the hour. The 23 is military time, specifying that the job should run in the 2300 hour window (in this example, 5 minutes after the hour). The three stars (* * *) signify that the job should run every day of the month, every month of the year, and every day of the week.

Exit the cron table file. If your default editor is vi, then type wq to exit. When you exit crontab, your cron table is saved for you. To view your cron entries, use the -l (list) option of the crontab command:

```
$ crontab -l
```

To remove your cron table completely, use the r option:

```
$ crontab -r
```

Before running the previous command, you should save your cron table in a text file, as shown:

```
$ crontab -l > saved.cron
```

In this way, you can refer to the saved file, in the event that you didn't mean to delete your cron table.

Tip   "I once worked with a DBA who thought crontab -r meant "read the cron table." Do not ever make that mistake. It's always good to back up your crontab to a text files so the schedule is safe for these type of issues with the crontab -l > crontab.backup. This can also be used to load into other servers.

Setting Default Editor

The default editor invoked to modify the cron table is dependent on the value of your VISUAL OS variable. In my current environment, the VISUAL variable is set to vi:

```
$ echo $VISUAL
vi
```

If the VISUAL OS variable isn't set, then the value of EDITOR is used to define the default editor. Make sure that either VISUAL or EDITOR is set to your editor of choice. If neither VISUAL nor EDITOR is set, your system will default to the ed editor. In this scenario, you will be presented with the following prompt:

```
26
<blank prompt>
```

Press the Q key to exit from ed. You can have the VISUAL or EDITOR variable automatically set for you when you log in to the system. You can also manually set the editor with the export command. The following example sets the default editor to vi:

```
$ export EDITOR=vi
```

Consider putting the prior line of code in a startup file (such as .bashrc) so that your editor is set consistently.

Loading the cron Table from a File

The other way to modify your cron table is to load it directly with a file name. This will allow you to save your contab jobs and have them be the same on each server by just loading it directly, using the following syntax:

```
$ crontab <filename>
```

Here, the crontab utility will load the contents of the specified file into your cron table. The recommended steps to modify your cron table with this method are as follows:

1. Before modifying your cron table, first populate a file with the cron table's current contents; for example,

   ```
   $ crontab -l > mycron.txt
   ```

2. Next, make a copy of the previously created file (mycron.txt). This allows you to revert back to the original file, in the event that you introduce errors and cannot readily figure out what is incorrect. This also provides you with an audit trail of changes to your cron table:

   ```
   $ cp mycron.txt mycron.jul29.txt
   ```

3. Now, edit the mycron.txt file with your favorite text editor:

    $ vi mycron.txt

For example, to schedule a script named backup.bsh to run daily, at 11:05 PM, add the following lines:

```
#-------------------------------------------------------------------------
# File backup, dk: 20-jan-14, inserted.
5 23 * * * /home/oracle/bin/backup.bsh
#-------------------------------------------------------------------------
```

4. When you are finished making edits, load the contents of mycron. txt into the cron table, as shown:

    $ crontab mycron.txt

If your file does not conform to the cron syntax, you will receive an error such as the following:

```
"mycron.txt":6: bad day-of-week
errors in crontab file, cannot install.
```

In this situation, either correct the syntax error, or reload the original copy of the cron table.

EXAMPLE OF A TYPICAL CRON TABLE

Listed here is a sample entry from a cron table on a database server:

```
#-------------------------------------------------------------------------
# min(0-59) hr(0-23) dayMonth(1-31) monthYear(1-12) dayWeek(0/7-6)
commandOrScript
#-------------------------------------------------------------------------
# RMAN backups, dk: 01-may-12, updated.
1 16 * * * /u01/oracle/bin/rmanback.bsh INV >/u01/oracle/bin/log/bck.log 2>&1
#-------------------------------------------------------------------
# Tablespace check, sp: 17-dec-12, created.
5 * * * * /u01/oracle/bin/tbsp_chk.bsh INV 10 1>/u01/oracle/bin/log/tbsp.log 2>&1
#-------------------------------------------------------------------
```

Take note of a few aspects in this entry. Place a line at the top of every cron table (on every database server) that briefly explains the meanings of the date scheduling features:

```
# min(0-59) hr(0-23) dayMonth(1-31) monthYear(1-12) dayWeek(0/7-6)
commandOrScript
```

Separate each entry with a comment line. This makes the entry much more readable:

```
#-----------------------------------------------------------------
```

Additionally, include a brief note (with the initials of author or modifier), describing the cron job and when the edit was made:

```
# RMAN backups, dk: 01-jan-18, updated.
```

If you manage dozens of database servers (each with its own cron table), with multiple DBAs, you will need some mechanism (and it does not have to be sophisticated) for tracking who made changes and when.

Redirecting cron Output

Whenever you run a Linux shell command, by default the standard output (of the command) will be displayed on your screen. Also, if any error messages are generated, they will, by default, be displayed on your screen. You can use either > or 1> (they are synonymous) to redirect any standard output to an OS file. Additionally, you can use 2> to redirect any error messages to a file. The notation 2>&1 instructs the shell to send any error messages to the same location as standard output. Even with sending output of the execution of the script, make sure that the script has appropriate logging and reporting for success or failure either in a log file or database table.

When you create a cron job, you can use these redirection features to send the output of a shell script to a log file. For example, in the following cron table entry, any standard output and error messages generated by the backup.bsh shell script are captured in a file named bck.log:

```
11 12 * * * /home/oracle/bin/backup.bsh 1>/home/oracle/bin/log/bck.log 2>&1
```

If you do not redirect the `cron` job output, then any output will be e-mailed to the user that owns the `cron` table. You can override this behavior by specifying the `MAILTO` variable directly within the `cron` table. With the next few lines of code, the `cron` output will go to the `root` user:

```
MAILTO=oraclebkup
11 12 * * * /home/oracle/bin/backup.bsh
```

If you do not want the output to go anywhere, then redirect it to the proverbial bit bucket. The following entry sends the standard output and standard error to the `dev/null` device:

```
11 12 * * * /home/oracle/bin/backup.bsh 1>/dev/null 2>&1
```

Troubleshooting cron

If you have a `cron` job that is not running correctly, follow these steps to troubleshoot the issue:

1. Copy your `cron` entry, paste it into the OS command line, and manually run the command. Frequently, a slight typo in a directory or file name can be the source of the problem. Manually running the command will highlight errors such as these.

2. If the script runs Oracle utilities, make sure you source (set) the required OS variables within the script, such as `ORACLE_HOME` and `ORACLE_SID`. Oftentimes, these variables are set by startup scripts (such as `HOME/.bashrc`) when you log in. Because `cron` does not run a user's startup scripts, any required variables must be set explicitly within the script.

3. Ensure that the first line of any shell scripts invoked from `cron` specify the name of the program that will be used to interpret the commands within the script. For instance, `#!/bin/bash` should be the first entry in a Bash shell script. Because `cron` does not run a user's startup scripts (such as `HOME/.bashrc`), you cannot assume that your OS user's default shell will be used to run a command or script evoked from `cron`.

4. Make certain that the `cron` background process is running. Issue
    the following command from the OS to verify:

    ```
    $ ps -ef | grep cron
    ```

    If the `cron` daemon (background process) is running, you should
    see something similar to this:

    ```
    root      2969     1  0 Mar23 ?        00:00:00 crond
    ```

5. Check your e-mail on the server. The `cron` utility will usually
    send an e-mail to the OS account when there are issues with a
    misbehaving `cron` job.

6. Inspect the contents of the `var/log/cron` file for any errors.
    Sometimes, this file has relevant information regarding a `cron` job
    that has failed to run.

7. Verify the times that the job is set to run, and make sure that all of
    the columns line up with the date, time, etc.

Examples of Automated DBA Jobs

In today's often chaotic business environment, it is almost mandatory to automate jobs.
If you do not automate, you may forget to do a task; or, if performing a job manually, you
may introduce error into the procedure. If you do not automate, you could find yourself
replaced by a more efficient or cheaper set of DBAs.

When a script fails it makes sense to receive an e-mail, but too many successful job
e-mails can cause noise and miss a failure. However, not receiving an e-mail in success
or failure is really a failure since it is in a state of uncertainty. A way to report on scripts
that run for databases is a centralized report that shows success or failure from the
consolidated logs or queries from an output table. Reviewing a daily e-mail will validate
that all jobs are running properly.

DBAs automate a wide variety of tasks and jobs. Almost any type of environment
requires that you create some sort of OS script that encapsulates a combination of OS
commands, SQL statements, and PL/SQL blocks.

The following scripts in this chapter are a sample of the wide variety of different
types of tasks that DBAs automate. This set of scripts is, by no means, complete. Many of

these scripts may not be needed in your environment. The point is to give you a good sampling of the types of jobs automated and the techniques used to accomplish a given task.

Note   Chapter 3 contains basic examples of some core scripts that DBAs require. This section provides examples of tasks and scripts that DBAs commonly automate.

Starting and Stopping the Database and Listener

In case a database server was to reboot or restart, it is desirable to have the Oracle databases and listener automatically restart with the server. This process used to be part of a parameter in the /etc/oratab file for the database to automatically restart. It would be called in the dbstart and dbshut commands and was 'Y' for restart 'N' for manual intervention.

Now there is Oracle Restart, and it is especially useful for a multicomponent environment with RAC and ASM, but is simple to add databases as part of the restart. When the database is created using dbca, the database is added to Oracle Restart configuration. The same is true when you remove the database using dbca, the database is removed from Oracle Restart. If you use Oracle Net Configuration Assistant (netca) to create or delete a listener, netca will add or remove from the Oracle Restart.

There are a few ways to add a database and listener to the Oracle Restart if using a different method from dbca, either scripted or manual with creatdb steps. With the database software install, there is a version of Enterprise Manager Database Control that can only add databases and listeners to the Oracle Restart configuration. The srvctl utility will allow for adding, modifying, and deleting of databases and listeners with the commands. The commands can become part of the scripted creation of databases so this task becomes part of the steps and not a manual task that is done afterward.

For the listener, the GRID_HOME or ORACLE_HOME needs to be set, depending on if the listener is started in the GRID or ORACLE_HOME. The default listener is added with the following:

```
# cd $GRID_HOME/bin
# . /srvctl add listener
```

To add another listener, the name of the listener would be provided.

To add a database:

```
# cd $ORACLE_HOME/bin
# ./ srvctl add service -d o18c -o /u01/app/oracle/product/18.1.0/db_1
```

```
-o is the ORACLE_HOME directory
-d is the database name
```

To remove a database:

```
# srvctl remove database -d o18c
```

A service can also be disabled to still be available but not run with the automatic restart. To disable or enable a database:

```
# srvctl disable database -d o18c
```

The srvctl utility is part of the Oracle software and available in the ORACLE_HOME, so the grid infrastructure does not need to be installed in order to use this method for adding databases and services to Oracle Restart. Oracle Restart will make sure that the databases are automatically restarted with a server restart as long as they are enabled in the restart configuration.

Checking for Archivelog Destination Fullness

Sometimes DBAs and SAs do not adequately plan and implement a location for storing archivelog files on disk. In these scenarios, it is sometimes convenient to have a script that checks for space in the primary location and that sends out warnings before the archivelog destination becomes full. Additionally, you may want to implement within the script that the archivelog location automatically start an RMAN job to back up and delete the archivelogs to free up space.

Scripts such as this proves useful in chaotic environments that have issues with the archivelog destination's filling up at unpredictable frequencies. If the archivelog destination fills up, the database will hang. In some environments, this is highly unacceptable. You could argue that you should never let yourself get into this type of situation. Therefore, if you are brought in to maintain an unpredictable environment, and you are the one getting the phone calls at 2:00 AM, you may want to consider implementing a script such as the one provided in this section.

Before using the following script, change the variables within the script to match your environment. The script will send a warning e-mail when the threshold goes below the amount of space specified by the THRESH_GET_WORRIED variable and run a RMAN backup of the archivelogs.

```
#!/bin/bash
PRG=`basename $0`
DB=$1
USAGE="Usage: ${PRG} <sid>"
if [ -z "$DB" ]; then
  echo "${USAGE}"
  exit 1
fi
# source OS variables
. /var/opt/oracle/oraset ${DB}

# Set thresholds for getting concerned.
THRESH_GET_WORRIED=2000000 # 2Gig from df -k
MAILX="/bin/mailx"
MAIL_LIST="dkuhn@gmail.com "
BOX=`uname -a | awk '{print$2}'`
#
loc=`sqlplus -s <<EOF
CONNECT / AS sysdba
SET HEAD OFF FEEDBACK OFF
SELECT SUBSTR(destination,1,INSTR(destination,'/',1,2)-1)
FROM v\\$archive_dest WHERE dest_name='LOG_ARCHIVE_DEST_1';
EOF`
# The output of df depends on your version of Linux/Unix,
# you may need to tweak the next line based on that output.
free_space=`df -k | grep ${loc} | awk '{print $4}'`
echo box = ${BOX}, sid = ${DB}, Arch Log Mnt Pnt = ${loc}
echo "free_space         = ${free_space} K"
echo "THRESH_GET_WORRIED= ${THRESH_GET_WORRIED} K"
#
if [ $free_space -le $THRESH_GET_WORRIED ]; then
```

```
$MAILX -s "Arch Redo Space Low ${DB} on $BOX" $MAIL_LIST <<EOF
Archive log dest space low running backup now,
box: $BOX, sid: ${DB}, free space: $free_space
EOF

# Run RMAN backup of archivelogs and delete after backed up
rman nocatalog <<EOF
connect target /
backup archivelog all delete input;
EOF
else
  echo no need to backup and delete, ${free_space} KB free on ${loc}
fi
#
exit 0
```

If you are using an FRA for the location of your archivelog files, you can derive the archive location from the V$ARCHIVED_LOG view; for example,

```
SQL> select
  substr(name,1,instr(name,'/',1,2)-1)
from v$archived_log
where first_time =
 (select max(first_time) from v$archived_log);
```

There are also a few other ways to manage this space when using FRA, and it is definitely another reason to use FRA instead of just setting a directory. The threshold can be determined using SQL from v$recovery_file_dest instead of looking at the file system.

```
SQL> select name, space_limit, space_used from v$recovery_file_dest;
NAME SPACE_LIMIT   SPACE_USED
---------------------------------------------------------------------
/u02/oradata/FRA  1048576       48576
```

The FRA size can be increased to accommodate more archivelogs until the space is freed up by a backup and delete or purge of old backups. The FRA destination can also be changed. It is easier to automate the process of increasing the FRA size and running a backup to make sure that the archivelog directory does not fill up. The following can be inserted into the previous script before the RMAN script:

```
SQL> alter system set DB_RECOVERY_FILE_DEST_SIZE=20G scope=both;
```

Typically, a script to check the archive log destination runs once an hour. Here is a typical cron entry (this entry should actually be a single line of code but has been placed on two lines in order to fit on the page):

```
38 * * * * /u01/oracle/bin/arch_check.bsh DWREP
  1>/u01/oracle/bin/log/arch_check.log 2>&1
```

Truncating Large Log Files

Sometimes log files can grow very large and cause issues by filling up critical mount points. The listener.log will record information about incoming connections to the database. The alert.log is another file that records errors, changes, and activity of the database. With active systems, this file can quickly grow to several gigabytes. For many environments, the information in the listener.log file does not need to be retained. If there are Oracle Net connectivity issues, then the file can be inspected to help troubleshoot issues.

The listener.log and alert.log files are actively written to, so you should not just delete them. If you remove the file, the listener process will not re-create the file and start writing to it again; you have to stop and restart the listener to restart its writing to the listener.log file. The alert.log will get re-created but should be handled in the same way as the following example for the listener.log. You can, however, null out the listener.log file or truncate it. In Linux/Unix environments, this is done via the following technique:

```
$ cat /dev/null >listener.log
```

The previous command replaces the contents of the listener.log file with the contents of dev/null (a default file on Linux/Unix systems that contains nothing). The result of this command is that the listener.log file is truncated, and the listener can continue to actively write to it.

Listed next is a shell script that truncates the default listener.log file after making a backup for retention until overwritten next time it runs This script is dependent on setting the OS variable ORACLE_BASE. If you do not set that variable in your environment, you will have to hard-code the directory path within this script:

```
#!/bin/bash
#
if [ $# -ne 1 ]; then
  echo "Usage: $0 SID"
  exit 1
fi
# See chapter 2 for details on setting OS variables
# Source oracle OS variables with oraset script
. /etc/oraset $1
#
MAILX='/bin/mailx'
MAIL_LIST='dkuhn@gmail.com'
BOX=$(uname -a | awk '{print $2}' | cut -f 1 -d'.')
#
if [ -f $ORACLE_BASE/diag/tnslsnr/$BOX/listener/trace/listener.log ]; then
  cp $ORACLE_BASE/diag/tnslsnr/$BOX/listener/trace/listener.log $ORACLE_
BASE/diag/tnslsnr/$BOX/listener/trace/listener.bkup
  cat /dev/null > $ORACLE_BASE/diag/tnslsnr/$BOX/listener/trace/listener.log
fi
if [ $? -ne 0 ]; then
  echo "trunc list. problem" | $MAILX -s "trunc list. problem $1" $MAIL_LIST
else
  echo "no problem..."
fi
exit 0
```

The following cron entry runs the prior script on a monthly basis (this entry should all be on one line but has been placed on two lines in order to fit on the page):

```
30 6 1 * * /orahome/oracle/bin/trunc_log.bsh DWREP
  1>/orahome/oracle/bin/log/trunc_log.log 2>&1
```

Checking for Locked Production Accounts

Usually having a database profile should be in place that specifies that a database account become locked after a designated number of failed login attempts. For example, set the DEFAULT profile FAILED_LOGIN_ATTEMPTS to 5. Sometimes, however, a rogue user or developer will attempt to guess the production account password, and after five attempts, locks the production account. When this happens, an alert is needed to know about it as soon as possible so that it can be investigated for either a security incident or the issue for the user and then unlock the account.

The following shell script checks the LOCK_DATE value in DBA_USERS for a list of production database accounts:

```
#!/bin/bash
if [ $# -ne 1 ]; then
  echo "Usage: $0 SID"
  exit 1
fi
# source oracle OS variables
. /etc/oraset $1
#
crit_var=$(sqlplus -s <<EOF
/ as sysdba
SET HEAD OFF FEED OFF
SELECT count(*)
FROM dba_users
WHERE lock_date IS NOT NULL
AND username in ('CIAP','REPV','CIAL','STARPROD');
EOF)
#
if [ $crit_var -ne 0 ]; then
  echo $crit_var
  echo "locked acct. issue with $1" | mailx -s "locked acct. issue" dkuhn@sun.com
```

```
else
  echo $crit_var
  echo "no locked accounts"
fi
exit 0
```

This shell script is called from a scheduling tool, such as cron. For example, this cron entry instructs the job to run every 10 minutes (this entry should actually be a single line of code but has been placed on two lines in order to fit on the page):

```
0,10,20,30,40,50 * * * * /home/oracle/bin/lock.bsh DWREP
    1>/home/oracle/bin/log/lock.log 2>&1
```

In this way, an e-mail notification goes out when one of the production database accounts becomes locked. If the risk level is acceptable, as part of this script, there should be a step to unlock the account after a set amount of time, and it is recorded that there were the failed login attempts.

Checking for Too Many Processes

On some database servers, you may have many background SQL*Plus jobs. These batch jobs may perform tasks such as copying data from remote databases and large daily update jobs. In these environments, it is useful to know if, at any given time, there are an abnormal number of shell scripts or SQL*Plus processes running on the database server. An abnormal number of jobs could be an indication that something is broken or hung.

The next shell script has two checks in it: one to determine the number of shell scripts that are named with the extension of bsh and one to determine the number of processes that contain the string of sqlplus:

```
#!/bin/bash
#
if [ $# -ne 0 ]; then
  echo "Usage: $0"
  exit 1
fi
#
crit_var=$(ps -ef | grep -v grep | grep bsh | wc -l)
if [ $crit_var -lt 20 ]; then
```

```
  echo $crit_var
  echo "processes running normal"
else
  echo "too many processes"
  echo $crit_var | mailx -s "too many bsh procs: $1" dkuhn@gmail.com
fi
#
crit_var=$(ps -ef | grep -v grep | grep sqlplus | wc -l)
if [ $crit_var -lt 30 ]; then
  echo $crit_var
  echo "processes running normal"
else
  echo "too many processes"
  echo $crit_var | mailx -s "too many sqlplus procs: $1" dkuhn@gmail.com
fi
#
exit 0
```

The prior shell script, named proc_count.bsh, is run once an hour from a cron job
(this entry should actually be a single line of code but is placed on two lines in order to fit
on the page):

```
33 * * * * /home/oracle/bin/proc_count.bsh
  1>/home/oracle/bin/log/proc_count.log 2>&1
```

Verifying the Integrity of RMAN Backups

As part of your backup-and-recovery strategy, you should periodically validate the
integrity of the backup files. This is also included as part of using RMAN to back up the
database, but a separate job can run against them to validate for restore. RMAN provides
a RESTORE...VALIDATE command that checks for physical corruption within the backup
files. The following script starts RMAN and spools a log file. The log file is subsequently
searched for the keyword error. If there are any errors in the log file, an e-mail is sent:

```
#!/bin/bash
#
if [ $# -ne 1 ]; then
```

```
  echo "Usage: $0 SID"
  exit 1
fi
# source oracle OS variables
. /etc/oraset $1
#
date
BOX=`uname -a | awk '{print$2}'`
rman nocatalog <<EOF
connect target /
spool log to $HOME/bin/log/rman_val.log
set echo on;
restore database validate;
EOF
grep -i error $HOME/bin/log/rman_val.log
if [ $? -eq 0 ]; then
  echo "RMAN verify issue $BOX, $1" | \
  mailx -s "RMAN verify issue $BOX, $1" dkuhn@sun.com
else
  echo "no problem..."
fi
#
date
exit 0
```

The RESTORE...VALIDATE does not actually restore any files; it only validates that the files required to restore the database are available and checks for physical corruption.

If you need to check for logical corruption as well, specify the CHECK LOGICAL clause. For example, to check for logical corruption, the prior shell script would have this line in it:

```
restore database validate check logical;
```

For large databases the validation process can take a great deal of time (because the script checks each block in the backup file for corruption). If you only want to verify that the backup files exist, specify the VALIDATE HEADER clause, like so:

```
restore database validate header;
```

This command only checks for valid information in the header of each file that would be required for a restore and recovery.

Autonomous Database

The previous scripts and tasks when scheduled are just scratching the surface of automating jobs for the Oracle database. Processes that start to take the results of these scripts and apply the fixes and perform the next actions are getting to closer to automation. Oracle 18c database has may processes and hooks that allow for environments to configure even more automation. Oracle 18c itself is not an autonomous database, but in the Oracle Cloud environment, it becomes the Oracle Autonomous Database. This is what is being called the self-healing, self-patching and self-driving database.

In the Oracle Cloud, the databases are managed, backed up by automated processes, and, if needed, performs failover and basic troubleshooting to handle issues. Issues can be increase in processing power that is needed or additional storage. If the database is not heavily utilized, it can shrink back down to save costs. The database has information about when activities occur and through learning it can monitor performance issues and take measures to remediate.

A secure configuration along with security options are implemented by default in the Oracle Cloud. The Autonomous has enabled threat detection and encryption, which protect the data that it is storing. Patching is also automated so that when there is a vulnerability the patching process can apply the fix. These steps happen without manual intervention, and with a highly available environment the database experiences no downtime.

In this cloud environment, what is a DBA to do? There are plenty of opportunities with development, data integrations, and quality, and other areas of security and business intelligence that add value to the enterprise based. Also, is this not what we have been discussing to automate basic tasks and ways to remediate issues for more consistent, stable database environments?

There are plenty of features of the database that can be used to manage other areas of the business, and even new features of the database that should be built into applications. The DBAs can be the ones to help drive this. The chapter is not going to into detail in the Oracle Cloud because it is still the Oracle 18c database that we have been talking about. The difference is the location or hardware that is running the database. The Oracle Cloud and Oracle Cloud Machine (in your data center) provide the monitoring, support, and automation of the processes for provisioning and patching databases to backup.

The Oracle Cloud databases can even be managed the same as an on-premise database with tools that DBAs are already familiar with such as SQL Developer and Cloud Control (formally known as Enterprise Manager). Users are managed through the cloud services, and DBAs can help manage these resources and provide input for migrations to the cloud environments.

As the Autonomous Database continues to gather information about the activity for performance and security, it provides changes in query plans and indexes to improve and detect anomalies for security prevention controls. The Oracle 18c database is being used to transform how database environments are being implemented. The databases are just services that can be supplied on demand for business needs. The processes and steps to make that service available need to have fewer manual steps and more automated processes along with remediation.

Summary

Automating routine database jobs is a key strategy of the successful DBA. Automated jobs ensure that tasks are repeatable and verifiable and that you are quickly notified when there are any problems. For example, your job as a DBA greatly depends on successfully running backups and ensuring that the database is highly available. This chapter includes several scripts and examples that detail how to run routine jobs at defined frequencies.

Oracle provides the Oracle Scheduler utility (implemented via the DBMS_SCHEDULER PL/SQL package) for scheduling jobs. This tool can be used to automate any type of database task. You can also initiate jobs based on system events or on the success/failure of other scheduled jobs

If you are a DBA who works in a Linux/Unix shop, you should familiarize yourself with the cron utility. This scheduler is simple to use and is almost universally available. Even if you do not use cron for your current assignment, you are sure to encounter its use in future work environments.

Most of these scripts just check and alert, and the next step is to actually automate an action if something needs to be addressed or fixed. The corrective action could be unlocking the account or adding space to the FRA for the archivelog space in order to immediately handle the issue and allow for time to review and validate the action.

At this point in the book, you have learned how to implement and perform many tasks required of a DBA. With this knowledge and understanding, the database is more familiar and tasks to automate are probably being listed right now. The knowledge will carry over to cloud migrations and managing databases in the cloud. Even if you manage just one database, no doubt you have been embroiled in a vast number of troubleshooting activities. The next chapter focuses on diagnosing and resolving many of the issues that a DBA encounters.

CHAPTER 21

Database Troubleshooting

Database troubleshooting is a vague and general term that is applied to a wide variety of topics. It can mean anything from investigating database connectivity issues to detailed performance tuning. In this chapter, the following troubleshooting activities will be covered:

- Assessing database availability issues quickly

- Identifying system performance issues with OS utilities

- Querying data dictionary views to display resource-intensive SQL statements

- Using Oracle performance tools to identify resource-consuming SQL statements

- Identifying and resolving locking issues

- Troubleshooting open-cursor issues

- Investigating issues with the undo and temporary tablespaces

The prior list does not encompass all the types of database troubleshooting and performance issues that you will encounter. Rather, it is a sampling of the database problems that you are likely to encounter and demonstrates useful techniques for resolving problems.

Quickly Triaging

When getting the call that there is an issue with the database, it is critical to be able to ask questions and know the right questions to ask. Understanding the issue is the first step and must be done quickly to get to other troubleshooting steps. DBAs are going to be called upon to troubleshoot database and non-database issues, server, connection and

© Michelle Malcher and Darl Kuhn 2019
M. Malcher and D. Kuhn, *Pro Oracle Database 18c Administration*,
https://doi.org/10.1007/978-1-4842-4424-1_21

network as these are all part of the database system what might only be seen is that the data are not being returned in fast enough or at all.

Here are a handful of questions that are useful:

- Is this in the application or with a direct connection to the database?

- Is this a new process, query, piece of code?

- How long has this been slow? Has it happened before or is this the first time?

- Is anything being returned?

- Do you have any error messages that you are receiving?

As the answers are coming in, you can be checking the alert logs, script output from the regular jobs, pinging the database and database server, and seeing if you are able to log in. This should give you a good start for troubleshooting the issue.

Tip   Keep in mind that you should automate jobs that perform tasks such as verifying the database availability (see Chapter 19 for examples of automating DBA tasks). Automated jobs help you proactively handle issues so that they do not turn into database downtime.

Checking Database Availability

The first few checks do not require logging in to the database server. Rather, they can be performed remotely via SQL*Plus and OS commands. Performing the initial checks remotely over the network establishes whether all the system components are working.

One quick check to determine whether the remote server is available, the database is up, the network is working, and the listener is accepting incoming connections is to connect via an SQL*Plus client to the remote database over the network. The initial testing could use a non-DBA account. Here is an example of connecting over the network to a remote database as the michelle user with a password of ora123; the network connect information is embedded directly into the connect string (where dwdb1 is the server, 1521 is the port, and dwrep1 is the database service name):

```
$ sqlplus michelle/ora123@'dwdb1:1521/dwrep1'
```

If a connection can be made, then the remote server is available, and the database and listener are up and working. At this point and with the questions that were asked, we can verify if the connectivity issue has to do with the application or with something other than the database.

If the prior SQL*Plus command does not work, try to establish whether the remote server is available. In this example, the `ping` command is issued to the remote server, named `dwdb1`:

```
$ ping dwdb1
```

If `ping` works, you should see output such as this:

```
64 bytes from dwdb1 (192.168.254.215): icmp_seq=1 ttl=64 time=0.044 ms
```

If `ping` does not work, there is probably an issue with either the network or the remote server. If the remote server is not available, it is time to contact a system administrator or network administrator.

If `ping` does work, then check to see if the remote server is reachable via the port that the listener is listening on. The `telnet` command to accomplish this:

```
$ telnet IP <port>
```

In this example, a network connection is attempted to the server's IP address on the 1521 port:

```
$ telnet 192.168.254.215 1521
```

If the IP address is reachable on the specified port, you should see "Connected to . . ." in the output, like so:

```
Trying 192.168.254.216...
Connected to ora04.
Escape character is '^]'.
```

If the `telnet` command does not work, contact the SA or the network administrator.

If the `telnet` command does work, and there is network connectivity to the server on the specified port, then use the `tnsping` command to test network connectivity to the remote server and database, using Oracle Net. This example attempts to reach the DWREP1 remote service:

```
$ tnsping DWREP1
```

If successful, the output should contain the OK string, like so:

```
Attempting to contact (DESCRIPTION = (ADDRESS = (PROTOCOL = TCP)(HOST = DWDB1)
(PORT = 1521)) (CONNECT_DATA = (SERVICE_NAME = DWREP1)))
OK (20 msec)
```

If tnsping works, it means that the remote listener is up and working. It does not necessarily mean that the database is up, so you may need to log in to the database server to investigate further. If tnsping does not work, then the listener or the database is down or hung.

To further investigate issues, log in directly to the server to perform additional checks, such as a mount point filling up. Hopefully, if there was another issue, one of the logs or monitoring scripts reported it; however, the checks on the server might be necessary at this point.

ORACLE INSTANT CLIENT

Sometimes you are working with SAs and developers who sneed to test remote connectivity to a database but who do not have access to an Oracle installation with the SQL*Plus executable. In these situations, recommend that they download and use Oracle Instant Client or even SQLDeveloper (no client needed). It has a very small footprint and takes just a few minutes to install. Here are the steps:

1. Download the Instant Client from the Technology Network area of the Oracle web site (http://otn.oracle.com).

2. Create a directory for storing the files.

3. Unzip the files to that directory.

4. Set the LD_LIBRARY_PATH and PATH variables to include the directory to which the files were unzipped.

5. Connect to a remote database, using the easy connect syntax:

```
$ sqlplus user/pass@'host:port/database_service_name'
```

This process allows you to access SQL*Plus without having to perform a large and cumbersome Oracle install. Instant Client is available for most hardware platforms (Windows, Mac, Linux, and Unix). SQLDeveloper will take the database name, host, and port to be able to log in just as the instant client and this might prove to be a useful tool for them, too.

Investigating Disk Fullness

To further diagnose issues (such as running low on disk space), you need to log in directly to the remote server. Typically, you will need to log in as the owner of the Oracle software (usually the `oracle` OS account). When first logging in to a box, one issue that will cause a database to hang or have problems is a full mount point. The `df` command with the human readable -h switch assists with verifying disk fullness:

```
$ df -h
```

Any mount point that is full needs to be investigated. If the mount point that contains ORACLE_HOME becomes full, then you'll receive errors such as this when connecting to the database:

```
Linux Error: 28: No space left on device
```

To fix issues with a full mount point, first identify files that can be either moved or removed. Generally, start by looking for old trace files; often, there are old files that can be safely removed.

Locating the Alert Log and Trace Files

The default alert log directory path has this structure:

```
ORACLE_BASE/diag/rdbms/LOWER(<db_unique_name>)/<instance_name>/trace
Or in SQLPlus for the directory
SQL> show parameter background
```

Note You can override the default directory path for the alert log by setting the DIAGNOSTIC_DEST initialization parameter.

Usually, the db_unique_name is the same as the instance_name. In RAC and Data Guard environments, however, the db_unique_name is often different from the instance_name. You can verify the directory path with this query:

```
SQL> select value from v$diag_info where name = 'Diag Trace';
```

The name of the alert log follows this format:

```
alert_<ORACLE_SID>.log
```

You can also locate the alert log from the OS (whether or not the database is started) via these OS commands:

```
$ cd $ORACLE_BASE
$ find . -name alert_<ORACLE_SID>.log
```

In the prior find command, you will need to replace the <ORACLE_SID> value with the name of your database.

As shown in Chapter 3, it is advisable to set up an OS function that helps you navigate to the location of the alert log. Here is such a function (you will have to modify this to match your environment):

```
function bdump {
  if [ "$ORACLE_SID" = "O18C" ]; then
    cd /orahome/app/oracle/diag/rdbms/o18c/O18C/trace
  elif [ "$ORACLE_SID" = "O12c" ]; then
    cd /orahome/app/oracle/diag/rdbms/o12c/O12C/trace  elif [ "$ORACLE_SID"
    = "O11R2" ]; then
    cd /orahome/app/oracle/diag/rdbms/o11r2/O11R2/trace
  fi
}
```

You can now type bdump and will be placed in the working directory that contains the database alert log. Once you have found the correct file, inspect the most recent entries for errors, and then look for trace files in the same directory:

```
$ ls -altr *.tr*
```

If any of these trace files are more than several days old, consider moving or removing them.

Removing Files

Needless to say, be very careful when removing files. When trying to resolve issues, the last thing you want to do is make things worse. Accidentally removing one critical file can be catastrophic. For any files you identify as candidates for deletion, consider moving (instead of deleting) them. If you have a mount point that has free space, move the files there, and leave them for a couple of days before removing them.

Tip   Consider using the Automatic Diagnostic Repository Command Interpreter (ADRCI) utility to purge old trace files. For more details, see the Oracle Database Utilities Guide, which is available for download from the Technology Network area of the Oracle web site (`http://otn.oracle.com`).

If you have identified files that can be removed, first create a list of the files that will be removed before you actually delete them. Minimally, do this before removing any file:

```
$ ls -altr <file_name>
```

After viewing the results returned by the `ls` command, remove the file(s). This example uses the Linux/Unix `rm` command to permanently delete the file:

```
$ rm <file_name>
```

You can also remove files based on the age of the file. For example, say you determine that any trace files more than 2 days old can be safely deleted. Typically, the `find` command is used in conjunction with the `rm` command to accomplish this task. Before removing files, first display the results of the `find` command:

```
$ find . -type f -mtime +2 -name "*.tr*"
```

If you are satisfied with the list of files, then add the `rm` command to remove them:

```
$ find . -type f -mtime +2 -name "*.tr*" | xargs rm
```

In the prior line of code, the results of the `find` command are piped to the `xargs` command, which executes the `rm` command for every file found by the `find` command. This is an efficient method for deleting files based on age. However, be very sure you know which files will be deleted.

Another file that sometimes consumes large amounts of space is the `listener.log` file. Because this file is actively written to by the listener process, you cannot simply remove it. In Chapter 19, there is an example of this job, and this job can either be executed or look to see if it is running. If you need to preserve the contents of this file to inspect for connection issues, first copy it to a backup location (that contains free disk space), and then truncate the file. In this example the listener.log file is copied to ora01/backups, and then the file is truncated, as follows:

```
$ cp listener.log /u01/backups
```

Next, use the cat command to replace the contents of the listener.log with the /dev/null file (which contains zero bytes):

```
$ cat /dev/null > listener.log
```

The file needs to be replaced with nothing (/dev/null) instead of removing the file and letting a new one get created since this file is attached to a process, the listener. Replacing the file will allow the writes to continue to the file with the process running. This is also what needs to be done with the alert.log.

Inspecting the Alert Log

When dealing with database issues, the alert.log file should be one of the first files you check for relevant error messages. You can use either OS tools or the ADRCI utility to view the alert.log file and corresponding trace files.

Viewing the Alert Log via OS Tools

After navigating to the directory that contains the alert.log, you can see the most current messages by viewing the end (furthest down) of the file (in other words, the most current messages are written to the end of the file). To view the last 50 lines, use the tail command:

```
$ tail -50 alert_<SID>.log
```

You can continuously view the most current entries by using the f switch:

```
$ tail -f alert_<SID>.log
```

You can also directly open the alert.log with an OS editor (such as vi):

```
$ vi alert_<SID>.log
```

Sometimes, it is handy to define a function that will allow you to open the alert.log, regardless of your current working directory. The next few lines of code define a function that locates and opens the alert.log with the view command in either an 11g or a 10g environment:

```
#-----------------------------------------------------------#
# view alert log
  function valert {
  if [ "$ORACLE_SID" = "O18C" ]; then
    view /orahome/app/oracle/diag/rdbms/o18c/O18C/trace/alert_O18C.log
elif [ "$ORACLE_SID" = "O12C" ]; then
    view /orahome/app/oracle/diag/rdbms/o12c/O12C/trace/alert_O12C.log
    elif [ "$ORACLE_SID" = "O11R2" ]; then
    view /orahome/app/oracle/diag/rdbms/o11r2/O11R2/trace/alert_O11R2.log
  fi
  } # valert
#-----------------------------------------------------------#
```

Usually, the prior lines of code are placed in a startup file so that the function is automatically defined when you log in to a server. Once the function is defined, you can view the alert.log by typing this command:

```
$ valert
```

When inspecting the end of the alert.log, look for errors that indicate these types of issues:

- Archiver process hung, owing to inadequate disk space

- File system out of space

- Tablespace out of space

- ORA- 600 or 7445 errors

- Running out of memory in the buffer cache or shared pool

- Media error indicating that a data file is missing or damaged

- Error indicating an issue with writing an archivelog; for example,

```
ORA-19502: write error on file "/ora01/fra/o18c/archivelog/...
```

For a serious error message listed in the alert.log file, there is almost always a corresponding trace file. For example, here is the accompanying message for the prior error message:

```
Errors in file /orahome/app/oracle/diag/rdbms/o18c/O18C/trace/O18C_
ora_5665.trc
```

Inspecting the trace file will often (but not always) provide additional insight into the issue.

Viewing the alert.log, Using the ADRCI Utility

You can use the ADRCI utility to view the contents of the alert.log file. Run the following command from the OS to start the ADRCI utility:

```
$ adrci
```

You should be presented with a prompt:

```
adrci>
```

Use the SHOW ALERT command to view the alert.log file:

```
adrci> show alert
```

If there are multiple Oracle homes on the server, then you will be prompted to choose which alert.log you want to view. The SHOW ALERT command will open the alert.log with the utility that has been set as the default editor for your OS. On Linux/Unix systems, the default editor is derived from the OS EDITOR variable (which is usually set to a utility such as vi).

Tip   When presented with the alert.log, if you are unfamiliar with vi and want to exit, first press the Escape key, then press and hold down the Shift key while pressing the colon (:) key. Next, type q!. That should exit you out of the vi editor and back to the ADRCI prompt.

You can override the default editor within ADRCI, using the SET EDITOR command. This example sets the default editor to emacs:

```
adrci> set editor emacs
```

You can view the last N number of lines in the alert.log with the TAIL option. The following command shows the last 50 lines of the alert.log:

```
adrci> show alert -tail 50
```

If you have multiple Oracle homes, you may see a message such as this:

```
DIA-48449: Tail alert can only apply to single ADR home
```

The ADRCI utility does not assume that you want to work with one Oracle home over another on a server. To specifically set the Oracle home for the ADRCI utility, first use the SHOW HOMES command to display all available Oracle homes:

```
adrci> show homes
```

Here is some sample output for this server:

```
diag/rdbms/o18c/O18C
diag/rdbms/o18cp/O18CP
```

Now, use the SET HOMEPATH command. This sets the HOMEPATH to diag/rdbms/e64208/E64208:

```
adrci> set homepath  diag/rdbms/o18c/O18C
```

To continuously display the end of the file, use this command:

```
adrci> show alert -tail -f
```

Press Ctrl+C to break off continuously viewing the alert.log file. To display lines from the alert.log that contain specific strings, use the MESSAGE_TEXT LIKE command. This example shows messages that contain the ORA-27037 string:

```
adrci> show alert -p "MESSAGE_TEXT LIKE '%ORA-27037%'"
```

You will be presented with a file that contains all the lines in the alert.log that match the specified string.

Tip   See the Oracle Database Utilities Guide for full details on how to use the ADRCI utility.

Identifying Bottlenecks via OS Utilities

In the Oracle world, there is sometimes a tendency to assume that you have a dedicated machine for one Oracle database. Furthermore, this database is the latest version of Oracle, fully patched, and monitored by a sophisticated graphical tool. This database environment is completely automated and kept trouble free through the use of visual tools that quickly pinpoint problems and efficiently isolate and resolve issues. If you live in this ideal world, then you probably do not need any of the material in this chapter.

Let me paint a slightly different picture. An environment in which one machine has a dozen databases running on it. There's a MySQL database; a PostgreSQL database; and a mix of Oracle version 11g, 12c, and 18c databases. Furthermore, many of these old databases are on nonterminal releases of Oracle and are therefore not supported by Oracle Support. There are no plans to upgrade any of these unsupported databases because the business cannot take the risk of potentially breaking the applications that depend on these databases. Note: the security risk to the business should also be understood at this point; nevertheless, multiple database platforms are a possibility.

So, what does one do in this type of environment when somebody reports that a database application is performing poorly? In this scenario, it is often something in a different database that is causing other applications on the box to behave poorly. It may not be an Oracle process or an Oracle database that is causing problems.

In this situation, it is almost always more effective to start investigating issues by using an OS tool. The OS tools are database agnostic. OS performance utilities help pinpoint where the most resources are consumed, regardless of database vendor or version.

In Linux/Unix environments, there are several tools available for monitoring resource usage. Table 21-1 summarizes the most commonly used OS utilities for diagnosing performance issues. Being familiar with how these OS commands work and how to interpret the output will allow you to better diagnose server performance issues, especially when it is a non-Oracle or even a non-database process that is tanking performance for every other application on the box.

Table 21-1. *Performance and Monitoring Utilities*

Tool	Purpose
vmstat	Monitors processes, CPU, memory, and disk I/O bottlenecks
top	Identifies sessions consuming the most resources
watch	Periodically runs another command
ps	Identifies highest CPU- and memory-consuming sessions; used to identify Oracle sessions consuming the most system resources
mpstat	Reports CPU statistics
sar	Displays CPU, memory, disk I/O, and network usage, both current and historical
free	Displays free and used memory
df	Reports on free disk space
du	Displays disk usage
iostat	Displays disk I/O statistics
netstat	Reports on network statistics

When diagnosing performance issues, it is useful to determine where the OS is constrained. For instance, try to identify whether the issue is related to CPU, memory, or I/O, or a combination of these.

Identifying System Bottlenecks

Whenever there are application performance issues or availability problems, seemingly (from the DBA's perspective), the first question asked is, "What's wrong with the database?" Regardless of the source of the problem, the onus is often on the DBA to establish whether the database is behaving well. I usually approach this issue by determining which system-wide resources are being consumed. There are two Linux/Unix OS tools that are particularly useful for displaying system-wide resource usage:

- vmstat

- top

The vmstat (virtual memory statistics) tool is intended to help you quickly identify bottlenecks on your server. The top utility provides a dynamic, real-time view of system resource usage. These two utilities are discussed in the next two sections.

Using vmstat

The vmstat utility displays real-time performance information about processes, memory, paging, disk I/O, and CPU usage. This example shows using vmstat to display the default output, with no options specified:

```
$ vmstat
procs -----------memory---------- ---swap-- -----io---- --system-- ----cpu----
 r  b   swpd   free   buff  cache   si   so   bi   bo   in   cs us sy id wa
14  0  52340  25272   3068 1662704    0    0   63   76    9   31 15  1 84  0
```

Here are some general heuristics you can use when interpreting the output of vmstat:

- If the wa (time waiting for I/O) column is high, this is usually an indication that the storage subsystem is overloaded.

- If b (processes blocked) is consistently greater than 0, then you may not have enough CPU processing power.

- If so (memory swapped out to disk) and si (memory swapped in from disk) are consistently greater than 0, you may have a memory bottleneck.

By default, only one line of server statistics is displayed when running vmstat (without supplying any options). This one line of output gives average statistics calculated from the last time the system was rebooted. This is fine for a quick snapshot. However, if you want to gather metrics over a period of time, use vmstat with this syntax:

```
$ vmstat <interval in seconds> <number of intervals>
```

While in this mode, vmstat reports statistics, sampling from one interval to the next. For example, if you wanted to report system statistics every 2 seconds, for 10 intervals, you'd issue this command:

```
$ vmstat 2 10
```

You can also send the vmstat output to a file. This is useful for analyzing historical performance over a period of time. This example samples statistics every 5 seconds, for a total of 60 reports, and records the output in a file:

```
$ vmstat 5 60 > vmout.perf
```

Additionally, the vmstat utility can be used with the watch tool. The watch command is used to execute another program on a periodic basis. In this example, watch runs the vmstat command every 5 seconds and highlights on the screen any differences between each snapshot:

```
$ watch -n 5 -d vmstat
Every 5.0s: vmstat                                          Thu Aug  9 13:27:57 2007
procs -----------memory---------- ---swap-- -----io---- --system-- ----cpu----
 r  b   swpd   free   buff  cache  si  so   bi   bo   in   cs us sy id wa
 0  0    144  15900  64620 1655100   0   0    1    7   16    4  0  0 99  0
```

When running vmstat in watch -d (differences) mode, you'll visually see changes on your screen, from snapshot to snapshot. To exit watch, press Ctrl+C.

Note that the default unit of measure for the memory columns of vmstat is kilobytes. If you want to view the memory statistics in megabytes, then use the S m (statistics in megabytes) option:

```
$ vmstat -S m
```

Tip Use the man vmstat or vmstat --help command for further documentation on this utility.

Using top

Another tool for identifying resource-intensive processes is the top command. Use this utility to quickly identify which processes are the highest consumers of resources on the server. By default, top will repetitively refresh (every 3 seconds) information regarding the most CPU-intensive processes. The simplest way to run top is as follows:

```
$ top
```

Here is a fragment of the output:

```
top - 13:34:32 up 19 min,  2 users,  load average: 0.05, 0.16, 0.24
Tasks: 176 total,   1 running, 175 sleeping,   0 stopped,   0 zombie
Cpu(s): 2.0%us,  0.7%sy,  0.0%ni, 91.6%id,  5.7%wa,  0.0%hi,  0.0%si,  0.0%st
Mem:    787028k total,   748744k used,    38284k free,      1836k buffers
Swap: 1605624k total,    31896k used, 1573728k free,    377668k cached

  PID USER      PR  NI  VIRT  RES  SHR S %CPU %MEM    TIME+  COMMAND
 4683 root      20   0  279m  14m 7268 S  2.0  1.9  0:01.61 gnome-terminal
 3826 root      20   0  218m 9944 4200 S  1.7  1.3  0:02.80 Xorg
 3592 oracle    -2   0  601m  18m  15m S  0.7  2.4  0:09.36 ora_vktm_o12c
```

The process identifiers (PIDs) of the top-consuming sessions are listed in the first column (PID). You can use this information to see if a PID maps to a database process (see the next section, "Mapping an OS Process to an SQL Statement," for details on mapping a PID to a database process).

While top is running, you can interactively change its output. For example, if you type the redirection character (>), this will move the column that top is sorting one position to the right. Table 21-2 lists some key features that you can use to alter the top display to the desired format.

Table 21-2. *Commands to Interactively Change the* top *Output*

Command	Function
Spacebar	Immediately refreshes the output
< or >	Moves the sort column one position to the left or to the right. By default, top sorts on the CPU column.
D	Changes the refresh time
R	Reverses the sort order
Z	Toggles the color output
H	Displays the Help menu
F or O	Chooses a sort column

Type q, or press Ctrl+C, to exit top. Table 21-3 describes several of the columns displayed in the default output of top.

Table 21-3. *Column Descriptions of the* top *Output*

Column	Description
PID	Unique process identifier
USER	OS username running the process
PR	Priority of the process
NI	Nice value or process. Negative value means high priority; positive value means low priority.
VIRT	Total virtual memory used by process
RES	Nonswapped physical memory used by process
SHR	Shared memory used by process
S	Process status
CPU	Processes percentage of CPU consumption since last screen refresh
MEM	Percentage of physical memory the process is consuming
TIME	Total CPU time used by process
TIME+	Total CPU time, showing hundredths of seconds, used by process
COMMAND	Command line used to start a process

You can also run top using the b (batch mode) option and send the output to a file for later analysis:

```
$ top -b > tophat.out
```

While running in batch mode, the top command will run until you kill it (with Ctrl+C) or until it reaches a specified number of iterations. You could run the previous top command in batch mode, with a combination of nohup and & to keep it running, regardless of whether you were logged in to the system. The danger there is that you might forget about it and eventually create a very large output file (and an angry SA).

If you have a particular process that you are interested in monitoring, use the p option to monitor a PID or the U option to monitor a username. You can also specify a delay and the number of iterations by using the d and -n options. The following example monitors the oracle user with a delay of 5 seconds, for 25 iterations:

```
$ top -u oracle -d 5 -n 25
```

Tip Use the man top or top --help command to list all the options available in your OS version.

Mapping an Operating System Process to an SQL Statement

When identifying OS processes, it is useful to view which processes are consuming the greatest amount of CPU. If the resource hog is a database process, it is also useful to map the OS process to a database job or query. To determine the ID of the processes consuming the most CPU resources, use a command such as ps, like so:

```
$ ps -e -o pcpu,pid,user,tty,args | sort -n -k 1 -r | head
```

Here is a snippet of the output:

```
14.6 24875 oracle    ?       oracleo18c (DESCRIPTION=(LOCAL=YES)(ADDRESS=...
 0.8 21613 oracle    ?       ora_vktm_o18c
 0.1 21679 oracle    ?       ora_mmon_o18c
```

From the output, you can see that the OS session 24875 is the top consumer of CPU resources. The output also indicates that the process is associated with the o12c database. With that information in hand, log in to the appropriate database, and use the following SQL statement to determine what type of program is associated with the OS process 24875:

```
SQL> select
  'USERNAME : ' || s.username|| chr(10) ||
  'OSUSER   : ' || s.osuser  || chr(10) ||
  'PROGRAM  : ' || s.program || chr(10) ||
  'SPID     : ' || p.spid    || chr(10) ||
  'SID      : ' || s.sid     || chr(10) ||
  'SERIAL#  : ' || s.serial# || chr(10) ||
```

```
  'MACHINE  : ' || s.machine || chr(10) ||
  'TERMINAL : ' || s.terminal
from v$session s,
     v$process p
where s.paddr = p.addr
and    p.spid  = &PID_FROM_OS;
```

When you run the command, SQL*Plus will prompt you for the value to use in place of &PID_FROM_OS. In this example, you'll enter 24875. Here is the relevant output:

```
USERNAME : MV_MAINT
OSUSER   : oracle
PROGRAM  : sqlplus@speed2 (TNS V1-V3)
SPID     : 24875
SID      : 111
SERIAL#  : 899
MACHINE  : speed2
TERMINAL : pts/4
```

In this output the PROGRAM value indicates that an SQL*Plus session is the program consuming the inordinate amount of resources on the server. Next, run the following query to display the SQL statement associated with the OS PID (in this example, the server process identifier [SPID] is 24875):

```
SQL> select
  'USERNAME : ' || s.username || chr(10) ||
  'OSUSER   : ' || s.osuser   || chr(10) ||
  'PROGRAM  : ' || s.program  || chr(10) ||
  'SPID     : ' || p.spid     || chr(10) ||
  'SID      : ' || s.sid      || chr(10) ||
  'SERIAL#  : ' || s.serial#  || chr(10) ||
  'MACHINE  : ' || s.machine  || chr(10) ||
  'TERMINAL : ' || s.terminal || chr(10) ||
  'SQL TEXT : ' || sa.sql_text
from v$process p,
v$session s,
v$sqlarea sa
```

```
where p.addr = s.paddr
and s.username is not null
and s.sql_address = sa.address(+)
and s.sql_hash_value = sa.hash_value(+)
and p.spid= &PID_FROM_OS;
```

The results show the resource-consuming SQL as part of the output, in the SQL TEXT column. Here is a snippet of the output:

```
USERNAME : MV_MAINT
OSUSER   : oracle
PROGRAM  : sqlplus@speed2 (TNS V1-V3)
SPID     : 24875
SID      : 111
SERIAL#  : 899
MACHINE  : speed2
TERMINAL : pts/4
SQL TEXT : select a.table_name from dba_tables a,dba_indexes b,dba_objects c...
```

When you run multiple databases on one server and are experiencing server performance issues, it can sometimes be difficult to pinpoint which database and associated process are causing the problems. In these situations, you have to use an OS tool to identify the top resource-consuming sessions on the system.

In a Linux/Unix environment, you can use utilities such as ps, top, or vmstat to identify top-consuming OS processes. The ps utility is handy because it lets you identify processes consuming the most CPU or memory. The previous ps command identified the top-consuming CPU processes. Here, it is used to identify the top Oracle memory-using processes:

```
$ ps -e -o pmem,pid,user,tty,args | grep -i oracle | sort -n -k 1 -r | head
```

Once you have identified a top-consuming process associated with a database, you can query the data dictionary views, based on the SPID, to identify what the database process is executing.

OS WATCHER

Oracle provides a collection of scripts that gather and store metrics for CPU, memory, disk, and network usage. On Linux/Unix systems, the OS Watcher tool suite automates the gathering of statistics, using tools such as `top`, `vmstat`, `iostat`, `mpstat`, `netstat`, and `traceroute`. This utility also has an optional graphical component for visually displaying performance metrics.

You can obtain OS Watcher from Oracle's MOS web site. For the Linux/Unix version, see MOS note 301137.1 or the document titled "OS Watcher User Guide." For details on the Windows version of OS Watcher, see MOS note 433472.1.

Finding Resource-Intensive SQL Statements

One of the best ways to isolate a poorly performing query is to have a user or developer complain about a specific SQL statement. In this situation, there is no detective work involved. You can directly pinpoint the SQL query that is in need of tuning.

However, you do not often have the luxury of a human letting you know specifically where to look when investigating performance issues. There are a number of methods for determining which SQL statements are consuming the most resources in a database:

- Real-time execution statistics
- Near real-time statistics
- Oracle performance reports

These techniques are described in the next several sections.

Monitoring Real-Time SQL Execution Statistics

You can use the following query to select from the V$SQL_MONITOR to monitor the near real-time resource consumption of SQL queries:

```
SQL> select * from (
select a.sid session_id, a.sql_id
,a.status
,a.cpu_time/1000000 cpu_sec
```

```
,a.buffer_gets, a.disk_reads
,b.sql_text sql_text
from v$sql_monitor a
    ,v$sql b
where a.sql_id = b.sql_id
order by a.cpu_time desc)
where rownum <=20;
```

The output for this query does not fit easily onto a page. Here is a subset of the output:

```
SESSION_ID  SQL_ID         STATUS     CPU_SEC  BUFFER_GETS  DISK_READS
----------  -------------  ---------  -------- -----------  -----------
SQL_TEXT
---------
       139  d07nngmx93rq7  DONE        331.88  5708                3490 select
count(*)
       130  9dtu8zn9yy4uc  EXECUTING   11.55   5710                 248 select
task_name
```

In the query, an inline view is used to first retrieve all records and organize them by CPU_TIME, in descending order. The outer query then limits the result set to the top 20 rows, using the ROWNUM pseudocolumn. You can modify the previous query to order the results by the statistic of your choice or to display only the queries that are currently executing. For example, the next SQL statement monitors currently executing queries, ordered by the number of disk reads:

```
SQL> select * from (
select a.sid session_id, a.sql_id, a.status
,a.cpu_time/1000000 cpu_sec
,a.buffer_gets, a.disk_reads
,substr(b.sql_text,1,35) sql_text
from v$sql_monitor a
    ,v$sql b
where a.sql_id = b.sql_id
and    a.status='EXECUTING'
order by a.disk_reads desc)
where rownum <=20;
```

The statistics in V$SQL_MONITOR are updated every second, so you can view resource consumption as it changes. These statistics are gathered by default if an SQL statement runs in parallel or consumes more than 5 seconds of CPU or I/O time.

The V$SQL_MONITOR view includes a subset of statistics contained in the VSQL, VSQLAREA, and V$SQLSTATS views. The V$SQL_MONITOR view displays real-time statistics for each execution of a resource-intensive SQL statement, whereas VSQL, VSQLAREA, and V$SQLSTATS contain cumulative sets of statistics resulting from several executions of an SQL statement.

Once the SQL statement execution ends, the runtime statistics are not immediately flushed from V$SQL_MONITOR. Depending on activity in your database, the statistics can be available for some time. If you have a very active database, however, the statistics can potentially be flushed soon after the query finishes.

Tip   You can uniquely identify the execution of an SQL statement in V$SQL_MONITOR from a combination of the following columns: SQL_ID, SQL_EXEC_START, SQL_EXEC_ID.

You can also query views such as V$SQLSTATS to determine which SQL statements are consuming an inordinate amount of resources. For example, use the following query to identify the ten most resource-intensive queries, based on CPU time:

```
SQL> select * from(
select s.sid, s.username, s.sql_id
,sa.elapsed_time/1000000, sa.cpu_time/1000000
,sa.buffer_gets, sa.sql_text
from v$sqlarea sa
    ,v$session s
where s.sql_hash_value = sa.hash_value
and   s.sql_address    = sa.address
and   s.username is not null
order by sa.cpu_time desc)
where rownum <= 10;
```

In the prior query, an inline view is used to first retrieve all records and sort the output by CPU_TIME, in descending order. The outer query then limits the result set to the top 10 rows, using the ROWNUM pseudocolumn. The query can be easily modified to sort by a column other than CPU_TIME. For instance, if you want to report resource usage by BUFFER_GETS, simply substitute BUFFER_GETS for CPU_TIME in the ORDER BY clause. The CPU_TIME column is calculated in microseconds; to convert it to seconds, it is divided by 1,000,000.

Tip Keep in mind that V$SQLAREA contains statistics that are cumulative for the duration for a given session. So, if a session runs an identical query several times, the statistics for that connection will be the total for all the runs of a query. In contrast, V$SQL_MONITOR shows statistics that have accumulated for the current run of a given SQL statement. Therefore, each time a query runs, new statistics are reported for that query in V$SQL_MONITOR.

Running Oracle Diagnostic Utilities

Oracle provides several utilities for diagnosing database performance issues:

- Automatic workload repository (AWR)
- Automatic database diagnostic monitor (ADDM)
- Active session history (ASH)
- Statspack

AWR, ADDM, and ASH were introduced many years ago, in Oracle Database 10g. These tools provide advanced reporting capabilities that allow you to troubleshoot and resolve performance issues. These new utilities require an extra license from Oracle. The older Statspack utility is free and requires no license.

All these tools rely heavily on the underlying V$ dynamic performance views. Oracle maintains a vast collection of these views, which track and accumulate metrics of database performance. For example, if you run the following query, you will notice that for Oracle Database 18c, there are approximately 760 V$ views:

```
SQL> select count(*) from v$fixed_table where name like 'V$%';
```

```
  COUNT(*)
----------
       767
```

V$FIXED_TABLE provides information about the dynamic performance views including the underlying X$ tables and GV$ views for RAC environments.

The Oracle performance utilities rely on periodic snapshots gathered from these internal performance views. Two of the most useful views, with regard to performance statistics, are the V$SYSSTAT and V$SESSTAT views. The V$SYSSTAT view offers more than 800 types of database statistics. This V$SYSSTAT view contains information about the entire database, whereas the V$SESSTAT view contains statistics on individual sessions. A few of the values in the V$SYSSTAT and V$SESSTAT views represent the current usage of the resource. These values are

- Opened cursors current

- Logins current

- Session cursor cache current

- Work area memory allocated

The rest of the values are cumulative. The values in V$SYSSTAT are cumulative for the entire database, from the time the instance was started. The values in V$SESSTAT are cumulative per session, from the time the session was started. Some of the more important performance-related cumulative values are these:

- CPU used

- Consistent gets

- Physical reads

- Physical writes

For the cumulative statistics, the way to measure periodic usage is to note the value of a statistic at a starting point, then note the value again at a later point in time and capture the delta. This is the approach used by the Oracle performance utilities, such as AWR and Statspack. Periodically, Oracle will take snapshots of the dynamic wait interface views and store them in a repository.

The following sections detail how to access AWR, ADDM, ASH, and Statspack via the SQL command line.

> **Tip**   You can access AWR, ADDM, and ASH from the Enterprise Manager. If you have access to the Enterprise Manager, you will find the interface fairly intuitive and visually helpful.

Using AWR

An AWR report is good for viewing the entire system's performance and identifying the top resource-consuming SQL queries. Run the following script to generate an AWR report:

```
SQL> @?/rdbms/admin/awrrpt
```

From the AWR output, you can identify top resource-consuming statements by examining the "SQL Ordered by Elapsed Time" or "SQL Ordered by CPU Time" section of the report. Here is some sample output:

```
SQL ordered by CPU Time              DB/Inst: O18C/o18c  Snaps: 1668-1669
-> Resources reported for PL/SQL code includes the resources used by all SQL
   statements called by the code.
-> %Total - CPU Time     as a percentage of Total DB CPU
-> %CPU   - CPU Time     as a percentage of Elapsed Time
-> %IO    - User I/O Time as a percentage of Elapsed Time
-> Captured SQL account for   3.0E+03% of Total CPU Time (s):          0
-> Captured PL/SQL account for  550.9% of Total CPU Time (s):          0

    CPU                    CPU per      Elapsed
  Time (s) Executions   Exec (s) %Total  Time (s)  %CPU   %IO          SQL Id
---------- ------------ ---------- ------ ---------- ------ ----- --------------
     3.2            1      3.24  930.5      10.5   30.9  74.9  93jktd5vtxb98
```

Oracle will automatically take a snapshot of your database once an hour and populate the underlying AWR tables that store the statistics. By default, 7 days of statistics are retained.

You can also generate an AWR report for a specific SQL statement by running the awrsqrpt.sql report. When you run the following script, you will be prompted for the SQL_ID of the query of interest:

```
SQL> @?/rdbms/admin/awrsqrpt.sql
```

Using ADDM

The ADDM report provides useful information on which SQL statements are candidates for tuning. Use the following SQL script to generate an ADDM report:

```
SQL> @?/rdbms/admin/addmrpt
```

Look for the section of the report labeled "SQL Statements Consuming Significant Database Time." Here is some sample output:

```
FINDING 2: 29% impact (65043 seconds)
-------------------------------------
SQL statements consuming significant database time were found.

   RECOMMENDATION 1: SQL Tuning, 6.7% benefit (14843 seconds)
      ACTION: Investigate the SQL statement with SQL_ID "46cc3t7ym5sx0" for
```

The ADDM report analyzes data in the AWR tables to identify potential bottlenecks and high resource-consuming SQL queries.

Using ASH

The ASH report allows you to focus on short-lived SQL statements that have been recently run and that may have only executed for briefly. Run the following script to generate an ASH report:

```
SQL> @?/rdbms/admin/ashrpt
```

Search the output for the section labeled "Top SQL." Here is some sample output:

```
Top SQL with Top Events            DB/Inst: O18C/o18c   (Jan 30 14:49 to 15:14)
```

SQL ID	Planhash	Sampled # of Executions	% Activity
Event	% Event Top Row Source		% RwSrc
dx5auh1xb98k5	1677482778	1	46.57
CPU + Wait for CPU	46.57 HASH JOIN		23.53

The previous output indicates that the query is waiting for CPU resources. In this scenario, the problem may be that another query is consuming the CPU resources.

When is the ASH report more useful than the AWR or ADDM report? The AWR and ADDM output shows top-consuming SQL in terms of total database time. If the SQL performance problem is transient and short-lived, it may not appear on the AWR and ADDM reports. In these situations, an ASH report is more useful.

Using Statspack

If you do not have a license to use the AWR, ADDM, and ASH reports, the free Statspack utility can help you identify poorly performing SQL statements. Run the following script as SYS to install Statspack:

```
SQL> @?/rdbms/admin/spcreate.sql
```

The prior script creates a PERFSTAT user that owns the Statspack repository. Once crated, then connect as the PERFSTAT user, and run this script to enable the automatic gathering of Statspack statistics:

```
SQL> @ ?/rdbms/admin/spauto.sql
```

After some snapshots have been gathered, you can run the following script as the PERFSTAT user to create a Statspack report:

```
SQL> @?/rdbms/admin/spreport.sql
```

Once the report is created, search for the section labeled "SQL Ordered by CPU." Here is some sample output:

```
SQL ordered by CPU  DB/Inst: 018C/o18c  Snaps: 30-31
-> Total DB CPU (s):          1,432
-> Captured SQL accounts for  100.5% of Total DB CPU
-> SQL reported below exceeded  1.0% of Total DB CPU
```

CPU Time (s)	Executions	CPU per Exec (s)	%Total	Elapsd Time (s)	Buffer Gets	Old Hash Value
1430.41	1	1430.41	99.9	1432.49	482	690392559

Module: SQL*Plus
select a.table_name from my_tables

Tip   See the ORACLE_HOME/rdbms/admin/spdoc.txt file for Statspack documentation.

Detecting and Resolving Locking Issues

Sometimes, a developer or application user will report that a process that normally takes seconds to run is now taking several minutes and does not appear to be doing anything. In these situations, the problem is usually one of the following:

- Space-related issue (e.g., the archive redo destination is full and has suspended all transactions).

- A process has a lock on a table row and is not committing or rolling back, thus preventing another session from modifying the same row.

In this scenario, first check the alert.log to see if there are any obvious issues that have occurred recently (such as a tablespace's not being able to allocate another extent). If there is nothing obvious in the alert.log file, run an SQL query to look for locking issues. The query listed here is a more sophisticated version of the lock-detecting script introduced in Chapter 3. This query shows information such as the locking session SQL statement and the waiting SQL statement:

```
SQL> set lines 80
SQL> col blkg_user form a10
SQL> col blkg_machine form a10
SQL> col blkg_sid form 99999999
SQL> col wait_user form a10
SQL> col wait_machine form a10
SQL> col wait_sid form 9999999
```

```
SQL> col obj_own form a10
SQL> col obj_name form a10
SQL> col blkg_sql form a50
SQL> col wait_sql form a50
--
SQL> select
 s1.username      blkg_user, s1.machine      blkg_machine
,s1.sid           blkg_sid, s1.serial#       blkg_serialnum
,s1.process       blkg_OS_PID
,substr(b1.sql_text,1,50) blkg_sql
,chr(10)
,s2.username      wait_user, s2.machine      wait_machine
,s2.sid           wait_sid, s2.serial#       wait_serialnum
,s2.process       wait_OS_PID
,substr(w1.sql_text,1,50) wait_sql
,lo.object_id     blkd_obj_id
,do.owner         obj_own, do.object_name obj_name
from v$lock           l1
    ,v$session        s1
    ,v$lock           l2
    ,v$session        s2
    ,v$locked_object lo
    ,v$sqlarea        b1
    ,v$sqlarea        w1
    ,dba_objects      do
where s1.sid = l1.sid
and s2.sid = l2.sid
and l1.id1 = l2.id1
and s1.sid = lo.session_id
and lo.object_id = do.object_id
and l1.block = 1
and s1.prev_sql_addr = b1.address
and s2.sql_address = w1.address
and l2.request > 0;
```

The output from this query does not fit well on one page. When running this query, you will have to format it so that it is on your screen. Here is some sample output, indicating that the SALES table is locked and that another process is waiting for the lock to be released:

```
BLKG_USER  BLKG_MACHI  BLKG_SID BLKG_SERIALNUM BLKG_OS_PID
---------- ----------  -------- -------------- ------------------------
BLKG_SQL                                            C WAIT_USER  WAIT_MACHI
--------------------------------------------------- - ---------- ----------
WAIT_SID WAIT_SERIALNUM WAIT_OS_PID
-------- -------------- ------------------------
WAIT_SQL                                            BLKD_OBJ_ID OBJ_OWN
--------------------------------------------------- ----------- ----------
OBJ_NAME
----------
MV_MAINT   speed2              32              487 26216
update sales set sales_amt=100 where sales_id=1       MV_MAINT    speed2
     116            319 25851
```

This situation is typical when applications do not explicitly issue a COMMIT or ROLLBACK at appropriate times in the code. This leaves a lock on a row and prevents a transaction from continuing until the lock is released. In this scenario, you can try to locate the user that is blocking the transaction and see if the user needs to click a button that says something like "Commit your changes." If that is not possible, you can manually kill one of the sessions. Keep in mind that terminating a session may have unforeseen effects (such as rolling back data that a user thought was committed).

If you decide to kill one of the user sessions, you need to identify the SID and serial number of the session you want to terminate. Once identified, use the ALTER SYSTEM KILL SESSION statement to terminate the session:

```
SQL> alter system kill session '32,487';
```

Again, be careful when killing sessions. Ensure that you know the impact of killing a session and thereby rolling back any active transactions currently open in that session.

The other way to kill a session is to use an OS command such as KILL. In the prior output, you can identify the OS processes from the BLKG_OS_PID and WAIT_OS_PID columns. Before you terminate a process from the OS, ensure that the process is not critical. For this example, to terminate the blocking OS process, first check the blocking PID:

```
$ ps -ef | grep 26216
```

Here is some sample output:

```
oracle   26222 26216  0 16:49 ?        00:00:00 oracleo12c
```

Next, use the KILL command, as shown:

```
$ kill -9  26216
```

The KILL command will unceremoniously terminate a process. Any open transactions associated with the process will be rolled back by the Oracle process monitor.

Resolving Open-Cursor Issues

The OPEN_CURSORS initialization parameter determines the maximum number of cursors a session can have open. This setting is per session. The default value of 50 is usually too low for any application. When an application exceeds the number of open cursors allowed, the following error is thrown:

```
ORA-01000: maximum open cursors exceeded
```

Usually, the prior error is encountered when

- OPEN_CURSORS initialization parameter is set too low

- Developers write code that does not close cursors properly

To investigate this issue, first determine the current setting of the parameter:

```
SQL> show parameter open_cursors;
```

If the value is less than 300, consider setting it higher. It is typical to set this value to 1,000 for busy OLTP systems. You can dynamically modify the value while your database is open, as shown:

```
SQL> alter system set open_cursors=1000;
```

If you are using an spfile, consider making the change both in memory and in the spfile, at the same time:

```
SQL> alter system set open_cursors=1000 scope=both;
```

After setting OPEN_CURSORS to a higher value, if the application continues to exceed the maximum value, you probably have an issue with code that is not properly closing cursors.

If you work in an environment that has thousands of connections to the database, you may want to view only the top cursor-consuming sessions. The following query uses an inline view and the pseudocolumn ROWNUM to display the top 20 values:

```
SQL> select * from (
select a.value, c.username, c.machine, c.sid, c.serial#
from v$sesstat  a
    ,v$statname b
    ,v$session  c
where a.statistic# = b.statistic#
and   c.sid        = a.sid
and   b.name       = 'opened cursors current'
and   a.value      != 0
and   c.username IS NOT NULL
order by 1 desc,2)
where rownum < 21;
```

If a single session has more than 1,000 open cursors, then the code is probably written such that the cursors are not closing. When the limit is reached, somebody should inspect the application code to determine if a cursor is not being closed.

Tip   It is recommended that you query V$SESSION instead of V$OPEN_CURSOR to determine the number of open cursors. V$SESSION provides a more accurate count of the cursors currently open.

Troubleshooting Undo Tablespace Issues

Problems with the undo tablespace are usually of the following nature:

- ORA-01555: snapshot too old

- ORA-30036: unable to extend segment by ... in undo tablespace 'UNDOTBS1'

    The prior errors can be caused by many different issues, such as incorrect sizing of the undo tablespace or poorly written SQL or PL/SQL code. Snapshot being too old can also occur during exports due to updates to very large tables, and normally seen when either the undo retention or size is not properly set. For an export, it is an easy fix to rerun at a quieter time.

Determining if Undo Is Correctly Sized

Suppose you have a long-running SQL statement that is throwing an ORA-01555: snapshot too old error, and you want to determine if adding space to the undo tablespace might help alleviate the issue. Run this next query to identify potential issues with your undo tablespace. The query checks for issues that have occurred within the last day:

```
SQL> select to_char(begin_time,'MM-DD-YYYY HH24:MI') begin_time
,ssolderrcnt     ORA_01555_cnt, nospaceerrcnt  no_space_cnt
,txncount        max_num_txns, maxquerylen     max_query_len
,expiredblks     blck_in_expired
from v$undostat
where begin_time > sysdate - 1
order by begin_time;
```

Here is some sample output. Part of the output has been omitted to fit this on the page:

BEGIN_TIME	ORA_01555_CNT	NO_SPACE_CNT	MAX_NUM_TXNS	BLCK_IN_EXPIRED
01-31-2013 08:21	0	0	51	0
01-31-2013 08:31	0	0	0	0
01-31-2013 12:11	0	0	629	256

The ORA_01555_CNT column indicates the number of times your database has encountered the ORA-01555: snapshot too old error. If this column reports a nonzero value, you need to do one or more of the following tasks:

- Ensure that code does not contain COMMIT statements within cursor loops.
- Tune the SQL statement throwing the error so that it runs faster.
- Ensure that you have good statistics (so that your SQL runs efficiently).
- Increase the UNDO_RETENTION initialization parameter.

The NO_SPACE_CNT column displays the number of times space was requested in the undo tablespace. In this example, there were no such requests. If the NO_SPACE_CNT is reporting a nonzero value, however, you may need to add more space to your undo tablespace.

A maximum of 4 days' worth of information is stored in the V$UNDOSTAT view. The statistics are gathered every 10 minutes, for a maximum of 576 rows in the table. If you have stopped and started your database within the last 4 days, this view will only contain information from the time you last started your database.

Another way to get advice on the undo tablespace sizing is to use the Oracle Undo Advisor, which you can invoke by querying the PL/SQL DBMS_UNDO_ADV package from a SELECT statement. The following query displays the current undo size and the recommended size for an undo retention setting of 900 seconds:

```
SQL> select
  sum(bytes)/1024/1024                    cur_mb_size
 ,dbms_undo_adv.required_undo_size(900) req_mb_size
from dba_data_files
where tablespace_name =
  (select
    value
   from v$parameter
   where name = 'undo tablespace');
```

Here is some sample output:

```
CUR_MB_SIZE REQ_MB_SIZE
----------- -----------
      36864       20897
```

The output shows that the undo tablespace currently has 36.8GB allocated to it. In the prior query, you used 900 seconds as the amount of time to retain information in the undo tablespace. To retain undo information for 900 seconds, the Oracle Undo Advisor estimates that the undo tablespace should be 20.8GB. In this example, the undo tablespace is sized adequately. If it were not sized adequately, you would have to either add space to an existing data file or add a data file to the undo tablespace.

Here is a slightly more complex example of using the Oracle Undo Advisor to find the required size of the undo tablespace. This example uses PL/SQL to display information about potential issues and recommendations for fixing the problem:

```
SQL> SET SERVEROUT ON SIZE 1000000
SQL> DECLARE
 pro    VARCHAR2(200);
 rec    VARCHAR2(200);
 rtn    VARCHAR2(200);
 ret    NUMBER;
 utb    NUMBER;
 retval NUMBER;
BEGIN
  DBMS_OUTPUT.PUT_LINE(DBMS_UNDO_ADV.UNDO_ADVISOR(1));
  DBMS_OUTPUT.PUT_LINE('Required Undo Size (megabytes): ' || DBMS_UNDO_ADV.
  REQUIRED_UNDO_SIZE (900));
  retval := DBMS_UNDO_ADV.UNDO_HEALTH(pro, rec, rtn, ret, utb);
  DBMS_OUTPUT.PUT_LINE('Problem:   ' || pro);
  DBMS_OUTPUT.PUT_LINE('Advice:    ' || rec);
  DBMS_OUTPUT.PUT_LINE('Rational:  ' || rtn);
  DBMS_OUTPUT.PUT_LINE('Retention: ' || TO_CHAR(ret));
  DBMS_OUTPUT.PUT_LINE('UTBSize:   ' || TO_CHAR(utb));
END;
/
```

If no issues are found, a 0 will be returned for the retention size. Here is some sample output:

```
Finding 1:The undo tablespace is OK.
Required Undo Size (megabytes): 64
Problem:   No problem found
Advice:
Rational:
Retention: 0
UTBSize:   0
```

Viewing SQL That Is Consuming Undo Space

Sometimes, a piece of code does not commit properly, which results in large amounts of space being allocated in the undo tablespace and never being released. Sooner or later, you will get the ORA-30036 error, indicating that the tablespace cannot extend. Usually, the first time a space-related error is thrown, you can simply increase the size of one of the data files associated with the undo tablespace.

However, if an SQL statement continues to run and fills up the newly added space, then the issue is probably with a poorly written application. For example, a developer may not have appropriate commit statements in the code.

In these situations, it is helpful to identify which users are consuming space in the undo tablespace. Run this query to report on basic information regarding space allocated on a per-user basis:

```
SQL> select s.sid, s.serial#, s.osuser, s.logon_time
,s.status, s.machine
,t.used_ublk, t.used_ublk*16384/1024/1024 undo_usage_mb
from v$session   s
    ,v$transaction t
where t.addr = s.taddr;
```

If you want to view the SQL statement associated with a user consuming undo space, then join to V$SQL, as shown:

```
SQL> select s.sid, s.serial#, s.osuser, s.logon_time, s.status
,s.machine, t.used_ublk
,t.used_ublk*16384/1024/1024 undo_usage_mb
```

```
,q.sql_text
from v$session        s
    ,v$transaction t
    ,v$sql            q
where t.addr = s.taddr
and s.sql_id = q.sql_id;
```

If you need more information, such as the name and status of the rollback segment, run a query that joins to the V$ROLLNAME and V$ROLLSTAT views, like so:

```
SQL> select s.sid, s.serial#, s.username, s.program
,r.name undo_name, rs.status
,rs.rssize/1024/1024 redo_size_mb
,rs.extents
from v$session        s
    ,v$transaction t
    ,v$rollname       r
    ,v$rollstat       rs
where s.taddr = t.addr
and t.xidusn   = r.usn
and r.usn      = rs.usn;
```

The prior queries allow you to pinpoint which users are responsible for space allocated within the undo tablespace. This can be especially useful when there is code that is not committing at appropriate times and is excessively consuming undo space.

Handling Temporary Tablespace Issues

Issues with temporary tablespaces are somewhat easy to spot. For example, when the temporary tablespace runs out of space, the following error will be thrown:

```
ORA-01652: unable to extend temp segment by 128 in tablespace TEMP
```

When you see this error, you need to determine if there is not enough space in the temporary tablespace or if a rare runaway SQL query has temporarily consumed an inordinate amount of temporary space. Both of these issues are discussed in the following sections.

Determining if Temporary Tablespace Is Sized Correctly

The temporary tablespace is used as a sorting area on disk when a process has consumed the available memory and needs more space. Operations that require a sorting area include

- Index creation

- SQL sorting operations

  Temporary tables and indexes

- Temporary LOBs

- Temporary B-trees

There is no exact formula for determining if your temporary tablespace is sized correctly. It depends on the number and types of queries, index build operations, and parallel operations, and on the size of your memory sort space (PGA). You will have to monitor your temporary tablespace while there is a load on your database to establish its usage patterns. Since TEMP tablespaces are temporary files, they are handled differently than the data files and details are found in a in different view. Run the following query to show both the allocated and free space within the temporary tablespace:

```
SQL> select tablespace_name
,tablespace_size/1024/1024 mb_size
,allocated_space/1024/1024 mb_alloc
,free_space/1024/1024      mb_free
from dba_temp_free_space;
```

Here is some sample output:

```
TABLESPACE_NAME    MB_SIZE    MB_ALLOC    MB_FREE
---------------    -------    --------    -------
TEMP                   200         200        170
```

If the FREE_SPACE (MB_FREE) value drops to near 0, there are SQL operations in your database consuming most of the available space. The FREE_SPACE (MB_FREE) column is the total free space available, including space currently allocated and available for reuse.

If the amount used is getting near your current allocated amount, you may need to allocate more space to the temporary tablespace data files. Run the following query to view the temporary data file names and allocated sizes:

```
SQL> select name, bytes/1024/1024 mb_alloc from v$tempfile;
```

Here is some typical output:

```
NAME                                     MB_ALLOC
---------------------------------------- ----------
/u01/dbfile/o18c/temp01.dbf                   400
/u01/dbfile/o18c/temp02.dbf                   100
/u01/dbfile/o18c/temp03.dbf                   100
```

When first creating a database, if you have no idea as to "correct" size of the temporary tablespace, usually size this tablespace at approximately 20GB. If I'm building a data warehouse–type database, I might size the temporary tablespace at approximately 80GB. You will have to monitor your temporary tablespace with the appropriate SQL and adjust the size as necessary.

You can also create multiple TEMP tablespaces to be used for different applications and users. If there is an application that seems to be consuming all of the TEMP tablespace, create another TEMP tablespace, such as TEMP2, and assign it to that application user. This will isolate the problem, until the code, sorting, and index creation can be researched and fixed.

Viewing SQL That Is Consuming Temporary Space

When Oracle throws the ORA-01652: unable to extend temp error, this may be an indication that your temporary tablespace is too small. However, Oracle may throw that error if it runs out of space because of a one-time event, such as a large index build. You will have to decide whether a one-time index build or a query that consumes large amounts of sort space in the temporary tablespace warrants adding space.

To view the space a session is using in the temporary tablespace, run this query:

```
SQL> SELECT s.sid, s.serial#, s.username
,p.spid, s.module, p.program
,SUM(su.blocks) * tbsp.block_size/1024/1024 mb_used
,su.tablespace
```

```
FROM v$sort_usage     su
   ,v$session        s
   ,dba_tablespaces tbsp
   ,v$process         p
WHERE su.session_addr = s.saddr
AND   su.tablespace    = tbsp.tablespace_name
AND   s.paddr          = p.addr
GROUP BY
 s.sid, s.serial#, s.username, s.osuser, p.spid, s.module,
 p.program, tbsp.block_size, su.tablespace
ORDER BY s.sid;
```

If you determine that you need to add space, you can either resize an existing temp file or add a new one. To resize a temporary tablespace temp file, use the ALTER DATABASE TEMPFILE...RESIZE statement. The following command resizes a temporary data file to 12GB:

```
SQL> alter database tempfile '/u01/dbfile/o18c/temp02.dbf' resize 12g;
```

You can add a data file to a temporary tablespace, as follows:

```
SQL> alter tablespace temp add tempfile '/u02/dbfile/o18c/temp04.dbf' size 2g;
```

Summary

A senior DBA must be adept at efficiently determining the source of database unavailability and performance problems. The ability to identify and resolve problems defines a professional-level DBA. Anyone can google a topic (there is nothing worse than being on a trouble call with a manager who is googling and recommending random solutions). Besides confirming that the proper Oracle version is being googled, finding the appropriate solution and confidently applying it in a production database environment is how you add tremendous value.

Diagnosing issues sometimes requires some system and network administrator skills. Additionally, an effective DBA must know how to leverage the Oracle data dictionary to identify problems. As part of your strategy, you should also proactively monitor for the common sources of database unavailability. Ideally, you will be aware of the problem before anybody else and will proactively solve the issue.

No book can cover every troubleshooting activity. This chapter includes some of the most common techniques for identifying problems and dealing with them. Often, basic OS utilities will help you ascertain the source of a hung database. In almost every scenario, the `alert.log` and corresponding trace files should be inspected. Finding the root cause of a problem is often the hardest task. Use a consistent and methodical approach, and you will be much more successful in diagnosing and resolving issues.

This chapter tries to convey techniques and methods that will help you survive even the most chaotic database environments. To summarize these thoughts, a DBA's manifesto, of sorts:

- Automate and monitor through scripts and schedulers. Be the first to know when something is broken.

- Strive for repeatability and efficiency in processes and scripts. Be consistent.

- Keep it simple. If a module is more than a page long, it is too long. Do not implement a script or feature that another DBA will not be able to understand or maintain. Sometimes, the simple solution is the correct solution.

- Remain calm regardless of the disaster. Be respectful.

- Do not be afraid to seek or take advice. Welcome feedback and criticism. Listen to others. Entertain the thought that you might be wrong.

- Take advantage of graphical tools, but always know how to implement a feature manually.

- Expect failure, predict failure, prepare for failure. You do not know what will go wrong, but you do know something will go wrong. Be happy that you prepared for failure. The best lessons are painful.

- Test and document your operating procedures, backup, and restores. This will help you stay calm(er) and focused when in stressful database-down situations.

- Do not write code to implement a feature that the database vendor has already provided a solution for (replication, disaster recovery, backup and recovery, and so on).

- Become proficient with SQL, procedural SQL, and OS commands. These skills separate the weak from the strong. The best DBAs posses both SA and developer expertise.

- Continually investigate new features and technology. Learning is a never-ending process. Question everything, reevaluate, and look for a better way. Verify your solutions with repeatable, peer-reviewed tests. Document and freely share your knowledge.

- Know what questions to ask to understand a problem or situation better.

- Look to assist in database migrations to the cloud, to move to the right database, and to take advantage of autonomous database processes.

- Do what it takes to get the job done. You compete with the world now. Work harder and smarter.

The job of a DBA can be quite rewarding. It can also be very painful and stressful. Hopefully, the techniques documented in this book will get you from being mostly stressed to an occasionally happy state.

CHAPTER 22

Pluggable Databases

New with Oracle Database 12c is Oracle Multitenant. This feature allows you to create and maintain many pluggable databases within an overarching multitenant container database. Following is a concise introduction to pluggable terminology.

A multitenant container database (CDB) is defined as a database capable of housing one or more pluggable databases (PDB). A container is defined as a collection of data files and metadata that exist within a CDB. A PDB is a special type of container that can be easily provisioned by cloning another database. If need be, a PDB can also be transferred from one CDB to another.

A CDB is going to be the container for the resources of the database, and you should view it as the database for the processes, full memory, and CPU allocation. There is one set of processes that will start up with each CDB, and the memory is allocated to the CDB to be used by each PDB. There is resource management that we will get into later that will allow for certain allocation of memory and CPUs to each of the PDBs; otherwise it is shared as needed across all of the PDBs in the one CDB.

Instead of having multiple database instances on a server, one or a few CDBs can be created to contain all of the PDBs. PDBs are separate from each other with data and users so that they do not each need their own CDB for isolation.

Every CDB contains a master set of data files and metadata known as the root container. Each CDB also contains a seed PDB, which is used as a template for creating other PDBs. Each CDB consists of one master root container, one seed PDB, and one or more PDBs.

A pluggable enabled CDB must be created with the ENABLE PLUGGABLE DATABASE clause. A database that was not created in this manner (a non-CDB) cannot contain PDBs. A non-CDB was the only type of database available prior to Oracle Database 12c and can currently still be created this way. When using the dbca utility a CDB with a PDB is the default setting. Each CDB consists of the following elements:

M. Malcher and D. Kuhn, *Pro Oracle Database 18c Administration*,
https://doi.org/10.1007/978-1-4842-4424-1_22

- One root container, named CDB$ROOT. The root contains the master set of data dictionary views, which have metadata regarding the root as well as every child PDB within the CDB.

- One static seed container, named PDB$SEED. This container exists solely as a template for providing data files and metadata used to create new PDBs within the CDB.

- Zero, or one or more, PDBs (with a maximum of 4096). Each PDB is self-contained and functions like an isolated non-CDB database. Additionally, each PDB contains its own data files and application objects (users, tables, indexes, and so on). When connected to a PDB, there is no visibility to the root container or any other PDBs present within the CDB.

New with Oracle Database 12c, there is a CDB level of data dictionary views that overarch the DBA/ALL/USER-level views. The CDB-level views report across all containers (root, seed, and all pluggable databases) in a CDB. For instance, if you wanted to view all users within a CDB database, you would do so from the root container, by querying CDB_USERS. If you are not using a CDB, then DBA_USERS is still an accurate view for reporting all user information. Many of the data dictionary views now contain a new column, named CON_ID, which is a unique identifier for each container within the CDB. The root container has a CON_ID of 1. The seed has a CON_ID of 2. Each new pluggable database created within the CDB is assigned a unique sequential container ID.

Table 22-1 defines terms used in a pluggable database environment. Refer back to this table as you read through this chapter.

Table 22-1. *Summary of Pluggable Database Terms*

Term	Meaning
Container database (CDB), multitenant database	A database capable of housing one or more pluggable databases, processes, and shared resources
Pluggable database, (PDB)	A set of data files and metadata that can be seamlessly transferred from one CDB to another, user databases for applications
Root container	A master set of data files and metadata containing information regarding all containers within a CDB. The root container is named CDB$ROOT.
Container	A collection of data files and metadata. Can be root, seed, or a pluggable database.
Seed pluggable database	A template of data files and metadata used to create new pluggable databases. The seed pluggable database is named PDB$SEED.
Plugging	Associating the metadata and data files of a pluggable database with a CDB
Unplugging	Disassociating the metadata and data files of a pluggable database from a CDB
Cloning	Creating a pluggable database from a copy of another database (seed, PDB, or non-CDB)
CON_ID	A unique identifier for each container within a CDB. The CDB-level views contain a CON_ID column that identifies the container with which the information being viewed is associated.
CDB data dictionary views	Views that contain metadata regarding all pluggable databases within a CDB. These views only display meaningful information when queried via a privileged connection from the root container. The pluggable databases must be open for use.
non-CDB database	An Oracle database created without the pluggable database feature enabled (the only type of database that was available prior to 12c)

The goal of this chapter is to make you proficient in administering a container/pluggable database environment. By the end of this chapter, you should understand how to create a pluggable environment, provision PDBs, connect and navigate within PDB, and transfer PDBs from one CDB to another. The foundation for this starts with understanding the pluggable architecture. Figure 22-1 might be oversimplified but represents the overall view of the database with the CDB and PDBs. It provides the basic view of the multitenant architecture.

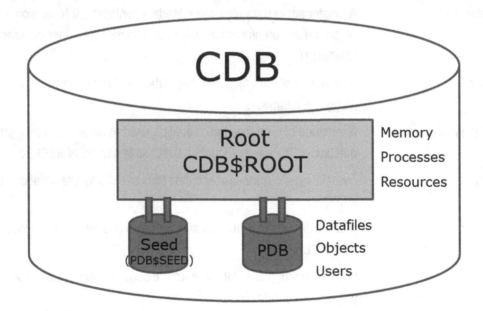

Figure 22-1. *Overview of Oracle Multitenant, recommended one CDB with one PDB*

Note   Oracle Multitenant is an extra cost option available with the Enterprise Edition. However, it is available for use with one pluggable database for all editions. It is recommended to create one CDB and one PDB even if not planning on using the option and creating more PDBs. Figure 22-1 shows how this architecture would look even without using the option. Setting up the database this way will allow for future use of multitenant option without having to migrate. Check the Oracle licensing guide for details.

Understanding Pluggable Architecture

PDBs have some important architectural differences with a non-CDB database environment. Figure 22-2 displays a container database, named CDB, which contains a root container, a seed database, and two PDBs named SALESPDB and HRPDB.

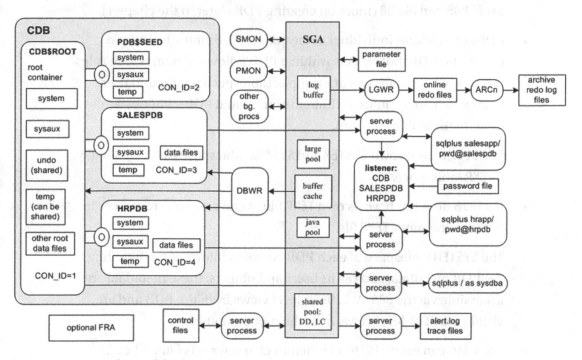

Figure 22-2. *Pluggable database architecture*

Take a minute to inspect Figure 22-2. If you are a curious DBA, most likely dozens of thoughts immediately come to mind. The following list highlights some key points to understand about the new architecture in Figure 22-2:

- A connection to the CDB database is synonymous with connecting to the CDB$ROOT root container. The main purpose of the root container is to provide the resources and house metadata for any associated PDBs.

- You can access the root container via the SYS user, just as you would a non-CDB database. In other words, when logged in to the database server, you can use OS authentication to connect directly to the root container without specifying a username and password (sqlplus / as sysdba).

919

- The seed PDB (PDB$SEED) only exists as a template for creating new PDBs. You can connect to the seed, but it is read-only, meaning you cannot issue transactions against it.

- Besides the two default containers (root and seed), for this particular CDB, two additional PDBs have been manually created, named SALESPDB and HRPDB (more on creating PDBs later in the chapter).

- PDBs exist within individual namespaces. PDBs must be unique within the CDB, but objects within a PDB follow the namespace rules of a non-CDB database. For example, tablespace names and user names have to be unique within the individual PDBs, but not across other PDBs within the CDB.

- Each PDB has its own SYSTEM and SYSAUX tablespaces and, optionally, a TEMP tablespace.

- If a PDB does not have its own TEMP file, it can consume resources in the root container TEMP file.

- The SYSTEM tablespace of each PDB contains information regarding the PDB metadata, such as its users and objects; these metadata are accessible via the DBA/ALL/USER-level views from the PDB and are visible via CDB-level views from the root container.

- The CDB can house PDBs of different character sets (since 12.2).

- You can set the time zones for the CDB and all associated PDBs, or you can set the time zone individually per PDB.

- The CDB instance is started and stopped while connected as SYS to the root container. You cannot start/stop the CDB instance while connected to a PDB (separation of duties from system DBAs and application DBAs).

- There is one initialization parameter file that is read by the instance when starting. A privileged user connected to the root container can modify all initialization parameters. In contrast, a privileged user connected to a PDB can only modify parameters applicable to the currently connected PDB.

- When connected to a PDB and modifying initialization parameters, these modifications only apply to the currently connected PDB and persist for the PDB across database restarts. The ISPDB_MODIFIABLE column in V$PARAMETER shows which parameters are modifiable while connected as a DBA to a PDB. (There are additional security permissions for locking parameters and configurations.)

- Application users can only access the PDBs via a network connection. Therefore, a listener must be running and listening for service names corresponding to associated PDBs. If a listener is not running, then there is no way for an application user to connect to a PDB.

- The individual PDBs are not stopped or started per se (not in the terms of a database instance). When you start/stop a PDB, you are not allocating memory or starting/stopping background processes. Rather, PDBs are either made available or not (open or closed).

- There is one set of control files for the CDB. The control files are managed while connected to the root container as a privileged user.

- There is one UNDO tablespace for the CDB. All PDBs within the CDB use the same UNDO tablespace (if RAC, then one active undo tablespace per instance).

- There is one thread of redo (per instance) that is managed while connected to the root container as a user with appropriate privileges. Only privileged connections to root can enable archiving or switching online logs. Connections of SYSDBA privileged users to PDBs cannot alter online redo or archiving settings.

- There is one alert log and set of trace files for a CDB. Any applicable database messages for associated PDBs are written to the common CDB alert log.

- Each container is assigned a unique container ID. The root container is assigned a container ID of 1; the seed database is assigned a container ID of 2. Each subsequently created PDB is assigned a unique sequential container ID.

- There is one FRA for the CDB. Separate directories are not created for PDBs within the FRA. RMAN backup files, control files, and online redo logs are placed in a directory associated with the CDB and are not segregated by PDB. Backup files can be separated out if only backing up the PDB but are still in the same FRA.

- The Flashback Database feature is turned on and off via a privileged connection to the root container. You cannot enable flashback at the PDB level.

- AWR, ADDM, and ASH reports are issued across all PDBs in the CDB. Resource consumption is identified per PDB.

- When resolving SQL performance issues, queries are associated with a particular PDB via the CON_ID column in views such as V$SQL and V$SQLAREA.

- Security options such as Database Vault can be enabled at a PDB level. The privileges in CDBs and PDBs provide another level of security and separation of duties.

The prior list is long with a ton of information, but once you digest the nuances of a PDB environment, you will be able to effectively implement and manage this technology. One of the main points here is that you can have dozens or more securely isolated PDBs housed within one CDB with only one instance (memory and background processes), one thread of redo, and one set of control files to manage. There is also much more to discuss in this chapter to fill in more details.

Paradigm Shift

It is fairly common for a specific application to request that its database objects (users, tables, indexes, and so on) be placed in a database isolated from other applications. Reasons cited for doing this are often security issues or performance concerns. Before the advent of PDBs, think about how you solved the requirement of separate environments for various applications and development teams. Two common solutions employed are as follows:

- Create a separate database for each team/application that needs an environment. Sometimes this approach is implemented with one database per server, which often translates into additional hardware and licensing costs.

- Create separate environments within one database. Usually this is achieved through separate schemas and distinct tablespaces. This approach requires that there not be any database object naming collisions between applications, for example, with objects such as user names, tablespace names, and public synonyms.

Starting with Oracle Database 12c, PDBs give you another tool for addressing the prior needs. PDBs provide the security isolation requirement; there is no direct access from one PDB to another. Even a user connected with SYSDBA privileges to a given PDB has no direct SQL access to other PDBs within the CDB. This is just like with non-CDB databases. From a security and application perspective, you have totally isolated PDBs within the larger CDB.

As a DBA, instead of having to implement and maintain dozens of individual databases and associated operational tasks (such as provisioning new databases, installs, upgrades, tuning, availability, monitoring, replication, disaster recovery, and backup and recovery), you can manage any number of PDBs as if they were one database. From the root container perspective, it is similar to managing one non-CDB database.

Another significant advantage of the pluggable architecture is that a PDB can easily be cloned or transferred from one CDB to another. This allows for more options when performing tasks such as provisioning new databases, upgrading databases, load balancing, or moving application data from one environment to another (such as from a development database to a test database). Creating a new environment can be done by cloning another PDB. And, moving a PDB from a CDB simply requires that you unplug (via SQL commands) the PDB from the CDB and then associate the metadata and data files (plug in) with a new CDB.

As mentioned, a few times in previous chapters, the new database structure should be a CDB with at least one PDB. This supports the new shift to have one CDB manage many PDBs with centralized resource management and planning.

PDB IN THE ORACLE CLOUD: EXADATA EXPRESS

A great way to test, develop, and start a migration to the cloud is to use the Exadata Express offering in the Oracle Cloud. This is a PDB on Exadata. It has everything you can do in a PDB, basically a Platform as a Service (PaaS) with features of Exadata, Enterprise Edition of the database available. This is not only a good way to test some applications but to get used to administration of a PDB without having to worry about anything else.

The infrastructure and CDB are already taken care of, and provisioning of the PDB just takes a few minutes. Maintenance scripts and applications can quickly be tested along with using a cloud service for the database.

This entry point for PDBs and Oracle Cloud is a great to get familiar with the needed services and administration of the PDBs. Add users, objects, and data to spend time exploring the PDB data dictionary in the cloud.

Backup and Recovery Implications

A pluggable environment has some interesting backup and recovery architectural aspects. The following list highlights these features:

- While connected to the root container with SYSDBA or SYSBACKUP privileges, you have the option of backing up all the data files within the CDB (root, seed, and all PDBs) via one backup command. You also have the choice of performing backup and recovery tasks at a PDB level of granularity.

- While connected directly to a PDB with SYSDBA or SYSBACKUP privileges, you can only back up and recover data files associated with the currently connected PDB; you cannot view or operate on the root container data files or other PDB data files.

- An incomplete recovery of the entire CDB must be performed with a connection to the root container with SYSDBA or SYSBACKUP privileges. All data files within the CDB (root container and associated PDBs) are unavailable during an incomplete recovery of the entire CDB.

- A direct connection to a PDB with SYSDBA or SYSBACKUP privileges can perform an incomplete recovery only on the currently connected PDB without affecting any other PDBs within the CDB.

- Because there is a shared UNDO tablespace, any point-in-time incomplete recoveries of a PDB will also have to temporarily restore the root container's UNDO tablespace to an auxiliary database location so that it can participate in the point-in-time recovery of the PDB.

This means that as a root-level DBA, you can treat backup and recovery operations as if they were one database. From the pluggable perspective, if need be, you can perform backup and recovery per PDB.

Note   See Chapters 18 and 19 for examples of using RMAN to back up, restore, and recover in a pluggable environment.

Tuning Nuances

Tuning in a pluggable environment presents new challenges but will seem familiar to tuning on a server with several database instances. The advantage is here is a CDB that has the resources and a view into the other PDBs that are plugged in consuming the resources. Performance tuning can start at the PDB level and continue to the CDB to understand the other PDB activities. Also, there are ways to manage the resources for the PDBs based on different service levels, priority, or data tiers for the PDB.

The AWR, ADDM, and ASH reports now show resource usage at the PDB level; this will allow you to focus your tuning efforts on the appropriate PDB. For any homegrown tuning SQL queries that you have written, you will need to modify these to report on the CDB-level views where appropriate. Likewise, when analyzing SQL statements, you will have to consider which PDB the SQL statement is executing within.

The previous sections of this chapter place an emphasis on discussion of the pluggable architecture. Before creating a CDB, it is critical that you understand these architectural underpinnings; hence, the lengthy introduction to this topic. Now that you have a pluggable foundation, you are ready to turn theoretical concepts into usable and sustainable database technology. The first real task at hand is to create a CDB.

PLUGGABLE SHIPPING CONTAINERS: STRENGTH IN NUMBERS

Security: PDBs within a CDB are similar to the shipping containers present on a large merchant ship. Each container is securely isolated and self-contained. If you were to find yourself inside a particular shipping container, you would not necessarily be aware of any other containers on the mother ship. The captain (SYS connection to the root container) is aware of all the containers on the vessel and can view the contents of each container via the shipping manifest (CDB-level metadata views).

Granularity: If need be, repair and maintenance can be performed at the container level. Likewise, you can take PDBs offline for maintenance or move without affecting any other PDBs within the CDB.

Synergy: Each container efficiently shares the ship's communal resources, such as the engine, crew, and navigation systems. This is similar to PDBs sharing a common SGA, UNDO tablespace, FRA, parameter file, and redo logs and archivelogs as well as background processes and control files. Economies of scale are generated through sharing a mutual database infrastructure; hardware, and human resource (DBA) costs are spread across many databases.

Provisioning: For this analogy, assume that you can easily replicate a shipping container (perhaps with a giant three-dimensional scanner/printer); this would allow you to create containers as copies of existing containers. Similarly, PDBs can quickly and efficiently be created from existing databases (seed, PDB, or non-CDB).

Transferability: When required, a shipping container can be easily transferred to another form of transportation (another ship, a freight train, or piggyback on a semi-truck). In the same way, PDBs can be easily unplugged and plugged into other CDBs. It does not necessarily matter if the destination CDB is the same version and type as the source CDB.

Creating a CDB

To use the pluggable database feature, you have to specifically create a pluggable enabled CDB. There are several different techniques for creating a CDB:

- Using the dbca utility

- Generating the required scripts with the DBCA, and then manually running the scripts to create a CDB

- Manually issuing the SQL CREATE DATABASE command using RMAN to duplicate an existing CDB

The next two sections focus on showing you how to create a database with the CREATE DATABASE command and the DBCA. For details on using RMAN to duplicate a CDB or pluggable database, see *RMAN Recipes for Oracle Database 12c*, Second Edition, by Darl Kuhn, Sam Alapati, and Arup Nanda (Apress, 2013).

Using the Database Configuration Assistant (DBCA)

You can use the DBCA utility to create a CDB through either a graphical interface or the command-line mode. When using the graphical interface, you'll be prompted as to whether or not you want to create a CDB.

This example walks you through using the command-line mode. First, ensure that your ORACLE_SID, ORACLE_HOME, and PATH variables are set for your CDB environment (see Chapter 2 for details on setting OS variables); for example,

```
$ export ORACLE_SID=CDB
$ export ORACLE_HOME=/u01/app/oracle/product/18.1.0.1/db_1
$ export PATH=$ORACLE_HOME/bin:$PATH
```

Now, use the DBCA to create a CDB. When using the command-line mode of the DBCA, you must specify the createAsContainerDatabase clause. The following bit of code creates a database named CDB:

```
dbca -silent -createDatabase -templateName General_Purpose.dbc -gdbname CDB
-sid CDB -responseFile NO_VALUE -characterSet AL32UTF8 -memoryPercentage 30
-emConfiguration LOCAL -createAsContainerDatabase true
-sysPassword foo -systemPassword foo
```

The prior code must be entered on one line (it only appears here on multiple lines in order to fit on the page). The SID that you provide (in this example, CDB) must not exist in your oratab file. On Linux systems the oratab file is usually located in the /etc directory. On other Unix systems (such as Solaris), the oratab file is generally located in the /var/opt/oracle directory.

After pressing the Enter key, you should see some output similar to this:

```
Copying database files
...
9% complete
41% complete
Creating and starting Oracle instance
43% complete
48% complete
...
```

It will take the DBCA assistant several minutes to create the new CDB. Ensure that you have enough disk space available when creating this database (approximately 5GB should be enough). After the DBCA is finished running, you should have a fully functional CDB database and can start creating PDBs within it.

Generating CDB Create Scripts via DBCA

You can use the DBCA to generate the scripts required to create a CDB, and then you have the option of manually running the scripts to carry out the process. This next bit of code invokes the DBCA utility from the command line and generates the scripts needed to create a CDB named CDB1:

```
dbca -silent -generateScripts -templateName General_Purpose.dbc -gdbname CDB1
-sid CDB1 -responseFile NO_VALUE -characterSet AL32UTF8 -memoryPercentage 30
-emConfiguration LOCAL -createAsContainerDatabase true
-sysPassword foo -systemPassword foo
```

The prior code must be entered on one line when executed. Here is a snippet of typical output:

```
Database creation script generation
1% complete
.....
100% complete
Look at the log file "/orahome/app/oracle/admin/CDB1/scripts/CDB1.log"...
```

After the DBCA is finished running, change the directory to the location of the newly generated scripts:

```
$ cd $ORACLE_BASE/admin/CDB1/scripts
```

Now, display the scripts in the directory:

```
$ ls
```

Here is some sample output:

```
CDB1.log                cloneDBCreation.sql        lockAccount.sql
CDB1.sh                 init.ora                   postDBCreation.sql
CDB1.sql                initCDB1Temp.ora           postScripts.sql
CloneRmanRestore.sql    initCDB1TempOMF.ora        rmanRestoreDatafiles.sql
tempControl.ctl
```

To create the database, run the CDB1.sh script:

```
$ CDB1.sh
```

The prior shell script calls CDB1.sql, which subsequently invokes the RMAN utility. RMAN creates the required data files from a backup and also creates a database named CDB1. You should be able to start the database after you've set your ORACLE_SID OS variable to contain the name of the freshly created CDB.

Creating Manually with SQL

First, ensure that your ORACLE_SID, ORACLE_HOME, and PATH variables are set for your CDB environment (see Chapter 2 for details on setting OS variables); for example,

```
$ export ORACLE_SID=CDB
$ export ORACLE_HOME=/u01/app/oracle/product/18.1.0.1/db_1
$ export PATH=$ORACLE_HOME/bin:$PATH
```

Next, create a parameter initialization file in the ORACLE_HOME/dbs directory. Make certain you set the ENABLE_PLUGGABLE_DATABASE parameter to TRUE. Here, it shows an OS text editor to create a file named initCDB.ora and placed within it the following parameter specifications:

```
db_name='CDB'
enable_pluggable_database=true
audit_trail='db'
control_files='/u01/dbfile/CDB/control01.ctl','/u01/dbfile/CDB/control02.ctl'
db_block_size=8192
db_domain="
memory_target=629145600
memory_max_target=629145600
open_cursors=300
processes=300
remote_login_passwordfile='EXCLUSIVE'
undo_tablespace='UNDOTBS1'
```

Now, use an OS text editor to create a file named credb.sql, and place within it an appropriate CREATE DATABASE statement:

```
SQL> CREATE DATABASE CDB
    MAXLOGFILES 16
    MAXLOGMEMBERS 4
    MAXDATAFILES 1024
    MAXINSTANCES 1
    MAXLOGHISTORY 680
    CHARACTER SET US7ASCII
    NATIONAL CHARACTER SET AL16UTF16
DATAFILE
'/u01/dbfile/CDB/system01.dbf' SIZE 500M
    EXTENT MANAGEMENT LOCAL
UNDO TABLESPACE undotbs1 DATAFILE
'/u01/dbfile/CDB/undotbs01.dbf' SIZE 800M
SYSAUX DATAFILE
'/u01/dbfile/CDB/sysaux01.dbf' SIZE 500M
DEFAULT TEMPORARY TABLESPACE TEMP TEMPFILE
```

```
'/u01/dbfile/CDB/temp01.dbf' SIZE 500M
DEFAULT TABLESPACE USERS DATAFILE
'/u01/dbfile/CDB/users01.dbf' SIZE 50M
LOGFILE GROUP 1
        ('/u01/oraredo/CDB/redo01a.rdo') SIZE 50M,
        GROUP 2
        ('/u01/oraredo/CDB/redo02a.rdo') SIZE 50M
USER sys    IDENTIFIED BY foo
USER system IDENTIFIED BY foo
USER_DATA TABLESPACE userstbs DATAFILE
  '/u01/dbfile/CDB/userstbsp01.dbf' SIZE 500M
ENABLE PLUGGABLE DATABASE
SEED FILE_NAME_CONVERT = ('/u01/dbfile/CDB','/u01/dbfile/CDB/pdbseed');
```

There are a few clauses of the CREATE DATABASE statement relevant only to PDBs. For instance, the ENABLE PLUGGABLE DATABASE clause is required if you want to create a PDB within the CDB. The USER_DATA TABLESPACE clause specifies that an additional tablespace be created within the seed database; this tablespace will also be replicated to any PDBs that are cloned from the seed database. Also, the SEED FILE_NAME_CONVERT specifies how the seed database files will be named and in what directories they will be located.

Next, ensure you have created any directories referenced in the parameter file and the CREATE DATABASE statement:

```
$ mkdir -p /u01/dbfile/CDB/pdbseed
$ mkdir -p /u01/dbfile/CDB
$ mkdir -p /u01/oraredo/CDB
```

Now, start up your database in nomount mode, and run the credb.sql script:

```
$ sqlplus / as sysdba
SQL> startup nomount;
SQL> @credb.sql
```

If successful, you should see this:

```
Database created.
```

Oracle recommends that you use the `catcon.pl` Perl script to run any Oracle supplied SQL scripts for a CDB. Therefore, to create the data dictionary for a CDB, use the `catcon.pl` Perl script. First change directories to the `ORACLE_HOME/rdbms/admin` directory:

```
$ cd $ORACLE_HOME/rdbms/admin
```

Now use `catcon.pl` to run the `catalog.sql` script as SYS:

```
$ perl catcon.pl -u sys/foo -s -e -d $ORACLE_HOME/rdbms/admin -b catalog1
catalog.sql > catcon-catalog.log
```

Next, use `catcon.pl` to run the `catproc.sql` script as SYS:

```
$ perl catcon.pl -u sys/foo -s -e -d $ORACLE_HOME/rdbms/admin -b catproc1
catproc.sql > catcon-catproc.log
```

After you have created the data dictionary, as the S schema, create the product user profile tables:

```
$ perl catcon.pl -u system/foo -s -e -d $ORACLE_HOME/sqlplus/admin -b pupbld1
pupbld.sql >catcon-pupbld.log
```

At this point, you should have a fully functional CDB database and can start creating PDBs within it.

Verifying That a CDB Was Created

To verify whether a database was created as a CDB, first connect to the root container as SYS:

```
$ sqlplus / as sysdba
```

You can now confirm that the CDB was successfully created via this query. If a database was created as a CDB, the CDB column of V$DATABASE will contain a YES value:

```
SQL> select name, cdb from v$database;
```

Here is some sample output:

```
NAME      CDB
--------- ---
CDB       YES
```

At this point, you should have two containers in your CDB database: the root container and the seed pluggable database. You can check with this query:

```
SQL> select con_id, name from v$containers;
```

Here is some sample output:

```
CON_ID NAME
------ --------------------
     1 CDB$ROOT
     2 PDB$SEED
```

You should also have data files associated with the root and the seed database. You can view the data files associated with each container via this query:

```
SQL> select con_id, file_name from cdb_data_files order by 1;
```

Here is some output:

```
CON_ID FILE_NAME
------ -------------------------------------------------------
     1 /u01/app/oracle/oradata/CDB/system01.dbf
     1 /u01/app/oracle/oradata/CDB/sysaux01.dbf
     1 /u01/app/oracle/oradata/CDB/undotbs01.dbf
     1 /u01/app/oracle/oradata/CDB/users01.dbf
     2 /u01/app/oracle/oradata/CDB/pdbseed/system01.dbf
     2 /u01/app/oracle/oradata/CDB/pdbseed/sysaux01.dbf
```

Note that if you had selected from DBA_DATA_FILES instead of CDB_DATA_FILES, you would only see the four data files associated with the root container (the container you are currently connected to); for example,

```
SQL> select file_name from dba_data_files;

FILE_NAME
-----------------------------------------------------
/u01/app/oracle/oradata/CDB/system01.dbf
/u01/app/oracle/oradata/CDB/sysaux01.dbf
/u01/app/oracle/oradata/CDB/users01.dbf
/u01/app/oracle/oradata/CDB/undotbs01.dbf
```

Administrating the Root Container

When you manage a CDB, for the most part, you are connecting to the root container as SYS and performing tasks as you would with a non-CDB database. However, there are several points to be aware of that are specific to maintaining a CDB. The following tasks can only be performed while connected to the root container with SYSDBA privileges:

- Starting/stopping instance

- Enabling/disabling archive log mode

- Managing instance settings that affect all databases within the CDB, such as overall memory size

- Backup and recovery of all data files within the database

- Managing control files (adding, restoring, removing, and so on)

- Managing online redo logs

- Managing the root UNDO tablespace

- Managing the root TEMP tablespace

- Creating common users and roles

These topics are discussed in the following sections.

Connecting to the Root Container

Connecting to the root container as SYS allows you to perform all the tasks you normally associate with database administration. You can connect as SYS locally from the database server through OS authentication or a network connection (which requires a listener and password file). It is recommended that there are roles that are set up for CDB administrators to be able to use individual accounts and not log in via SYS. Logins on the server would be needed only when performing the server tasks otherwise connection to the CDB through a network connection should be what is allowed for security and compliance.

Through Network

If you're initiating a remote connection through the network, then you need to first set up a listener on the target database server and create a password file (see Chapter 2 for details). Once a listener and password file are established, you can connect remotely over the network, as shown:

```
$ sqlplus user/pass@connection_string as sysdba
SQL> show user cond_id, conname user

USER is "user"


CON_ID
-----------
1

CON_NAME
---------------
CDB$ROOT
USER is "user"
```

For details on how to implement a listener in a pluggable environment, see the section "Managing a Listener in a PDB Environment" later in this chapter.

Displaying Currently Connected Container Information

From SQL*Plus there are a couple of easy techniques for displaying the name of the CDB that you are currently connected to. This example uses the SHOW command to display the container ID, the name, and the user:

```
SQL> show con_id con_name user
```

You can also display the same information via an SQL query:

```
SQL> SELECT SYS_CONTEXT('USERENV', 'CON_ID') AS con_id,
SYS_CONTEXT('USERENV', 'CON_NAME') AS cur_container,
SYS_CONTEXT('USERENV', 'SESSION_USER') AS cur_user
FROM DUAL;
```

Here is some sample output:

```
CON_ID               CUR_CONTAINER        CUR_USER
-------------------  -------------------  --------------------
1                    CDB$ROOT             USER
```

Starting/Stopping the Root Container

You can only start/stop the CDB while connected as a privileged user to the root container. The procedure for starting and stopping the root container is the same as for a non-CDB database. To start a CDB, first connect as SYS, and issue the startup command:

```
$ sqlplus / as sysdba
SQL> startup;
```

Starting the CDB database does not open any associated PDBs. You can open all PDBs with this command:

```
SQL> alter pluggable database all open;
```

To shut down a CDB database, issue the following command:

```
SQL> shutdown immediate;
```

Just as with a non-CDB database, the prior line shuts down the CDB instance and disconnects any users connected to the database. If any pluggable databases are open, they are closed, and users are disconnected.

Creating Common Users

There are two types of users in a pluggable environment: local and common. A local user is nothing more than a regular user that is created in a PDB. The local type of user in a PDB behaves the same as a user in a non-CDB environment. There is nothing special about administering local users. You administer them as you would a user in a non-CDB environment.

A common user is a new concept in Oracle Database 12c and only pertains to a pluggable database environment. A common user is one that exists in the root container and in every PDB. This type of user must be initially created in the root container and is automatically created in all existing PDBs as well as in any PDBs created in the future.

Tip   The SYS and SYSTEM accounts are common users that Oracle creates automatically in a pluggable environment.

Common users must be created with the string C## or c## at the start of the username. For instance, the following command creates a common user in all PDBs:

```
SQL> create user c##dba identified by foo;
```

Common users must be granted privileges from within each pluggable database. In other words, if you grant privileges to a common user while connected to the root container, this does not cascade to the PDBs. If you need to grant a common user a privilege that spans PDBs, then create a common role, and assign it to the common user.

What use is there for a common user? One situation would be the performance of common DBA maintenance activities across PDBs not requiring SYSDBA-level privileges. For example, you want to set up a DBA account that has the privileges to create users, grants, and so on, but you don't want to use an account such as SYS (which has all privileges in all databases). In this scenario, you would create a common DBA user and also create a DBA common role that contains the appropriate privileges. The common role would then be assigned to the common DBA.

Creating Common Roles

Much like you can create a common user that spans all PDBs, you can, in the same manner, create a common role. Common roles provide a single object to which you can grant privileges that are valid within all pluggable databases associated with the root container.

A common role is created in the root container and is automatically created in all associated PDBs as well as any PDBs created in the future. Like common users, common roles must start with the C## or c## string; for example,

```
SQL> create role c##dbaprivs container = all;
```

Next, you can assign privileges, as desired, to the common role. Here, the DBA role is assigned to the previously created role:

```
SQL> grant dba to c##dbaprivs container = all;
```

Now, if you assign this common role to a common user, the privileges associated with the role are in effect when the common user connects to any pluggable database associated with the root container:

```
SQL> grant c##dbaprivs to c##dba container = all;
```

Creating Local Users and Roles

A local user is a user that is only for that contain and "local" to the container. This is especially used for application users and users that are only authorized in specific PBDs. There is not really any difference between database users and local users, and these are users without "C##" for the CDB.

You can create a local user in a PDB by specifying the CONTAINER clause or without it. Connect to the PDB where the local users are to be created for:

```
SQL> CREATE USER pdbsys IDENTIFIED BY pass CONTAINER=CURRENT;
SQL> CREATE USER appuser IDENTIFIED BY pass;
```

Roles are also common or local. All Oracle supplied roles are common but can be granted to a local user.

Reporting on Container Space

To report on all containers (root, seed, and all PDBs) within a CDB, you must follow this procedure:

- Connect to the root container as a user with privileges to view the CDB-level views.

- Make sure your query uses the CDB-level views where appropriate.

- Ensure that any PDBs you wish to report on are open. If the PDBs are not open, then no information will be displayed.

Here is a query that uses the CDB-level views to report basic space usage information relating to all containers within a CDB:

```
SQL> SET LINES 132 PAGES 100
SQL> COL con_name        FORM A15 HEAD "Container|Name"
SQL> COL tablespace_name FORM A15
SQL> COL fsm             FORM 999,999,999,999 HEAD "Free|Space Meg."
SQL> COL apm             FORM 999,999,999,999 HEAD "Alloc|Space Meg."
--
SQL> COMPUTE SUM OF fsm apm ON REPORT
SQL> BREAK ON REPORT ON con_id ON con_name ON tablespace_name
--
SQL> WITH x AS (SELECT c1.con_id, cf1.tablespace_name, SUM(cf1.
bytes)/1024/1024 fsm
          FROM cdb_free_space cf1
               ,v$containers   c1
          WHERE cf1.con_id = c1.con_id
          GROUP BY c1.con_id, cf1.tablespace_name),
     y AS (SELECT c2.con_id, cd.tablespace_name, SUM(cd.bytes)/1024/1024 apm
          FROM cdb_data_files cd
               ,v$containers   c2
          WHERE cd.con_id = c2.con_id
          GROUP BY c2.con_id
                   ,cd.tablespace_name)
SELECT x.con_id, v.name con_name, x.tablespace_name, x.fsm, y.apm
FROM x, y, v$containers v
WHERE x.con_id         = y.con_id
AND   x.tablespace_name = y.tablespace_name
AND   v.con_id         = y.con_id
UNION
SELECT vc2.con_id, vc2.name, tf.tablespace_name, null, SUM(tf.
bytes)/1024/1024
FROM v$containers vc2, cdb_temp_files tf
WHERE vc2.con_id  = tf.con_id
GROUP BY vc2.con_id, vc2.name, tf.tablespace_name
ORDER BY 1, 2;
```

Here is some sample output:

CON_ID	Container Name	TABLESPACE_NAME	Free Space Meg.	Alloc Space Meg.
1	CDB$ROOT	SYSAUX	42	780
		SYSTEM	7	790
		TEMP		88
		UNDOTBS1	206	230
		USERS	4	5
2	PDB$SEED	SYSAUX	2	640
		SYSTEM	5	260
		TEMP		87
**********	***************	***************	---------------	----------------
sum			266	2,880

Make sure any PDBs you want to report on are open before attempting to query the CDB-level views. If a PDB is not open, it will not appear in the report output. A PDB is set to be open by default; for reference, here is the statement again to open all pluggable databases:

```
SQL> alter pluggable database all open;
```

Tip   Reporting on tablespace and data file usage for an individual pluggable database is not significantly different from reporting on the space in a non-CDB database. First, connect directly to the pluggable database as a user that has privileges to select from the DBA-level views. Then, run a report that queries the space-related views. See Chapter 4 for a query for reporting on space usage in a non-CDB.

Switching Containers

Once you connect as a common user to any container within the database (either the root or a PDB), you can use the ALTER SESSION command to switch to another container for which you have been granted access. For example, to set the current container to a PDB named SALESPDB, you would do as follows:

```
SQL> alter session set container = salespdb;
```

You can switch back to the root container by specifying the CDB$ROOT:

```
SQL> alter session set container = cdb$root;
```

You do not need a listener to be up and running or a password file to switch containers. As long as the common user has privileges, then the user is successfully switched to the new container context. Having the ability to switch containers is especially useful when you need to connect to a PDB to troubleshoot issues and then connect back to the root container.

Creating a Pluggable Database Within a CDB

After you have created a CDB, you can start creating PDBs within it. When you instruct Oracle to create a PDB, under the covers, it is actually copying data files from an existing database (seed, PDB, or non-CDB) and then instantiating the CDB with the new PDB's metadata. The key here is to correctly reference what database you want Oracle to use as a template for creating the new PDB.

There are several tools for creating (cloning) a PDB: namely the CREATE PLUGGABLE DATABASE SQL statement, the DBCA utility, and Enterprise Manager Cloud Control. This chapter focuses on using SQL and the DBCA utilities. If you understand how to create PDBs using SQL and DBCA, you should easily be able to use the Enterprise Manager screens to achieve the same objectives.

With the CREATE PLUGGABLE DATABASE statement, you can use any of the following sources to create a PDB:

- Seed database

- Existing PDB (either local or remote)

- Non-CDB database

- Unplugged PDB

With the DBCA, you can create a PDB from any of the following sources:

- Seed database

- RMAN backup

- Unplugged PDB

In the following sections, all the CREATE PLUGGABLE DATABASE variants of creating a PDB are covered. With the DBCA, I only show how to create a PDB from the seed database. You should be able to modify that example for your various needs.

Cloning the Seed Database

The CREATE PLUGGABLE DATASE statement can be used to create a PDB by copying the seed database's data files. To do this, first connect to the root container database as the SYS user (or a common user with create PDB privileges):

```
$ sqlplus sysuser/pass@CDB1 as sysdba
```

The following SQL statement creates a pluggable database named SALESPDB:

```
SQL> CREATE PLUGGABLE DATABASE salespdb
ADMIN USER salesadm IDENTIFIED BY foo
FILE_NAME_CONVERT = ('/u01/app/oracle/oradata/CDB/pdbseed',
                     '/u01/app/oracle/oradata/CDB/salespdb');
```

After running the prior code, you should see some output similar to this:

```
Pluggable database created.
```

Note If you are using OMF, you do not need to specify the FILE_NAME_CONVERT clause when creating a pluggable database, because Oracle automatically determines the names and locations of the pluggable database data files.

Note that the FILE_NAME_CONVERT clause in this example has two strings. One specifies the location of the seed database data files:

```
/u01/app/oracle/oradata/CDB/pdbseed
```

The second string is the location where you want the new PDB's data files created:

```
/u01/app/oracle/oradata/CDB/salespdb
```

You will have to modify these strings to the appropriate values for your environment.

There are several options available when using the CREATE PLUGGABLE DATABASE statement to create a PDB. Table 22-2 summarizes the meanings of the various clauses.

Table 22-2. *Pluggable Database Creation Options*

Parameter	Description
ADMIN USER	A local user that is created and used for administrative tasks. This user is assigned the PDB_DBA role.
MAXSIZE	Maximum amount of storage a pluggable database can consume; if not specified,then there is no limit to the amount of storage a PDB can use
MAX_SHARED_TEMP_SIZE	Maximum amount of shared temporary tablespace that can be used by sessions connected to the PDB
DEFAULT TABLESPACE	Specifies the default permanent tablespace assigned to new users created withinthe pluggable database.
DATAFILE	Path and file name of the data file associated with the default tablespace
PATH_PREFIX	Specifies that any new data files added to the pluggable database must exist within this directory or its subdirectories
FILE_NAME_CONVERT	Specifies the location of the seed database data files and the location where an if theyshould be copied

Cloning an Existing PDB

You can create a PDB from an existing PDB within the currently connected (local) CDB, or you can create a PDB as a copy of a PDB from a remote CDB. These two techniques are detailed in the next two sections.

Local

In this example an existing PDB (SALESPDB) is used to create a new PDB (SALESPDB2). First, connect to the root container, and place the existing source PDB in read-only mode:

```
$ sqlplus sysuser/pass@CDB1 as sysdba
SQL> alter pluggable database salespdb close;
SQL> alter pluggable database salespdb open read only;
```

Now, run the following SQL to create the new PDB:

```
SQL> CREATE PLUGGABLE DATABASE salespdb2
FROM salespdb
FILE_NAME_CONVERT = ('/u01/app/oracle/oradata/CDB/salespdb',
                     '/u01/dbfile/CDB/salespb2')
STORAGE (MAXSIZE 6G MAX_SHARED_TEMP_SIZE 100M);
```

In the prior example the data files (associated with SALESPDB) in the /u01/app/oracle/oradata/CDB/salespdb directory are used to create data files in the /u01/dbfile/CDB/salespdb2 directory. The destination directory will be created for you if it does not preexist. You can also specify governing restrictions on the cloned PDB such as limiting its maximum size to 6GB and the maximum amount of shared resources it can consume in the shared temporary tablespace to 100MB.

Remote

You can also create a PDB as a clone of a remote PDB. First, you need to create a database link from the CDB to the PDB that will serve as the source for the clone. Both the local user and the user specified in the database link must have the CREATE PLUGGABLE DATABASE privilege.

This example shows a local connection as SYS to the root container. This is the database in which the new PDB will be created:

```
$ sqlplus sysuser/pass@CDB1 as sysdba
```

In this database, create a database link to the PDB in the remote CDB. The remote CDB contains a PDB named SALESPDB, with a user that has been created with the CREATE PLUGGABLE DATABASE privilege granted to it. This is the user that will be used in the database link:

```
create database link salespdb
connect to mv_maint identified by foo
using 'speed2:1521/salespdb';
```

Next, connect to the remote database that contains the PDB that will be cloned:

```
$ sqlplus sysuser/foo@speed2:1521/salespdb as sysdba
```

Close the PDB and open it in read-only mode:

```
SQL> alter pluggable database salespdb close;
SQL> alter pluggable database salespdb open read only;
```

Now, connect to the destination CDB as SYS, and create the new PDB as shown by cloning the remote PDB:

```
$ sqlplus sysuser/pass@CDB1 as sysdba

SQL> CREATE PLUGGABLE DATABASE salespdb3
FROM salespdb@salespdb
FILE_NAME_CONVERT = ('/u01/app/oracle/oradata/CDB/salespdb',
                     '/u01/dbfile/CDB2/salespdb3');
```

Cloning from a Non-CDB Database

There are three ways of creating a PDB from an existing non-CDB:

- Using the DBMS_PDB package to generate metadata and then create PDB with CREATE PLUGGABLE DATABASE SQL statement

- Data Pump (using the transportable tablespace feature)

- GoldenGate replication

The following example uses the DBMS_PDB package to create a PDB from a non-CDB. For details on Data Pump and GoldenGate, see the Oracle Database Utilities Guide and GoldenGate-specific documentation, respectively, available from the Technology Network area of the Oracle web site (http://otn.oracle.com).

Note   When using the DBMS_PDB package to convert a non-CDB to a PDB, the non-CDB must be Oracle12c or higher.

First, place the non-CDB in read-only mode:

```
SQL> startup mount;
SQL> alter database open read only;
```

Then, run the DBMS_PDB package to create an XML file that describes the structure of the non-CDB database:

```
BEGIN
  DBMS_PDB.DESCRIBE(pdb_descr_file => '/orahome/oracle/ncdb.xml');
END;
/
```

After the XML file is created, shut down the non-CDB database:

```
SQL> shutdown immediate;
```

Next, set your oracle OS variables (such as ORACLE_SID and ORACLE_HOME), and connect to the CDB database that will house the non-CDB as a PDB:

```
$ sqlplus / as sysdba
```

Now, you can optionally check to see if the non-CDB is compatible with the CDB in which it will be plugged. When you run this code, provide the directory and name of the XML file that was created previously:

```
SQL> SET SERVEROUTPUT ON
SQL> DECLARE
hold_var boolean;
begin
hold_var := DBMS_PDB.CHECK_PLUG_COMPATIBILITY(pdb_descr_file=>'/orahome/
oracle/ncdb.xml');
if hold_var then
  dbms_output.put_line('YES');
else
  dbms_output.put_line('NO');
end if;
end;
/
```

If there are no compatibility issues, a YES is displayed by the prior code; a NO is displayed if the PDB is not compatible. You can query the contents of the PDB_PLUG_IN_VIOLATIONS view for details on why a PDB is not compatible with a CDB.

Next, use the following SQL to create a PDB from the non-CDB. You must specify details such as the name and location of the previously created XML file, the location of the non-CDB data files, and the location where you want the new data files created:

```
SQL> CREATE PLUGGABLE DATABASE dkpdb
USING '/orahome/oracle/ncdb.xml'
COPY
FILE_NAME_CONVERT = ('/u01/dbfile/dk/',
                     '/u01/dbfile/CDB/dkpdb/');
```

If successful, you should see this:

```
Pluggable database created.
```

Now, connect as SYS to the newly created PDB as SYS:

```
$ sqlplus sys/foo@'speed2:1521/dkpdb' as sysdba
```

As a last step, run the following script:

```
SQL> @?/rdbms/admin/noncdb_to_pdb.sql
```

You should now be able to open the PDB and begin using it.

Unplugging a PDB from a CDB

Before plugging a PDB into another CDB, it must first be unplugged. Unplugging translates to disassociating a PDB from a CDB and generating an XML file that describes the PDB being unplugged. This XML file can be used in the future to plug the PDB into another CDB.

Here are the steps required to unplug a PDB:

1. Close the PDB (which changes its open mode to MOUNTED)

2. Unplug the pluggable database via the ALTER PLUGGABLE DATABASE ... UNPLUG command

First, connect to the root container as the SYS user, and then close the PDB:

```
$ sqlplus sysuser/pass@CDB1 as sysdba
SQL> alter pluggable database dkpdb close immediate;
```

Next, unplug the PDB. Make sure you specify a directory that exists in your environment for the location of the XML file:

```
SQL> alter pluggable database dkpdb unplug into
'/orahome/oracle/dba/dkpdb.xml';
```

The XML file contains metadata regarding the PDB, such as its data files. This XML is required if you want to plug the PDB into another CDB:.

Note   Once a PDB is unplugged, it must be dropped before it can be plugged back into the original CDB.

Plugging an Unplugged PDB into a CDB

Before a PDB can be plugged: into a CDB, it must be compatible with a CDB in terms of data file endianness and compatible database options installed. The character set can be different in the PDB compared to the PDB starting with 18c. You can verify the compatibility via the DBMS_PDB package. You must provide as input to the package the directory and name of the XML file created when the PDB was unplugged. Here is an example:

```
SQL> SET SERVEROUTPUT ON
SQL> DECLARE
hold_var boolean;
begin
hold_var := DBMS_PDB.CHECK_PLUG_COMPATIBILITY(pdb_descr_file=>'/orahome/
oracle/dba/dkpdb.xml');
if hold_var then
  dbms_output.put_line('YES');
else
  dbms_output.put_line('NO');
end if;
end;
/
```

If there are no compatibility issues, a YES is displayed by the prior code; a NO is displayed if the PDB is not compatible. You can query the contents of the PDB_PLUG_IN_VIOLATIONS view for details on why a PDB is not compatible with a CDB.

Plugging in a PDB is done with the CREATE PLUGGABLE DATABASE command. When you plug a PDB into a CDB, you must provide some key pieces of information, using these two clauses:

- USING clause: This clause specifies the location of the XML file created when the PDB was unplugged.

- COPY FILE_NAME_CONVERT clause: This clause specifies the source of the PDB data files and the location where the PDB data files will be created within the destination CDB.

To plug in a PDB, connect to the CDB as a privileged user, and run the following:

```
SQL> CREATE PLUGGABLE DATABASE dkpdb
USING '/orahome/oracle/dba/dkpdb.xml'
COPY
FILE_NAME_CONVERT = ('/u01/app/oracle/oradata/CDB1/dkpdb',
                     '/u01/dbfile/CDB2/dkpdb');
```

You can now open the PDB and begin using it.

Using the DBCA to Create a PDB from the Seed Database

You can use the DBCA utility to create a PDB from the seed database by specifying the −createPDBFrom DEFAULT clause. Here is an example that creates a pluggable database named HRPDB within a CDB named CDB:

```
$ dbca -silent -createPluggableDatabase -sourceDB CDB -pdbName hrpdb
-createPDBFrom DEFAULT
-pdbAdminUserName adminplug -pdbAdminPassword foo
-pdbDatafileDestination /u01/dbfile/CDB/hrpdb
```

The prior lines of code must be entered on one line. Also, if the PDB destination directory does not exist, the DBCA will automatically create it. As the command progresses, you should see output similar to this:

```
Creating Pluggable Database
4% complete
12% complete
...
Completing Pluggable Database Creation
100% complete
Look at the log file "/orahome/app/oracle/cfgtoollogs/dbca/CDB.log" for
further details.
```

As a last step, you should inspect the log file and ensure that there were no issues with the creation of the PDB.

Checking the Status of Pluggable Databases

After creating a PDB, you may want to check its status. You can view the status of all PDBs within a CDB while connected in the root container. For instance, a user with DBA privileges can report on the status of all PDBs via this query:

```
SQL> select pdb_id, pdb_name, status from cdb_pdbs;
```

Here is some sample output:

```
    PDB_ID PDB_NAME              STATUS
---------- -------------------- -------------
         2 PDB$SEED             NORMAL
         3 SALESPDB             NORMAL
         4 HRPDB                NORMAL
```

This next query reports on whether or not the pluggable databases are open:

```
SQL> select con_id, name, open_mode from v$pdbs;
```

Here is some sample output:

```
CON_ID NAME                           OPEN_MODE
---------- ------------------------------ ----------
        2 PDB$SEED                       READ ONLY
        3 SALESPDB                       READ WRITE
        4 HRPDB                          READ WRITE
```

If you run the prior queries while connected directly to a PDB, no information will be displayed in CDB_PDBS. Also, the V$PDBS will only display information for the currently connected PDB.

Administrating Pluggable Databases

You can perform many database administrative tasks while connected directly to the PDB. You can open/close a PDB, check its status, show currently connected users, and so on. You can administer a pluggable database as a privileged connection to the root container, or you can perform tasks while connected as a privileged user directly to the PDB itself.

Keep in mind that when you connect as SYS to a PDB within the CDB, you can only perform SYS-privileged operations for the PDB to which you are connected. You cannot start/stop the container instance or view data dictionary information related to other PDBs within the CDB. Separation of duties for a PDB to just be able to administer one or more PDBs and another team or DBAs would be taking care of the CDB administration.

Connecting to a PDB

You can connect to a PDB as SYS either locally or over the network. To make a local connection, first connect to the root container as a common user with privileges on the PDB, and then use the SET CONTAINER command to connect to the desired PDB:

```
SQL> alter session set container=salespdb;
```

The prior connection does not require a listener or password file; a connection over the network requires both. This next example makes a network connection via SQL*Plus and specifies the host, listener port, and service name of the PDB when connecting via SQL*Plus:

```
$ sqlplus pdbsys/foo@speed2:1521/salespdb as sysdba
```

If you are unsure how to set up a listener and a password file, see Chapter 2. If you use the DBCA utility to create the PDB, the listener for the PDB will be set up. For instructions on how to register a PDB service name with the listener, see the next section.

Managing a Listener in PDB Environment

Recall from Chapter 2 that a listener is the process that enables remote network connections to a database. Most database environments require a listener in order to operate. When a client attempts to connect to a remote database, the client provides three key pieces of information: the host the listener is on, the host port the listener is listening on, and a database service name.

Each database has one or more service names assigned to it. By default, there is usually one service name that is derived from the database's unique name and domain. You can manually create one or more service names for a database. DBAs sometimes create more than one service so that resource usage can be controlled or monitored for each service. For example, a service may be created for a sales application, and a service may be created for the HR application. Each application connects to the database via its service name. The service connection information appears in the SERVICE_NAME column of the V$SESSION view for each session.

If you start a default listener with no listener.ora file in place, the PMON background process will automatically register any databases (including any pluggable) as a service:

```
$ lsnrctl start
```

Eventually, you should see the databases (including any PDBs) registered with the default listener.

Note   When starting the listener, if there is a listener.ora file present, the listener will attempt to statically register any service names that appear in the listener.ora file.

By default, the PDBs are registered with a service name that is the same as the PDB name. The default service is typically the one that you would use to make connections:

```
$ sqlplus pdbsys/foo@speed2:1521/salespdb as sysdba
```

You can verify which services are running by connecting as SYS to the root container and querying:

```
SQL> select name, network_name, pdb from v$services order by pdb, name;
```

You can also verify which services a listener is listing for via the lsnrctl utility:

```
$ lsnrctl services
```

Oracle recommends that you configure an additional service (besides the default service) for any applications that need to access a PDB. You can manually configure services by using the SRVCTL utility or the DBMS_SERVICE package. This example shows how to configure a service via the DBMS_SERVICE package. First, connect as SYS to the PDB that you want to create the service in via the default service:

```
$ sqlplus pdbsys/foo@speed2:1521/salespdb as sysdba
```

Make sure the PDB is open for read-write mode:

```
SQL> SELECT con_id, name, open_mode FROM v$pdbs;
```

Next, create a service. This code creates and starts a service named SALESWEST:

```
SQL> exec DBMS_SERVICE.CREATE_SERVICE(service_name => 'SALESWEST',
network_name => 'SALESWEST');
SQL> exec DBMS_SERVICE.START_SERVICE(service_name => 'SALESWEST');
```

Now, application users can connect to the SALESPDB pluggable database via the service:

```
$ sqlplus appuser/pass@speed2:1521/saleswest
```

Caution   If you have multiple CDB databases on one server, ensure that the PDB service names are unique across all CDB databases on the server. It is not advisable to register two PDB databases with the exact same name with one common listener. This will lead to confusion as to which PDB you are actually connecting to.

Showing the Currently Connected PDB

From SQL*Plus, there are a couple of easy techniques for displaying the name of the PDB that you are currently connected to. This example uses the SHOW command to display the container ID, the name, and the user:

```
SQL> show con_id con_name user
```

Here is some sample output:

```
CON_ID
-------------------------------
3

CON_NAME
-------------------------------
SALESPDB

USER is "SYS"
```

You can also display the same information via an SQL query:

```
SELECT SYS_CONTEXT('USERENV', 'CON_ID') AS con_id,
SYS_CONTEXT('USERENV', 'CON_NAME') AS cur_container,
SYS_CONTEXT('USERENV', 'SESSION_USER') AS cur_user
FROM DUAL;
```

Here is some sample output:

```
CON_ID      CUR_CONTAINER    CUR_USER
----------  ---------------- ----------
3           SALESPDB         SYS
```

Keep in mind that the SYS_CONTEXT function can be used to display other useful information, such as the SERVICE_NAME, DB_UNIQUE_NAME, INSTANCE_NAME, and SERVER_HOST; for example,

```
SELECT
 SYS_CONTEXT('USERENV', 'SERVICE_NAME') as service_name,
 SYS_CONTEXT('USERENV', 'DB_UNIQUE_NAME') as db_unique_name,
```

```
 SYS_CONTEXT('USERENV', 'INSTANCE_NAME') as instance_name,
 SYS_CONTEXT('USERENV', 'SERVER_HOST') as server_host
from dual;
```

Starting/Stopping a PDB

When you start/stop a PDB, you are not starting/stopping an instance. Rather, you are making the PDB either available or unavailable, open or closed. You can change the open mode of a PDB from either a connection to the root container as SYS or a direct connection to the PDB as SYS.

From Root Container

To change the open mode of a PDB from the root container, do as follows:

```
SQL> alter pluggable database salespdb open;
```

You can also start a pluggable database in a particular state, such as read-only:

```
SQL> startup pluggable database salespdb open read only;
```

To close a PDB, you can specify the name of the PDB:

```
SQL> alter pluggable database salespdb close immediate;
```

You can also open or close all pluggable databases while connected to the root container. In a live production system, this is not recommended since these can all be different applications, and unless server maintenance was being performed, there might not be a reason to close all PDBs.

```
SQL> alter pluggable database all open;
SQL> alter pluggable database all close immediate;
```

From Pluggable

To open/start a pluggable database, connect to the pluggable database as SYS:

```
$ sqlplus pdbsys/foo@salespdb as sysdba
SQL> startup;
```

To shut down the database, issue the following command:

```
SQL> shutdown immediate;
```

Modifying Initialization Parameters Specific to a PDB

Oracle allows some initialization parameters to be modified while connected as a privileged user to a PDB. You can view these parameters via the following query:

```
SQL> SELECT name
FROM v$parameter
WHERE ispdb_modifiable='TRUE'
ORDER BY name;
```

Here is a snippet of the output:

```
NAME
-------------------------------
sort_area_size
sql_trace
sqltune_category
star_transformation_enabled
statistics_level
```

When you make initialization parameter changes while connected directly to a PDB, these changes only affect the currently connected PDB. The parameter changes do not affect the root container or other PDBs. For example, say you wanted to change the value of OPEN_CURSORS. First, connect directly to the PDB as a privileged user, and issue the ALTER SYSTEM statement:

```
$ sqlplus pdbsys/foo@speed2:1521/salespdb as sysdba
SQL> alter system set open_cursors=100;
```

The prior change modifies the value of OPEN_CURSORS only for the SALESPDB PDB. Furthermore, the setting of OPEN_CURSORS for SALESPDB will persist across database restarts.

Renaming a PDB

Occasionally, you may be required to rename a PDB. For instance, the database may have been originally misnamed, or you may no longer be using the database and want to append an _OLD to its name. To rename a pluggable database, first connect to it as a SYSDBA-privileged account:

```
$ sqlplus pdbsys/foo@invpdb as sysdba
```

Next, stop the PDB and restart it in restricted mode:

```
SQL> shutdown immediate;
SQL> startup restrict;
```

Now, the pluggable database can be renamed:

```
SQL> alter pluggable database INVPDB rename global_name to INVPDB_OLD;
```

Limiting the Amount of Space Consumed by PDB

You can place an overall limit on the amount of disk space a PDB can consume. It is possible that the max size of the PDB datafiles would do this, but this is if there are multiple tablespaces and datafiles. The sizing of the databases should be available through ASM diskgroups or filesystem sizing.

In this example an overall limit of 100GB is placed on a pluggable database. First, connect to the pluggable database as SYS:

```
$ sqlplus pdbsys/foo@speed2:1521/salespdb as sysdba
```

Then, alter the pluggable database's' maximum size limit. This command limits the size of the pluggable database to a maximum of 100GB:

```
SQL> alter pluggable database salespdb storage(maxsize 100G);
```

The space is not the only resource that can be limited by PDB. CPU and memory can be limited by using the parameters in the PDB or using resource management plans. As a privileged user in the PDB, you can alter the system to set CPU_COUNT equal to less than over all CPU_COUNT for the CDB. This will not allow the PDB to use more than those CPU resources. The same is for memory in setting the memory limit parameters in the PDB, again less than the CDB. Connect to the PDB and use the following alter statements:

```
SQL> alter system set CPU_COUNT = 2 scope  =  both;
SQL> alter system set SGA_TARGET = 16GB scope = both;
```

Restricting Changes to SYSTEM at PDB

In administering the PDB, the parameters can be changed as described at the PDB level. You can also change these parameters for a PDB at the CDB level. The changes can be restricted so that only CDB administrators can modify these settings for the PDB. This will allow the CDB DBAs to know how many PDBs are in the CDB and manage it. The changes will be kept even while the sysdba user in each PDB can have the DBA permissions in the PDB and administer the PDB.

This is done with PDB_LOCKDOWN. The lockdown profile is created, set for a PDB, and the commands are added to the profile to restrict PDB DBAs from changing the configurations, such as those set with CPU, memory, etc.

In the CDB here is a quick overview of creating PDB_LOCKDOWNs:

```
SQL> CREATE LOCKDOWN PROFILE pdbprofile1;
SQL> ALTER SYSTEM SET PDB_LOCKDOWN=pdbprofile1;
```

And you can view the parameters in PBD_LOCKDOWN:

```
SQL> SHOW PARAMETER PDB_LOCKDOWN
```

Oracle 18c has dynamic lockdown profiles that allow for additional parameter settings, resource manager plans, and options. They are dynamic because they do not require that the PDB to be restarted and take effect immediately.

Viewing PDB History

If you need to view when a PDB was created, you can query the CDB_PDB_HISTORY view, as shown:

```
SQL> COL db_name FORM A10
SQL> COL con_id FORM 999
SQL> COL pdb_name FORM A15
```

```
SQL> COL operation FORM A16
SQL> COL op_timestamp FORM A10
SQL> COL cloned_from_pdb_name FORMAT A15
--
SQL> SELECT db_name, con_id, pdb_name, operation,
        op_timestamp, cloned_from_pdb_name
FROM cdb_pdb_history
WHERE con_id > 2
ORDER BY con_id;
```

Here is some sample output:

```
DB_NAME    CON_ID PDB_NAME        OPERATION      OP_TIMESTA CLONED_FROM_PDB
---------- ------ --------------- -------------- ---------- ---------------
CDB             3 SALESPDB        CREATE         04-DEC-12  PDB$SEED
CDB             4 HRPDB           CREATE         10-FEB-13  PDB$SEED
```

In this way, you can determine when a PDB was created and from what source.

Dropping a PDB

Occasionally, you may need to drop a PDB. You may want to do so because you do not need the PDB anymore or because you are transferring (unplugging/plugging) to a different CDB and you want to drop the PDB from the original CDB. If you need to remove a PDB, you can do it in two ways:

- Drop the PDB and its data files.

- Drop the PDB and leave its data files in place.

If you never plan on using the PDB again, then you can drop it and specify that the data files also be removed. If you plan on plugging the PDB into a different CDB, then (of course) don't drop the data files, as doing so removes them from disk.

To drop a PDB, first connect to the root container as a privileged account, and close the PDB:

```
SQL> alter pluggable database dkpdb close immediate;
```

This example drops the PDB and its data files:

```
SQL> drop pluggable database dkpdb including datafiles;
```

If successful, you should see this message:

```
Pluggable database dropped.
```

This next example drops a PDB without removing the data files. You may want to do this if you're moving the pluggable database to a different CDB:

```
SQL> drop pluggable database dkpdb;
```

In this manner, the PDB is disassociated from the CDB, but its data files remain intact on disk.

Refreshable Clone PDB

In Oracle 18c, PDBs can be refreshed from the source PDB periodically. This helps for clones that take a long time and updates the PDB in another CDB for failover, load-balance and only needing to manage two CDBs. The roles can also be reversed, making the source PDB the clone and the clone the source PDB. This basically replaces Data Guard failover for a PDB.

The PDB is created with a refresh mode and configures the clone. This allows for automatic refreshes of the clone PDB and sets intervals for it to happen. A manual refresh can be triggered as well. To create the clone:

```
SQL> CREATE PLUGGABLE DATABASE pdbclone1 REFRESH MODE EVERY 5 MINUTES
```

Change the refresh mode to manual:

```
SQL> ALTER PLUGGABLE DATABASE pdbclone1 REFRESH MODE MANUAL;
```

The clone can be switched using the following in the clone PDB container:

```
SQL> ALTER PLUGGABLE DATABASE REFRESH MODE MANUAL FROM pdb1@CDB1_dblink
SWITCHOVER;
```

Databases in the Cloud

Oracle databases can be created the different cloud platforms. There are templates, containers, and other ways to install the Oracle software as part of Infrastructure as a Service (IaaS) or Platform as a Service (PaaS) to create the databases and administer the environment.

Oracle Autonomous Database Cloud is the autonomous database offering from Oracle in their public cloud. It is powered by Oracle 18c and was first the Autonomous Data Warehouse Cloud (ADWC) and is now including the Autonomous Transaction Processing Database (ATP). This self-driving database provides several automated processes for maintenance, performance, and security in form of patching. The advantage of using the Oracle Cloud is the Oracle software and options come available and implemented, ready to use. The Express Edition gives you a PDB that was discussed earlier in the chapter. The creation of CDB service and multiple PDBs would be recommended for a cloud implementation. The access in the cloud may not include server access and why connections with sysdba users over the network is important for the CDB and PDB. The other tasks for managing users, objects, and other containers are going to be the same in the cloud or on-premise.

The Autonomous Database can literally be taken for a test drive, and understanding the CDB and PDB concepts with users and administration is going to simplify the testing in the cloud and support any migration and future environment in the cloud.

Summary

New with Oracle Database 12c, a PDB is a collection of data files and metadata that exist within a CDB. PDBs have several interesting architectural features:

- When connected to a PDB, you have no visibility to other PDBs that exist within the CDB. It is as if you are connected to an isolated database.

- Multiple PDBs share common database resources (memory structures, background processes, and so on) within the CDB. From the root container level, you can manage many DBA databases as if they were one database.

- You can shut down a PDB without affecting other PDBs within the CDB.

- New PDBs can be quickly created by cloning the seed database, an existing PDB, or a non-CDB.

- PDBs can be created and set up with an automatic refresh.

- PDBs can be easily transferred from one CDB to another by unplugging from one CDB and plugging the PDB into another CDB.

These features provide new ways in which you can create and manage databases. The main advantage of PDB technology is that it allows you to consolidate many databases into one overarching database. This generates economies of scale, in that more databases can be implemented and maintained on fewer servers with less support personnel. As a DBA, understanding this technology and how to implement it makes you all the more valuable to your company. The database environment that is configured on-premise is available in the cloud. Understanding how to administer the database on-premise will apply to management in the cloud. Having the PDB level of the database allows for separate administration that does not need to administer the CDB or database server.

Even with the autonomous database in the Oracle Cloud, the DBA is still needed to work through application data, integrations, and strategies for data security. Always enough to do when you understand databases, data, and how to use them.

Index

A

Active session history (ASH), 894, 897–898
ADD LOGFILE GROUP statement, 172–173
ADRCI utility, 881
ADR_HOME directory, 6
Advanced row compression, 258
ADVISE FAILURE command, 780–782
alert.log file, 878–881
alias command, 90
ALTER DATABASE BACKUP
    CONTROLFILE TO TRACE
    statement, 146
ALTER DATABASE command, 783
ALTER DATABASE DATAFILE
    statement, 140
ALTER DATABASE DATAFILE ... OFFLINE
    FOR DROP, 140
ALTER DATABASE DROP LOGFILE
    MEMBER statement, 176
ALTER DATABASE MOVE DATAFILE
    command, 142
ALTER DATABASE RENAME FILE
    statement, 143–144
ALTER SEQUENCE statement, 380
ALTER SESSION command, 154, 940
ALTER SYSTEM KILL SESSION
    statement, 901
ALTER SYSTEM SWITCH LOGFILE
    statement, 173
ALTER TABLE statement, 251

ALTER TABLE ... MOVE statement, 283
ALTER TABLE...SHRINK SPACE
    statement, 283
ALTER TABLESPACE statement, 127–128,
    138, 144
ALTER TABLESPACE ... ADD DATAFILE
    statement, 137
ALTER TABLESPACE ... OFFLINE
    IMMEDIATE, 139
ALTER TABLESPACE ... OFFLINE
    NORMAL statement, 139
ALTER USER command, 209–210
APP_DATA_LARGE tablespace, 120
APP_DATA_SMALL tablespace, 120
ARCHIVE_LAG_TARGET initialization
    parameter, 165
Archivelog mode
    architectural decisions, 179–180
    archive log destination, 188–190
    backing up archive redo log files, 190
    disabling, 187
    enable, 186–187
    Redo file location
        FRA, 185–186
        LOG_ARCHIVE_DEST_N
            database, 181
            user-defined disk location, 181–182
Archive redo log file, 179
ASM cluster file system (ACFS), 149
AUTOALLOCATE clause, 123

© Michelle Malcher and Darl Kuhn 2019
M. Malcher and D. Kuhn, *Pro Oracle Database 18c Administration*,
https://doi.org/10.1007/978-1-4842-4424-1

AUTOEXTEND feature, 123

Autoincrementing (identity) column, 253–255

Automatic database diagnostic monitor (ADDM), 306, 894, 897

Automatic diagnostic repository command interpreter (ADRCI), 877

Automatic segment space management (ASSM), 120

Automatic storage management (ASM), 124, 126

disk groups, 153

tablespaces, 148–149

Automatic workload repository (AWR), 306, 894, 896–897

Automating jobs

cron utility, 838

background process, 848

cron daemon process, 847

crontab entry, 850–851

default editor, 852

editing cron table, 851, 852

enabling access, 849

etc/crontab file, 847

files and directory, 848

loading, 853–854

redirecting output, 855–856

root user, 847

troubleshooting, 856–857

var/spool/cron directory, 847

DBA

locked production accounts, 864–865

OS script, 857

reboot/restart database, 858–859

redo log destination, 859, 861

RMAN backups, 866–868

SQL*Plus process, 865

truncating large log files, 862–863

Linux/Unix environment, 838

Oracle Scheduler utility

COPY_JOB procedure, 844

CREATE_JOB procedure, 840

vs. cron, 845–846

deleting, 845

DISABLE procedure, 843

ENABLE procedure, 843

JOB_CLASS parameter, 840

logging history, 842

modification, 842

orahome/oracle/bin directory, 839

PL/SQL package, 839

REPEAT_INTERVAL parameter, 840

run, 844

stopping, 843

view details, 841

Autonomous Database

Oracle Cloud, 869

patching, 868

secure configuration, 868

Autonomous data warehouse cloud (ADWC), 961

Autonomous transaction processing database (ATP), 961

autotrace tool, 278

B

BACKUP command, 695, 707, 722, 795

BACKUP AS COPY command, 796, 806

backup.bsh script, 855

Backup retention policy

CLEAR command, 716

delete obsolete backups, 716

recovery window, 715

redundancy, 715

TO NONE command, 716

BACKUP...VALIDATE
command, 756, 795

Bash Shell Backslash, 86

Bash shell environment, 85

BASIC compression algorithm, 719

BasicFiles, 412

   LOB Column, 413

   SecureFile migration, 428

   vs. SecureFiles, 411

   space, 436

bdump, 91

BIGFILE clause, 133

Binary file (BFILE), 240, 408, 439

Binary large object (BLOB), 240, 408, 434

Bitmap index, 327

Bitmap join index, 328–329

Block-level recovery, 794–795

Bottlenecks identification

   OS utilitity

      database application, 882

      Linux/Unix environments, 882

      mapping, OS process, 888, 890

      performance and monitoring, 883

      top command, 885, 887

      vmstat utility, 884–885

B-tree index, 309, 318–321

BUILD DEFERRED clause, 603

C

cat command, 878

CATALOG command, 714

CB_RAD_COUNTS view, 403

CDB_USERS, 195

Central MV Log, 639–641

CHANGE FAILURE command, 782

Character data type

   CHAR, 235

   NVARCHAR2 and NCHAR, 236

   VARCHAR2, 234–235

Character large object (CLOB), 408, 432

Check constraint, 295–296

CHECK LOGICAL clause, 755, 867

CLEAR command, 719

CLOB command, 240

Clustered table, 232

Cold-backup strategy

   archivelog mode database, 659

   noarchivelog mode database

      backup copies, 652

      backup location, 650

      database locations and names, 651

      disk space, 650

      flashback database, 649

      restart database, 652

      shut down database, 651

      with Online Redo Logs, 652–653

      without Online Redo Logs, 653–655

   RMAN scenario, 659

   scripts

      cbdir variables, 656

      coldback.sql script, 657

      coldrest.sql script, 658

Comma-separated-value (CSV) files, 557

Common roles creation, 937

Common user creation, 936–937

Complete recovery

   block-level recovery, 794–795

   control files, 682, 684–687

   data file

      mount mode database, 792–793

   entire database

      backup control file, 789

      current control file, 788

Complete recovery (*cont.*)
    nondefault location, 793–794
    pluggable database, 796–797
    restore-and-recovery scenario
        database open, 680
        data file data file, 677
        mount mode, 677
        online logs, 676
        RECOVER DATABASE
          statement, 681
        RECOVER DATAFILE statement, 679
        RECOVER TABLESPACE, 681
        RMAN, 679
        SYSTEM tablespace, 681
    tablespace
        mount mode, 790
        read-only, 790
        temporary restore, 791
    testing
        Backup preview, 785–786
        media recovery, 786–787
Complete refreshable MV
    architectural components, 590–591
    CREATE MATERIALIZED VIEW...AS
        SELECT statement, 587
    CREATE MATERIALIZED VIEW system
        privilege, 587
    CREATE TABLE system privilege, 587
    DBMS_MVIEW package, 590
    REFRESH procedure, 590
    SEGMENT CREATION IMMEDIATE
        clause, 588
    USER_MVIEWS data dictionary, 588
    USER_OBJECTS view, 588
    USER_SEGMENTS view, 588–589
Compressed data, 257
Concatenated index, 322–323
CONFIGURE command, 707, 722–723, 731

CONFIGURE ARCHIVELOG DELETION
    command, 717
CONFIGURE CHANNEL
    command, 708
CONFIGURE...CLEAR
    commands, 726
conn.bsh script, 102–103
Constraints
    definition, 231
    disabling, 297–299
    enabling, 299–301
    foreign key constraints,
        creation, 293–294
    NOT NULL constraint, 296
    primary key constraints,
        creation, 289–290
    specific data conditions,
        checking, 295–296
    types, 289
    unique key constraints,
        creation, 291–292
Container database (CDB), 163
    creation
        DBCA, 927–928
        scripts, 928–929
        SQL, 929, 931–932
        verification, 932–933
CREATE ANY VIEW privilege, 352
CREATE CONTROLFILE
    statement, 146–147
CREATE DATABASE
    command, 118, 386
CREATE GLOBAL TEMPORARY TABLE
    statement, 286
CREATE OR REPLACE method, 362
CREATE SCHEMA statement, 206
CREATE SYNONYM
    command, 366–367

CREATE TABLE statement, 242, 356
CREATE TABLE AS SELECT (CTAS)
    statement, 263, 567
CREATE TABLESPACE statement,
    122, 132, 450–452
CREATE USER SQL statement, 202
CREATE VIEW statement, 352
cron utility
    background process, 848
    cron daemon process, 847
    crontab entry, 850
    default editor, 852
    editing cron table, 851
    enabling access, 849
    etc/crontab file, 847
    files and directory, 848
    load, 853
    redirecting output, 855
    root user, 847
    troubleshooting, 856
CROSSCHECK command, 717
CTIME column, 219

D

Database buffer cache, 80
Database Configuration Assistant
    (DBCA), 927
    CREATE DATABASE
        statement, 72
    find command, 71
    graphical mode, 70
    mydb.rsp file, 71
    OS command line, 70
    rman utility, 72
    silent mode, 70–71
    utility, 39
Database directory object, 502

Database environment
    OS command prompt, 84–87
    rerunning commands
        Bash shell, 93
        command-line editor, 95–96
        Ctrl+P and Ctrl+N, 94
        history command, 94–95
        ls - altr command, 96
        reverse search, 95
        set - o command, 95
        up and down arrow keys
            scrolling, 94
    shell aliases, 89–90
    shell function, 91–93
    shell scripts
        conn.bsh, 102–103
        dba_fcns, 98–99
        dba_setup, 97–98
        filesp.bsh, 103, 105–106
        lock.sql, 108–109
        login.sql, 106
        tbsp_chk.bsh, 99–102
        top.sql, 107
        users.sql, 110–111
    SQL prompt, 87–89
    SQL scripts (see SQL scripts)
Database index
    application behavior, 334–335
    bitmap index creation, 327
    bitmap join index creation, 328–329
    B-tree index creation, 318–321
    concatenated index creation, 322–323
    existing index invisible, 333
    foreign key columns
        index determination, 344–346
        index implementation, 342–343
        table locks, 346–347
    function-based index creation, 324

Database index (*cont.*)

guidelines for index creation, 348–349

index maintenance

display DDL, 336

drop index, 341

monitor index, 339–340

rebuild index, 337–338

rename index, 336

UNUSABLE index, 338–339

invisible index creation, 332–333

key-compressed index creation, 330

parallelism, 331

proactive index creation, 305

reactive index creation, 306–307

redo generation avoidance, 331–332

reverse-key index creation, 329–330

robustness

index placement in
tablespace, 315–316

index size, 311–313

index type, 308–310

naming standards, 317

portable scripts creation, 316

separate tablespace
creation, 313–315

storage parameters, 315

ROWID, 303

unique index creation, 325–326

Database intelligence, 83

Database offline, incomplete recovery, *see*
Incomplete recovery

Database online, complete recovery, *see*
Complete recovery

Database point-in-time recovery
(DBPITR), 805, *see also* Incomplete
recovery,

Database Upgrade Assistant
(DBUA), 26–27

Database writer writes blocks (DBWn), 79

Data definition language (DDL), 127, 364

Data dictionary

architecture

dynamic performance, 387, 389

read-only view, 384

static view, 384–387

DBMS_STATS package, 400

derivable documentation, 393–394

metadata

database issues, 389

logical and physical structure, 389

Oracle database, 390

relationship, 391

SQL queries, 392

TABLESPACE_NAME column, 392

tablespaces, 389

object dependency, 402, 404–405

primary key and foreign key, 401–402

SQL query, 383

table row count, 398, 400

user information, 394–396

Data files

data dictionary views, 117

offline data file operations, 142

re-creating the control file and OS
commands, 145–147

SQL and OS commands, 143–145

online data file operations, 142

Data Manipulation Language (DML), 385

Data pump

additional dump files, 543

architecture

components, 503

exports and imports information, 500

Linux/Unix systems, 502

ps command, 501

status table, 502

COMPRESSION parameter, 545
consistent export files, 535–537
database directory object, 502
data export
    access to the directory, 506
    directory object, creation, 505–506
    export information, database, 508
data pump jobs
    database alert log, 553
    data dictionary views, 552
    interactive command mode
      status, 554
    log file, 551
    OS utilities, 554
    status table, 553
data remapping, 539–541
DBMS_DATAPUMP and DBMS_
    METADATA built-in PL/SQL
    packages, 500
DDL file, 544–545
DISABLE_ARCHIVE_LOGGING
    parameter, 548
dump files, 534
ENCRYPTION parameter, 546–547
exclude objects, 532
expdp and impdp utilities, 500
export and import
    entire database, 511–513
    Linux server, 516
    schema level, 513–514
    Solaris box, 516
    table level, 514–515
    tablespace level, 515
    transferring data, 516
export job components, 503
file size estimation, 533
filtering data and objects, 526
import job components, 504

interactive command mode
    KILL_JOB command, 550
    running job and view, 549
    STOP_JOB parameter, 550
log file suppresion, 541
master process, 501
old exp/imp utilities, 499
parallelism, 541–542
parameter file, 509–510
PL/SQL packages, 504
REUSE_DUMPFILES parameter, 543
status table, 501
substantial functionality, 499–500
TABLE_EXISTS_ACTION and
    CONTENT parameters, 537–538
table import, 509
table-level compression, 546
table renaming, 539
testing database, 517
transferring data, 516
    copying data files, 519–521
    export and import, network, 516
user clone, 535
utility, 272
VIEWS_AS_TABLES parameter, 548
worker process, 501
Data recovery advisor, 779
Data types
    characters
      CHAR, 235
      NVARCHAR2 and NCHAR, 236
      VARCHAR2, 234–235
    Date/Time, 237–238
    JSON, 241
    LOB, 240
    numeric, 236–237
    RAW, 238
    ROWID, 239

DATE data type, 237

Date/Time data type, 237–238

DBA/ALL/USER_CONSTRAINTS views, 326

DBA/ALL/USER_EXTENTS, 279, 282

DBA/ALL/USER_INDEXES views, 321

DBA_DEPENDENCIES view, 403

dba_fcns script, 98–99

DBA_ROLE_PRIVS view:, 227

DBA_SCHEDULER_JOBS, 845

DBA_SEQUENCES view, 378

dba_setup script, 97–98

DBA_SYS_PRIVS view, 224

DBA_TAB_PARTITIONS view, 469

DBA_USERS_WITH_DEFPWD view, 199, 200

DB_CREATE_FILE_DEST, 753

DB_FLASHBACK_RETENTION_TARGET parameter, 818

DBMS_METADATA package, 127

DBMS_SCHEDULER package, 840, 846

DBMS_SPACE package, 279, 280

DBMS_STATS package, 483

DBMS_UNDO_ADV package, 905

DB_WRITER_PROCESSES parameter, 171

DDL_LOCK_TIMEOUT parameter, 266

DDL LOGGING, 265

DEFAULT_PWD$ view, 198

Default user, 193–195

Deferred segment creation, 252

DELETE statement, 275–276, 717

DELETE NOPROMPT OBSOLETE command, 716

DELETE OBSOLETE command, 716

Deterministic, 324

DEVDB database, 820

DICT_COLUMNS view, 394

DICTIONARY view, 393

DIRECTORY parameter, 506

DISABLE procedure, 843

Displaying archivelog mode, 187

DISTINCT clauses, 307

DML statements, 307

DOP_JOB procedure, 845

DROP CATALOG command, 761

Drop database, 73

DROP SEQUENCE statement, 379

DROP SYNONYM statement, 370

DROP TABLE command, 273, 287

DROP TABLESPACE statement, 130

DROP USER statement, 213–214

DROP VIEW statement, 365

DUAL table, 405

dump directory, 92

DUPLICATE DATABASE command, 819

E

ECHO command, 735–736, 849

ENABLE procedure, 843

ENABLED column, 843

ENABLE PLUGGABLE DATABASE clause, 915

Environment seperation, applications, 923

Exadata Express, 924

EXCLUDE command, 742

EXPLAIN_MVIEW procedure, 607

Export command, 41

EXTENT MANAGEMENT LOCAL clause, 123

External table, 232

   advanced transformation

      CREATE TABLE statement, 569

      embedded transformation, 570

EXA_INFO table, 570

exa_trans function, 569

pipelined function, 568

rec_exa_type, 568

CSV file, 557

architectural components, 560

CREATE TABLE...ORGANIZATION
EXTERNAL statement, 561

database object creation, 562

directory object and granting
access, 561

EXADATA_ET, 563

ex.csv file, 561

loading regular table, 566

SQL generation, 563

steps to access, 560

view metadata, 565–566

data selection, 557

definition, 557

vs. SQL*Loader, 558

text files, 570

unloading and loading data

advantage, 572

components, 573

definition, 572

directory object, 574

dump file, 574

dump file compression, 577

dump file encryption, 577

elapsed time reduction, parallel
process, 575

inline SQL, 579

INV table, 574

INV_DW, 575

ORACLE_DATAPUMP access
driver, 578

F

Fast Recovery Area (FRA), 697

Fast refreshable MV

architectural components, 594, 596

complex query, 607–610

implementation steps, 592

log, 592

MLOG$_<base table name>, 594

Oracle features, 597

<base table name>_PK1, 594

PRIMARY KEY clause, 592

records, adding, 595

ROWID clause, 592

RUPD$_<base table name>, 594

SALES table, 592

SELECT statement, 592

USER_MVIEWS view, 596

USER_OBJECTS, 593

FAST_START_MTTR_TARGET, 171

filesp.bsh script, 103, 105–106

Filtering data and objects

constraint and trigger DDL, 531

exclude objects, 532

EXCLUDE parameter, 528–530

include objects, 532

INCLUDE parameter, 531

percentage data, 528

query, 526–528

statistics, 530

table and index, 531

find command, 16, 18, 877

Flashback database feature, 816

FLASHBACK TABLE statement, 275

Flashback table operations, 813

Foreign keys, 334

check index, 344–346

constraints, 293–294

Foreign keys (*cont.*)
  index on, 342–343
  table locks, 346–347
FORMAT command, 707
Full-table scans, 303
Function-based index, 324

G

Gap-free sequences, 376
GET_DDL function, 272, 364, 370
Graphical installer, Oracle binaries
  components and utilities, 30
  DISPLAY variable, 31, 33
  install X software and networking
      utilities, PC, 31
  runInstaller utility, 31, 34
  scp command, 32
  secure networking, 31
  ssh utility, 33
  startx command, 31
  troubleshoot, 31, 35
  xhost command., 31, 33
  X Window System
      emulation, 31
groupadd command, 10
GROUP BY clauses, 307
groupdel command, 11
groupmod command, 11

H

Hash clustered table, 232
Heap-organized table
  creation, 242, 244–246
  description, 232
High-water mark, 278
history command, 94

Hot-backup strategy
  ALTER DATABASE BEGIN BACKUP
      statement, 662
  archivelog mode, 661
  archive redo logs, 664, 672
  back up location, 661
  backup location, 661
  control files, 664
  frozen SCN, 674
  NLS_DATE_FORMAT
      parameter, 663
  Online Redo Logs, 663
  OS utility, 662
  script
    hotback.sql script, 666
    ORACLE_HOME OS variable, 665
    ORACLE_SID OS variables, 665
    SQL*Plus hbdir variable, 665, 667
  split-block issue, 669
    redo stream, 669–671
    restore and recovery, 672
  tablespaces out of backup
      mode, 663

I, J

Incomplete recovery
  archive redo logs/unarchived online
      redo log, 688
  cancel-based incomplete
      recovery, 688–689
  database back, 688
  data pump dump file, 812
  DBPITR, 805
  log sequence-based recovery, 809
  OPEN RESETLOGS clause, 690
  RESTORE DATABASE UNTIL
      command, 805

restore point, 811

SCN based incomplete
recovery, 688

SCN-based recovery, 810

steps, 805

testing environment, 688

time based incomplete recovery, 688

time-based recovery, 808–809

TSPITR, 806

type of, 808

user-managed incomplete
recovery, 688

INCREMENT BY setting, 380

Index-organized tables (IOTs), 232, 288

INDEX_STATS view, 321

Infrastructure as a Service
(IaaS), 35–36, 961

Init.ora Scenario, 158–159

INTERVAL data type, 238

interval partition type, 445

inventory.xml file, 21

Invisible columns, 250

Invisible index, 332–335

ISDATE function, 270

ISNUM function, 269

K

Key-compressed index, 330

L

Large objects (LOB)

BasicFiles *vs.* SecureFiles, 411

BFILE, 408, 439

BLOB, 408, 434

chunks, 409

CLOB, 408, 432

column

adding columns, 420

BasicFiles, 413

cache descriptions, 421

In- and Out of Line, 422

moving columns, 420

partition, 417

removing column, 421

SecureFiles, 416

tablespace, 415

index, 409

locators, 409

LONG and LONG RAW, 407

metadata, 431

NCLOB, 408

oracle data types, 409

SecureFiles, 412

BasicFiles migration, 428

deduplication, 425

degrees of compression, 424

encryption feature, 426

space, 435

VARCHAR2 data type, 407

LELLISON user, 227

Linux/Unix, 763

LIST BACKUP command, 765

LIST BACKUP SUMARY
command, 765

Listener.log file, 862

LIST FAILURE command, 779, 782

LOB data type, 240

Local user creation, 938

Locking issues, 899–902

lock.sql script, 108–109

LOG_ARCHIVE_FORMAT, 182

Log Archive Format String, 183

Log buffer, 80

login.sql script, 106

M

MAILTO variable, 856

Managing control files
    adding, 155–156
    ALTER SESSION statement, 154
    binary file, 151
    data dictionary, 152
    Init.ora Scenario, 158–159
    moving, 159–160
    names and locations, 155
    remove, 160–162
    spfile or init.ora file, 152
    Spfile Scenario, 156–157

Manipulating storage
    data file paths and names, 522–523
    REMAP_TABLESPACE feature, 523
    segment and storage
        attributes, 525–526
    tablespace metadata, 522
    TRANSFORM parameter, 524

man tar command, 24

Materialized view (MV)
    complete refreshable (*see* Complete
        refreshable MV)
    compressing, 600
    database performance report, 582
    data dictionary view, 585–586
    DDL view, 611
    dropping, 611
    encrypting columns, 600–601
    fast refreshable (*see* Fast
        refreshable MV)
    groups
        adding to refresh group, 645
        CHANGE function, 642
        creation, 642
        DBA_RGROUP and DBA_RCHILD
          views, 644

        DBMS_MVIEW *vs.* DBMS_
          REFRESH, 643–644
        dropping, 645
        INTERVAL calculation, 642
        refreshing, 643
        removing from refresh
          group, 645
    indexes, 598
    logs
        CREATE TABLE privilege, 619
        creating, 620–621
        dropping, 626
        Indexing columns, 622
        master table, 619
        moving, 625
        Oracle internal trigger, 619
        row count, 624
        shrinking space, 623–624
        terminology and features, 620
        viewing space, 622–623
    master tables, 581
    modification
        ALTER MATERIALIZED VIEW...
          MOVE TABLESPACE
          statement, 619
        base table DDL, 612
        ON PREBUILT TABLE clause,
          615–616
        parallelism, 618
        recreation, 613–614
        redo logging, 617–618
        underlying table
          preservation, 614
    never refreshable, 605
    ON COMMIT refreshable, 604
    partitioning, 599
    prebuilt table, 602
    query rewrite, 606–607

refresh
    efficient performance, 630
    interval, 629
    manual, 627
    ORA-12034 error handling, 631
    progress determination, 632
    real-time refresh progress, 633–634
    remote (*see* Remote MV refreshes)
    viewing last refresh times, 632
    within time period, 634–635
  SALES table, 581
  SALES_DAILY, 583
  sales table, 582
  tablespace, 598
  terminology, 584–585
  unpopulated, 603
MAX SQL function, 448
Media recovery testing, 786–787
MESSAGE_TEXT LIKE command, 881
MHURD user, 227
m kdir command, 50, 112
MV_CAPABILITIES_TABLE, 610
My Oracle Support (MOS), 16, 26, 28

N

NCLOB command, 240
Nested table, 232
Net configuration assistant
    (netca), 58, 858
Never refreshable MV, 605
NEXT clause, 629
NLS_DATE_FORMAT, 734–735
NOCOMPRESS clause, 135
NOLOGGING feature, 260, 617
NORESETLOGS clause, 146
NOT NULL constraint, 296
NOVALIDATE clause, 300

Numeric data type, 236–237
NVARCHAR2 and NCHAR data type, 236

O

Object table, 232
Offline and online data files, tablespaces,
    138–141
ON COMMIT DELETE ROWS, 286
ON COMMIT refreshable MV, 604
Online redo logs
  ADD LOGFILE GROUP statement, 172
  ALTER DATABASE ADD LOGFILE
    MEMBER statement, 175
  archivelog mode, 163
  back up, 165
  configuration, 164
  FAST_START_MTTR_TARGET
    value, 171
  GoldenGate/Streams, 162
  log writer, 162
  MAXLOGFILES value, 171
  mechanisms, 164–165
  moving/renaming, 176–177
  optimal number determination,
    169–170
  Oracle LogMiner utility, 162
  recovering transactions, 162
  remove, 175–176
  resizing and dropping, 172–174
  round-robin fashion, 163
  size, 168–169
  useful views, 167
  V $INSTANCE_RECOVERY, 169
  V $LOG_HISTORY, 168
  V $LOG View, 167
  V$LOGFILE View, 167
ON PREBUILT TABLE clause, 612, 615

opatch utility, 28

OPEN_CURSORS parameter, 902–903

OPEN RESETLOGS
command, 690, 802, 830

Optimal flexible architecture (OFA)
automatic diagnostic repository, 6–7
directory structure and file names, 3
Oracle base directory, 4–5
Oracle home directory, 5
Oracle inventory directory, 4
Oracle network files directory, 6

OR Operation, results, 328

Oracle autonomous database cloud, 961

ORACLE_BASE variable, 4

Oracle binaries installations
database, 7–8
existing copy
binaries copy, OS utility, 22, 24
Oracle home attachment, 24
free disk space, 11
graphical installer (*see* Graphical
installer, Oracle binaries)
graphical or silent install, 15
interim patches, 28–29
memory and swap space, 11
OFA (*see* Optimal Flexible
Architecture (OFA))
operating system software, 11
operating system version and
kernel, 11
oraInst.loc file creation, 14
OS Groups and user creation, 8–11
reinstallation, 27–28
software, 26–27
software download page, 12
system architecture, 11
troubleshoot issues, 20–21
unzip the files, 13

Oracle B-tree hierarchical index, 319

Oracle (circa version 8), 323

Oracle database
architecture, 77
one server database
advantages and
disadvantages, 77
applications and users, 76
architecture, 74
multiple applications and users, 75
multiple databases, 75
multiple pluggable databases, 76
OS authentication, 64–65
starting database, 65–66
phases, 67
startup command, 67–68
stopping database, 68
SHUTDOWN command, 68, 69

Oracle Database 12c, 374

Oracle Database 12c Release 1
Scenario, 16–20

Oracle enterprise management
tool, 114

ORACLE_HOME directory, 28

Oracle index type, 309–310

Oracle internal trigger, 619

Oracle listener
database connection, 61–62
manual configuration, 59–61
netca, 58–59

ORACLE_LOADER Driver, 572

Oracle managed files (OMF)
tablespaces, 132–133

Oracle Multitenant, 918

Oracle Scheduler utility
COPY_JOB procedure, 844
CREATE_JOB procedure, 840
vs. cron, 845

deleting, 845

DISABLE procedure, 843

ENABLE procedure, 843

JOB_CLASS parameter, 840

logging history, 842

modification, 842

orahome/oracle/bin directory, 839

PL/SQL package, 839

REPEAT_INTERVAL parameter, 840

run, 844

stopping, 843

view details, 841

Oracle universal installer (OUI), 1, 14, 26

Oracle wallet, 428, 578, 601

oraInst.loc file, 14

ORDER BY clauses, 307

OS techniques, 84

OVERFLOW clause, 288

P, Q

P_0 PROCESSES, 256

PARALLEL clause, 256

PARALLEL_THREADS_PER_CPU, 257

Partitioned table, 232

Partitioning

  benefits, 441

    indexes

    architecture, 487–488

    global index, 490–492

    LOCAL clause, 487

    partial, 492–493

    prefixed *vs.* nonprefixed, 490

    ROWID values, 486

    tablespace, 488

    types, 489

    USER_IND_PARTITIONS table, 487

    USER_PART_INDEXES, 489

maintenance

  ADD PARTITION clause, 474–477

  dropping, 482

  exchange, 476, 478

  existing table, 472, 474

  manipulating data, 485

  merging, 480–481

  metadata, 468

  moving, 469–470

  removing rows, 484

  renaming, 479

  splitting, 479–480

  statistics, 483

  updated rows, 471

modifying specific strategy, 496

OLTP databases, 443

Oracle partitioning terminology, 442

parallelism, 441

pruning, 494

table creation

  based on date, 458–461

  based on number, 461–462

  composite partitioning, 455–457

  MAX SQL function, 448, 449

  NUMBER implementation, 446–448

  parent table, 462–466

  PARTITION BY HASH

    clause, 454–455

  PARTITION BY LIST clause, 453–454

  PARTITION BY RANGE clause, 446

  PARTITION BY SYSTEM clause, 467

  strategies, 445

  TIMESTAMP implemention, 449

  virtual column, 466

tables, 443–444

PCTTHRESHOLD, 288

PERFSTAT user, 898

ping command, 873

Platform as a Service (PaaS), 35, 924, 961
PL/SQL function, 539
    role, 228
Pluggable architecture, advantage, 923
Pluggable databases (PDB)
    administrative tasks, 951
    architecture, 919–922
    backup and recovery, 924–925
    clone, 960
    connection, 951–952
    creation
        DBCA, 949–950
        existing PDB, 943
        non-CDB, 945–947
        options, 943
        plugging, 948–949
        remote PDB, 944–945
        seed database, 942
        sources, 941
        status check, 950–951
        unplug, 947–948
    dropping, 959–960
    Exadata Express, 924
    history view, 958–959
    initialization parameters, 956
    listener, 952–953
    lockdown profile, 958
    renaming, 957
    shipping containers, 926
    SHOW command, 954, 955
    space limit, 957–958
    start/stop
        pluggable database, 955
        root container, 955
    terms, 917
    tuning, 925
Process monitor (PMON), 60
Primary key constraints, 289–290

Process identifiers (PIDs), 886
Program global area (PGA), 80
ps command, 847
ps utility, 890
PURGE_LOG procedure, 842
PURGE_MVIEW_FROM_LOG
        procedure, 641
pwd command, 95

R

RAW data type, 238
README.txt, 29
Read-only tables, 251
RECOVER command, 695, 777, 788, 799
RECOVER DATABASE command, 788
RECOVER DATABASE UNTIL
        command, 807
RECOVER DATAFILE commands, 792
RECOVER TABLE command, 811
RECOVER TABLESPACE command, 789
RECOVER TABLESPACE UNTIL
        command, 806
Recovery manager (RMAN), 43
RECYCLEBIN feature, 275
Reference partition type, 445
Referential integrity constraints, *see*
        Foreign keys
REMAP_SCHEMA parameter, 518
Remote MV refreshes
    architectures, 636–638
    base table information, 638
    central MV Log, 639–641
    master database, 635
    setup, 635
RENAME statement, 364
REPAIR FAILURE command, 781–782
REPORT command, 766

REPORT SCHEMA command, 739

RMAN REPORT SCHEMA command, 792

RESETLOGS, 146, 687

RESTORE command, 695, 777, 788, 807

RESTORE CONTROLFILE
command, 801

RESTORE DATABASE
command, 787, 805–806

RESTORE DATABASE UNTIL
command, 805

RESTORE DATAFILE command, 792

RESTORE...PREVIEW command, 785, 786

RESTORE TABLESPACE command, 789

RESTORE...VALIDATE command,
756–757, 786

RESTORE...VALIDATE HEADER
command, 786

Reverse-key index, 309, 329–330

REVOKE statement, 226

$RMAN_BACKUP_JOB_DETAILS, 770

RMAN backups
command initialisation
ECHO command, 735–736
NLS_DATE_FORMAT, 734–735
SHOW ALL command, 736
corruption
BACKUP...VALIDATE
command, 756
RESTORE...VALIDATE
command, 756–757
VALIDATE command, 754–755
execution
archive redo logs, 740–741
autobackup, 737
backup sets vs. image copies, 738
control file, 739–740
data files, 739
data files (not backed up), 743

EXCLUDE command, 742
FRA, 741–742
full backup vs. incremental
level=0, 737
parallelism, 745
repository, 745–746
skip offline or inaccessible
files, 744
SKIP READONLY command, 743
spfile, 740
tablespaces, 738–739
incremental backup features
block change tracking, 753–754
incremental level, 750–751
updating backup, 751–753
output
cron, 762
data dictionary, 764–765
Linux/Unix, 763
shell script (rmanback.bsh), 762
SPOOL LOG command, 764
pluggable databases, 747
root container, 747–748
SYSDBA/SYSBACKUP
privileges, 748–749
recovery catalog
back up, 760
creation, 757–759
DROP CATALOG command, 761
synchronization, 760
target database register, 759
version, 761
report
LIST, 765–766
REPORT command, 766–767
SQL, 767–772
types of, 733

RMAN CATALOG command, 146

RMAN configuration
    architectural components
        auxiliary database, 696
        backup/back up, 696
        backup piece file, 696
        backup set, 696
        channel(s), 695
        DBA, 695
        FRA, 697
        image copy, 696
        media manager, 697
        memory buffers (PGA or SGA, 695)
        Oracle server processes, 695
        PL/SQL packages, 695
        recovery catalog, 696
        RMAN client, 695
        snapshot control file, 697
        target database, 695
    architectural decision
        archive redo log destination and file
            format, 705
        archive redo logs' deletion
            policy, 717–718
        backing up, 711
        BACKUP...FORMAT, 707
        backup retention policy (*see* Backup
            retention policy)
        backup sets/image copy, 719
        backup user specification, 704
        binary compression, 722
        block change tracking, 721
        CONFIGURE command, 731
        CONFIGURE CHANNEL...FORMAT,
            708–709
        control file autobackup, 709
        CONTROL_FILE_RECORD_KEEP_
            TIME initialization parameter, 714
        cron utility, 727, 732

        CROSSCHECK command, 731
        default location, 706–707
        DELETE NOPROMPT
            OBSOLETE, 732
        ECHO parameter, 731
        encryption algorithm, 723
        FRA, 707
        implementation, 701–703, 729–730
        incremental backups, 720–721
        incrementally updated
            backups, 721
        informational output, 725–726
        media manager, 713
        miscellaneous settings, 724–725
        NLS_DATE_FORMAT OS
            variable, 731
        online/offline backups, 705
        oraset variable, 731
        parallelism degree, 718
        recovery catalog, 712–713
        remotely/locally, 704
        snapshot control file, 711–712
        specifying location of, 710
    OS variables, 699
    PATH variable, 699
    rman and sqlplus, 699
    SQL statements, 724
    types of
        archivelog backups, 698
        block change tracking, 698
        full backup, 697
        incremental level 0
            backup, 697
        incremental level 1
            backup, 698
        incrementally updated
            backup, 698
RMAN duplicate database, 518

RMAN restore and recovery
  complete recovery (*see* Complete
    recovery)
  control file
    Autobackup, 802
    recovery catalog, 801
    specific backup piece file, 803
  data recovery advisor
    change failure, 782
    listing failure, 779–780
    repairing failure, 781–782
    suggesting corrective action,
      780–781
  DBA, 774
  flashback table feature
    recycle bin feature, 813
    RESTORE POINT, 816
    SCN, 815–816
    SHOW RECYCLEBIN
      statement, 814
    TIMESTAMP, 816
    undo tablespace, 815
  incomplete recovery
    archived redo log file, 807
    Data Pump dump file, 812
    DBPITR, 805
    log sequence-based recovery, 809
    RESTORE DATABASE UNTIL
      command, 805
    restore point, 811
    SCN-based recovery, 810
    SQL query, 806
    steps, 805
    time-based recovery, 808–809
    TSPITR, 806
    type of, 808
  media recovery, 775
  RECOVER command, 777
  redo log file, 777
    default location, 800
    nondefault Location, 800–801
  RESTORE command, 777
  server, 819
    building block, 819
    control file, 824
    control file aware, 824
    copy, 821
    database, origination, 821
    database recover, 828
    database rename, 831–834
    data file, control file and dump/
      trace file, 823
    data file location, 826
    init.ora file creation, 823
    mount mode, 824
    nomount mode, 824
    online redo logs, 829
    oracle binaries install, 822
    OS variable, 822
    temp file, 831
  spfile, 803–804
  SQL*Plus, 773
  steps, 778
  stop/start Oracle, 783
ROLLBACK statement, 276
Root container
  administration, 934
  name display, 935–936
  network connection, 935
  space report, 938–940
  start/stop, 936
Row identifier (ROWID), 303
  data type, 239, 285
ROWNUM pseudocolumn,
    892–893, 903
runInstaller command, 16

S

SALESPDB pluggable database, 748–749

Scalable sequence, 375

Schemas *vs.* users, 205–206

scp command, 32

script command, 763

SecureFile

    advanced features

        deduplication, 425

        degrees of compression, 424

        encryption feature, 426

    vs. BasicFiles, 411

    LOB column, 416

    space, 437

SEGMENT SPACE MANAGEMENT
    AUTO clause, 123

SELECT statement, 364

Sequence

    autoincrementing column, 374–375

    creation, options, 372

    definition, 371

    dropping, 379

    metadata, 378

    pseudocolumns, 373

    renaming, 379

    resetting, 379–381

    single/multiple sequence, 377–378

    unique values, 376–377

service command, 847

Service name (SID), 61

SET_ATTRIBUTE procedure, 842

SET CONTAINER command, 951

SET EDITOR command, 880

SET HOMEPATH command, 881

SET NEWNAME command, 793, 826

SET_SCHEDULER_ATTRIBUTE
    procedure, 842

SET SQLPROMPT command, 87

setup.exe command, 16

SHOW command, 722

SHOW ALERT command, 880

SHOW ALL command, 736

SHOW HOMES command, 881

SHUTDOWN command, 153, 783

SHUTDOWN IMMEDIATE
    statement, 68, 783

SKIP INACCESSIBLE command, 744

SKIP OFFLINE command, 744

SKIP READONLY command, 743

Skip-scan feature, 323

Smoke test, 209

Spfile, 740

    parameter, 182–184

    scenario, 156–157

SPOOL LOG command, 764

SQL, 767–772

SQL*Plus, 336

    drop database, 73

    Oracle database

        CREATE DATABASE
          statement, 50, 52

        data dictionary creation, 56

        initialization file, 47

        OFA structures, 56

        OS variables, 46

        TEMP tablespace, 53

    Oracle listener, 61

    OS variables

        LD_LIBRARY_PATH, 40

        manually intensive approach, 41

        ORACLE_HOME, 40

        ORACLE_SID, 40

        oraenv, 43

        oraset file, 45

        oratab file, 42

        PATH variable, 40

PASSWORD command, 210
password file, 62
variables, 89
SQL scripts
.bashrc file, 113
directories creation, 112
HOME/bin directory, 112
HOME/scripts directory, 112
startup file configuration, 113
SQL TEXT column, 890
STARTUP command, 153, 783
STARTUP NOMOUNT command, 387, 801
START WITH clause, 629
startx command, 31
STATE column, 355
Statspack, 898
Status table, 502
STOP_JOB procedure, 843
Storage area network (SAN), 314
SWITCH command, 793
SWITCH_DIR variable, 861
Synonyms
creation, 366–367
definition, 366
dropping, 370
generates synonyms, 368
metadata, 369–370
public synonyms, 367–368
renaming, 370
types, 365
USER2's EMP table, 365
SYSAUX tablespace, 119
SYS_CONTEXT function, 395–396
SYSDBA role, 196
SYS vs. SYSTEM, 196
SYSOPER role, 196
SYSTEM schema, 196
SYSTEM tablespace, 119, 207

System change number (SCN), 162, 168
System global area (SGA), 66
system partition type, 445
SYSTEM schema, 932

T

Tables
character data type
CHAR, 235
NVARCHAR2 and NCHAR, 236
VARCHAR2, 234–235
constraints (see Constraints)
creation
autoincrementing (identity)
column, 253–255
compressing table data, 257, 259–260
default parallel SQL execution,
256–257
deferred segment creation, 252
factors, 241
from a query, 263
guidelines, 244
heap-organized table, 242, 244–246
invisible columns, 250
IOTs, 288
read-only tables, 251
redo creation, avoid, 260–261, 263
temporary table, 286–287
virtual columns, 246, 248–249
Date/Time data type, 237–238
definition, 231
displaying table DDL, 271
dropping, 273
LOB data type, 240
modification
adding column, 267
altering column, 268, 270

Tables (*cont.*)

    dropping unused column, 270

    locking, 266–267

    renaming column, 270

    renaming table, 267

  numeric data type, 236–237

  RAW data type, 238

  removing data from table, 275

  restoring dropped table, 274–275

  ROWID data type, 239

  types, 232

  viewing and adjusting high-water mark

    lowering method, 282

    performance-related issues, 278–279

    readjusting, 283

    rebuilding table, 283–284

    selecting from data dictionary
extents view, 282

    space detecting methods, 278–282

Tablespace point-in-time recovery
(TSPITR), 806

Tablespaces

  ampersand variables, 125

  APP user, 120

  best practices for creating and
managing, 126–127

  bigfile features, 133

  CREATE TABLESPACE statement, 122

  database space usage, 135–136

  data dictionary views, 117

  default table compression, 134–135

  dropping, 129, 131

  human resources application, 121

  inventory application, 121

  logical storage objects and physical
storage, 118, 121

  N OLOGGING clause, 177–178

  objects, 117

  Oracle managed files, 132–133

  read-only mode, 128

  read/write mode, 128

  reasons, separate tablespaces, 121

  rename, 127

  resize, 137–138

Tablespaces partitions

  CREATE TABLESPACE
statement, 450–452

  data files, 452

  single tablespace, 451

  storage clauses, 453

TAIL option, 881

tar command, 23

TARGET parameter, 695

tar -tvf <tarfile name> command, 23, 24

tbsp_chk.bsh script, 99–102

telnet command, 873

TEMP tablespace, 119

Temporary table, 232

Temporary tablespace, 313

Temporary tablespace issues, 908–911

THRESH_GET_WORRIED
variable, 860

TIMESTAMP data type, 238

tnsping command, 874

TO NONE command, 716

top.sql script, 107

Transparent network substrate
(TNS), 61

Troubleshooting

  automating job, 856–857

  bottlenecks (*see* Bottlenecks
identification)

  locking issues

    COMMIT/ROLLBACK, 901

    KILL command, 902

    OS command, 902

output, 901
   space-related issue, 899
   SQL statement, 899
open-cursor issues, 902–903
oracle installation issues, 21
OS Watcher tool, 891
SQL statement
   ADDM report, 897
   ASH report, 897
   AWR report, 896
   diagnosing database, 894–895
   monitoring real-time statistics,
      891, 893–894
   Oracle performance utility, 895
   Statspack, 898
   V$SYSSTAT and V$SESSTAT
      views, 895
temporary tablespace issues
   determination, 909
   SQL view, 910
triaging
   ADRCI utility, 880
   alert log and trace files, 875–876
   database availability, 872–874
   OS tools, 878
   removing files, 876, 878
undo tablespace issues
   determination, 904–906
   SQL view, 907–908
TRUNCATE statement, 275–277

U

unalias command, 90
UNDO tablespace, 119
   issues, 904–906
UNIFORM SIZE [size] clause, 123
UNION clauses, 307

Unique index, 325–326
Unique key constraint creation
   methods, 291
Unpopulated MV, 603
UNTIL SCN clause, 810
unzip command, 13
USE_CURRENT_SESSION parameter, 844
userdel command, 11
USERENV namespace, 395
User-managed backups and recovery
   archivelog mode database
      complete recovery (see Complete
         recovery)
      incomplete recovery (see
         Incomplete recovery)
   cold-backup strategy (see Cold-backup
      strategy)
   hot backup strategy (see Hot backup
      strategy)
usermod command, 11
USER_ROLE_PRIVS view, 227
Users
   ALTER USER command, 209–210
   choosing name, 201–202
   configuration, 204–205
   creation, 200
      CREATE USER SQL statement, 202
      OS authentication, 203–204
      schemas, 205–206
   DBA-created accounts, 198
   DBA role, 196
   DBA_USERS_WITH_DEFPWD
      view, 200
   default, 193–195
   default permanent tablespace and
      temporary tablespace, 206–209
   DEFAULT_PWD$ view, 198
   different user logging in, 210–211

Users (*cont.*)

DROP USER statement, 213–214

grouping and assigning
privileges, 226–227

limiting database resource
usage, 221–223

modifying users, 212

object privileges, 225–226

password change, 196–198

password check, 199–200

password security, 215–218

password strength, 219–221

SQL statements, 197

SYS account, 197

SYSDBA role, 196

SYSOPER role, 196

system privileges, 224–225

SYSTEM schema, 196

USERS tablespace, 119, 787

users.sql script, 110–111

USER_TABLES view, 385

V

V$CONTROLFILE_RECORD_SECTION:,
152

V$DATABASE_BLOCK_CORRUPTION,
755, 795

V$LOG_HISTORY, 168

V$SESSTAT view, 895

V$SQL_MONITOR view, 893

V$SQLSTATS view, 893

V$SYSSTAT view, 895

VALIDATE command, 754, 795

VALIDATE DATABASE command, 780

VALIDATE HEADER clause, 867

VARCHAR2 data type, 234–235

view command, 879

Views

creation, 352–354

definition, 362–363

dropping, 365

INSTEAD OF triggers, 358–359

invisible column, 360–361

read-only views, 355

renaming, 364

SQL query, 363–364

updatable join view, 356–358

updation, 354–355

uses, 352

WITH CHECK OPTION, 354

Virtual columns, 246, 248–249

virtual partition type, 445

VRMAN_OUTPUT view, 764

V$CONTROLFILE view, 155

W

WITH CHECK OPTION, 355

WITHOUT VALIDATION
clause, 478

X, Y, Z

xargs command, 877

xhost command, 31, 33, 35

Printed in the United States
By Bookmasters